UNITED STATES ARMY IN WORLD WAR II

The Mediterranean Theater of Operations

CASSINO TO THE ALPS

by

Ernest F. Fisher, Jr.

MILITARY INSTRVCTION

CENTER OF MILITARY HISTORY

UNITED STATES ARMY

WASHINGTON, D.C., 1993

Library of Congress Cataloging in Publication Data

Fisher, Ernest F   1918–
   Cassino to the Alps.

   (United States Army in World War II: The Mediterranean theater of operations; 4)
   Bibliography: p.
   Includes index.
   1. World War, 1939–1945—Campaigns—Italy. 2. Italy—History—German occupation, 1943–1945. I. Title. II. Series: United States. Dept. of the Army. Office of Military History. United States Army in World War II. D769.A533 vol. 11, pt. 4 [D763.18] 940.54′12′7308s

               [940.54′21]   76–43097

First Printed 1977—CMH Pub 6–4–1

For sale by the Superintendent of Documents, U.S. Government Printing Office
Washington, D.C. 20402

UNITED STATES ARMY IN WORLD WAR II

Maurice Matloff, General Editor

Advisory Committee

(As of 1 March 1976)

Otis A. Singletary
University of Kentucky

Edward M. Coffman
University of Wisconsin

Harry L. Coles
Ohio State University

Frank Freidel, Jr.
Harvard University

Peter Paret
Stanford University

Russell F. Weigley
Temple University

Maj. Gen. Robert C. Hixon
United States Army Training and
Doctrine Command

Brig. Gen. Edward B. Atkeson
United States Army War College

Brig. Gen. William C. Louisell, Jr.
United States Army Command and
General Staff College

Col. Thomas E. Griess
United States Military Academy

Center of Military History

Brig. Gen. James L. Collins, Jr., Chief of Military History

Chief Historian	Maurice Matloff
Chief, Historical Services Division	Col. Walter L. McMahon
Chief, Histories Division	Col. James F. Ransone, Jr.
Editor in Chief	Joseph R. Friedman

. . . to Those Who Served

Foreword

From September 1943, when Allied troops came ashore near Salerno, until German surrender in May 1945, 312,000 Allied soldiers were killed, wounded, or missing in Italy. Was a campaign that from the first faced the bleak prospect of coming to a dead end against the forbidding escarpment of the Alps worth that cost? Was the objective of tying down German troops to avoid their commitment in northwestern Europe all that the campaign might have accomplished?

The answers to those questions have long been sought but, as is the nature of history, must forever remain conjecture. What is established fact, as this volume makes clear, is the tenacity and intrepidity displayed by American and Allied soldiers in the face of a determined and resourceful enemy, harsh weather, sharply convoluted terrain, limited numbers, and indefinite goals in what many of them must have looked upon as a backwater of the war.

This volume relates the story of the last year of their struggle. Three volumes previously published tell of the campaign in northwest Africa, the conquest of Sicily and covert politico-military negotiations leading to surrender of the Italian armed forces, and the campaign from the Allied landings on the mainland through the bitter disappointment of the amphibious assault at Anzio. This volume is thus the capstone of a four-volume series dealing with American military operations in the western Mediterranean.

Washington, D.C.
1 April 1976

JAMES L. COLLINS, JR.
Brigadier General, USA
Chief of Military History

The Author

Ernest F. Fisher, Jr., graduated from Boston University in 1941, and in World War II served in Europe with the 501st Parachute Infantry, 101st Airborne Division. He returned to Boston University and received an M.A. in 1947 and in 1952 a Ph.D. degree in history from the University of Wisconsin. From 1954 to 1959 Dr. Fisher was a historian with Headquarters, U.S. Army, Europe. Since 1960 he has been a member of the staff of the Center of Military History. He is a retired colonel in the Army of the United States.

Preface

"Wars should be fought," an American corps commander noted in his diary during the campaign in Italy, "in better country than this."[1] It was indeed an incredibly difficult place to fight a war. The Italian peninsula is only some 150 miles wide, much of it dominated by some of the world's most precipitous mountains. Nor was the weather much help. It seemed to those involved that it was always either unendurably hot or bone-chilling cold.

Yet American troops fought with remarkable courage and tenacity, and in company with a veritable melange of Allied troops: Belgians, Brazilians, British, Canadians, Cypriots, French (including superb mountain troops from Algeria and Morocco), Palestinian Jews, Indians, Italians, Nepalese, New Zealanders, Poles, South Africans, Syro-Lebanese, and Yugoslavians. The combatants also included the United States Army's only specialized mountain division, one of its last two segregated all-Negro divisions, and a regimental combat team composed of Americans of Japanese descent.

Despite the forbidding terrain, Allied commanders several times turned it to their advantage, achieving penetrations or breakthroughs over some of the most rugged mountains in the peninsula. To bypass mountainous terrain, the Allies at times resorted to amphibious landings, notably at Anzio. Thereafter German commanders, forced to reckon with the possibility of other such operations, had to hold back forces to protect their long coastal flanks.

The campaign involved one ponderous attack after another against fortified positions: the Winter Line, the Gustav Line, the Gothic Line. It called for ingenuity in employing tanks and tank destroyers over terrain that to the armored soldier seemed to be one vast antitank ditch. It took another kind of ingenuity in devising methods to get at the enemy in flooded lowlands along the Adriatic coast.

It was also a campaign replete with controversy, as might have been expected in a theater where the presence of various nationalities and two fairly equal partners imposed considerable strain on the process of coalition command. Most troublesome of the questions that caused controversy were: Did the American commander, Mark Clark, err in focusing on the capture of Rome rather than conforming with the wishes of his British superior to try to trap retreating German forces? Did Allied

---

[1] Martin Blumenson, *Salerno to Cassino*, UNITED STATES ARMY IN WORLD WAR II (Washington, 1969), p. 234, quoting Maj. Gen. John P. Lucas.

commanders conduct the pursuit north of Rome with sufficient vigor? Indeed, should the campaign have been pursued all the way to the Alps when the Allies might have halted at some readily defensible line and awaited the outcome of the decisive campaign in northwestern Europe?

Just as the campaign began on a note of covert politico-military maneuvering to achieve surrender of Italian forces, so it ended with intrigue and secret negotiations for a separate surrender of the Germans in Italy.

This volume is chronologically the final work in the Mediterranean theater subseries of the UNITED STATES ARMY IN WORLD WAR II series. It follows *Salerno to Cassino,* previously published.

The present work was originally projected as two volumes in the series. The first, entitled The Drive on Rome, was to cover the period from the fall of Cassino and the Anzio breakout to the Arno River north of Rome, a campaign that lasted from early May to late July 1944. The second, entitled The Arno to the Alps, was to carry the story through to the end of the war.

Dr. Sidney T. Mathews, first to be designated to write The Drive on Rome, left the Center of Military History after preparing several chapters that proved valuable guides to research. Ultimately, the present author received the assignment and worked for many months on that volume under the original concept. Thereafter, the decision was made to combine what was to have been two separate narratives into a single volume.

An entirely new approach thus had to be devised, one that involved considerable further research. The result is the present publication, which covers one of the lengthiest and most agonizing periods of combat in World War II.

As with other volumes in this series, many able individuals have helped bring this work to completion. Foremost among these has been the former head of the European and Mediterranean Sections of the Center of Military History, Charles B. MacDonald. His superlative skill in developing a lucid narrative of military operations and his patience with my efforts to acquire a modicum of that skill have been pillars of strength during the preparation of this volume. To Mr. Robert Ross Smith, Chief of the General Histories Branch, goes a generous share of the credit for refining and clarifying many aspects of the combat narrative. A very special thanks is also due Dr. Stetson Conn, former Chief Historian, who designated me for this task and encouraged me along the way. The arduous assignment of typing and retyping many versions of the manuscript with skill and patience fell largely to Mrs. Edna Salsbury. The final version was typed by Mrs. Robert L. Dean.

The excellent maps accompanying the volume are the work of several able cartographers and draftsmen: Mr. Arthur S. Hardyman and Mr. Wayne Hefner performed the difficult and tedious task of devising the layouts, and Mr. Grant Pierson, Mr. Howell Brewer, and Mr. Roger Clinton demonstrated professional skill in the drafting. Mrs. Lois Aldridge, formerly of the World War II Records Division of the National Archives and Records Service, helped me find my way through the wealth of source material. Equally valuable was the assistance rendered by Mr. Detmar Finke and Miss Hannah Zeidlik of the General Reference Branch of the Center of Military History. The author is also grateful for the comments of the distinguished panel that read and reviewed the manuscript. The panel included General Lyman L. Lemnitzer, former Deputy Chief of Staff to the Allied commander in Italy; Dr. Robert Coakley, Deputy Chief Historian; Col. John E. Jessup, Jr., Chief, Histories Division; and Martin Blumenson and Dr. Jeffrey Clarke, fellow historians. To General Mark Wayne Clark I owe a special debt of gratitude for generously allowing me to use his diary in the preparation of this volume and for making helpful comments on the finished manuscript. The final editing and preparation of the volume for publication was the work of Mr. David Jaffé, assisted by Mr. Duncan Miller. Finally, a very special note of thanks to my wife, Else, who throughout has been a close, steadfast, and patient source of encouragement.

The author's debt to all those without whose guidance and support this volume would never have come to completion does not diminish in the least his sole responsibility for all errors of fact and interpretation.

Washington, D.C.   ERNEST F. FISHER, JR.
1 April 1976

Contents

PART ONE

The Spring Offensive

PART TWO

Breakout From the Beachhead

PART THREE

Drive to Rome

PART FOUR

Rome to the Arno

PART FIVE

The Gothic Line Offensive

PART SIX

In the Northern Apennines

PART SEVEN

The Last Offensive

PART EIGHT

Pursuit to the Alps

Maps

Maps I–XVI Are In Accompanying Map Envelope

Illustrations

Illustrations are from Department of Defense files, with the exception of the photograph on page 212, which is from *Yank Magazine,* and that on page 348, which was supplied by William G. Bell of the Center of Military History.

The U.S. Army Center of Military History

The Center of Military History prepares and publishes histories as required by the U.S. Army. It coordinates Army historical matters, including historical properties, and supervises the Army museum system. It also maintains liaison with public and private agencies and individuals to stimulate interest and study in the field of military history. The Center is located at 1099 14th Street, N.W., Washington, D.C. 20005–3402.

PART ONE

THE SPRING OFFENSIVE

War is a matter of vital importance to the State; the province of life or death; the road to survival or ruin. It is mandatory that it be thoroughly studied.

SUN TZU, *The Art of War*

CHAPTER I

Spring in Italy—1944

An hour before midnight on 11 May 1944, 1,660 guns opened fire. Shells crashed along a 25-mile front from the slopes of Monte Cassino to the Tyrrhenian Sea. The crash and roar of artillery turned high ground beyond the Rapido and Garigliano Rivers into an inferno of flame and steel. The Allied Armies in Italy (AAI) with this preparatory fire had launched Operation DIADEM, a full-scale offensive that was destined to carry the U.S. Fifth and the British Eighth Armies from southern Italy to the Alps, where the Germans would at last lay down their arms.

Spring in 1944 came early to Italy. On the reverse slopes of a hundred hills overlooking the valleys of the Rapido and the Garigliano Rivers, as Allied and German infantrymen emerged from their dugouts to stretch and bask in the warm sunshine, they could look back on several months of some of the hardest fighting yet experienced in World War II.

The campaign in southern Italy had grown out of the Allied capture of Sicily, which had helped to bring about the overthrow of the Italian dictator, Benito Mussolini, and contributed to the surrender of Italy. Early in September 1943, first elements of the British Eighth Army had come ashore near Reggio in Calabria on the southernmost tip of the Italian mainland. Six days later additional British forces landed in Taranto from warships. On the same day the U.S. Fifth Army hit the beaches of Salerno and soon engaged in a bitter struggle against a tenacious enemy. [1]

In southern Italy, the Allies found awaiting them not demoralized Italians but a well-equipped and determined German foe. Fighting alone at that point, the Germans had moved swiftly to occupy Rome, liberate an imprisoned Mussolini, disarm the Italian military forces, and occupy the entire country.

For the next seven months the British and American armies advanced slowly northward from their respective beachheads against a stubborn enemy fighting skillfully in mountainous terrain. Battles at the Volturno River and at the historic Benedictine abbey of Monte Cassino together with an unsuccessful attempt to cross the Rapido River exacted a heavy toll on both opponents.

By the end of March 1944, the German armies between the Adriatic and Tyrrhenian Seas below Rome had fought the Allies to a virtual stalemate. They were also containing a beachhead at Anzio, some thirty miles south of Rome, where Anglo-American troops under the U.S. VI Corps had come ashore in January 1944. With this

---

[1] For details concerning this and the following periods see Albert N. Garland and Howard M. Smyth, *Sicily and the Surrender of Italy* (Washington, 1965), and Martin Blumenson, *Salerno to Cassino* (Washington, 1968), both volumes in the UNITED STATES ARMY IN WORLD WAR II series.

beachhead and a modest bridgehead beyond the Garigliano River in hand, as well as a tenuous toehold on the slopes of Monte Cassino, Allied leaders believed they held the key that would open the way to Rome and central Italy.

The main Allied front stretched a hundred miles—from the Gulf of Gaeta on the Tyrrhenian Sea northeastward across the Apennines to the Adriatic. (*Map I*)* The Central Apennines had thus far confined the campaign largely to the coastal flanks. In the wild, mountainous region in the center lies the Abruzzi National Park, a desolate wilderness with few roads and trails, defended only by weak and scattered German outposts. There small Allied detachments harassed the enemy and maintained contact between the widely separated main forces on the flanks.

Monte Cassino, keystone of the German defenses in the Liri valley, towered above the Rapido River at the threshold of the relatively broad valley of the Liri River, which led enticingly toward Rome. From mid-January to mid-March the U.S. Fifth Army had fought unsuccessfully to drive German paratroopers and infantrymen from the ruins of Cassino and from the rocky slopes of Monte Cassino itself. Near the Tyrrhenian coast the British 10 Corps had crossed the Garigliano River to establish an 8-mile bridgehead near Minturno.

In the Anzio beachhead the Allied troops in early March had brought the last German counterattacks to a halt

---

* Maps I–XVI are in inverse order inside back cover.

along a front approximately thirty miles long—from the coast about twelve miles northeast of Anzio southward as far as the bank of the Mussolini Canal. The beachhead enclosed by that front extended at its deepest about fifteen miles from Anzio northeastward toward the German strongpoint of Cisterna, the distance along the coast being approximately twenty-two miles. Thus there were two fronts in Italy in the spring of 1944, and Rome, the objective that had eluded the Allies for seven hard months, seemed still beyond reach.

Allied Strategy

On 26 May 1943 the Combined Chiefs of Staff (CCS), composed of the Chiefs of Staff of the British and the American military services, had instructed General Dwight D. Eisenhower, then Allied commander in the Mediterranean, to launch the major Allied assault against the Germans in northwestern France early in 1944. That strategic concept would dominate the over-all conduct of the Italian campaign from its Sicilian beginnings in July 1943 until the end of the war. Even before the Allies landed in Sicily, the Italian campaign had been allotted a secondary role. Diversion of enemy strength from the Russian front as well as from the expected decisive area of operations—the Channel coast—was the basic goal of Allied strategy in the Mediterranean. The campaign in Italy was envisioned mainly as a great holding action, although engaging and destroying German divisions as well as seizing air bases near Foggia in southern Italy for Allied use in bombing

Germany were important considerations. [2]

Few Allied strategists held any brief that the war could be won solely by a drive either through the length of Italy or into the Balkan peninsula. Yet some British leaders, notably Prime Minister Winston S. Churchill and General Sir Alan Brooke, Chief of the Imperial General Staff, sought to invest the Italian campaign with a larger role than did most of the Americans. Churchill envisioned an eventual Allied thrust into the mid-Danube basin, where centuries before his distinguished ancestor, the Duke of Marlborough, had won lasting fame at Blenheim. A determined man, Churchill would long cling to this theory even when the weight of strategic argument and events moved against him.

From its inception, therefore, the Italian campaign played a larger role in the strategic and political aspects of British war planning than it did with American planning. Until the Allied landings in northwestern France in June 1944 much of British strategic thinking would be focused on Italy, the scene from September 1943 to June 1944 of the only active land campaign in western Europe. There was, more-

over, an emotional factor involved with the British, a factor not shared by the Americans because it stemmed from Britain's immediate and distant past. When the British came ashore in southern Italy in September 1943, it was for them only partial compensation for their forced withdrawal from the Continent at Dunkerque more than three years before. Not since the Napoleonic wars in the early 19th century had British arms been driven so ingloriously from the mainland of Europe. For Americans only General Douglas MacArthur's flight from and ultimate return to the Philippines would have anywhere near a comparable emotional meaning.

During a top-level Anglo-American planning conference at Quebec in August 1943 (QUADRANT), the CCS had drawn up a blueprint for an Italian campaign. Operations in Italy were to be divided into three phases. The first was expected to culminate in the surrender of Italy and the establishment of Allied air bases in the vicinity of Rome. The second phase would be the capture of Sardinia and Corsica. The third called for the Allied armies to maintain pressure against the Germans in northern Italy to help create conditions favorable for both the cross-Channel invasion (OVERLORD) and the entry of Allied forces into southern France (later designated ANVIL, and still later DRAGOON).

During the months that the Allied armies battled their way to the line marked by the Garigliano, Rapido, and Sangro Rivers, British and American planning staffs in London and Washington continued a debate that would prove to be among their most acrimonious during the war and would affect

---

[2] Unless otherwise indicated, the discussion on Allied strategy is based upon the following publications: Field Marshal, the Viscount Alexander of Tunis, *Despatch*, 19 Apr 47, published as "The Allied Armies in Italy from 3 September 1943, to 12 December 1944," in the *Supplement to The London Gazette* of 6 June 1950 (hereafter cited as Alexander *Despatch*); Maurice Matloff, *Strategic Planning for Coalition Warfare, 1943–44*, UNITED STATES ARMY IN WORLD WAR II (Washington, 1959); and John Ehrman, "History of the Second World War, United Kingdom Series," Vols. V and VI, *Grand Strategy* (London: Her Majesty's Stationery Office, 1956).

all planning for operations in Italy until late 1944. The basic issue was whether exploiting the Italian campaign to the Alps and possibly beyond (essentially the British position) or landing on the southern coast of France with a subsequent advance up the Rhone Valley (basically the American position) would best assist the main Allied enterprise: the cross-Channel invasion of northwestern France.

The question was debated at the SEXTANT–EUREKA Conference in Cairo and Teheran in November–December 1943. Although the conference yielded a victory for the American view that OVERLORD and ANVIL were to be the main Allied tasks for 1944, the British left Cairo convinced that the Americans had also agreed to turn Operation ANVIL into something more elastic that would not seriously affect the campaign under way in Italy.[3]

To the Americans the decisions made at Cairo and Teheran meant that, in addition to remaining a secondary operation (or even tertiary, considering ANVIL), the Italian campaign would also be governed by a limited objective strategy—attainment of the so-called Pisa-Rimini Line, a position considerably short of the Po Valley and the towering Julian and Karawanken Alps, toward which the British continued to direct their gaze and their hopes. The American view reflected a long-held conviction that the Allies should concentrate on driving along the most direct route into the heart of the Third Reich rather than on nibbling away at enemy forces

with a series of peripheral operations of indeterminate length that could deflect Allied strength from the main thrust.

Yet, as is so often the case, the fortunes of battle would force modification of the carefully contrived international agreements. For when it appeared in late March that the Allied armies could not reach Rome before early June, the British and American high commands agreed than an ANVIL concurrent with OVERLORD was impracticable. The American Joint Chiefs of Staff reluctantly acknowledged that to open a new front—ANVIL—in the Mediterranean before the issue in Italy had been decided would be risky, difficult, and perhaps impossible. They also recognized the advantages of a strengthened OVERLORD. Those could be realized only at the expense of ANVIL. Bowing to the inevitable, the JCS on 24 March agreed to postpone ANVIL and to transfer from the Mediterranean to OVERLORD all the amphibious means beyond that required for a one-division lift. But the specter of ANVIL had not been effectively exorcized and would continue to haunt the planning staffs of the Allied armies' headquarters in Italy for months to come.

German Strategy

Controversy over strategy also afflicted the German High Command. A lengthy debate over whether to defend the Italian peninsula south of Rome along its narrowest part or along a more extended line in the Northern Apennines had finally been resolved by the German head of state, Adolf Hitler, in favor of the advocate of the first proposition, Generalfeldmarschall Albert Kesselring, a former *General der*

[3] Matloff, *Strategic Planning for Coalition Warfare, 1943-44*, pp. 378–387. See also Arthur Bryant, *Triumph in the West* (New York: Doubleday, 1959), p. 77.

Flieger who had been promoted to the
rank of field marshal in 1940 immediately after the armistice with France.
Although Kesselring harbored no illusions about holding the Allies indefinitely below Rome, he reasoned that an
Allied breakthrough south of Rome
would be less disastrous than one in the
Northern Apennines into the Po Valley
and the agricultural and industrial
heartland of Italy. [4] Furthermore,
strong German forces in Central Italy
might discourage or thwart an Allied
amphibious operation across the Adriatic and into the Balkans, from which
the Germans drew critical supplies of
raw materials for their industry. These
forces would also keep Allied air bases
in Italy farther away from Germany.

The Germans would adhere to the
decision to hold the front south of
Rome as long as militarily possible. Not
even the establishment of the Anzio
beachhead and the failure of the Germans to drive the Allies back into the
sea prompted Hitler or Kesselring to
change this strategy, even though the
beachhead seriously threatened the
Germans' defensive lines across the
waist of the peninsula farther south.

As the first signs of spring came to
Italy in 1944, few on the German side
could deny that the high tide of German arms had already started to ebb,
but Adolf Hitler refused to read the

FIELD MARSHAL KESSELRING

portents. Still in possession of most of
the European continent, he firmly resolved to defend it, even though he
knew that the Allies had yet to commit
the bulk of their forces. German armies
were not only to defend the interior of
Fortress Europe, but also all its outlying
peninsulas and islands.

Given Hitler's resolve, the Armed
Forces Operation Staff (*Wehrmachtfuehrungsstab, WFSt*) had little choice but to
accept the German situation early in
1944 as one of strategic defense along
interior lines but without the advantages that normally stem from interior
lines. The numerous unengaged Allied
forces in the Mediterranean, the Near
and Far East, Africa, the United Kingdom, Iceland, and the United States
could be, the Germans believed, committed at any time against the periph-

---

[4] Italian industry, centered largely in the north,
in mid-June 1944 accounted for about 15 percent
of the total German-controlled armaments output.
See the following Foreign Military Studies, pre-
pared by former German officers from 1945–54:
Production after September 1943, MS # D–003;
Activities of German Chief of Military Economy in
Italy, 1941–45, MS # D–029; German Use of Italian
Munitions Industry, MS # D–015. Filed in Modern
Military Branch, National Archives and Records
Service.

ery of Europe and forced the Germans to keep reserves spread thinly over the entire Continent.[5]

Competition for reinforcements among the various theaters of operations, particularly from the German Army High Command (*Oberkommando des Heeres*, OKH) for new divisions to stem the advance of the Red Army on the Eastern Front, came to a head about 1 April 1944. Hitler reacted by directing the Armed Forces High Command (*Oberkommando der Wehrmacht*, OKW) to prepare a study showing the location, strength, mobility, organization, and composition of all German military forces. The study disclosed that the western theaters had a total of forty-one divisions sufficiently trained and equipped to fight in the east. Of these, twenty were already committed on the various defensive fronts and twenty-one were being held in general reserve behind the invasion-threatened northwest coastal regions of Europe. No economy of force could be achieved by a general retirement elsewhere or by evacuating offshore positions, since such movements would involve establishing long and more vulnerable land fronts that would require even larger defensive forces. [6]

The Germans clearly had no alternative to a wholly defensive strategy throughout 1944. Only by practicing the utmost economy could the German command manage to husband forces that could be shifted from one theater to another in case of unexpected emergencies. The *Wehrmachtfuehrungsstab* (*WFSt*) realized that Germany had to pin its hopes on the accomplishment of a more formidable objective: "While stubbornly defending every foot of ground in the East, we must beat off the impending invasion in the West as well as all possible secondary landings in other theaters. Then, with the forces released by this victory, we can recover the initiative and force a decision in the war." [7] This was a rational strategy but given Hitler's decision to attempt to defend Italy south of Rome, a strategy unlikely to succeed.

Allied Command and Organization

When General Dwight D. Eisenhower left the Mediterranean Theater in December 1943 to become Allied commander in northwestern Europe, General Sir Henry Maitland Wilson assumed command of Allied Forces in the theater. Experience in the diplomatic and military fields as Middle East commander made Wilson an excellent choice for a theater with troops of many nationalities and where delicate relationships with several neutral nations were involved. For example, the British Chiefs of Staff had hopes of eventually bringing Turkey into the war, but it was important to keep Axis-oriented Spain out of it. There were

---

[5] Information in this section, unless otherwise noted, is based upon *Oberkommando der Wehrmachtfuehrungsstab, Kriegstagebuch (OKW/WFSt, KTB), Ausarbeitung, die OKW-Kriegsschauplaetze im Rahmen der Gesamtkriegsfuehrung*, 1.I–31.III.44, vols. IV(1), IV(2), edited by Helmuth Greiner and Percy Ernst Schramm (Frankfurt a/Main: Bernard and Graefe, 1961), (hereafter cited as Greiner and Schramm, eds., *OKW/WFSt, KTB*).

[6] *Ibid.*, pp. 56–57. According to General Walter Warlimont, deputy chief of the OKW operations staff, distribution of this study was canceled for security reasons.

[7] Greiner and Schramm, eds., *OKW/WFSt, KTB*, pp. 56–57.

also. partisan movements to be sustained in the Balkans.

Wilson's deputy was Lt. Gen. Jacob L. Devers, the senior American officer who also served as Commanding General, North African Theater of Operations, U.S. Army (NATOUSA), later changed to Mediterranean Theater (MTOUSA). Maj. Gen. Thomas B. Larkin was Commander of Services of Supply, MTOUSA, and responsible for the logistical services to the U.S. Army elements in the theater, while logistical support of the British forces in Italy was the responsibility of Allied Armies in Italy (AAI) headquarters. British logistical functions in rear areas were exercised by Headquarters, North African District. Both Allied logistical systems furnished support for the various national contingents under Allied command in the theater.

In over-all command of the Allied ground forces in Italy was General Sir Harold R. L. G. Alexander, whose conduct of the British retreat in Burma had led Prime Minister Churchill, after Alexander's return from the Far East, to make him Commander in Chief of the British forces in the Near East. During the Allied campaign in Tunisia, in 1943, Alexander had become Eisenhower's deputy. [8]

The British contingent of the AAI, the Eighth Army, was commanded by Lt. Gen. Sir Oliver Leese, who early in World War II served with distinction as head of the British 30 Corps in the

GENERAL WILSON

North African campaign. In sharp contrast to General Leese's outwardly casual manner was the vigor and intensity of Lt. Gen. Mark W. Clark, who since January 1943 had led the American contingent, the U.S. Fifth Army. Clark enjoyed the unique opportunity of having organized and trained the army he commanded through many months of combat. A former instructor at the Army War College, Clark had served as Chief of Staff of the Army Ground Forces. In June 1942 he went to England to command the U.S. II Corps, and the next month he took command of the U.S. Army Ground Forces in the European Theater of Operations. He left that post in October to become Deputy Commander, Allied Forces in North Africa, under Eisenhower.

General Clark's chief of staff, Maj. Gen. Alfred M. Gruenther, had come to London in August 1942 as deputy to Eisenhower's own chief of staff, Maj.

---

[8] Alexander had commanded the British 18th Army Group in North Africa, 18 Feb 43–15 May 43. On Sicily and in Italy his headquarters was known as 15th Army Group, 10 Jul 43–11 Jan 44; Allied Forces in Italy, 11–18 Jan 44; Allied Central Mediterranean Force, 18 Jan–9 Mar 44; and Allied Armies in Italy (AAI), 9 Mar–12 Dec 44.

GENERALS LEESE, ALEXANDER, AND CLARK

Gen. Walter Bedell Smith. Gruenther continued to hold that position when Eisenhower moved to North Africa. In January 1943 at Clark's request he was assigned to head the Fifth Army staff. As his operations officer, Clark had picked a close friend and long-time associate, Col. Donald W. Brann, formerly chief of staff of the 95th Infantry Division.

Lt. Gen. Ira C. Eaker, a former commander of the Eighth U.S. Air Force in the United Kingdom, was Commander in Chief of the Mediterranean Allied Air Forces (MAAF). British Air Marshal Sir John Slessor was his deputy and commander of all British air formations in the theater. [9]

For operations, Eaker's forces were divided into three Anglo-American commands: the Mediterranean Allied Tactical Air Forces (MATAF), under Maj. Gen. John K. Cannon, who also commanded the U.S. Twelfth Air Force; the Mediterranean Allied Coastal Air Force (MACAF), under Air Vice Marshal Sir Hugh P. Lloyd; and the Mediterranean Allied Strategic Air Force (MASAF), under Maj. Gen. Nathan F. Twining, who also commanded the U.S. Fifteenth Air Force. General Cannon's tactical command comprised the U.S. Twelfth Air Force (less elements assigned to the MACAF) and the British Desert Air Force (DAF). Eaker's operational control of the MASAF was limited in that Twining's primary operational responsibility lay with the U.S. Strategic Air Force, based in England under the command of Lt. Gen. Carl Spaatz. Allied naval forces in the Mediterranean theater remained throughout the campaign under the command of Admiral Sir John Cunningham with the senior American naval officer being Admiral H. Kent Hewitt, also the commander of the U.S. Eighth Fleet.

Once primary American attention and resources shifted to the cross-Channel attack, and the Mediterranean thea-

GENERAL GRUENTHER

ter came under a British commander in January 1944, the CCS placed the theater under the executive direction of the British Chiefs of Staff. Thus General Wilson was responsible to the Combined Chiefs through the British Chiefs of Staff, an arrangement that would give the British Prime Minister greater opportunity to intervene in the shaping of strategy for the theater.

The Germans

In May 1944 all German-occupied territory in central Italy was nominally under the control of Generalfeldmarschall Albert Kesselring. His appointment as Commander in Chief, Southwest (*Oberbefehlshaber, Suedwest*), had been an attempt to create a joint com-

---

[9] History AFHQ, Part III, pp. 652–53.

mand similar to those in other theaters controlled by the Armed Forces High Command (*Oberkommando der Wehrmacht,* OKW). Kesselring was responsible to the OKW through the Armed Forces Operation Staff (*Wehrmachtfuehrungsstab,* WFSt) for operations and nominally had full tactical authority over all units of the Army, Navy, Luftwaffe, and *Waffen-SS* in Italy. The *Naval Command, Italy* and the *Luftflotte II,* senior naval and air commands in the theater, were not, however, unequivocally under Kesselring's command and remained directly subordinate to their service chiefs in Germany. Only in the event of "imminent danger" to the strategic situation would Kesselring's orders be binding on these two commands, and in such an event Kesselring was to keep the naval and Luftwaffe headquarters in Germany constantly informed of his actions.[10] Actually, Kesselring's prestige as the senior Luftwaffe officer in Italy and his close personal relations with the naval commander, Vice Adm. Wilhelm Meendsen-Bohlken, enabled the field marshal to secure the full support of both headquarters without ever having to invoke his powers under the "imminent danger" clause.[11]

Kesselring's other title, commander of *Army Group C,* provided him with command over a conventional entity in the administration, training, and supply hierarchy of the German Army. In this capacity he reported directly to the Army High Command (*Oberkommando des Heeres,* OKH).[12]

In the spring of 1944 Kesselring had under his over-all command the *Tenth Army,* at the main front, led by Generaloberst' Heinrich Gottfried von Vietinghoff, genannt Scheel, and at Anzio the *Fourteenth Army* under Generaloberst Eberhard von Mackensen, and the provisional *Armee Abteilung von Zangen,* a rear-area catchall organization in northern Italy built around the *LXXVII Corps* headquarters and named for its commander, General der Infanterie Gustav von Zangen. Its unconventional composition sprang from a dual function as a reservoir for replacements and theater reserves and as the responsible agency in its sector for coast-watching, construction of rear area defenses, and antipartisan warfare.

As with any drama, whether historical or theatrical, the setting is one of the key elements in its development. For over two millennia Italy's boot-shaped peninsula has provided a colorful and challenging stage for historical drama. The peninsula's uniqueness lies partly in the variety and challenging

---

[10] The order containing Kesselring's appointment as Commander in Chief, Southwest, and the delineation of his authority, dated 6 November 1943, may be found in English translation in ONI. Fueher Directives, 1943–45, p. 103.

[11] MS # C–064 (Kesselring), p. 35.

[12] OKW was, in certain respects, nominally superior to the three branch high commands: Army, Luftwaffe, and Navy. The OKW was responsible through its chief, Generalfeldmarschall Wilhelm Keitel, to Adolf Hitler in his capacity as Commander in Chief of the German Armed Forces. During the period covered by this volume, however, Hitler also held the position of Commander in Chief of the Army. Staff functions affecting military operations were, moreover, divided horizontally and geographically between the OKW and the nominally lower-level OKH. Concerning Italy, for example, the chief of the WFSt of OKW, rather than the chief of staff of OKH, was Hitler's chief adviser for operations. See MSS #'s T–101 (Winter *et al.*), The German Armed Forces High Command, and T–111 (Halder *et al.*), The German High Command, both in CMH.

nature of terrain surpassing anything the Allied armies would encounter in northwestern Europe during World War II.

When staff officers at Allied Mediterranean headquarters studied the maps of Italy, they noted, as had other commanders since Hannibal's day, that the peninsula's most striking geographic feature is the high, rugged Apennine mountain chain which divides the country into three rather clearly defined compartments—the eastern coastal plain, the central mountain region, and the western coastal plain.

The eastern coastal region is a narrow, largely treeless plain bordering the Adriatic Sea and extending northward approximately 200 miles from the Gargano peninsula, the spur of the Italian boot, to the Po Valley. In the summer the entire region is dry and dusty, and in winter frequent rains turn much of it into a vast quagmire. The coast is generally low and sandy, fringed by lagoons and backed by the narrow plains from which rise deeply scarred hills. Along the plain run only one main highway and one railroad, as well as a negligible number of fair secondary roads. From the plain a series of flat-top ridges extend westward into the Central Apennines. These ridges are separated by numerous streams flowing through narrow, steep-sided alluvial valleys that cut across the Allies' projected axis of advance. This configuration would make large-scale deployment of tracked and wheeled vehicles off the roads almost impossible, and was only one of several drawbacks that had eliminated the east coast from consideration by Allied planners as the major area of effort for the spring offensive.

The Central Appenines, which by their size and sharply folded structure largely determine the shape and form the backbone of the peninsula, consist of numerous parallel ridges alternating with flat-bottomed valleys, all running in a northwest-southeasterly direction. The upper courses of the Tiber and Arno Rivers flow through the broad, alluvial valleys parallel to these ridges before cutting narrow canyons through the mountains and turning westward to the sea. The ridges are not continuous but are interrupted by deep transverse water gaps and by prominent saddles several thousand feet below crest elevation. In the Central Apennines the highest point is the Gran Sasso d'Italia (9,583 feet high). Southward the peaks gradually decrease to approximately 3,000 feet in the vicinity of Benevento, about thirty miles northeast of Naples. The lower slopes of the mountains are usually terraced and planted with vineyards and with citrus and olive groves, while the upper slopes generally support a thin cover of evergreen or scrub oak.

Within this central mountain region rugged heights and deep ravines severely restrict cross-country movement. As with the east coast corridor, only one railroad and one highway run through the area, thus presenting a formidable obstacle to east-west movement of any military significance. South of a line running from Rome northeast to Pescara, four good roads enter the mountains from the east, but only two continue on to the western half of the country. Furthermore, all roads are flanked by high, rugged terrain and can easily be blocked by demolitions or defended by small forces. Narrow and tortuous with very steep gradients, the roads are frequently blocked by landslides during the rainy season and in winter by snow. North of the Rome-Pescara line, roads crossing the Apennines are more frequent, but they cross even higher passes and from mid-December to mid-March are often blocked by heavy snows. Military operations in this region would require units well trained in mountain warfare, which were in short supply among the Allied forces in Italy.

The grim logic of the inhospitable terrain left Allied commanders little choice in their selection of sites for major military operations—the peninsula's western half, including the Liri valley and the coastal plain. Although the western coastal plain shares many of the disadvantages of the other regions, from the Allied point of view it was the most favorable of the three, for its long, exposed left flank could easily be turned by Allied sea power. The plain extends northwestward 100 miles from the mouth of the Garigliano River to San Severo, a small port about twenty miles west of Rome. Less than a mile wide at its northern and southern extremities, the plain broadens to a maximum of eight miles along the lower Tiber. At the foot of the Alban Hills just south of Rome lie the Pontine Marshes. Crisscrossed with drainage ditches and irrigation canals, the region, although seeming to offer a favorable maneuver area for military forces, was actually quite unfavorable for the deployment of wheeled or tracked vehicles on a wide front. South of the marshes to the lower reaches of the Garigliano River, the coastal plain resembles the 20-mile stretch northwest of

Rome in that it offers more favorable terrain for the deployment of armored formations than do the Pontine Marshes.

Another major geographic feature of the region west of the Central Apennines is the Liri valley, which also offers a favorable route into central Italy and Rome. The gateway to this valley, leading through the mountains southeast of Rome, lies at the junction of the Liri and the Garigliano and Rapido Rivers. In 1944 the Germans had closed this gateway with a series of formidable defensive positions across the Liri valley and anchored on both flanks by two great mountain bastions, Monte Majo and Monte Cassino. Located south of the valley, Monte Majo rises to approximately 3,000 feet and sends steep-sided spurs into the Liri valley. To the north the vast bulk of the Monte Cairo massif, southernmost peak of a great spur of the Central Apennines, towers to a height of 5,000 feet. From the summit of this mountain a ridge thrusts southwestward, terminating abruptly in Monte Cassino. The Allied commander in Italy, General Alexander, had long believed Monte Cassino to be the key to the gateway leading into the Liri valley. Before this gateway, like a moat beneath a castle wall, flows the Rapido. Throughout the winter of 1943–44 the U.S. Fifth Army had tried in vain to blast open this gate. Now once again Alexander turned his attention toward a new strategic concept which this time he hoped would lead the Allies into the Liri valley and place them irresistibly on the road to Rome.

Rome, the immediate objective of the Allied armies in Italy, lies in a gap carved through a range of hills that separate the upper Tiber basin from the sea. North of the city rise the Sabatini Mountains; south of it, the Alban Hills. This was the region of Latium, cradle of the ancient Roman republic.

The western half of the peninsula is also well served by a network of good roads, particularly in the vicinity of Rome, to which, for many centuries, all roads in Italy have led. In the coastal corridor the roads cross numerous stream beds, many of which are either dry or easily forded during the summer, but in winter and early spring often become raging torrents. Elsewhere the roads frequently pass through narrow defiles, providing ideal sites for demolitions and mines, something at which the Germans were particularly adept.

In this region numerous villages nestled in the valleys, sprawled along the main roads, or perched like miniature fortresses on the hilltops. Solidly built of native stone, the latter villages provided excellent observation points as well as cover for troops.

The mountainous terrain, the narrow, twisting roads, the intensively cultivated plains and valleys all combined to compartmentalize the countryside and relegate armor largely to the role of self-propelled artillery in support of the infantry. Already in the advance to the banks of the Sangro and Rapido Rivers the Allies had experienced, but not yet fully mastered, the difficulties peculiar to fighting over this kind of terrain. The greatest problem was searching out a skillfully camouflaged enemy, who frequently withheld his fire until the last moment. Whereas the attacker might readily ascertain that an orange grove or vineyard harbored enemy troops, it was generally impossible to determine their exact location and strength without actually entering the area and risking heavy losses. After several costly encounters, the Allies had adopted the tactic of backing off and battering the suspected area with artillery or mortar fire before moving in to mop up, yet this was slow and costly in terms of matériel. Since deployment off the roads was often difficult and frequently impossible, and since the enemy used demolitions, mines, and ambush cunningly, the tactical problem of keeping losses to a minimum while advancing along the roads would be one of the most difficult and persistent encountered by the Allied forces throughout the entire campaign.

CHAPTER II

Preparing for a New Offensive

The German Defenses

The Germans had closed the gateway to the Liri valley with formidable defenses along two lines, or, more properly, zones, that they had constructed across the peninsula from Ortona on the Adriatic to the mouth of the Garigliano River on the Tyrrhenian Sea. One of these two lines the Germans had named Gustav.[1] Crossing Italy at its narrowest, the line incorporated some of the best defensive terrain on the peninsula. It extended almost a hundred miles northward to the Adriatic coast, which it reached at a point some two miles northwest of Ortona.[2]

The most heavily fortified part of the Gustav Line was the central sector, opposite the Eighth Army. Anchored on Monte Cairo, the 5,415-foot summit of the mountain massif forming the Liri valley's northern wall, this sector of the Gustav Line followed the high ground southeast to Monte Cassino, then ran south along the west banks of the Rapido and Gari Rivers across the entrance to the Liri valley and a terminus on the southern slopes of Monte Majo.[3] From Monte Majo's eastern foothills the line continued south of the village of Castelforte, where it turned southwestward along high ground north of Minturno and thence on to the sea.

With steep banks and swift-flowing current the Rapido was a formidable obstacle, and the Germans had supplemented this river barrier with numerous fieldworks. Along the river's west bank stretched a thick and continuous network of wire, minefields, pillboxes, and concrete emplacements. Between the Rapido and the Cassino-Sant'Angelo road, the Germans had dug many slit trenches, some designed to accommodate no more than a machine gun and its crew, others to take a section or even a platoon.

The entire fortified zone was covered by German artillery and mortar fire, given deadly accuracy by observers located on the mountainsides north and south of the Liri valley. Allied forward observers and intelligence officers estimated that there were about 400 enemy guns and rocket launchers located

---

[1] Phonetic designation for the letter "G" in German alphabet.

[2] MS # T-1a (Westphal *et al.*), CMH; Situation map, 7-10 May 44, *AOK 10, KTB, Lagekarten, 4-20.V.44.*

[3] Considerable confusion appears to have existed during these and earlier operations as to which stream was the Rapido and which the Gari. Based upon a 1:25,000 map of Italy, the Gari, beginning just south of Cassino town, meets the Rapido flowing from Sant'Elia through Villa, making a bend to the east of Cassino about a mile north of Sant'Angelo. It is doubtful whether the map is accurate, since a stream flows through Cassino town. Therefore, since "rapido" could approximately be applied to either stream and the current of both is extremely fast, the author has chosen the name Rapido to designate the major river in the area.

north of Highway 6 in the vicinity of the villages of Atina and Belmonte, respectively, nine and six miles north of Cassino. Of these the British believed that about 230 could fire into the Cassino sector, and about 150 could fire in support of the defenders of Monte Cassino and Cassino town.

Opposite the Fifth Army sector, however, only a small portion of the Gustav Line was still a part of the defensive positions that the Germans had selected in the autumn of 1943, for south of the Liri valley the front followed a line where the British 10 Corps had established a bridgehead beyond the Garigliano during the winter fighting. This meant that in some areas facing the Fifth Army the Germans were holding a defensive line not of their own choosing and that in some sectors (the French, for example) the Allies rather than the Germans possessed high ground overlooking the enemy positions. [4]

The Gustav Line was a zone of mutually supporting firing positions—a string of pearls, Kesselring called them. While those sectors of the line located in the Liri valley and along the coastal corridor were relatively deep defensive zones, ranging from 100 to 3,000 yards in depth, those in the mountains were much thinner, partly because the rocky terrain made it extremely difficult to dig or build heavier defenses, but mainly because the local German commanders doubted that the Allies, unable to use armor and artillery there, would choose to attack through such forbid-

ding terrain. In any event, an attack over the mountains, they believed, would be relatively easy to stop. [5]

Except for barbed wire, railroad ties, and steel rails, the materials used in constructing the Gustav Line positions were readily obtainable on the site. Whenever possible the Germans utilized the numerous stone houses of the region as shelters or firing positions. Locating machine guns or an antitank gun in the cellar, enemy troops piled crushed stone and rubble on the ground floor to provide overhead protection. If bombs or shells destroyed the upper part of the house, the additional rubble would simply reinforce this cover. Allied troops would frequently fail to detect these cellar positions, sometimes not until hours after a position had been overrun and the Germans had opened fire on the rear and flanks of the assaulting troops.

Firing positions for infantry weapons were mostly open but usually connected by trenches to covered personnel shelters. The shelters ranged from simple dugouts covered with a layer of logs and earth to elaborate rooms hewn out of solid rock, the latter often used as command posts or signal installations. Invariably well camouflaged, most infantry shelters were covered with rocks, earth, logs, railway ties, or steel rails.

Behind the Gustav Line the Germans had constructed the other defensive zone—the *Fuehrer Riegel*, or the Hitler

---

[4] Situation map, 7–10 May 44, *AOK 10, KTB, Lagekarten, 4–20.V.44.*

[5] MS # C–064 (Kesselring); MS # C–071 (Vietinghoff *et al.*). Unless otherwise cited the following section is based upon these references. See also Engr Rpt w/atchd map, 13 Apr 44, in files, *XIV Panzer Corps, 1a/Nr. 211/44 g.Kdos, KTB, Anlagen 1.IV–30.IV.44.*

Line.[6] This line lay from five to ten miles behind the Gustav Line. Beginning on the Tyrrhenian coast near Terracina, twenty-six miles northwest of the mouth of the Garigliano and the southern gateway to the Anzio beachhead, the Hitler Line crossed the mountains overlooking the coastal highway and the Itri-Pico road from the northwest and west, and thence the Liri valley via Pontecorvo and Aquino to anchor at Piedimonte San Germano on the southern slope of the Monte Cairo massif. Although essentially a switch position, as its name implied, the line was made up of fieldworks similar to those in the Gustav Line and was, at least in the Liri valley sector, as strong as or, in some instances, even stronger than the latter.

Manning the German defense system on the southern front was the equivalent of about nine divisions. One of these was in reserve; the remainder were divided among two regular and one provisional corps headquarters. All were under the command of the *Tenth Army*. The *XIV Panzer Corps*, commanded by Generalleutnant Fridolin von Senger und Etterlin, held a sector of the Gustav Line extending from the Tyrrhenian coast across the Aurunci Mountains to the Liri and a junction with General der Gebirgstruppen (General of Mountain Troops) Valentin Feuerstein's *LI Mountain Corps*. Along

the panzer corps' front were the *94th Infantry Division* in the coastal sector, and the *71st Infantry Division* in the Petrella massif. A composite *Kampfgruppe* made up of a regimental group detached from the *305th Infantry Division* and a regiment from the *15th Panzer Grenadier Division* lay between the *71st Division* and the Liri River. The remainder of the *15th Panzer Grenadier Division* was in corps reserve and watching the coast.[7]

In the *LI Mountain Corps* sector the *44th Infantry (H u. D) Division*[8] manned the valley positions, and the elite *1st Parachute Division* continued to hold the Monte Cassino sector, including the town of Cassino. In the mountains north of the Monte Cairo massif the *5th Mountain Division* and the *144th Jaeger Division* held the corps' left wing to a junction with Generalleutnant Friedrich Wilhelm Hauck's provisional corps, *Group Hauck*. The latter held a quiet sector about eight miles southeast of the Pescara River on the Adriatic coast with the *305th* and the *334th Infantry Divisions* and the *114th Jaeger Division* in reserve. In front of the Allied beachhead at Anzio lay the *Fourteenth Army* with its five divisions divided between the *I Parachute Corps* and the *LXXVI Panzer Corps*. One of these five divisions was located along the coast northwest of Rome as a precaution against an Allied amphibious landing attempt.

As a mobile strategic reserve under *Army Group C's* control, Kesselring held

---

[6] Colloquially, the German word *Riegel* means the bar of a door; in military parlance it is generally used in the combination *Riegelstellung* which is best translated as "switch position." When the Allied threat to the *Fuehrer Riegel* increased, the Germans renamed it the *Senger Riegel* after General Fridolin von Senger und Etterlin, commander of the *XIV Panzer Corps*, through whose sector a major portion of the line ran.

[7] As the *15th Panzer Division*, this unit had been destroyed in Tunisia. It had been reconstituted as the *15th Panzer Grenadier Division* in Sicily.

[8] The designation H u. D refers to an honorary title given the division: *Reichsgrenadierdivision "Hoch und Deutschmeister."*

the *3d* and *90th Panzer Grenadier Divisions* and the *26th Panzer Division* in the vicinity of Rome, and, some thirty miles to the north near Viterbo, the *29th Panzer Grenadier Division*. In northern Italy, serving mainly as a coast defense force, was *Army Group von Zangen,* consisting of the *162d (Turkomen) Infantry Division,* the *356th Infantry Division,* the *278th Infantry Division,* and the *188th Mountain Division,* none of which were first-rate units. Except for von Zangen's group, all of the reserve divisions were first-rate and could, if committed soon enough, have an important influence on the outcome of the fighting. Yet their dispositions, partly determined by Kesselring's reaction to Allied deception plans, made it unlikely that they could, or would, be able to reach the southern front in time to influence the tide of battle. For the most part, however, Kesselring's veteran divisions were located in defensive zones well sited in relation to terrain that favored the defense. If properly manned, the Gustav and Hitler Lines well merited Kesselring's confidence that the gateway to the Liri valley and to Rome was reasonably secure.

Alexander's Concept

To open the gateway, Alexander laid before his army and corps commanders, on 22 February 1944, guidelines for a co-ordinated attack by the British Eighth and the U.S. Fifth Armies. In the first battle for Rome, which had lasted from January to March, the American Fifth Army had carried the burden of the main effort at Monte Cassino and along the Garigliano River. This time General Alexander had de-

cided that it would be the Eighth Army's responsibility to accomplish what the Fifth had failed to do, break through the enemy's defenses into the Liri valley and lead a drive to the line Civitavecchia-Viterbo-Terni north of Rome.

On the Eighth Army's left, between the Liri River and the Tyrrhenian coast, the Fifth Army was to attack through the Aurunci Mountains and along the coast. That part of the Fifth Army in the Anzio beachhead was to burst forth from the confines of the beachhead and push back the German *Fourteenth Army* in order to cut off and destroy the right wing of the German *Tenth Army* as it fell back from the main attack along the southern front.[9]

Behind this concept lay General Alexander's conviction, based upon unusually good intelligence of the enemy's strength and dispositions, that the Liri valley, at the foot of the western margin of the Central Apennines, and the Anzio beachhead on the western coastal plain provided the only satisfactory areas for major offensive operations wherein he could effectively utilize Allied air and armored superiority. The central sector facing the Liri valley, which until March had been held by General Clark's Fifth Army, was now assigned to General Leese's Eighth Army, while Clark's Army was shifted to a relatively narrow sector between the Liri valley and the Tyrrhenian Sea.

---

[9] Memo, Alexander to Wilson, 22 Feb 44, Future Operations in Italy, AFHQ microfilm, Job 10–A, reel 1–c, G–3 Plans/20, Italy Opns Policy; ACMP Appreciation No. 1, 22 Feb 44, AFHQ film, Job 47–B, reel 156–G, Ph/9, Post Husky Administration & Maintenance; Opn. Order #1, Hqs. AAI, 5 May 1944. See also W.G.F. Jackson, *The Battle for Italy* (New York: Harper and Row, 1967), p. 223.

Clark also retained command of the Anzio beachhead.

The source of the extraordinarily good intelligence that supported General Alexander's conviction arose from a fortuitous circumstance that had led eventually to the breaking of the Germans' major operational code. Since early 1940 the British had been deciphering and reading the Germans' Enigma Code—the code by which all major command radio traffic was sent. The advantages this gave the Allies in the North African campaign moved General Alexander to remark in 1943 that "the knowledge not only of the enemy's precise strength and disposition but also how, when, and where he intends to carry out his operations has brought a new dimension into the prosecution of the war." Planning for the spring offensive, therefore, would take place under the most favorable circumstances for the Allied command. Unknown to the Germans, every major radio message to and from the OKW and OKH to Kesselring's army group and his two field armies was deciphered within minutes of its transmission and then relayed via special liaison units, attached to army groups and field armies, to the commanders and the relatively few officers on their staffs privy to the secret.[10]

After the failure of an Allied assault on Monte Cassino in February, General Alexander had concluded that he would have to develop a local superiority of at least three to one in infantry in order to have a reasonable chance of

breaking through the enemy's defenses. To achieve this superiority in the critical Liri valley sector, he had ordered major regrouping of Allied forces on 5 March. For ease in administration and supply, all British-equipped divisions, which included Dominion, Indian, and Polish units, would be brought into the Eighth Army, and all American-equipped divisions would remain in the Fifth Army. Thinning out the eastern sector of the front from the Central Apennines to the Adriatic, Alexander gave responsibility for the entire Adriatic sector to the British 5 Corps, under direct command of Headquarters, AAI.[11]

While these changes were being made, the Mediterranean Allied Tactical Air Force (MATAF) began, on 19 March, a large-scale interdiction operation against German rail, road, and sea communications throughout an area from the so-called Pisa-Rimini Line to the southern battlefront. Appropriately designated STRANGLE, the operation was designed to choke off the enemy's supplies during the period preceding the spring offensive. By the end of March all rail lines from Rome to the southern front were cut off. North of Rome rail traffic was generally unable to approach closer than within 125 miles of the capital. This program of interdiction was to be continued

---

[10] Quoted in F.W. Winterbotham, *The Ultra Secret* (London: Weidenfeld and Nicholson, 1974), p. 187.

[11] Operations of British, Indian, and Dominion Forces in Italy, 3 September 1943 to 2 May 1945, Part II, The Campaign in Central Italy, 26 March to 10 August 1944, Sec. B, Eighth Army Advance to Rome, British Historical Section, Central Mediterranean, copy in Military History Research Collection, Carlisle, Pa.; *Fifth Army History,* Part V, *The Drive to Rome* (Florence, Italy: L'Impronta Press, 1945), p.2.

LIRI VALLEY

through the first day of DIADEM, the code name of the Allied offensive.[12]

A Cover Plan

To conceal the large-scale shifting of divisions behind the Allied front, the AAI staff devised a cover and deception plan designated NUNTON. Its purpose was to confuse the enemy on the location of the forthcoming Allied of-

fensive—to come either from the Anzio beachhead or from the southern front—in the hope that Kesselring in his uncertainty would be led to hold his reserves well back from the main front when the attack came.[13]

When in late March it became apparent that the efforts of the New Zealand corps at Cassino had already tipped off the Germans on the importance the Allies attached to the sector west of the Apennines, AAI modified its deception

[12] See Wesley Frank Craven and James Lea Cate, eds., "Army Air Forces in World War II," vol. III, *Europe: Argument to V-E Day* (Chicago: University of Chicago Press, 1951), p. 387 (hereafter cited as Craven and Cate, eds., *AAF III*).

[13] Operations of British, Indian, and Dominion Forces in Italy, Part II, Sec. B.

plan somewhat. Henceforth the plan would attempt to convince the enemy that the Allies intended to launch another amphibious operation, this time in the vicinity of Civitavecchia, some forty miles north of Rome. The surprise achieved by the Anzio operation suggested that the Germans would be specially alert for any sign of a similar operation, and therefore more likely to be taken in by this deception than by indications of a major offensive from the beachhead area. The Germans, the Allied planners hoped, would therefore view the opening of the spring offensive along the Garigliano and Rapido Rivers as a strong demonstration designed to draw their attention from the coastal flank.[14] The scenario for the cover plan called for the two divisions of the 1st Canadian Corps, then in Eighth Army reserve, and the 36th Infantry Division, in Fifth Army reserve, to simulate heavy radio traffic and take other measures to create the impression that they were engaged in amphibious training in the Naples-Salerno area.

Disposition of the Allied Armies

Foul weather and the normal delays attending the shifting of large numbers of troops in mountainous terrain had deferred completion of the regroupment of the two armies until the end of March. At the beginning of April the Eighth Army's sector extended 75 miles northeastward from the southernmost edge of the Liri valley, along a line

from the highest peak of the Maiella, over the summit of the Gran Sasso massif of the Central Apennines, thence to the slopes of the hills overlooking the eastern coastal plain held by the British 5 Corps. General Leese's striking force, the British 13 Corps, commanded by Lt. Gen. Sidney C. Kirkman, held the left of this line astride the Liri valley with four divisions. In army reserve, prepared either to pass through or to enter the corps front, was Maj. Gen. E.L.M. Burns' I Canadian Corps with two infantry divisions and an armored brigade. To the 13th Corps' right and assembled for what was expected to be the final assault against Monte Cassino, was Lt. Gen. Wladyslaw Anders' 2 Polish Corps, also controlling two infantry divisions and an armored brigade— but with this difference, the Polish divisions contained only two brigades. The armored brigade was to support either division. The British 10 Corps, with the equivalent of two divisions, was next in line.

Holding a quiet front across the wild and desolate Central Apennines on the Eighth Army's right wing, Lt. Gen. Sir R.L. McCreery's 10 Corps included a miscellaneous group of units representing the equivalent of four independent brigades, an infantry and an armored division. On the Adriatic flank were veterans of the Tunisian Campaign, the British 5 Corps with two infantry divisions and an armored brigade. This corps was to serve as a containing force and be prepared to follow up any enemy withdrawal.[15]

The U.S. Fifth Army held a relatively narrow front extending 12 miles from a

---

[14] For text of plan, see AAI Opns Plan 53, 18 Apr 44, in Operations of the British, Indian, and Dominion Forces in Italy, Part II, Sec. A, Allied Strategy, App C–2.

[15] Alexander *Despatch*, p. 47.

GENERAL COULTER   GENERAL SLOAN

point just east of the village of Scauri on the Tyrrhenian coast. Curving northward as far as Tremensuoli, the front then ran eastward along a range of hills north of the Garigliano River as far as the town of Minturno. From there the front line continued east through the village of Rufo, northeast across the Ausente valley to a point just southwest of Castelforte about six miles northeast of Minturno, thence east of the Monte Majo massif and across the forward slopes of Monti Turlitto, Juga, and Ornito to the Garigliano. It followed that river's east bank to the interarmy boundary along the southern edge of the Liri valley.

On the left of this front was the U.S. II Corps, commanded by Maj. Gen. Geoffrey Keyes, a cavalryman who had gained considerable experience in armor as deputy to Lt. Gen. George S. Patton, Jr., in North Africa. Keyes had assumed command of the II Corps in Sicily. During April Keyes' corps con-

sisted of two newly arrived infantry divisions—the 85th and 88th, commanded respectively by Maj. Gens. John B. Coulter and John E. Sloan. The arrival of these divisions in Italy was, as General George C. Marshall remarked after the war, "the great psychological turning-point in the building of a battleworthy army." [16] These were the first U.S. divisions to enter combat consisting largely of wartime draftees, making the coming offensive, at least the II Corps' part of it, the first real test of the U.S. Army's wartime training and replacement system. It was particularly fitting that this test be made under General Clark's command, for as G–3 and later as Chief of Staff of the Army Ground Forces in 1942 he had played an important role in the creation of the system. Beginning on 10 April two regiments of the 85th Division assumed responsibility for the left half

---

[16] General Marshall Intervs, 25 Jul 49, in CMH files.

of the Minturno bridgehead, while one regiment of the 88th Division covered the remainder of the corps front to the left boundary of the French-held Monte Juga bridgehead north of the Garigliano.

The French Expeditionary Corps (FEC) on the II Corps' right had been formed in Italy during the previous winter. Armed and equipped in North Africa by the U.S. Army, the FEC was under the command of General Alphonse Juin, Algerian-born graduate of St. Cyr, the French national military academy. [17] During the winter fighting the French corps had incurred 7,836 casualties in an attempt to envelop Monte Cassino from the north. Although the maneuver had failed to bring about the capture of that key position, French mountain troops had amply demonstrated their skill and worth with the capture of Monte Belvedere and Monte Abate. Allied commanders could expect that they would do equally well when faced once again with similar mountainous terrain.

For the first half of April the 4th Moroccan Mountain Division, recently arrived from Corsica, held the entire corps front, while the 2d Moroccan Infantry and 3d Algerian Infantry Divisions rested or engaged in mountain training in the vicinity of Salerno. In the middle of the month the 2d Moroccan Division returned to the front to take over a part of the bridgehead from the 4th Moroccan Division. In the second half of April, Juin's corps also

received the French 1st Motorized Infantry Division, which included many early Free French recruits, who after the fall of France had rallied to the banner of General Charles de Gaulle.

During April three groups of Tabors, totaling about 12,000 men, arrived in Italy from North Africa. The Tabors—units somewhat larger than battalion strength and made up of goums, or companies—were recruited from the mountain tribes of French North Africa. Usually referred to as goumiers, the men were professional soldiers and skilled in mountain warfare. [18]

To control the Tabors, the First Goum Headquarters was attached to FEC on 13 April. By the beginning of May Juin's corps numbered 99,000 officers and men—a formidable organization. Among the reinforcements were sufficient engineers to permit the release of American units previously attached to the FEC. After April only U.S. armor and artillery units, the latter under the command of the 13th Field Artillery Brigade, would still be used in significant numbers in support of Juin's corps. [19]

---

[17] See Marcel Vigneras, *Rearming the French*, THE UNITED STATES ARMY IN WORLD WAR II (Washington, 1957), for the background of the FEC.

[18] A group of Tabors was the equivalent of a battalion; a goum the equivalent of a company. A goumier was a Moroccan irregular soldier, usually recruited from the Berber tribesmen of the Atlas mountains and under the command of French officers and noncommissioned officers. A Tabor usually included a headquarters, one heavy weapons goum, and three goums with a total strength of about 65 officers and NCO's and 859 native NCO's and men, with 247 horses and mules. A group was composed of a headquarters and three Tabors with a total strength of about 3,100. In February 1944 the Goums Moroccains, under the command of Brig. Gen. Augustine Guillaume, was composed of the 1st, 3d, and 4th Groups of Tabors, in all about 10,000 men.

[19] Operating as the French Expeditionary Corps' artillery as long as the corps remained in Italy, the

GENERAL KEYES

GENERAL CRITTENBERGER

In preparation for the coming offensive, the Fifth Army also received some small but important reinforcements for mountain warfare. Two battalions of U.S. pack artillery (75-mm. pack howitzers) and two additional Italian pack mule companies were assigned to the army. The veteran 36th Infantry Division lay in army reserve, recuperating from the bloody battles of the past winter.

Since February, the U.S. VI Corps at Anzio had been commanded by Maj. Gen. Lucian K. Truscott, Jr., former commander of the 3d Infantry Division.

13th Field Artillery Brigade, under the command of Brig. Gen. Carl C. Bank, eventually moved with the French units when they left Italy for southern France, during Operation DRAGOON. From the Mediterranean to the Rhine, the brigade would function as the I French Corps' artillery with both French and American units under its control.

Truscott's corps held the beachhead with five and one-half divisions: the British 1st and 5th, the U.S. 3d, 34th, and 45th Infantry Divisions, and Combat Command A (CCA) of the U.S. 1st Armored Division. In addition to these, Truscott had the 36th Engineer Combat Regiment and the 1st Special Service Force, the latter an elite Canadian-American regiment-sized combat command composed of men trained as parachutists, rangers, and commandos. Truscott had four of his infantry divisions in line and one in reserve along with the armored combat command.

Lt. Gen. Willis D. Crittenberger, commander of the newly arrived IV Corps headquarters, was like his fellow U.S. corps commanders in Italy a former cavalryman. An outstanding instructor at the U.S. Army Command and General Staff College at Fort Leavenworth, Crittenberger had also served as chief of staff of the 1st Armored Division, commanding general of the 2d Armored Division, and later commanding general of the II Armored Corps.

Crittenberger brought the IV Corps headquarters to Italy on 26 March, where for the next seven weeks it would remain in command of the coastal sector near Naples. Because of the relatively narrow army sector Clark would not commit the corps until June, when the VI Corps was withdrawn to take part in the Seventh Army's operation in southern France.

Both Allied armies were multinational in their make-up. The U.S. Fifth Army reflected the wartime coalition of the United States, Britain, and France. The British Eighth Army was even more of a polyglot assemblage. Serving under General Leese's command were soldiers of such diverse nationalities as Polish, Nepalese, Belgian, Greek, Syro-Lebanese, and Yugoslav. Added to this variety were troops from the United Kingdom and the other widespread members of the British Commonwealth—Canada, New Zealand, South Africa, Newfoundland, India, and Ceylon. There were also men from Basutoland, Swaziland, Bechuanastan, as well as from the Seychelles, Mauritius, Rodriques, and West Indian Islands. As a recently announced cobelligerent, Italy also provided a few miscellaneous units. [20]

The manpower strength of the British Eighth Army, including the 5 Corps, totaled some 265,371 officers and men. This was considerably smaller than the 350,276 making up the U.S. Fifth Army and would help account for the somewhat different approaches to tactical problems on the part of the two army commanders. [21]

Planning the Offensive

The code name DIADEM given to the coming offensive of the AAI staff implied that it was expected to be the crowning touch to months of frustrating campaigning by the Fifth and Eighth Armies, respectively, from Salerno and Calabria to the banks of the Rapido and the Sangro. Although the capture of Rome, the first of the two axis capitals, was one of DIADEM's obvious strategic goals, the offensive's real purpose was to keep as many German divisions as possible engaged in Italy as the Mediterranean theater's contribution to OVERLORD—the forthcoming invasion of northwestern France. Just before the spring offensive began, Alexander, in his order of the day, would hint at this connection with the words: "To us in Italy has been given the honor to strike the first blow." [22]

General Alexander, with a record of distinguished service on the western front in World War I, shared the determination of all British authorities, from the Prime Minister on down, to avoid, if at all possible, "the costly

---

[20] Alexander *Despatch* p. 42 and App. E.

[21] Operations of British, Indian, and Dominion Forces in Italy, Part V, Sec. III; *Fifth Army History*, Part V, App. B. Exact over-all, (present for duty) strength figures at any given time are difficult to determine. The figures given are therefore necessarily approximate and give only a basis for comparison with enemy strength figures which are also approximate.

[22] Alexander, Order of the Day, AAI, May 1944.

frontal assaults which had characterized the campaigns of 1915–1918."[23] It was logical for the Allied armies commander in Italy to opt for a strategy that would eschew the concentration of all his forces at one point for one massive onslaught against the enemy's lines. Instead the coming offensive was conceived of in terms of the campaign in North Africa. Drawing upon a boxing analogy which he would frequently employ in the months to come, General Alexander described the coming offensive in terms of a one-two punch, with the Eight and Fifth armies throwing the first punch on the southern front and the Fifth Army's VI Corps following up with the second punch—a left hook from the Anzio beachhead. On the southern front the Eighth Army was to play the major role with a breakthrough into the Liri valley, followed by an advance along the axis of Highway 6 to Valmontone twenty miles southeast of Rome and a junction with the U.S. VI Corps attacking out of the beachhead. From his reading of the Ultra messages Alexander knew that the Valmontone area was a potentially weak point in the Germans' defenses. The Fifth Army was, meanwhile, to turn the southern flank of the enemy's defenses opposite the Eighth Army by securing the Ausonia defile, five miles northwest of Castelforte, extending northward about three miles to the Liri valley, and then advancing four miles to the northwest, via Esperia, to the southern edge of the valley.[24]

General Alexander evidently intended for Valmontone rather than Rome to be the major tactical focal point of the spring offensive, as had been the case in the first battle for Rome in January. Converging on Valmontone, the two Allied armies, Alexander believed, would trap and possibly destroy a major portion of the German *Tenth Army*. His plan to use the Fifth Army reserve, the 36th Infantry Division, either to reinforce the southern front or, on short notice, to move to the beachhead suggests the importance he attached to his "one-two punch" concept.[25]

Planning for Operations in the Liri Valley

For some time it had been apparent, not only to Alexander but also the Eighth Army's staff, that the Liri valley offered the only terrain in the Allied sector where that Army's superiority in artillery, armor, and aircraft could be exploited to best advantage. Moreover the valley offered the shortest and best road to central Italy and to Rome. Along the valley's southern edge runs the river which gives the valley its name. A tributary, the Gari, flows due south for nine miles across the valley's entrance to join the Liri about a mile north of Sant'Ambrogio. A neck of land enclosed by these two rivers, shortly before they join some six miles south of Cassino to form the Garigliano, was called the Liri "appendix" by Allied staff officers. From the tip of the

[23] John Ehrman, "Lloyd George and Churchill as War Ministers," pp. 101–15, in *Transactions of the Royal Historical Society*, Fifth Series, vol. 11 (London, 1961).

[24] See General Alexander's notes for the conference held at AAI headquarters on 2 April 1944, in Operations of British, Indian and Dominion Forces in Italy, 3 Sep 43 to 2 May 45, Part I, The Conquest of Southern Italy, App. B–1.

[25] *Ibid.*

appendix to the road junction of Ceprano, near the junction of the Liri and
Sacco Rivers, the valley is about twenty
miles in length. Forming a rather broad
and open plain opposite the Eighth
Army's front, the valley gradually narrows to the northwest, becoming undu-
lating and well-wooded toward Ceprano. In the spring of 1944 the valley's fertile soil supported abundant
crops, especially vineyards, their vegetation the more luxuriant because they
were untended.

Except for Highway 6, the Roman-
built Via Casilina, which hugs the valley's northern wall, there were in 1944
few roads in the valley suitable for
modern military traffic. Communications were further hampered by the
ability of the enemy in the flanking hills
to observe all movement in the valley
below. Numerous transverse gullies, the
most important of which was the Forme
d'Aquino, cut across the valley and
would create additional problems as the
Eighth Army advanced.

Allied commanders had long agreed
that the flanking high ground must
first be seized before any large-scale
operations could be undertaken in the
Liri valley. In a move General Clark
had tried during the winter, General
Leese decided to send an attack into the
foothills of the Monte Cairo massif, of
which Monte Cassino is the most prominent and best known feature, simultaneously with an attack across the Rapido to isolate and capture the town of
Cassino. The Monte Majo massif, the
high ground south of the valley, was to
be dealt with by the FEC, the Fifth
Army's right flank corps. In keeping
with British practice, Leese issued no
operation order. Instead on 11 April he

simply gave his corps commanders a
short directive, then elaborated his plan
verbally in a series of command conferences between that date and D-day. [26]

Leese divided his attack into two
phases, the first aimed at the Gustav
Line and the second aimed at the Hitler
Line. During the opening phase, the
Polish corps was to isolate Monte Cassino from the north and northwest and
thereby dominate Highway 6 to facilitate the advance of the 13 Corps,
fighting its way south of the highway
from the Rapido. Only after the latter
corps had gained control of the highway were the Poles to attempt to storm
and capture the monastery itself. While
the Polish corps cut off the Germans
defending Monte Cassino, the 13 Corps
was to establish a bridgehead across the
Rapido River just south of Cassino.
Moving out from the bridgehead, the
corps was to isolate the town at the foot
of Monastery Hill by cutting the highway and joining up with the Polish
troops southwest of Cassino. Finally, 13
Corps was to clear the town and open
up the highway from the front to the
point of contact with the Polish corps,
before advancing on the Hitler Line,
the enemy's second line of defense in
the Liri valley. [27]

In the attack's second phase the
Polish corps was to advance four miles
westward across the flanks of the

[26] Operations of the British, Indian, and Dominion Forces in Italy, Part II, The Campaign in
Central Italy. Unless otherwise indicated the following section is based upon this reference.

[27] The 2 Polish Corps had its origin in the 1st
Carpathian Infantry Brigade which had served with
distinction during 1941–42 in North Africa. Lt.
Gen. Wladyslaw Anders, the corps' commander,
had formed the Polish Army of the East after the
Soviet Union had allowed the Poles to emigrate to
Iran.

mountains north of the highway to the town of Piedimonte San Germano, the Hitler Line's northern anchor. The 10 Corps was meanwhile to cover the Poles' right flank and to feint in the direction of Atina, a road junction in the mountains about ten miles north of Cassino. The 10 Corps was also to be prepared to provide reinforcements to other units as the battle progressed.

When the offensive began, the I Canadian Corps was to be prepared either to reinforce the attack if necessary or to pass through the 13 Corps to exploit a breakthrough of the enemy's defenses. The 6th South African Armoured Division, its motor brigade detailed temporarily to the 2d New Zealand Division in 10 Corps, was also in army reserve.

To accomplish its tasks the 13 Corps had an armored and three infantry divisions; the 2 Polish Corps, two infantry divisions and one armored brigade; and the 10 Corps, an infantry division, an Italian battle group (*Gruppo Combattimento*) equivalent to about a regiment, an infantry brigade, and two armored car regiments. The Eighth Army had, therefore, an attack force with the strength equivalent to about seven infantry and three armored divisions as opposed to the four divisions (a parachute, a mountain, and two infantry divisions) that the *Tenth Army* had opposite the Eighth Army's front. This ratio was approximately the superiority which Alexander believed was necessary.

To support its thrust into the Liri valley the Eighth Army had assembled 1,060 guns of all types. About 300 of these were to fire in support of the 2 Polish Corps in its assault on Monte Cassino. The remainder were sited in

support of the 13 Corps sector. By way of comparison, the Germans were believed to have no more than 400 guns and rocket launchers supporting the units manning the Gustav Line in the valley.

As the army's attack developed, artillery reconnaissance aircraft were to carry out a daily average of twelve missions to provide almost continuous surveillance of the battle area. Once the offensive got under way the main air effort during daylight was to be directed against enemy artillery and mortar positions in the valley and in the Atina area north of Cassino; by night the aircraft were to concentrate on the enemy line of communications. On the first day of the offensive fighter-bombers were to attack enemy command posts and all traffic observed behind the German lines.

To direct this air support Eighth Army had established three miles southeast of Cassino on Monte Trocchio, overlooking the front, a static forward air control post known as Rover David. Fighter-bombers circling the general area were to call in at stated intervals and be assigned targets of opportunity, thus reducing to a minimum the time lag between a request for help and the response. Within the army the 13 Corps and the 2 Polish Corps were to have first priority on air support. This support would be shifted to the 1st Canadian Corps when it began its exploitation role following the expected breakthrough of the enemy's first line of defense in the Liri valley.

Developing the Fifth Army Plan

A chain of steep rugged peaks rising to heights from 3,000 to 5,000 feet, the

Aurunci Mountains facing the Fifth Army extended in a northwestwardly direction toward Rome and averaged fifteen miles in width. One side of the mountain chain is bounded by a narrow coastal corridor along the Tyrrhenian Sea, the other by the relatively broad Liri valley. At the towns of Gaeta and Terracina, respectively ten and twenty-six miles from the mouth of the Garigliano River, the coastal corridor narrows to little more than the width of a road as the mountains drop abruptly to the sea. Elsewhere the high ground recedes more gradually and yields either to the flat, waterlogged Fondi and Pontine plains or to a fruitful coastal strip between Formia and Minturno. Inland are such formidable peaks as Monte Petrella and its surrounding massif, whose steep sides tower hundreds of feet above the low-lying coastal plain. Yet even in these hills are to be seen fertile farms offering a welcome contrast to the bare rock that abounds elsewhere.

Along the Fifth Army's far left flank ran Highway 7, the Via Appia, the only really good road in the army's zone and its vital supply artery. Crossing the Garigliano below Minturno, the highway parallels the coast for about ten miles as far as Formia before turning northwestward into the mountains to Itri and Fondi, respectively six and eighteen miles from Formia. After skirting the coastal marshes to a bottleneck at Terracina—a town straddling Highway 7 as it passes between the mountains and the sea—the highway breaks out of the mountains onto the level Pontine plain and continues thirty-one miles to the town of Cisterna, major strongpoint of the German forces op-posing the Anzio beachhead. From there the road begins a gradual ascent of the southwestern flanks of the Alban Hills and thence to Rome.

Within the Aurunci Mountains the wild, roadless Petrella massif presented the most formidable terrain of all. Only a few trails, created by generations of charcoal makers and shepherds, run along its steep slopes and through its narrow valleys. From the south and east access to the region by large military formations is virtually impossible. The coastal plain rises gradually past isolated Monte Campese to the foot of the massif, which in turn rises sharply from the plain. East of the massif a steep escarpment overhangs the Ausonia corridor, through which ran a road from the coastal highway northward to the Liri valley. At the village of Spigno, on a shoulder of the escarpment, a trail ascended to the northwest with a 51 percent grade for the steepest quarter-mile and then curved north and west of Monte Petrella for about seven miles to a mountain basin called the Fraile.

The massif's northern and western slopes are more accessible. A good mule trail led southwest from Esperia, four miles northwest of Ausonia, to the Fraile, approximately six miles away; and from the Itri-Pico road, a three-mile trail, which the Germans had been improving, ran as far as the Piano del Campo, a level upland plain about four miles north of Itri. While men and mules could penetrate to the key peak of the massif from several directions, motor movement was out of the question. A poor road cut northwest from the town of Castelforte to the town of Ausonia, north of which it joined a second-class road that followed Ausente

GENERALS BRANN (*left*) AND CLARK

Creek from Sant'Ambrogio through Esperia to Pico and San Giovanni Incarico. From Pico there are two routes,
one running northwest through Pas-
tena and Ceccano and the other southwest through Lenola, Valle Corsa, and
Amaseno.

The German rear areas were well
served by two lateral roads, one branch-
ing off the coastal highway west of
Minturno and following the Ausonia
corridor northward some eighteen
miles through the towns of Ausonia
and San Giorgio a Liri to Cassino; the
other, Highway 82, running northward

from Itri twelve miles to Pico and on to
the Liri valley.

As unlikely and uninviting a picture
as this terrain presented to the Fifth
Army commanders and staff, to bold
and innovative minds it would offer
tactical and strategic opportunities as
alluring as those more apparent ones in
the Liri valley. This favorable development, when combined with the known
German troop dispositions and the
strong initiative shown by the Fifth
Army commander within the Allied
command structure in Italy, would have
a far-reaching effect on the course of

the forthcoming spring offensive.

As was British custom, Alexander's staff had drawn up the general order for Operation DIADEM in nothing like the minute detail usually found in American field orders. The British practice was to provide only broad operational guidelines for subordinate commanders. For American staffs and commanders such broad directives created problems. So much freedom of action did the British practice afford subordinate commanders that they sometimes carried out an operational plan quite at variance with the senior commander's original intent. Clark, his staff, and his corps commanders enjoyed the same latitude in preparing Fifth Army's part in Operation DIADEM. While following in principle the guidelines laid down in Alexander's order, the plan drawn up at the end of March by the Fifth Army operations officer, Brig. Gen. Donald W. Brann, provided room for significant deviations from the original concept.[28]

In accordance with this concept Leese's Eighth Army was to make the main attack across the Rapido River to capture Cassino town and Monte Cassino and open up the Liri valley. The Fifth Army was to concentrate on an envelopment of the Cassino-Rapido line from the left through the Aurunci Mountains to help the Eighth Army accomplish its mission. Yet the Fifth Army staff saw in the envelopment maneuver an opportunity to greatly enhance the army's role in the offensive. Monte Majo, rather than Monte Cassino, might well become the key to a

breakthrough into the Liri valley. Clark, convinced that his neighbor on the right lacked sufficient aggressiveness to lead the Allied offensive up the Liri valley where the German defenses were strongest, was determined that Fifth Army should lead the way.[29]

Instead of repeating the past winter's practice of costly frontal attacks, one that had cost the Fifth Army heavy casualties, Brann believed that the Germans' defenses in the Liri valley could best be unhinged by a flanking attack led by the FEC through the Aurunci Mountains south of the Liri. Thus far Brann's concept differed little from Alexander's. If as Brann envisioned, the U.S. II Corps, after first blocking the Formia corridor, would pass through the FEC and continue the attack on a narrow front toward Monte d'Oro, some seventeen miles northwest of Monte Majo, the possibility loomed large that the Fifth Army and not the Eighth Army would, as Clark expected, lead the way toward Rome. It seemed to Brann that the Eighth Army's primary role should be to maintain sufficient pressure against the defenses at the mouth of the Liri valley to prevent the enemy from reinforcing the mountain sector opposite the Fifth Army's right wing.[30]

At Fifth Army headquarters the G–3 planning subsection, headed by Lt. Col.

---

[28] Memo, Gen Brann for Gen Clark, 24 Mar 44, Truscott Papers.

[29] At the time of the original attempt to break into the Liri valley during the winter campaign, General Keyes had urged that the mountain mass above Sant'Angelo and south of the valley be taken before an attempt was made to cross the Rapido. At that time the suggestion was not accepted by General McCreery, the British 10 Corps commander. See Blumenson, *Salerno to Cassino*, p. 326.

[30] Memo, Brann for Clark, 24 Mar 44, Truscott Papers.

Abraham M. Lazar, worked out the details of Brann's plan. Lazar and his staff recognized that the main objective in the first phase of the attack should be Monte Majo, the dominating feature opposite the army's right wing and the southernmost of the two anchors of the German defenses across the Liri valley. After Monte Majo, the next objective on that wing would be Monte d'Oro, whose summit would provide observation over the second line of German defenses in the Liri valley.[31]

There were several advantages in concentrating on Monte Majo first, not the least of which was that German defenses there appeared to be less than formidable. Although the terrain was forbidding, it was just the type the 4th Moroccan Mountain Division of the FEC had been trained to operate in. Once the French had occupied Monte Majo, they could exploit the excellent observation from its summit over the Liri valley and the enemy's first line of defenses there. The one major drawback in the plan was obvious: a dearth of roads, which posed serious problems in supply and artillery support. The planners, however, believed that mule pack trains and jeeps might suffice until roads and trails could be improved.[32]

Generals Juin and Keyes agreed in commenting on the draft plan that the army's main effort should be made along the Monte Majo–Monte d'Oro axis to outflank the enemy's Liri valley positions. Yet both objected to the failure to provide for an advance over the central part of the Aurunci Mountains, the Petrella massif, and to the proposal

that, once the Formia corridor had been sealed off, the II Corps should pass through the FEC to continue the attack. Juin and Keyes both wanted to broaden the base of the Army's offensive to include a thrust across the Petrella massif either to open the coastal road (Highway 7) or to assist the French corps' advance toward Monte d'Oro.[33]

Juin's chief of staff, General Marcel Carpentier, conveyed this dissent to Brann, pointing out that the projected route of advance from Monte Majo to Monte d'Oro, one to two miles wide and served by a single road, was too narrow to accommodate two corps, that a wider envelopment, including an attack through the Petrella massif as far as the Itri-Pico road, was necessary to outflank the enemy's deep defensive zones in the Liri valley. General Carpentier proposed, instead, that the FEC move through the Aurunci Mountains, while the U.S. II Corps broke through the enemy's coastal defenses, to open Highway 7.[34] This modification would further enhance the role played by the Fifth Army in the coming offensive at the expense of Alexander's concept of subordinating everything to expediting the Eighth Army's thrust up the Liri valley.

These proposals reflected Juin's conclusions after he reviewed the winter operations at Cassino. Only an outflanking maneuver through the mountains south of the Liri—an envelopment far

---

[31] Fifth Army G–3 Planning Study, 26 Mar 44.
[32] *Ibid.*

[33] Maréchal Alphonse Juin, *La Campagne d'Italie* (Paris: Editions Grey Victor, 1962), pp. 91–100.
[34] Marcel Carpentier, "Le corps expéditionnaire francais en Italie," *Revue de Défense Nationale*, new series (November 1, 1945), p. 579; Juin, *La Campagne d'Italie*, pp. 91–100.

wider than that contemplated by either
Alexander or Clark—would, Juin believed, force a German withdrawal in
the Liri valley. The longer Juin studied
the area in front of his corps the more
convinced he became that the decisive
objective for the first phase of the Fifth
Army's offensive should be the enemy's
second lateral route of communications,
the Itri-Pico road connecting the coastal
highway near Formia with the Liri
valley. By controlling this route the FEC
would be able in the second phase to
strike northward against the deep flank
and rear of the enemy forces in the
valley, an envelopment so deep that the
Germans would be forced to withdraw
completely from the Liri valley to avoid
being trapped there.[35]

With this objective in mind Juin
recommended to Clark a double envelopment by the two Allied armies—the
Fifth Army from the south by way of
the Aurunci Mountains and Pico and
the Eighth Army from the north by
way of Atina, an important road junction nine miles north of Cassino.[36] This
approach was quite different from that
originally outlined by General Alexander. To achieve the envelopment
from the south, Juin wanted to send his
corps along the Monte Juga-Pico axis,
first breaking through the enemy positions at Monte Majo, then quickly exploiting along several ridges running
northwest from Monte Majo before
clearing the area between Ausonia and
Coreno to the north and the Colle di

Teto to the south. The II Corps,
meanwhile, would be clearing the lower
Garigliano and opening the approach
roads and assembly areas required for
an exploitation through the Petrella
massif.

The FEC commander further cautioned against concentrating the Fifth
Army's efforts on frontal attacks astride
the two available roads in the army
zone—the narrow Ausonia-Pontecorvo-
Pico road and the coastal highway—for
they were under enemy observation
and covered by strong defenses. An
advance along the roads to take the
towns of Esperia and Formia would, he
warned, involve heavy fighting and "put
us at the mercy of the enemy" regardless of Allied strength. Juin instead
urged upon Clark a rapid push by two
corps through the lightly defended
mountain sectors. This push would cut
enemy communications and bypass defenses along the roads, thereby preparing the way for later advances along
them.

To make the exploitation phase of
the offensive across the roadless mountains, Juin expected to form a provisional mountain corps consisting of the
4th Moroccan Mountain Division and
the Tabors. This force was to advance
northwest ten miles from Castelforte to
establish a strong base in the vicinity of
Monte d'Oro four miles south of Pontecorvo in the Liri valley. From there the
force could either attack the enemy's
second line of defense or, if the II
Corps required help, turn south toward
Itri and Highway 7. After Esperia had
been cleared, the 4th Moroccan Mountain Division, in company with another
division, would attack the enemy's second line of defense in the vicinity of

---

[35] Juin, *La Campagne d'Italie*, pp. 91–100.

[36] *Mémoire du General Juin en date du 4 Avril 1944
sur les futures operations du C.E.F. dans les monts
Aurunci, pièce Nr. 116, in FEC Journal de Marche*
(annexes), 1 April–22 July 1944, vol. I, roll No. 10.
Unless otherwise indicated, the following section is
based upon this document.

Pico. General Juin thus anticipated a wide envelopment of objectives, combined with pressure along the Esperia road.

Once established around Pico, the FEC could attack either toward Ceprano or Frosinone, important road junctions on Highway 6 and seventeen and twenty-eight miles, respectively, west-northwest of Cassino. In Juin's opinion, his corps, if reinforced by a fourth division and relieved on the right by the Eighth Army's advance in the Liri valley, would be able to continue in the direction of Frosinone instead of yielding its zone to the II Corps as Brann had originally proposed. Unalterably opposed to the single axis concept, Juin pointed to the confusion and lost time that would result if the II Corps attempted to relieve the FEC after it had reached the enemy's second line of defense.

Instead Juin suggested that Keyes' corps cut the Ausonia-Formia road and take Spigno on the eastern edge of the Petrella massif. If Keyes used Spigno as a base for a thrust across the mountains, his corps could, in Juin's opinion, better assist the FEC advance toward the Germans' second line of defense. In the coastal area the II Corps should, Juin believed, follow up the attack from Spigno by occupying and clearing Highway 7 and thereby opening up a supply route to support further advances in the mountains.

Agreeing in principle with Juin's proposals, Keyes indicated that he would use the 88th Division to make the main effort on his right. He would make a secondary effort with the 85th Division in the coastal sector on the corps' left flank.

Clark approved Juin's and Keyes' recommendations. To Brann's plan for a breakthrough by the FEC over Monte Majo and the sealing off of the Formia corridor by the II Corps, Clark added Juin's proposals to broaden the base of the army's offensive by making a two-corps attack across the Petrella massif to cut the Itri-Pico road, the Germans' main lateral supply route, and to make a wider envelopment of their defenses in the Liri valley.[37]

While still embodying Alexander's concept of an envelopment of the Germans' Liri valley defenses, the Fifth Army operations plan, as eventually published, gave Clark's army a far more significant role than Alexander's guidelines had originally suggested. If Clark's forces broke through the mountain sector south of the Liri on a two-corps front, as Juin and Keyes believed they would, a real possibility existed that the Fifth rather than the Eighth Army might lead the way to central Italy and Rome.

This objective was of particular importance to General Clark whose Fifth Army had lost an opportunity to lead the way to Rome in January when a combination of weather, terrain, and German resistance had halted the Allies in the first battle for that city. Eighth Army was to play the role Fifth Army had played then, but Clark was determined that his army would succeed this time, for the Eighth faced obstacles that had stalled the first drive on Rome, while Fifth Army was now concentrated on what had seemed to be the enemy's most vulnerable sector.

---

[37] Interv, Mathews with Clark, 10–21 May 49, CMH.

Artillery and air plans in support of the Fifth Army called for isolating the battle area by interdicting roads and trails and destroying bridges with artillery and air bombardment.[38] Artillery fires were to remain normal until H-hour, when a 40-minute concentration, including counterbattery fire, was to be placed on known enemy positions and artillery. Fire missions for 240-mm. howitzers were to be carried out under corps' direction. The 240-mm. howitzers were to join medium 155-mm. guns in interdicting critical road junctions in the Itri and Pico areas.

Besides the field artillery support, the Fifth Army would have reinforcing fires from the 8-inch guns of an American cruiser lying just offshore. These guns were to direct their fire against those targets in the coastal sector beyond the range of corps artillery. In the offensive's early phases the Navy was to fire interdiction missions in the Terracina area and against suitable targets such as the towns of Itri and Sperlonga, depots along the Itri-Pico road, 170-mm. gun positions near Itri, and the highway between Itri and Formia. The naval guns were to be available on call at least until D plus 5 and were to fire a minimum of five missions of about 100 rounds each on suitable firing days.

Clark's modification of Alexander's operational concepts was manifested in yet another way—by an effort to revise air support priorities that Alexander had set up for the two armies. Since the AAI commander deemed Leese's Eighth Army to be making the main effort, Alexander had divided the available air support between the two armies on a 70–30 ratio in favor of the Eighth Army. After the Eighth Army had initiated the second phase of the offensive by breaking through the enemy's defenses in the Liri valley, air support priority was to be shifted to the Fifth Army's VI Corps on the Anzio beachhead. Within the Allied armies, air control sections were to designate all targets. In co-ordination with the XII Tactical Air Command (TAC), the air sections were to determine the priority targets within each army's zone of operations. Convinced the major role in the eventual breakthrough on the southern front would be the Fifth rather than the Eighth Army's, Clark sought to persuade Alexander to split the available air support equally between the two armies. At a final meeting of army commanders on 1 May at Alexander's headquarters at Caserta—a meeting marked by bickering and mounting tension—Clark argued his point in vain.[39] Alexander refused to alter the arrangement, insisting that there would be adequate air support for both armies. He even declined a mollifying suggestion from General Cannon, American commander of the XII TAC, that the zones of the two armies be treated as one front with aircraft free to attack targets in both zones during the same mission. He would retain for himself, Alexander said, the decision to change the air support priorities. In any case he would allot air support in **keeping with the developing situation.**[40]

---

[38] II Corps AAR, May–Jun 44; *Fifth Army History*, Part V, pp. 27–31. The following section is based upon these references unless otherwise indicated.

[39] Clark Diary, 30 Apr 44; Interv, Mathews with Clark, 13 May 49, CMH; AAI Plan for Operation DIADEM, FO 1, 5 May 44.

[40] Interv, Mathews with Alexander, 10–15 Jan 49, CMH: AAI FO 1, 5 May 44.

On one point there was general agreement: the offensive should begin at night in order to conceal movement of the French beyond the Garigliano and the British beyond the Rapido. Accordingly, H-hour was set for 2300, since the moon, four days from its last quarter, would not rise until 2331. This would allow for half an hour of preparatory artillery fire before the infantry began to move. In order to assure adequate moonlight for French and British troop movements, Alexander had first selected 10 May as D-day, for it fell within the period of the rising moon. But when the Eighth Army reported that it would not be ready on that day, Alexander postponed D-day twenty-four hours.[41]

At the 1 May conference, Alexander and his army commanders also agreed that the attack should be postponed in the event or threat of heavy rain. Any postponement, however, would be for only twenty-four hours at a time, and, to make allowance for any adjustments a delay would entail, would have to be decided by 1000 on D-day.[42]

Because Alexander decided not to designate an army group reserve, he restricted Clark's use of the 36th Division, the Fifth Army reserve. Clark was to commit the 36th only with Alexander's permission.[43]

Both the decision on committing the 36th Division and the timing of the

Anzio attack, Alexander believed, should depend on the degree of progress the offensive had made on the southern front. In any case, the 36th Division was not to be sent to Anzio nor was the beachhead breakout attack to be launched until the two Allied armies had penetrated the enemy's first line of defense on the southern front—the Gustav Line—and had demonstrated that they would need no additional strength for an assault against the second line of defense, the Hitler Line.[44]

Another factor in the timing of the breakout from the beachhead was the status and disposition of Kesselring's reserve. Only after Allied intelligence had evidence that Kesselring had shifted his army group reserve to the support of the southern front was Truscott to strike. The attack from the beachhead was, in Alexander's view, "his most important weapon of opportunity, to be launched when the situation was fluid."[45] If this operation went according to plan, Alexander expected that the VI Corps' attack from the beachhead toward Valmontone on Highway 6 would possibly block the route of withdrawal for a large percentage of the German forces on the southern front and result in the destruction of the *Tenth Army's* right wing.[46]

Alexander was aware during the last weeks before the offensive that Clark's strategic views differed sharply from his own. Nevertheless, the Allied commander and his staff remained con-

---

[41] Conf min, 1 May 44, AAI files. See also *Fifth Army History*, Part V, p. 23. Standard Army Time (from 0200, 2 April 1944) was B Time, two hours ahead of Greenwich Standard Time (Z).

[42] Conf min, 1 May 44, AAI files.

[43] AAI FO 1, 5 May 44; Lt Gen John Harding, AAI COS, Remarks at Fifth Army Commanders Conference, 5 May 1944, Army Records Center, St. Louis, Mo.

[44] Interv, Mathews with Alexander, 10–15 Jan 49, CMH.

[45] Harding, Remarks at Fifth Army Commanders Conf, 5 May 44.

[46] Interv, Mathews with Alexander, 10–15 Jan 49, CMH.

vinced that Leese's Eighth Army, after breaking through the German defenses in the Liri valley, would lead the way up Highway 6 toward Rome. The AAI commander believed furthermore that at best the FEC's projected attack over the Aurunci Mountains would be a secondary and supporting effort, keeping pressure against the Germans in that area and preventing them from shifting troops to the point of main effort, the Liri valley. He did not count on the French colonial troops to break through readily on Monte Majo or for the II Corps to advance rapidly across the Petrella massif.[47]

Alexander's final operation order as published on 5 May still assigned to the Eighth Army the major role in the offensive and sketched the Fifth Army's mission in only general terms. This gave Clark and his commanders the flexibility they wanted in order to enhance their army's role as much as they wished. Concerning the unspoken yet real question in everyone's mind, namely, which army would take Rome, the order remained silent. Yet it was hard to see how it would be possible for any but the Fifth Army to be first in Rome, and it was Clark's understanding that Alexander expected that the prize would fall to the Americans.[48] On the direction the breakout was to take, however, Alexander's order was quite clear. Attacking from the beachhead, the VI Corps was to cut Highway 6 in the vicinity of Valmontone, thereby blocking the supply or withdrawal of the enemy's *Tenth Army* on the southern front. After the two portions of the

Fifth Army linked up, the entire army was presumably to continue northwestward alongside the Eighth Army; for the order outlining Operation DIADEM read that the Fifth Army was to drive the enemy north of Rome, capture the Viterbo airfields forty miles to the north and the port of Civitavecchia, then continue northwestward up the narrow coastal plain.[49]

With the prospect of capturing Rome looming large in his mind, Clark displayed no inclination on the eve of DIADEM to worry about the availability of forces beyond the Tiber, something that American emphasis on France, rather than Italy, would eventually call into question. As far as he was concerned, the important thing was that for the first time in the Italian campaign the full resources of both Allied armies were to be used in a co-ordinated effort. With an over-all Allied strength of twenty-five divisions as opposed to nineteen enemy divisions, superiority in artillery, overwhelming domination of the air, sufficient reserves, and the troops rested and ready, the Allied commanders could view the prospects of the coming offensive with confidence.[50]

---

[47] *Ibid.*

[48] AAI Opns O No. 1, 5 May 44, in *Fifth Army History,* Part V, App. 1.

[49] *Ibid.*

[50] Of the 25 Allied divisions under Alexander's control, 17 were deployed on the main southern front, and opposing them on the same front the Germans had 6 divisions. The U.S. VI Corps controlled six divisions on the Anzio beachhead, and were opposed there by eight German divisions. On the Adriatic sector, east of the Central Apennines, the British had two divisions and the Germans three. The Germans had one division in strategic reserve and one in army reserve. Some writers point out that while the Allies had twenty-five divisions, the Germans had twenty-three, but reach the latter figure by adding in the four divisions in *Army Group von Zangen* in northern Italy, units that were not available for the defense of the southern front.

German Preparations

In making preparations to meet an expected Allied offensive, the German armies in Italy were left largely to their own resources. Since the increasing pressures against the front in Russia and the growing danger of a cross-Channel invasion precluded any significant reinforcement of Kesselring's command above the normal replacement flow, support from Hitler and the OKW was limited for the most part to exhortations to stand firm. The best the OKW could do for Kesselring was to postpone indefinitely the scheduled transfer from Italy to France of the *Parachute Panzer Division "Hermann Goering,"* a unit of the OKW reserve located near Leghorn, well over 200 miles away from the southern front.[51]

Nevertheless, from March through April 1944, in spite of the efforts of the Allied air forces through Operation STRANGLE to prevent German reinforcements from reaching the front, German troop strength and matériel in Italy had increased, though modestly. Although no major units had moved into the theater, the flow of replacements and recovered wounded exceeded a casualty rate reduced by the April lull in the fighting, and the assigned strength of the German army units rose from 330,572 on 1 March to 365,616 on 1 May 1944.[52]

In addition to assigned strength, the *Tenth* and *Fourteenth Armies* on 1 May 1944 also had approximately 27,000 men attached from the Luftwaffe and the *Waffen-SS*. One division and miscellaneous small Luftwaffe ground units in von Zangen's group accounted for an estimated 20,000 more. Thus, on 1 May 1944 the total German ground strength, including army, SS, and Luftwaffe ground units, assigned to the Italian theater numbered approximately 412,000 men. But this force was scattered from the fronts south of Rome to the Alpine passes far to the north.

Although most German units in 1944 were plagued by a shortage of well-trained junior officers and noncommissioned officers, units in Italy had yet to suffer seriously from a growing manpower shortage afflicting German forces elsewhere. Several expedients, such as the "combing out" of overhead units and using foreign auxiliaries for housekeeping and labor duties, enabled the Germans to meet their manpower requirements. For these reasons, in early 1944 *OB Suedwest* commanded forces superior in quality to the average German unit in other OKW theaters of operation.[53]

Nineteen of the 23 divisions in Kesselring's *Army Group C* as of 1 May 1944 were considered suitable for the defensive missions they might be required to accomplish. The German commanders deemed only two of these divisions

---

[51] Greiner and Schramm, eds., *OKW/WFSt, KTB,* pp. 478–80. This division hereafter will be referred to as the *Hermann Goering Division.*

[52] Strength Rpt, *Staerke des Feldheeres,* 25 May 44, *OKW/Generalstab des Heeres/Organizationabteilung* (hereafter cited as *OKW/Org.Abt.*), KTB Anlagen, 5 May 44–9 May 45. A study of *Tenth* and *Fourteenth Armies'* war diaries disclosed that the 1 April figures shown in the documents cited actually apply to 1 May, and they are so quoted. All of the figures

used in this paragraph refer to "assigned strength" and are therefore somewhat higher than "present for duty" figures.

[53] For a contemporary comparison between *Tenth Army* divisions and those of other German theaters, see Trip Rpt, 7 Apr 44, *Fahrbemerkungen des Heeres OB Armeekommando 10* (hereafter referred to as *AOK 10, KTB 6, Anlagen 1.10–14.44*).

qualified for any offensive mission, 11 for limited attacks, 6 for sustained defensive action, and 4 for small-scale defensive action. Thus approximately half of the divisions, an unusually high proportion at that stage of the war, were rated capable of some offensive action.[54]

The relative quiet on the battlefronts in April had enabled Kesselring to disengage several of his better divisions—among them the *26th Panzer* and the *29th* and *90th Panzer Grenadier Divisions*—for movement to the rear for rest and rehabilitation. Together with the *Hermann Goering Division* and several other divisions of lesser quality that were training, fighting partisans, or guarding the coasts, these disengaged formations made up the general and theater reserves available to Kesselring.[55]

In the disposition of his general reserves Kesselring had to consider three important factors. First, the existence of two fronts south of Rome made it desirable to place reserves so that they could be quickly shifted to either front. Second, thanks to the Allied deception plan, so vulnerable did he regard the coastal sectors north as well as south of the Anzio beachhead that he believed a number of powerful and highly mobile units were necessary to back up the weak forces guarding that area of the coast. Finally, the possibility that the Allies might try to cut the few roads between Rome and the southern front by means of an airborne landing in the vicinity of Frosinone, some fifty miles southeast of Rome, required a division in that area. Although Kesselring made strenuous efforts to satisfy all three requirements, whatever success he achieved was bought at the cost of dividing some of his best divisions among two or more widely separated groups.[56]

The Germans clearly had been taken in by the Allied deception plan. In the area selected by the Allies for their main effort—the Liri valley—the enemy had underestimated Allied strength by seven divisions. For example, opposite the *XIV Panzer Corps* in the Allied bridgehead beyond the Garigliano General Juin had managed to assemble four times the number of troops his adversaries had estimated to be under his command. On the other hand, German intelligence credited the Allies with much larger reserves than they actually had and believed that three divisions were in the Salerno-Naples area engaged in landing exercises preparatory for another amphibious operation. Kesselring had disposed his forces on that assumption. A minimum number of troops was in line and several reserve divisions were positioned along the coast to counter expected landings. That was to prove a vital factor in the early battles of the coming offensive.

While some ground combat troops in Italy belonged to the Luftwaffe, as, for example, the *Hermann Goering Division*,

---

[54] Status Rpt for 1 May 44, *Zustandsberichte des OB Suedwest, 1 Jun 44, OKW/Org.Abt. KTB 1944.*

[55] Since the location of these general reserves seemed to point to their commitment on the southern front, some confusion arose later as to whether they were army or army group reserves. But since in most cases Kesselring's or OKW's permission was required for the commitment even of units in corps reserve, the distinction is unimportant.

[56] Greiner and Schramm, eds., *OKW/WFSt, KTB,* II(I), pp. 478–81; MS # T–1b (Westphal *et al.*), CMH.

actual German air strength was negligible. Compared with the approximately 4,000 operational aircraft the Allies could muster in Italy and on the nearby islands, the Luftwaffe had only 700 operational aircraft in the central Mediterranean area. Of this number less than half were based in Italy.[57] Of these only a small percentage would ever rise to challenge the overwhelming Allied air forces or to harass Allied ground movements. German air commanders were carefully husbanding their few aircraft for those occasions that might give some promise of success against a new Allied amphibious landing or, in conjunction with the greater air strength in Germany and France, against the expected Allied invasion attempt in northwestern Europe.[58]

[57] British Air Ministry Pamphlet 248, *The Rise and Fall of the German Air Force, 1933–45* (London: Air Ministry [A.C.AS. 1], 1948, pp. 265–71.

[58] *Ibid.*

CHAPTER III

DIADEM'S First Day—11 May

Behind the German Front

An atmosphere of uncertainty prevailed on the German side of the front. Although German commanders reminded one another daily that an Allied attack could begin at any time, they had no specific information, as was evident from the absence of most senior officers from the front when the offensive began. Only a few hours before it started, General von Vietinghoff, the *Tenth Army* commander, left for Germany to receive a decoration for valor from the hands of his Fuehrer. About the same time, the chief of staff of the *XIV Panzer Corps* departed for a week's home leave. Two weeks earlier General-major Siegfried Westphal, Field Marshal Kesselring's ailing chief of staff, had gone to Germany on convalescent leave; and General von Senger, the panzer corps commander, was still away on a 30-day home leave that had begun in mid-April. Thus the Allied offensive was destined to strike a corps occupying a critical sector without its regular commander and chief of staff, an army minus its commanding general, and an army group without its chief of staff, an extraordinary situation.[1]

For the Germans the daylight hours on 11 May passed uneventfully; no

THE BATTLE FOR MONTE CASSINO
12 May 1944

ALLIED GAINS
AXIS OF ALLIED ADVANCE
AXIS OF ALLIED RETREAT
GUSTAV LINE

Contour interval 100 meters

0   1 MILES
0   1 KILOMETERS

M. Finnemann

MAP 1

prisoners were taken and Allied artillery fire was sporadic, as it had been for several days. Heavy motor movements in the Eighth Army's rear opposite the *Tenth Army*'s left wing only

---

[1] Britt Bailey (MS #R-50), The German Situation in Italy, 11 May–4 June 44, copy in CMH (hereafter cited as MS #R-50 [Bailey]). Allied knowledge of the German situation was thanks, in large measure, to the interception of the German Enigma

Code. As a matter of fact, the Allies first learned of Vietinghoff's absence after intercepting a radio message from Kesselring ordering Vietinghoff to return at once to his command in Italy. See Winterbotham, *The Ultra Secret*, pp. 114–15.

MONTE CASSINO (*Allied view*).

confirmed the belief that the Allies had yet to complete preparations for their offensive.

Monte Cassino and the Rapido

An hour before midnight on 11 May the massed artillery of two Allied armies—1,060 guns on the Eighth Army front and 600 on the Fifth Army's—opened fire from Cassino to the Tyrrhenian Sea. On the Fifth Army front beyond the lower reaches of the Garigliano the infantry divisions of the U.S. II Corps and of the French Expeditionary Corps began moving up the slopes of the hills leading to their objectives. Three-quarters of an hour later the Eighth Army opened its attack as the British 13 Corps moved toward preselected crossing sites on the Rapido River. At 0100, two hours after the Fifth Army had begun to move, the Polish 2 Corps attacked enemy positions on Monte Cassino. (*Map 1*)

In the early hours of the offensive the two Polish divisions—the 3d Carpathian and the 5th Kresowa—fought their separate ways across Monte Cassino's rocky flanks to capture two features: "The Phantom Ridge," some

1,800 yards northwest of the abbey, and Point 593, high ground about 1,000 yards northwest of the abbey. But the Germans, well-entrenched and long familiar with the ground, quickly recovered from the preparatory artillery bombardment to inflict heavy casualties on the Polish troops. After daybreak exposed the attackers to enemy gunners, losses became so severe that the Poles were unable to withstand a series of counterattacks that began shortly after daylight. At 1400 on the 12th, General Anders, the corps commander, ordered his troops to withdraw during the night under cover of darkness to their line of departure northeast of Monte Cassino. Almost half of their number had been killed or wounded.[2]

Making the main attack in the valley below, General Kirkman's 13 Corps fought on through the night to establish a bridgehead beyond the fog-shrouded Rapido. General Kirkman had planned to establish a bridgehead west of the Rapido with the British 4th Division on the right and the 8th Indian Division on the left. After consolidating a position beyond the Rapido, the 4th Division was to swing to the northwest to effect a junction with the Polish corps on Highway 6 at a point about three miles west of Cassino. On the left, the Indians were, after securing their bridgehead, to clear the so-called Liri Appendix, the tongue of land between the Rapido and Liri Rivers, then exploit northwestward to the Hitler Line. The 78th Division, in corps reserve, was to be prepared either to

cover the Indian division's left flank or to exploit through one of the assault divisions. Until the infantry had broken through the enemy's first line of defense, the Gustav Line, the armor (the 6th Armoured Division and the 1st Canadian Armoured Brigade, on whose superior numbers and firepower British commanders had placed great reliance) could be used only for fire support.

At 2345, as the two infantry divisions launched their assault boats, the river's swift current swept many downstream and capsized others. Enemy automatic weapons fire, slashing through the dense smoke and fog, caused numerous casualties and made control difficult. Fortunately the earlier counterbattery fire had done its work well, for the assault troops encountered little enemy artillery fire at the crossing sites. Even so, by daybreak the corps had secured only a shallow bridgehead.

Although the engineers began work on bridges as soon as the infantry had reached the far bank, the 4th Division's bridgehead was too shallow to give the engineers the necessary cover from enemy small arms fire, and at first light the work was abandoned. In the 8th Indian Division's sector, however, engineers managed to complete two pontoon bridges by morning. With these in place, the Indians rushed reinforcements across to expand their bridgehead by late afternoon into the village of Sant'Angelo in Tiodice, about two miles south of Cassino.

The 13 Corps' gains by nightfall on the 12th were, nevertheless, disappointing. Only about half of the objectives set for the offensive's first two hours were in Allied hands. Yet something had been achieved. For the first time

[2] Operations of the British, Indian, and Dominion Forces in Italy, Part II, The Campaign in Central Italy. Unless otherwise indicated this section is based upon this reference.

TERRAIN FACING THE U.S. II CORPS. *Santa Maria Infante (lower left), Pulcherina (center foreground), and Monte Fammera (background).*

the Allies had succeeded in placing two vehicular bridges across the Rapido.[3]

Santa Maria Infante and the S-Ridge

Unlike the Eighth Army, the Fifth Army, in DIADEM's first hours, had no deep and swift-flowing river to cross nor, except in the French sector, high mountains to scale. Instead, the Americans would launch their phase of the Allied offensive from assembly areas on the reverse slopes of a range of hills

paralleling the Garigliano River some two to three miles to the west. The French would actually have the advantage of attacking from mountain positions west of the river that overlooked the German lines. For this favorable state of affairs the Fifth Army was indebted to the success of the British divisions of the 10 Corps, which, in the previous January, had established a bridgehead beyond the Garigliano extending from Monte Juga in the bend of the river southwest to Minturno, about five miles away.

By evening of 11 May the American

---

[3] *Ibid.*

assault units had moved into their assembly areas between the towns of Minturno and Tremonsuoli, a mile and a half to the west. An overcast obscured the stars, and fog drifted through the narrow valleys. All was in readiness. It was, noted the 88th Division's G–3, "a quiet night, nothing special to report."[4]

Holding the 88th Division's objectives were the right flank regiment of Generalleutnant Wilhelm Raapke's *71st Light Infantry Division* and the left flank regiment of Generalmajor Bernhard Steinmetz's *94th Infantry Division*. The 88th Division's attack would thus strike the enemy along an interdivisional boundary, usually a weak point in the front.[5]

Not only would the enemy be hit at a vulnerable point, but the II Corps' attack would be backed up by massive artillery support. In addition to organic artillery, the 85th and 88th Divisions would be supported by the 6th, 36th, and 77th Field Artillery Groups, controlling a total of nine firing battalions.[6]

Corps artillery also was to execute counterbattery missions and harassing and interdiction fire. The 36th Division artillery with more than three battalions was to fire in direct support of the 85th Division, and the 6th Field Artillery Group, with two battalions, in direct support of the 88th Division.

In comparison, the Germans had about three battalions of light artillery in the Ausonia corridor west of the village of Santa Maria Infante and Monte Bracchi, a mile to the northeast; three battalions of light and a battalion of medium artillery in the Formia corridor astride the coastal highway; several batteries of dual-purpose 88-mm. guns near Itri and along the Itri-Sperlonga road—an equivalent total of six battalions of light and one battalion each of medium and heavy artillery. The enemy also had numerous self-propelled light caliber guns and not more than six rocket projectors.[7]

To counter fire from the enemy's long-range 170-mm. guns, corps artillery, during the night of 10 May, moved a 155-mm. gun battery and a single 240-mm. howitzer across the Garigliano River and into prepared positions within 1,500 yards of the front. Throughout the 11th a heavy smoke screen concealed these new positions from enemy observation. When the Americans began the preliminary bombardment that night they were able to bring the 170-mm. guns under effective counterbattery fire, and so the enemy's heavy artillery was silent on the first day of the offensive.[8]

From H-hour, or until the assault troops closed with the enemy, the sixteen American battalions of light artillery were to fire on German frontline positions. Thereafter the fire was to shift to enemy command posts, reserves, and supply routes. Although the greater weight of artillery fire support

---

[4] II Corps G–3 Jnl, 11–12 May 44.

[5] Unless otherwise indicated this account is based upon the official records of the 85th and 88th Divisions and those of the II Corps, supplemented by after-action interviews with key participants by members of the Fifth Army Historical Section.

[6] Directly under corps' control was a battalion each of 240-mm. howitzers and 8-inch howitzers, a battalion each of 155-mm. and 4.5-inch guns, four battalions of 155-mm. howitzers, and five battalions of 105-mm. howitzers. *Fifth Army History*, Part V, pp. 56–57. Also see II Corps Artillery AAR, 25 Mar–5 June 44.

[7] II Corps Arty AAR, 25 Mar–5 Jun 44: MS # T-1b (Westphal *et al.*).

[8] II Corps Arty AAR, 25 Mar–5 Jun 44.

available to Fifth Army had been assigned to the FEC, the II Corps would have, in addition to the fire support already described, considerable help available from 11 to 16 May from an offshore cruiser firing against previously located targets.[9]

As the American infantry began to advance toward the *94th Infantry Division*'s positions, the American artillery hammered the German front for an hour. Shells interrupted enemy communications, but had little effect on the German infantry, deeply dug in.

Making the main effort of the 88th Division and, in effect, the main effort of the II Corps, the 351st Infantry, commanded by Col. Arthur S. Champeny, moved toward the village of Santa Maria Infante. After taking the village and the adjacent high ground, the regiment was to attack across the Ausonia road and mount the Petrella escarpment. The 349th Infantry, commanded by Lt. Col. Joseph B. Crawford, was to support this attack by taking Monte Bracchi, overlooking Santa Maria Infante a mile to the northeast. Col. James C. Fry's 350th Infantry on the right was to take Monte SS Cosma e Damian,[10] a small hill mass just west of the town of Castelforte, to advance and occupy Monte Rotondo and Monte Cerri, about one and two miles, respectively, to the northwest, in order to protect the division flank. (*Map II*)

For men of the 350th Infantry ascending the slopes of Monte Ciannelli, one of the several hills making up Monte Damiano, resistance was at first surprisingly light; but forty-five minutes after the attack began, when the leading battalion sought to continue beyond Monte Cianelli, heavy fire erupted from the village of Ventosa on the northern slope of the hill. It took repeated attacks, plus commitment of the battalion reserve company, to gain Ventosa by dawn.

On the left, the 350th Infantry's 2d Battalion moved northward against Hill 316, another summit in the Monte Damiano hill mass. Shortly after midnight, when machine gun fire stopped one of Company F's platoons, the platoon leader, S. Sgt. Charles W. Shea, continued forward alone to attack the enemy guns. Crawling up to one gun, he tossed grenades into the position, forcing four enemy soldiers to surrender, and then attacked a second, capturing its two-man crew. Though a third gun took him under fire, he rushed it as well and killed all three Germans in the position. With these guns silenced, the 2d Battalion's attack gathered momentum and soon reached the summit of Mount Damiano.[11]

Just before daylight the right flank regiment of Raapke's *71st Division* launched a company-sized counterattack against the 2d Battalion on Monte Damiano's southern slope, but the American infantrymen held their ground. Since the 88th Division's commander, General Sloan, was anxious to avoid exposing his right flank, he ordered Colonel Fry to halt his men on Monte Damiano until the French could take the high ground north of Castelforte.

---

[9] *Ibid.*
[10] Hereafter referred to as Monte Damiano.

[11] Shea received the first Medal of Honor awarded in the 88th Division, and was commissioned a 2d lieutenant.

Within thirteen hours after the beginning of the offensive, Fry's regiment had captured its first objective at a cost of two men killed and 55 wounded. This baptism of fire would prove to be the only real success along the entire II Corps front during the first twenty-four hours of the offensive.

Nowhere across the American front on that first day would the agonizing adjustment of a new and untried division to the challenge of combat be more vividly illustrated than in the experience of men of the 351st Infantry as they attacked a well-entrenched battalion of the *94th Infantry Division* astride the road leading from Minturno to the regimental objective of Santa Maria Infante. At his headquarters in Minturno, the regimental commander, Colonel Champeny, had erected a sand table model of the terrain in order to familiarize his men with the ground over which they would soon fight. All unit commanders had reconnoitered the area from the air and from well-sited observation points along the regimental front. One platoon leader commented that "never had an infantry outfit a better chance to study thoroughly the plan and terrain before an attack."[12]

Although Champeny's patrols had probed the enemy's outposts nightly, the infantrymen actually knew considerably less about the disposition and strength of the German defenses than they did about the terrain. They had located several automatic weapons emplacements, mine fields, and barbed wire obstacles but still lacked an accu-

rate picture of the German positions. Possibly overoptimistic, Champeny expected to capture Santa Maria Infante within two hours after the attack began. He directed his supply officer to be prepared to feed the men a hot breakfast in the village before they continued the advance toward the Petrella escarpment.

Colonel Champeny selected the 2d Battalion, commanded by Lt. Col. Raymond E. Kendall, to lead the attack, while the 3d Battalion advanced in echelon to the right rear, and the 1st remained in reserve. From an assembly area south of the cemetery about half a mile northwest of Minturno, Colonel Kendall planned to advance with two companies abreast. One company would move along each side of the main road that leads from Minturno via Santa Maria Infante to the road running through the Ausonia corridor from the coastal highway to Ausonia, where the corridor narrows to a mile and a half defile bearing that name. The two companies were first to occupy twin knobs (wistfully dubbed "Tits" by the infantrymen) which flanked the road about 350 yards beyond the line of departure, then to continue astride the road into Santa Maria Infante.

The road ran along the crest of a ridge some 125 yards wide connecting the base of a triangular wedge of hills just south of the Ausonia defile with an apex at Monte Bracchi. From an S-curve near the cemetery the road wound along the ridge for almost a mile until it reached the southern outskirts of Santa Maria Infante, where it forked. The right fork led northeast to a dead end at the village of Pulcherini, perched high up the slope of Monte

---

[12] 351st Inf S–3 Jnl, 10–12 May 44.

Bracchi, while the left fork wound through the hamlet of Tame, a cluster of houses about 400 yards west of Santa Maria Infante, and thence to a junction with the road running through the Ausonia corridor northward from the coast to Ausonia.

Many spurs cutting the flanks of the ridge provided the enemy with excellent defensive positions against frontal attack. On one of the spurs, 700 yards southeast of Santa Maria Infante and overlooking a sunken road that traversed the slope, the Germans had developed a strongpoint, in a group of stone cottages, of well-sited and camouflaged machine guns and mortars— unfortunately not known to Champeny's men. In the early hours of the attack that position proved a formidable and deadly challenge to the untried infantrymen.

About 2230 the two assault companies, their movement masked by the roar of supporting artillery fire, moved beyond the Minturno cemetery toward positions immediately in front of the Tits. As the men advanced they laid white tape to help maintain contact in the darkness. Apparently anticipating a short operation, many of the men discarded their combat packs along the way.

Company F on the left, commanded by Capt. Carl W. Nelson, ran into its first obstacle just beyond the cemetery; a string of concertina wire blocked the way. Since the supporting artillery still kept the Germans under cover, it was a simple matter to cut the wire and continue to the base of the left Tit. There the company halted to await completion of the artillery preparation. Hardly had the friendly fires ceased

when the leading platoons came under heavy small arms fire from an S-shaped ridge off to their left in the zone of the neighboring 85th Division. Caught in the open under intense fire for the first time, the company quickly dispersed into small one- or two-squad groups.

Within thirty minutes after the jump-off, Company F's attack had degenerated into a series of poorly co-ordinated platoon and squad actions. One after another of the platoon radios broke down, the leaders lost contact with their men, and darkness and fog shrouded the battlefield in a blanket of confusion that even bravery and good intentions were unable to penetrate. Early in the attack Captain Nelson lost communication with his battalion commander and, aside from his command group, had contact at that point with only one squad. At dawn he finally regained control of his support and weapons platoons, as well as an attached heavy machine gun platoon. That part of Company F not in touch with Nelson separated into three small isolated groups, each independently and fruitlessly seeking to press the attack.

Moving forward at a trot, one group of approximately twenty men led by S. Sgt. Peter Pyenta soon encountered more barbed wire. As the men tried to bypass it, fire from automatic weapons emplaced west of the ridge road cut down half the group. Fighting back with rifles and hand grenades, the survivors managed to silence the enemy guns, but with only nine men left and no information available concerning the rest of the company, Sergeant Pyenta withdrew his men to a point about 150 yards north of the Minturno cemetery.

1st Lt. Jack L. Panich, a platoon

leader, fared little better. Having lost control of all but one of his squads, he continued to press forward west of the road until he came upon T. Sgt. Robert A. Casey, another platoon leader, who also had lost contact with most of his men. Consolidating their small forces, Panich and Casey, with about ten men between them, continued to climb the slope of the ridge behind a stone wall that shielded them from machine gun fire coming from the crest. Spotting two of the enemy guns, most of the men took shelter in a large shell crater in order to provide covering fire while Lieutenant Panich along with four men crawled toward the guns. Reaching an open communications trench, apparently connecting the machine gun positions with the crews' sleeping quarters, Panich and his men hurled grenades until their supply was exhausted.

Still the German guns fired. The engagement was at an impasse until Panich, learning that Casey (in command of the covering force) had been wounded, was prompted to withdraw. Leading his own and Sergeant Casey's men toward the rear, the Lieutenant came upon Sergeant Pyenta and his small group near the cemetery. They joined forces, and, carrying their wounded, both groups withdrew to the company's former assembly area behind the cemetery.

A third group led by 1st Sgt. Paul N. Eddy came under several short rounds of supporting artillery fire and ran into brief fire fights with individual enemy skirmishers along the road, but continued to advance until halted by machine gun fire, apparently from the same guns that had stopped the other two groups. Failing to silence the guns with rifle grenades, the infantrymen dug in.

There they vainly awaited reinforcements until night came again on the 12th, when they too withdrew to the vicinity of the cemetery.

Captain Nelson, with about 100 men he had assembled, had, in the meantime, managed to slip through the enemy's defenses west of the road more by accident than design. Screened by a stone terrace on the west slope of the ridge, Nelson and his men continued to move forward, despite brief delays occasioned by machine gun and mortar fire. Nelson himself knocked out one machine gun position with a rifle grenade, and his men captured two mortars and overran fifteen half-dressed enemy soldiers in their dugouts. By dawn of the 12th, Nelson's small force had reached Tame, the cluster of houses about 400 yards west of Santa Maria Infante. There Nelson and his men established a strongpoint based on a culvert under the main road leading from Minturno to the Ausonia corridor.

Company E experienced similar confusion and dispersion while advancing on the right of the road leading into Santa Maria Infante from Minturno. Two of the company's platoons, followed by Colonel Kendall, the battalion commander, and his command group, climbed the forward slope at the right Tit and occupied the crest against short-lived resistance. The platoon on the right advanced rapidly through grain fields for about 150 yards to the sunken road traversing the slope of one of the spurs cutting the flank of the ridge. Crossing the road, the infantrymen deployed as skirmishers and assaulted over the crest of the spur; but machine gun fire from both flanks drove them back to the shelter of the sunken road.

On the left two squads of the other platoon, which had lagged behind, also sprinted forward and gained the sunken road. Moving cautiously, the two squads continued to within seventy-five yards of a house near the crest of the spur, when a machine gun opened fire from the house and forced them to halt.

The third squad, separated from the rest of the platoon, ran into mortar fire on the forward slope of the Tit. The men took cover until Capt. Robert K. Carlstone, the Company E commander, arrived and urged them forward. Although wounded by a shell burst shortly after his arrival, Carlstone refused evacuation until he could arrange for supporting artillery fire and turn the company over to the weapons platoon leader, 1st Lt. Harold V. McSwain.

As McSwain assumed command of Company E, Colonel Kendall, disturbed at the company's lack of progress, arrived on the forward slope of the right Tit. Striding upright among men who were crouching behind any shelter they could find, Colonel Kendall prodded a few of them good-naturedly with his swagger stick. "Come on, you bastards," he called out, "you'll never get to Rome this way!" [13] The very presence of Kendall—a tall, strapping figure—was enough to get the men moving again. Calling for more artillery fire on the crest of the spur, Kendall ordered his reserve company forward to join Company E.

Taking over direction of the attack, Lieutenant McSwain led Company E's support platoon to the sunken road, where he established contact with the

platoon about 150 yards to his left. But after a survey revealed a confused situation, he decided to reorganize his force before continuing. As the men waited under the intermittent glare of enemy flares, and as mortar fire and grenades shattered the ground around them, the moon broke through the overcast to illuminate the hillside with a pale light.

Learning that the attack had stalled, Colonel Kendall this time personally took command of the company. After requesting tanks to support the 2d Platoon advance along the main road, he himself led the 1st Platoon against the enemy's positions, apparently based upon houses on the crest of the spur.

As the lead squad of the 1st Platoon clambered over a stone wall and started to move toward the westernmost of the three houses, machine gun fire cut down all but three of the twelve men. The three survivors scrambled back to the sunken road. At the same time a second squad led by Kendall plodded up the slope toward the second house, the men firing as they advanced. Kendall successively fired every weapon he could lay his hands on—a carbine, an M1, and a bazooka. When his third bazooka rocket struck the house, he urged two of his men to charge the position. But again a machine gun opened fire, apparently from the house. Both men scrambled for cover.

At that point Kendall, calling on the rest of his men to follow, dashed forward. He personally destroyed the enemy gun and killed two of its crew while the survivors fled across the crest of the hill. As Kendall paused for a moment to hurl a grenade into the position, another enemy machine gun

[13] Sidney T. Mathews, Fifth Army His Sec, 1944, Combat Interview, CMH; 351st Inf AAR.

opened fire. Kendall fell mortally wounded, but as he did so he clutched the grenade to his body to prevent it from harming his companions. Kendall was dead, but the survivors of the 1st Platoon and a few men from the 2d and 3d Platoons at last had a precarious foothold on the spur.[14]

When word of the battalion commander's death reached Maj. Edwin Shull, the battalion executive officer, he assumed command and also moved forward to where most of Company E was dug in above and below the sunken road. After trying in vain to get the men moving again, Major Shull called for additional artillery fire on the objective and waited for new instructions from the regimental commander.

Since the attack had opened up, Company E had lost 89 men killed or wounded, roughly half of its starting strength. One enemy machine gun on the spur had been destroyed, but the accurate fire of about nine others still kept most of the men huddled in the cover of the sunken road.

The tank support requested by Kendall failed to arrive until 0300, when a platoon of five mediums from Company C of the supporting 760th Tank Battalion reached Company E's left flank. After a mine disabled the lead tank, the column halted behind the left Tit. An attempt to get the tanks moving again failed when the second tank also struck a mine. A third effort to get the tanks forward came to naught when another mine disabled yet a third tank. At 0500 Champeny re-

quested division headquarters to send him another platoon of tanks.

Until the additional armor arrived, Colonel Champeny ordered Company G (2d Battalion's reserve), assembling behind the right Tit in response to Kendall's earlier order, to reinforce Company E. Although Company E commander, 1st Lt. Theodore W. Noon, Jr., led his men as far as the sunken road, when they tried to storm the enemy positions beyond, machine gun fire from the westernmost house on the spur brought them to a halt.

Lieutenant Noon nevertheless rallied his men and returned to the assault. With one platoon he sought to envelop the enemy from the left, but even though his men advanced to within thirty yards of the house, they too were forced to fall back to the sunken road. Noon then tried to knock out the gun himself. With two of his men providing covering fire, he rushed the house. Hurling grenades and firing his pistol point-blank at the enemy position, Lieutenant Noon destroyed the gun, but not before the two men covering him were killed. Noon then withdrew to the sunken road.[15]

As daylight neared it was evident that the 351st Infantry's attack had failed to make significant headway toward Santa Maria Infante. About ninety men from Company F were on the outskirts of Tame but were confined to a small perimeter around the culvert and posed no serious threat to the Germans. Except for that group none of Champeny's units had been able to breach the defenses astride the Minturno road.

Shortly before daybreak, to get the

---

[14] For this action Colonel Kendall was posthumously awarded the DSC.

[15] For this action Noon was awarded the DSC.

stalled attack under way, Colonel Champeny ordered his reserve battalion (commanded by Maj. Charles P. Furr) to move along the west side of the Minturno road, pass through Company F, and envelop Santa Maria Infante from the left.

With Company K leading, Major Furr's battalion advanced beyond the left Tit, but there it came to a halt in the face of ubiquitous German machine gun fire. Furr then ordered Company I to swing further to the left in an effort to envelop the German defenses. He ordered Company K to regroup and support the envelopment with a renewed frontal assault.

Informed that elements of the 85th Division on his left had by that time occupied the S-Ridge, Major Furr anticipated little difficulty from that direction. Yet hardly had Company I begun its maneuver when the tragic inaccuracy of the information became apparent. Machine guns from the S-Ridge joined with guns to the front, as well as a bypassed machine gun somewhere along the road to the battalion's right rear, to strike Furr's companies from three directions. Again the attack ground to a halt.

The regimental commander realized at that point that until the enemy's positions on the S-Ridge were destroyed, any attempt to envelop the German defenses from the left was doomed to failure. The nature of the terrain and divisional boundaries precluded a wider envelopment maneuver from the left; therefore when Colonel Champeny asked permission to divert his attack to take the crest of S-Ridge his request was denied. A staff officer at division headquarters assured him

that the 338th Infantry of the neighboring 85th Division would soon take the ridge. Unfortunately that regiment was having as much difficulty on the slopes of the S-Ridge as was the 351st before Santa Maria Infante.

At that point Champeny called on his attached tank company to help smash a way up the Minturno road. Working throughout the rest of the night, the regimental mine platoon by daylight had succeeded in clearing the road to a point just beyond the Tits. Around noon a second platoon of five tanks, advancing along the road, destroyed two machine gun positions, but when the tanks tried to continue their advance, concealed antitank guns, firing from the outskirts of Santa Maria Infante, knocked out three and forced the others to withdraw behind the Tits. Several hours later a third platoon of tanks also attempted to force its way further along the road, only to encounter a similar fate. Concentrated fire by the guns of the 913th Field Artillery Battalion on the suspected location of the German guns about 700 yards east of the town likewise failed either to destroy the guns or to drive the Germans from their positions.

At the culvert near Tame, meanwhile, the Germans at the first light of day on the 12th discovered Captain Nelson's small force and quickly surrounded it. Throughout the day a beleaguered Company F fought back, its ammunition rapidly dwindling. At one point enemy self-propelled guns, advancing along the road from Spigno toward Tame, pounded the company with point-blank fire. All appeared lost until American artillery observers, soaring above the battlefield in small observation aircraft, spotted the German vehicles and, with well-directed fire from the supporting artillery battalion, destroyed two and drove the rest to cover.

Although the immediate threat to Company F was thus removed, as the hours passed the situation of the besieged force at the culvert worsened. By nightfall on the 12th food and ammunition were virtually exhausted, and Captain Nelson received an order from Major Shull to withdraw after dark to the vicinity of the Minturno cemetery. Nelson agreed to try but doubted whether he could do it. On that despairing note Nelson's radio fell silent.

Shortly after sundown several enemy soldiers approached the culvert position shouting "kamerad." Not suspecting a ruse, Nelson's men scrambled from their shelter to accept their surrender. Suddenly, from all sides German soldiers closed in. Except for five men who feigned death in their foxholes, the encircled men surrendered. That action effectively liquidated the 351st Infantry's only penetration of the German front. Despite heavy supporting fire—the 913th Field Artillery Battalion alone had fired 4,268 rounds—the enemy at nightfall on the 12th still held Santa Maria Infante.

As was evident from the German automatic weapons fire from the S-Ridge that had plagued the troops of the 351st Infantry during the assault on Santa Maria Infante, men of General Coulter's 85th Division on the left wing of the II Corps also faced determined resistance. Corps had ordered Coulter to capture the high ground overlooking the Ausonia corridor on the corps' left wing. Immediate objectives were the S-Ridge, the southern extension of the

ridge on which Santa Maria Infante was located; San Martino Hill, an isolated rise just north of the Capo d'Acqua Creek about three-quarters of a mile beyond the American forward positions; and the Domenico Ridge, the latter a group of low hills to the south of the San Martino feature overlooking the village of Scauri and the coastal highway. Control of the latter ridge would give the Americans terrain dominating the junction of the coastal highway and the road running through the Ausonia corridor, the enemy's first lateral line of communications and the road toward which the Minturno–Santa Maria Infante road led.

On the 85th Division's left wing Col. Brookner W. Brady's 339th Infantry, attacking with three battalions in line (in reserve, a fourth attached from Col. Oliver W. Hughes' 337th Infantry), advanced toward San Martino Hill and the Domenico Ridge. Antipersonnel mine fields and heavy fire from well-placed enemy automatic weapons made the going slow from the start. The best Brady's infantrymen could accomplish was to win tenuous footholds on the lower slopes of their objectives.[16]

On the 85th Division's right wing the 338th Infantry, commanded by Lt. Col. Alfred A. Safay, was to capture the S-Ridge, whose terraced sides were dotted with isolated stone cottages and an occasional grove of olive trees, with the

---

[16] During this action 1st Lt. Robert T. Waugh of Company G led his platoon in an assault against six enemy bunkers. Lieutenant Waugh advanced alone against the first bunker, threw phosphorous grenades into it, and then killed the defenders as they attempted to flee. He repeated this procedure with the remaining bunkers. For this and subsequent gallantry in the offensive, Lieutenant Waugh was awarded the Medal of Honor.

village of Solacciano perched on the ridge's seaward nose. Under cover of the artillery preparation, Safay's regiment began moving toward the S-Ridge at 2300 with two battalions abreast.

The 1st Battalion on the right, commanded by Maj. Vernon A. Ostendorf, struck at Hills 109 and 131, the latter the most imposing height along the S-Ridge and the site of the machine guns that later were greatly to plague the neighboring 351st Infantry in the attack against Santa Maria Infante. For the first two hours the two lead companies advanced through olive groves and grain fields up the southern slopes of the S-Ridge until halted midway to their objectives by a combination of antipersonnel mines and automatic weapons fire. Although one platoon from each company briefly gained the crest, they were pinned down there by heavy fire. Unable to get reinforcements forward and aware that the platoons could hardly hope to hold in the event of counterattack, the company commanders ordered withdrawal halfway down the forward slope.

On Major Ostendorf's left, the 3d Battalion, commanded by Lt. Col. William Mikkelson, encountered a growing volume of fire while advancing toward the village of Solacciano and high ground just east of the village. Experiencing their first hostile fire, the two lead companies advanced cautiously and slowly throughout the night. At daylight the battalion reached the outskirts of Solacciano where heavy automatic weapons fire forced a halt. During the day the 3d Battalion fought its way into the village to seize two houses, but even that limited gain came at a high price. By nightfall Mikkelson could

muster only 200 effectives to defend his forward position at Solacciano.

Like Colonel Champeny's men on the right, Colonel Safay's infantry, in spite of heavy artillery fire support, had been stalled by well-entrenched automatic weapons fire. Because these weapons had neither been silenced nor wrested from the Germans, Safay's men had little more to show for their first day of battle on the slopes of S-Ridge than had Colonel Champeny's in their approach to Santa Maria Infante.

The 349th Infantry, which General Sloan had held in reserve on Hill 105, about 1,600 yards northeast of Minturno and overlooking the Ausente Creek, had early on 12 May sent its 1st Battalion to occupy first phase objectives on the forward slope of the Casale Hill, some 1,200 yards southeast of Santa Maria Infante. There the battalion would remain until the afternoon of the 14th, when it again moved forward, this time to occupy Monte Bracchi by nightfall.

Everywhere the Germans had held. The fighting had hurt them severely, but as the first day ended this fact was hardly discernible to the Americans.

The massive artillery support of the II Corps' attack had taken a sharp toll. When, for example, General Steinmetz, commander of the *94th Division,* attempted to reinforce his troops on San Martino Hill with a company from his reserve, American artillery fire cut the company to pieces while the troops were assembling for their approach march. The heavy artillery fire had also played havoc with the enemy's line of communications between the division rear area and the front line, virtually isolating one from the other. Though that left what was essentially only a thin crust of resistance, it was one that proved remarkably tough in the face of renewed American assault the next day.

With the coming of daylight on the 12th, Allied fighter and medium fighter-bombers, according to plan, began a daylong attack against enemy headquarters, lines of communications, and supply dumps in an effort to complete the isolation of the battlefield begun earlier by Operation STRANGLE. Artillery spotter and control aircraft were especially effective throughout the day in locating enemy batteries and directing both friendly artillery and tactical bombers against them. Even Kesselring's and Vietinghoff's headquarters came under attack. Allied planes destroyed the *Tenth Army* field headquarters in the first hours of the offensive and severely damaged *Army Group C*'s command post near Frascati in the Alban Hills south of Rome.[17]

The Capture of Monte Majo

General Juin envisioned the role that his French Expeditionary Corps would play in the early stages of the Allied offensive as participation in a series of three battles, to be fought in several phases and all aimed at eventually turning the enemy's second major defensive line south of Rome, the Hitler Line.

The first objective was a breakthrough over the Monte Majo massif to win footholds on the massif's two parallel ridges. Juin expected his troops to capture Monte Majo within the first five hours of the offensive. To protect the right flank of this thrust, the French would, as a preliminary action, have to

drive the Germans from relatively strong positions on the high ground overlooking the axis of attack. The high ground consisted of three terrain features—Cerasola Hill, Hill 739, and Monte Garofano—rising from a high plateau named Massa di Ruggero.[18]

General Juin planned to exploit a breakthrough in the Monte Majo massif with drives along parallel northwest-running ridges to seize the Ausonia defile at the northern end of the Ausonia corridor. With that defile in hand, Juin expected to turn his corps westward toward Monte Fammera, northernmost summit of the Petrella massif. Monte Fammera would provide the needed foothold for an advance deep into the massif.

The objective of the second battle was to be a blocking action east of the town of Esperia, and included the capture of the town and nearby Monte d'Oro, a dominant height overlooking the Liri valley. If successful this operation would sever communications between the *XIV Panzer Corps* and the *LI Mountain Corps*, the latter opposing the British Eighth Army at Monte Cassino and in the Liri valley.

In the third battle, Juin planned to send his forces first against Monti del Montrono and della Commundo, overlooking the road junction of Pontecorvo in the Liri valley. From there he would be able to send a column northwestward to envelop the town of Pico, another road junction on the Germans' second lateral route of communications between the Tyrrhenian coast and the Liri valley. Meanwhile, a provisional

---

[17] Craven and Cate, eds., *AAF III*, p. 387.

[18] *C.E.F., État Major, Mémoires du Avril* (24 Apr 44), *pièce Nr. 117.* The following paragraphs are based upon this document.

TERRAIN IN FRENCH CORPS SECTOR SHOWING CASTELFORTE AND MONTE MAJO *(background)*.

corps under Maj. Gen. Francois Sevez was to approach the town from the southeast.

Judging it to be best qualified for the demanding requirements of mountain warfare, General Juin selected Maj. Gen. André W. Dody's 2d Moroccan Division to spearhead the thrust through the Monte Majo massif. General Sevez's 4th Moroccan Mountain Division, recently arrived in Italy from occupation duty on Corsica, was to attack on Dody's right but minus a substantial portion of its infantry, which Juin brigaded with General Guillaume's

goumiers to form a provisional mountain corps under General Sevez. Upon this task force Juin placed the main burden of the drive west from Monte Fammera and toward the enemy's second lateral communications road, a drive to be launched once Dody's Moroccans had captured the Ausonia defile. In all three battles, enemy strongpoints were to be bypassed whenever possible in order to maintain the momentum of the attack and to sustain and exploit the surprise that Juin expected to gain at Monte Majo.

Juin's G–2 knew that the left wing of

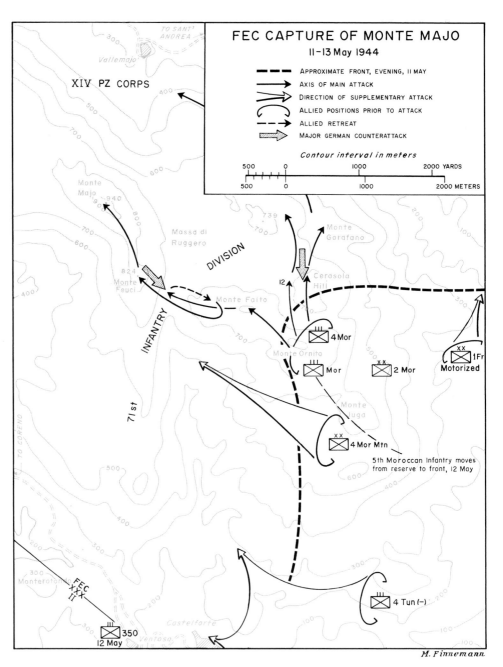

FEC CAPTURE OF MONTE MAJO
11-13 May 1944

━━━ APPROXIMATE FRONT, EVENING, 11 MAY
──▶ AXIS OF MAIN ATTACK
⟩⟩▶ DIRECTION OF SUPPLEMENTARY ATTACK
↺ ALLIED POSITIONS PRIOR TO ATTACK
--▶ ALLIED RETREAT
⟹ MAJOR GERMAN COUNTERATTACK

Contour interval in meters

500   0   1000   2000 YARDS
500   0   1000   2000 METERS

TO SANT' ANDREA

Vallemajo

XIV PZ CORPS

Monte Majo 940

Massa di Ruggero

DIVISION

739

Monte Garafano

824 Monte Feuci

Monte Faito

Cerasola Hill

12

INFANTRY

4 Mor

Monte Ornito

Mor

2 Mor

1 Fr Motorized

71st

Monte Juga

4 Mor Mtn

5th Moroccan Infantry moves from reserve to front, 12 May

TO CORENO

FEC XXX II

Monteratanio

Castelforte

4 Tun (-)

350
12 May

Ventosa

M. Finnemann

MAP 2

Senger's *XIV Panzer Corps* stretched from the Ausonia corridor across the Monte Majo massif into the Liri valley. In the mountain sector the corps front was thinly held by the *71st Division,* under the command of General Raapke. This was a light infantry division with a strength of 10,000 men, supported by eighty artillery pieces, a few Italian assault guns, and a dozen self-propelled antitank guns—a relatively small force when compared with Juin's corps of approximately 90,000 men. Some thirty miles to the rear Senger held about forty tanks as part of his corps reserve.

Interrogation of a German noncommissioned officer captured a week before the offensive revealed that a few miles behind the Gustav Line Senger had directed preparation of a switch position that he designated the Orange Line. Actually, existence of the line proved later to have been limited largely to operations maps. Extensive aerial reconnaissance also disclosed that the enemy had virtually no defenses along that part of the Hitler Line extending through the Aurunci Mountains southwest of the village of Sant' Oliva, about three miles south of the road junction of Pontecorvo in the Liri valley. It appeared that Kesselring expected to rely upon the formidable mountains themselves as constituting a sufficient barrier.

In darkness, for the moon would not rise for another half hour, the infantrymen of the 2d Moroccan Mountain Division began moving at 2300 on 11 May from their assembly areas on Monte Juga toward assault positions on the eastern slopes of the Monte Majo massif, there to await completion of the bombardment of the enemy's positions in the forbidding heights far above. For the next half hour the Moroccans waited while shells from some 400 guns, including those of the U.S. 13th Artillery Brigade, smashed into the rocky slopes.[19]

A week earlier Allied registration fires had prompted the German commander, General Raapke, to move most of his artillery into alternate positions so that the Allied guns inflicted few losses on his batteries. Dispersed in well-covered dugouts and too close to the French lines to be hit by the artillery, Raapke's infantrymen also remained virtually unscathed by the preparatory fire. As on the II Corps front, the principal effect of the Allied fire was to disrupt wire communications and isolate scattered infantry positions.

During the first two hours of the attack, the Moroccan infantrymen fought their way to within 300 yards of the summit of Monte Ornito, a 2,000-foot peak about two miles southeast of Monte Majo, the division's objective. The Moroccans had just reached their new positions when local reserves of the *71st Division*'s *191st Grenadier Regiment* counterattacked. (*Map 2*)

Failure of the artillery to make punishing inroads on the enemy infantry all too soon became apparent. Although by midmorning of the 12th a regiment of the 2d Moroccan Mountain Division fought its way to the crest of Monte Faito, a mile and a half southeast of

---

[19] In this account the author has drawn upon two sources: Sidney T. Mathews, "The French in the Drive on Rome," prepared in CMH for publication in *Fraternité d'Armes Franco-Américaine,* a special issue of the *Revue Historique de l'Armée* (Paris, 1957); and Juin, *La Campagne d'Italie,* pp. 101–12.

Monte Majo, with light losses, the troops were still over a mile short of Monte Majo, which General Juin had confidently expected to take within the first five hours of the offensive. What was more important, German defenders had thwarted a supporting attack on the right aimed at the high ground—Cerasola Hill, Hill 739, and Monte Garofano—overlooking the route the Moroccans would have to take from Monte Faito to Monte Majo.

Despite the failure to take the high ground indispensable for a successful attack on Monte Majo, the division commander, General Dody, tried to resume the advance toward the objective. Yet hardly had the men begun to move when fire from the heights on the right brought them to a halt.

Still determined to press on, General Dody ordered a regrouping, but before the men could move out again, a German battalion, reinforced by troops earlier driven off Monte Faito, counterattacked. Only with the help of massed artillery fire were the Moroccans able to repulse the threat, but the action left them too disorganized immediately to renew their attempt to take Monte Majo.

Although Generalmajor Friedrich Wentzell, chief of staff and acting commander of the *Tenth Army* in General von Vietinghoff's absence, and General der Artillerie Walter Hartmann, acting commander of the *XIV Panzer Corps* in Senger's absence, informed Field Marshal Kesselring of the unexpected severity of the French attack against the Monte Majo sector—unexpected, because the Germans had no idea of the size of Juin's force assembled in the bend of the Garigliano—the army

group commander remained convinced that it was nothing more than a supporting operation for what he considered to be the main Allied effort in the Liri valley. Until Kesselring determined that this was not so and that there was to be no amphibious landing on his Tyrrhenian flank, he would refuse to authorize commitment of reserves to shore up the *71st Infantry Division*'s sector. The best he would do was to authorize the movement of two reserve battalions into supporting positions behind the *94th* and *71th Divisions*' sectors. He retained for himself, however, the right to say when either of the battalions might be committed. General Raapke, Kesselring insisted, should create additional reserves by the familiar expedient of thinning out less threatened sectors. Hartmann saw no alternative, therefore, to ordering the *71st Division* commander to use his reserve battalion of panzer grenadiers. It was that battalion whose counterattack had just thrown the Moroccans off balance.[20]

It seemed at this point that the French attack had stalled because of the same kind of resistance encountered by the U.S. II Corps on their left and by the British 13 Corps on their right. The failure to take the division objective as planned could be attributed directly to the failure to control the high ground on the right of the corps zone of operations.

To revitalize the attack, General Dody proposed to the corps commander that he take advantage of the coming darkness to move on Monte Majo without first clearing the high ground. General Juin rejected this pro-

[20] MS # R–50 (Bailey), CMH.

posal, for he was convinced that even if Dody's troops managed to slip past the high ground during the night, the enemy would emerge at daylight to harass their flank. Instead Juin ordered Dody to employ his reserve regiment in a night attack to clear the high ground on the right, first against Cerasola Hill and then against the other two hills in turn. Shortly after the attack began, Dody's assault forces were to move out once again from Monte Faito toward Monte Majo. This, Juin insisted confidently, would carry the objective.

General Juin's confidence permeated Dody's staff, and in a few hours the units were in position to renew the attack. At 0320 on 13 May, all artillery attached to Dody's division, except for two battalions supporting the troops on Monte Faito, began to fire on Cerasola Hill. Forty minutes later, as the reserve regiment began to advance, the artillery fire shifted to Hill 739 and finally to Monte Garofano. At the last minute, before the Moroccan infantry began their ascent, a detachment of combat engineers rushed forward with bangalore torpedoes to blow gaps in barbed wire blocking the path of the advance.

The artillery apparently did its job well, for, as the riflemen climbed the slope, German reaction was almost nonexistent. Reducing the few positions that had escaped the bombardment, the Moroccans moved quickly on to the next objective, Hill 739, and then to the third, Monte Garofano. Within two and a half hours the regiment had occupied all three objectives, capturing 150 enemy soldiers in the process, and even advanced a few hundred yards farther to occupy yet another hill mass overlooking the village of Vallomajo in the shadow of Monte Majo.

Success was not to be so readily achieved on the left, where the regiment making the 2d Moroccan's main effort tried to get moving shortly after 0400, first toward an intermediate objective, Monte Feuci, about midway between Monte Faito and the objective, then on to Monte Majo. Almost immediately the regiment ran into a counterattack by the *71st Division*'s lone reserve battalion. Even though the Moroccans held, employing mortar and artillery fire with deadly effect to drive the Germans back, the action checked the French advance.

Three more times before daylight and again at 0900 the German battalion tried to recapture Monte Faito with no success. Now the French, rather than the Germans, occupied the high ground on the right, which hampered the counterattacks from Monte Feuci just as it had earlier hampered French efforts to attack toward that feature. French gunners, with the observation advantage that daylight brought, had turned the last counterattack into a costly failure. Broken by heavy casualties, the enemy battalion fell back in disorder. Covered by an artillery preparation, the Moroccan infantrymen reached the crest of Monte Feuci by 1130; not a shot was fired against them.

The destruction of Raapke's reserve battalion, after the heavy punishment the troops in the main line of resistance had already taken, meant that no means existed for holding the Monte Majo sector of the Gustav Line. As the French regrouped, a radio operator intercepted a German radio message saying: "Feuci has fallen. Accelerate the general withdrawal." When a platoon-sized patrol left Monte Feuci a few minutes later to test German defenses on Monte Majo, the results appeared to confirm the German message, for the patrol found not a German there. In late afternoon a battalion came forward to occupy the division objective and to raise on an improvised flagstaff a French tricolor large enough to be seen from Monte Cassino to the Tyrrhenian Sea.

Breaking through to Monte Majo on 13 May, the Moroccans had breached the Gustav Line at one of its deepest, albeit most weakly defended, points. The feat had unhinged the entire left wing of the *XIV Panzer Corps*. It also had split General Raapke's *71st Division* and opened the way for further advances along the parallel ridges running northwest toward Ausonia, San Giorgio, and Esperia and for a thrust across the Ausonia defile to Monte Fammera. Most importantly for the Eighth Army, it had put the FEC in a position to bring pressure against the right flank of the German defenses in the Liri valley.

It was to this latter threat that Field Marshal Kesselring now directed his attention. Kesselring at last realized that his southern front and not his Tyrrhenian flank between Rome and Civitavecchia was the point of greatest danger. Accordingly, late on the 13th, he ordered the *90th Panzer Grenadier Division* to begin moving from its coast-watching position near the mouth of the Tiber southeastward to the southern front. Despite Allied air attacks against all enemy traffic, the last unit of the division managed to depart in the early hours of the 14th. Traveling mostly at night, the *200th Panzer Grenadier Regiment* was the first unit to reach the southern front, some seventy-five miles away, early on 14 May. As the regiment arrived it was committed on the *71st Division*'s left in an effort to stem the French advance from Monte Majo toward the town of San Giorgio on the southern edge of the Liri valley.[21]

---

[21] Greiner and Schramm, eds., *OKW/WFSt, KTB*, IV (1), pp. 489–90.

CHAPTER IV

Collapse of the Gustav Line

Despite the Allied command's long-held conviction that Monte Cassino would have to fall before there could be any appreciable success in the Liri valley, it now seemed, with the French breakthrough of the Gustav Line, that Monte Majo instead of Monte Cassino might be the key, not only to the Fifth Army's advance through the mountains south of the Liri but also to the Eighth Army's penetration of the enemy's defenses in the valley itself. Northeast of Monte Cassino the 2 Polish Corps had withdrawn to its line of departure as of the night of 11 May, leaving the *1st Parachute Division* still master of the ruined abbey and its neighboring ridges, but General Raapke had been forced to commit his last reserves in a vain attempt to prevent the FEC from taking Monte Majo. The threat to Monte Majo and the need to reinforce that sector during the night of 12 May doubtless had been a factor in the German failure to prevent the British 13 Corps from widening and deepening its foothold beyond the Rapido. Thus by morning on the 13th the British 4th Division at last succeeded in bridging the river. With three pontoon bridges in operation—southeast of Cassino the 8th Indian Division had succeeded in building two the previous night—the 13 Corps soon had a secure bridgehead, varying in depth from 1,000 to 2,500 yards.

The Eighth Army had accomplished what the Fifth Army had failed to do during the winter campaign: establish and reinforce a bridgehead beyond the Rapido. Although Monte Cassino remained in German hands, the 13 Corps had managed to construct bridges over which it could reinforce its units at will. Since the assault divisions had incurred considerable casualties, General Leese authorized the corps commander (General Kirkman) to commit his reserve division, the 78th, on 14 May and at the same time warned General Anders (the 2 Polish Corps commander) to be prepared to resume his attack on Monte Cassino the next day. The 78th Division was to move out as soon as possible after dawn in order to pass through the British and Indian divisions south of Cassino and Highway 6 and make contact with the Polish troops—hopefully, sometime on the 15th—at a point on the highway southwest of Monte Cassino.[1]

While the 78th Division assembled east of the Rapido preparatory to crossing into the 4th Division's zone, the XII Tactical Air Command flew 520 sorties in support of the British 4th and Indian 8th Divisions. In spite of clear weather and undisputed mastery of the skies, the strafing and bombing attacks failed to silence enemy batteries firing

---

[1] Operations of British, Indian, and Dominion Forces in Italy, Part II, Sec. B. Unless otherwise noted this and the following section are based upon this reference.

from well-concealed positions in the vicinity of Atina, approximately seven miles north of Monte Cassino.

The artillery fire, plus stiffening resistance to efforts to expand the bridgehead, as well as the first indications of growing traffic congestion on the few available roads—a problem that would eventually harass the Eighth Army in the Liri valley almost as much as would the enemy—so delayed the 78th Division that it was unable to get into position to fulfill its exploitation role. Although the 4th British and 8th Indian Divisions continued to push ahead, it became clear by nightfall that the corps would be unable to reach the highway by the morning of the 15th. That prompted General Leese to postpone the Polish attack on Monte Cassino. The Eighth Army had penetrated the Gustav Line but had not broken through.

German Countermeasures

In preventing an Allied breakthrough in the Liri valley on the 14th, the Germans had paid a high price. That night Generalleutnant Bruno Ortner, the commanding general of the *44th Division*, reported to the *LI Mountain Corps* headquarters that because of heavy losses and fragmentation of units within his division his front would have to be heavily reinforced or else he would have to withdraw into the Hitler (Senger) Line, at the latest during the night of 15 May.[2]

In response, General Feuerstein, the corps commander, authorized neither course. The only major reinforcement available in the corps area was the *90th*

Panzer Grenadier Division, but part of it had already been committed on the *XIV Panzer Corps'* left flank to reinforce the faltering *71st Infantry Division.* On the 15th, however, Feuerstein ordered the *361st Panzer Grenadier Regiment,* the second of the *90th Panzer Grenadier Division's* two motorized infantry regiments, to bolster the defense of Ortner's front on the Pignataro sector, about three miles southwest of the town of Cassino on the Cassino–San Giorgio road, but the regiment would arrive too late to prevent the Indian infantry, supported by armor, from capturing the village of Pignataro and breaking through the German lines about a half mile northwest of the town by midnight the same day.[3]

Meanwhile, on the *XIV Panzer Corps* front opposite the Fifth Army, General Hartmann, the acting corps commander, prepared countermeasures against the U.S. II Corps. He despaired of restoring his front against the French, but remained confident that, at least for the present, he could continue to hold opposite the Americans. Although the American 85th Division had penetrated the *94th Division's* front between the S-Ridge and the Domenico Ridge and had won a foothold in the village of Solacciano, Hartmann believed that those minor penetrations could be eliminated. It was therefore with some expectation of success that he ordered the *94th Division* commander, General Steinmetz, to launch counterattacks to pinch them off.[4]

---

[2] *LI Mtn Corps, Ia KTB,* Nr. 2, 14 May 44, *LI Mtn Corps Doc. No. 55779/1.*

[3] *Ibid.,* 15 May 44; G.W.L. Nicholson, "Official History of the Canadian Army in the Second World War," vol. 11, *The Canadians in Italy, 1943–1945* (Ottawa: Edmund Clothier, G. M. C., O.O., D.S.P., 1956), p. 406.

[4] MS # R–50 (Bailey), CMH.

Less sanguine than the corps commander, General Steinmetz, on the night of 12 May, nevertheless counterattacked on his right wing, from the S-Ridge to the coastal corridor; but except for some slight gains on the Domenico ridge the Germans failed to regain the lost ground. Accurate concentrations of American artillery fire had broken up the counterattacks and forced them back with heavy casualties that Steinmetz could ill afford. The *94th Division* commander now recognized that unless his troops could be reinforced before the next American onslaught, his thin, brittle front would soon crack. He had no alternative but to act on a suggestion General Hartmann had earlier given the *71st Division* commander: create his own reserves in the customary manner. In view of the strength of the Allied offensive across the entire corps front on 12 May, such a do-it-yourself scheme for obtaining needed reserves was patently the counsel of despair.[5]

The II Corps' Attack Renewed

General Steinmetz's despair contrasted sharply with General Clark's reaction to the results of operations on his own front. Sensing a breakthrough by the Fifth Army, Clark was impatient with what he deemed to be a lack of aggressiveness and flexibility in the II Corps' attack. That lack was particularly apparent when contrasted with the élan and drive shown by the FEC in its thrust into the Monte Majo massif. Though aware that the latter was composed of veteran, professional mountain troops, while 85th and 88th Divisions

were mainly conscripts engaging in their first combat operation, in view of the strength concentrated by the II Corps before the enemy's positions at Santa Maria Infante, Clark believed that Sloan's 88th Division should have cleared the village by noon on 12 May.[6]

Contrary to the impression created by the stubborn enemy resistance, General Keyes (II Corps commander) believed, as did General Steinmetz, that the German front was near the breaking point. Convinced that one more effort would pierce the Gustav Line, Keyes called both of his division commanders to corps headquarters early on the 13th to plan for a continuation of the attack.

The 88th Division commander, General Sloan, presented a reassuring picture of the situation on his right wing, where the 350th Infantry held the village of Ventosa and Hill 316, key points on the regimental objective of Monte Damiano. Troops from the 350th Infantry were also building up on Monte Ceracoli, and infantry with a platoon of tanks in support had thrust north of that feature toward the Ausonia corridor.[7]

Unfortunately, progress on the 88th Division's right wing had far exceeded that on the left, which was one of the causes of Clark's concern. Along both sides of the Minturno–Santa Maria Infante road the troops of the 351st Infantry still faced strong opposition. Numerous strongpoints near the village of Pulcherini on the western slope of Monte Bracchi, on the Spur, at Santa Maria Infante, and on the S-Ridge

---

[5] Greiner and Schramm, eds., *OKW/WPSt, KTB,* pp. 488-91.

[6] Clark Diary, 13 May 44.

[7] Memo, Hq. II Corps, 13 May 44, sub: Conference of Corps and Division Commanders at 0730, in II Corps G–3 Jnl.

southwest of Tame were holding up
General Sloan's left wing as well as
General Coulter's right.

On the credit side, losses incurred by
the two divisions in the early hours of
the offensive had been quickly made up
by replacements held in readiness in
division rear areas. As an experiment,
each division had been assigned sufficient overstrength to permit the creation of replacement detachments in
support of each regiment. Having
trained with their assigned unit, these
men could be quickly integrated when
replacements were needed, so that the
two U.S. divisions were prepared to
continue their attacks on 13 May with
almost the same numbers as on the
11th, the day the offensive began.

Keyes continued to place the main
burden of the renewed effort on
Sloan's 88th Division, which was to
resume its attack during the afternoon
of the 13th. The corps commander also
shifted the interdivisional boundary
slightly to the left to give the 88th
Division, which was to continue its drive
on Santa Maria Infante, the additional
task of clearing the northern end of the
S-Ridge (Hills 109, 128, and 126), but
leaving Hill 131 in the 85th Division's
sector. Thus, the division bore responsibility for eliminating the machine guns
that had been so troublesome on the
351st Infantry's left flank. Coulter's
85th Division, meanwhile, was to consolidate its recently won positions at Solacciano and on the San Martino Hill and
protect the corps' left flank by maintaining strong pressures on the Domenico Ridge.[8]

In making plans at the division level

to resume the attack, General Sloan
decided to shift the boundary of Colonel Crawford's 349th Infantry westward
to include the sector of the 1st Battalion, 351st Infantry. This freed the 1st
Battalion, still relatively fresh, to try to
take Santa Maria Infante from the left
flank. The battalion was to capture Hill
109 on the S-Ridge, then swing northward along the ridge through Tame to
envelop Santa Maria Infante from the
northwest. While this battalion maneu-
vered on the left, the 2d and 3d
Battalions, astride the Minturno road,
were to maintain pressure by holding
attacks against the Spur and Hill 103.
On the left, Coulter's 85th Division was
to help with a renewed attack by Colonel Safay's 338th Infantry against Hill
131.

Shortly after the conference, General
Clark arrived at Keyes' command post.
Concluding that the Germans had been
thrown off balance by the magnitude of
the Allied offensive, the Fifth Army
commander directed Keyes to press his
attack throughout the night, with the
88th Division driving through Santa
Maria Infante, crossing the Ausonia
corridor, and capturing the village of
Spigno on the edge of the Petrella
massif preparatory to a thrust across
the mountains, as the French were even
then preparing to do from Monte
Majo. Back at his own headquarters at
Caserta that afternoon, Clark noted
confidently in his diary that "we should
have Spigno tonight."[9]

While the divisions prepared to renew their efforts on the afternoon of
the 13th, three U.S. fighter-bombers
attacked Santa Maria Infante, already

[8] Ibid.

[9] Clark Diary, 14 May 44.

reduced to Cassino-like ruins. As if in response, the enemy made one of his rare air raids over Allied lines. At 1330 three out of a flight of twenty-two FW–190's eluded Allied air patrols and bombed and strafed the 85th Division sector in the vicinity of Minturno-Tremonsuoli, but damage was light and casualties few.

Although the 351st Infantry commander, Colonel Champeny, had designated 1630 as the jump-off hour, a slow approach march by the 1st Battalion to its line of departure at the base of the S-Ridge was followed by a series of delays that for several hours jeopardized the operation. Taking longer to launch its attack because it had a greater distance to move from an assembly area near the cemetery than had the other battalions, the 1st Battalion also had difficulty in co-ordinating its plans with those of Colonel Safay's 338th Infantry, which was preparing to attack Hill 131, the southernmost knob of the S-Ridge. The battalion was further delayed when enemy mortar fire pinned down the commander and several of his staff while they were on reconnaissance, separating them from their units and killing the heavy weapons company commander. Not until six hours after the time originally set for the attack did the battalion at last begin to move toward Hill 109, 300 yards northwest of Hill 131. Learning of the 1st Battalion's failure to reach its line of departure on time, Champeny postponed the regimental attack first for half an hour, then for another thirty minutes, and finally for an additional hour.[10]

[10] Unless otherwise indicated the following tactical narrative is based upon official records of the 85th and 88th Divisions and the II Corps.

Unfortunately, word of the postponements failed to reach the 2d Battalion, assembled east of the Minturno road. Ordered to pin down the defenders of Santa Maria Infante by an attack against the Spur, the battalion moved out as originally planned at 1630. As the lead companies approached the sunken road on the eastern slope of the Spur, where the attack on the 12th had halted, the Germans from the vicinity of Santa Maria Infante and Pulcherini brought down a heavy volume of artillery and small arms fire. The men nevertheless reached the crest of the Spur, where continued heavy fire drove them to cover and prevented them from going further.

On the left, in the 85th Division's sector, a tank-infantry team, composed of two platoons from Company I, 338th Infantry, and about ten tanks from Company C, 756th Tank Battalion, with which Colonel Safay planned to cover the left flank of Colonel Champeny's attack, also failed to get word of the postponement. Tanks and infantry moved toward Hill 131 on the S-Ridge, but the former were soon wallowing helplessly in a small gully at the foot of the hill. Unassisted, the two infantry platoons nevertheless quickly overran the enemy on Hill 131, capturing about forty Germans but losing over half the American riflemen in the process. When the Germans struck back almost immediately with a sharp local counterattack, they forced the survivors to fall back to their original positions down the slope. By evening only sixteen men remained of the original infantry force that had attacked Hill 131.

When, after two hours, the 1st Battalion, 351st Infantry, still failed to appear, Colonel Champeny, apparently unaware of the 338th Infantry's setback on Hill 131, decided to wait no longer. He ordered the 3d Battalion to maintain its pressure against Hill 103 along the left side of the Minturno road in support of the 2d Battalion, already battling on the Spur.

Beginning at 1825, the 2d Chemical Battalion and the 913th Field Artillery Battalion, assisted by guns of corps artillery, fired several hundred rounds of smoke, white phosphorous, and high explosives on the villages of Santa Maria Infante and Pulcherini. On the heels of this preparatory fire, the 3d Battalion's two forward companies began to move toward Hill 103, about 500 yards west of the Spur. Company L was to pin down the enemy from the front, while Company I worked around the western slope to envelop the enemy from the crest. Meanwhile, Company K was to provide supporting fire from positions just west of the road leading to Santa Maria Infante.

As Company I attempted to begin its envelopment, 30 to 40 rounds of 88-mm. fire fell into the battalion sector. Heavy and accurate mortar fire also blanketed the area, forcing the lead companies to fall back in disorder to their starting positions. Company K was down to half its strength, Company I lost one-third of its effectives, and Company L also incurred heavy losses. The battalion S–3 reported despairingly to the regimental commander: "Two years of training [have] gone up in smoke . . . my men . . . about half of them—almost all my leaders." [11]

Close on that misfortune, the long-

delayed 1st Battalion began assembling for its attack on Hill 109. The commander, Maj. Harold MacV. Brown, decided on a frontal attack in a column of companies, with Company C leading the way. Once Company C reached the crest, the next company in line was to pass through and move northward along the crest to clear Hill 126 on the northern end of the ridge.

Shortly after midnight, following a 10-minute artillery preparation, men of Company C, advancing with two platoons forward, began to pick their way up the southern slope of Hill 109. Midway up the slope men of this company, as had other 1st Battalion troops, came under mortar and machine gun fire from Hill 131. Also like these other troops, they too believed Hill 131 to be in friendly hands. The company commander (1st Lt. Garvin C. MacMakin) ordered his men to dig in where they were while he brought his reserve platoon forward and surveyed the situation.

During MacMakin's absence his executive officer, assuming that the fire on his troops from Hill 131 was coming from American guns, disregarded the advice of fellow officers and set out alone toward the hill. Shouting repeatedly, "We're Americans, stop your fire!" he approached to within a few yards of the German positions. A short burst of enemy fire cut him down.

To Lieutenant MacMakin it was obvious at this point that something had gone wrong with Colonel Safay's attack on the left. He decided to hold his men where they were until somebody had cleared Hill 131.

Colonel Champeny, in turn, informed his division headquarters that

---

[11] Telephone Log, 351st Inf Jnl, 13 May 44.

he was "catching hell from Hill 131," and requested permission to go into the 85th Division's zone and clear it himself. Until the hill was taken, Champeny pointed out, his regiment simply would be unable to move. General Coulter, the 85th Division commander, denied permission, apparently wary of the hazards of violating unit boundaries in the darkness. Coulter declined even to approve neutralizing artillery fire against the hill, since the fire might endanger his own men on the forward slope of the S-Ridge.

Colonel Champeny, convinced that he could not take Hill 109 and outflank Santa Maria Infante while Hill 131 remained in enemy hands, ignored the refusal. He took it on himself to order Major Brown to seize the hill with the reserve company of his 1st Battalion.[12]

Lieutenant MacMakin of Company C had in the meantime brought up his reserve platoon. With the men of this platoon in position to cover the flank that faced Hill 131, he decided to try again to take Hill 109. With two platoons abreast, MacMakin started up the hill. This time, to his surprise, hardly any German resistance developed. His men quickly gained the crest and found there only a small enemy rear guard, eager to surrender.

Even as MacMakin's infantrymen deployed on Hill 109 and while it was still dark, Major Brown's reserve company started to climb Hill 131. There too the Americans were in for a surprise. The company encountered only scattered bursts of machine gun fire and reached the top of the hill with few losses. By that time the men found only empty dugouts, probably abandoned by a rear guard that had just slipped away unobserved in the darkness. The only Germans remaining were on the reverse slope—they were dead, victims of the first day's artillery fire.

The Germans Fall Back on the Right

The unexpected ease with which the men of the 351st Infantry's 1st Battalion finally captured Hills 109 and 131 was, without their knowing it, a direct dividend of the French breakthrough in the Monte Majo sector on the afternoon of the 13th. As the French had widened their breach in the Gustav Line during the rest of the day and through the night, General Hartmann, the acting *XIV Panzer Corps* commander, ordered Steinmetz to pull back his left wing about a mile and to anchor it on Monte Civita, two miles northwest of Santa Maria Infante, where contact could be re-established with Raapke's battered *71st Division*.[13]

During the night General Steinmetz withdrew across the Ausonia corridor, leaving a rear guard behind. In an effort to strengthen his center, he also pulled back his troops from the coastal salient on his right flank near Monte Scauri. Because neither Sloan nor Coulter hampered its movement, Steinmetz's division by morning had managed to establish itself in the Gustav Line's rearmost positions along the high ground extending from Monte Scauri northward to a point east of Castellonorato along the crests of hills overlooking the Ausonia corridor from the west

---

[12] Msg 118, 132335, CO, 351st Inf, to CG, 88th Div, in 88th Div G–3 Jnl, 11–15 May 44, vol. 4, incl. 7.

[13] MS # R–50 (Bailey), CMH. Unless otherwise indicated this section is based upon this reference.

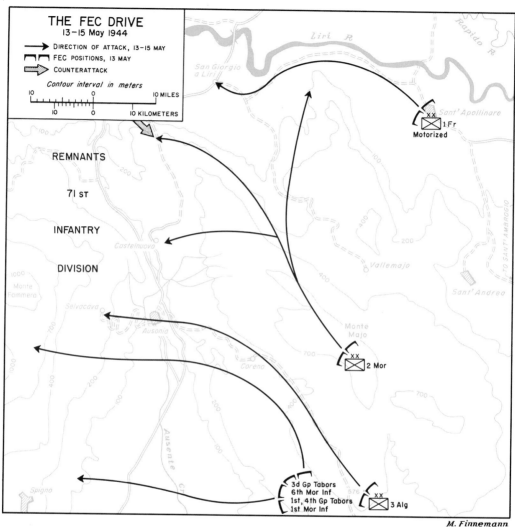

THE FEC DRIVE
13–15 May 1944

→ DIRECTION OF ATTACK, 13–15 MAY
⌐⌐ FEC POSITIONS, 13 MAY
⇨ COUNTERATTACK

Contour interval in meters

MAP 3

to the eastern slope of Monte Civita. From there Steinmetz's *94th Infantry Division* linked up with the *71st Division*'s right flank. The French continued to widen their gap in the Monte Majo massif and advance toward San Giorgio on the southern flank of the Liri valley, while the *94th Infantry Division*, on the *XIV Panzer Corps*' right flank, would try

to stabilize its front along the new line. (*Map 3*)

As the two Allied armies prepared to continue their offensive on the 14th, the Germans found control over their front line increasingly difficult to maintain because individual combat units, dispersed by Allied breakthrough and penetrations, had lost both leaders and communications. Steinmetz was sure that unless Kesselring released considerable reinforcements, his, Steinmetz's, division would be unable to achieve more than to hold the Americans briefly short of the Hitler Line (*Senger Riegel*). A withdrawal into the second line of defense appeared inevitable and would most likely have to be set up by the night of 15 May.[14]

The Fall of Santa Maria Infante

The U.S. II Corps commander, General Keyes, meanwhile had learned from reconnaissance reports during the night of 13 May that the enemy had demolished a bridge on the road leading from Ausonia to the coast and the first lateral communications route behind the enemy front. That confirmed Keyes' suspicions that Steinmetz was preparing to fall back to new positions west of the road. Keyes promptly directed Sloan to move his men as rapidly as possible into Santa Maria Infante **and then on to occupy the Monte Bracchi, Rotondo, and Cerri, the high** ground to the northeast of the village. A day earlier Clark had told Keyes to strike across the Ausonia corridor and seize Spigno as rapidly as possible. But the hard fighting and uncertainty as to the extent of the enemy withdrawal since the 11th had left both troops and corps commander unprepared for a headlong pursuit of the enemy. Instead, Keyes ordered Sloan to send strong patrols into the corridor to locate the enemy.[15] (*Map III*)

Before dawn on the 14th, the 349th Infantry's 1st Battalion advanced in a column of companies to occupy Monte Bracchi. Meeting little resistance and capturing only a few stragglers, the battalion gained the summit within eight hours. The remaining battalions of the regiment, in the meantime, moved up the Minturno road behind the 351st Infantry into an assembly area southeast of Santa Maria Infante, whence they were prepared to exploit the capture of the village by advancing through the 351st Infantry, across the Ausonia corridor, and onto the Petrella massif.[16]

While the 1st Battalion of the 349th Infantry scaled Monte Bracchi, the 3d Battalion of the 351st at last closed in on Santa Maria Infante, defended now by only a small rear guard. By early afternoon, after a house-to-house fight, the village was cleared.

A small but nevertheless important role in the battle for Santa Maria Infante had been played by sixty local Italian peasants who had volunteered to serve as carriers during the battle. Of these sixty, twenty-three had been killed by enemy fire and several wounded.[17]

On the 88th Division's right flank, Colonel Fry's 350th Infantry had secured its initial objectives from the Ausente Creek around to Castelforte. After the adjacent French unit had cleared the north side of the Castelforte road, the regiment attacked on the 13th from the vicinity of Monte Damiano to occupy Monte Rotondo. Although interrogation of prisoners had revealed that the objective was lightly held, rugged terrain and a particularly stubborn

---

[14] *Ltr, Gen Kdo LI Mtn Corps, Ia 484/44g.Kdos, 14.v.44 to AOK 10,* in *AOK 10 KTB Nr. 6, Band V, Anlagen 723,* 11–20 May 44, *AOK 10,* Doc. 53271/8.

[15] II Corps G–3 Jnl, 11–13 May 44.

[16] *Ibid.,* 11–16 May 44.

[17] WD Hist Div, *Small Unit Actions* (Washington, 1946), p. 57.

AMERICAN TROOPS ENTERING THE RUINS OF SANTA MARIA INFANTE

rear guard forced Colonel Fry's men into a 3-hour struggle before they could occupy the height.[18]

Colonel Fry had then turned his attention to Monte Cerri, the regiment's second objective. Some 2,000 yards southwest of Monte Rotondo, Monte Cerri had been reported free of enemy by an earlier patrol. Fry gave the job of occupying the feature to a reserve company located on Monte Ceracoli, only a mile away from the objective.

What followed poignantly illustrated the demoralizing effect that the sounds and rumors of battle can have on

inexperienced troops waiting anxiously in reserve. When the regimental commander's order reached the company commander, he refused to move out with his unit. Promptly relieving him, Colonel Fry sent Maj. Milton A. Matthews, his S–3, to take command of the company. The men, Major Matthews found upon arrival on Monte Ceracoli, were thoroughly demoralized. Matthews explained to them that a patrol had reported the objective abandoned; however, only one officer and one noncommissioned officer reluctantly agreed to follow him. Only after considerable urging and cajoling was Matthews able to persuade the men to advance.

As the company neared Monte Cerri, an 18-man German rear guard opened

[18] 88th Div G–2 Rpt No. 51, 141300B May 44, in 88th Div G–3 Jnl, vol. 3, incl. 7; II Corps G–3 Jnl, May 44. Unless otherwise indicated the following is based upon the latter reference.

fire, giving the lie to the patrol's optimistic report. Nevertheless, the company kept moving. It quickly gained the summit and dispersed the enemy rear guard at a cost of only two men slightly wounded. This small success restored the company's morale.

By early afternoon on 14 May, after almost three days of fighting that had cost the 88th Division almost 2,000 casualties, German withdrawal across the Ausonia corridor enabled the weary infantrymen to walk unopposed onto most of their objectives. After almost three days of infantry probes by two fresh divisions, supported by heavy and accurate artillery fire and supplemented by wide-ranging fighter-bombers from which only darkness brought relief, the losses among the defending German units had been heavy. That evening General Steinmetz reported that since the night of 11 May his *94th Division* had lost 40 percent of its combat strength and could hardly hope to hold at length in the positions across the forward slopes of the Petrella massif and the coastal heights. He was convinced that the Americans would soon move against Monte Civita and the villages of Castellonorata and Spigno, the three remaining key positions in that part of the *XIV Panzer Corps* sector of the Gustav Line opposite the Fifth Army.[19]

Monte Civita was the first of the new positions to be occupied by the Americans. General Sloan sent Fry's 350th Infantry toward Spigno and Crawford's 349th Infantry to take Monte Civita, the nearest summit in the Petrella massif beyond the Ausonia corridor. Reaching the base of Monte Civita by dark on the 14th, the regiment's forward battalion paused to rest. Resuming the attack that night, the American infantrymen encountered little resistance as they occupied the south peak of the 1,800-foot height by morning. There they surprised and captured 23 men from an artillery unit that was still firing on American positions in the valley below.[20]

Colonel Fry's 350th Infantry meanwhile advanced on Spigno. Widely dispersed, uncertain of enemy strength, Fry's regiment moved cautiously. Upset at what seemed to be a lack of drive, the army commander, General Clark, threatened disciplinary action against whoever was responsible for the delay in capturing Spigno. General Keyes therefore sent the 351st Infantry forward to relieve the 350th Infantry. Passing through Fry's lines on the morning of the 15th, the 351st Infantry attacked toward Spigno, capturing the town within a few hours.[21]

Clark's thoughts now were already ranging far beyond Spigno, for that morning he ordered Keyes to send the 88th Division with all possible speed from Spigno directly west across the mountains toward Itri, nine miles away, and the road junction on the second of the enemy's two lateral communications routes, while Coulter's 85th Division followed the withdrawal of that part of the *94th Division* on the seaward side of the Aurunci Mountains. Echeloned to the left rear, the 85th Division was to follow only as far as Monte Campese, the high ground about two miles west

[19] MS # R–50 (Bailey), CMH.

[20] 349th Inf Opns Report, May 44.
[21] *Ibid.*; II Corps G–3 Jnl, 11–16 May 44.

of Castellonorato and overlooking the coastal highway.

Looking ahead to a breakout from the Anzio beachhead, Clark planned first to move the uncommitted 36th Division there within three days, then to shift the 85th Division and increments of the II Corps headquarters to Anzio as preliminaries to moving the entire corps there. General Crittenberger's IV Corps, then at Pozzuoli on the coast just west of Naples, was to take over the II Corps sector.[22]

It was evident at this point that Clark was still thinking in terms of making the major breakthrough to the Anzio beachhead through the Aurunci Mountains sector rather than along the coastal corridor where the German defenses appeared more formidable. Because of those defenses, both Clark and Keyes had rejected a frontal attack along the axis of the coastal road (Highway 7) as too costly. Keyes directed Coulter instead to break through to that part of the Gustav Line based upon the town of Castellonorato, on the seaward fringe of the high ground, thereby outflanking the strong positions on the coastal plain. To provide additional strength for that attack, Keyes attached the 349th Infantry and the 337th Field Artillery Battalion to the 85th Division.[23]

Its buildings clustered beneath the ruins of an ancient fortress perched atop a steep hill, Castellonorato was the lone stronghold remaining in that part of the Gustav Line. Yet since German positions on Hill 108, approximately a

mile and a half northwest of Solacciano, midway between Minturno and Castellonorato, dominated the route of approach to Castellonorato, General Coulter had first to clear the hill before he could move against the town.

During the morning of 14 May, the 85th Division commander regrouped his regiments before attacking Hill 108 in early afternoon. Holding the 339th Infantry on the S-Ridge as a base of fire, he moved the 338th from the San Martino Hill to occupy the Cave d'Argilla, high ground about half a mile farther north, overlooking the approach to Hill 108. To the 337th Infantry, which except for one battalion had been in reserve since the beginning of the offensive, he gave the mission of taking first Hill 108 and then Castellonorato. The attached 349th Infantry was to cover the attack by advancing on the right, with the 337th Field Artillery Battalion firing in support.[24]

Attack on Castellonorato

Colonel Hughes, commander of the 337th Infantry, decided to employ a tank-infantry team composed of the 2d Battalion with two platoons of tanks, as Colonel Safay had done the day before in his ill-fated attack on the division's right flank. After taking Hill 108, Hughes planned to use the armor to probe the enemy's defenses before making a final thrust into Castellonorato. The 3d Battalion was to follow closely in reserve, while the 1st Battalion remained attached to the 338th Infantry.

[22] Clark Diary, 15 May 44; Fifth Army G–3 Jnl, 15–16 May 44; Fifth Army OI 18, 15 May 44.
[23] II Corps G–3 Jnl, 11–16 May 44.

[24] 88th Div Directive (sgd Sloan), 15 May 44; 85th Div FO 6 (sgd Coulter), 15 May 44; II Corps G–3 Periodic Rpt (sgd Col Butchers, G–3), 15 May 44.

Hardly had the attack on Hill 108 jumped off on the afternoon of the 14th when a hitch developed. As engineers tried to prepare a fording site for the tanks to cross a small stream near Capo d'Acqua, a hamlet about 2,200 yards east of the objective, heavy fire from the vicinity of Castellonorato forced them to take cover. The tanks had to remain on the east bank where they could provide the infantry with only long-range support. Even so, that support proved sufficient at the start, for the infantrymen forded the creek and gained the crest of the hill on which the hamlet was located against little opposition; but when the men tried to continue down the reverse slope, the story was different. Heavy machine gun fire drove them back across the crest.

Here the attack was stalled for several hours until engineers at last succeeded in preparing a crossing site for the tanks, ten of which immediately forded the stream and joined the infantry to provide the impetus the attack needed. As the tanks rumbled down the reverse slope of Hill 108, part of the enemy surrendered while the rest fled toward Castellonorato.

With the capture of Hill 108, the way was clear for Colonel Hughes' reserve battalion to make a final attack on the town, but the setbacks encountered earlier forced a postponement until the following morning. On the 15th, shortly before the assault on Castellonorato was to begin, aircraft from the XII TAC roared over the front. Beyond a bomb line laid down only a thousand yards ahead of the infantry, a flight of six fighter-bombers struck the objective. While smoke and dust hung heavily

over the town, Hughes' men quickly entered, but despite the aerial bombardment it still took several hours of street fighting to clear the place. By midnight Castellonorato was free of the enemy.

While the 337th fought for Castellonorato, a battalion from the 338th Infantry moved down from the Cave d'Argilla and quickly occupied Monte Penitro, situated over one mile to the west and overlooking the Ausonia corridor road a mile northeast of Highway 7. Routing a small enemy detachment, the battalion also captured the village of Penitro and continued down the Ausonia road to Santa Croce, a hamlet located at the junction of the road with the coastal highway. The capture of Castellonorato, Monte Penitro, and the Santa Croce road junction carried the 85th Division—with it the II Corps—all the way through the Gustav Line on the seaward slope of the mountains. Thus outflanked, the enemy's defenses astride Highway 7 on the coastal plain near Monte Scauri were no longer tenable.[25]

The Germans Prepare To Withdraw

Recognizing the portent of this penetration for the entire German right wing, the acting *XIV Panzer Corps* commander, General Hartmann, issued the usual injunction to General Steinmetz to contain the breach at all costs, at the same time reporting to the *Tenth Army* headquarters that without reinforcements a clear American breakthrough,

[25] 337th Inf Rpt of Opns, 14–15 May 44; 338th Inf Rpt of Opns, 14–15 May 44; 85th Div Rpt of Opns, 14–15 May 44.

comparable to that which had already taken place in the French sector, was inevitable. Hartmann urged either reinforcing the *94th Division* with a separate panzer grenadier regiment that was patrolling the coast on the Gaeta peninsula or authorizing the corps to fall back about two miles immediately to the Dora switch position. Despite those recommendations, General von Vietinghoff, the army commander, newly returned from his leave, authorized nothing more than withdrawal during the night of 15 May of the *94th Division*'s artillery.[26]

While failing to obtain permission to withdraw all of the *94th Division*, General Hartmann nevertheless saw the authorization for artillery displacement as a harbinger of eventual approval. Relaying the instructions to Steinmetz, Hartmann hinted that orders for such a move would soon be forthcoming.

To support the crumbling front and cover the expected general withdrawal, Steinmetz managed to assemble three infantry companies from the now untenable Monte Scauri salient, along with a platoon of heavy antitank guns from the vicinity of Formia, five miles west of Scauri. Those units he rushed into positions southwest of Castellonorato. Yet Steinmetz's center continued to give way. A real danger began to loom that the Americans might overrun the Dora Line even before the Germans could occupy it. For Steinmetz, the only bright spot was the arrival within his lines of survivors from a company that had fought out of an encirclement on Hill 79, south of San Martino Hill.

Keyes Reinforces His Left

General Hartmann was not alone in recognizing the portents of the capture of Hill 108 and the fall of Castellonorato. General Keyes too realized their significance. He also realized that at this point the more favorable terrain of the mountain slopes overlooking the coastal corridor rather than the inhospitable Aurunci Mountains offered the best opportunity for exploiting the II Corps' success in the Gustav Line. Accordingly, during the night of 15 May, Keyes gave first priority on artillery and armored support to the 85th Division, thereby transforming what was to have been the secondary attack on the left into the main attack. Thenceforth the momentum of the II Corps was directed along the axis of the Castellonorato-Maranola road, the latter village located two and a half miles due west of Castellonorato. Keyes hoped thereby to outflank Formia, four miles up the coastal highway, which controlled the road junction leading to the enemy's second line of lateral communications, Route 82. Indications are that Keyes had not consulted Clark on this decision, for the latter had authorized use of the 85th Division only as far as Monte Campese, and Maranola lies a mile to the northwest and Formia over two miles to the southwest.[27]

By early morning of 16 May, the French Expeditionary Corps as well as the U.S. II Corps had broken through the Gustav Line between the Liri valley and the Tyrrhenian Sea. Earlier, following its success against the *71st Division* at Monte Majo on the 13th, the FEC, on

---

[26] MS # R–50 (Bailey), CMH. Unless otherwise indicated the following is based upon this reference.

[27] Clark Diary, 15 May 44.

the Fifth Army's right wing, had fought across the Ausonia corridor, captured the Ausonia defile leading into the Liri valley, and advanced over the northern half of the Petrella massif into the heart of the Aurunci Mountains. The net effect of the successful II Corps–FEC strike had been to outflank the strongest parts of the Gustav Line, those along the Tyrrhenian coast and in the Liri valley.

A total of more than 3,000 casualties—1,100 of which were incurred during the first forty-eight hours of the offensive by the 85th Division—surpassed the II Corps' losses in the hard fought battle for Monte Cassino during the preceding winter campaign. The replacement system employed by both the 85th and 88th Divisions nevertheless enabled the corps to make up the losses quickly and maintain the momentum of the offensive.[28]

Progress in the Liri Valley

The Eighth Army, meanwhile, had also begun to move. On the 14th General Leese had assembled the 1st Canadian Corps behind the 13 Corps' left wing preparatory to sending the Canadians across the Rapido to take part in the forthcoming exploitation toward the Hitler Line. Even as the U.S. II Corps was battering through the Gustav Line's last defenses on the night of 15 May, so too in the Liri valley the British 13 Corps broke through the last of the Gustav Line's positions. That

night the Canadian corps began crossing the Rapido.[29]

The next day the 78th Division completed its passage of the 4th Division's lines and launched its long-delayed attack to cut Highway 6 southwest of Cassino. During the day the 78th Division made such good progress that General Leese ordered the Polish corps on Monte Cassino to resume its postponed attack the following morning.

Accordingly, early on the 17th, the British in the valley and the Poles in the mountains launched a pincers attack against the surviving enemy positions on Monte Cassino and in the town at its base. By afternoon the 78th Division had cut the highway southwest of Monte Cassino and the Poles and seized the Colle Sant'Angelo Ridge north of the abbey. Only two escape routes— along the Monte Cassino–Massa Albeneta Ridge and the flanks of the hills overlooking the highway—remained open. The Cassino position was now clearly untenable. Field Marshal Kesselring acknowledged this fact by ordering General Vietinghoff to withdraw from that position the *1st Parachute Division*. Within minutes after Kesselring's order was radioed to the *Tenth Army* on the night of the 17th, British Intelligence had deciphered the message and in turn radioed the welcome news to Churchill, Alexander, and the U.S. Chiefs of Staff.[30]

Throughout the day aircraft of the Mediterranean Allied Air Forces flew about 200 sorties in support of the

---

[28] 85th Div G–1 Rpt of Opns, May 44; 88th Div LO Rpt to G–3, 15 May 44; 88th Div G–1 Rpt of Opns, May 44.

[29] Operations of British, Indian, and Dominion Forces in Italy, Part II, Sec. B. Unless otherwise indicated the following section is based upon this reference.

[30] See Winterbotham, *The Ultra Secret*, p. 116.

MONTE CASSINO MONASTERY SHORTLY AFTER ITS CAPTURE

Polish attack on Monte Cassino. Targets were enemy mortar and artillery positions in the vicinity of Villa Santa Lucia, Passa Corno, and Piedimonte Roccasecca (features north and west of Monte Cassino), as well as the command posts of the *1st Parachute* and *90th Panzer Grenadier Divisions* and some troops assembling for a counterattack to cover the planned withdrawal of parachutists. The counterattack came that night from the neighborhood of the Villa Santa Lucia, a mountain village about two miles northwest of the abbey and was aimed at the Polish troops on the Colle Sant'Angelo Ridge. It enabled the Germans, as the Polish corps commander, General Anders, had feared, to withdraw over the remaining escape routes. Consequently, on the morning of the 18th, when a patrol from the 12th Podolski Lancers, advancing along

a ridge from the Colle d'Onufrio southeast of the abbey, reached its objective, it found only thirty badly wounded German soldiers with several medical orderlies quietly awaiting capture in the massive ruins of the abbey. At 1020 the Polish lancers hoisted their standard over Monte Cassino, thus ending the fourth in a series of battles for the height which had begun on 17 January 1944 when the U.S. 36th Infantry Division had fought its way across the Rapido.

With the capture of Monte Majo by the French on 13 May, of Spigno and Castellonorato by the Americans on the 15th, and, finally, on the 18th, of Monte Cassino by the Poles, the Allies could claim a complete collapse of the Gustav Line. General Leese's Eighth Army was now poised to move against the towns of Pontecorvo, Aquino, and

Piedimonte San Germano, strongpoints in that sector of the Hitler Line astride the Liri valley. Two days earlier General Clark's Fifth Army had begun its exploitation to the Hitler Line. That meant an advance across the Aurunci Mountains and the seaward slopes in order to reach that part of the enemy's second line of defense lying between the Tyrrhenian Sea and the Liri valley.

The German Reaction

From the very start of the Allied offensive, Field Marshal Kesselring, despite considerable effort on the part of his staff, had been unable to obtain an accurate picture of the situation on his southern front. He bitterly demanded that his senior commanders on that front, Vietinghoff and Senger, hastily summoned from their leaves in Germany in response to the emergency, give him the needed information. "It is intolerable," he fumed at one point, "that a division is engaged in combat for one and a half days without knowing what is going on in its sector." Fighting a desperate defensive battle, the *Tenth Army* had captured only a few Allied prisoners while losing over 2,000 of its own men as prisoners of war. Little wonder that German division commanders were unable to give their superiors a clear picture of the forces pressing against their positions.[31]

Not until the 14th had Vietinghoff determined that eleven and not six Allied divisions, as German intelligence

officers had originally believed, were trying to break through his front. He also suspected that Alexander was holding twelve additional divisions in readiness for exploitation of any penetration.[32]

Shortly after the beginning of the offensive the Germans had identified at the front a number of Allied divisions previously presumed to be in rear areas. Yet they still believed as late as the 14th that the U.S. 36th Infantry, Canadian 1st Infantry, and South African 6th Armoured Divisions were in the vicinity of Naples, possibly preparing for another amphibious landing. Field Marshal Alexander's deception plan had done its work. *OB Suedwest's* G–2 also believed that on the island of Corsica one American and three French divisions were being held in readiness as a forward echelon of a large strategic reserve in North Africa, earmarked for landings either in southern France or on the Ligurian coast of Italy. When on 15 May German agents in Bari reported an unusually large concentration of Allied ships in that port, concern arose briefly at Kesselring's headquarters that the Allies might launch an amphibious attack against the Adriatic flank in co-ordination with a breakout attempt from the Anzio beachhead.[33] The ships actually were bringing in supplies for the British forces in Italy.

Because of this faulty estimate of Allied troop dispositions, a problem that would plague the German com-

---

[31] Telecon, Lt Col v. Ingelheim, *Ia, OB Suedwest*, to *AOK 10*, 0955, *15.V44*, in *AOK 10 KTB Nr. 6, Band V, Anlagen 725*, Doc. 53271/8. Through intercepts of Enigma messages, the Allied command was well aware of the disarray at Kesselring's headquarters. See Winterbotham, *The Ultra Secret*, p. 116.

[32] Comments on Inspection of *LI Mtn Corps* by *Tenth Army* CINC, 14 May 44, in *AOK 10, Ia KTB Nr. 6, Band V, Anlagen 719*, 11–20 May 44, *AOK 10*, Doc. 53271/8.

[33] Greiner and Schramm, eds., *OKW/WFSt, KTB*, p. 489.

mand in Italy throughout the campaign, Kesselring and his staff persistently worried about the possibility of an amphibious landing somewhere along the Tyrrhenian flank. Partly this concern was the fruit of the Allied deception plan which deliberately sought to foster concern in the enemy. Consequently, during the first critical days of the Allied offensive, Kesselring had been unwilling to authorize more than piecemeal commitment of his reserves, and had forfeited his only opportunity for checking the Allied armies before their offensive acquired an irresistible momentum.

Not until 15 May did the Germans identify the Canadian 1st Infantry Division and the South African 6th Armoured Division opposite the entrance to the Liri valley. Only then did Kesselring belatedly realize that the supposed Allied concentration in the vicinity of Naples no longer existed. His apprehension alleviated, on the 16th he ordered the *26th Panzer Division,* as he had earlier the *90th Panzer Grenadier Division,* to move from the vicinity of Rome southeastward into the *Tenth Army*'s sector.[34] Since Kesselring rated those divisions, together with the *29th Panzer Grenadier Division,* as among his best, the shift indicated an even greater awareness of the seriousness of the Allied gains on the southern front. Yet Kesselring hesitated to release control of the *26th Panzer Division* to Vietinghoff, holding it instead as a part of

Army Group C's reserve even as the division began to move southward.[35]

Over the next few days *Army Group C* alerted additional units—among them the *1027th Grenadier* and *8th Grenadier Regiments* of the *3d Panzer Grenadier Division*—for movement to the *Tenth Army*'s sector. In the *Tenth Army* Vietinghoff ordered the *305th* and *334th Divisions* on the army's Adriatic flank to shift units to the Liri valley. Movement of those reinforcements, however, was considerably delayed by Allied air attacks.[36]

At Supreme Headquarters in Germany, Hitler had on the 15th been briefed on the renewed fighting on the distant Italian front. He immediately ordered the *16th SS Panzer Grenadier Division* to move from Germany to reinforce the OKW reserves in northern Italy. Yet like his commander in Italy, Hitler remained uncertain about actual Allied intentions there. He therefore placed strong restrictions on the employment of the reserve units; they were to be used only in event of an Allied landing on the Ligurian coast, a possibility that the German command in Italy had already begun to discount. Such hesitancy on the part of both the OKW and *Army Group C* in reacting to the gathering momentum of the Allied offensive boded ill for re-establishing a stabilized front south of Rome, as in the previous winter.

---

[34] MS # R–50 (Bailey), CMH.

[35] *Ibid.*
[36] Greiner and Schramm, eds., *OKW/WFSt, KTB,* p. 490.

CHAPTER V

Breakthrough on the Southern Front

The Eighth Army's Advance to the Hitler Line

With both Allied armies having broken through the Gustav Line, Field Marshal Alexander's next concern was to close with and assault the Hitler Line, the enemy's second line of defense, before the Germans could dig in. The Hitler Line, especially in the Liri valley, was formidable and if fully manned could be even more of an obstacle than the Gustav Line.

The main defenses extended from the hill town of Piedimonte San Germano, about four miles west of Cassino at the northern edge of the Liri valley, in a westerly direction to the vicinity of Aquino, then turned southward paralleling a secondary road for two and a half miles as far as Pontecorvo. Between Aquino and Pontecorvo the defensive zone varied in depth from 500 to 1,000 yards. Supplementing some of the natural obstacles found on the valley floor, such as the Forme d'Aquino, a tributary of the Liri, was a discontinuous antitank ditch, created by blowing craters that were rapidly filled by the high water table. There were also antitank mine fields with belts of barbed wire in the front and rear. Covered by fields of fire from automatic weapons, these wire belts would present a tough obstacle to engineers and infantry seeking to clear paths through the mines for armor. Scattered along the forward edge of the defensive zone were numerous prefabricated armored pillboxes, capable of holding two men and a light machine gun. The line's main defensive zone consisted of an intricate system of reinforced concrete gun emplacements and satellite weapons pits, all linked by tunnels or communications trenches. Adding to antitank defenses were nine Panther tank turrets on concrete bases with underground living quarters for the crews. The turrets had a 360° traverse, and two or three mobile antitank guns were echeloned to their flanks. A total of sixty-two antitank guns, of which twenty-five were self-propelled, were available. Deep shelters, having concrete roofs five inches thick and covered with up to twenty feet of earth, gave the defenders excellent protection against air and artillery bombardment.[1]

As formidable as the positions were they were weakened by the failure of the Germans to clear fields of fire through lush, untended vegetation that had grown up since the spring. Yet a greater handicap was the lack of an adequate number of troops to man the positions.

---

[1] MS # D–170 (Rothe); Map, 1:25,000, *Stellungskarte Abschnitt 90 Pz. Gren Div, LI Mtn Corps, KTB Anlagen, Taetigkeitsbericht der Abt. Ia/Stopi, 10,V–30.VI.44;* Situation map, 5–6 Apr 44, *AOK 10, KTB Anlagen VI, Lagekarten, 1.IV–14.IV.44.*

In the Liri valley the Hitler Line would be defended by the *1st Parachute Division,* in the Piedimonte San Germano area, and the *90th Panzer Grenadier Division,* which since the 16th had replaced the battered *44th Infantry Division,* in the sector between Aquino and Pontecorvo. The parachute and infantry divisions had already incurred heavy casualties in defense of the Gustav Line. The latter division, for example, now encompassed in addition to its organic units a motley collection of dismounted panzer troops as well as various engineer units, all pressed into service as infantrymen. The sector of the Hitler Line south of the Liri valley between Pontecorvo and Pico was held by the recently committed *26th Panzer Division.*

General Alexander hoped that the French Expeditionary Corps, advancing rapidly through the mountains overlooking the valley from the south, and the Polish corps, advancing along the flanks of the mountains overlooking the valley from the north, might be able to turn the Hitler Line from the north and south and force the Germans to withdraw, as they had from the Gustav Line, thereby sparing the Eighth Army the necessity of making a set-piece frontal attack against the strongest sectors of the line in the valley.[2]

Meanwhile, early on the 18th, General Leese, hoping to overwhelm the Germans before they reached the shelter of the Hitler Line, sent the British 78th Division hurrying seven miles west along Highway 6 to capture the town of Aquino, located on the near bank of

the Forme d'Aquino and on a secondary road about a mile and a half south of the main highway. The division reached the town in the afternoon and immediately attacked. But the Germans, veterans of the defense of Monte Cassino, had already occupied the Hitler Line positions and repulsed the attack with heavy fire. Reluctant to continue during the night, the British settled down to await armored support, plus a thrust by the 1st Canadian Division toward Pontecorvo. (*Map IV*)

Early on the 19th a ground fog offered welcome concealment to the attacking troops. The 78th Division got off to a good start, but unlike Joshua, Leese was unable to halt the sun in its course. When the sun burned the fog away, the advancing troops found themselves on open terrain with little cover and exposed to heavy and accurate fire from well-sited enemy antitank guns. The fire drove the accompanying armor from the field and left the infantry alone to face heavy automatic weapons and mortar fire. Under those conditions the infantry was unable to continue and fell back to its line of departure. In the meantime, the 1st Canadian Division's attack toward Pontecorvo stalled partly for lack of sufficient artillery support, which had been largely engaged in backing up the assault on Aquino. Traffic congestion, aggravated by a paucity of roads and trails, added to the problem.

The failure of the initial assaults on Aquino and Pontecorvo dashed General Alexander's hope of outracing the Germans to their second line of defense. There now seemed no alternative to an all-out set-piece attack against the Hitler Line.

---

[2] Operations of the British, Indian, and Dominion Forces in Italy, Part II, Sec. B. Unless otherwise indicated the following is based upon this reference.

The Fifth Army's Advance to the Hitler Line

The terrain in the Fifth Army's zone was far more rugged than that in the Liri valley, yet General Clark's troops experienced less trouble than did General Leese's in advancing to and closing with the Hitler Line. While few roads or trails crossed the Aurunci Mountains, neither did the mountains harbor many enemy troops. Aerial reconnaissance, supported by prisoner of war interrogations, had disclosed such a dearth of enemy that the Fifth Army's two corps could approach their tasks of crossing the wilderness of rock and scrub oak with considerable confidence.

Their first goals were the road junctions of Itri and Pico, key points on the enemy's second lateral line of communications (Route 82), and, in the case of Pico, a strongpoint in the Hitler Line, which, opposite the Fifth Army, extended some twenty miles from its anchor at Terracina on the Tyrrhenian coast northeastward across the mountains via Fondi to Pico, on the southern edge of the Liri valley. Capture of Itri, the II Corps' objective, would give Keyes control over Highway 7 and the southern half of the enemy's second lateral route of communications. The key to Itri was Monte Grande, a dominating height just northwest of the town. Twelve miles north of Monte Grande lies Pico, the second important road junction and immediate goal of the FEC. An integral part of the German defense system, Pico was a hinge of that part of the Hitler Line passing through Piedimonte, Aquino, and Pontecorvo.

On 15 May Clark had directed Keyes, in co-ordination with Juin's drive across the Aurunci Mountains, to send the II Corps as rapidly as possible to capture Itri and then attack the sector of the Hitler Line between Fondi and Terracina. Clark directed Juin to make his major effort against a sector of the enemy's defenses south of Pico, where Clark believed it to be the weakest opposite the Fifth Army front.[3]

Spigno, on the southern shoulder of the Petrella massif, lay within the II Corps zone, but Keyes agreed on 16 May to share the village with the French as a point of departure for the advance across the mountains. The steep, tortuous road leading across the escarpment to the village soon became jammed with American infantry, French colonial troops, mules, and motor vehicles of many types, all winding westward through billowing clouds of dust.[4]

The II Corps was to advance in parallel columns: Sloan's 88th Division through the Aurunci Mountains and, echeloned to the left, Coulter's 85th Division moving across the seaward slopes of the mountains toward Maranola and Formia, the latter on the coast about seven miles southwest of Castellonorato.[5] General Sloan selected Colonel Champeny's 351st Infantry to lead the 88th Division across the mountains. Champeny's route of march was across the southern half of the Petrella massif to Monte Sant'Angelo and Ruazzo, about three and six miles, respectively, west of Spigno.

---

[3] Fifth Army G–3 Jnl, 15–19 May 44; *Fifth Army History,* Part V, pp. 69–72.

[4] II Corps CG Diary, 161345B May 44.

[5] II Corps Directive, 16 May 44; II Corps G–3 Rept of Opns No. 237, 16 May 44; II Corps Diary, 161345B May 44. All in 88th Div G–3 Jnl, 16–20 May 44, vol. 3, incl. 7.

Guided by two local peasants, the two lead battalions started out early on the 16th for Monte Sant'Angelo. Moving rapidly, the battalions soon outdistanced their telephone lines, and even radios could function satisfactorily only after the setting up of intermediate relay stations on the mountaintops. By noon Champeny's infantrymen, encountering only scattered and light resistance, had reached Monte Sant'Angelo. Although the regimental commander wanted to pause there for a rest, an urgent radio message from corps prompted him to rush his men westward during the late afternoon toward their second objective, Monte Ruazzo.[6]

As the two battalions of the 351st Infantry moved toward Route 82, the Itri-Pico road, Senger, the *XIV Panzer Corps* commander, strengthened his positions along that road with a scratch force of self-propelled guns and motorized infantry, a force hardly able to do more than check the Americans briefly as they emerged from the mountains.

On 17 May, as the seriousness of Senger's situation in the mountains became evident at *Army Group C* headquarters at Frascati, in the Alban Hills some ten miles south of Rome, Kesselring, still glancing anxiously over his shoulder at his coastal flank and the Anzio beachhead, finally decided to do something about the *Tenth Army's* right wing. The German commander authorized Vietinghoff to shift a reconnaissance battalion from the Liri valley to reinforce Steinmetz's hard-pressed infantry in the Aurunci Mountains. "Otherwise," Kesselring remarked to the *Tenth Army* commander, "Steinmetz will

not be able to get the situation in the mountains straightened out."[7]

On the morning of the 17th, Colonel Champeny's men gained the summit of Monte Ruazzo. Pausing only briefly, they resumed their advance in the late afternoon toward Monte Grande, the high ground overlooking Itri. When early the next morning the Americans approached the Itri-Pico road, they ran head on into fire from a force of tanks and self-propelled guns hastily assembled by General Senger to defend the road. Surprised by the heavy fire, Champeny's men had no choice but to halt, for their artillery was too far to the rear to be of help. Only when the regiment's reserve battalion arrived and artillery came within supporting distance could the 351st Infantry resume its advance.[8]

Forward displacement of the 88th Division's artillery depended upon the progress of the neighboring 85th Division advancing across the seaward slopes of the Aurunci Mountains, the only area where roads and trails were to be found over which the guns and their prime movers might pass. While General Sloan's division threaded its way over the mountains toward the Itri-Pico road, General Coulter's 85th Division advanced in two columns along the corps' left wing. One column moved astride the coastal highway toward Formia and the other, slightly ahead of the first, crossed the seaward slopes of the Aurunci Mountains toward Maranola, at the foot of Monte Campese and

---

[6] 88th Div G–3 Jnl, 16–20 May 44, vol. 3, incl. 7.

[7] Telecon, *OB AOK 10* with Kesselring, 2030B 17 May 44, in *AOK 10, Ia KTB Nr. 6, Band V, Anlagen 777*, 11–20 May 44, *AOK 10*, Doc. 53271/1.
[8] 88th Div G–2 Rpt 55, 181600B May 44, in 88th Div G–3 Jnl, vol. 3, incl. 7.

VIEW OF ITRI

about three miles west of Castellonorato. On the afternoon of the 17th the
337th Infantry, 85th Division, after scaling Monte Campese, descended its
northwestern ridge to take Maranola
before dusk. That move cut the only
lateral road leading to Formia, about
two miles to the southwest.[9]

Meanwhile, Juin's Moroccans and Algerians closed in on Pico. After crossing

the northern flanks of the Aurunci
Mountains from the Ausonia corridor
on the 17th, the French reached the
outskirts of Esperia, whence they overlooked the Liri valley. Early the next
morning, as the Eighth Army began its
race for the Hitler Line in the Liri
valley, the Algerians swarmed out of
the mountains and into Esperia, while
elements of General Sevez's provisional
mountain corps moved to within artillery range of Pico. In the mountains
five miles west of Esperia, between
Monte Faggeto and the Sierra del Lago,

---

[9] II Corps G–3 Rpt 237, 16 May 44 and 88th Div
G–2 Rpt 55, 181600B May 44, both in 88th Div G–3
Jnl.

some French units had actually made two slight penetrations of a lightly defended sector of the Hitler Line.[10]

It was no longer possible for the Germans to establish a line east of their second lateral communications road. Furthermore, most German troop movements in the rear had become almost as hazardous as those in the front. During daylight hours, flights of fighter-bombers of the XII TAC freely roamed the skies, bombing and strafing virtually everything that moved behind the German lines, and depriving the enemy of the tactical moblity so vital to his defense. The Allied aircraft, after completing the destruction of Itri, knocked out two bridges northeast of the town and one to the southwest of Pico.[11]

As the Americans drew near Itri and Monte Grande and the French closed in on Pico, Vietinghoff's chief of staff, General Wentzell, told General Westphal, Kesselring's chief of staff, that Raapke had reported that his *71st Division* had only 100 infantry effectives left.[12] Westphal promised an allocation of replacements as soon as possible, but it was too late. On the afternoon of the 18th Kesselring himself belatedly recognized that loss of the *XIV Panzer Corps'* mountain sector was only a matter of hours away, which meant that Vietinghoff had to withdraw the *Tenth Army's* entire right wing or face envelopment.

Pivoting on Pico, which was to be held, that sector between Pico and Itri was to be withdrawn slowly west of the lateral road connecting the two towns. To reinforce the *Tenth Army's* right flank, which could be exposed by the maneuver, Kesselring was forced a second time to dip into his reserves. He directed the *Fourteenth Army* (Mackensen) to release to Vietinghoff the following day the *29th Panzer Grenadier Division* from the *Fourteenth Army's* reserve.[13] Like the recently committed *26th Panzer Division,* this too was one of *Army Group C's* better units.

Their confidence in the mountains as an obstacle to the Allied advance shattered, the Germans were also in for some surprises along the Tyrrhenian coast, where the 337th Infantry's capture of Maranola had outflanked their positions east of Formia. Thus the 338th Infantry, advancing astride Highway 7, was able to catch up with and eventually overtake its neighboring regiment in the mountains on the right. The 338th Infantry captured Formia against only scattered resistance on the afternoon of the 18th and continued on to the important junction of the coastal highway with the Itri-Pico road, less than a mile away. There was no opposition. Acting on Kesselring's orders to Vietinghoff, General von Senger had already ordered a withdrawal to a line extending about four miles southwest from Itri to Monte Moneta. From that line, which was only a delaying position, the Germans were to fall back to a line between Fondi and Terracina, the remaining strongpoints of the Hitler Line on the *Tenth Army's* right flank. Only a

---

[10] II Corps G–3 Periodic Rpt 258, 171600B May 44 and G–3 Periodic Rpt 259, 181600B May 44, both in 88th Div G–3 Jnl, vol. 3, incl. 7; Juin, *La Campagne d'Italie,* pp. 118–21.
[11] Hq XII TAC, ISUM, 170600B May 44, in 88th Div G–3 Jnl, vol. 3, incl. 7.
[12] Telecon, *AOK 10* C/S with Gen Westphal, 181210B May 44, in *AOK 10, Ia KTB Nr. 6, Band V, Anl. 801,* 11–20 May 44, *AOK 10,* Doc. 53271/8.

[13] MS # C–064 (Kesselring), pp. 53–55.

U.S. INFANTRY APPROACHING ITRI

rear guard remained at Itri and on Monte Grande.

The withdrawal in the coastal corridor came none too soon, for the 88th Division's leading regiment the (351st Infantry) was about to cut the last escape route along Highway 7. During the afternoon and evening of the 18th the 351st Infantry's reserve battalion arrived before Itri and the 601st and 697th Artillery Battalions, moving up from Maranola, drew within range of the Germans even as they were preparing to withdraw to their first delaying positions between Itri and Monte Moneta.

At that point, Colonel Champeny's infantrymen, well supported by artillery, attacked at dawn on the 19th. Opposed only by a rear guard, the Americans easily occupied Monte Grande by midmorning.[14]

The first pack train to reach Colonel Champeny's 351st Regiment in three days arrived after a 14-mile march across the mountain trails from Spigno. The ninety mules making up the train brought the weary infantrymen their

[14] Msg, Leggin 6 to CG 88th Div, 191210B May 44; Hq, 88th Div Directive to CO Leather, 182100B May 44, both in 88th Div G–3 Jnl, vol. 3, incl. 7, 16–20 May 44.

GERMAN PRISONERS CAPTURED AT ITRI

first resupply of rations, ammunition, and signal equipment since they had begun their march on the afternoon of the 15th.[15]

While the men cut the Itri-Pico road and dug in atop Monte Grande, advance patrols of Colonel Crawford's 349th Infantry, which had moved up from Maranola during the night, entered Itri and found it leveled. By early afternoon on the 19th the regiment

had captured or driven away a few Germans lurking in the ruins.

All across the II Corps front the enemy was breaking contact and withdrawing toward the Hitler Line. Anticipating that the withdrawal would lead Clark to consider the possibility of a linkup by the II Corps with the Anzio beachhead, General Keyes directed General Sloan to form a task force consisting of a motorized infantry battalion, reinforced by self-propelled artillery, tanks, and engineers. The force was to be prepared to capture Fondi,

---

[15] Msg, 351st Inf to II Corps, 191945B May 44, in 88th Div G–3 Jnl, vol. 3, incl. 7.

seven miles northwest of Itri, and block a secondary route from the coast to the Liri valley—the Lenola–Valle Corsa road where it passes through a narrow defile four miles north of Fondi—as preliminaries to an assault on the Hitler Line and a thrust to the beachhead.[16]

Meanwhile, General Coulter had sent the 91st Reconnaissance Squadron southwest along the coast to the 18th century Neapolitan seaside stronghold of Gaeta. Ranging freely and virtually unopposed, the squadron entered the port on the 19th. From Gaeta the force pushed northwestward eight miles along coastal roads to enter Sperlonga the next day.

As General Sloan assembled his mobile task force for the drive on Fondi and possible exploitation toward the Anzio beachhead, General Clark weighed the choices before him. Only one day earlier he had directed Keyes to hold all but one regiment of Coulter's division at Formia to await movement by sea to Anzio. Should the entire II Corps attempt a breakthrough of the Hitler Line between Fondi and Terracina and then continue on to Anzio, or should Keyes merely close up to the line without attacking while Clark withdrew the 85th Division and other elements of the II Corps for movement to the Anzio beachhead by water?

Clark hesitated. On the 18th he had received a message from Alexander, who was understandably concerned about the Eighth Army's progress in the Liri valley and uncertain just how vigorously the Germans would defend the Hitler Line. He ordered Clark to be

prepared to change the axis of his army's advance to the north. He was to be ready to send the II Corps as well as the FEC toward the Ceprano road junction of Routes 6 and 82 in the Liri valley to threaten the German line of communications in the valley. Next day General Alexander became painfully aware about how staunchly the Germans would defend the Hitler Line. The British 78th Division was thrown back at Aquino and the French were halted before Pico by elements of the *26th Panzer Division,* which Kesselring had ordered to replace the battered *71st Division* on that part of the front.[17]

Although Clark shared Alexander's uncertainty about how strongly the Germans would attempt to hold the Hitler Line, the Fifth Army commander understandably had less concern for the Eighth Army's problems in the Liri valley than for his own. Clark's attention was focused on the Hitler Line between Fondi and Terracina. If the II Corps were to link with the beachhead, Keyes would have to break through soon. The Fifth Army staff had estimated that it would require four days to move the 36th Division to Anzio by sea and almost a week to shift the 85th Division and other parts of the II Corps. Such a delay would afford the Germans a welcome respite. When, on the 20th, the 91st Reconnaissance Squadron, after having taken Gaeta the day before, probed brusquely into Fondi and, before retiring, found the town weakly defended—no troops of the *29th Panzer Grenadier Division* destined for that part of the front had

[16] Msg, Hq II Corps (sgd Col R.L.J. Butchers, II Corps' G–3) to 85th Div, 191645B May 44, in 88th Div G–3 Jnl, vol. 3, incl. 7.

[17] Mathews, "The French in the Drive on Rome," *Fraternité d'Armes Franco-Américaine,* pp. 133–34.

yet arrived—Clark had his answer. He decided, notwithstanding Alexander's concern for Eighth Army's difficulties in the Liri valley, to take advantage of the enemy's apparent weakness along the coastal flank and throw the weight of Keyes' corps into a drive up the narrow coastal corridor toward a junction with the beachhead. Juin's corps would, Clark believed, be sufficient to force the Germans to relax their defense opposite the Eighth Army.[18]

Breakthrough of the Hitler Line

Clark's decision to disregard Alexander's operational concept was not the first time, nor would it be the last, that the American commander, taking advantage of rapidly changing opportunities, followed a course of action at variance with that originally envisioned by Alexander. In this instance, after being advised by Clark of the change, Alexander did not object. He had held as loose a rein on Montgomery in the Western Desert. This was the Allied commander's style of command. It had brought success to the Alexander-Montgomery team in North Africa, and Alexander expected that it would work in Italy with an equally independent subordinate. In any case, the Fifth Army was advancing toward the long-sought junction with the Anzio beachhead, and the Eighth Army was preparing to launch a major set-piece attack against the Hitler Line.[19] In prepara-

tion for that attack General Leese had shifted the burden from the British 13 Corps (78 Division) to the 1st Canadian Corps, which was to make the main effort in the sector immediately north of Pontecorvo. The former was to maintain pressure against Aquino and be prepared to advance abreast of the Canadians after the breakthrough.

Alexander had selected the night of 21 May, or early on the 22d, for the beginning of the attack, indicating that he expected the operation in the Liri valley to coincide with the beginnings of the U.S. VI Corps' breakout offensive from the Anzio beachhead.[20]

Meanwhile, on the 19th the Polish corps, on the 13 Corps' right, had advanced four miles beyond Monte Cassino to capture an enemy strongpoint, the Villa Santa Lucia. From there the Poles prepared to continue their progress the next day toward the northern anchor of the Hitler Line at Piedimonte San Germano.

Preparing for his imminent set-piece attack on the Hitler Line, General Leese brought forward units from his reserve. The 8th Indian Division, which had been relieved earlier by the 1st Canadian Infantry Division, began moving on the 19th from east of the Rapido to an assembly area behind the Canadian corps' sector. Concurrently, the British 6th Armoured Division also departed the army reserve to take part in the exploitation of the expected breakthrough of the Hitler Line. With those units under way, together with

---

[18] Hqs, Fifth Army Opns Instr 19, 18 May 44; Clark Diary, 20 May 44; *Fifth Army History,* Part V, pp. 79–80.

[19] Gen Clark's personal comments on MS, Oct 1973, in CMH files; Nigel Nicolson, *Alex, the Life of Field Marshal, Earl Alexander of Tunis* (New York: Atheneum, 1973), p. 160.

[20] Operations of British, Indian, and Dominion Forces in Italy, Part II, Sec. B. Unless otherwise indicated the following section is based upon this reference. See also Nicholson, *The Canadians in Italy,* pp. 411–12.

the normal supply traffic in support of the offensive, the few roads and trails behind the army front soon became congested with monumental and virtually uncontrollable traffic jams.

Traffic control problems were not, however, peculiar to the Eighth Army. On the same day that General Keyes assembled his forces for an assault on the Hitler Line at a point between Fondi and Terracina, he directed the troops still on the mountains to move at once southward through Itri. That order precipitated a traffic jam near the Itri road junction of Routes 7 and 82, as the infantry from the 88th Division, descending the mountains on the 19th became intermingled with elements of the 88th Division's motorized task force assembling to move on Fondi. For almost eight hours a tangle of motor vehicles, pack trains, and troops blocked the main road and held Sloan's task force east of the Itri junction more effectively than the enemy could then have done. Not until the following morning was the snarl untangled.[21]

Once again, as in the early hours of the May offensive when the FEC's capture of Monte Majo had been the break that had loosened up the entire German defenses, the French were to be the first to break through the enemy line. On the 20th, despite heavy fog and stubborn resistance from elements of the *26th Panzer Division,* the 3d Algerian Infantry Division, reinforced with armor, penetrated the Hitler Line southwest of Pico and drove the enemy from the heights overlooking the town

from the south. That evening the Algerians gained a foothold in the town itself. The Germans held off the attacking troops until the afternoon of the 22d, but the pressure was too great. Fighting on throughout the night, the Algerians drove the last of the enemy from the town by morning of the 23d.[22]

As Clark had foreseen, it would be the French breakthrough at Pico that would soon pay important dividends both in the Liri valley and on the Tyrrhenian flank, for in the attempt to hold Pico, Vietinghoff had been forced to bring up substantial parts of the *15th* and *90th Panzer Grenadier Divisions* from the Liri valley where they might have manned the Hitler Line against the Eighth Army. Moreover, Senger's preoccupation with the defense of Pico had prevented him from countering the threat posed by Keyes' II Corps to that part of the Hitler Line between Fondi and Terracina.[23]

In General Alexander's opinion, the critical stage of the spring offensive had been reached on the morning of 23 May. The French had captured Pico, the hinge and vital connecting link between the sector of the Hitler Line that lay across the Liri valley and that still blocked the way to the II Corps' junction with the Anzio beachhead. Also on the 23d, the Eighth Army's 1st Canadian Corps was about to launch an all-out set-piece attack against the Pontecorvo sector of the Hitler Line, while on the coastal flank astride Highway 7 the Fifth Army's II Corps was about to

[21] Msg, 88th Div to Engrs, 192030B May 44; CO Recon Trp to LO, 200220B May 44; Msg, 85th Div (Capt Butner) to II Corps, 200215B May 44. All items in 88th Div G–3 Jnl, vol. 3, incl. 7.

[22] Mathews, "The French in the Drive on Rome," pp. 134–35; Juin, *La Campagne d'Italie,* pp. 124–28.
[23] Mathews, "The French in the Drive on Rome," p. 134.

enter Terracina. And that same morning the Fifth Army's VI Corps had begun its long-awaited breakout offensive from the Anzio beachhead.

For the assault on the Hitler Line the Eighth Army commander had assigned the 1st Canadian Corps a sector extending northward from the Liri to a point near Aquino, which remained the objective of the British 13 Corps. General Leese's over-all concept envisioned a breakthrough of the Hitler Line by the Canadian corps at Pontecorvo, while the FEC, after capturing Pico, would thrust toward Ceprano to menace the enemy's line of communications in the upper Liri valley. The 5th Canadian Armoured Division was, in the meantime, to be prepared to exploit the breakthrough at Pontecorvo by an advance toward Ceprano.[24]

Behind a rolling barrage fired by 810 guns, the Canadians launched their attack against Pontecorvo at dawn on the 23d. Taking cover in the deep shelters in the sector opposite the Canadians were four grenadier and two engineer battalions, as well as a field replacement battalion, all under the command of the *90th Panzer Grenadier Division.* The *1st Parachute Division,* with two parachute infantry regiments in line, awaited the British 13 Corps' attack at Aquino.

Meanwhile, the haze that had covered the valley in the morning had changed to rain, turning the battlefield, already pocked by heavy artillery fire, into a morass. Only after severe fight-

ing did the Canadians by nightfall at last blast a hole in the Hitler Line about a mile northeast of Pontecorvo. By daylight on the 24th the enemy was gone from the town.

Casualties were heavy, especially in the 1st Division's 2d Brigade, which led the attack. In the Allied attack a total of 513 men were killed or wounded, yet the enemy incurred even heavier losses. The Canadians took 540 prisoners and estimated even a larger number to be killed or wounded. Only at Aquino did the Germans throughout the 23d and the 24th repulse all assaults against the Hitler Line, but thereby they denied the Eighth Army the only good road in the valley, Highway 6.

While the 78th Division fought on at Aquino, the Canadian corps swept through Pontecorvo on the 24th and by nightfall had advanced five miles beyond to the near bank of the Melfa River, a southward-flowing tributary of the Liri. That night the Canadians forced a crossing of the river. Ceprano, the goal of both the French and the Canadians, lay only five miles away.

Meanwhile, throughout the 25th, the German delaying action at Aquino and Piedimonte San Germano continued to deny the Eighth Army use of Highway 6. Thus blocked, the Canadian 5th Armoured Division and the British 6th Armoured Division, as well as all other traffic in support of the offensive, had to take the already overcrowded and rapidly deteriorating secondary roads and trails in the valley, so that traffic jams continued to cause delay and confusion as the Canadians widened their bridgehead beyond the Melfa. Covered by a rare air strike the Germans, during the night of 25 May, took

[24] Operations of British, Indian, and Dominion Forces in Italy, Part II, Sec. B; Nicholson, *The Canadians in Italy,* pp. 414–25. Unless otherwise indicated the following is based upon these references.

advantage of the slow Allied advance to evacuate both Aquino and Piedimonte San Germano, but they failed to demolish two bridges in Aquino that the British were quick to use.

After the fall of Piedimonte San Germano, the Polish corps was pinched out of line by the British 10 Corps, operating on the army's right flank. The latter continued to follow up the enemy's withdrawal, the same assignment it had been executing since the beginning of the offensive.

Junction With the Beachhead

While the Eighth Army achieved its breakthrough in the Liri valley, in the mountains to the south of the valley the U.S. Fifth Army continued its efforts to exploit the penetration of the Hitler Line made by the FEC on the Pico sector and to achieve a breakthrough with the II Corps. General Clark, anxious to keep the enemy from withdrawing troops from the southern front in order to counter the VI Corps' breakout offensive from the beachhead, sought to maintain heavy pressure against the Germans in the mountains and in the Liri valley. He directed General Juin on 22 May to exploit the imminent fall of Pico by a thrust against the southern flank of the Liri valley with a two-pronged drive northward toward Ceprano, a road junction on Highway 6 seven miles north of Pico, and northwestward via Valle Corsa to Castro dei Volsci to Pofi, some nine miles northwest of Pico. This phase of the Fifth Army's offensive began early the next day at the same time the breakout offensive began at Anzio. When, however, the Eighth Army be-

gan to show considerable progress in its attack on the Hitler Line in the Liri valley, the French drive shifted more toward the northwest in the direction of Castro dei Volsci in order to envelop the Germans opposing the Eighth Army. On the 24th Valle Corsa, five miles south of Castro dei Volsci, fell to the French and San Giovanni Incarico, on Route 82 four miles north of Pico, fell on the next day. Thereafter, the enemy fought only delaying actions in an attempt to hold open his routes of escape opposite the U.S. II Corps on the west and the Eighth Army on the east.

The II Corps had still to contend with a ten-mile stretch of the Hitler Line overlooking the coastal highway between Fondi and Terracina. Except for strongpoints at both places, the Germans had developed few defenses in that sector and preferred, as in the mountains between Pico and Fondi, to rely primarily on the rugged terrain. Before joining up with the U.S. VI Corps in the Anzio beachhead, the II Corps would have to cross an area varying in width from ten to twenty miles, from an irregular coastline to the left flank of the FEC, three miles north of Fondi. The area extended northwest from the Itri-Pico road over thirty miles of desolate mountains, deep gorges, and marshy coastal plains to Sezze, an isolated village overlooking the beachhead from the Lepini Mountains to the northeast.

South of Itri a hilly region four miles wide and ten miles long parallels the coast as far as Sperlonga, about seven miles east of Terracina. The hills fall away in the west into a triangle-shaped coastal marsh, which the Germans, by flooding, had made even more of an obstacle. The base of the triangle stretches along the coast from Sperlonga to Terracina with an apex at Fondi.

When General Sloan's 88th Division attacked Fondi, it found the town defended only by survivors of General Steinmetz's battered *94th Infantry Division* and the modest reinforcements that Senger and Vietinghoff had managed to scrape together locally. The formidable *29th Panzer Grenadier Division,* which Kesselring on the 19th had ordered sent to the Fondi area, still had not arrived because General von Mackensen, the *Fourteenth Army* commander, had been slow to release the division. Facing an imminent Allied offensive from the Anzio beachhead, Mackensen was understandably anxious to husband his remaining reserves.

Once before, in October 1943, one of Kesselring's army commanders (that time, Vietinghoff) had apparently dragged his heels in obeying orders to send the *16th Panzer Division* to repel the British landing at Termoli. Then events had vindicated Vietinghoff's insubordination. Would events do the same for Mackensen?[25] The traffic jam between Itri and Fondi might have delayed General Sloan's forces long enough to have enabled the *29th Panzer Grenadier Division* to occupy the Terracina-Fondi sector before the Americans attacked had not the men of Colonel Crawford's 349th Infantry, preceded by elements of the 91st Reconnaissance Squadron, managed to slip by the bottleneck.[26] The advance owed much to

the presence of Brig. Gen. Paul W. Kendall, the 88th Division assistant commander, who had been acting as General Sloan's alter ego: first with the 350th Infantry during the fight for Monte Damiano on 11 and 12 May and later with the 351st Infantry in the dash from Spigno to Monte Grande. He would continue to act in this capacity as the 349th Infantry raced for Fondi. By noon on the 20th the regiment had come within two miles of the town.[27]

Fondi—the ancient Roman Fundi, near where the Republic's legions under Quintus Fabius Maximus had checked Hannibal's army during the First Punic War—provided in May 1944, as it had in the 3d century, B.C., a natural defensive position, this time guarding access to the enemy's third lateral line of communications leading northward across the mountains to the Liri valley. Pillaged twice in the 16th century, the town was to fare somewhat better in the 20th, for the very swiftness of the 349th Infantry's advance would carry the American infantrymen through the position before German reinforcements could dig in.

A patrol of the 91st Reconnaissance Squadron having drawn heavy fire from Fondi early on the 20th, Lt. Col. Walter B. Yeager (commander of the 349th Infantry's 3d Battalion) was alert to the hazards of a frontal assault on the town. Leaving only a holding force south of Fondi, Yeager led his troops, accompanied by a platoon of tanks, off the main road and into the hills overlooking the town from the northeast. As Yeager had suspected, the local German commander, apparently antici-

---

[25] See Blumenson, *Salerno to Cassino,* pp. 190–91; MS # C–064 (Kesselring).

[26] 349th Inf Rpt of Opns, May 44.

[27] II Corps G–3 Jnl, May 44.

pating an Allied thrust along the main road instead of through the mountains, had concentrated his meager defenses astride Highway 7. An assault down the slopes made quick work of the enemy garrison.[28]

Leaving a company to outpost the town, Yeager continued with the rest of his men toward Monte Passignano, just over a mile to the north. By evening the battalion was securely established on the high ground and had settled down for a well-earned rest while patrols probed north and west in search of the foe. The swift blow at Fondi had cost the 349th Infantry 6 dead and 13 wounded, but in the process, the 3d Battalion had pierced the Hitler Line at one of the two remaining strongpoints within the II Corps sector and had denied to the enemy his last good lateral communications short of the Anzio beachhead.[29]

While the breakthrough at Fondi was the more decisive, a thrust by the 88th Division far into the mountains northeast of the town appeared more spectacular. Even as Yeager attacked Fondi on the 20th, Colonel Fry's 350th Infantry began what became a ten-mile march northwestward to Monte Alto, deep within enemy territory. There Fry's men overran scattered German positions, killing 40 enemy soldiers and taking 65 prisoners at a cost of 30 American casualties, most of whom were wounded and evacuated over the difficult mountain trails on litters borne by the German prisoners.[30]

Fry's bold thrust created such a deep

salient within the *Tenth Army*'s right wing that it would take the rest of the Fifth Army three days to catch up. Until the rest of the 88th Division could cover Fry's flanks, he was dependent for supplies on an unprotected line of communications maintained by pack mule trains plodding over trackless mountain terrain. German patrols ambushed and destroyed one train of forty animals and frequently harassed others. To protect his line of communications, General Sloan on the 21st sent the 349th and 351st Infantry Regiments along Fry's right flank, where they remained until the left flank of the FEC would draw abreast two days later.[31]

Along the coastal flank, the 85th Division, with the 337th Regiment leading the way, continued to move toward Terracina. Finding the narrow coastal highway frequently blocked by demolitions, the corps commander ordered General Coulter to mount a small-scale amphibious operation to bypass the obstacles in the hope of accelerating the advance. Keyes had confidence in such a maneuver, since a similar tactic had had some success in the closing days of the Sicilian campaign.[32]

Late in the afternoon of the 21st the 1st Battalion, 338th Infantry, boarded a fleet of DUKW's at the port of Gaeta and moved parallel to the coast toward Terracina, but so choppy was the sea that the small armada eventually gave up and limped into port at Sperlonga,

[28] *Ibid.*

[29] 88th Div G–3 Jnl, vol. 3, incl. 7; 349th Inf Rpt of Opns, May 44.

[30] 350th Inf Jnl, May 44.

[31] II Corps Opns Rpt, May–Jun 44.

[32] Fifth Army G–3 Jnl, 21–22 May 44; 88th Div G–3 Jnl, 16–20 May 44, vol. 3, incl. 7; Paul L. Schultz, *The 85th Division in World War II* (Washington: The Infantry Journal Press, 1959), p. 49; Msg, Harpool 3, 220445B May 44, in II Corps G–3 Jnl, 30 Apr–31 May 44. Unless otherwise cited the following section is based on the above sources.

HIGHWAY 7

AERIAL VIEW OF TERRACINA

several miles short of Terracina. The *ad hoc* seaborne infantrymen had nothing to show for their pains—and they were many—except a renewed appreciation for the terra firma they knew so well.

Upon arrival at Sperlonga most of the DUKW's were found to be unseaworthy. One sank and three others broke down on reaching shore; twelve others, the battalion commander insisted, would never make it to Terracina. Abandoning the amphibious venture, the 1st Battalion moved inland to join the rest of the 338th Infantry in reserve southwest of Fondi.

Magnificently situated on an eminence of gleaming limestone, Terracina anchored the Hitler Line in the II Corps sector and appeared to be an ideal defensive position. From a high, finger-like ridge the mountains overlooking the town drop sharply into the sea. At several places cliffs overhang the main road, which runs along a narrow strip often less than a hundred yards wide between the mountains and the sea. An ancient Roman fortress town, Terracina marks the traditional boundary between southern and central Italy.

Because the Germans considered

Terracina easily defensible from the landward side, they had concentrated their permanent defensive works against a seaborne attack, which after the Anzio landing had seemed the greater danger. The fiasco at Sperlonga, however, ended any threat from that quarter.

The 337th Infantry's 1st Battalion, advancing slowly along the heavily cratered and mined coastal highway, moved to within a mile of Terracina before machine gun and small arms fire forced a halt. Again, as at Fondi, the Americans took to the hills overlooking the road. Leaving their artillery support behind and marching across the seaward slopes, they gained high ground northeast of Terracina, the summit of Monte Sant'Angelo, on the morning of the 22d.[33]

Establishing themselves near the ruins of a temple to Jupiter Auxur, the infantrymen of the 1st Battalion paused to gaze northwestward across the Pontine Marshes toward the dim outline of the Alban Hills, the last major terrain feature south of Rome. If on that picturesque height any of the men chose to meditate upon the vanished glories of antiquity in their immediate vicinity, they were rudely cut short by heavy fire from a battalion of the *29th Panzer Grenadier Division* that had arrived belatedly during the night. Faced with an overwhelming volume of fire, Colonel Hughes withdrew his men to the base of Monte Sant'Angelo, where they were joined by the 3d Battalion, while artillery, which had drawn to within supporting distance, opened fire

on Terracina and the western slopes of Monte Sant'Angelo.[34] (*Map 4*)

Behind heavy preparatory artillery fire and with the newly arrived 3d Battalion in reserve, the 1st Battalion returned to the attack during the afternoon of the 22d. This time the Germans contested every foot of the ground, but despite intense mortar fire from the hills northwest of Terracina, the men of the 337th Infantry had by nightfall fought their way back to the top of Monte Sant'Angelo and moved down the reverse slope as far as a cemetery a mile north of the town. After thirty-six hours of virtually uninterrupted fighting, the 1st Battalion, too exhausted to continue, was relieved after dark by the 3d Battalion. Resuming the attack, the 3d Battalion by midnight had infiltrated beyond the cemetery into the outskirts of Terracina.[35]

As the 337th Infantry prepared to renew the assault on Terracina on the 23d, two battalions of the 338th Infantry advanced over Monte San Stefano toward Monte Leano, four miles northwest of the town. Their mission was to block Highway 7 where it ran along the foot of Monte Leano, thereby cutting the German route of withdrawal from Terracina. Threatened with encirclement, the German garrison in Terracina left behind a small rear guard and, during the night of 23 May, withdrew northwestward in the darkness.

The Tenth Army Withdraws

To Kesselring and his staff the overall German situation in Italy was far

---

[33] Fifth Army G–3 Jnl, 21–22 May 44, Tel Msg from II Corps, 220515B May 44, Jnl X5-22-12.

[34] 337th Inf, 85th Div, Opns Rpt, May 44, pp. 4–5.

[35] *Ibid.*

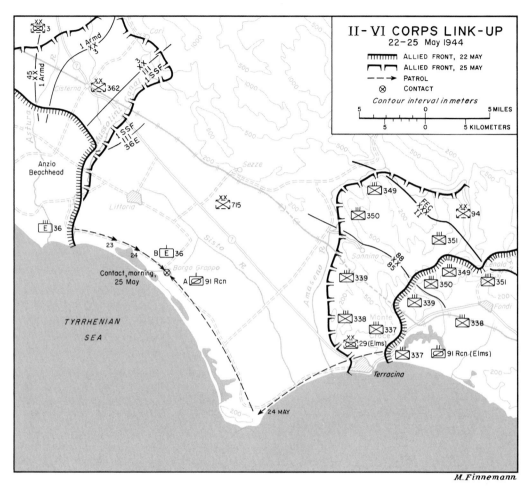

MAP 4

from reassuring. In the Liri valley, the Eighth Army had pierced the Hitler Line. The Fifth Army's two-pronged drive by the U.S. II Corps and the FEC toward the Anzio beachhead and upper reaches of the Liri valley, respectively, threatened to envelop the entire left wing of Mackensen's *Fourteenth Army* and the right wing of the *Tenth Army*. Furthermore, the Allied beachhead al-

ready had begun to erupt. The pending fall of Terracina would open the main coastal highway all the way to the beachhead, while the FEC—driving beyond Pico toward Lenola, thirteen miles northeast of Terracina and a key strongpoint on a road to Frosinone, on Highway 6 some fifty miles southeast of Rome—threatened to split the two German armies. Should the Germans fail to

halt the Fifth Army at either Terracina
or at Lenola, a breakthrough to the
beachhead and probably to the Caesar
Line, the last German defensive position below Rome, was a certainty.[36]

At Supreme Headquarters (OKW) in
Germany, some officers recommended
to Hitler that Kesselring be directed to
abandon his front south of Rome,
others that he employ all of his remaining air strength in an effort to hold his
positions. One of the latter, General der
Artillerie Walter Warlimont, deputy
chief of the OKW operations staff,
declared that failure to commit the
Luftwaffe would doom Kesselring's
chances of holding Rome. Determined
to husband remaining air power for the
expected Allied invasion of northwestern France, Hitler refused to accept
that reasoning. He chose instead to
allow Kesselring to continue as he was
doing: defend as long as possible on
favorable terrain before falling back
under pressure to another line, all the
while exacting as heavy a toll as possible
from the attacking Allied forces, instructions known to Alexander and his
army commanders through the deciphered Enigma messages.[37]

The Americans, in the meantime,
had launched their final thrust to the
beachhead. Early on the 24th patrols of
the 85th Division's 337th Infantry entered Terracina, and in midmorning
Clark's chief of staff reported, "Terracina is ours."[38] While General Coulter's
engineers cleared the road through the

town, a patrol from the 91st Reconnaissance Squadron moved cautiously
across the Pontine Marshes to the village of Borgo Grappo, where shortly
after daylight on 25 May the troopers
met an engineer patrol from the U.S.
VI Corps. Two weeks after the beginning of the May offensive on the
Rapido-Garigliano front and 125 days
after the Allied landings at Anzio, the
troops from the southern front, having
successively broken through the Gustav
and Hitler Lines, had linked with those
from the beachhead.[39]

With the French capture of Pico and
the beginning of the breakout offensive
from the Anzio beachhead on the 23d,
and the fall of Pontecorvo to the Canadians and of Terracina to the Americans on the 24th, Vietinghoff's *Tenth
Army* had no alternative to a full-scale
withdrawal across the southern front.
Beginning the night of the 25th, the *LI
Mountain Corps*, opposite the Eighth
Army, fell back beyond the Melfa River
and withdrew from the Liri valley
northward along the several roads
through the mountains that parallel
Highway 6 to the north. Opposite the
Fifth Army's II Corps and the FEC, the
XIV Panzer Corps withdrew northward
through the Ausonia Mountains into
the Sacco River valley, which joins the
Liri valley about three miles northeast
of Pico.

A combination of increasingly difficult terrain, congested roads, and a
caution born of weariness and heavy
casualties slowed the Eighth Army's
pursuit, while the tremendous significance attached to the capture of Rome
had its influence on the Fifth Army's

[36] Greiner and Schramm, eds., *OKW/WFSt, OKW,*
pp. 491–92.

[37] *Ibid.;* Winterbotham, *The Ultra Secret,* p. 117.

[38] 337th Inf Opns Rpt, May 44; Fifth Army
Sitreps, 11–30 May 44; Msg, Gruenther to Clark,
Ref 167, 240925B May 44.

[39] II Corps G–3 Jnl, May 44.

next operations. Meanwhile, large quantities of supplies from Naples moved in long truck columns along Highways 6 and 7 to support the final drive on Rome. Operation DIADEM was about to enter a new phase.[40]

---

[40] Gen Clark's personal comments on MS, Oct 1973, in CMH files.

PART TWO

BREAKOUT FROM THE BEACHHEAD

From . . . the general endeavour to attain a relative superiority, there follows another endeavour which must consequently be just as general in its nature: this is the *surprise* of the enemy. It lies more or less at the foundation of all undertakings, for without it the preponderance at the decisive point is not properly conceivable.

CLAUSEWITZ, *On War*

CHAPTER VI

The Anzio Beachhead

Italian Lands vs. German Blood

As the Allied force used its strong right arm to punch its way from the southern front toward the Hitler Line, the left arm, which for several weeks had been gathering strength within the confines of the Anzio beachhead, remained flexed for a sharp hook against General Mackensen's *Fourteenth Army,* keeping vigil over the beachhead. In accord with General Alexander's order of 5 May, the attack from the beachhead was to be launched on 24-hours' notice at any time after D plus 4. The Allied armies commander had reserved for himself the final decision as to the exact time.[1] It was to constitute the hoped-for fulfillment of Alexander's— as well as Churchill's—original strategic concept behind Operations DIADEM and SHINGLE, a one-two punch designed to trap and annihilate a large portion of Kesselring's armies south of Rome before moving in to capture the capital of Mussolini's crumbling empire. This strategy rested upon the premise that it was more profitable to destroy enemy units than to take ground. It would not be enough merely to push back enemy armies but to wipe them out to such an extent that they would have to be replaced from other theaters to avoid a rout. Yet the lure of Rome for all Allied commanders in Italy threatened to undermine that premise.[2]

This strategy had yet to receive full acceptance within the Fifth Army, although the original mission in Operation SHINGLE had included a thrust from the beachhead to cut the *XIV Panzer Corps'* line of communications.[3] As far as General Clark was concerned, the question of which direction Truscott's corps was to take once it had broken out of the beachhead had yet to be answered. In any case, since it was a corps within Clark's army that was involved, Clark intended the decision to be his, not Alexander's.

The question of the timing of the breakout offensive depended to a certain extent upon its direction; thus timing remained a subject of controversy and some confusion until the very eve of the offensive, although the formal order from Headquarters, AAI, on 5 May had clearly stated, as noted earlier, that the decision on timing was to be Alexander's.

The question of which direction the offensive was to take following the breakout had been a matter of contro-

---

[1] Hq AAI, Opns 0 1, 5 May 44.

[2] Brigadier C. J. C. Molony, "History of the Second World War," *The Mediterranean and Middle East, Volume V, The Campaign in Sicily and the Campaign in Italy, 3rd September 1943 to 31st March 1944* (London: Her Majesty's Stationery Office, 1973), p. 833.

[3] Martin Blumenson, "General Lucas at Anzio," in *Command Decisions* (Washington, 1960), p. 301; Clark's comments on MS, in CMH files.

versy within Allied planning circles ever since January 1944, when the Allies had first come ashore at Anzio. The controversy had polarized about the persons of Alexander and Clark and stemmed largely from differing views on the role of the Anzio beachhead. From its very inception Clark had opposed the very concept of Anzio and during the planning stage had recommended dropping it. This view was also held by U.S. Army Chief of Staff General George C. Marshall. Thus Anzio was a British project, although carried out in large part by Americans. This anomaly may have had something to do with the later disagreement between Clark and Alexander.[4]

General Alexander originally had envisioned the beachhead as a base for a thrust northwest along the axis of Highway 7 into the Alban Hills, while the main Allied forces drove the enemy from the southern front up the Liri valley into a trap formed by the VI Corps athwart the enemy's line of communications in the Rome area. In developing plans to implement that concept early in 1944, General Clark had reversed the roles of the participating forces. He was then convinced that the VI Corps should be limited to pinning down the German *Fourteenth Army* opposite the beachhead, thereby preventing Kesselring from shifting reinforcements southward to assist the *Tenth Army,* which was then opposing the Fifth Army's attempt to break into the Liri valley.[5]

Throughout the winter of 1943-1944 the matter had been allowed to simmer quietly, but with the coming of spring and revival of plans for a May offensive, the controversy had boiled again. Although Alexander had shifted his attention from the Alban Hills and Rome southeastward some twenty miles to Valmontone and Highway 6, his original concept—trapping a major part of Vietinghoff's *Tenth Army* between a blocking force striking out from the beachhead and the main force advancing from the southeast—remained unaltered.

On the other hand, the Fifth Army commander's views had changed significantly. In April, after Alexander had regrouped the two Allied armies, General Leese's Eighth Army rather than General Clark's Fifth stood before the entrance to the Liri valley, leading Clark to wonder whether the British rather than the Americans might reach Rome first. The U.S. VI Corps, therefore, seemed to offer Clark a chance to counter this geographical advantage in a race for the Italian capital. If Truscott's VI Corps could break out of the beachhead and strike directly northward into the Alban Hills, the Americans might win that race. Moreover, in addition to winning the race Clark was very much concerned about reaching Rome before the beginning of OVERLORD, as George Marshall had frequently and pointedly urged him to do.

General Clark, no longer considering the beachhead a holding action as he had during the winter, saw Truscott's corps as the potential spearhead of a Fifth Army drive on Rome. The Alban Hills had become in Clark's eyes a gateway rather than a barrier to Rome.

---

[4] See Forrest C. Pogue, *George C. Marshall, Organizer of Victory* (New York: Viking Press, 1973), p. 331.

[5] *Ibid.,* pp. 326–27; Mark W. Clark, *Calculated Risk* (New York: Harper & Brothers, 1950), pp. 283–86.

Moreover, as long as the enemy held the hills in strength a threat remained to the flank of any thrust from the beachhead in the direction of Valmontone and Highway 6. Clark believed that his forces should secure the Alban Hills before attempting to cut off the *Tenth Army's* right wing at Valmontone.[6]

General Clark, just as he had earlier modified Alexander's directive for the offensive along the southern front, now laid the groundwork for another, even more important unilateral change, this time in Alexander's guidelines for the VI Corps' breakout offensive from the Anzio beachhead. Clark directed Truscott to prepare a plan for an offensive to be launched on forty-eight hours' notice along one of four possible axes: northwestward along the coastal corridor, across the Alban Hills directly toward Rome, northwestward through Cisterna to Valmontone on Highway 6, or eastward to Sezze in the Lepini Mountains, overlooking the beachhead from that direction. On 2 April, during a conference with his army commanders, General Alexander had opted for an attack toward Valmontone in the hope of cutting the enemy's line of communications with the main front. Yet Clark's instructions to Truscott had carefully avoided specifying a choice among the possible axes of attack from the beachhead, for General Clark failed to share the belief that significant numbers of Germans would be cut off by a thrust to Valmontone and Highway 6. There were, in Clark's opinion, just too many alternate routes of escape available to the Germans. Alexander's desire

for the thrust on Valmontone had, in Clark's view, been dictated mainly by an expectation that it would help to loosen up German resistance opposite the Eighth Army and enable the latter to accelerate its advance up the Liri-Sacco valley. For Clark that was insufficient to justify the risks to his Fifth Army inherent in Alexander's plan.[7]

On 5 May Alexander visited the VI Corps headquarters where Truscott laid before him the four alternate plans which the corps staff, as directed by Clark, had developed during the two preceding months. The plans went by the code names of GRASSHOPPER, BUFFALO, TURTLE, and CRAWDAD.

GRASSHOPPER outlined an attack toward the east in the direction of Littoria-Sezze with the object of making contact with the Fifth Army's main force advancing northwestward. Only if troops on the southern front appeared to be bogged down and in need of help to achieve a junction with the beachhead was GRASSHOPPER to be mounted. Operation BUFFALO, which most closely corresponded to SHINGLE's and DIADEM's original strategic concepts, called for a thrust northeastward through Cisterna, Cori, and Artena to Valmontone. Its objective was to block Highway 6 and thereby cut off the retreat of the *Tenth Army's* right wing. The destruction of a significant part of the *Tenth Army* would open the road to Rome along Highway 6. Operation TURTLE called for an attack astride the Via Anziate (the Anzio-Rome road) and the Rome railroad, northward through Carroceto and Campoleone to a junction with High-

---

[6] Clark's comments on MS, in CMH files.

[7] *Ibid.*

GENERAL TRUSCOTT

way 7 about a mile south of Lake
Albano in the Alban Hills. Operation
CRAWDAD outlined a drive through
Ardea, twelve miles northwest of Anzio,
roughly paralleling the coast southwest
of the Alban Hills. In terms of distance,
CRAWDAD afforded the shortest route to
Rome, but the road network was less
favorable than that offered by Highway
7. After looking over the four plans,
General Alexander quickly dismissed all
but BUFFALO. The drive on Valmontone, he declared, was the only operation likely to produce "worthwhile results."[8]

While BUFFALO was eminently suited
to Alexander's strategic concept, it con-
flicted sharply with the idea taking
shape in Clark's mind. The Fifth Army
commander had no faith in the plan.
When Truscott informed him of Alexander's visit and of his comments on

[8] Truscott Personal Radios Sent files, Feb–Jun
1944.

the breakout plans, Clark immediately
telephoned the Allied commander to
express irritation over what he interpreted as an unwarranted interference
with the Fifth Army's command channels.[9] Clark insisted that he wanted to
keep his own plans flexible and not be
tied to "pre-conceived ideas as to what
exactly was to be done." Rejecting Alexander's apparent assumption that Operation BUFFALO would trap a large part
of the German *Tenth Army,* Clark added
that he did not "believe we have too
many chances to do that—the Boche is
too smart." Clark agreed that Truscott
should give BUFFALO first priority in his
operational planning, but he insisted
that the VI Corps commander should
be free to continue to develop other
plans as well. The Fifth Army commander declared with some logic that
he had to be "prepared to meet any
eventuality" and keep his "mind free of
any commitment before the battle
started."[10]

Even before these exchanges Clark
had become suspicious that there might
be "interests brewing for the Eighth
Army to take Rome." But as he was to
note later, "We not only wanted the
honor of capturing Rome, but we felt
that we more than deserved it . . . My
own feeling was that nothing was going
to stop us on our push toward the
Italian capital. Not only did we intend
to become the first army in fifteen
centuries to seize Rome from the south,
but we intended to see that the people
back home knew that it was the Fifth

[9] Clark Diary, 8 May 44; Clark's comments on
MS, in CMH files.
[10] Clark Diary, 8 May 44; Sidney T. Mathews,
"Clark's Decision to Drive on Rome," in *Command
Decisions* (Washington, 1960), pp. 353–54.

Army that did the job and knew the price that had been paid for it." These considerations were for Clark "important to an understanding of the behind-the-scenes differences of opinion that occurred in this period. Such controversies, he observed years later, were conceived in good faith as a result of honest differences of opinions about the best way to do the job."[11] Alexander, however annoyed he may have been, generally kept his feelings to himself. Not only did he not reproach Clark in his dispatches but even failed to mention their disagreement. Such was the character of the Allied armies' commander.[12]

German Plans

Fundamental differences over strategy between Alexander and Clark concerning the direction the VI Corps' offensive was to take had a counterpart within the German command where opposing concepts, especially between Kesselring and Mackensen, the *Fourteenth Army* commander, exacerbated relations between the two men. Field Marshal Kesselring believed that the Allied forces on the beachhead would attempt to break out in the direction of Valmontone in an effort to cut Highway 6 and sever the line of communications to the southern front. General von Mackensen, for his part, believed that once free of the beachhead, the VI Corps would advance into the Alban Hills along the axis of Highway 7, next to the coastal road, the most direct road

to Rome.[13] Thus did the *Fourteenth Army* commander anticipate the strategy even then taking form in Clark's mind.

This disagreement between the army group and *Fourteenth Army* commanders was further complicated by Hitler's intervention in the development of strategic and tactical plans in Italy, about which he was deeply concerned even though far from the front, and even though Italy was a secondary theater. Anticipating the time when the Allies would attempt to break out of the Anzio beachhead, Hitler as early as mid-March, had instructed Kesselring to study the possibility of employing the so-called false front tactic, which, Hitler recalled, the French and Germans had successfully used near Rheims in the last year of World War I. More recently, the U.S. VI Corps had used it in repelling German counterattacks at Anzio in mid-February. This tactic may be described as follows: just before attacking forces began their preparatory artillery fire, the defenders would evacuate the forward positions for previously prepared positions in the rear of the main line of resistance. After the offensive had spent itself and the attackers were thrown off balance, the defenders' reserves, waiting securely in the rear, were to counterattack and destroy the foe.

On 1 April Kesselring responded to Hitler's instructions with a plan of his own. He had already directed Mackensen, he said, to begin an extensive thinning of the *Fourteenth Army*'s forward battle positions and to dispose his defenses in greater depth. Forward po-

[11] Clark, *Calculated Risk,* p. 352; Clark Diary, 5 May 44.

[12] Nicolson, *Alex,* pp. 252–53.

[13] CMDS (Br), The German Operations at Anzio, 22 January to 31 May 1944.

sitions were to be held in strength sufficient only to compel the Allied forces to attack with all their heavy weapons. While the Allied attack wore itself out against numerous strongpoints arranged in depth throughout the main battle position, German losses would be held to a minimum. Even if the Allied forces penetrated the main line of resistance, there would still be time, Kesselring believed, to bring up his reserves for a counterattack.

Taking a mildly critical view of Hitler's tactical suggestions, Kesselring pointed out an inherent weakness. How could one determine early enough that a given Allied artillery bombardment presaged an offensive so that forward positions might be evacuated in time? To delay too long risked having those positions overrun and thereby exposing the main defenses; yet a premature withdrawal could mean loss of the entire main line of resistance. Moreover, Kesselring argued, it would be difficult to deceive the Allies for any length of time as to the real location of the main line of resistance.

Hitler, too, was concerned about the possibility that Mackensen's secondary defenses might be destroyed by artillery when the Allied attack rolled over his forward positions. When the *Fourteenth Army*'s chief of staff, Generalmajor Wolf-Ruediger Hauser, visited the Fuehrer's headquarters early in April, Hitler indicated that he wanted Mackensen to consider shifting his secondary position even farther to the rear.

As finally drawn, Kesselring's defense plan represented a compromise with Hitler's concepts. It called for temporary evacuation of the forward areas and occupying previously prepared blocking positions as soon as preparations for a full-scale Allied attack were identified, but only near the strongpoints of Aprilia (called "the Factory"), Cisterna, and Littoria, in the northern, central, and southern sectors, respectively. Defenders elsewhere were to hold in place.

Although the Germans at first believed that waterlogged terrain would limit large-scale employment of armor in the beachhead until well into the spring of 1944, by March they had begun to suspect that another breakout offensive by the Allied forces would not be long in coming. As the ground began to dry out toward the end of April, expectations increased.

Early in April the *Fourteenth Army* commander reported a significant increase in Allied artillery registration fires and frequent use of smoke over the port of Anzio and other Allied debarkation points. Anticipating that the activity possibly foreshadowed the expected offensive from the beachhead, Kesselring ordered the planned withdrawal, but when April passed with no such attack, he concluded that the Allied offensive would begin not in the beachhead but either on the southern front or possibly with another amphibious landing. He therefore ordered the *Fourteenth Army*'s troops back to their original positions.

The Terrain

The Anzio beachhead sprawled over a large coastal plain which in Roman times had been a fertile farming region, but which through the centuries had become a vast malarial swamp. Reclaiming this pestilential region, known as the Pontine Marshes, had long been a dream of Italian agronomists. In the decade immediately preceding the war much of the area had been partially drained and had become one of the agricultural show places of Mussolini's government.

A complex grid of drainage canals and ditches cut the plain into a series of compartments, severely restricting cross-country movement of military vehicles. The most formidable of the barriers were the 240-foot-wide Mussolini Canal and the Colletore delle Acqua Medie, or West Branch of the Mussolini Canal; the former flowed generally from north to south along the beachhead's right flank and the latter flowed southeastward from the direction of the Alban Hills to join the Mussolini Canal about seven miles from the coast. The smooth, sloping banks of these canals dropped into water that varied in depth from ten to twenty feet. Most of the smaller canals were from twenty to fifty feet wide.

Approximately triangular in shape, the Anzio beachhead encompassed much of the plain west of the Mussolini Canal, generally better drained than that to the east of the canal. Except for the few roads along the tops of dikes, the region around Littoria, fifteen miles east of Anzio, had reverted to its ancient state, a virtually impassable marsh. From Terracina, at the southeastern edge of the plain, Highway 7 runs northwest for thirty miles to the town of Cisterna, fifteen miles inland and northeast from the port of Anzio. A section of the Naples-Rome railroad parallels the highway for a short distance before crossing the highway at Cisterna. The Allied beachhead lay southwest of both the highway and the railroad.

The apex of the triangle, whose base rested upon a 20-mile stretch of coastline, pointed like an arrowhead toward Cisterna. Around a large administrative building in the center of Cisterna, mostly in ruins as a result of months of artillery fire, the Germans had built a ring of mutually supporting strongpoints, which had become the hinge of their forward defensive lines.

Inland from Cisterna the coastal plain narrows, rising to a gently rolling corridor about three miles wide and extending from Cisterna in a north-northeasterly direction fourteen miles to Valmontone on Highway 6, at the upper end of the Sacco River, a tributary of the Liri. Dotted with vineyards and orchards and cut by occasional wide, southward-running ravines, the corridor offers terrain generally favorable for military operations. Flanking to the southeast are the steep-sided Lepini Mountains, rising to heights of over 3,000 feet. In the vicinity of the ancient fortress town of Cori, six miles northwest of Cisterna, the slopes of the mountains are covered by olive groves which give way on the higher elevations to bare rock and scrub oak. Footpaths and cart trails similar to those encountered by the II Corps in the Petrella massif offer the only access to that inhospitable region.

Northwest of the corridor are the Alban Hills, whose highest summits are somewhat lower than those of the Lepini Mountains. Thousands of years ago this circular hill mass had been formed by a volcano. Two of the highest hills are the Rocca di Papa and

CASSINO TO THE ALPS

Monte Cavo, both rising hundreds of feet above the crater floor. Over the years the southeastern rim of the crater eroded to form an elongated ridge about four miles in length, averaging 2,000 feet in height. Rising like a wall behind the town of Velletri, located at a point halfway up the ridge where Highway 7 leaves the coastal plain and enters the hills, the ridge bears the lyrical name of Monte Artemisio. From both Velletri and the ridge behind it the Germans had excellent observation over both the beachhead and the corridor leading from Cisterna to Valmontone.

Extending like fingers from the southern slopes of the Alban Hills and onto the coastal plain, steep-sided ridges formed by ancient lava flows ran past the towns of Velletri and Lanuvio, the latter located five miles to the west of the former. The sides of the ridges were covered with modest vineyards and groves of chestnut trees, but the crests were open and usually cultivated in a patchwork of grain fields.

The Opposing Forces

Reflecting the fluctuations imposed by attack and counterattack in the weeks since the landing at Anzio, the Allies' forward positions by mid-May traced a meandering line across the landscape. From the sea on the southwest they led to a ridge south of the Moletta River, thence to the Anzio-Aprilia-Albano road. From the road the front curved northeastward about five miles to the hamlet of Casale Carano, thence followed the Carano Canal for a short distance before turning southeast to parallel the Cisterna-Campoleone-Rome railroad for some seven miles as

far as the west bank of the Mussolini Canal. At the canal the front turned south and followed its west bank for nine miles to the sea. Blocking the most likely avenues of enemy attack across the front were numerous mine fields emplaced by the Allied troops during the winter battles.

Of the U.S. units on the beachhead in February—the 3d and 45th Divisions, the 1st Armored Division's Combat Command A, the 1st Special Service Force (an American-Canadian regimental-sized force), the reinforced 509th Parachute Regiment, and the 6615th Ranger Force (three battalions)—only the paratroopers had left the beachhead by mid-May. The survivors of the ranger force had been integrated into the 1st Special Service Force. Those losses had been more than made up in late March by the arrival of the 34th Infantry Division, a veteran of the winter fighting at Cassino. On 28 March that division began relieving the 3d Division, which had been on the front for sixty-seven consecutive days. The 1st Armored Division was also brought up to full strength with the arrival in April of CCB, its second combat command, and other elements of the division.

The British too had shifted some of their units. In early March the 5th Division had replaced the 56th, and the latter, together with some British commandos, left the beachhead. The 1st Division remained, but its 24th Guards Brigade was relieved by the 18th Guards Brigade, the former moving to Naples for rest and reorganization.

By the beginning of April all Allied units had been brought to full strength. The VI Corps, including the two British divisions, mustered a combat strength of approximately 90,000 men. As planning for the beachhead offensive got under way, Allied units were holding the front from left to right in the following order: the British 5th and 1st Divisions, the U.S. 45th and 34th Divisions, and the 36th Engineer Regiment. In corps reserve were the 3d and 36th Divisions (the latter having arrived on the beachhead by sea on 22 May), the 1st Armored Division, and the 1st Special Service Force.[14]

The Germans too, after the repulse of their winter attack, had begun to regroup their forces. In mid-March a Jaeger division[15] was moved to the Adriatic coast to strengthen the front there, and the *Hermann Goering Division* was withdrawn to Tuscan bases near Leghorn for rest and reorganization. About the same time, the *26th Panzer* and *29th Panzer Grenadier Divisions* had also been withdrawn from the *Fourteenth Army* into army group reserve in the Rome area.[16]

Facing the Allied beachhead were five divisions divided into two corps. From right to left there were in line the following units: the *I Parachute Corps,* commanding the *4th Parachute, 65th Infantry,* and *3d Panzer Grenadier Divisions,* and the *LXXVI Panzer Corps* with the *362d* and *715th Infantry Divisions.*

The heavy winter fighting had left most of the divisions somewhat under-

strength. Although General von Mackensen's army would never regain its February strength, replacements had continued to trickle in. By mid-April the *Fourteenth Army* had grown to 70,400 men, still considerably less than the approximately 90,000 Allied soldiers assembled on the beachhead.

The *Fourteenth Army's* artillery units, long-time targets of Allied air attacks, had also incurred heavy losses. Mackensen's artillery had been further plagued by chronic delays in the arrival of ammunition, delays occasioned more by shortages of transport than by lack of supply in dumps. Furthermore, most Allied guns lay beyond range of the self-propelled howitzers and dual-purpose antiaircraft guns which made up the bulk of the *Fourteenth Army's* artillery. Mackensen's artillery could fire effective counterbattery only with a few 100-mm. guns, although Kesselring had promised that additional heavy pieces were on the way: twelve 210-mm. howitzers and seven batteries of 122-mm. guns from the OKW artillery reserve in France and a railway artillery battery of 320-mm. guns from northern Italy. He also promised to increase ammunition allocations, although in view of German transportation problems that was hardly likely to come about.

Allied Preparations

As the Germans awaited the Allied blow, the leader of the force that was to make the main effort, General Truscott, commander of the U.S. VI Corps, still awaited a decision as to the direction his force was to take once breakout from the beachhead had been achieved. Yet despite General Clark's determination to keep the matter open, Truscott

---

[14] DA Hist Div, "American Forces in Action," *Anzio Beachhead (22 January–25 May 1944)* (Washington, 1947), p. 106.

[15] "Jaeger" denotes a light infantry division as contrasted with a standard infantry division.

[16] GMDS (Br), The German Operations at Anzio, 22 January to 31 May 1944, pp. 94–95. Unless otherwise cited the following is based upon this source.

focused his attention on the plan he deemed most likely to be adopted, the one General Alexander had favored— Operation BUFFALO.

Vital to BUFFALO's success, Truscott reasoned, were rapid capture of the enemy's main stronghold at Cisterna and swift occupation of the town of Cori, halfway up the western slopes of the Lepini Mountains. Until those two objectives were in hand, the enemy would control the road network leading to BUFFALO's objective, Valmontone on Highway 6.

On 6 May, the day following General Alexander's visit to VI Corps headquarters, General Truscott outlined for his division commanders a two-phase attack designed to gain those objectives. In the first phase the corps was to drive northeastward to build up along the X-Y Line, a line forming a large arc two miles north and east of Cisterna and extending from Highway 7 as far as the main road from Cisterna to Cori.[17] In the second phase the corps was to capture Cori, then to advance northward via Guilianello toward Artena, a road junction about three miles south of Valmontone. From Artena the drive was to continue with a thrust to cut Highway 6, capture Valmontone, and cut the *Tenth Army*'s line of communications.

The armored strength of the VI Corps' offensive was to be provided by the 1st Armored Division, commanded by Maj. Gen. Ernest N. Harmon, a vigorous and able leader given to blunt speaking. The 1st Armored Division had fought in North Africa but, after

GENERAL HARMON

the division landed on the Italian mainland in September 1943, mountainous terrain had denied it more than a minor role in the advance from Salerno to Cassino. During the winter, division headquarters and CCA had joined the VI Corps in the Anzio beachhead, while CCB remained behind with the II Corps on the southern front in order to exploit a projected Fifth Army breakthrough into the Liri valley. In the end, CCB also had to come to Anzio by sea.

A so-called "heavy" armored division, one of three formed in the U.S. Army before a decision to scale down the tank strength of armored divisions, the 1st Armored Division had a TO&E strength of 232 medium tanks and 14,620 officers and men, making it a formidable force with a tank strength a third again greater than a German

_____

[17] VI Corps FO 25, 6 May 44. Unless otherwise cited this section is based upon this source.

panzer division. In addition, the division had an attached tank destroyer battalion, an antiaircraft battalion, and, to supplement its three organic 105-mm. (howitzer) self-propelled artillery battalions, the attached 69th Field Artillery Battalion of 105-mm. self-propelled howitzers. To supplement the division's armored infantry regiment for the offensive, General Truscott attached the 135th Infantry from the 34th Division. There were also two companies from the 83d Chemical Battalion, equipped with 4.2-inch mortars capable of firing smoke and high-explosive shells,[18] one company each from the 109th Combat Engineer and self-propelled 636th Tank Destroyer Battalions, and a detachment of the 6617th Mine Clearing Company.

General Harmon's division and the 3d Infantry Division, formerly Truscott's own division, were to lead the breakout offensive. One of the U.S. Army's oldest and most distinguished divisions, the 3d had taken part in the North African and Sicilian campaigns. After Truscott had moved up to corps command, the division came under the command of Maj. Gen. John W. O'Daniel, whose rough features and barracks-yard voice had prompted the nickname "Iron Mike."

For his part, General Harmon objected strongly to pairing an armored

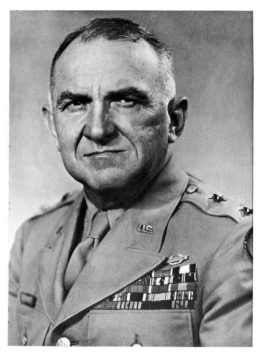

GENERAL O'DANIEL

and an infantry division for the breakout attempt. Better to follow the conventional pattern, he argued, of holding the armor in reserve as a tool for exploiting an infantry breakthrough. He confided that view to two staff officers of the Fifth Army's G-3 plans section who visited his headquarters on the eve of the offensive. Harmon told his visitors that he expected to lose 100 tanks in the first thirty minutes of the offensive. It was, he declared, "a crazy idea."[19] Actually, General Truscott recognized that his decision to use the armored division in the first stage of

---

[18] This mortar had been developed from the Stokes Mortar of World War I and had first seen action during the Sicilian campaign in the summer of 1943. After the Chemical Corps adapted the mortar to fire HE, it became an important and useful infantry support weapon with a maximum range of 4,397 yards. See Leo P. Brophy, Wyndham D. Miles, and Rexmond C. Cochrane, *The Chemical Warfare Service: From Laboratory to Field*, U.S. ARMY IN WORLD WAR II (Washington, 1959).

[19] Interv, Sidney T. Mathews with Lt Col T. J. Conway (Chief, Plans Subsection, G-3, Hq Fifth Army, 16 Dec 44–May 45), 27 Jun 50, CMH.

the offensive ran counter to current armored doctrine, but he saw the weight of the armor as affording the best possibility of breaking the long-held German positions in the Cisterna sector.[20]

Under Truscott's plan the 1st Armored Division was, during the offensive's first phase, to advance from positions southwest of Cisterna along a line roughly parallel to Le Mole Canal to cut the railroad northwest of Cisterna, push on to Highway 7, then to the X-Y Line. In the second phase, the division was to move first to a phase line designated the O-B Line, which crossed the corridor between the Alban Hills and the Lepini Mountains three miles south of Velletri. The division's left flank was to keep the Velletri-based enemy north of that line, while the rest of Harmon's troops were, on Truscott's order, to swing northeast and continue the drive on Artena and Valmontone. Maj. Gen. Fred L. Walker's 36th Infantry Division was to move up from corps reserve to take Cori and to reinforce the armored division's attack on Artena.

To the 3d Division, General Truscott gave the crucial task of first isolating, then capturing Cisterna. Unlike Harmon, O'Daniel had complete confidence in the plans for the forthcoming offensive and in the ability of his division to seize Cisterna and continue to the final objective. General O'Daniel's zeal may have been enhanced by an opportunity to even a score with the enemy following a futile attempt by the division to storm Cisterna in January.

While the 3d Division attacked the enemy's center, the division's right flank

was to be covered by Brig. Gen. Robert T. Frederick's American-Canadian 1st Special Service Force, advancing from positions just west of the Mussolini Canal to cut Highway 7 southeast of Cisterna and occupy that part of the X-Y Line in that sector. Thereafter, Frederick's men were to be prepared, on corps order, to seize the heights of Monte Arrestino, overlooking Cori from the south, then move northward across the Lepini Mountains to cut Highway 6 east of Valmontone.

On the 1st Armored Division's left, Maj. Gen. William W. Eagles' 45th Division, holding the sector between the Spaccasassi Canal and the Carano Canal, was to cover the left flank of the offensive by an advance as far as the first phase line, which in Eagles' sector ran generally in a northerly direction just west of the village of Carano, some five miles southwest of Cisterna and on the bank of the Carano Canal. As the main attack moved on beyond Cisterna, the division was to keep the enemy in its zone occupied by vigorous patrolling.

Meanwhile, Maj. Gen. Charles W. Ryder's 34th Division, holding the front across the corps center from Le Mole Canal to the Nettuno-Cisterna road, was to screen the final preparations for the offensive and to assist in gapping American mine fields and barbed wire barriers for the attacking units. When relieved from that assignment, the division, less the regiment attached to the armor, was to regroup and prepare to relieve elements of either the 1st Armored Division or the 1st Special Service Force if either should be unable to continue the offensive after reaching the first phase line.

General Truscott had also prepared a

---

[20] Interv, author with Truscott, Mar 62, CMH.

deception plan, Operation HIPPO, designed to deceive the enemy as long as possible as to the offensive's true direction by a strong demonstration on the beachhead's far left flank a few hours before the breakout offensive began. The job of executing HIPPO fell to the British 1st and 5th Divisions, holding that sector of the beachhead perimeter from the Tyrrhenian coast northeastward to the left flank of the 45th Division. Since they were to be withdrawn after the capture of Rome, the two British divisions were to operate under direct control of the Fifth Army without an intervening corps command.[21]

To support the offensive, the VI Corps assembled an impressive groupment of corps artillery: three battalions of 155-mm. howitzers, a battalion of 8-inch howitzers, and a battery of 240-mm. howitzers. Two British artillery regiments were also attached to corps. Except for a battalion of 105-mm. howitzers that Truscott had attached to the 1st Armored Division, corps artillery was to fire in general support of the offensive. Three battalions of 90-mm. antiaircraft artillery from the 35th Antiaircraft Artillery Brigade were to be prepared to fire on ground targets. With a high muzzle velocity and flat trajectory, antiaircraft guns would be particularly useful against enemy armor and pillboxes. Finally, on D-day, as had been the case when the offense began along the Garigliano, the guns of two cruisers lying offshore were to engage prearranged targets opposite the British sector.[22]

Several weeks before the anticipated date of the offensive, Truscott directed his corps artillery to begin a daily firing schedule designed to uncover the enemy's defensive fires and further mislead the Germans as to the actual start of the offensive. In view of the defensive strategy that Hitler had urged upon his commanders in Italy such deception was of paramount importance. But this, of course, was unknown to General Truscott. Each morning from different parts of the beachhead guns of various batteries opened a series of barrages, with their time, length, and method of firing frequently changed. At first the Germans replied with large-scale defensive fires, but after a time apparently concluded that the barrages were only another spendthrift American harassment and made little response. This assumption was destined to pay off with a delayed reaction when the Allied artillery preparation for the offensive actually began.[23]

Truscott's breakout was also to be supported by aircraft from the XII TAC, flying from bases in the vicinity of Naples. Before the offensive, fighter-bombers were to step up their operations against the enemy's line of communications, especially southeast of Rome. Long-range artillery positions and supply installations in the Alban Hills near Frascati and Albano as well as at Velletri and Valmontone were to be bombed and strafed almost daily.[24]

Beginning at 0625 on D-day and continuing until 1930, fighter-bombers of the XII TAC were to fly twenty-

---

[21] Hq VI Corps AAR, 1–31 May 44.
[22] VI Corps FO 26, 6 May 44.

[23] Lucian K. Truscott, *Command Missions* (New York: E. P. Dutton and Co., 1954), pp. 368–70.
[24] Hq, VI Corps FO 26, 6 May 44, Air annex.

eight preplanned missions, mostly against artillery positions and troop bivouacs. The airmen were also to provide fighter cover to protect ground forces from hostile air attack, even though for some time the Luftwaffe had been virtually driven from Italian skies. Once the ground forces began their offensive, seventy-two fighter-bombers were to attack enemy positions along the rail line extending northwest from Cisterna, then bomb and strafe enemy artillery in an effort to limit defensive fires in the offensive's early phases. Four fighter-bombers were to attack the town of Cori, and a group of heavies was to hit Velletri and Sezze with demolition and fragmentation bombs.[25]

Fighter-bombers were to provide close support as the offensive continued, with a forward controller located at the VI Corps command post directing the aircraft to targets of opportunity. Aircraft flying prebriefed missions to specific targets were, upon entering the corps zone, to check in immediately with the forward air controller. If there were no emergency targets, the controller was to release the aircraft to go about assigned missions. Fighter-bombers were also to fly armed reconnaissance along Highways 6 and 7 south of Rome and over the road network between the two highways.[26]

The freedom of movement long enjoyed by the Allies behind their shield of air supremacy was again demonstrated by the ease with which the Fifth Army, despite numerous small-scale enemy air attacks and harassing artillery fire, assembled over a period of several weeks sufficient supplies at Anzio to sustain the forthcoming offensive. Improvement of the VI Corps' counterbattery fires and antiaircraft defenses and the cumulative effect of the XII TAC's attacks against German artillery positions eventually reduced the effectiveness of enemy action against VI Corps' supply dumps to a negligible factor.[27]

During the winter most of the VI Corps' supply problems had been caused by a chronic shortage of shipping. As the weather gradually improved and more craft became available, particularly small craft suitable for offshore unloading of Liberty ships, the problems eased. Transportation battalions were soon discharging five or six Liberty ships at a time. During March a peak volume of 157,274 tons was unloaded at the beachhead.[28]

By mid-May enough stocks to support the VI Corps and its attached units for forty days of offensive operations had been cached in dumps dispersed over the beachhead. The supplies were in addition to those usually maintained to support ten days of normal operations. To save time and personnel after the offensive got under way, several quartermaster truck companies were brought ashore, their vehicles fully loaded with ammunition. Once ashore,

---

[25] *Ibid.*
[26] *Ibid.*

[27] Wide dispersion of supply dumps helped account for the low loss rate. Of the nine million gallons of POL shipped to the beachhead, for example, less than 1 percent was lost to enemy action. See William M. Ross and Charles F. Romanus, *The Quartermaster Corps: Operations in the War Against Germany,* U.S. ARMY IN WORLD WAR II (Washington, 1965), pp. 96–114. See also Fifth Army G–4 Jnl, May 44, and DA Hist Div, *Anzio Beachhead,* pp. 107–11.
[28] Fifth Army G–4 Jnl, May 44.

the trucks moved quickly into concealed positions to await D-day.[29]

Final Moves

Before Truscott could determine the exact H-hour for the offensive, he first had to resolve the conflicting operational requirements of armored and infantry divisions. The infantry, being particularly vulnerable to small arms and mortar fire, quite naturally preferred to begin the attack before daylight. On the other hand, the armored division's tank gunners had to have enough daylight to see the cross-hairs in their gunsights. Since Truscott's staff believed that the infantry could substitute smoke for darkness and that the armored division could find no substitute for its requirements, H-hour was set for one hour after dawn.[30]

Getting the assault units undetected into positions close to their line of departure, about two or three miles south of the Cisterna-Rome railroad and between the Spaccasassi Creek and the Mussolini Creek, posed a special problem, for the Germans enjoyed superb observation of the entire beachhead area from their vantage points in the flanking hills and mountains. To solve the problem Allied staffs worked out detailed movement schedules for the infantry and artillery to be accomplished during the last two nights before the offensive began.[31] Movement of the armor into forward assembly areas was accompanied by tying the movement to the artillery deception plan. For several weeks preceding the offensive, as the artillery fired a daily barrage, the tanks, with no attempt at concealment, rumbled noisily toward the German lines, firing point-blank, then turning and scurrying to the rear. Noting that the tanks always stopped short of their own infantry's forward positions, the Germans soon ceased to react to the maneuver. Each day, once the ground had begun to dry out in mid-May, a few of the tanks slipped off the roads into previously prepared positions. The tactic was repeated until a substantial armored assault force had been assembled close behind the front.[32]

While the VI Corps made final preparations for the offensive, General Clark in his headquarters at Caserta remained concerned over the direction the offensive should take once the corps had broken out of the beachhead. On the morning of 19 May, Truscott and members of his staff went at Clark's request to the army headquarters. There Clark raised the suggestion that BUFFALO's initial objectives, Cisterna and Cori, be taken as planned, but then, instead of moving to Highway 6, the VI Corps might regroup and turn northwestward into the Alban Hills. Frederick's 1st Special Service Force, in the meantime, could continue toward Artena and Valmontone, the original objectives of Operation BUFFALO. Only after Truscott pointed out that Frederick's force alone was not strong enough for this task did Clark drop the sugges-

---

[29] Ibid.

[30] VI Corps G-3 Jnl, May 44; Truscott Personal File; Interv, Mathews with Gen Harmon, 14 Dec 48, CMH.

[31] Truscott, Command Missions, pp. 367–68.

[32] Monograph, "American Armor at Anzio," The Armored School, Ft. Knox, May 49, pp. 87–88.

tion.[33] Yet the suggestion reflected Clark's concern about what effect the enemy's presence on the Alban Hills might have on the VI Corps' advance toward Valmontone and Highway 6. During the conference Clark also informed Truscott that Alexander might order the breakout offensive to begin two days later—on the 21st. Returning to the beachhead on the 19th, Truscott directed part of his corps and divisional artillery to begin displacing forward that night into their previously prepared positions. Until he received more definite word on the jump-off date, that was the only move he sanctioned.[34]

Alexander himself visited Clark's headquarters the next day. Poor weather predicted for the 21st, Clark told him, might delay the VI Corps its needed tactical air support; he recommended postponing the offensive at least twenty-four, perhaps even forty-eight, hours. Anxious to have the breakout offensive coincide as closely as possible with the Eighth Army's assault against the Hitler Line, Alexander readily agreed. When he radioed the news to Truscott, Clark indicated the possibility of a postponement to the 23d but promised final word by late afternoon of the 21st.[35]

Postponing the offensive for even twenty-four hours created an awkward and a potentially dangerous situation for the VI Corps. The postponement meant that some units would have to remain in forward assembly areas

longer than the forty-eight hours that Truscott intended, increasing the possibility that the Germans might detect their presence and conclude that an offensive was about to begin.

The Germans, meanwhile, were apparently nervous. Throughout the nights of the 20th and 21st the enemy increased his patrolling and artillery fire across the front. One patrol penetrated the 179th Infantry's outpost line in the 45th Division sector on the corps' left flank but withdrew in the face of heavy mortar fire without taking a prisoner.[36]

At 1715 on the 21st final word on the date of the offensive arrived at Truscott's headquarters. "Operation BUFFALO will be launched at 0630 hours on 23 May," Clark radioed. "I will arrive at Advanced Command Post about noon on Monday [22 May]."[37]

That night the VI Corps' combat units moved into their assigned assembly areas, while the 109th Engineer Battalion and the 34th Division's engineers began the tedious and hazardous work of clearing gaps through Allied mine fields. The front remained relatively quiet, disturbed only by occasional German shelling that killed three men at a road junction near the 3d Division headquarters and caused minor casualties in the 45th Division's area.

By daylight on 22 May, all units had reached their jump-off positions. Throughout a lovely spring day that invited lounging in the sunshine, the troops instead crouched in dark dugouts, the ruins of farmhouses, and scattered groves of trees along the

[33] Truscott, *Command Missions*, pp. 370–71; Clark's comments on MS, in CMH files.
[34] Truscott, *Command Missions*, pp. 370–71; *Fifth Army History*, Part V, p. 108.
[35] Clark, *Calculated Risk*, pp. 352–53; Clark Diary, 20 May 44.

[36] VI Corps G–3 Jnl, May 44.
[37] Msg, Clark to Truscott, 211705B May 44, Truscott Personal Radios Received files, Feb–Jun 44.

drainage canals to avoid being seen by enemy observers. In the meantime, Clark, leaving his chief of staff in charge of the Fifth Army main headquarters at Caserta, moved to the beachhead with his staff, where the army commander established a command post in a tunnel beneath the Villa Borghese, located on a small hill overlooking Anzio harbor.

General Clark confidently awaited the start of the offensive, yet as he did so he was troubled with misgivings over what he termed his "political problems." Three considerations were uppermost in his mind: he wanted above all to be first in Rome and to be there before the imminent invasion of northwestern Europe crowded the Italian campaign off the front pages of the world's newspapers; he was also understandably anxious to avoid destructive fighting within the hallowed city; and, finally, he was persuaded that to follow the strategy Alexander preferred would deny the Fifth Army the first goal and quite possibly the second.[38]

General Clark had by that time convinced himself that to follow Alexander's strategic concept was pointless. To do so, Clark believed, would shift the burden from the Eighth to the Fifth Army which had already incurred heavy casualties since the spring offensive had begun. "I was determined that the Fifth Army was going to capture Rome," he later recalled, "and I was probably overly sensitive to indications that practically everybody else was trying to get into the act. These indications mounted rapidly in the next few days, and I had my hands full."[39] Thus it was that General Clark's rejection of Alexander's strategic concepts for the beachhead offensive cast a threatening shadow over Operation BUFFALO and, with it, Alexander's (and Churchill's) expectations of trapping a major part of the German *Tenth Army* between the British Eighth and the U.S. Fifth Armies south of Rome.

---

[38] Clark, *Calculated Risk*, pp. 351–52.

[39] *Ibid.*, p. 357; Clark's comments on MS, in CMH files.

CHAPTER VII

The First Day

While the Americans tried to rest during the night of 22 May, the British launched the diversionary attack from their positions on the beachhead's far left flank. Shortly after dark and closely following preparatory artillery fire, a brigade of the British 1st Division lunged at the enemy's defenses west of the Anzio-Albano road. The British advanced only about 300 yards before automatic weapons and mortar fire forced a halt. Two hours later, a brigade of the 5th Division, supported by tanks, joined the fight with an attack along the coast toward the settlement of L'Americano. The fighting continued that night and next day until the brigades, after dark, returned to their starting positions.[1]

General Clark arose at 0430, breakfasted in his van, then joined General Truscott in a forward observation post where, surrounded by their staffs, the two commanders awaited the commencement of the corps artillery preparation. Beginning at H-hour minus thirty minutes, the artillery fired for five minutes on the enemy's main line of resistance across the entire front. For the next twenty-five minutes the divisional artillery joined in with fire directed against all known enemy gun positions. A heavy pall of smoke soon shrouded the landscape. Although a light rain cleared the air to a degree, visibility at dawn was limited to about 300 yards.[2]

When the artillery fire lifted, Clark and his companions heard the rumble of engines as sixty fighter-bombers from the XII TAC appeared over the front on their way to attack enemy positions about 3,000 yards in front of the corps and along the railroad running northwest from Cisterna. Encountering heavy overcast in the target area, the aircraft turned about and attacked Cisterna, their alternate target. Leaving the enemy strongpoint shattered and burning, the bombers flew southeast to attack the towns of Littoria and Sezze as well. Although the poor weather conditions limited air activity, the XII TAC would manage to fly 722 sorties during the first day of the offensive.[3]

A General Hazard

In actions along most of the VI Corps front on 23 May one weapon played a leading role in determining the course of the fighting—the mine (both Allied and German). Since the beginning of the Italian campaign, troops of both the U.S. Fifth and the British Eighth Armies had incurred numerous casualties both from enemy mines and their own—the latter when patrols, raiding parties, or advancing

---

[1]*Fifth Army History*, Part V, p. 108.

[2]Clark Diary, 23 May 44.
[3]VI Corps G–2 Jnl, 23 May 44, Summary of Air Action; DA Hist Div, *Anzio Beachhead*, p. 119; Craven and Cate, eds., *AAF III*, pp. 384–96.

troops moved unwittingly into indiscriminately laid or poorly charted mine fields. Commanders at all echelons constantly sought to develop methods of eliminating losses from friendly mine fields, but the basic problem remained, particularly in the Anzio beachhead where, during the heavy German counterattacks in February and early March, the front lines had frequently fluctuated. At the start of the breakout offensive, uncharted or poorly charted mine fields were destined to prove the single most harassing and disruptive battlefield obstacle, especially for the tanks of the 1st Armored Division. [4]

Bearing in mind that ever since the division's earliest experience, mines rather than enemy antitank guns had thus been the tanks' greatest hazard, the division commander, General Harmon, had demanded maximum effort in locating and clearing lanes through all mine fields, enemy and friendly. The engineers proposed to do the job by blasting gaps through known or suspected mine fields with 400-foot lengths of steel pipe filled with explosive material—long, unwieldy contraptions which the engineers had named "Snakes." The Snakes were to be towed forward and then pushed into position by tanks; once in place, they would be detonated by machine gun fire from the tanks. In tests the resulting explosions had produced 15-foot-wide gaps in mine fields and had detonated mines buried as deep as five feet. [5]

The decision on whether to employ the Snakes, Harmon left to his combat command commanders. Col. Maurice W. Daniel of CCA opted for them, but Brig. Gen. Frank Allen, Jr., of CCB chose to depend upon mine detectors in the hands of his engineers. Allen was concerned lest a premature detonation of the Snakes by enemy fire spoil the element of surprise. He wanted to hold his Snakes for the more extensive mine fields that he expected would be found near the railroad running northwestward from Cisterna. [6]

Harmon's Plan

Truscott had assigned to Harmon's armor the comparatively open terrain west of Cisterna on the 3d Division's left flank. The zone widened from about three miles at the line of departure (two miles south of the railroad) to about nine miles along the first phase line, the X-Y Line six miles to the north. The Mole Canal, extending northward from the beachhead and at a near right angle to the railroad, divided the zone into approximately two equal parts, the canal actually being just inside CCA's portion. General Harmon assigned the left and slightly wider part to Colonel Daniel's CCA and the right, from the canal's east bank to the divisional boundary, to Allen's CCB. (*Map V*)

General Harmon had devised for his division a scheme of maneuver involving a three-phase attack with the two

---

[4] Hq 15th AGp, *A Military Encyclopedia, Based on Operations in the Italian Campaign, 1943–45*, pp. 311–14.

[5] There were important limitations to the use of Snakes. They were useful only against minefields protecting prepared positions. If towed assembled for any distance over rough ground, they broke up.

On the other hand, if moved unassembled into position, more time was required to assemble them than to cross mine fields by other means or to bypass them altogether.

[6] Interv, Mathews with Lt Col Robert R. Linville, 9 May 50, CMH.

combat commands abreast. During the first phase, the combat commands were to pass through the 34th Division to occupy the line of the railroad three miles northwest of Cisterna; they were then to pause to allow the engineers to prepare crossings and open a path through the expected extensive mine fields.

Both combat commands were to advance from the railroad to seize, first, a low ridge line about a quarter of a mile beyond, then fan out to occupy the X-Y Line. From that first phase line the division was to reconnoiter aggressively toward Giulianello and Velletri, respectively seven miles northwest and north of Cisterna, while getting ready to respond to a corps order to continue the offensive as far north as the second, or O–B phase line. From there the armor was to continue northward into the Velletri gap toward the town of Artena, within three miles of Highway 6 and the goal of the attack's third phase.[7] So read the plans on paper, but in actual fact the bulk of the division was destined never to reach Highway 6. Clark had other plans for it which he would not disclose until Cisterna had fallen.

The assault echelon in each of the combat commands consisted of a battalion each of medium and light tanks, 2 battalions of infantry—2 from the 6th Armored Infantry with CCB and 2 from the 135th Infantry supporting CCA—and 2 companies of tank destroyers. Each combat command had a battalion of medium tanks in reserve. Two armored artillery battalions supported CCA and 3 supported CCB; 3

field artillery battalions and an antiaircraft battalion were in general support.[8]

Colonel Daniel had chosen the 3d Battalion, 1st Armored Regiment, to lead the attack in his sector and General Allen the 13th Armored Regiment's 2d Battalion to lead in his. Each was to advance with two companies of tanks abreast, followed at a 200-yard interval by infantry accompanied by light tanks. The interval was designed to protect the infantry from enemy artillery fire, which most likely would be aimed at the medium tanks leading the attack. On the other hand, the 200-yard interval would keep the infantry close enough to the armor to prevent bypassed enemy groups from attacking the tanks from the rear.[9]

The Attack Begins

The weather on the 23d seemed to favor the American ground operations. Throughout the day a persistent haze, combined with an Allied smoke screen, would so limit observation from the hills overlooking the beachhead that German artillery would prove to be generally ineffective. The few German guns disclosing their presence were soon silenced by concentrations fired by the 27th Field Artillery Battalion. That battalion also helped Harmon's tanks to maintain their course over the haze-shrouded terrain by firing at 20-minute intervals three rounds of red smoke aimed at a point a little over a mile beyond the front and in the center of the division sector. The remaining two

[7] 1st Armd Div FO 10, 19 May 44, and CCA and CCB FO's of same date.

[8] *Ibid.*
[9] *Ibid.*

battalions of division artillery also placed supporting fires 1,300 yards ahead of the assault elements. As predetermined lines were reached, the artillery shifted its fires forward at the request of the assault commander. [10]

The British diversionary attacks on the 1st Armored Division's left helped cover the noise of Harmon's tanks as they began moving toward their line of departure shortly after midnight. Beginning at 0430 in CCA's sector, two engineer guides led four tanks, each towing a 400-foot Snake into the two gaps prepared earlier through an American mine field along the line of departure. For over an hour engineers toiled in the darkness within the narrow confines of the gaps to connect the unwieldy lengths of pipe. Thirty minutes before H-hour (set for 0630) Daniel's tanks began pushing the Snakes through the gaps into their final positions. Several times enemy fire struck dangerously close to both tanks and Snakes, but the Snakes failed to detonate. By H-hour they were in place in the enemy mine fields.

As CCA's tanks approached the line of departure, commanders of the leading tanks ordered their machine gunners to detonate the Snakes. Shattering explosions followed, blasting wide paths through the mine fields. Other tanks moved through to push additional Snakes into position. As the smoke and dust from the second detonations drifted through the air, Colonel Daniel's tanks advanced through two gaps

---

[10]Unless otherwise noted, the following narrative is based on the official records of the 1st Armored Division and subordinate units and on combat interviews and small unit action reports prepared by Sidney T. Mathews.

25 feet wide and extending over 700 feet into the German defenses.

In the left half of CCA's sector two medium tank companies of the 3d Battalion, 1st Armored Regiment, advanced along both sides of the Bove Canal, one of several canals paralleling the axis of advance. Following each company in close support came a platoon of tank destroyers and engineers.

Company H led the 3d Battalion attack along the left side of the canal. In the van was a platoon of five tanks, with three volunteers from the 135th Infantry crouching atop each. Moving swiftly toward a slight rise about a quarter of a mile beyond the line of departure, the platoon opened fire on the first of two enemy strongpoints. Apparently still stunned by the detonation of the Snakes and prevented by tank fire from manning their guns, fifteen surviving enemy soldiers quickly surrendered as the tank-riding infantrymen leaped to the ground and swarmed over their position. While the tanks moved on, the infantrymen hurried their prisoners to the rear along the shelter of the Bove Canal's steep banks. To the right of the canal, tanks from Company I employed similar tactics to destroy a second enemy strongpoint.

With two strongpoints out of the way, CCA's tanks rolled on toward the railroad embankment about a mile away. Two hundred yards behind them came the 1st Armored Regiment's light tanks.

As CCA's mediums penetrated deeper into the German defenses, individual enemy infantrymen, armed with the bazooka-like *Panzerfaust*, vainly attacked the leading vehicles. A tactical formation developed by the armored division during the North African campaign was largely responsible for the enemy's failure. The tanks were echeloned so that only the lead tank was exposed to enemy fire. As soon as a German soldier fired a *Panzerfaust,* all of the tanks in the formation shot at the suspected position. Only a few of these encounters were needed to convince most German tank fighters to withhold their fire rather than risk certain death. In the few instances when a *Panzerfaust* found its target, the rockets exploded harmlessly against sandbags bracketed with steel rods to the front and sides of the hulls.

On the right of the Bove Canal, Company I's medium tanks pushed ahead of the rest of the battalion. Assisted by the accompanying tank destroyers and fire from the supporting artillery battalion, the tanks silenced several antitank guns positioned in the shadow of the railroad embankment. By 1100 the company was within 200 yards of the railroad, the first objective.

As the company neared the railroad, the accompanying forward artillery observer spotted eight enemy tanks a thousand yards to the north, presumably assembling for a counterattack. Two artillery battalions, responding to his call with heavy concentrations, set two tanks afire and prompted the others to withdraw. The threat removed, Company I's tanks crossed the remaining 200 yards and at noon gained the railroad. Quite unexpectedly, the tankers found no mines, nor did they experience any difficulty in negotiating the embankment's steep sides; moreover, antitank fire beyond the railroad was feebler than anticipated. By 1300

all of the company's tanks, followed by the 1st Battalion, 135th Infantry, had crossed the railroad and occupied high ground 500 yards to the north. [11]

Left of the Bove Canal mines prevented Company H from matching Company I's progress. After advancing about a thousand yards beyond the line of departure, Company H ran into an unsuspected enemy mine field. Four tanks were immediately disabled and a fifth returned to the rear with wounded crewmen. Continuing forward, the 135th Infantry's 2d Battalion, with its bodyguard of light tanks, cut around the disabled medium tanks and crossed the mine fields, the light tanks inexplicably failing to set off explosions. Beyond the mine field, infantry and tanks confronted an enemy strongpoint. Supported by direct fire from the light tanks, infantrymen of Company E assaulted it with grenades and bayonets. With hands held high, twenty enemy soldiers poured from the position.

No sooner were those prisoners hustled to the rear than the tank-infantry force ran into another belt of antipersonnel and antitank mines. While enemy small arms and mortar fire from somewhere to the front picked at the area, an engineer detachment hurried forward to clear a path. The field having been gapped by 1130, the infantry and light tanks resumed their advance to within 400 yards of the railroad. Concerned about likely enemy strength beyond the railroad, the infan-

---

[11] Technical Sgt. Ernest H. Dervishian and Staff Sgt. George J. Hall of the attached 135th Infantry (34th Division) won the Medal of Honor during the fighting on the 23d for "conspicuous gallantry and intrepidity at risk of life above and beyond the call of duty."

try commander halted his men to await arrival of the medium tanks that were still trying to extricate themselves from the first mine field.

By early afternoon both wings of Colonel Daniel's CCA were either within striking distance of the railroad or had already crossed it and occupied a low ridge 500 yards to the north. At that point General Harmon directed Daniel to move the 135th Infantry's 2d Battalion up to the railroad on the division's left, where the battalion was to tie in with the 45th Division to cover the 1st Armored Division's left flank while the main body of CCA crossed the railroad.

While the armored regiment's Companies H and I completed their crossings of the railroad and headed toward the ridge beyond, supporting artillery either kept the enemy at arm's length or cowering under cover. In the course of the move, Company H encountered only scattered resistance and quickly moved onto its portion of the objective, but on the right, it was Company I's turn to fight. The tanks had to knock out several well-emplaced antitank guns before gaining the ridge. As the two infantry battalions and their accompanying light tanks followed to join the mediums on the high ground for the night, division artillery dispersed an enemy force detected assembling in a draw a mile north of the railroad.

General Harmon's left wing under Colonel Daniel's command had, by nightfall, gained its objectives with relatively few losses, but Allen's CCB, on the right, had fared less well. Antitank mines were the cause. Nowhere along the VI Corps front on that first day did mines take a greater toll than in CCB's

sector. The reason was that General Allen had decided to hold his Snakes in reserve; he depended instead upon infantrymen and engineers from the 34th Division to clear gaps through known or suspected mine fields just beyond the line of departure.

Assigned a sector flanked on the left by the Mole Canal and on the right by the Femminamorta Canal and divided by a third, the Santa Maria Canal, CCB was to breach the German defenses south of the railroad and seize part of the low ridge a quarter of a mile beyond. To make the assault, Lt. Col. James S. Simmerman's 2d Battalion, 13th Armored Regiment, began to move from its assembly area shortly before H-hour. With Company D on the left of the Santa Maria Canal and Company F on the right, the battalion advanced along two unimproved roads toward the line of departure. As in CCA, behind the medium tank companies came the infantry, accompanied by light tanks. Following Company D was the 6th Armored Regiment's 3d Battalion accompanied by an attached platoon of light tanks; behind Company F came the same regiment's 1st Battalion, also with a platoon of light tanks.

Colonel Simmerman's battalion crossed the line of departure at the appointed time, but within half an hour exploding antitank mines disabled ten medium tanks—three from one company and seven from the other. The tanks had apparently run into an uncharted antitank mine field hastily laid by U.S. troops sometime during the hectic winter defense of the beachhead. Although the 34th Division's mine-clearing detachments had labored through the night, often under harassing fire, to clear paths through the mine fields, they had missed this one.

Under considerable pressure to keep the attack moving, Colonel Simmerman decided not to delay until mine-clearing detachments could come forward to complete their job, nor did he call for Snakes. Instead, in the hope that the mine field was not extensive and that the first explosions would be the last, he told the other tank commanders to keep moving by maneuvering as closely as possible around the disabled vehicles. His hope was short-lived. As the second wave of tanks attempted to proceed they too fell victim to mines. Simmerman at that point had no choice but to delay until mine-clearing detachments could come forward.

When news of Simmerman's difficulties reached General Allen, the CCB commander chose to believe, as had Simmerman at first, that the tanks had encountered no extensive mine field but only a few scattered mines. Anxious to hold onto his Snakes for possible use later, he authorized sending them forward only after engineers had determined that the tanks had in fact come on an extensive mine field. It was 0915, almost three hours after the start of the attack, before the medium tanks began the arduous task of towing the unwieldly lengths of steel pipe forward and then pushing them into position.

Meanwhile, the two infantry battalions had closed up behind the crippled tanks. In hope of maintaining the momentum of the attack, the armored infantrymen following Company D bypassed the tanks and advanced to within a thousand yards of the railroad before fire from two enemy strong-

points forced a halt. The battalion commander, Lt. Col. Robert R. Linville, tried to get tank destroyers and towed 57-mm. antitank guns forward to support an assault on the strongpoints. But these were as vulnerable to antitank mines as were medium tanks.

Following Company F on the right, Lt. Col. Lyle S. Deffenbaugh's infantrymen (1st Battalion, 6th Armored Infantry Regiment) also passed through the antitank mine field only to run into an antipersonnel mine field backed by an enemy strongpoint that forced a halt after an advance of only 500 yards. There the infantrymen remained until the engineers cleared a path through the antitank mine field and enabled the surviving medium tanks of Company F to come forward. First silencing a nest of enemy antitank guns that opened fire from a draw to the right front, Company F's tanks churned through the antipersonnel mine field, and the infantry followed safely in their tracks. Together tanks and infantry eliminated the enemy strongpoint. With the medium tanks again leading, the attackers moved a few hundred yards closer to the railroad, only to be stopped once again by a mine field 1,200 yards short of their objective.

By midday CCB's left wing was within a quarter of a mile of the railroad, but the right still had more than half a mile to go. The gains had cost 23 medium tanks and seven tank destroyers. Most were recoverable, yet they were nevertheless lost to the attack. While the crews of eight tank recovery vehicles toiled through the afternoon and far into the night to move the disabled tanks to the rear for repair, the division commander (General Harmon) replaced CCB's losses with twenty-three tanks from his reserve.

Time was running short if CCB was to reach the railroad before dark, as Harmon had insisted. Although General Allen gave his approval to using the Snakes if necessary to get the attack moving, so narrow and circuitous were the paths cleared through the first mine field that the tank crewmen almost despaired of getting through with the long, unwieldy steel pipes.

As that slow process went on, the commander of Company F, Capt. John Elliott, impatient at the delays, decided to try to bypass the second mine field that blocked his tanks on the right wing of CCB's attack. Sideslipping 500 yards to the northeast, the company's tanks, followed by infantry, by midafternoon finally located the field's eastern limits, but, before they could proceed, a concealed German antitank gun knocked out the lead tank, while enemy artillery fire forced the American infantrymen to cover. Only after Captain Elliott had sent a platoon to the rear of the troublesome antitank gun to silence it were tanks and infantry able to continue. They reached the railroad as darkness was settling over the beachhead. While the tanks took cover for the night south of the railroad, the armored infantrymen crossed the railroad embankment and outposted the high ground a few hundred yards beyond.

Colonel Linville's infantrymen (3d Battalion, 6th Armored Infantry) on CCB's left wing meanwhile had been unable to overcome the two enemy strongpoints south of the railroad. Not until late afternoon, when tank destroyers, towed antitank guns, and the pla-

toon of light tanks that had originally accompanied the infantry came forward, did the attack on the positions begin to make headway. The strongpoint finally fell to a frontal assault launched by two infantry companies, assisted by another enveloping from the left. Only then, as nightfall came, was the infantry able to cross the railroad and outpost the ridge 500 yards to the north.

For all the day's mishaps, the tanks and infantry of the 1st Armored Division's two combat commands by nightfall had fought their way across the railroad to their first objective, the low ridge to the north. During the night both commands consolidated their positions while self-propelled supporting artillery displaced forward.

Not since the fighting for Monte Trocchio during January of 1944 had the division incurred so many casualties in one day. Of the total of 173 casualties, 35 had been killed, 137 wounded, and 1 was missing in action.[12]

From the German viewpoint, the 1st Armored Division's penetration had occurred within the sector of the *LXXVI Panzer Corps* almost adjacent to the boundary with the *I Parachute Corps.* The armored attack pierced the main line of resistance on the right wing and center of the *362d Infantry Division* to a depth of almost a mile. (As in several cases on the southern front when the Allied offensive had opened there, the beachhead offensive caught the com-

---

[12]9th MRU, Fifth Army Battle Casualties, 10 Jun 45. During the fighting on the 23d, 2d Lt. Thomas W. Fowler of the 1st Armored Division performed with "conspicuous gallantry and intrepidity at risk of life above and beyond the call of duty," for which he was subsequently awarded the Medal of Honor.

mander of the *362d Division* away from his post, on leave in Germany, visiting a son badly wounded in Russia.)[13] CCA's thrust had pushed back two under-strength battalions of the *956th Infantry Regiment*, while CCB's had done the same to the *954th Infantry*. On the *362d Division*'s left wing south of Cisterna the third regiment, the *955th Infantry*, the only one with a battalion in reserve, had in the meantime achieved greater success in facing the attack of the U.S. 3d Infantry Division.

The Attack on Cisterna

In striving to take the rubble-strewn strongpoint of Cisterna—vital to General Truscott's plans since the main roads leading to Velletri, Cori, and Valmontone passed through the town—General O'Daniel's 3d Division was to fix the defenders of Cisterna frontally with one regiment while the other two enveloped the objective from the right and left, after which the center regiment was to penetrate the town. Once Cisterna was in hand, the division was to continue to Cori, there to anchor the VI Corps' right flank on the high ground behind the village, then turn north toward Highway 6 and Valmontone. General Frederick's Canadian-American 1st Special Service Force was to operate along the division's right flank.

In addition to the *362d Division*'s left regiment, located west of the main highway into Cisterna from the southwest, the 3d Division faced the right wing of the *715th Division*, reinforced by a panzer grenadier regiment. Since that division held the line from the same

road all the way around the eastern arc of the beachhead to the coast, its regiments were thinly spread. General O'Daniel's men faced four enemy battalions on line, with approximately three in reserve.

Just as mines seriously deterred the 1st Armored Division's attack, so they also posed a major hazard for the 3d Division. Only on the division's right wing, where the 15th Infantry under Col. Richard G. Thomas sought to envelop Cisterna from the southeast, would mines cause no appreciable delay.[14]

In making a wheeling maneuver to get behind Cisterna, Colonel Thomas recognized that his regiment would be turning away from General Frederick's 1st Special Service Force, on the 15th Infantry's right flank, and thus creating a gap between the two forces. To cover that gap Thomas formed a special task force around Company A, which he drew from his regimental reserve. Commanded by Major Michael Paulick, the task force included a platoon each of medium and light tanks from the 751st Tank Battalion and a section from the 601st Tank Destroyer Battalion. The force also included the regimental battle patrol, a platoon of machine guns, a section of mortars, a platoon from the cannon company, and a squad of engineers. Moving close along the right flank of the 2d Battalion, which was to constitute the regiment's right wing, Paulick's task force was to cross the Cisterna Canal and drive northeastward

---

[13]MS # C–064 (Kesselring).

[14]Unless otherwise noted the tactical narrative is based upon official records of the 3d Division and its subordinate units, plus combat interviews and small unit action narratives prepared by Sidney T. Mathews of the Fifth Army Historical Section.

to cut Highway 7, in the process taking several road junctions and clearing the Boschetta di Mosca woods, the latter less than a mile short of Highway 7.

Striking swiftly at H-hour (0630) Company A with fire support from the attached tanks and tank destroyers quickly enveloped and seized a bridge over the Cisterna Canal, but every attempt to advance beyond the bridge brought down a hail of small arms fire from a group of houses some 600 yards away along a road leading from the hamlet of Borgo Podgora into Cisterna. The company commander tried to set up a base of fire with one platoon and send a second to outflank the enemy position, but the German fire was too intense. When the attached tanks and tank destroyers tried to move against the position, accurate fire from well-sited antitank guns knocked out two tanks and one tank destroyer.

At that point Major Paulick sought to break the impasse by sending his three surviving tanks on a wide flanking maneuver into the 1st Special Service Force's zone on the right. The necessary permission obtained, the tanks turned back to cross the Cisterna Canal until they were well to the rear of the enemy-held houses. Firing point-blank at the houses, the tanks enabled a platoon of Company A to attack the position from the front. Unable to withstand the fire, the Germans withdrew as the infantry closed in. That resistance broken, the main body of Task Force Paulick moved on with little difficulty into the Boschetta di Mosca, there to dig in for the night within half a mile of Highway 7 southeast of Cisterna.

After dark the regimental battle patrol sent three men to a road junction 200 yards beyond the woods. The men reached the junction just in time to observe a column of about sixty German soldiers apparently on their way to establish a strongpoint in the vicinity of the woods. Undetected, the three men quickly withdrew to the main body of the battle patrol and set up an ambush. When the German column came within range, the entire battle patrol opened fire, killing 20 and capturing 37.

Two of the 15th Infantry's battalions meanwhile had launched the regiment's main attack between the location of Task Force Paulick and Cisterna, with the 2d Battalion on the right making steady progress from the start. While the infantrymen advanced toward the first objective, a wooden area about half a mile beyond the line of departure, the attached platoon of medium tanks encountered no antitank mines; from the first the infantry had effective close-in fire support.

As the troops neared the woods, the battalion commander, in a maneuver designed to draw fire and force the enemy to disclose his positions, sent Company F across an open field 500 yards east of the woods. At the same time, Company E, accompanied by the tank platoon, made the main assault directly against the woods. At that point the tanks did run into mines, but so close to the woods that they were still able to support the infantry by fire.

With ammunition running short and anxious to take advantage of the supporting tank fire's keeping the enemy under cover, Company E's commander ordered his men to fix bayonets and charge. In one of the few verified bayonet assaults by American troops during World War II, the men dashed into the woods and swarmed over the German positions. They killed 15 of the enemy and captured 80, while an undetermined number broke from the far side of the woods and fled. Company F, meanwhile, crossed the open field east of the woods to join Company E in rounding up enemy stragglers.

The first objective taken, the battalion commander called for an artillery concentration on the area between the woods and the highway and committed his reserve, Company G, with orders to pass north of the woods and capture a road junction 500 yards away on the Cisterna–Borgo Podgora road. Meeting only light resistance, Company G reached the junction at 1800 and then turned east to the Cisterna Canal, there to capture more than a hundred Germans who had taken refuge from artillery fire in deep dugouts along the side of the canal. Since those shelters were useless as fighting positions, the Germans had little choice when U.S. infantrymen suddenly appeared but to surrender.

Although Colonel Thomas had intended both his assault battalions to cut Highway 7 southeast of Cisterna before dark, the opening moves of the 2d Battalion had taken too much time, and a lapse in communications between the battalion and regimental headquarters imposed a further delay. The battalion at last headed for the highway in late afternoon, but progress was so slow that darkness found the men still short of that objective.

On the 15th Infantry's left wing, the 3d Battalion, in the meantime, had crossed the line of departure in a column of companies, with Company L

leading and taking advantage of the cover of a shallow ditch about half a mile east of the American-held settlement of Isola Bella. The company's objective was a group of houses around which the Germans had developed a formidable strongpoint southwest of a road junction 700 yards away. As the men emerged from the ditch, a blast of small arms and mortar fire from the strongpoint forced them back. Only after a fire fight lasting several hours and with supporting fire from tank destroyers did Company L capture the position, and then but 40 effectives remained of an original strength of 180 men. Other enemy positions still blocked the way, and Company L was too depleted to continue.

At noon the battalion commander relieved Company L with what many in the 3d Division hoped would be a decisive innovation in infantry combat— a regimental "battle sled team" towed by a platoon of medium tanks. The battle sled was General O'Daniel's idea, one in which he took special pride. It was an open-topped narrow steel tube mounted on flat runners and wide enough to carry one infantryman in a prone position. Serving as protection against shell fragments and small arms fire, the steel tubes were to transport infantrymen through enemy fire in what O'Daniel looked on as portable foxholes. Early in May, a battle sled team of sixty men had been organized in each of the division's three regiments.[15]

With each of five tanks towing twelve

---

[15]Donald G. Taggert, ed., *History of the Third Infantry Division in World War II* (Washington: Infantry Journal Press, 1947), p. 148.

CISTERNA

ISOLA BELLA. *Cisterna and Alban hills in background.*

battle sleds, the 3d Battalion, with Companies I and K following, renewed its attack in early afternoon. The tanks had advanced only a short distance when they came upon a drainage ditch too wide and too deep to negotiate. The men in the battle sleds had to dismount and continue the attack on foot. Thus ended the first and, as it turned out, sole test of the division commander's proud innovation. The medium tanks that had towed the sleds nevertheless continued to support the infantrymen by fire. Progress was steady, yet it took time to root the enemy from one strongpoint after an-

other. Consequently, as darkness fell the 3d Battalion, like the 2d, was still well short of cutting Highway 7 southeast of Cisterna.

Whereas mines had caused the 15th Infantry, on the 3d Division's right wing, little trouble, they were much more of an obstacle in the center, where the 7th Infantry, under Col. Wiley H. Omohundro, attacked. Not decisive, the mines nevertheless served to deny the infantry companies much of their needed tank support in front of Cisterna in what General O'Daniel expected would be the hardest fighting on his division's front.

GENERAL O'DANIEL'S BATTLE SLEDS

In direct defense of the major stronghold of Cisterna, the Germans had constructed their most formidable defenses, controlled from a regimental command post located in a wine cellar deep underneath a large building in the center of the town. Other cellars and numerous tunnels honeycombed the ground beneath the town, sheltering its garrison from the 3d Division's preparatory artillery fire and aerial bombardment. When those fires ceased, the Germans quickly emerged to man firing positions from which they could contest every foot of ground.

The 7th Infantry commander, Colonel Omohundro, was to send two battalions abreast in a northeasterly direction along the axis of the Isola Bella–Cisterna road to break through the enemy defenses south of Cisterna and draw up to the town. That accomplished, Omohundro, on division order, was to send his reserve battalion to take the settlement of La Villa, on the railroad a mile northwest of Cisterna, and then seize a ridge just east of La Villa, cut Highway 7 in the vicinity of the Cisterna cemetery, and occupy a portion of the X-Y phase line. The remainder of the regiment was, on division order, to clear the Germans from the rubble of Cisterna. A company each from the 751st Tank Battalion and the 601st Tank Destroyer Battalion, as well as a battery from the 10th Field Artillery Battalion (105-mm. howitzers, towed), were to be in direct support of the regiment throughout.

No sooner had leading troops of the 7th Infantry's 3d Battalion crossed their line of departure (about three miles southwest of Cisterna) at 0630 than automatic weapons fire from two positions about half a mile northeast of Isola Bella drove them to cover. Two and a half hours after the attack began the two advance companies were still, in the words of Omohundro's S–3, "pinned down." To that report General O'Daniel growled, "We have no such words in our vocabulary now." The division commander added threateningly in words meant more for Omohundro than his harried S–3, "You're supposed to be at the railroad track by noon. You'll get a bonus if you do, something else if you don't."[16] What Omohundro's infantrymen most needed at that point was close-in fire support, but an uncleared antitank mine field kept the attached medium tank platoon and a platoon of tank destroyers too far away to have effect.

To get the attack moving again, a slow, painstaking, and costly infantry advance in the face of enemy fire seemed the only way. Taking advantage of every scrap of cover and concealment, especially numerous drainage ditches, the 3d Battalion, with Company L leading, laboriously started to move. It took the men three hours to advance one mile to within grenade-throwing

range of the enemy strongpoint that had held up the attack all morning. Unable or unwilling to resist once Company L got that close, sixteen surviving Germans raised their hands in surrender. Their capitulation enabled Company L to move quickly onto its first objective, the Colle Monaco, a low rise about a quarter of a mile northeast of Isola Bella, while Company I in the meantime slipped around to the left to seize a nose of adjacent high ground 500 yards away. Moving too far to the west, Company I encountered a storm of enemy fire that forced the men to take such cover as they could find. The battalion commander committed Company K on Company I's right, but that move proved of little help after enemy fire killed first the company commander and then his executive officer. By midafternoon, the 3d Battalion had penetrated the German position to a depth of almost a mile, but, in doing so, had incurred such heavy casualties that the momentum of its attack was lost.

On the 7th Infantry's right wing, the 2d Battalion had even less to show in its advance astride the Isola Bella–Cisterna road. Scheduled to jump off at H-hour, the battalion had to delay for twenty minutes because of enemy artillery fire. The assault companies, supported by a platoon of medium tanks, had advanced only 200 yards beyond the shelter of a drainage ditch that marked the line of departure before small arms fire from two strong points approximately 600 yards away drove the men to cover. To get the attack moving again, tanks came forward to deal with those positions, but the maneuver collapsed when antitank mines disabled all of the tanks. The Company E com-

[16] 3d Div G–3 Jnl, 230925B May 44.

mander then decided to envelop one of the strongpoints by sending an infantry platoon on a wide swing to the west. Advancing slowly in cover afforded by a drainage ditch, the platoon, after two hours of crawling through the ditch, approached to within striking distance of the enemy. Assaulting the first strongpoint with rifle fire and grenades, the men quickly overran and destroyed it, but the effort left the platoon with but eighteen men.

Meanwhile, Company F, fighting east of the Isola Bella–Cisterna road, had a much easier experience. Attacking the other strongpoint, Company F had the support of an attached platoon of tank destroyers that somehow experienced no difficulty with mines. In only forty minutes, Company F overcame the enemy position.

Regrouping his men, the 2d Battalion commander called for more tanks to replace those lost earlier to mines, but the regiment had none to spare. without tank support, no recourse remained but to resume the attack with the firepower at hand, this time toward the Colle Maraccio, a group of low hills about 1,300 yards north of the Colle Monaco. The two assault companies had advanced a quarter of a mile when heavy automatic weapons fire forced another halt.

When word of the 7th Infantry's continuing difficulties reached the division commander, he authorized additional artillery support and a smoke screen behind which Omohundro's regiment was to try again before dark to break the impasse. While his regiment regrouped, Colonel Omohundro moved his reserve battalion into a blocking position east of Isola Bella.

The new drive was to begin at 1645 behind a 15-minute preparation fired by four battalions of artillery. As the fire lifted, the 2d Battalion began to advance. Apparently demoralized by losses during the morning action, the adjacent 3d Battalion failed to move.

With two companies abreast, the 2d Battalion advanced along both sides of the Isola Bella road. Although antitank mines again prevented two surviving tanks and a platoon of tank destroyers from accompanying the infantry, when two enemy tanks suddenly appeared several hundred yards to the front, the American armor was close enough to bring the enemy vehicles under fire. One German tank burst into flame and the other withdrew. That threat removed, the 2d Battalion continued to advance, although the commander was concerned that unless the 3d Battalion soon drew abreast, his leading companies might be cut off. By 2300 the lead company was within 600 yards of Cisterna.

The 3d Battalion in the meantime remained throughout the afternoon on the Colle Monaco. At last convinced that the commander was no longer able to control either himself or his unit, the executive officer, Maj. Lloyd B. Ramsey, assumed command and made plans for a two-company attack to start shortly after nightfall at 2100. When the armored support Ramsey requested failed to appear, he postponed the attack to 2130, but before that hour arrived, enemy tanks made a second appearance. Leading a small infantry force, several German tanks approached to within 250 yards of Ramsey's right front. Although the tanks failed to attack, their presence was enough to prompt Ramsey to cancel his plans and go on the defensive for the night while awaiting reinforcement by the regiment's reserve battalion. By the end of the first day, only the 2d Battalion of Omohundro's 7th Infantry had made any significant penetration of the enemy's defense, that to within 600 yards of Cisterna. Antitank mine fields had severely limited the close-in fire support so desperately needed by the infantry in the first hours if the momentum of the attack was to be maintained. Moreover, the day's gains had been as costly as they were disappointing. Of the regiment's more than 200 casualties, 54 men had been killed.

As with the 7th Infantry, antitank mines also affected progress of the 30th Infantry, constituting the 3d Division's left wing and main effort alongside the 1st Armored Division. This was the regiment comprising the left pincer of General O'Daniel's enveloping maneuver to isolate Cisterna. The regiment was first to cut the railroad, then the highway to the northwest of the town, and finally to move on Cori along with the 15th Infantry on the right. The sector assigned extended at the line of departure for 2,500 yards astride the Femminamorta Canal but narrowed to about 800 yards at the railroad, a little over a mile away.

Like Colonel Omohundro on his right, the regimental commander, Col. Lionel C. McGarr, also planned to attack with two battalions abreast. In direct support of each was a platoon of the 751st Tank Battalion. The 30th Infantry was further strengthened by attachment of a company from the 601st Tank Destroyer Battalion, whose vehicles were to be employed as self-propelled assault guns.

Believing the enemy's defenses to be weakest opposite his left wing, Colonel McGarr sought to exploit this situation by choosing his most experienced commander, Lt. Col. Woodrow W. Stromberg of the 2d Battalion, to lead the effort there. Because the battalion's sector was quite narrow, McGarr told Stromberg to attack in a column of companies, leapfrogging them periodically to keep the freshest forward.

On the right, where the sector was much broader and the defenses apparently stronger, McGarr ordered the 3d Battalion to attack with three companies abreast and attached a company from the 1st Battalion as a reserve. He also placed all of the attached tank destroyers and the regimental cannon company of 105-mm. howitzers in direct support.

At 0630 Company G led Stromberg's 2d Battalion in a column of companies west of the Femminamorta Canal and advanced toward Hill 77, about 1,200 yards northwest of Ponte Rotto, an enemy-held settlement at a road junction and bridge over the canal a mile and a half southwest of Cisterna. Even before the company crossed the line of departure, automatic weapons fire, punctuated with shelling by mortars and artillery, forced the men to take cover in a nearby drainage ditch. At the same time, mines halted the tanks too far from the action to be of much assistance.

Since the drainage ditch led in the direction Company G wanted to go, it provided a confined though adequate covered approach and enabled the infantrymen to reach and overrun Hill 77. Then they moved 300 yards beyond to the foot of Hill 81, about 600 yards beyond the line of departure. Since that put Company G almost halfway to the railroad, Colonel Stromberg sent Company E to seize the hill.

That accomplished with reasonable facility, Stromberg directed Company F to destroy a troublesome strongpoint on a knoll just east of Hill 81. By 0900, less than three hours after the attack began, that mission too was accomplished. Yet for all the relative ease of the advance, Colonel Stromberg hesitated to continue to the railroad without first dealing with several bypassed pockets of resistance. That both flanks were exposed also made him wary of continuing. It took much of the rest of the day for Company G to clear the pockets of resistance, while Company E, from blocking positions on Hills 81 and 77, covered the battalion's flanks. As time passed, Colonel Stromberg grew ever more apprehensive about continuing alone to the railroad, particularly when reports revealed that Company G was down to 26 men and Company E to 40. Only Company F, last in line in the battalion column of companies, had incurred relatively few casualties and was in a condition to continue the attack.

Anxious that the 30th Infantry secure its objectives before morning, General O'Daniel authorized Colonel McGarr to commit his reserve battalion to exploit the 2d Battalion's limited success.[17] With that assurance of support, Colonel Stromberg, as darkness settled over the battlefield, sent Company F on toward the railroad. When the company reached a point only a hundred

yards from the railroad bridge over the Femminamorta Canal, intermittent small arms fire began to strike the column. Unable to locate the enemy positions in the darkness, the company dug in and settled down for the night. Not until daylight came was the reserve battalion destined to reach the company's position.

On the 30th Infantry's right wing, the 3d Battalion met little resistance at first, but that was before the supporting tanks and tank destroyers bogged down in the mine fields. From that point resistance increased, so that by midafternoon the battalion had lost its momentum. As night fell the leading company, unable to keep pace with Company F west of the canal, had reached a point only about half a mile north of the Ponte Rotto road junction. Shortly after dark the troops dug in where they were, placed concertina wire and mines across the road, and settled down to await dawn.

Thus, although the armored half of the VI Corps' attack had made considerable progress toward seizing the first day's objectives on schedule, the infantry half (the 3d Division) had lagged. In spite of abundant artillery support, frequent harassment of the enemy's rear throughout the day by tactical aircraft, and, most importantly, the element of surprise that Truscott had succeeded in maintaining until the offensive began, a well dug-in enemy had responded to the 3d Division's attack with considerable small arms fire and had held the infantrymen to relatively modest gains. Some indication of the effectiveness of the enemy's defensive fires could be seen in the high losses incurred by the division on the first day. Of a total of

[17] VI Corps G–3 Jnl, 231450B May 44.

1,626 casualties, 107 were killed in action, 642 wounded, 812 missing, and 65 captured.[18]

Action on the Corps' Flanks

Even as the 1st Armored and 3d Infantry Divisions attacked in their sectors, General Eagles' 45th Division had launched a limited objective attack to stabilize the VI Corps' left flank. While one regiment made a vigorous demonstration on the far left in the vicinity of the Anzio-Campoleone railroad, the 45th Division's other two regiments attacked along an axis running northwest of the village of Carano, a little over five miles southwest of Cisterna.

Mine fields, fortunately, were not the problem here that they were elsewhere. Both regiments moved rapidly toward objectives along the road leading northwest from Carano to the Cisterna-Rome railroad. The supporting tanks worked closely with the infantry, the two arms fighting together as a smooth-working team. By midafternoon, Col. Robert L. Dulaney's 180th Infantry, on the left, had reached its objectives about one mile northwest of Carano after overrunning a battalion of the *29th Panzer Grenadier Regiment* and capturing the battalion commander in his command post. On the 180th Infantry's right, the 157th Infantry, commanded by Col. John H. Church, attacked toward distant objectives along the railroad and in the process encountered a sharp German riposte.

Although General Eagles was unaware of it at the time, the quick penetration by his division seriously threatened the left flank and rear of the *3d Panzer Grenadier Division*, comprising the left wing of the *I Parachute Corps*. The panzer grenadier division commander reacted by counterattacking with the only force at his disposal: 15 Tiger tanks from the *508th Panzer Battalion.*[19] About the time Colonel Dulaney's 180th Infantry was digging in on its objectives, a force of Tigers variously estimated by American observers to number between fifteen and twenty-four attacked Colonel Church's 157th Infantry. The German tanks pushed through one battalion and opened fire on the rear of another.

To counter that threat, General Truscott ordered forward a battalion of armored infantry from the 1st Armored Division's reserve, but before the infantrymen could arrive, division and corps artillery, including 8-inch howitzers, responded with a devastating blast of shelling. It was too much for the Germans. The tanks withdrew, leaving behind several of their number as flaming hulks. By nightfall, fighting had cost the division a total of 458 casualties, of whom 30 were killed, 169 wounded, 31 captured, and 228 missing.[20]

Meanwhile, on the opposite flank of the American offensive, General Frederick's 1st Special Service Force had begun its part of the operation with an advance by its 1st Regiment toward

---

[18] 9th MRU, Fifth Army Battle Casualties, 10 Jun 45, CMH. As a result of the fighting on the 23d three members of the 3d Division were awarded the Medal of Honor: Privates 1st Class John W. Dutko (posthumously), Patrick L. Kessler, and Henry Schauer.

[19] MS # R–50 (Bailey), CMH.

[20] 9th MRU, Fifth Army Battle Casualties, 10 Jun 45, CMH. For action during this fight Technical Sgt. Van T. Barfoot was awarded the Medal of Honor.

Highway 7 and the railroad. Despite German small arms and machine gun fire, the lead regiment quickly overran the enemy's forward positions and by noon had pushed across Highway 7 to within a thousand yards of the railroad. General Frederick held the regiment there to allow units of the neighboring 15th Infantry on the left to pull abreast.

The pause afforded the Germans time to assemble a counterattacking force of tanks and infantry beyond the railroad embankment. Shortly after dark, twelve Mark IV tanks and an estimated platoon of enemy infantry suddenly struck. Within an hour the Germans had rolled through the 1st Special Service Force's outpost line and threatened to break through to the rear. "All hell has broken loose up here," Frederick's G-3 reported. "The Germans have unleashed everything. They got four of our M-4's and three M-10 tank destroyers. We need more M-4's and TD's." Maj. William R. Rossen, the assistant corps G-3, promised to "see if we can get some stuff up right away."[21]

Help arrived, but not before part of one company had been cut off and captured. The rest of the regiment fell back about half a mile south of the highway. Despite the early gains, won largely by exploitation of the elements of shock and surprise, the Germans lacked the necessary reserve strength to take advantage of their success and under heavy artillery fire fell back north of the railroad. The withdrawal gave General Frederick an opportunity to regroup his battered force, reoccupy some of the lost ground, and count his

losses. The 1st Regiment had lost 39 men killed, over 100 wounded, and 30 captured. During the night, General Truscott, in order to give the regiment some respite from its exertions that day, ordered the 34th Division's 133d Infantry to send one battalion to relieve the 1st Special Service Force's 1st Regiment and outpost a line north of the highway and another to protect the flank along the Mussolini Canal.

For Generalleutnant der Panzertruppen Traugott Herr, at the command post of his *LXXVI Panzer Corps,* the situation map throughout 23 May provided little reason for satisfaction despite the brief successes of the counterattacks against the American flanks. The stronghold of Cisterna in the panzer corps center still held, but the magnitude of the attack meant to General Herr that the Allies had indeed begun their long-awaited breakout offensive.[22]

In response to pleas during the afternoon from the commander of the hard-pressed *715th Infantry Division,* opposite the 1st Special Service Force, General Herr requested approval by *Fourteenth Army* headquarters to withdraw the division's left wing about 1,200 yards to the line of the railroad, which southeast of Cisterna lay beyond the highway. That move would enable Herr to anchor his left flank on higher ground, the foothills of the Lepini Mountains, and establish a stronger defensive line parallel to the Tyrrhenian coast.

In line with that reasoning, yet unwilling to make the decision without

---

[21] VI Corps G-3 Jnl, 23–24 May 44.

[22] Unless otherwise noted German material is based upon MSS #'s R-50 (Bailey), T-1a and T-1b (Westphal *et al.*), and C-064 (Kesselring).

approval of higher authority, General von Mackensen relayed the proposal to Field Marshal Kesselring, along with the additional information that the Americans (the 1st Special Service Force) had already cut Highway 7 southeast of Cisterna and the railroad (1st Armored Division) northwest of the town. Still concerned about an Allied thrust against the German right flank along the coast, Mackensen also pointed out that approval of the panzer corps commander's proposal would release some troops to reinforce the Cisterna sector while avoiding the risk of weakening other parts of the front in a quest for reinforcements.

As in the case of the southern front, Kesselring would sanction no withdrawal. Hold in place, the army group commander directed, and stabilize the *LXXVI Panzer Corps* with local reserves. To pull back the left wing of Herr's corps might create a gap in the mountains north of Terracina between the corps and the *Tenth Army*'s right flank, thereby enabling the U.S. Fifth Army to separate the two German armies. New positions along a line between Cisterna and Sezze, Kesselring believed, also would be less economical in men and weapons, and pulling back would deny the *Fourteenth Army* an opportunity to mount further counterattacks against the American right flank in hope of pinching off the penetration of the army's lines about the beachhead.

Kesselring also dismissed Mackensen's concern for his right flank along the beachhead's northwestern front; the attack there by the British divisions, the field marshal correctly believed, had been only a diversion. He suggested, instead, that Mackensen shift elements of the *92d Infantry Division* from the *I Parachute Corps* sector southward to reinforce the central sector of the *LXXVI Panzer Corps* near Cisterna.

That Mackensen was unwilling to do. The *Fourteenth Army* commander was convinced that the Americans had yet to reveal the direction of the main thrust from the beachhead, and that when it came it would develop near his right wing in the Aprilia-Albano sector, the gateway into the Alban Hills. (Actually, General Clark was even then considering the possibility of shifting the axis of Truscott's beachhead offensive in that very direction.) Shifting troops to the Cisterna sector would, Mackensen reckoned, leave the Albano gateway open. In any case, the *92d Infantry Division* was his only uncommitted division. Recently formed and only partially trained, he regarded it as unfit for intensive fighting.

In response to the 1st Armored Division's pushing back the *362d Division*'s right wing beyond the railway, the only action Mackensen took was to direct General der Flieger Alfred Schlemm, commander of the *I Parachute Corps,* to transfer a panzer reconnaissance battalion from the vicinity of Albano to reinforce the *362d*'s right. Until that battalion completed its move shortly after nightfall on the 23d, the *LXXVI Panzer Corps* would have to draw upon its own local reserves.

In the fight against both the 1st Armored Division and the 3d Infantry Division, the acting *362d Division* commander by midafternoon had already committed his last reserves: one engineer and two infantry battalions. On the left, the commander of the *715th Infantry Division* had committed his remaining infantry reserves and some tanks in the counterattack against the 1st Special Service Force along Highway 7.

Both divisions had incurred heavy losses during the day. The *362d Division*, bearing the brunt of the American attack, had lost 50 percent of its combat strength; two regiments of the *715th Division* had lost 40 percent of their's. In both divisions equipment losses, especially in antitank guns, had been correspondingly heavy.

By early evening of the 23d, Field Marshal Kesselring realized that, contrary to all his expectations, the situation at the beachhead had taken a most unfavorable turn. The Allied offensive itself, however, had been no surprise to him. He had been expecting it for over a week, though he had been uncertain as to the exact timing.

What had surprised him was Mackensen's failure, with the forces at his disposal, to contain the breakout. The penetration by the 1st Armored Division into the *362d Division*'s sector, Kesselring recognized, threatened the *Fourteenth Army*'s entire position and also that of the *Tenth Army*, whose slow withdrawal from the southern front would be jeopardized should the *Fourteenth Army*'s front collapse. That evening Kesselring hinted to Vietinghoff, the *Tenth Army* commander, that he should be thinking about a withdrawal to the Caesar Line south of Rome.

Both Kesselring and Mackensen agreed that somehow Herr's *LXXVI Panzer Corps* had to be reinforced, but they differed as to how it should be done. The army group commander clung to his conviction that the corps front could be reinforced in place by

thinning out quiet sectors. In that vein, he ordered Mackensen to move to the threatened sector all available antitank gun companies from the *I Parachute Corps*. That Mackensen did, but he still delayed transferring other units from the *I Parachute Corps* to the *LXXVI Panzer Corps* front. In response to Kesselring's urging, he did order the *I Parachute Corps* to assemble a fusilier battalion in the Alban Hills as a reserve under army control for possible commitment in the Cisterna sector. Mackensen also directed a battalion of the *12th Parachute Regiment* to the central sector but countermanded the order after Schlemm, the *I Parachute Corps* commander, played upon his fear that the British attack on the northern flank of the beachhead might increase in strength and be supplemented by an amphibious landing along the coast.

Concerned lest the American armored penetration along the intercorps boundary turn the left flank of the *I Parachute Corps*, Mackensen directed Schlemm to withdraw his corps during the night of the 23d, in accord with the army's original defense plan, to a secondary defense line about half a mile behind his forward positions. Meanwhile, General Herr, the *LXXVI Panzer Corps* commander, awaiting authority to withdraw, went ahead hopefully with plans to shift units from the *715th Division*'s relatively quiet coastal flank to bolster the division's front just east of Cisterna. That action, he hoped, would prevent the Americans from splitting the division from the rest of the corps and pinning it against either the coast or the Lepini Mountains. Moreover, the Americans preparing to assault Terracina would, if they broke through there, soon threaten the division's rear.

Unlike Kesselring, Mackensen still believed that General Clark intended a main effort along the more direct road to Rome—that is, against the *I Parachute Corps*—and that he might also launch an amphibious landing in the army's rear. He also still looked with deep concern at the British divisions close to the coast. Until the morning of the 24th, these misplaced concerns denied timely reinforcement of the central sector at Cisterna, the real focus of General Truscott's offensive. Thus, unknown to Truscott at the time, the cover plan HIPPO had accomplished exactly what those who planned it had intended.

The first day of the breakout offensive had been costly for the Americans, and there had been no breakthrough of the enemy's defenses. Yet decisive advances had been made, and Generals Clark and Truscott, following the day's action on the operation maps in their command post, were satisfied. Had they been aware of the growing differences between Field Marshal Kesselring and General von Mackensen over defense strategy, their satisfaction might have been even greater.

CHAPTER VIII

Breakout From the Beachhead

As Operation BUFFALO entered the second day, General Harmon's 1st Armored Division prepared to exploit its success beyond the railroad. His two combat commands were to cross Highway 7 to occupy the X–Y Line, or first phase line, about a mile and a half northeast of the railroad. Thereafter, on corps' order, the axes of the combat commands were to diverge: Colonel Daniel's CCA, on the left, was to turn northward toward Velletri to occupy the O–B, or second, phase line, some four miles northwest of Cisterna, and block the enemy believed to be in the vicinity of Velletri; Allen's CCB, on the right, was to swing northeast of Cisterna in the direction of Giulianello, a village seven miles beyond Cisterna and midway between Velletri and Cori, to occupy the O–B Line in that sector. If all went well General Allen's command would become the armored spearhead of the drive through the corridor toward Valmontone and Highway 6, Operation BUFFALO's ultimate objective, about thirteen miles away.[1]

As the advance resumed at 0530 on the 24th, Colonel Linville's 6th Armored Infantry Regiment led the way for CCB, with the 2d and 3d Battalions forward. A company each of medium

and light tanks supported each battalion. Leading both battalions were two companies of dismounted armored infantrymen, each supported by an attached machine gun section.

Between the railroad and Highway 7, leading northwestward out of Cisterna, tall reeds and dense brush covered the terrain, which, near the highway, became increasingly compartmentalized by gullies and ravines. Not unusual during the advance through the dense vegetation was an experience of a company commander from the 3d Battalion. Following his platoons on foot, 1st Lt. Mike Acton almost bumped into an enemy officer who suddenly stepped out of a thicket. Acton and the German drew their pistols at the same time. Acton's weapon jammed; the German fired but missed. A quick-thinking runner in Lieutenant Acton's headquarters section shot the German officer.

Progressing slowly toward the highway the two battalions, often without physical or visual contact, fought their way through or around small groups of enemy soldiers well concealed in the reeds and brush. To speed the attack and draw the enemy out into the open, General Allen ordered medium tanks from the 2d Battalion of Colonel Simmerman's 13th Armored Regiment to take the lead. Followed closely by Linville's infantry and harassed only by scattered and poorly directed artillery fire, Simmerman's tanks moved northeastward along a narrow dirt road that

---

[1] This narrative is based upon official records of the 1st Armored Division; Sidney T. Mathews' MS, "The Beachhead Offensive;" and published works such as Taggert, ed., *The History of the Third Infantry Division in World War II*, and George F. Howe, *The Battle History of the 1st Armored Division, "Old Ironsides"* (Washington: Combat Forces Press, 1954).

provided the only cleared corridor through the thick vegetation to within a hundred yards of Highway 7. A platoon and an infantry detachment remained behind to mop up any bypassed enemy.

In moving to within assault distance of the highway, CCB's tanks and infantry had overrun the *954th Infantry Regiment*'s main battle position. The burden of defense in the sector fell thereafter upon the men of the *362d Artillery Regiment,* with the help of a few survivors of the *954th*. As the tanks resumed their attack German artillery, deployed along the west side of Highway 7, fought back at point-blank range. The guns included 88–mm. dual-purpose pieces that destroyed six tanks before the defenders fell back on the artillery regiment's secondary firing positions. Yet the 1st Armored Division's tanks overran those positions too, before an enemy panzer reconnaissance battalion, which had taken the entire night to move from the vicinity of Albano, could reinforce the sector.

By noon the medium tanks were in position on their objective, the X–Y Line, a low ridge beyond Highway 7. Scarcely had they gained the objective when antitank guns located on high ground to the northwest opened fire. In response to a call from Colonel Simmerman for artillery support, the 91st Field Artillery Battalion fired 130 rounds, knocking out at least one piece and destroying a building concealing another. The artillery support was in a way a mixed blessing, since for two hours short rounds fell intermittently among the medium tanks despite repeated demands by Colonel Simmerman that the firing cease. Eventually

the gunners determined which piece was faulty.

A similar error also temporarily checked Colonel Linville's 6th Armored Infantry following the tanks. When small arms fire from enemy positions on a knob overlooking the highway from the east pinned down the infantry just west of the highway, short rounds from artillery trying to dislodge the enemy fell among the American infantry. The rounds continued to fall even after the enemy had ceased firing and had apparently withdrawn. Not until 1400 did the infantry reach the highway and proceed across the road to join the tanks on CCB's objective.

Having crossed Highway 7, CCB had cut one of the two major roads serving the Germans in Cisterna. That accomplished—and with it what appeared to be a critical penetration of the enemy's *362d Division*—General Harmon passed on to General Allen the corps' order to proceed with the second phase of the breakout offensive. Accordingly General Allen sought control of the remaining road, that leading northeastward to Cori. He told Lt. Col. Frank F. Carr to move with his battalion of light tanks to the high ground at the Colle di Torrechia, near a road junction some two miles northeast of Cisterna overlooking the road to Cori. At the same time, Allen sent the 13th Armored Regiment's reconnaissance company ahead to screen Carr's left flank and maintain contact with elements of Colonel Daniel's CCA, which were engaged in forcing what remained of the *362d Division*'s right wing beyond the Mole Canal.

Carr's light tanks gathered quickly in an assembly area just south of the railroad, but soon ran into successive delays along the railroad embankment: first a mine field, then long-range artillery fire, and finally tanks of the combat command's reserve crowding onto the same crossing site over the railroad. It took Carr's tanks two hours to reach Highway 7 and regroup in a wooded area beyond.

Under cover of prearranged artillery concentrations fired by the 91st Field Artillery Battalion, the tanks turned eastward toward the Colle di Torrechia. Rolling toward that objective, they encountered little resistance as they overran a Tiger tank, its 88-mm. gun in full working order. Faced with such a swarm of light tanks, the German crew apparently decided against giving battle and escaped on foot into the underbrush. Soon after dark a battalion of armored infantry joined the tanks to help hold the Colle di Torrechia, while a battalion of medium tanks took up positions about half a mile behind the advance elements to give depth to the defense.

Meanwhile, on the 1st Armored Division's left Colonel Daniel's CCA, advancing to the northwest astride Highway 7, experienced similar success. Such heavy losses had the *362d Division* incurred that even with reinforcement by the panzer reconnaissance battalion that General von Mackensen belatedly ordered transferred from the *I Parachute Corps,* the division could do no more than execute a fighting withdrawal. As night fell CCA's 81st Reconnaissance Battalion had reached a position within four miles of Velletri from which a sortie toward the town could be made the next morning to determine how well defended it was. The *362d Divi-*

sion's front was split, with the troops in front of Cisterna separated from the rest of the division. The stronghold of Cisterna now almost isolated, its defenders awaiting the inevitable—not passively, however, for there was still plenty of fight left in them, as the infantrymen of the 3d Division were soon to learn.

While the advance of CCB's light tanks to the Colle di Torrechia was in effect a partial envelopment of the enemy stronghold of Cisterna, the job of completing the envelopment of the town still belonged to General O'Daniel's 3d Division, whose 30th Infantry, closer to the town, was doing the job on the west, the 15th Infantry on the east. The 7th Infantry in the division's center was to pin the enemy in Cisterna and later reduce the town. At the same time the regiment was to assist the 30th Infantry in the envelopment. With its reserve battalion, the 7th Infantry was to take the settlement of La Villa, a mile northwest of Cisterna, and cut Highway 7 in the vicinity of the Cisterna cemetery. The battalion thereby would serve as a blocking force against the Germans in Cisterna lest they interfere with the 30th Infantry's wheeling movement to get in behind the town, while at the same time affording a starting line for an attack to take the Cisterna defenses in flank.

At 0400 on the 24th, the 3d Division's artillery fired for fifteen minutes in front of the 7th Infantry's left wing. Four hours later the artillery repeated the performance. Meanwhile, the reserve battalion, the 1st, had moved up in the darkness in rear of the positions gained in the first day's fighting.

Following the second artillery preparation, the 1st Battalion began to advance in a column of companies and reached high ground within 400 yards of the railroad after experiencing nothing more disturbing than an occasional round of enemy shellfire. Yet when Company C, in the lead, started to move across flat, exposed ground leading to the railroad, rifle and machine gun fire erupted from the edge of a wood close to La Villa. The battalion commander, Lt. Col. Frank M. Izenour, then committed another company in a flanking maneuver against this opposition, enabling Company C to get moving again behind the fire support of the battalion's 81-mm. mortars. Passing through a cut in the railroad embankment in the face of only occasional German small arms fire, the company moved quickly into La Villa. In the hamlet the men searched in vain for a tunnel that the division G–2 believed led to Cisterna.

Continuation of the attack to cut Highway 7 and gain the Cisterna cemetery was delayed when a company of tanks and a platoon of tank destroyers that were to assist failed to arrive. When at last seven tanks appeared, Colonel Izenour ordered Company B to get on with the attack. As it turned out, not even those tanks were needed. In half an hour, by 1600, Company B and the tanks were astride Highway 7 at the cemetery with no sign of the enemy.

Colonel McGarr's 30th Infantry, in the meantime, had been building up to the railroad and the highway to the northwest to get into position for the enveloping maneuver. The advance involved a thrust by Company F, which had led the regiment's attack on the first day to within a hundred yards of the railroad, and by the fresh 1st Battalion, to which Company F was temporarily attached.

At dawn on the 24th, Company F on the left and Company B on the right, each supported by a platoon of heavy machine guns, advanced toward a group of low hills, west of the Femminamorta Canal, that overlooked the railroad from the south. From the high ground the two companies would be able to cover the move of the rest of the 1st Battalion across the railroad on the other side of the canal.

The 41st Field Artillery Battalion fired several concentrations before the infantry moved out, but the Germans responded to the new attack with automatic weapons and mortar fire from positions near a group of ruined stone houses atop two knobs south of the railroad. Rather than attempt what might have been a costly frontal attack against the positions, Company F swung far to the left in an outflanking maneuver. That move carried the western knob and enabled Company B to clear the eastern knob quickly. By 1100 Company F and the entire 1st Battalion had closed up to the railroad.

The 30th Infantry's 3d Battalion, astride the Ponte Rotto road, found even easier going. Hearing movements before daylight in the vicinity of an enemy strongpoint along the Femminamorta Canal, men of Company L deduced that the Germans might be withdrawing. In an attempt to catch them before they got away, the company hastened along the canal toward the position, but too late. At the strongpoint Company L found only twenty-four enemy dead. Moving on to a second position nearby, the company found that, too, abandoned.

In midafternoon, as the 1st Battalion prepared to cross the railroad and seize the high ground just beyond, the 3d Battalion made ready to develop the enveloping maneuver by advancing to a road junction a mile and a half northeast of Cisterna on the forward slopes of the Colle di Torrechia, not far from the objective of the light tanks of Colonel Carr's battalion of the 1st Armored Division's CCB. Indeed, had not the infantry battalion incurred delays, the two forces might have arrived on their adjacent objectives at approximately the same time. While the 3d Battalion's move constituted the left arm in the envelopment of Cisterna, it was also designed to put the 30th Infantry in position to assist the 15th Infantry in a drive early the next morning on Cori.

Although the 3d Battalion, 30th Infantry, began to move about 1630, darkness had fallen when the men crossed the highway and passed through the cemetery. Unwittingly, the troops had cut across the rear of a battalion of the 7th Infantry just as that battalion launched an attack on Cisterna. As German mortar fire began to fall, confusion in the cemetery increased. Untangling the two forces took considerable time, so that it was close to daylight before the 3d Battalion, 30th Infantry, in an unopposed march through the darkness, could reach the road junction near the Colle di Torrechia. A projected continuation of the attack at 0630 on the 25th against Cori would have to be delayed.

With the 3d Battalion thus delayed, not until midnight did the 30th Infan-

try's 1st Battalion receive an order to follow. That battalion reached the objective soon after daylight, there to find preparations for mounting an attack on Cori hampered by persistent German shelling apparently directed at the light tanks of the 1st Armored Division's CCB assembled nearby on another part of the Colle di Torrechia. It would be late on the 25th before the 30th Infantry could launch its drive on Cori.

Constituting the other arm of the maneuver to envelop Cisterna, the 15th Infantry in the meantime had mounted an attack with its 2d Battalion driving due north to cross Highway 7 and the railroad, skirting Cisterna to the east, and advancing to the Cisterna-Cori road. While the 1st Battalion and Task Force Paulick, closing the gap between the division and the 1st Special Service Force, remained along Highway 7 in positions gained on the first day, the 3d Battalion was to follow the 2d and once across the railroad was to swing east to occupy the Maschia San Biagio, a wooded area a mile and a half east of Cisterna, thereby protecting the 2d Battalion's flank.

At 0730 Company G led the 2d Battalion's attack, advancing fairly readily across Highway 7 to the railroad despite harassing machine gun fire from somewhere near the railroad embankment. As the men started to cross the embankment, fire from small arms and self-propelled guns in the outskirts of Cisterna drove them back. To get the attack moving again, the battalion commander sent Company F along the shelter of the steep banks of the San Biagio Canal, a small tributary of the Cisterna Canal, to outflank the enemy from the right, but German fire halted that maneuver too.[2] The 39th Field Artillery Battalion fired several concentrations in order to silence the enemy fire, but a second try at crossing the railroad met continued opposition.

During the early afternoon the battalion commander sideslipped his companies to the right in an effort to avoid the fire coming from Cisterna. He also committed a third company as prelude to a new assault. Prevented by antitank fire from bringing tanks and tank destroyers close enough to the railroad embankment to give the infantry close support, he gained permission to move the destroyers into the 1st Special Service Force's sector on the right. From there the destroyers tried to place flanking fire on the troublesome enemy positions, but again the effect on the volume of enemy fire was negligible.

A visit in midafternoon to the 15th Infantry command post by the division commander, General O'Daniel, brought a promise of additional artillery support to help get the attack moving again; but a new attempt shortly before nightfall, this time supported by five artillery battalions, made no headway. Only after another heavy artillery preparation did the infantrymen finally cross the railroad and advance to the edge of a wood about 700 yards to the north—only to be forced back 200 yards by fire from small arms and tanks. By that time darkness had fallen.[3]

Taking advantage of the darkness, engineers built ramps on the steep sides

of the railroad embankment so that the tanks and tank destroyers might cross. After joining the infantry, the tank destroyers before daylight on the 25th knocked out the strongpoints that had been holding up the 2d Battalion for almost twenty-four hours. At the first light of the new day, the 2d Battalion began to move again while remnants of the enemy's *955th Regiment* retreated deeper into the ruins of Cisterna. In early morning of the 25th the battalion reached the Casa Montaini, a farm near the Cori road about half a mile northeast of Cisterna and within hailing distance of troops of the 30th Infantry on the Colle di Torrechia. That action completed the encirclement of Cisterna.

Even as the 3d Division's two flank regiments were getting on with that encirclement, the division commander, General O'Daniel, deemed the enemy so weakened that he had no need to delay delivering the *coup de grace* to Cisterna itself. While the 7th Infantry's 2d Battalion, attacking frontally against the Cisterna defenses, gained little ground during the second day, O'Daniel believed that, by hitting the enemy from the flank position held by the regiment's 1st Battalion at the cemetery alongside Highway 7, the 7th Infantry might yet take the town in one quick thrust. He told the regimental commander, Colonel Omohundro, to use his 3d Battalion. That was the unit that had failed to follow orders on the first day, but the battalion had a new commander, its former executive officer, Major Ramsey, and a quick, successful seizure of Cisterna might fully restore the confidence of officers and men alike.

Colonel Omohundro planned to be-

---

[2] The intrepid performance of Pvt. James H. Mills, Company F, 15th Infantry, during this attack was subsequently recognized by the award of the Medal of Honor.

[3] For his role in the attack Sgt. Sylvester Antolak, Company B, 15th Infantry, was awarded the Medal of Honor posthumously.

PATROL MOVING THROUGH CISTERNA

gin the assault on Cisterna with a renewed frontal attack by the 2d Battalion to serve as a diversion. Once that attack began, supporting artillery was to deliver a 30-minute barrage on the town, whereupon Ramsey's 3d Battalion was to strike from the cemetery southeastward down Highway 7. A smoke screen was to conceal the start of the 3d Battalion's attack.

While preparations for the attack were under way, a patrol reconnoitered from the cemetery as far as Cisterna's western outskirts but there encountered considerable machine gun and mortar fire. That response was the first hint that the town might be less readily

taken than General O'Daniel had believed, and that the 3d Battalion might have a hard fight, something for which that unit the day before had shown little inclination.

The first hitch in Omohundro's plan developed when the 2d Battalion delayed its attack until a supporting platoon of tank destroyers could get forward. Scheduled to attack at 1930, the battalion did not move until shortly after the tank destroyers finally arrived at 2130. Since the 2d Battalion was to attack first, the 3d Battalion at the cemetery also had to postpone its attack, which meant there would be no further need for a smoke screen: the

7th Infantry was to hit Cisterna by night.

This unforeseen delay was the second in a series of unfortunate circumstances that had begun earlier in the day when Major Ramsey, the 3d Battalion's new commander, was wounded and evacuated to the rear. The commander of the Weapons Company, Capt. Glenn E. Rathbun, took his place. At 2145, with Company K on the left, Company D on the right, and Company L in reserve behind Company I, the battalion at last began to move through the Cisterna cemetery toward a line of departure just beyond it. An attached tank platoon and three tank destroyers were in direct support. It was then that the third in the series of mishaps occurred: the unfortunate intermingling in the cemetery with the leading battalion of the 30th Infantry and the delay of several hours before the battalions could be separated and control restored.

Even more trouble awaited the unfortunate 3d Battalion. As the men finally crossed the line of departure, heavy enemy shelling and several short rounds from U.S. artillery fell among them. That left the men badly shaken. At dawn on the 25th the battalion was only 200 yards beyond its line of departure, still about 700 yards short of the first buildings of Cisterna. When Colonel Omohundro ordered the battalion to renew the attack, withering automatic weapons fire stopped the men as soon as they attempted to move. Casualties were heavy, among them the commander of Company K, the company's third commander in four days. The attack collapsed and with it General

O'Daniel's hope of quickly redeeming the battalion.

Paradoxically, the diversionary attack by the 2d Battalion into the face of the main defenses at Cisterna had been making better progress. The battalion at first ran into stubborn resistance from Germans concealed in a group of ruined houses on both sides of the railroad. Each house had to be laboriously reduced; but with the help of well co-ordinated mortar and artillery fire, the men fought through the night and gradually worked their way forward. When the two leading companies reached the railroad embankment, they called for supporting fires to lift, then rushed across at six points. Weary from the night's fighting, the companies dug in just beyond the embankment and less than 200 yards from the fringe of Cisterna. The 2d Battalion's success and the 3d Battalion's failure were destined to dictate a change in plan for the final assault into the town.

Action on the Flanks

As the 3d Division encircled Cisterna on the 24th, the 133d Infantry, serving as a screen for the 1st Special Service Force on the division and corps right, headed slowly northward, its right flank anchored on the Mussolini Canal. That night the 1st Special Service Force assembled behind the 133d Infantry and prepared to pass through its lines the next morning in a thrust toward Monte Arrestino, overlooking Cori from the southeast.

On the opposite flank, the 45th Division, after gaining its assigned objectives on the 23d, continued to hold its position northwest of Carano. Yet again that was to be no passive operation, for at dusk on the 24th the Germans counterattacked with a reinforced battalion supported by tanks. Moving south along the west bank of the Carano Canal, the enemy struck the right flank of the 180th Infantry's 2d Battalion astride the Carano road. Under cover of heavy mortar and artillery fire and taking advantage of lush vegetation, the enemy infantry crept to within 100 yards of the American lines before being discovered. Hurling grenades at the Americans, the Germans rushed forward. During ensuing hand-to-hand fighting, the defenders were supported by eight battalions of artillery firing at the enemy's lines of communications. Although the counterattack forced back the 180th Infantry's front slightly, the lost ground was regained by midnight, and patrols that night reported that the enemy had withdrawn from the division's immediate front.

While the U.S. 45th Division lost and then regained ground on the Carano sector, the British 5th and 1st Divisions on the beachhead's western flank along the coast yielded to counterattacking enemy units from the *4th Parachute* and *65th Infantry Divisions* the slight gains made by the diversionary attack on the 23d. Falling back to their original front, the British held.

The German Reaction

The counterattacks mounted by the *I Parachute Corps* during the 24th reflected the emphasis which the *Fourteenth Army* commander, General von Mackensen, had placed since the beginning of the Allied breakout offensive on his right wing between the Alban Hills and the Tyrrhenian coast. The limited success of the counterattacks in holding that sector of the *Fourteenth Army* front was the only encouragement for Mackensen on the second day of the Allied offensive. Yet, since it at last had become undeniable that the Allied main effort was at Cisterna, the limited successes on the parachute corps front hardly brightened a day filled with gloom.[4]

Little time had passed during the morning of 24 May before General von Mackensen discerned that the thrusts by the American armor northwest of Cisterna and the infantry on either side of the town were about to drive wedges between the *362d Division* and its two neighboring divisions—the *3d Panzer Grenadier Division* on the right and the *715th Division* on the left. The counterattacks against the U.S. 45th Division and the two British divisions were expected to ease the pressure somewhat on the right. Yet the extreme left wing of the *715th Division* was still behind the Mussolini Canal and unless allowed to withdraw was likely to be pinned against the Tyrrhenian coast.

Field Marshal Kesselring at last agreed to pulling back the *715th Division*'s left wing to the railroad, which parallels the coast approximately ten miles inland. To the approval, however, Kesselring attached the proviso that any forces thereby freed from contact with the Americans were to reinforce the defenders of Cisterna. The proviso bore little relationship to the situation on the ground, for even by nightfall of the 24th the American advances had

---

[4] Unless otherwise indicated, the German account is based upon MSS#'s T-1b (Westphal *et al.*) and R-50 (Bailey).

virtually severed contact between the *715th Division* and the rest of the panzer corps.

As pressure against the *715th Division* increased during the afternoon of the 24th, General von Mackensen made up his mind to exceed the authority granted by Kesselring and withdraw the entire division to a secondary line extending eastward from Cisterna toward the Lepini Mountains. When Mackensen learned in late afternoon that troops of the U.S. 3d Division were on the fringe of Cisterna and that the 1st Special Service Force had penetrated the *715th Division*'s center, he authorized withdrawal of the division as soon as darkness provided concealment from Allied fighter-bombers.

As the *715th Division* began to withdraw that night, the commander of the *362d Division*, Generalleutnant Heinz Greiner, returned to his command from his emergency leave in Germany. Taking stock of the obviously critical situation, Greiner concluded that if the garrison of Cisterna was to have any chance at escape he had to mount some kind of counterattack. While harboring no illusions about what a counterattack by his depleted forces could accomplish, he nevertheless hoped he might throw the Americans off balance long enough for reinforcements to arrive from the *I Parachute Corps* and for the garrison to slip out of Cisterna.

Even that faint hope had disappeared when, in late afternoon, contingents of the U.S. 1st Armored Division plunged toward the Colle di Torrechia. Either abandon Cisterna or lose all the men there, Greiner believed, but Field Marshal Kesselring refused withdrawal. General von Mackensen nevertheless

went beyond his authority for the second time that day and told Greiner to pull the men back. When General Greiner that afternoon tried to pass on the word, it was too late. The garrison's radio had ceased to function. In Greiner's words, "*Cisterna antwortete nicht mehr*" ("Cisterna no longer answered").[5]

To the German command it was now clear that only the arrival of division-size reinforcements could prevent a collapse of the *Fourteenth Army*'s center. Three divisions from the army group reserve already having departed to reinforce the *Tenth Army* on the southern front, the only major reserve force remaining was the *Hermann Goering Division*, which on the 23d had begun a march south from the Ligurian coast, over 150 miles away. Having overestimated Allied amphibious capabilities, Kesselring and the German High Command had hesitated until the last minute before deciding to use that division.

As for a shift of forces within the *Fourteenth Army*, even after it was clear that the Allied offensive was actually aimed at the left wing of the *LXXVI Panzer Corps*, General von Mackensen ordered only piecemeal transfer of small units. Why shift units and invite trouble elsewhere when he was convinced his army lacked sufficient forces to accomplish its defensive mission? As late as 19 May he had bitterly protested Kesselring's transfer to the southern front of the *26th Panzer* and *29th Panzer Grenadier Divisions* from the army group reserve, a reserve on which Mackensen believed he had first claim and without which he judged he had no hope of

---

[5] Heinz Greiner, Glt a.D., *Kampf um Rom—Inferno am Po* (Kurt Vowinckel, Verlag, Neckargemuend, 1968), p. 50.

containing the Allied offensive. The presence of the *92d Infantry Division*, guarding the coast just south of the Tiber, was of little consequence as a reserve force for it was as yet an untried unit, composed largely of men still undergoing training. At that point he doubted that he could even count on being given the *Hermann Goering Division*, if and when it arrived at the front south of Rome, for he strongly suspected that it too would go to the *Tenth Army*. To Mackensen, Field Marshal Kesselring's inability to halt the offensive was proof that his belief that it could be stopped was misguided optimism. Relations between the two German commanders had become so strained as to approach the breaking point.

The Third Day

Against the backdrop of futility on the German side, all units of General Truscott's VI Corps planned to renew their assaults on the third day of the offensive, 25 May, and exploit the impressive gains already achieved—the 1st Special Service Force to take Monte Arrestino, the 3d Division to take Cisterna while at the same time driving northeastward on Cori, the 1st Armored Division to pursue the drive on Velletri and northeastward toward Valmontone via Cori and Giulianello, and the 45th Division to continue to anchor the left flank of the American force.

Throughout the night of 24 May General Truscott shifted his units preparatory to continuing the offensive the next morning. To close a gap created by the diverging axes of the 1st Armored Division's two combat commands, Truscott gave the 34th Division control of a five-mile sector north of Cisterna behind the armor. With two regiments, the division was to block any attempt by the enemy to exploit open space between the armored columns and permit the armor to move more freely in exploiting the German collapse below Cori. During the night contingents of corps artillery began displacing forward to areas south and west of Isola Bella in order to better support the continuation of the main attack.

On the extreme right flank of the corps the 36th Division engineers, who since the 23d had remained in corps reserve, had readied task forces to move southward to contact the II Corps advancing from Terracina. That night the engineers crossed the Mussolini Canal and pushed down along the coastal road through territory recently abandoned by the *715th Division*. The link-up with the Americans from the Garigliano front was to occur on the morning of the 25th.

As the two fronts joined, the 1st Armored Division was advancing beyond the second phase line. Combat Command A continued to move toward Velletri against steadily increasing resistance. A combination of rugged terrain, well-sited antitank guns, and a counterattack led by Mark V tanks held the Americans four miles south of the town. The day's fighting cost Colonel Daniel's combat command seventeen tanks damaged or destroyed.

On Daniel's right General Harmon had in the meantime moved from reserve a task force under Col. Hamilton H. Howze. The task force was composed of Lt. Col. Bogardus S. Cairn's 3d Battalion, 13th Armored

Regiment; the 2d Battalion, 6th Armored Infantry; the 3d Battalion, 135th Infantry; Companies B and D, 1st Armored Regiment; and Companies B of the 635th and 701st Tank Destroyer Battalions. Colonel Howze assembled the unit during the night of 24 May near Torrechia Nuova in readiness for an advance toward the road junction of Giulianello the following day.

Striking across country, the medium tanks of Howze's task force by 1300 reached and blocked the Cori-Giulianello road about 2,500 yards south of Giulianello. When an infantry column arrived late in the afternoon, tanks and infantry moved together to clear the village before dark. Meanwhile, General Allen's Combat Command B prepared to accompany and support the 3d Division's 15th Infantry as it moved from the Colle di Torrechia toward the village of Cori on the western slope of the Lepini Mountains.

The Enemy Situation

The 1st Armored Division's thrust up the Valmontone corridor to Giulianello had irretrievably separated the *362d* and *715th Divisions*. Large groups of the enemy, cut off and without effective control, surrendered. By midday on 25 May, 2,640 prisoners had passed through the Fifth Army's cages at Anzio since the offensive began on the 23d. The penetration also threatened to cut off the left wing of the *715th Division*, attempting to withdraw along secondary roads and trails southwest of the Lepini Mountains. The division, having exhausted its mortar ammunition and lost most of its mortars as well as its light and heavy machine guns,

was in desperate straits. Contact with the attached panzer grenadier regiment, constituting the division's center, had been lost completely; communications with other subordinate units were little better. A 100-man *Kampfgruppe*, commanded by an artillery battery commander, constituted the division's right wing north of the Cisterna-Cori road. Supporting the *Kampfgruppe* were an artillery battery, firing at point-blank range, and a platoon of 88-mm. antiaircraft guns. On 25 May that was all that stood between the Americans and Cori.[6]

Two infantry battalions, unsupported by heavy weapons, were scattered in hasty positions in the hills to the northwest of Cori. A rifle company and the heavy weapons company, all that remained of a battalion on the division's left flank, had been ordered to reinforce these battalions, but it was doubtful whether the reinforcements would be either sufficient or in time to check the onrush of the Americans. Also, transfer of even those modest forces would leave the Monte Arrestino sector held only by the equivalent of three rifle companies.

Meanwhile, an infantry regiment from the *92d Infantry Division,* guarding the coast just south of the mouth of the Tiber, had been sent to reinforce the *715th Division.* That regiment had been last reported marching from Giulianello toward Cori. Without motor transport, the regiment had had to leave behind its heavy support weapons and even its field kitchens, and was not expected to reach Cori until noon on the 25th.

---

[6] MS # R–50 (Bailey). The following account is based on this source.

The Attack on Cori

Although General O'Daniel, the 3d Division commander, had originally expected the 15th Infantry to attack toward Cori no later than 0530 on the morning of 25 May, the 1st and 3d Battalions (the latter having relieved the 2d) reached their assembly points along the Cisterna-Cori road only by mid-morning. The 3d Battalion had a greater distance to move from its positions south of Cisterna, and the line of march was made hazardous by numerous antipersonnel mines. Those factors prevented the battalion from reaching its line of departure before the 1st Battalion started for Cori at 1000.

With the regimental battle patrol covering the battalion's right flank, Company C led the way toward Cori across the increasingly hilly terrain that merged gradually into the slopes of the Lepini Mountains. On the left (north) of the Cisterna-Cori road moved the 3d Battalion of the 15th Infantry. Neither battalion encountered appreciable opposition. Reaching the fringe of Cori at twilight, both battalions sent patrols into the town to probe the ruins of the village. Although the patrols found no sign of the enemy, the battalion commander decided to await daylight before moving in.

The 15th Infantry had found no enemy in Cori because the reinforcements from the *92d Division* had never arrived. The night of the 24th, as the regiment had marched along the Giulianello-Cori road, the men had encountered elements of the *715th Division* withdrawing in the opposite direction to escape being cut off by the American thrust toward Cori. German command-

ers were unable to straighten out the resulting confusion before daylight exposed the crowded road to the eyes of a pilot of a reconnaissance aircraft from the XII TAC. Calling for assistance, the pilot soon had all available aircraft bombing and strafing the concentration of men and vehicles.

The Capture of Cisterna

As the remainder of the 3d Infantry Division advanced north and east of Cisterna, the 7th Infantry, charged with the task of taking the enemy strongpoint, prepared to close in for the kill. The failure of the attack against the town's north flank on the 24th and the relative success of the 2d Battalion's frontal advance the same day prompted the regimental commander, Colonel Omohundro, to give the job of taking the town to the 2d Battalion. The commander, Lt. Col. Everett W. Duvall, started the assignment by sending his reserve, Company F, around the right flank of the positions gained earlier just beyond the railroad embankment.

Attacking before daylight on 25 May, Company F quickly secured a foothold in the southwestern part of the town. Upon arrival of two medium and eight light tanks from the 751st Tank Battalion to provide fire support, Duvall ordered the company to continue toward the center of town, while Company G cleared the enemy from the southeastern section. Colonel Duvall intentionally sent the two companies on divergent axes lest in the close quarters of the rubble-filled streets one should fire upon the other.

While Company G proceeded methodically with a task that amounted to

DISARMING GERMAN PRISONERS AT CISTERNA

mopping up, the men of Company F picked their way slowly toward the center of town against machine gun and mortar fire that grew in intensity. The Germans had prepared what had apparently once been the town hall for a last-ditch defense, ringing it with antitank mines and covering all approaches with machine guns protected by rubble-covered emplacements. On the west side a well-sited antitank gun covered the entrance to an inner courtyard.

Despite support of the light and medium tanks, the attack against the town hall made little headway. Not until late afternoon, when a squad managed to emplace a machine gun atop a ruin overlooking the entrance to the court-yard, did the siege take a turn for the better. From that position, the gunner drove off the crew manning the troublesome antitank gun. A medium tank immediately came forward, destroyed the gun, and, with men of Company F close behind, rolled through the entrance into the town hall's inner courtyard. All resistance collapsed. In the gathering twilight of the 25th, three days after the breakout offensive had begun, the American infantrymen swarmed into the ruins to rout out the survivors, including the commander of the *955th Infantry Regiment*.

That night General Truscott could look back with some satisfaction on the capture of Cisterna and the imminent fall of Cori. On his right wing, the 1st

Special Service Force, having gained Monte Arrestino's rugged and deserted summit, was poised for a drive across the Lepini Mountains toward the upper Sacco valley and Highway 6. The objectives of Operation BUFFALO's second phase had been gained. Truscott's VI Corps had broken out of a six-month confinement in the beachhead, and BUFFALO's ultimate objective, Valmontone and Highway 6, lay some ten miles away. The Anzio beachhead no longer existed but had become instead the extended left flank of the U.S. Fifth Army. Fifth Army's troops were much closer to Rome than were those of the British Eighth Army, still some forty miles southeast of Valmontone.

German Countermoves

The sharp deterioration of *Army Group C's* situation was remarked at OKW as early as the evening of the 24th. The link-up of the Fifth Army's main forces and the beachhead, the Eighth Army's steady advance in the Liri valley, and the VI Corps' breakout at Cisterna led the German High Command to conclude that there was no alternative to withdrawal of the entire army group into the Caesar Line. Early in April the Germans had started constructing that secondary defense line between the Anzio beachhead and Rome from the Tyrrhenian coast north of Anzio, across the southern flanks of the Alban Hills to Highway 6 near Valmontone, thence over the Ernici Mountains to Sora on the Avezzano road. Despite the fact that more than 10,000 Italian laborers, under the direction of German army engineers, had worked on the defenses, the line was far from finished. From Campo Iemini,

on the Tyrrhenian coast about seventeen miles southwest of Rome, across the southern slopes of the Alban Hills as far as the town of Labico on Highway 6, some two miles east of Valmontone, the line was complete; but elsewhere it was nothing more than a penciled line on situation maps.[7] German records refer to the Caesar Line as the *C-Stellung,* or C-Position; Allied staffs simply assumed the "C" stood for "Caesar"—a logical deduction considering its location. A second line, the *Campagna Riegel,* or switch position, lay between the *C-Stellung* and Rome, but was of little significance.

To screen the Caesar Line, the Germans had put up an almost continuous barbed wire obstacle, which in some sectors attained a depth of ninety feet. They had also placed mines to block the most favorable routes of approach. While infantry firing positions and shelters in the Caesar Line resembled those along the Gustav Line, few defenses were in such depth. In the opinion of General von Mackensen, the *Fourteenth Army* commander, the Caesar Line was suitable for no more than a delaying action.[8]

The German High Command operations staff nevertheless recommended to Hitler on the evening of the 24th, even before the fall of Cisterna and the crossing of the Melfa River by contingents of the Eighth Army, that both German armies begin at least a partial withdrawal into the Caesar Line. The *Fourteenth Army's* right wing was to remain in place as far as Cisterna, while

---

[7] MSS #'s C–061 (Mackensen *et al.*) and D–211 (Bessel). See also Greiner and Schramm, eds., *OKW/ WFSt, KTB,* IV (1), pp. 480–81.

[8] Greiner and Schramm, eds., IV(1), pp. 492–94.

the left wing (the *LXXVI Panzer Corps*), in co-ordination with the *Tenth Army's* right wing (the *XIV Panzer Corps*), withdrew gradually to gain as much time as possible for the occupation and preparation of the unimproved portions of the line. The operations staff also proposed that the remnants of the *71st* and *94th Infantry Divisions* be employed in the Caesar Line as security detachments until they could be brought up to strength with replacements. In addition to the *Hermann Goering Division,* which on the 23d had started shifting southward from its bases near Leghorn, the *356th Infantry Division* was also to move south from the vicinity of Genoa. [9]

During the regular noon situation briefing on the 25th, Hitler substantially accepted those proposals and, thanks to British Intelligence, the Allied command in Italy was soon privy to this decision. The area immediately north of the Alban Hills on both sides of Highway 6—in short, Operation BUF-FALO's general objective—was, Hitler and his advisers agreed, the most threatened sector. That was exactly the conclusion that Clark hoped that the Germans would reach. Moreover, his G–2 had also informed him that the Germans would attempt to reinforce with the *Hermann Goering* and *356th Infantry Divisions.* Both Clark and Kesselring, however, would underestimate the ability of Allied aircraft to delay movement of those divisions.

---

[9] The latter division's place was to be taken by the *42d Jaeger Division.* The *16th SS Panzer Grenadier Division,* on occupation duty in northern Italy, was to be billeted along the coastal region vacated by the two divisions though not to be committed to a coastal defense role. Additional divisions from northern Europe were to be moved into Italy to reconstitute the theater's strategic reserves.

In any case, Hitler insisted, the Caesar Line had to be held. Uncompleted sectors of the line were to be improved at once by using labor companies, security detachments, and local inhabitants. Delaying action in front of the line was to be aimed at inflicting such crippling losses that the Allied forces would be stopped even before reaching the line. Such an order bore little relationship to the reality of the tactical situation and would not reach *Army Group C* until the afternoon of the 26th, too late to do much about it.

In the meantime, Kesselring and Mackensen turned their attention to General Herr's battered *LXXVI Panzer Corps* on the *Fourteenth Army's* faltering left wing. The harried corps commander had no knowledge of the exact location of the *715th Division* but guessed that it might be scattered among the towns of Cori, Norma, and Sezze in the Lepini Mountains. As for Greiner's *362d Division,* it was in better shape. One regiment had been destroyed at Cisterna. Survivors of the remaining two were withdrawing in the direction of Velletri and Valmontone. [10]

To Kesselring it was evident that a dangerous gap had opened on Herr's front, and that Truscott's corps would soon move through to threaten Highway 6 near Valmontone. To close the gap Kesselring ordered the *Fourteenth Army* commander to commit the reconnaissance battalion of the *Hermann Goering Division* as soon as it arrived, the battalion to serve as a blocking force along a four-mile front between Lariano at the foot of the Alban Hills to an anchor on Monte Ilirio, about two miles

---

[10] MS # R–50 (Bailey). Unless otherwise indicated the following section is based upon this source.

northeast of Giulianello. Kesselring also told Mackensen to have patrols of the *362d Division* try to re-establish contact with the *715th Division*.

Mackensen readily agreed that he might be able to close the gap with the reconnaissance battalion, but pointed out that it would be too thinly spread for any offensive action. As for the *362d Division*, it was already overextended and probably would be unable to maintain contact with the *715th Division*, even if patrols should succeed in locating the division. Mackensen had little confidence that either measure could do much to stem the American thrust toward Valmontone and Highway 6.

Mackensen, nevertheless, transmitted both orders to his panzer corps commander. Meanwhile, the corps was to establish a new defense based on former artillery positions south of the Velletri-Giulianello road. That road had to be kept open if the integrity of the *LXXVI Panzer Corps* was to be maintained, yet even as the order was given, the armored spearhead of the U.S. VI Corps had reached the fringe of Giulianello.

Turning to his right wing, Mackensen ordered Schlemm to begin withdrawing his *I Parachute Corps* into the Caesar Line. The positions there were to be held at all costs.[11]

As the situation on the *Fourteenth Army's* left wing deteriorated on the 25th, Kesselring directed Mackensen to shift additional antitank guns from the *I Parachute Corps* to the *LXXVI Panzer*

Corps front. Mackensen had already transferred 48 heavy antitank guns, 8 88-mm. guns, and about half of the parachute corps' remaining assault guns to the panzer corps, leaving only 1 company of antitank guns and 8 assault guns in the parachute corps. Of the *508th Panzer Battalion's* original 38 Tiger tanks only 17 remained, and those too had been moved to the panzer corps.

General von Mackensen decided that he could make no further withdrawals from the parachute corps without seriously weakening his right wing. He still believed, as he had since the beginning of the Allied offensive on the 23d, that eventually the Allied main effort was going to erupt against that right wing. The only reserve left to the *I Parachute Corps*, in any case, was the newly organized *92d Infantry Division*, with a coastal defense mission west of Rome; and because of the condition of the roads and the shortage of transport, Mackensen doubted whether it would be possible to shift the division to Herr's front. All that Mackensen could hope to add to oppose the American thrust toward Valmontone was the panzer reconnaissance battalion of the *Hermann Goering Division* and, if found, the disorganized remnants of the *715th Division*.

General von Vietinghoff, the *Tenth Army* commander, was also concerned about keeping open Highway 6 through Valmontone as long as possible, for, while he had other routes available to him, the Valmontone junction was important for a withdrawal of the *Tenth Army's* right wing. The integrity of Herr's corps was thus vital to Vietinghoff's plans for extricating Senger's corps from the converging Allied

[11] *CINC AOK 14, Ia Nr. 1470/44 g.K chefs,* 26 May 44, in *AOK 14 Ia KTB Nr. 3, Anl. 462,* 1–31 May 44, *AOK 14, 59091/3.*

armies. Meanwhile, the *Tenth Army* continued to fall back to a new delaying position anchored on the Sacco River near Castro dei Volsci.

PART THREE

DRIVE TO ROME

If I know that the enemy can be attacked and that my troops are capable of attacking him, but do not realize that because of the conformation of the ground I should not attack, my chance of victory is but half.

SUN TZU, *The Art of War*

CHAPTER IX

Stalemate Along the Caesar Line

Clark's Decision

On the afternoon of 24 May General Clark asked General Truscott, "Have you considered changing the direction of your attack to the northwest—toward Rome?"

General Truscott, whose attention was still focused on Valmontone and Highway 6, replied that he had, but only in the event that Mackensen shifted a significant part of the still formidable *I Parachute Corps* from the Alban Hills into the Valmontone Gap. Since such a concentration might delay the VI Corps long enough to allow the Germans to slip through Valmontone, Truscott thought that under those circumstances "an attack to the northwest might be the best way to cut off the enemy withdrawal north of the Alban Hills." To meet such a contingency, his staff had kept plan TURTLE current—an attack to the northwest directly toward Rome.[1]

Clark's question was for Truscott the first indication since the meeting at Army headquarters a few days before the breakout offensive began that the Fifth Army commander was still seriously considering modification of Operation BUFFALO. Although Clark said nothing further at the moment, Truscott was puzzled over Clark's apparent desire to tinker with an operation that seemed to be moving rapidly to a successful conclusion.[2]

In spite of Truscott's confidence in the operation, Clark continued to question the validity of what he considered to be Alexander's strategic concept. Seeing the attack toward Valmontone as simply the result of a "long-standing . . . preconceived idea" promoted by Alexander's chief of staff, Lt. Gen. Sir John Harding, General Clark believed it was "based upon the false premise that if Highway 6 were cut at Valmontone a German army would be annihilated." The many alternate roads leading northward out of the Sacco-Liri valley, he believed, would enable the *Tenth Army* to bypass a trap at Valmontone. Clark became more and more convinced that instead of continuing a major effort toward Valmontone and Highway 6, he should be driving straight for Rome.[3]

Clark's conviction was strengthened by his estimate of the enemy's dispositions. According to G–2 reports, rem-

---

[1] Truscott, *Command Missions*, p. 374; Interv, author with Gen Truscott, 1 Mar 62, CMH.

[2] Interv, author with Gen Truscott, 1 Mar 62, in CMH files; Ltr, Gen Truscott to CMH, 3 Nov 1961, in CMH files.

[3] Clark Diary, 26 May 44.

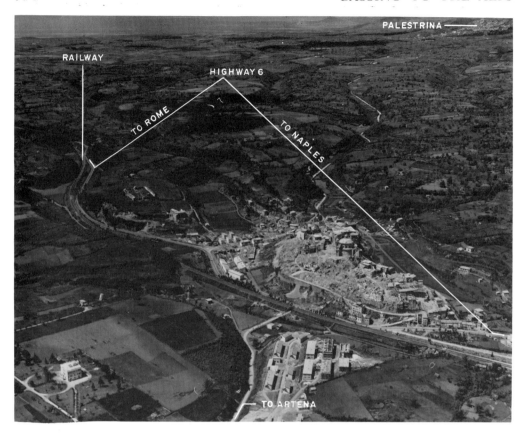

AERIAL VIEW OF VALMONTONE AND HIGHWAY 6

nants of the *362d Division* had with-drawn from Cisterna into the sector between Velletri and Valmontone, and Kesselring had ordered the *Hermann Goering Division* into the Valmontone Gap. General Clark also suspected that Mackensen would shift units from the *Fourteenth Army's* right flank toward Valmontone, and would thereby signif-icantly thin out the *I Parachute Corps'* defense in the Alban Hills. Earlier German actions along the Gustav Line, where forces had been transferred from the mountains in order to but-tress defenses athwart natural routes of

advance, tended to support his reason-ing.[4]

Even if the VI Corps managed to break through to Valmontone—which Clark saw as unlikely in view of the reported enemy build-up there—Clark concluded that the lengthening line of communications extending from Anzio toward Valmontone would become in-creasingly vulnerable to German forces in the Alban Hills. Without further staff discussion on the subject, Clark decided to modify Operation BUFFALO signifi-

---

[4]Fifth Army G–2 Jnl, May 44.

cantly and turn the bulk of Truscott's corps northwestward into the Alban Hills.[5]

On 25 May Clark directed his G–3, General Brann, to inform General Truscott of the new objective. "We will capture Rome," Clark said confidently, ". . . it is just a matter of time."[6]

Visiting his subordinate commanders on the morning of 25 May, and unaware of the impending change in plan, Truscott was pleased with what he saw. The 1st Armored Division was within four miles of Velletri. The 3d Division was closing in on Cori. Frederick's 1st Special Service Force was nearing the summit of Monte Arrestino on the VI Corps' right flank. All shared Truscott's confidence that by the following morning the VI Corps "would be astride the German line of withdrawal through Valmontone."[7]

Returning to his command post about noon, Truscott found General Brann waiting for him. "The Boss wants you to leave the 3d Infantry Division and the Special Force to block Highway 6," Brann said, "and mount that assault you discussed with him to the northwest as soon as you can."[8]

Truscott was dumbfounded. There was as yet no indication, he protested, that the enemy had significantly weakened his defenses in the Alban Hills. That was, he insisted, the only condition that would justify modifying BUF-FALO. Nor, unlike Clark, did Truscott have evidence of an important enemy build-up in the Valmontone area, except for an identification of reconnaissance elements of the *Hermann Goering Division*. This was no time, the corps commander argued, to shift the main effort of his attack to the northwest toward the *I Parachute Corps* where the enemy was still strong. The offensive should continue instead with "maximum power into the Valmontone Gap to insure destruction of the German Army."[9]

When Truscott said he wanted to talk with Clark before abandoning BUF-FALO, Brann said that was impossible. The Army commander had left the beachhead and was out of reach of radio. There was no point arguing; the "Boss" had said attack to the northwest and that was an order. Truscott told his staff to prepare to implement the order.[10]

Later that afternoon, apparently disturbed that his protest might indicate an unwillingness to pursue the new course, Truscott called Brann and expressed enthusiasm for the new plan. "I feel very strongly that we should do this thing. We should do it tomorrow. May not be able to get it organized before noon. I have preparations going on . . ."[11] Yet despite that turnabout, Truscott actually believed Clark's decision to be basically wrong. He determined nevertheless to carry it out wholeheartedly, and he intended for his division commanders to do the same.[12]

[5] Interv, Mathews with Lt Col T. J. Conway, 27 Jun 50.

[6] Fifth Army G–3 Jnl, May 44; Clark Diary, 25 May 44.

[7] Truscott, *Command Missions*, pp. 374–75.

[8] VI Corps G–3 Jnl, 25–27 May 44, entry 251740B May 44.

[9] Truscott, *Command Missions*, pp. 375–76.

[10] *Ibid.*

[11] VI Corps G–3 Jnl, 25–27 May 44, entry 251740B.

[12] Interv, author with Truscott, Mar 62, CMH.

The test came shortly before midnight when Truscott met with his commanders in the VI Corps command post to tell them of the change. It was a gloomy gathering, for rumors of the change had already reached the divisions. Although Truscott presented the new plan with zeal, he failed to change the prevailing mood. Generals Harmon and O'Daniel were especially bitter, for they deemed they were on the threshold of success. The decision was unjustifiable, they argued, because their divisions would soon be astride Highway 6 and in possession of Valmontone from which they could make a rapid advance along the highway to Rome.[13]

Without minimizing the problems inherent in the change in direction, Truscott eloquently defended Clark's concept. The German *Tenth Army*'s retreat from the southern front and Kesselring's shift of reserves from the north, Truscott declared, had led Clark to believe that "in the Valmontone Gap the going will grow increasingly more difficult." Nor would cutting Highway 6 guarantee destruction of the *Tenth Army*, for the German troops could withdraw over alternate routes. Although Truscott conceded that Allied forces would eventually have to break through the defenses at Valmontone, he endorsed Clark's theory that an attack northwestward into the Alban Hills would enable the Fifth Army to outflank those defenses and open the road to Rome more quickly. "It is," Truscott said stoutly, "an idea with which I am heartily in accord."[14]

The VI Corps, General Truscott announced, was to attack the next day on a three-mile front with two divisions abreast, the 34th and the 45th, to occupy a general line between Campoleone and Lanuvio, respectively four and eight miles west of Velletri. Since the divisions were to attack on a relatively narrow front and in some depth, the attack would be powerful and capable of punching a hole in the last enemy defenses south of Rome.[15] (*Map VI*)

Those defenses, Truscott continued, were manned by Schlemm's *I Parachute Corps*—composed of the *4th Parachute*, the *65th Infantry*, and the *3d Panzer Grenadier Divisions*, significantly weakened, Truscott's G–2 had assured him, by shifts to reinforce the Cisterna and Valmontone sectors. Elements of the *334th Infantry Division* had also been identified, and an additional battalion of paratroopers could be expected; otherwise, between Velletri and Campoleone to the southwest there was only a "hodgepodge of units," much like those encountered when the corps had first landed at Anzio. Moreover, the *362d Division*, which had defended the Cisterna sector, was believed to be virtually destroyed, and the *715th Division* had been severely hurt.[16]

This latter estimate was reasonably accurate. Yet the analysts overlooked the fact that even though the *I Parachute Corps* lacked many tanks, assault guns, and antitank pieces, the corps' three divisions still represented a strong

---

[13] VI Corps Division Commanders' Meeting, 25 May 44.

[14] *Ibid.*; Interv, author with Gen Truscott, Mar 62, CMH.

[15] VI Corps Division Commanders' Meeting, 25 May 44.

[16] *Ibid.*

and as yet uncommitted force, well entrenched in the only completed portion of the Caesar Line.

Moreover, the situation labeled a "hodgepodge of units" prevailed not to the southwest of Velletri, but more nearly described that on the sector around Valmontone. Even as the U.S. VI Corps began to shift its main attack from the northeast to the northwest, General O'Daniel's reinforced 3d Division continued to push toward Valmontone and Highway 6. That development so disturbed Field Marshal Kesselring that he abandoned all plans for reinforcing the *Tenth Army*. Instead he began to send everything he could lay his hands on—a rocket launcher unit from the *334th Division*, an infantry regiment from the *90th Division*, and an antiaircraft artillery battery—toward Valmontone and Highway 6 to reinforce the *Fourteenth Army*'s left wing, and to cover the *Tenth Army*'s right flank.[17] Until division-sized reinforcements might arrive, these forces were indeed a hodgepodge of units, and through most of the 27th were all that stood between Truscott's VI Corps and it's original objective.

Buffalo Buried—Almost

By shifting the direction of the VI Corps offensive, Clark had of course altered Operation BUFFALO significantly, but he had not completely buried it.[18] A force sizable enough to justify Kesselring's concern continued in the direction of Highway 6 and Valmontone.

While General O'Daniel's 3d Division made up the bulk of this force, it also included Frederick's 1st Special Service Force, operating on the right flank, as well as Howze's armored task force on the left. Operation BUFFALO had been downgraded to a secondary operation, and, if the enemy could bring in sufficient force in time, might become essentially defensive rather than offensive.[19] To be sure, Clark planned eventually to augment O'Daniel's force with Keyes' II Corps after it had completed its task in the mountains to the south, but it was questionable whether this augmentation could be made in time to accomplish Operation BUFFALO's strategic objective.

Led by a battalion of the 15th Infantry, the 3d Division at first encountered little opposition. It was a mild May day and, since the enemy had seemingly vanished, the troops began to react to the balmy weather, so much that an irate division staff officer was prompted to upbraid his counterpart on the staff of the offending regiment. "Today your troops up there seem[ed] to be relaxing without helmets, arms . . . picking daisies, and enjoying the spring air. What do you think—that the war is over?"[20]

The vernal interlude was rudely shattered that afternoon when a flight of American fighter-bombers, mistaking the 3d Division's columns for fleeing enemy troops, attacked without warning. About five P-40's first bombed the columns, then returned to strafe the scattered infantrymen. As the planes disappeared in the distance, they left

---

[17] Greiner and Schramm, eds., *OKW/WFSt, KTB*, IV(1), pp. 493–94.

[18] See, Mathews, "The Drive on Rome," in *Command Decisions*, p. 360.

[19] *Ibid.*

[20] 3d Inf Div G-3 Jnl, 270300B May 44, Cobra 3 to Si3, 30th Inf.

behind over a hundred men killed or
wounded and a number of vehicles
destroyed, including several loaded with
ammunition.[21]

The tragic mistake was especially
costly to smaller units, such as the 10th
Field Artillery Battalion. Two battery
commanders were killed and a third
battery commander, the communications officer, the assistant S-2, and the
antitank officer wounded.[22] Even as the
units were caring for their casualties,
other Allied aircraft bombed Cori,
which had been in American hands
since early morning. It took engineers
five hours to clear a path through
rubble blocking the main road in the
town.[23]

The mistaken bombing prompted the
division commander, General O'Daniel,
to substitute the 7th Infantry for the
15th Infantry and to send the 30th
Infantry to cover the flanks. One battalion of the 30th Infantry moved northwestward from Giulianello to screen the
left and a second marched eastward
from Giulianello to screen the right.
Following a narrow twisting road toward the village of Rocca Massima, the
second battalion surprised and captured
the village's garrison, a German infantry company. Meanwhile, the 7th Infantry passed through the 15th and continued on toward Artena, where after
dark the regiment halted in hills southwest of the town.[24]

Screening the 3d Division's left flank,

Colonel Howze's task force advanced
that afternoon far beyond Giulianello,
and as darkness approached one tank
company came to a halt within 800
yards of Highway 6, not far from
Labico, a village about two miles northwest of Valmontone. When the tanks
approached the highway, enemy antitank fire destroyed three and forced
the remainder to fall back into cover.[25]

Despite the setback, General O'Daniel
was markedly encouraged by the progress on the 26th. That evening he
observed to the VI Corps commander,
"This area is very soft . . . . I'm convinced we could go into Rome, if we
had more stuff up here."[26] Truscott
shared O'Daniel's optimism and urged
him to occupy the Artena-Valmontone
area and cut the highway before daybreak. Willing to give O'Daniel an additional tank battalion to do the job,
Truscott reminded him, "Highway 6
must be . . . cut and the gap between
Artena and the Alban Hills must be
kept closed."[27]

In giving vent to such optimism and
ambition, neither O'Daniel nor Truscott
was affording sufficient weight to a
disturbing portent that had developed
in late afternoon as the 7th Infantry
approached Artena. The German
troops pushed back by the men of the
7th Infantry were from the reconnaissance battalion of the *Hermann Goering
Division*. General O'Daniel displayed a
more realistic interpretation of the im-
plication in that intelligence when in the
evening he told Colonel Howze to

[21] *Fifth Army History*, Part V, pp. 120–22; Taggert,
ed., *History of the Third Infantry Division in World War
II*, p. 173; 3d Div G–3 Jnl, 261955B May 44.
[22] 3d Div G–3 Jnl, 261955B May 44; 10th FA Bn
Opns Rpt, May 44.
[23] 10th FA Bn Opns Rpt, May 44.
[24] 3d Div G–3 Jnl, 26 May 44.

[25] Col Hamilton Howze, MS "The Rome Operation" (hereafter cited as Howze MS).
[26] VI Corps G–3 Jnl, 26–28 May 44.
[27] VI Corps G–3 Jnl; 263310B May 44.

withdraw his tank company near Highway 6 at Labico and tie the company in with the task force's main position along the railroad west of Artena.

Nevertheless, even if the presence of the enemy reconnaissance battalion did presage early commitment of the entire *Hermann Goering Division*, a chance still remained that the reinforced 3d Division might yet get to Valmontone ahead of the German reinforcements and, as Truscott had urged, close "the gap between Artena and the Alban Hills." If that could be accomplished, Operation BUFFALO's original goal might be partially achieved despite General Clark's decision to shift the VI Corps' main effort northward into the Alban Hills.

Presence of the enemy reconnaissance battalion did indeed indicate that Field Marshal Kesselring was planning to commit the *Hermann Goering Division* at Valmontone, although except for the reconnaissance battalion, he intended waiting until the entire division arrived before committing the rest of the division. Yet that would be difficult to do, for, hard hit by Allied aircraft en route, units of the division, often without much of their heavy equipment, trickled in. Alarmed at the pace of the American advance, the division commander, Generalmajor Wilhelm Schmalz, took it on his own to reinforce the reconnaissance battalion with the other units as they arrived.

When word of what was happening reached army group headquarters, Kesselring sent a sharply worded order to disengage the division immediately and hold it in an assembly area north of Valmontone. The order reached General Schmalz on the morning of the

27th. Convinced that if he followed the order the Americans would quickly cut Highway 6, General Schmalz ignored it. Kesselring, he believed, was unaware of the true situation and, once he understood it, would endorse Schmalz's decision.[28]

In the meantime, Kesselring apparently came to the same conclusion, for later in the morning he removed all restrictions on commitment of the *Hermann Goering Division*. The *Fourteenth Army* commander, General von Mackensen, then ordered Schmalz to counterattack at noon. Although Schmalz had issued such an order, he found American artillery fire so punishing and the ground over which the attack had to move so exposed that he later postponed the attack until 1930, hopeful that gathering darkness would enhance the chance of success. Unfortunately for Schmalz's plan notification of delay failed to reach all units.[29]

That development explains why the Germans launched a virtually suicidal counterattack that afternoon. Shortly after noon, Colonel Howze's outposts along the railroad west of Artena reported what seemed to be enemy infantry advancing through the wheat fields in full view of the American positions. Doubting that the Germans would actually be so foolhardy, the men in the outposts asked if they might possibly be Americans. "Hell, no, shoot them up!" Colonel Howze himself bellowed into the phone. Leaving his command post, the task force commander raced forward in his jeep "to get in on the

---

[28] MS # C–087b (Schmalz and Bergengruen), *Einsatz der Division Hermann Goering in Italien*, 26 Mai–5 Juin 44, CMH.
[29] *Ibid.*

show." When he reached his front line, Howze could scarcely believe his eyes, ". . . the jerries walking and crawling through the wheat on the hillsides only 1,500 yards away." Here was the long-expected *Hermann Goering Division* "coming in to face us." Howze's tanks opened fire with devastating results. Gazing out over the carnage, Howze mused, "Why over the hills in daylight? . . . another mystery."[30]

The remainder of the *Hermann Goering Division* attacked at 1930, striking hard at Task Force Howze's left flank. Slipping through a wooded area on the left and firing from the shelter of the trees, a German self-propelled gun destroyed two of Howze's tanks. At the same time, accurate artillery fire hit the American positions, falling primarily on men of the 1st Battalion, 6th Armored Infantry, and perilously close to Howze's command post. Even as the infantrymen sought cover, a "terrific pounding of 155's"—short rounds from their own supporting guns—hit their positions. As if to compound the confusion, a group of 160 replacements arrived just as the bombardment began. Bewildered and frightened, the men flung themselves to the ground; over half of them were killed or wounded. The infantry battalion commander and all three of his artillery observers exposed themselves selflessly at the radio transmitter in futile efforts to halt the American fire, but they were killed during the barrage. Taking advantage of the artillery fire and confusion among the Americans, Schmalz's troops penetrated the 6th Armored Infantry's

lines, but the surviving infantry halted them short of a breakthrough.

Under the circumstances, Colonel Howze decided to refuse his embattled left by withdrawing the company holding the flank. After night came the company pulled back about 1,500 yards, while the supporting artillery—the U.S. 91st Armored Field Artillery Battalion and the British 24th Royal Artillery Field Regiment—hurled salvo after salvo beyond the lines. In the face of that fire, the Germans desisted. Early the following morning Howze sent his infantry back into the abandoned positions.

In the meantime, the 15th Infantry early on the 27th had again taken the lead in the attack on Artena. Although the regiment entered the town by 0900, the men were unable to clear the last resistance until late afternoon, about three hours before the German strike against Task Force Howze. The surviving Germans in Artena withdrew a mile north to the Artena railroad station where they hastily constructed field fortifications blocking the way to Valmontone—only a tempting mile and a half away.[31]

Although the *Hermann Goering Division*'s counterattack had failed to hold the ground gained on the 27th, and the Americans had taken Artena, the Germans had thrown O'Daniel's force sufficiently off balance to force a postponement of the drive toward Valmontone and Highway 6. Relieving Task Force Howze, the 7th Infantry attacked through the day of the 28th—advancing over the same grain fields through which the Germans had attacked on the

---

[30] Howze MS. Unless otherwise cited, the following is based upon this source.

[31] VI Corps G–3 Jnl, 270900 and 271610 May 44.

27th—but gained only a few hundred yards before coming to a halt in the face of heavy enemy fire.[32]

Late on the 28th the 1st Battalion, 6th Armored Infantry, followed the next day by the 91st Armored Field Artillery, withdrew from the task force and returned to the 1st Armored Division, then preparing to join the drive on Rome through the Alban Hills. The remainder of Howze's task force then reverted to 3d Division reserve. By noon on the 29th General O'Daniel's troops held a line across the Valmontone corridor from the northeastern corner of the Alban Hills east to the Lepini Mountains. The right was held by General Frederick's 1st Special Service Force, the center of the line by the 7th, and the left by the 30th Infantry, with the 15th Infantry in reserve. The 91st Cavalry Reconnaissance Squadron had moved up on the right to patrol the hills between the 1st Special Service Force and the FEC, advancing through the Lepini Mountains toward Colleferro, some five miles east of Artena.[33]

At this point General Clark decided to halt the drive toward Valmontone briefly until General O'Daniel's troops could be reinforced, for, in his words, "Valmontone and the high ground to the north and to the west is so strongly held and in the enemy's main defense position that to send one division to the north alone would meet with disaster."[34] General Clark gave yet another reason for his decision. The thrust toward Valmontone had exposed the VI Corps' right flank, and an enemy division—the *715th*—was facing it. As it turned out that decision, in reality, constituted no threat, for its remnants were even then desperately attempting to escape northward before being trapped between the Americans and the French.

In General Juin's corps, operating on the Fifth Army's right flank across the northwestern slopes of the Lepini Mountains, Clark had a strong force which, if used boldly, might be able to cut the enemy's LOC—Highway 6— several miles east of Valmontone. Recognizing this opportunity, and faced with the very real prospect of being pinched out of line by the U.S. VI Corps and the Eighth Army, Juin proposed on 28 May that his corps debouch from the mountains into the Sacco valley. Thus would the French outflank the enemy east of Valmontone then drive toward Tivoli in the Sabine Hills east of Rome. Alexander, unlike Clark, did not favor such a maneuver, and forbade the French to cross the Sacco River.[35]

General Alexander objected mainly because he wanted to keep Highway 6 clear for the approaching Canadian Corps on the Eighth Army's left wing. Yet the Canadians, after taking Ceprano on the 27th and on the following day pushing on to the outskirts of Arce some forty miles southeast of Valmontone, would not reach Frosinone until the 31st. Meanwhile Juin sent his corps over the northern and northwestern

[32] Taggert, ed., *History of the Third Infantry Division in World War II*, pp. 175–76.

[33] Fifth Army G–3 Jnl, 27–28 May 44; Msg, Brann to Gruenther, 28 May 44; *Fifth Army History*, Part V, pp. 121–22.

[34] Clark Diary, 30 May 44.

[35] Pierre Le Goyet, *La Participation Française à la Campagne d'Italie, 1943–44* (Paris: Imprimerie Nationale, 1969), pp. 124–25; Juin, *La Campagne d'Italie*, pp. 132–35.

slopes of the Lepini Mountains toward a junction with the U.S. VI Corps near Artena. The 4th Moroccan Mountain Division then relieved the U.S. 88th Infantry Division on a sector extending westward to Sezze. Alexander's concern for keeping Highway 6 free for Leese's army was obviously overly sanguine, for it was evident to both Clark and Juin that it would be some time before the Eighth Army drew abreast.[36]

Yet reinforcement of the diluted drive on Valmontone was destined to come from another quarter. On 25 May General Keyes' II Corps had made contact with the VI Corps near Sezze about twelve miles southeast of Cisterna. As for the FEC, denied permission to strike out directly for Ferentino and Highway 6, it would continue in a northeasterly direction through the Lepini Mountains along the axis of the Carpineto Romano–Colle Ferro road which connects with Highway 6 five miles east of Valmontone. Once the French had reached that point Clark hoped to persuade Alexander to shift the interarmy boundary northward to allow Juin and his corps to cover the Fifth Army's right flank north of the highway as that army's II Corps advanced toward Rome along Highway 6 west of Valmontone.[37]

Meanwhile, back in London, Prime Minister Churchill, whose strategic concepts bore most heavily upon the unfolding campaign in Italy, fretted over the daily situation maps in the Cabinet War Room. As he saw it, unless the Americans soon captured Valmontone and cut Highway 6, the *Tenth Army*

might elude the trap the Anzio offensive had been designed to spring. Whether that strategic grand design rested upon military realities or upon ministerial fancy, Churchill cabled Alexander on 28 May urging him to move sufficient armor "up to the northernmost spearhead directed against the Valmontone-Frosinone road [Highway 6]. . . " To that Churchill added: "a cop [in the English school boy slang, to capture or nab a ball as in cricket] is much more important than Rome . . . the cop is the one thing that matters."[38] Later the same day the Prime Minister expressed his growing concern in yet another cable, which said in part: ". . . the glory of this battle . . . will be measured, not by the capture of Rome or the junction with the bridgehead [Anzio beachhead], but by the number of German divisions cut off. I am sure," the British leader reminded his commander in Italy, "that you will have revolved all this in your mind, and perhaps have already acted in this way. Nevertheless, I feel that I ought to tell you that it is the cop that counts."[39]

Alexander sought, apparently in vain, to put his Prime Minister's mind at ease, but Clark's earlier decision to divert the bulk of Truscott's VI Corps to the northwest had already taken the matter out of Alexander's (and Churchill's) hands. Years later Churchill would observe: ". . . the *Hermann Goering Division* . . . got to Valmontone first. The single American division sent by General Clark was stopped short of it

---

[36] *Ibid.*

[37] Clark Diary, 26 and 28 May 44; Clark, *Calculated Risk*, pp. 356–61.

[38] Winston S. Churchill, "The Second World War" series, *Closing the Ring* (Boston: Houghton Mifflin Company, 1951), p. 607.

[39] *Ibid.*

and the escape road [Highway 6] remained open. That was very unfortunate."[40]

"The most direct route to Rome"

In line with the shift of emphasis away from Valmontone toward Rome, General Truscott had planned to implement Clark's order by attacking with Ryder's 34th and Eagles' 45th Divisions on a three-mile front southwest of Velletri, to the Campoleone station. On the left, Eagles' division was to advance toward the railroad station, while Ryder's division on the right approached Lanuvio. Harmon's 1st Armored Division was to maintain pressure against Velletri until relieved by Walker's 36th Division, then in corps reserve. Instead of relieving the 3d Division north of Cisterna, as originally planned, the 36th Division was to replace the armor so as to free it for exploitation of any enemy soft spots uncovered between Lanuvio and the Campoleone station.

Throughout the night of 25 May American infantrymen moved by truck or on foot over the roads southwest of Cisterna into assembly areas in preparation for the offensive. "Considering the congested area and restricted road net," the corps commander later observed, "a more complicated plan would be difficult to conceive." When it became apparent early on the 26th that the units would be unable to reach their lines of departure before daylight, General Truscott delayed the attack an hour, until 1000, then another hour to 1100.[41]

During the morning army headquarters confirmed General Clark's oral orders of the previous day. The reason given was that "the overwhelming success of the current battle makes it possible to continue Operation BUF-FALO with powerful forces and to launch a new attack along the most direct route to Rome."[42]

Soon afterward, General Alexander visited the Fifth Army rear headquarters where General Gruenther, Clark's chief of staff, briefly explained the new plan. Alexander agreed that it seemed to be a good one. He also inquired whether Clark intended to continue his drive toward Valmontone. Gruenther assured him that Clark "had the situation thoroughly in mind, and that he could depend upon [Clark] to execute a vigorous plan with all the push in the world."[43]

Whether Alexander was satisfied with the answer or whether he chose, in view of the limitations peculiar to this multinational command, to accept it with his usual good grace made little difference, for he had been presented with a *fait accompli*. The bulk of the U.S. VI Corps had already launched a new offensive across the southern slopes of the Alban Hills—in General Clark's words, "the gateway to Rome."

While the two British divisions demonstrated west of the Anzio-Albano road in order to hold the Germans on that front, and the 1st Armored Division increased its pressure against Velletri, 228 guns began a 30-minute preparatory barrage at 1030, and the 34th and 45th Divisions prepared to jump

[40] *Ibid.*
[41] Truscott, *Command Missions*, pp. 375–76; VI Corps G–3 Jnl, 25–27 May 44.

[42] Fifth Army OI 24, 26 May 44.
[43] Clark, *Calculated Risk*, pp. 357–58.

off. [44] Attacking at 1100 with two regiments abreast through rolling wheatfields east of Aprilia, a road junction ten miles north of Anzio, the 45th Division encountered flanking automatic weapons fire from the direction of Aprilia, which lay in the British sector. For two hours the fire pinned down the troops, until a company of tanks came forward to silence the enemy guns. By nightfall the division had advanced a mile and a half and had netted some 170 enemy prisoners, including a battalion commander and three members of his staff. The day's action cost the 45th Division a total of 225 casualties, of whom 2 were killed, 203 wounded, and 20 missing. [45]

On the right the 34th Division advanced along the axis of the old Via Appia until its troops too were stopped by heavy machine gun fire. Supporting artillery fire eventually silenced the enemy guns, so that at the end of the day, the 34th Division was also about a mile and a half beyond its line of departure. The division paid for that modest success with a total of 118 casualties, of which 21 were killed and 94 wounded. [46]

Both divisions were within two miles of their respective objectives, the Campoleone railroad station and Lanuvio,

yet co-ordination between the two units had left much to be desired. Unfamiliar terrain and a virtually sleepless night of rapid marches from one sector to another help to explain it. Because of the lack of co-ordination, a wide gap had opened along the Cisterna-Campoleone-Rome railroad, the interdivision boundary. In spite of efforts of reconnaissance companies from both divisions to close the gap, scattered and bypassed enemy detachments continued to harass the inner flanks of the divisions for the next two days.

The next morning both divisions renewed their efforts; but unknown to the Americans, the enemy had withdrawn during the night behind a screen of automatic weapons, backed by roving tanks and self-propelled guns. At 0615, behind a 15-minute artillery preparation, the 45th Division attacked with two regiments forward. Not until early afternoon did any significant resistance develop. This came from a covey of German tanks located in a small woods beyond the Spaccasassi Canal, a southward-flowing drainage canal a thousand yards west of Carano. Armor supporting the attack quickly came forward, crossed the creek, and forced the Germans to withdraw. As darkness fell, the infantry joined the tanks and dug in for the night beyond the creek.

The 34th Division also attacked on a two-regiment front. All went well until enemy guns located along a low ridge, extending from the Presciano Canal in

---

[44] Stone buildings concealing enemy guns and command installations were targets for the 240-mm. howitzers and 155-mm. guns. Even four battalions of 90-mm. antiaircraft guns opened fire against terrestrial targets. See *Fifth Army History*, Part V, p. 123.

[45] 45th Div Opns Rpt, May 44; *Fifth Army History*, Part V, pp. 123-24; 45th Div G-3 Jnl, 262250B and 270350B May 44; Analysis of Battle Casualty Reports, U.S. Fifth Army, June 45.

[46] Although the artillery had played the primary role in destroying the enemy guns, the action of 1st Lt Beryl R. Newman (133d Infantry), who single-

handedly silenced three enemy machine guns, killed 2 enemy, wounded 2, and took 11 prisoners, had much to do with it. For this Lieutenant Newman received the Medal of Honor. See 34th Div Rpt of Opns, May 44, and U.S. Fifth Army Battle Casualty Rpts, Jun 45.

the west to the Prefetti Canal in the east, broke up the assault. No sooner had the attack failed than the Germans launched a tank-supported counterattack. After beating back the enemy force, the Americans settled down for the night at the foot of the ridge.

After two days of fighting, the main body of the VI Corps still was almost two miles short of Campoleone railroad station and the town of Lanuvio, the immediate objectives. Yet in spite of the slow progress, Truscott still believed the enemy front to be weakly held and alerted General Harmon to assemble his armor for an attack through the 45th Division's lines on the 29th. Walker's 36th Division had already relieved the armored division south of Velletri.

Truscott Commits His Armor

During the night of 28 May General Harmon assembled his armored division behind the VI Corps' left wing to exploit what appeared to the corps commander to be a potentially soft spot in the enemy's defenses opposite the 45th Division. The terrain there seemed to be favorable for the use of armor. To give Harmon a more extensive road net, Truscott, after co-ordinating with Fifth Army headquarters, shifted the corps' boundary slightly to the left into the British sector. At the same time, General Ryder's 34th Division, now screened on its right by the 36th Division, was to try once more to break through at Lanuvio, while General Eagles' 45th Division was to regroup and follow in the wake of Harmon's armor. That night General Eagles sent the 179th Infantry into the line east of the Albano road to screen the armored

division's preparations, and General Ryder prepared to launch the 135th Infantry, less one battalion, in a renewed attack against Lanuvio in the morning.

Before dawn on the 29th the 1st Armored Division moved to a line of departure about 1,200 yards south of Campoleone station, and at 1530 the division attacked. On its left was CCB, supported by the 180th Infantry, and on the right, CCA, supported by the 3d Battalion, 6th Armored Infantry. Offshore a French cruiser lent additional support, its guns firing at targets in the vicinity of Albano. To a staff officer of the 180th Infantry observing Harmon's armored units as they rolled forward, the attack "looked like a corps review."[47]

During the morning the armored units advanced easily against light resistance. CCB quickly cleared a rear guard from the Campoleone station and then continued northward along the sides of several scrub-covered gullies. After crossing the Albano road, CCA also wheeled northward. Early that afternoon, as the armor approached the outpost positions of the Caesar Line, opposition increased sharply. Heavy fire from enemy armor and artillery smashed against CCA's front and right flank, while at close range small detachments of enemy infantry armed with *Panzerfausts* harassed the American tanks. The tanks, nevertheless, continued to advance, too far in fact, for they bypassed many strongpoints that held up the infantry. That happened, for example, when men of the 180th Infantry tried to follow CCB's tanks into Campoleone station; enemy automatic

---

[47] 45th Div G-3 Jnl, 291030B May 44; VI Corps G-3 Jnl, 290920B May 44.

TANKS OF 1ST ARMORED DIVISION ASSEMBLING FOR ATTACK NEAR LANUVIO

weapons and artillery fire halted the accompanying foot soldiers.[48] In CCA's zone a tank-supported counterattack stopped the 2d Battalion, 6th Armored Infantry, and forced the battalion to fall back almost two miles, to a line a mile north of Campoleone station, there to hold for the night. Thus the enemy broke up the close partnership between infantry and armor that was vital in operations of this kind.

The capture of the station seemed to be all that Harmon's armored division had to show for its efforts on the 29th, which cost the division 133 casualties: 21 killed, 107 wounded, and 5 missing. In addition, enemy antitank fire destroyed 21 M-4 and 16 M-5 tanks. Unlike tanks damaged earlier by mines west of Cisterna, those hit by enemy guns and *Panzerfausts* were generally a total loss.[49]

The German Situation

In reality, the 1st Armored Division had accomplished more than was sug-

---

[48] 1st Armd Div AAR, May 44; 180th Inf Opns Rpt, May 44.

[49] 6th Armd Inf AAR, May 44; Fifth Army Battle Casualties, 10 Jun 45.

gested by the numerous burned-out hulks north of the Campoleone station. The attack had actually penetrated the *65th Division*'s center northeast of the railroad to a depth of almost two miles on a 1,500-yard front. Early that afternoon Mackensen had informed Kesselring that the division was in a precarious situation. Casualties were severe—over 400 killed and 150 taken prisoner—and there remained only six assault guns, a Tiger tank, and a few heavy antitank guns with which to repel further attacks by an entire U.S. armored division. All that Kesselring could do to help was to attach the remaining antiaircraft artillery from army group reserve to the *I Parachute Corps*. That reserve amounted to about fourteen batteries, all of which were to concentrate solely on antitank fire. At the same time, the army group commander ordered all available engineers to lay antitank mine fields in the path of the American armor.[50]

Meanwhile, Mackensen had begun to round up additional antitank weapons, ordering the *334th Division* to send its antitank guns to the *I Parachute Corps* sector at once. Mackensen also transferred to the corps the assault battalion of the army group weapons school as well as some antitank weapons from the *92d Division*, still in army group reserve. Yet few of these reinforcements managed to arrive on the 29th. Until they did the *65th Division* had to rely for support upon a battalion of the *11th Parachute Regiment*, backed up by several 88-mm. antiaircraft guns.[51]

In spite of directives from both OKW and Field Marshal Kesselring to the

effect that the Caesar Line had to be held at all costs, and not sharing *Army Group C*'s belief that Valmontone remained the focus of the U.S. Fifth Army's efforts, Mackensen had quietly directed the *I Parachute Corps* to reconnoiter a switch position just southeast of the Tiber. The reconnaissance was not, however, to include the city of Rome, for Mackensen hoped eventually to use Rome as a screen behind which his forces might retire to the north.[52]

Although the presence of three U.S. divisions in the attack against the *Fourteenth Army*'s right wing west of Velletri since noon on the 26th was known to Field Marshal Kesselring, only on the 28th did he begin to have misgivings that the American thrust toward Valmontone was the main effort and the attack toward the Alban Hills no more than a feint. The next day intercepted radio messages and front line reports identified the U.S. 1st Armored Division on the Albano-Lanuvio front. Only then did Kesselring conclude that the offensive toward Valmontone had become a secondary effort.[53]

Infantry Against Lanuvio

The new direction taken by the VI Corps' offensive had come as no surprise to General von Mackensen, the *Fourteenth Army* commander, for he had always assumed that the forces in the Anzio beachhead would eventually

---

[50] MS # R–50 (Bailey).

[51] *Ibid.*

[52] *Befehl, OB AOK 14, Ia Nr. 2164/44 g. Kdos,* 28 May 44, in *AOK 14, Ia KTB Nr. 3, Anl. 742a,* 1–31 May 44, *AOK 14, Doc. Nr. 5909/3.*

[53] *Ibid.; AOK 14, G–2 Rpt, Ic Nr. 1002/44 geh. Kdos,* 28 May 44, in *AOK 14 IC Rpts,* 1 Apr–30 Jun 44, *AOK 14 Doc. Nr. 5902/2; AOK 14, G–2 Rpt, Ic Nr. 2357/44,* 29 May 44, in *AOK 14, Ic Morgen-u. Tagesmeldungen,* 1 Apr–30 Jun 44, *AOK 14 Doc. Nr. 59092/4.*

move in that direction. He had accordingly arranged his defense to the detriment of the Cisterna sector of his front but to the advantage of the Caesar Line against which General Truscott's forces were now moving.[54]

Although unfinished, the Caesar Line could cause an attacking force some trouble. Behind it numerous self-propelled guns ranged the roads, firing repeated volleys before moving to escape the inevitable counterbattery fires. South of Lanuvio and opposite the 34th Division were two particularly challenging enemy strongpoints, San Gennaro Hill and Villa Crocetta, on the crest of Hill 209. Before them was a series of fire trenches five to six feet deep with machine guns and mortars covering every route of approach. Barbed wire fronted the trenches. Even to draw within striking distance of these formidable obstacles the American infantrymen would first have to cross open wheat fields, then attack up steep slopes in the face of heavy fire.[55]

On the morning of the 29th the 34th Division's 168th Infantry prepared to assault those positions. At dawn, behind a 30-minute artillery barrage directed mainly at the fire trenches and wire, the 1st and 2d battalions attacked, the former passing through the 3d Battalion, which was to remain in reserve. Two hours later Ryder observed that the assault had gone "pretty well on the left, slow on the right."[56]

What had held up the right were three enemy tanks and a self-propelled gun on San Gennaro Hill. Fire from those weapons halted an attack from

the southeast by the 2d Battalion's Company E, but the battalion's other two companies, unaware that Company E was pinned down, continued to struggle up the western slope of the objective. Reaching the railroad (the Velletri-Rome line) that crosses the forward slopes of Hill 209 and San Gennaro Hill, Company F turned eastward and, taking advantage of the shelter afforded by the railroad embankment, soon gained the crest of San Gennaro Hill. To the west and somewhat behind Company F, Company G moved cautiously along a dirt road just south of the railroad.[57]

Both companies at that point had dangerously exposed flanks. At 1445 some men from Company F straggled into Company G's area, saying that they had been driven from the San Gennaro Hill by a counterattack coming from vineyards on the eastern slope. At the same time, enemy fire from the rear began to hit Company G. The men nevertheless hurried forward to reinforce their companions on San Gennaro Hill. Sprinting through a hail of hand grenades and bursts of small arms fire, the men of Company G soon gained the crest, but before they could dig in properly on the exposed hilltop, heavy enemy mortar fire forced both Companies F and G to withdraw. The survivors of the two companies fought their way back down the hill through groups of infiltrating enemy soldiers. Shortly before dark the exhausted infantrymen reached the same gully in which they had spent the previous night. There they met the first arrivals

[54] MS # R–50 (Bailey).
[55] *Fifth Army History*, Part V, p. 127.
[56] VI Corps G–3 Jnl, 290820B May 44.

[57] VI Corps G–3 Jnl, 28–29 May 44; *Fifth Army History*, Part V, pp. 127–28.

of the 3d Battalion, coming to relieve them. Because the men were tired and the hour late, the battalion commanders decided not to attempt to retake the hill that night.[58]

Meanwhile, on the left of the regimental sector, the 1st Battalion had attacked the enemy defending the Villa Crocetta, about 1,200 yards southwest of San Gennaro Hill. Crawling through the grainfields on the forward slopes of Hills 203 and 216, the Americans reached a shallow ravine a few hundred yards southeast of the villa. When the men left the ravine to make the final assault, enemy machine gun and mortar fire drove them back and held them there. Prevented by enemy fire from either continuing the assault or withdrawing from the ravine, the troops had to wait until three tanks and four tank destroyers came forward to screen their withdrawal into a new assembly area, where they prepared to renew their assault that afternoon.[59]

Shortly before the attack on Villa Crocetta was to resume, General Truscott phoned the 34th Division command post to express his impatience with the delay in taking the division's objectives—San Gennaro Hill and the Villa Crocetta: General Ryder was forward with one of his regiments. When Ryder returned, the corps commander told a division staff officer, "tell him to crack this Lanuvio. It's holding up the whole thing."[60]

In resuming the attack early that afternoon, the 1st Battalion, 168th Infantry, was to try to envelop Villa Crocetta with tank-supported infantry. Before Companies A and C began a frontal assault, Company B with accompanying tanks was to swing left of the Villa Crocetta as far as Hill 203 before turning right to envelop the objective from the west. The appearance of the supporting armor on Hill 209 directly behind Villa Crocetta was to be the signal for Companies A and C to begin their attack from the southeast.[61]

The enveloping company moved out as planned and quickly secured Hill 203. Leaving a contingent of six men there, the company, still accompanied by tanks, moved down a slope on the right, crossed a shallow gully, and rather than envelop Villa Crocetta by taking Hill 209, actually overran the villa, forcing the enemy to flee.[62]

Unknown to General Ryder, the penetration at Villa Crocetta and the earlier abortive thrust on San Gennaro Hill had hit the Germans at a critical point, along the boundary between the *3d Panzer Grenadier* and the *362d Infantry Divisions*. Unless quickly contained, the thrusts might develop into a breakthrough of the Caesar Line southeast of Lanuvio. To forestall such a blow, Schlemm, the *I Parachute Corps* commander, ordered the *3d Panzer Grenadier Division*, the stronger of the two German units, to counterattack both American forces, the one which had taken Villa Crocetta and the one which had taken San Gennaro Hill but which, apparently without German awareness, it had abandoned in the face of heavy mortar fire.[63]

---

[58] *Ibid.*
[59] VI Corps G–3 Jnl, 290900B May 44; *Fifth Army History*, Part V, p. 128.
[60] VI Corps G–3 Jnl, 291205B May 44.

[61] *Fifth Army History*, Part V, p. 128.
[62] *Ibid.*, p. 129.
[63] MS # R–50 (Bailey).

Spearheaded by a rifle company, supported by four self-propelled guns, the counterattack overwhelmed the six men on Hill 203 and carried the Germans to a point from which they could fire on the rear of Company B at Villa Crocetta. Concerned lest they be cut off, the men of Company B withdrew to the original line of departure at the base of the hill. Having failed to observe the tanks, either at Villa Crocetta or on the original objective of Hill 209, Companies A and C had not begun their scheduled frontal attack on the villa. By nightfall the 168th Infantry's 1st Battalion was back to where the men had started from that morning. As if to add a final full measure to a day filled with frustration and disappointment, Anzio Annie, as the troops had nicknamed the German 280-mm. guns that for long had harassed the beachhead, fired sixteen harassing rounds before retiring. Meanwhile the two-division British force, its left flank resting on the coast, had followed up the German withdrawal and had kept abreast of the 45th and 1st Armored Divisions on the right but had exerted little pressure on the enemy.[64]

On the German side, General von Mackensen was pleased with the *I Parachute Corps'* defense; early that evening he notified Kesselring that Schlemm's counterattacks had eliminated both American penetrations, and that the Caesar Line remained firmly in Ger-

man hands. The local German commanders attributed their success in part to a delay on the part of the Americans in occupying and securing captured firing trenches and a failure to hold reserves in close supporting positions.[65]

In spite of the American setbacks between Campoleone and Lanuvio the VI Corps had made some gains from the 26th through the 29th. Yet in almost every case, the gains had been largely the result of voluntary German withdrawals. As Allied pressure mounted, the *I Parachute Corps*, pivoting on Velletri, had swung slowly back like a great gate toward high ground and the prepared positions of the Caesar Line. It appeared to Truscott at this point that the gate had been slammed shut against the Alban Hills. As night fell on the 29th the VI Corps' attempt to break through the Caesar Line on the most direct route to Rome seemed halted at every point.

The 1st Armored Division's Attack Reinforced

In spite of three days of frustrations General Truscott still counted on the fire power of General Harmon's armored division to blast open that gate. But to do it both men agreed that the 1st Armored Division had to have more infantry support. CCB was therefore reinforced with the 1st Battalion, 6th Armored Infantry, and CCA with the 2d Battalion, 135th Infantry. CCA also received the tanks of the 1st Armored Regiment's 2d Battalion.[66] Thus rein-

---

[64] *Fifth Army History*, Part V, p. 129; MS # R–50 (Bailey). The action on the 29th was highlighted by the example and sacrifice of Capt. William Wylie Galt (168th Infantry) who personally killed forty of the enemy before falling mortally wounded over the machine gun he had manned atop an armored tank destroyer. He was awarded the Medal of Honor posthumously.

[65] MS # R–50 (Bailey).

[66] 1st Armd Div AAR, May 44; Fifth Army G–3 Jnl, The Advance on Rome. Unless otherwise cited the following section is based upon these references.

forced, the armored division returned to the attack at 0630 on the 30th. Yet it soon became evident that the enemy had also taken advantage of the lull to garner strength, so much so that the reinforcing units even had to fight their way forward to join the armored units they were to support. The morning's operations again produced only negligible gains.

Harmon tried again in mid-afternoon with an artillery preparation followed by attacks by both combat commands. In CCA's sector well-sited enemy anti-tank guns and self-propelled artillery fired on every tank that moved. Under cover of this fire enemy infantry armed with *Panzerfausts* again slipped in to destroy several tanks. Beyond the Campoleone station, CCB's tanks and their supporting infantry managed to stay together and advance as far as the Campoleone Canal (Fosso di Campoleone), a little over a mile away, but they could go no farther. Again the armor had achieved no breakthrough, and the division's casualties the second day were even heavier than on the first—28 killed, 167 wounded, 16 missing. Equipment losses were less but still heavy: 23 tanks destroyed and several others damaged.

On the right of the armored division General Ryder's 34th Division also resumed its efforts on the 30th to break the Caesar Line in the vicinity of Lanuvio. Once again the infantry followed a heavy artillery preparation up the San Gennaro Ridge toward the battered Villa Crocetta. This time two of the six supporting tank destroyers reached the crest of Hill 209 behind the villa, but enemy fire destroyed one and the other, after almost overrunning an en-

emy fire trench, withdrew amid a shower of hand grenades. The infantry briefly gained Hill 203 just below the Villa Crocetta only to be forced back by heavy mortar and machine gun fire.[67]

The only gains made on the 30th were by the British as they crossed the Moletta River, on the far left flank. After repulsing a brief counterattack, they occupied Ardea, a road junction about two miles beyond the river. Yet again this advance was a result of German withdrawal into the Caesar Line.

By nightfall on 30 May there emerged from the intricate patterns of blue and red lines and unit symbols on the situation maps of every commander from corps to company one grim fact: General von Mackensen had succeeded in slamming shut the gate on the VI Corps' drive to Rome over the southwestern flanks of the Alban Hills. Clark himself telephoned Truscott and his commanders to express his keen disappointment with their efforts.[68]

Yet the total Fifth Army situation was less bleak than it appeared on the VI Corps front. For the past five days the U.S. II Corps and the French Expeditionary Corps, opposed only by the rear guards of the *XIV Panzer Corps*, had been moving through the Lepini Mountains toward the Valmontone corridor. By nightfall on the 30th the 85th Division had reached the former Anzio beachhead area, and the 88th Division, at this point under control of the IV Corps, had reached Sezze, about thirteen miles southeast of Cisterna. Two days before, at General Clark's direction

---

[67] 34th Div G-3, Jnl, May 44; VI Corps G-3 Jnl, 28–30 May 44.
[68] Clark Diary, 30 May 44.

General Keyes, the II Corps commander, had turned control of his
corps zone and the 88th Division over
to General Crittenberger's IV Corps for
mopping up operations in the Lepini
Mountains and, by early afternoon on
the 29th, had assumed command of
General O'Daniel's reinforced 3d Infantry Division in the vicinity of Artena.
For the next three days the 88th Division mopped up scattered enemy units
in the southwestern half of the Lepini
Mountains while awaiting relief by elements of the FEC. Meanwhile, since the
25th, the French had been advancing
along two axes: the 4th Moroccan
Mountain Division up the Amaseno-
Carpineto road to clear the northeastern half of the Lepini Mountains, and
the 2d Moroccan Infantry Division
south of the Sacco River. By the 30th
both columns were headed toward Colleferro, a junction with the American
forces, and relief of the U.S. IV Corps
in the Lepini Mountains.[69]

Under those circumstances General
Clark had grounds for believing that
"one or two more days of all-out attack"
in the Lanuvio-Campoleone sector,
combined with a new operation being
planned by the 36th Division northeast
of Velletri, "might crack the whole
German position in the Alban Hills
area . . . . If I don't crack this position in three or four days," Clark
observed, "I may have to reorganize,
wait for the 8th Army and go at it with
a coordinated attack by both armies . . . ."[70] To the Fifth Army
commander that was an unacceptable
alternative.

It was hardly a likely alternative in
any case, for the Eighth Army's 1st
Canadian Corps, after clearing Ceprano
on the 27th, had been experiencing
considerable difficulty in advancing astride Highway 6 toward the road junction of Frosinone, some ten miles to the
northwest. One thousand yards south
of Ceprano a 120-foot bridge had collapsed on the 28th just as the engineers
were about to declare it operational.
For the next twenty-four hours the 5th
Canadian Armoured Division, assembled along the highway to exploit Ceprano's fall, waited idly while the engineers hurriedly constructed a new
bridge across the upper Liri. On the
30th the armored division finally
crossed the river and resumed the
advance. As the tanks moved beyond
Ceprano, the terrain became increasingly hilly, and ahead lay several tributaries of the Sacco, each a formidable
obstacle to armor. The Germans had
destroyed every bridge over the river
and covered each crossing site with
artillery and mines. Under those circumstances, Lt. Gen. E.L.M. Burns, the
Canadian corps commander, brought
forward the Canadian 1st Infantry Division to lead the way. By the evening of
the 30th the forward elements of the
Canadian infantry were within sight of
Frosinone, yet still about twenty-five
miles southeast of Valmontone.[71]

To the Canadian right a strong rear
guard held up the British 13 Corps' 6th
Armoured and 78th Infantry Divisions
south of Arce, on the 27th, but on the
28th the impasse was broken when the
8th Indian Division made a wide flank-

---

[69] *Fifth Army History*, Part V, pp. 134–37.
[70] Clark Diary, 30 May 44.

[71] Operations of British, Indian, and Dominion
Forces in Italy, Part II, Sec. B; Nicholson, *The
Canadians in Italy*, pp. 439–46.

ing maneuver through the mountains north and northeast of Arce and that night forced the Germans to yield their strong defensive positions. The next day the Indians occupied Arce without opposition and began a cautious advance along Highway 82 toward Sora. Enemy artillery, demolitions, and a narrow, winding mountain road would all combine to slow down the Indians for the next few days. Meanwhile, the British 78th Division turned to the northwest and advanced north of and parallel to Highway 6 to cover and eventually pull abreast of the right flank of the Canadian corps as the Canadians led the Eighth Army toward Frosinone.[72]

---

[72] Nicholson, *The Canadians in Italy*, pp. 439–46.

CHAPTER X

Breaking the Stalemate

The operation being planned by the 36th Division and which bolstered General Clark's confidence that the Caesar Line would soon be broken was triggered by a startling discovery during the night of 27 May. Reconnaissance patrols from the 36th Division, probing the dark slopes of Monte Artemisio, a four-mile-long ridge running from northeast to southwest and overlooking Velletri from about a mile to the north, had found no sign of the enemy. Had they stumbled upon an undefended gap in the Caesar Line?

There was indeed a gap. It lay along the boundary between the *I Parachute* and the *LXXVI Panzer Corps*. It was attributable to two developments: holding the left flank of the parachute corps, the *362d Division* was responsible for the Velletri sector, but severe losses in the defense of Cisterna had left it few troops for defense of Monte Artemisio. Also the *Hermann Goering Division*, on the right flank of the adjacent panzer corps, had been drawn to the southwest in the direction of Valmontone by the American thrust toward Highway 6, so that contact between the *362d* and the *Hermann Goering Divisions* had never been firmly established. When General Schmalz, commander of the *Hermann Goering Division*, learned of the lack of contact, he sent patrols during the night of 27 May to try to reach the *362d Division*. The patrols roamed across Monte Artemisio's south-

ern slope for two miles before at last finding troops of the *362d Division* near a fork in the road just northeast of Velletri.

Aware of the hazards of such a gap to the over-all defense of the Caesar Line, General Schmalz sent an engineer platoon to occupy the Castel d'Ariano, a ruin located on Monte Artemisio's crest three miles north of Velletri and two miles west of Lariano. A few hours later an officer-led patrol from Schmalz's division also occupied a group of houses at the hamlet of Menta, on the intercorps boundary. Yet those modest forces represented no more than outposts and in no sense served to close the gap, for it was on that same night of 27 May that American patrols were active on Monte Artemisio and had nowhere encountered any German troops.[1]

Reports of the situation on Monte Artemisio prompted General Herr, the panzer corps commander, to order Schmalz to send trucks immediately to the *Hermann Goering Division's* assembly area northwest of Valmontone to transport to Monte Artemisio two infantry battalions delayed during the long march from Leghorn. Herr also ordered the battered *715th Division*, which had been withdrawn to the Tivoli area for reorganization, to send troops at

---

[1] MS # C–087b (Schmalz and Bergengruen), Einstatz der Division Hermann Goering in Italien, CMH.

once to Schmalz's sector. Unfortunately for the Germans, neither the two infantry battalions nor the reinforcements from the *715th Division* would arrive in time to close the breach.[2]

Not until the afternoon of the 29th, during a brief visit to the forward area of the parachute corps, did Field Marshal Kesselring learn of the gap. He immediately ordered Mackensen to close it. Mackensen passed along the field marshal's order, but he and his two corps commanders were satisfied that the job had already been done and took no further action. That night the army commander's report to army group made no mention of a gap on Monte Artemisio.[3]

The next day Kesselring learned how tenuous the link between the two corps actually was and telephoned Mackensen to express his displeasure. He brusquely pointed out that while one battalion might be sufficient to hold Monte Artemisio against probing attacks, an entire division could hardly hold it if the Americans focused on that part of the front. Mackensen nevertheless stuck to his conviction that the gap had been satisfactorily closed and that Monte Artemisio's rugged terrain and steep sides would make up for the paucity of forces.

Meanwhile, Mackensen had turned his attention to the northern flank of the Alban Hills between Lariano and Valmontone where, he rightly suspected, the Americans might soon attempt an outflanking maneuver. Indeed, General Keyes, the commander of the U.S. II Corps, which had just reached the Anzio area to take command of the force in the Artena sector between the Alban Hills and Valmontone, was even then planning such a move. To block it, Mackensen directed Herr to have the *Hermann Goering Division* attack at once in order to throw the Americans off balance, much as the division's reconnaissance battalion had done on the 26th. But the panzer corps commander was reluctant to commit the *Hermann Goering Division* to anything so ambitious, because Schmalz's entire division had yet to arrive. Herr suggested instead that Schmalz concentrate what units he had on the panzer corps' right flank with a view merely toward reinforcing German positions on the northern slope of the Alban Hills. Even as—unknown to the Germans—two regiments of the U.S. 36th Division began to climb Monte Artemisio the night of 30 May, Mackensen reluctantly accepted Herr's counterproposal.

Stratagem on Monte Artemisio

The 36th Division commander, General Walker, had informed the VI Corps commander, General Truscott, on the afternoon of 28 May of the gap on Monte Artemisio. The following day Walker called Truscott's chief of staff, Brig. Gen. Don E. Carleton, to tell him that 36th Division patrols were on the feature's forward slopes seeking a favorable passage over Monte Artemisio, thereby outflanking Velletri from the northeast. Agreeing that this was a fine idea, Carleton noted that if it could be done, "the Boche in there [Velletri] would find themselves in a tough situation, and the town might just cave in."[4]

---

[2] MS # R–50 (Bailey).
[3] *Ibid.*

[4] VI Corps G–3 Jnl, 28–29 May 44, 291530B May 44; Tel, C/S to CG, 36th Div, 281851B May 44.

Encouraged by Carleton's reaction, Walker summoned his staff officers to give them a planning concept that envisioned pinning down the enemy in Velletri with one regiment, the 141st, and with the 142d and 143d scaling Monte Artemisio.[5] The 142d was to establish roadblocks to close the northern escape routes from Velletri, while the 143d, after assisting in the capture of Monte Artemisio, moved northward into the Alban Hills to seize Monte Cavo and the Rocca di Papa, two hills providing excellent observation over the entire area.

For the plan to succeed, armor and artillery had to follow close behind the attacking infantry to help maintain roadblocks and protect the long flanks created by the thrust. Since there would also be a vulnerable line of communications extending eight miles over a ridge varying in height from two to three thousand feet, and since no more than mere footpaths and a few cart trails led over the mountain, success of the entire venture would also depend upon rapid improvement of one of the trails to enable tracked vehicles and jeeps to ascend behind the infantry regiments.[6]

Here was a job for the engineers. After studying aerial photographs and reconnoitering several promising trails, the 36th Division's engineers found a trail that apparently could be improved within a reasonable period. Meanwhile, Walker's infantry regiments had been making their preparations. On the

morning of the 30th, the 36th Division commander laid his completed plan of operations before the corps commander at the latter's command post.[7]

General Walker's plan was relatively simple. While the 141st Infantry engaged the Velletri garrison, the 142d Infantry, followed by the 143d, was to pass through the lines of the 141st during the night of 30 May and scale Monte Artemisio. After reaching the ridge, the 142d Infantry was to move southwestward to the Maschio dell'Artemisio, a knob two miles northwest of Velletri, while the 143d was to move northward along the ridge to capture the Maschio d'Ariano and Hill 931, the two highest points at the northeastern end of the ridge. The 141st Infantry was then to launch a frontal attack to capture Velletri and open Highway 7.[8] (*Map 5*)

After questioning Walker's engineer closely as to the feasibility of improving an existing cart trail up Monte Artemisio, Truscott okayed the plan. He also placed the separate 36th Engineer Regiment in direct support of Walker's division.[9]

The 36th Division had acquired considerable but costly experience in mountain operations at night at the hard fought battle of San Pietro the previous January. That experience would serve the division well in the coming operation. Would it be another San Pietro? General Walker thought not. He noted in his diary: "Our operations for tonight and tomorrow have promise of being spectacular. We are

---

[5] The 141st and 143d Infantry had incurred heavy casualties in January 1944 along the Rapido and again on Monte Cassino. See Blumenson, *Salerno to Cassino*, pp. 322–51, 367–78.

[6] Col Oran C. Stovall, Div Eng, typescript account of operation.

[7] *Ibid*; Walker Diary, 29–30 May 44.

[8] 36th Div Rpt of Opns, May–Jun 44; *Fifth Army History*, Part V, p. 142.

[9] Truscott, *Command Missions*, p. 377.

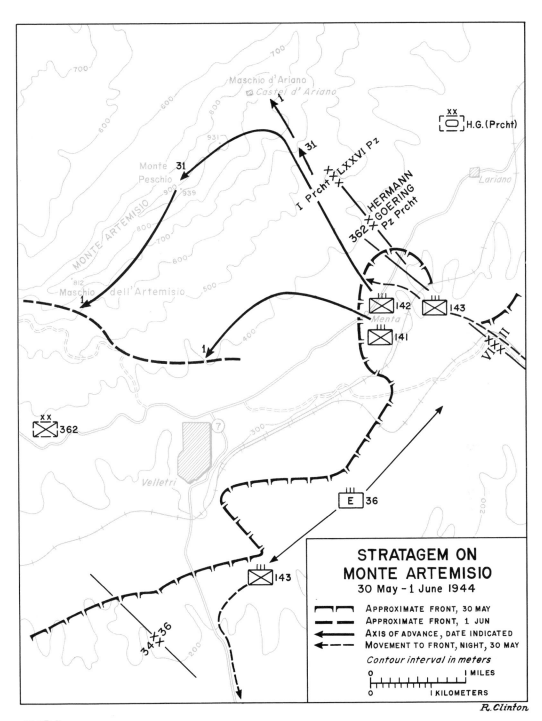

STRATAGEM ON
MONTE ARTEMISIO
30 May – 1 June 1944

	APPROXIMATE FRONT, 30 MAY
	APPROXIMATE FRONT, 1 JUN
	AXIS OF ADVANCE, DATE INDICATED
	MOVEMENT TO FRONT, NIGHT, 30 MAY

Contour interval in meters

0 _____ 1 MILES

0 _____ 1 KILOMETERS

R. Clinton

MAP 5

taking chances, but we should succeed in a big way." General Clark clearly shared his subordinates' confidence.[10]

About an hour before midnight, the 142d Infantry, in a column of battalions with the 2d Battalion leading, headed toward the dark outline of Monte Artemisio. Aided by a new moon that afforded just enough light to enable the troops to discern a trail, the leading company reached the base of the mountain at 0130. From there they picked their way slowly through leafy vineyards covering the lower slopes. Just as dawn began to blank out the stars, the head of the column crossed an open field and began to climb a steeper slope. Seeing the summit looming before them, the men quickened their pace. At 0635 the leading squads scrambled onto the crest of Monte Artemisio, there to surprise and capture three artillery observers, one of whom was taking a bath. Not a shot was fired. That fortunate state of affairs continued throughout the morning as the 142d Infantry turned southwest along the ridge toward the 2,500-foot Maschio dell'Artemisio.[11]

That afternoon Germans along the main road (Highway 7) leading west from Velletri spotted the Americans atop Monte Artemisio and opened fire with several self-propelled guns assembled in support of the defenders of Velletri. Despite that fire, mostly harassing, the 142d Infantry's leading battalion pressed on to reach the Maschio dell'Artemisio in early evening. From the crest the Americans looked down

on Velletri much as had advance guards of an Austrian army, under Prince von Lobkowitz, two centuries before when, instead of Germans, Spaniards under Don Carlos of Naples were defending Velletri; the Americans were not the first to have used this route to outflank the Velletri position.[12]

That night the 142d Infantry established roadblocks on two of the three roads left to the enemy troops in Velletri and by morning the town was virtually surrounded. Only one escape route (Highway 7) remained open to the Germans. When news of the 142d Infantry's success reached the Fifth Army headquarters, the frustration built up during the five days of virtual stalemate vanished and, in General Clark's words, "caused all of us to turn handsprings."[13]

Meanwhile, the 143d Infantry had followed the 142d to the crest and then had turned right to cover that flank. Moving northeastward along the ridge toward Hill 931 and the Maschio d'Ariano, the men of the 143d encountered considerable sniper fire, but by late afternoon had eliminated it. Only at the ruins of the Castel d'Ariano was it necessary to call upon artillery support to drive from the ruins the engineer platoon from the *Hermann Goering Division*, which General Schmalz had committed the night of the 27th. By dark the entire Monte Artemisio ridge was in American hands.[14]

The next morning a party of artillery observers accompanying the 143d In-

[10] Walker Diary, 30 May 44; Clark Diary, 30 May 44. See Blumenson, *Salerno to Cassino*, pp. 270–89, for detailed description of the San Pietro operation.
[11] 142d Inf Rpt of Opns, May 44.

[12] See Spenser Wilkinson, *The Defense of Piedmont, 1742–48* (London: Oxford, 1927), pp. 181ff.
[13] 142d Inf Rpt of Opns, May–Jun 44; Walker Diary, 31 May–1 Jun 44; Clark Diary, 31 May 44.
[14] Interv, Mathews with Col Paul D. Adams (CO 143d Inf), 27 Apr 48.

fantry were delighted to find that the summit of Maschio d'Ariano provided a 200° field of observation from the east to the southwest. Below lay supply arteries of much of the *Fourteenth Army*, especially those supporting the Lariano-Valmontone sector. Scores of tempting enemy targets crawled across the landscape beneath them. The only problem was to obtain enough batteries to do the firing and observers to direct them. Calls immediately went back to division and corps for every available artillery observer to come forward to help. Soon "forward observers were sitting around on the Maschio d'Ariano like crows on a telephone line, having a field day."[15]

"This was," General Truscott observed, "the turning point in our drive to the northwest."[16]

The German Reaction

Not until the afternoon of the 31st did the German *Fourteenth Army* headquarters become aware that the U.S. 36th Division was on top of Monte Artemisio. Dismayed, General von Mackensen quickly directed a series of countermeasures to restore his front. He ordered his two corps commanders to contain and destroy the American penetration at whatever cost, even if they had to use their last man and weapon. Corps' boundaries were to be ignored, Mackensen declared, for "in a situation of this kind, corps boundaries no longer have any meaning."[17]

In contrast to the earlier break-

through on the Cisterna sector, it was the *LXXVI Panzer Corps'* turn to help the *I Parachute Corps*. Mackensen directed Herr to backstop Schlemm's positions west of Monte Artemisio with an armored reconnaissance company which was to block a road leading northward from Monte Peschio, one of the several peaks on the Monte Artemisio ridge. Other armored reconnaissance detachments were to set up blocking positions along Highway 7 between Velletri and Lake Nemi. Meanwhile, a grenadier battalion from Herr's panzer corps was to try to pinch off the American salient by a counterattack directed against the 143d Infantry's positions on the northern end of the Monte Artemisio ridge. The corps commanders were to report the results of those measures to Mackensen by 0700 the next day, 1 June.[18]

The *Fourteenth Army* commander, fully engaged in attempting to contain the penetration along the intercorps boundary, failed to inform Field Marshal Kesselring of what had happened until late on the 31st. When Kesselring learned of the 36th Division's presence on Monte Artemisio, he was furious. Had he been notified promptly, he declared, one or two battalions might have been able to handle the situation, but now the penetration had grown to such proportions that no reserves then available to army group would be able to seal it off. As far as the army group commander was concerned, this was the last straw in his steadily deteriorating relations with his subordinate.[19] The

---

[15] 143d Inf Opns Rpt, Jun 44.

[16] Truscott, *Command Missions*, p. 377.

[17] *Befehl*, AOK 14, Ia Nr. 2338/44, g.Kdos, 31 May 44, in *AOK 14, Ia KTB Nr. 3, Anlage 487, 1–31 May 44, AOK 14, Doc. Nr. 59091/3.*

[18] *Ibid.*

[19] *Befehle, OB Suedwest, Ia Nr. 5914/44 g.Kdos, 1 Jun 44, in Heeresgruppe C/OB SW, Verschiedenes, Ia, Jan–Jun 44, Heeresgruppe C, Doc. Nr. 75138/1.*

feeling was apparently mutual, for General von Mackensen too had concluded that, figuratively speaking, the gap between him and the field marshal had become as large and menacing as that on Monte Artemisio. For the third time—there had been two other occasions in February—Mackensen placed his command at Kesselring's disposal. Having already obtained Hitler's permission to relieve Mackensen, Kesselring this time accepted Mackensen's request for relief. Five days later Mackensen would leave for Germany, after relinquishing his command to General der Panzertruppen Joachim Lemelsen.[20]

The countermeasures ordered by Mackensen had been tactically sound but by 1 June impossible of fulfillment. His blunder had been less in delaying to notify Kesselring of what had happened than in allowing the gap to develop in the first place.

Exploiting the Penetration

The successful penetration by the 36th Division on 31 May aided the other divisions of the VI Corps south of a line between Lanuvio and Campoleone, for it offered opportunities unforeseen during the past four days, a period which had been marked by grinding, costly, and frustrating fighting.[21] Seeing also a chance of outflanking the enemy in the Alban Hills, General Clark decided to shift the bur-

den of the drive on Rome to General Keyes' II Corps. This was the headquarters which two days earlier had assumed control of General O'Daniel's reinforced 3d Division, whose forces had been augmented by the arrival of the 85th Division.

Acknowledging that the II Corps, in the vicinity of Valmontone, would soon be astride Highway 6, Alexander, at Clark's request, adjusted the interarmy boundary to afford the Fifth Army exclusive use of Highway 6 between Valmontone and Rome, as well as the hills overlooking the highway from the north where Clark expected to employ the FEC. Thus Clark would be able to make the final drive on Rome with all three of the Fifth Army's corps along the axes of two main highways, 6 and 7, instead of only along Highway 7, as he had planned originally when sending Truscott's VI Corps into the Alban Hills.[22]

At the same time that Alexander was adjusting his interarmy boundary, Kesselring did the same. The German commander shifted the boundary of Vietinghoff's *Tenth Army* northwestward in order to give the *Fourteenth Army's* hard-pressed *LXXVI Panzer Corps* a narrower front. This Kesselring did by broadening the sector of the *XIV Panzer Corps* and placing the *29th Panzer Grenadier Division*, hitherto on the *LXXVI Panzer Corps'* left flank, under the control of the former corps.[23]

Before the II Corps could move on Rome, the corps had first to complete

---

[20] MSS #'s T–1a and T–1b (Westphal *et al.*), CMH.

[21] On the 31st, Pvt. Furman L. Smith, 135th Infantry, 34th Division, single-handedly held off an enemy counterattack until he fell mortally wounded, his rifle still in his hands. He was awarded the Medal of Honor posthumously.

[22] Alexander *Despatch*, p. 50.

[23] *Befehle, AOK XIV, Ia Nr. 2338/44 g.Kdos*, 31 May 44, in *AOK XIV, Ia KTB Nr. 3, Anlage 487*, 1–31 May 44, *AOK XIV Doc. Nr. 59091/3*.

Operation BUFFALO's original mission: to block Highway 6, capture Valmontone, and secure the high ground north of the town as well as the northeastern slopes of the Alban Hills. Thereafter, on Clark's order, the corps was to pursue the enemy northwestward astride Highway 6 toward Rome and, at the same time, send mobile forces southeastward along the highway to fall upon the flank and rear of those enemy forces retreating before the FEC and the British Eighth Army. Meanwhile, the FEC, having completed mopping up operations in the Lepini Mountains, was to secure the high ground in the vicinity of Segni on the northern slopes of those mountains and then cut Highway 6 near Colleferro before moving on northwestward to Cave and Palestrina, some ten miles away, to cover the II Corps' right flank and rear as it passed beyond Valmontone. Ultimate goal of the French was to seize a crossing of the Tiber east of Rome.[24]

Concurrently, the VI Corps was to attack along the axes of Highway 7 and the Via Anziate, the latter the main road running north from Anzio into the Alban Hills, to secure the southwestern half of the Alban Hills and cut the enemy's routes of withdrawal through Rome before sending forces southwestward to pin the Germans against the Tiber southwest of the city. On the VI Corps' left flank the British 1st and 5th Divisions, once again attached to Truscott's corps, were to follow up the enemy withdrawal toward the Tiber and help destroy those enemy forces trapped east of the river.[25]

The stage was at last set for the final drive on the Italian capital—a drive which was to become in effect an intra-army contest as to which corps—Truscott's VI or Keyes' II—would be first in Rome. On 31 May it had seemed to Clark that the odds favored Keyes, for, except for the 36th Division, all of Truscott's corps still faced the most heavily defended sector of the Caesar Line, that which stretched southwestward from Velletri to the sea. Moreover, the terrain would give Keyes' corps an advantage, for in front of the II Corps stretched the most favorable ground that corps had faced since the beginning of the May offensive along the Garigliano.

Between Highway 6 and the Via Prenestina to the north lay a belt of slightly rolling and intensively cultivated farmland varying in width from three to five miles and extending all the way to Rome. Unlike the former beachhead south of Cisterna, the firm, dry soil, infrequently cut by lateral drainage ditches, promised excellent footing for tanks. Supplementing the main highway, two excellent roads also ran through the corps zone to Rome: to the north of Highway 6 the Via Prenestina, and to the south, the Via Tuscolana, although the latter served the VI Corps for part of its length. To Keyes' troops these conditions represented a welcome respite from the craggy mountains and tortuous roads and trails encountered to the south. The only terrain obstacle of any consequence in the II Corps zone was the northern slopes of the Alban Hills, but the presence of the 36th Division on Monte Artemisio

---

[24] Hq, Fifth Army, OI 25, 31 May 44. See also Mathews, "The French in the Drive on Rome," *Revue Historique de l'Armee*, p. 139.

[25] Hq, Fifth Army, OI 25, 31 May 44.

would prevent the Germans from taking full advantage of that.[26] (*Map VII*)

As General Clark adjusted his forces for continuing the drive on Rome, the British Eighth Army was still slugging its way up the Liri valley and beyond. During the afternoon of 31 May infantry of the 1st Canadian Corps entered the important road center of Frosinone astride Highway 6 twenty-five miles southeast of Valmontone, while the British 13 Corps, having bypassed Arce to the southeast of Frosinone on Highway 82, pulled abreast on the right.[27] That meant that the Liri valley lay behind the two corps. From that point they were to continue northwestward up the valley of the Sacco River past Valmontone toward Tivoli, eighteen miles east of Rome. The 13 Corps was prepared to vary that route, should the army commander, General Leese, deem it propitious, in order to open additional roads leading generally northward through the Simbruini Mountains. The 10 Corps on the British right wing meanwhile was to continue to block passes in the Central Apennines to deny German intervention from the Adriatic front.

In altering the interarmy boundary north of Highway 6 to give the Fifth Army greater freedom of movement northwest of Valmontone, General Alexander, having abandoned all hope of trapping the *Tenth Army*, added the proviso that if it became necessary for both Allied armies to make a joint assault on the Caesar Line, the original boundary would be reinstated. In that event, the Eighth Army would attack abreast of the Fifth Army on a narrow front, with the 1st Canadian Corps astride Highway 6 and the British 13 Corps along an adjacent route, the Via Prenestina.

Once the Caesar Line was pierced and Rome fell, General Leese, the Eighth Army commander, planned to move the Canadian corps into army reserve, while the 13 Corps, passing east of Rome through Tivoli, was to lead the Army's advance northward. On the Eighth Army's far right the 10 Corps too was to drive generally northward along Highway 82 through Avezzano.

Preliminary Moves

To launch the new phase of the Fifth Army's drive on Rome, the II Corps commander, General Keyes, had little time to prepare elaborate plans. The 36th Division's presence on Monte Artemisio had apparently thrown the Germans off balance. It was important to move quickly for the Germans had long since demonstrated an almost uncanny ability to recover rapidly from reverses.[28]

Since the 36th Division's success on Monte Artemisio raised the possibility of quickly achieving a deep salient, Clark saw the need to act with dispatch to protect the 36th Division's right flank and rear. Convinced that General Keyes would need more strength than originally contemplated to accomplish that, he decided on the evening of the 31st to give the II Corps General Sloan's 88th Division, which he had intended to hold in army reserve.[29]

---

[26] II Corps Opns Rpt, Mar–Jun 44.
[27] Operations of British, Indian, and Dominion Forces in Italy, Part II, Sec. B.

[28] II Corps Opns Rpts, May–Jun 44.
[29] Clark Diary, 31 May 44.

For the drive on Rome General Keyes thus would control the 85th and 88th Divisions—the same ones with which he had broken the Gustav Line over two weeks before—plus the 3d Division, the 1st Special Service Force, and Colonel Howze's armored task force, the units that had been operating in the Valmontone corridor under General O'Daniel's command. This was a force about as formidable as that commanded by VI Corps when Clark turned it toward the Alban Hills.

Although General Keyes had no armored division, Howze's task force represented a powerful exploitation force, since it consisted of the 13th Armored Regiment (less one battalion), the 756th Tank Battalion, and several artillery, tank destroyer, engineer, and armored infantry units. Having rejoined the corps, the 91st Reconnaissance Squadron drew the mission of screening the right flank, pending further advance of the French Expeditionary Corps. General Frederick's 1st Special Service Force was also highly mobile, and each of the three infantry divisions had an attached medium tank battalion.

Before attempting to break into the Valmontone gap, Keyes first had to secure his left flank on the northeastern slope of the Alban Hills, both for his own protection and to cover the 36th Division's right flank. That was to be a responsibility of General Coulter's 85th Division (with the 349th Infantry attached from the 88th Division), which during the night of the 30th relieved a regiment of the 3d Division on the left wing of the corps in the vicinity of Lariano, midway between Artena and Velletri. The 85th Division was further reinforced with a company of tanks

from Howze's task force.[30]

An hour and a half after midday on the 31st, Coulter's infantrymen attacked across slopes dotted with thick chestnut and pine woods, terraced vineyards, and silvery-leaved olive trees. Advancing on either side of Lariano, the 1st and 3d Battalions, 337th Infantry, encountered little opposition. Bypassing the town, they occupied high ground to the northwest. The 2d Battalion, meanwhile, sent a reinforced company in a frontal assault against the town. Although the German defenders employed considerable small arms fire, the town was in hand by nightfall. During the night the 1st Battalion continued over two miles beyond Lariano to reach the Maschio d'Ariano at the northern end of the Monte Artemisio ridge, there to relieve the 36th Division's 143d Infantry.

The 337th Infantry's attack had dealt roughly with the battalions of the *Hermann Goering Division*, encircling a battalion of the *1st Panzer Grenadier Regiment* and driving back another from the *2d Panzer Grenadier Regiment*. Under cover of a company-size counterattack supported by seven tanks, the encircled battalion escaped during the night. Nonetheless, the 85th Division managed to hold on as anchor of the left flank of the II Corps on Monte Artemisio.[31]

Keyes' Plan

During the evening of 31 May, General Keyes outlined to his division com-

---

[30] 337th Inf Opns Rpt, May 44; 338th Inf Opns Rpt, May–Jun 44; 3d Inf Div Jnl, 31 May, 212100B May 44.
[31] MS # R–50 (Bailey), CMH.

manders his plan of attack to secure
Highway 6 in the vicinity of Valmontone before beginning the drive on
Rome. The main burden of the effort
was to be borne initially by the 3d
Division. This division was to capture
Valmontone before continuing to the
northwest to secure the corps' right
flank on high ground in the vicinity of
Palestrina, a few miles north of Valmontone, where the division was to
remain until relieved by the FEC. With
the flanks secured, the 88th Division,
accompanied by Task Force Howze,
was to advance as far as Highway 6,
west of Valmontone, then turn northwestward.[32] To the division's left Coulter's 85th Division was to cross the
Alban Hills' northeast slopes to the
vicinity of Frascati, about ten miles
southeast of Rome. Thereafter, Coulter
was to be prepared, on corps' order, to
swing one regiment abruptly to the left
to cut off those enemy troops opposing
the VI Corps. Once the FEC arrived to
relieve the 3d Division and cover the II
Corps' right flank and rear north of
Valmontone, General O'Daniel's division was to advance alongside the 88th
Division to screen the corps' right flank.

The II Corps Begins To Move

The main line of resistance of the
German *LXXVI Panzer Corps*, comprising the *Fourteenth Army*'s left wing, extended eastward from the northeastern
slope of the Alban Hills to Highway 6
at a point midway between Valmontone
and Labico, and thence to a junction
with the *XIV Panzer Corps* on the *Tenth*

Army's right wing a few miles east of
Valmontone. Manning the line from
the Alban Hills to the interarmy boundary were the *Hermann Goering Division*
and remnants of the *334th* and *715th
Infantry Divisions*. This force was more
impressive on paper than it was in
reality, for the only units actually in line
were two understrength panzer grenadier regiments and a *Kampfgruppe*, the
latter made up of miscellaneous artillery
units, most of which had lost their guns
to persistent Allied aircraft. With the
exception of antitank weapons, this
force nevertheless possessed adequate
supporting arms and services.[33]

Beginning at 0500 on 1 June the
85th and 3d Infantry Divisions—the
88th Division had yet to come into line
in the corps' center—began moving
toward their first objectives. Progress
was slow during the morning, especially
in the 3d Division sector. Only after
repelling several tank-led counterattacks
east of the Artena-Valmontone road
did the 15th Infantry finally succeed,
late in the day, in advancing the division's right as far as Highway 6. On the
left, Colonel Howze's armored task
force destroyed eight enemy antitank
guns while spearheading the 30th Infantry's attack. Task Force Howze in
turn lost three tanks, and snipers took a
heavy toll of tank commanders. To
make matters worse, darkness found
both tanks and infantry still short of the
highway northwest of Valmontone.
Colonel Howze summed up the day's
action by observing, "Our attack . . . went damned slowly."[34]

[32] II Corps AAR, Jun 44, The Rome Campaign.
Unless otherwise indicated the following is based
upon this document.

[33] MS # C–64 (Kesselring), CMH.
[34] 30th Inf Narr, Jun 44; Howze MS.

On the corps' left the 338th Infantry of Coulter's 85th Division ran into enemy well entrenched along a steep-sided railway embankment just northeast of Lariano. After a heavy fire fight the regiment drove the Germans from their positions, then wheeled slowly northwestward in the direction of Monte Ceraso, four miles away on the northeastern rim of the Alban Hills. When the maneuver opened a gap on the 338th Infantry's right flank, Coulter quickly closed it with the 349th Infantry.[35]

Meanwhile, a battalion of the 337th Infantry still on the Maschio d'Ariano, the northern knob of the Monte Artemisio ridge, came under fire from an enemy force that had been hastily assembled in the vicinity of a farm one mile to the northeast. Apparently belatedly trying to restore contact between the *Fourteenth Army*'s two corps, the enemy had infiltrated from the north through heavily wooded draws to isolate the 1st Battalion command post and capture an entire platoon of Company D. Later in the day the battalion rallied and drove the enemy off. The rest of the 337th Infantry advanced before dark as far as Monte Castellaccio, about two miles to the north, thus providing the II Corps a secure anchor for its left flank on high ground overlooking Highway 6 from the south.[36]

Southeast of Valmontone General Frederick's 1st Special Service Force reached Colle Ferro, a road junction a few miles southeast of Valmontone that was important to the enemy troops withdrawing before the FEC. Surprising the Germans, Frederick's men fell upon their right flank and took over 200 prisoners, thus virtually eliminating the enemy rear guard at that point, and assuring clear passage for the 3d Algerian Infantry Division, leading the FEC advance toward Highway 6.[37]

Although no breakthrough had developed, there were increasing signs with each passing hour that the enemy was growing progressively weaker. Later that afternoon outposts reported seeing a white flag flying over Valmontone and hearing the sounds of heavy motor traffic moving westward. Observers also reported two big explosions, apparently demolitions, in the vicinity of Cave on the Via Prenestina, midway between Genazzano and Palestrina.[38]

That night the commander of the 15th Infantry telephoned 3d Division headquarters near Giulianello, reporting the noise of heavy motor traffic across his front. "Why don't you put mortar fire on it?" General O'Daniel replied with some heat. "Get an AT gun up there and plaster the hell out of everything that comes along. You can block the road any place you want to. The important thing is to shoot every goddamn vehicle that comes by there."[39] Twenty minutes later the regimental commander telephoned again to say that Company E had just finished shooting up three truckloads of enemy soldiers on the road. "Good, Keep it up," O'Daniel replied, somewhat molli-

---

[35] 349th Inf Hist, Jun 44; 338th Inf Jnl, 1 Jun 44.

[36] 337th Inf Rpt of Opns, Jun 44; Orders, *AOK 14, Ia Nr. 2359/44, g/Kdos,* 1 Jun 44, in *AOK 14, Ia KTB Nr. 3, Anlage 484,* 1–31 May 44, *AOK 14, Doc. Nr. 5909/3; Fifth Army History,* Part V, p. 146.

[37] *Fifth Army History,* Part V, p. 146; Mathews, "The French in the Drive on Rome," p. 139.

[38] II Corps G–3 Jnl, 011855B Jun 44.

[39] 3d Inf Div G–3 Jnl, 012310 Jun 44, Tel CO 15th Inf to CG.

fied. "Don't let a single vehicle get through tonight—not one, understand?"[40]

With Highway 6 cut by fire, even though not physically blocked, the Germans were clearly in trouble. As General Clark had noted when arguing against General Alexander's preoccupation with Valmontone and Highway 6, other roads were available for the German *Tenth Army*'s withdrawal; nevertheless, a combination of the loss of Highway 6 and a continued American advance to the north would further restrict the *Tenth Army*'s escape routes from the Sacco Valley. Furthermore, if the left wing of General von Mackensen's *Fourteenth Army* collapsed, as appeared imminent, the Americans could hardly be stopped, and the *I Parachute Corps* would have to abandon its relatively strong Caesar Line positions in the Alban Hills.

Early on 1 June, even as the U.S. II Corps had begun to move, Field Marshal Kesselring had told the *Tenth Army*'s Chief of Staff, General Wentzell, to hasten the withdrawal of the *90th Panzer Grenadier Division* from the Sacco valley to secure the high ground north of Valmontone around Palestrina. That was to be a preliminary to the entire *XIV Panzer Corps* making a stand there. If the American II Corps swung northwestward toward Rome, as seemed likely, the *XIV Panzer Corps* would be in a position to harass the attackers' flank.[41]

If Kesselring's plan was to have any chance of success, the *Fourteenth Army*'s left wing had to hold either at Valmontone or on the high ground at Palestrina until the *90th Panzer Grenadier Division* could arrive. To those Germans on the scene there seemed to be little chance of that. Because of the American fire on Highway 6, the position at Valmontone was clearly untenable. Leaving only an 18-man rear guard in the town, the Germans withdrew to high ground, but the total strength then available for holding the new position was one infantry battalion supported by four Mark IV tanks, a smattering of assault guns and flak guns, and three light artillery batteries.[42]

At dawn on 2 June, General Keyes' II Corps renewed its attack, this time with General Sloan's 88th Division having taken over the center of the corps. That the Germans had pulled back during the night became quickly apparent. A patrol of the 3d Division's 30th Infantry led the way into Valmontone and by 1030 reported the town free of the enemy. To the left the 7th Infantry occupied Labico, on Highway 6 two miles northwest of Valmontone, and together the two regiments followed the retreating enemy toward the high ground around Palestrina, four miles to the north. By nightfall both regiments had seized footholds on the high ground against only light resistance.[43]

Two regiments of the 88th Division meanwhile moved toward Gardella Hill, a point of high ground overlooking Highway 6 about five miles northwest of Valmontone. Within a few hours the hill was occupied and the highway cut. Two battalions of the 351st Infantry then turned northwest astride the high-

[40] *Ibid*; 3d Div G–3 Jnl, Sitrep, 020730 Jun 44.

[41] Telecon, *AOK 10 C/A* w/Col Beelitz, *OB Suedwest* Opns Off, 011155B Jun 44, in *AOK 10, Ia KTB Nr. 7, Anlage 20*, 1–5 Jun 44, *AOK 10 Doc. Nr. 55291/2*.

[42] MSS #'s T–1a, T–1b, T–1c (Westphal *et al.*) and C–064 (Kesselring).

[43] II Corps G–3 Jnl, 021030B Jun 44.

3D DIVISION INFANTRY ENTERING VALMONTONE

way and entered the road junction town of San Cesareo, seven miles northwest of Valmontone. Along the way the men counted 12 destroyed or abandoned 88-mm. guns and 14 enemy vehicles. The 85th Division on the left made similar progress, one regiment coming abreast of the 351st Infantry near San Cesareo in later afternoon, another occupying Monte Fiori, two miles south of the town.[44]

By 2 June the II Corps had gained control of a six-mile length of Highway 6 and, more importantly, had compromised the positions on the high ground near Palestrina which the Germans had hoped to hold pending the arrival of the *90th Panzer Grenadier Division*. Conflicting reports reaching *Army Group C* headquarters throughout the day served to conceal the full extent of the peril to the German plan to employ that division defensively, but by nightfall Field Marshal Kesselring realized that more drastic steps were needed if what was developing as a full-scale

___

[44] II Corps AAR Jun 44, The II Corps Drive on Rome.

AMERICAN INFANTRYMEN ADVANCING ALONG HIGHWAY 6 TOWARD ROME

breakthrough at Valmontone was to be contained.[45]

To General von Vietinghoff, commander of the *Tenth Army* withdrawing before the British Eighth Army, Kesselring insisted that the *XIV Panzer Corps* counterattack the left flank of the Fifth Army's II Corps, now beginning to move up Highway 6. Vietinghoff responded emphatically that he had neither sufficient troops nor ammunition for a counterattack of any kind. The entire *XIV Panzer Corps*, for example, had only fourteen combat-ready tanks. Kesselring reluctantly took him at his word and both commanders had to accept the fact that Rome would soon be lost. During the night of 2 June, Vietinghoff ordered his *Tenth Army* to break contact with the British

[45] Telecon, *AOK 10* C/S with Colonel Beelitz, *OB Suedwest* Opns Officer, 011155B Jun 44, in *AOK 10, Ia KTB Nr. 7, Anlage 20*, 1–5 Jun 44, *AOK 10 Doc. Nr. 55291/2*; Telecon, C/S *AOK 10* w/*OB Suedwest*, 011220B Jun 44, *AOK 10 Doc. Nr. 55291/2*; MSS # T–1b (Westphal *et al.*) and C–064 (Kesselring). Unless otherwise indicated this section is based upon these references.

Eighth Army and retreat northward through the Simbruini Mountains to the Aniene River east of Rome.

As the full-scale withdrawal began, tension and sleepless nights began to take their toll among the senior German commanders. General von Vietinghoff, who for several months had been repeatedly incapacitated by chronic illness, turned over his command to his chief of staff, General Wentzell, and left for hospitalization in northern Italy. A few hours later Kesselring's chief of staff, General Westphal, collapsed from nervous exhaustion and was also evacuated.

The *Tenth Army*'s retreat through the mountains was well-conceived and skillfully executed, amply fulfilling Clark's earlier prediction that there were just too many escape routes open to the Germans. Yet an examination of the map suggests that a combination of a more vigorous follow-up by the Eighth Army of the Germans in the Liri valley, and a timely blockade of Highway 6 between Ferentino and Valmontone by the Fifth Army would have made that retreat far more costly.

The VI Corps Begins To Move

Since 26 May the VI Corps, west of the Alban Hills, had gained little ground and had incurred heavy casualties in some of the hardest fighting since the previous winter. Four of the five divisions (the 36th Division had been in corps reserve for much of the period and had sustained few losses during the ascent of Monte Artemisio) had suffered a total of 2,829 casualties, including 342 killed. Those were losses comparable to, and in some instances, surpassing those incurred during the

breakout offensive from the beachhead.[46]

That such a grim pattern of losses might still continue became evident on 1 June when the VI Corps resumed its efforts to break through the Caesar Line between Lanuvio and Campoleone. On a two-battalion front, the 179th Infantry led the 45th Division's advance astride the Albano road. The attack had penetrated the lines of an enemy infantry school regiment, a recent reinforcement to the *3d Panzer Grenadier Division*, but the 179th Infantry's heavy losses caused considerable disorganization in that regiment. By noon one company could muster only an officer and thirty-five men, and the other companies were little better off. The division commander, General Eagles, replaced the 179th with the 180th Infantry, so that the attack was renewed in the afternoon, but the second regiment had no more success than the first.[47]

To the 45th Division's right the 34th Division also resumed its efforts to capture the Villa Crocetta and the San Gennaro Ridge southeast of Lanuvio. After two hours of hard fighting, the 168th Infantry's 3d Battalion captured two hills on the ridge but was still short of complete control of the feature. On the 168th Infantry's left, the frustrating chronicle of the previous week was repeated as a platoon of the 109th Engineers struggled to within a stone's throw of the Villa Crocetta before a curtain of automatic weapons and mortar fire drove the men back down the

[46] See 9th Machine Records Unit Fifth Army American Battle Casualties, 10 Jun 45, CMH.

[47] 45th Div Opns Rpt, Jun 44; VI Corps G-3 Periodic Rpt, Jun 44; MS # T-1a (Westphal *et al.*).

hill through shattered olive groves to the line of departure.[48]

To the corps commander, General Truscott, it was apparent that his best prospects for breaking through the Caesar Line lay with the 36th Division. Since occupying Monte Artemisio before daylight of the 31st, that division had gradually extended its positions and had virtually surrounded Velletri. Only Highway 7 remained open as an escape route for the town's garrison, the survivors of General Greiner's *362d Infantry Division*. The 36th Division commander, General Walker, believed that the enemy, recognizing the hopelessness of the situation, would soon abandon Velletri.[49]

In reality, by early afternoon of 31 May, the *I Parachute Corps* commander, General Schlemm, had indeed decided that nothing was to be gained by prolonging the defense of Velletri, and accordingly had requested General von Mackensen's permission to withdraw. The *Fourteenth Army* commander readily assented, and that night, leaving behind a rear guard, Greiner withdrew his division along Highway 7 toward Lake Nemi, about five miles to the northwest of Velletri.[50]

As night fell on 1 June, the 36th Division entered Velletri, where the Americans captured 250 enemy soldiers at a cost of thirty-four casualties. With Velletri's fall, it seemed unlikely that the Germans could long hold the Lanuvio-Campoleone sector.[51]

Yet despite the 36th Division's suc-

cess, Field Marshal Kesselring had not yet authorized Mackensen to withdraw from the southern flanks of the Alban Hills. The army group commander believed that it was important, indeed vital, to the fortunes of the German forces that the *Fourteenth Army* hold as long as possible in order to enable the *Tenth Army* to make good its escape from the upper Liri-Sacco valley. If Mackensen were flung back too quickly on Rome the Allies might be able to separate the two German armies and seize the crossing sites of the Tiber north of Rome.[52]

Consequently, when the 34th and 45th Divisions resumed their efforts on 2 June, the Germans continued to hold except at the Villa Crocetta, which the 34th Division finally seized. Elsewhere between Lanuvio and Campoleone, the VI Corps made little headway.[53]

General Clark made no secret of his keen disappointment at Truscott's failure to break through west of Velletri. "I want to take ground, but Ryder and Eagles haven't gone any place today," Clark complained to Truscott's chief of staff.[54] They were engaged in a race against time, Clark added, and "my subordinates fail to realize how close the decision will be. If Kesselring manages to reinforce his positions in the Alban Hills with the *1st Parachute Division* and the *90th Panzer Grenadier* before I get there, they may turn the tide."[55]

[48] *Fifth Army History*, Part V, p. 151.
[49] 36th Div Rpt of Opns, May–Jun 44.
[50] MS # R–50 (Bailey).
[51] 9th MRU, Fifth Army American Battle Casualties, 10 Jun 45; 36th Div Rpt of Opns, May–Jun 44.

[52] Frido von Senger und Etterlin, *Neither Hope Nor Fear* (New York: E. P. Dutton & Co., Inc., 1964), p. 253.
[53] VI Corps G–3 Jnl, 1–2 Jun 44, 021745B Jun 44, Tel, CG 45th Div to CG VI Corps.
[54] *Ibid.*, 021840B Jun 44; Tel, Fifth Army Adv CP to CG VI Corps.
[55] Clark Diary, 2 Jun 44.

Although upset by the lack of progress west of Velletri, Clark was encouraged by the 36th Division's prospects at Velletri and on Monte Artemisio. "If the 36th goes," Clark observed to Truscott, "I feel that there should be a breakthrough."[56] Clark's confidence in Walker's division was well placed, for while Truscott's other division commanders fumed in frustration throughout 2 June, the 36th Division began a methodical exploitation of its capture of Velletri. At dawn the 142d and 143d Infantry Regiments led the way from Monte Artemisio across rolling farmland toward Monte Cavo and Rocca di Papa, which were four and a half miles away. Advancing along the only covered route of approach in its zone and taking fifty prisoners from the *Rome Police Battalion*, a scratch covering force hurriedly sent south from Rome, the 142d Infantry, gained a position directly east of Monte Cavo. To the right the 143d Infantry occupied Monte Tano, a mile and a half northeast of Monte Cavo. Meanwhile, the 141st Infantry, which had captured Velletri, advanced into the hills just east of Lake Nemi.[57]

The 36th Division's thrust opened Highway 7 as far as Lake Nemi and threatened the *362d Division's* left flank with envelopment. Even the commitment of a battalion of the *1099th Infantry Regiment* from the *92d Grenadier Division*, an untried unit in training along the coast near Rome, failed to stem what at that point amounted to a breakthrough along the *I Parachute*

Corps' left flank. To avoid envelopment, General Schlemm withdrew the *12th Parachute Regiment* from his center and shifted it to a sector extending northeast from Lake Nemi to the corps' left flank. Yet that unit, reduced by combat losses to about the strength of a battalion, could be expected to act as little more than a delaying force.

By nightfall on 2 June, Kesselring at last reluctantly acknowledged that the *Fourteenth Army* too had no alternative to withdrawal and authorized Mackensen to begin pulling back his entire front, with the exception of the far right along the Tyrrhenian coast where as yet the British divisions there had exerted little pressure. The *I Parachute Corps'* center and left were to withdraw about a mile and a half, and the *LXXVI Panzer Corps* was to pull back its right wing two miles and its left one mile. Kesselring further directed Mackensen to bring forward all of his field replacement battalions and, if necessary, to draw upon all available military transport—even that being used to supply foodstuffs for the civilian population of Rome—to move the reinforcements to the front.

That afternoon German artillery fire opposite the 34th and 45th Divisions' sector suddenly increased in volume and continued until dark. The fire served to mask the *I Parachute Corps'* preparations for a withdrawal that night. As darkness fell an unaccustomed quiet settled over the VI Corps front as the Germans broke contact and withdrew to new positions.[58]

Suspecting that a withdrawal was taking place, General Ryder, the 34th

[56] VI Corps G–3 Jnl, 020815B, 021415B, and 021840B Jun 44, Tels, Clark to Truscott.

[57] 142d Inf Opns Rpt, Jun 44; 141st Inf Narr, Jun 44.

[58] *AOK 14, Ia Nr. Anl. 2411/44*, 2 Jun 44, *AOK 14 Doc. Nr. 590912/44*.

Division commander, ordered his regimental commanders to send out strong combat patrols that night toward the enemy lines. Patrols from the 168th Infantry met no resistance as they entered Lanuvio's dark ruins shortly after midnight. At first light on 3 June the regiment began to move and by 0900 had completed the occupation of the town. The rest of the 34th Division then advanced on both sides of Lanuvio toward Genzano, a road junction with Highway 7 three miles to the northwest where the highway skirts Lake Nemi.[59]

That was the opportunity General Truscott had been waiting for, to commit General Harmon's 1st Armored Division as an exploitation force. Truscott planned to send the armor astride the Anzio road toward a junction with Highway 7 at the town of Albano. Harmon, who had never reconciled himself to Clark's decision to shift the VI Corps (and his division) from the Valmontone sector, once again protested against his new mission. This

was, he declared, "a hell of a place to put an armored division—on top of these mountains." Colonel Carleton, Truscott's chief of staff, replied that that was where the corps commander had said Harmon would go, and that ended the matter.[60]

Meanwhile, Truscott by phone urged the 45th Division commander to get his men moving as soon as possible. The 45th Division was to precede the armor toward Albano as far as the Velletri-Rome railroad northwest of Lanuvio, whereupon the armor was to pass through and, together with the 36th Division, lead the final drive to Rome.[61]

By the evening of 2 June both the II and VI Corps thus had broken through the Caesar Line. As dawn broke over the Alban Hills on the 3d, both corps were poised to begin the intra-army race to determine which would be first into Rome.

---

[59] VI Corps G–3 Jnl, 3–4 Jun 44; *Fifth Army History*, Part V, pp. 153–54.

[60] VI Corps G–3 Jnl, 021500B Jun 44, Tel, Carleton to Harmon.
[61] VI Corps G–3 Jnl, 3–4 Jun 44; *Fifth Army History*, Part V, pp. 153–54.

CHAPTER XI

The Fall of Rome

The German High Command realized only too well that the fall of Rome would have repercussions far beyond the Italian theater of war, and that Allied propaganda would take full advantage of the capture of the first of the Axis capitals. From the Allied point of view, a better prelude to the imminent invasion of France could scarcely have been desired. The Germans had only two choices: to evacuate Rome or to defend it street by street and house by house. The latter course would gain Kesselring a little time but would leave the city in ruins and invoke the certain condemnation of all Christendom.[1]

Since October 1943 the OKW planning staff had been considering alternately the possibility of either declaring Rome an open city, in the event of an Allied landing near the mouth of the Tiber, or of withdrawing the front to the environs of the city and thereby risking its destruction. On instructions from the OKW chief of staff, the subject had been placed in abeyance that winter, since Hitler had ordered the Bernhard Line in southern Italy held under all circumstances. In any case, the High Command believed that if the Allies landed near Rome, the local commanders would have to be governed by military necessity.

As for the concept of Rome as an open city, the only concession OKW was then prepared to make was to order that all monuments of historical or artistic value, as well as occupied hospitals, be spared destruction. Simultaneously, the High Command agreed to respect the Vatican's sovereignty and to place its territory off limits to all German military personnel.

When the Allies landed at Anzio in January 1944 the question of Rome's status, should the front approach the city, again became urgent. On 4 February Field Marshal Kesselring submitted to the OKW a list of measures to be accomplished in the event he had to give up the city. The army group commander recommended demolition of all bridges across the Tiber, all major electrical installations (except those required by the Vatican City), and all industrial and rail facilities outside the city (except those having no military role and serving only the civilian population). Within the city, Kesselring proposed demolition only of those industrial installations whose destruction could be accomplished without damage to neighboring structures. After clearing the matter with the German Foreign Minister, OKW approved Kesselring's recommendations, but with Hitler's own proviso forbidding destruction of the Tiber bridges within the city, for many of them had considerable historical and artistic merit.

On 11 March in a note verbale for

---

[1] Greiner and Schramm, eds., *OKW/WFSt, KTB*, IV, pp. 499–504. Unless otherwise indicated the following is based upon this source.

the German Ambassador to the Holy See, the Vatican reminded the Germans of their earlier assurances to spare from the ravages of war the Vatican City and Rome's famed monuments. The immediate effect of these representations was a 13 March order by the *Fourteenth Army*, in whose zone of responsibility Rome lay, directing all military personnel, except medical detachments and quartermaster, butcher, and bakery units, to leave the city. German soldiers could enter Rome only with special passes, and the Vatican City, including St. Peter's Church, was placed off limits. All military convoys were forthwith to be detoured around Rome. The German command hoped by these measures to remove all legitimate military targets from Rome and thereby give it the status of an open city within the meaning of the Hague Convention.

The next move came from the Allied side with a public statement by President Roosevelt on 19 April, in response to a message from President de Valera of neutral Ireland, requesting an Allied guarantee for the protection of the city of Rome. Roosevelt shrewdly observed in his reply that only the fact that Rome was in German hands had caused the question to be raised in the first place. Once the Germans had left Rome there would be no problem, for the Allies could easily guarantee its safety. The fate of Rome, Roosevelt concluded, therefore lay in German, not in Allied, hands. This equivocal reply left Rome's status still in doubt and the Allies free to take whatever action the military situation demanded.[2]

There the matter rested until after the Allied offensive had begun in mid-May. On 15 May the U.S. Department of State queried General Wilson, Allied Forces Commander, Mediterranean, on whether to declare Rome an open city, subject to reservation of transit rights for both belligerents.[3] Wilson replied with a firm negative. The Allied commander, echoing Roosevelt's earlier statement, pointed out that at this stage of the war, when German airpower was waning, such a declaration could be of advantage only to the enemy, since only the Allies were in a position to attack Rome. After they had captured the city they would have adequate means of defending it. Rome offered facilities essential to the continuation of the campaign beyond the Tiber, and Wilson was determined not to allow his hands to be tied by any declaration respecting the use of these facilities. The British chiefs of staff agreed with Wilson's position and added that military necessity alone must govern Allied policy toward Rome. If the Germans chose to defend the city, the Allies would "take appropriate measures to eject them."[4]

Although unwilling to commit themselves, the Allies had frequently assured Vatican authorities that the City State would "be accorded the normal rights of a neutral and [would] be treated as an independent neutral state."[5] Vatican property outside the city state would be given the same diplomatic immunity

---

[2] Msg OZ 2571, 15 May 44, AMSSO to AFHQ SHAEF SGS 370.2/2, vol. II.

[3] *Ibid.*

[4] Msg B 12688, AFHQ Adv CP to B/COS, 0100/4/28, 19 May 44, SACS; Msg 2770, Air Ministry to AFHQ SACS, Cable Log 26, ser. 28a.

[5] Ltr, Hq AAI, 27 May 44, Sub: Occupation and Preservation of Vatican and Other Religious Properties, AAI Plans Sec, 0300/7c/19.

accorded to Vatican authorities. Yet the Allied note contained an important qualification: during the forthcoming drive on Rome the diplomatic immunity of Vatican property would "not be allowed to interfere with military operations," a principle that had governed Allied operations at Monte Cassino, with ruinous consequences for the ancient monastery. The Holy See could take slight comfort in these assurances.[6]

Since these instructions, however, closely paralleled those that OKW had already given Kesselring, the Vatican City at least had statements from both sides that its neutrality would be respected, if at all possible. How effective these assurances would be if all Rome were to become a battleground continued to trouble Vatican authorities, for as long as Rome's status depended upon "military necessity" there was little real security for the Vatican itself.

Not until 3 June, when advance detachments of the U.S. Fifth Army drew within sight of Rome, did OKW authorize Kesselring to approach the Allies through the Vatican in an effort to obtain a joint agreement on declaring Rome an open city. This was in response to the field marshal's recommendations that, except for necessary services, there were under no circumstances to be military installations, troop billets, or troop movements within the city. There would be no demolitions, and electricity and water supply facilities would be maintained intact after the surrender of those still in German hands. Vatican authorities would be responsible for seeing that these measures were carried out and for arranging

direct contacts between officers of the two belligerents to work out the final details for declaring Rome an open city. If the Allies failed to respond to German overtures, Kesselring was free to act according to military necessity.

The AAI headquarters not only ignored these overtures but via Allied radio called upon Romans to rise and join the battle to drive the Germans from Rome. By this time the call was both pointless and rash, since within the city only isolated German units were desperately trying to reach the far bank of the Tiber before the Americans. Any attempt on the part of the civilian population to interfere might have led to destructive street fighting.[7]

On the heels of this radio appeal General Clark sent a message to his commanders repeating earlier Allied statements that if the Germans did not attempt to defend Rome there would be no combat within the city. The Fifth Army commander also declared that it was his "most urgent desire that Fifth Army troops protect both public and private property in the city of Rome." While every effort was to be made to prevent Allied troops from firing into the city, "the deciding factor would be the enemy's dispositions and actions." If the Germans opposed "our advance by dispositions and fires that necessitate Fifth Army troops firing into the city of Rome, battalion commanders, and all higher commanders [were] authorized to take appropriate action without delay to defeat the opposing enemy elements by fire and movement."[8]

---

[6] *Ibid.*, 0300/4a/28.

[7] MS # T–1b (Westphal *et al.*).
[8] II Corps G–3 Jnl, Jun 44, Fifth Army Msg from Clark, 3 Jun 44.

It was now the Germans' turn to make a unilateral declaration, as had the Belgian and French authorities four years earlier when the battlefronts threatened to overwhelm their capitals, that Rome was an open city within the meaning of the first category implied in the Hague Convention. The Allied command had left them little choice— either fight or get out. Since Rome lay within the zone of military operations, such a declaration amounted, as in the case of Brussels and Paris, to an "anticipatory surrender" of the city. Therefore, on the afternoon of 3 June the OKW instructed Kesselring to hold his front south and southeast of Rome only long enough to permit evacuation of the city's environs and withdrawal of the *Fourteenth Army* beyond the Tiber, which flows through Rome from north to south. Thereafter, he was authorized to withdraw the army north of Rome and west of the Tiber to the next favorable defense line.[9] That night *Army Group C* headquarters issued orders for the evacuation of Rome and the re-establishment of a new line north of the city and extending east and west astride the valley of the Tiber.

The Race for Rome

By daybreak on 3 June, both the II and the VI Corps were on the move. During the day the II Corps' left wing, made up of the 85th Division, with the 337th Infantry on the right and the 339th on the left, crossed the northeastern flanks of the Alban Hills toward Frascati, Kesselring's former headquarters. The 337th Infantry led the way,

passing north of Rocca Priora and taking first Monte Compatri, shortly thereafter, Monte Porzio Catone. After a brief skirmish on the slopes of Monte Compatri, the regiment counted thirty-eight prisoners who had been pressed into combat duty from the German Army cooks and bakers school near Rome. Darkness found the regiment descending the northern slopes of the Alban Hills into Frascati, and the prisoners heading toward the army's cages at Anzio.

In the corps' center, Company A of the 81st Armored Reconnaissance Battalion, followed by tanks of Howze's task force, led the 88th Division's advance along Highway 6 at a five- to seven-mile-an-hour pace. Hard-pressed to keep up, the infantry pulled abreast of the armor only after well-concealed enemy antitank guns opened fire on the tanks just beyond Colonna, a railway station about three miles west of San Cesareo. The tanks huddled in defilade until the infantry deployed and joined them in a co-ordinated assault on the enemy's hastily occupied positions. In the face of the American tank-infantry attack the Germans soon abandoned their guns and fell back along the highway toward the suburbs of Rome. Throughout the afternoon the 88th Division encountered gradually increasing opposition from similar rear guard detachments covering the enemy withdrawal.[10]

By the end of the day the II Corps' two leading divisions had scored impressive gains: south of Highway 6 the 85th Division had pushed back the

---

[9] Greiner and Schramm, eds., *OKW/WFSt KTB*, IV, pp. 505–06; MS # T–1b (Westphal *et al.*).

[10] 13th Armd Regt AAR, Jun 44; 1st Armd Div G–3 Jnl, Jun 44.

enemy rear guard five miles to the line of Monte Compatri–Colonna, while to the north of the highway the 88th Division, after brushing aside a small delaying force south of Zagarolo, located on a secondary road just west of Palestrina, had advanced halfway to the village of Pallavincini, seven miles west of Palestrina.

This setback in the vicinity of Zagarolo was especially worrisome to Field Marshal Kesselring, for, although he had already reconciled himself to the loss of Rome, he was still intent on extricating his forces located southeast of the city. The crossings of the Aniene River between Rome and Tivoli, rather than the city of Rome, was their best escape route, and to control these crossings he needed to delay the Allied forces between Palestrina and Zagarolo long enough to enable his forces to reach the Aniene first. To this end Kesselring diverted an assault gun battalion that Mackensen had ordered to Colonna on Highway 6 and sent it instead northward toward the vicinity of Zagarolo.[11]

During the day Allied aerial reconnaissance had reported considerable traffic streaming out of the Alban Hills in a northerly direction, apparently toward the crossings of the Aniene. The night before, the *Fourteenth Army* commander had ordered General Schlemm, commander of the *I Parachute Corps*, to withdraw the *11th Parachute Regiment* and the main body of the *4th Parachute Division*'s artillery from the army's right wing to the left where they were to

cover the withdrawal to the Aniene. By 0920 on 3 June one battalion of the parachute regiment had reached a road junction on the Via Tuscolana three miles northwest of Frascati, and a second took up positions at Due Torri, five miles west of a planned blocking point at Osteria Finocchio, until then held only by a detachment from the *29th Field Replacement Battalion* and sixty men from the *715th Division*. But this force was all that Mackensen had with which to cover that sector. Three additional reserve battalions were too far away to be of much help: one, a battalion of the *334th Division*, lay thirteen miles north of Tivoli; a second, a long delayed battalion of the *Hermann Goering Division*, still lay at Sutri, twenty miles north of Rome; and a third, the *26th Panzer Division*'s replacement battalion, was equally far to the rear. Nor was the *Tenth Army* in a position to send reinforcements to Mackensen's aid. Its *90th Panzer Grenadier Division*, with which Kesselring had expected to shore up the *Fourteenth Army*'s left wing, had been thrown off balance by Allied artillery fire after the division's arrival in the vicinity of Genazzano, five miles northeast of Valmontone. The division had, therefore, no choice but to remain on the defensive where it was and to concentrate on delaying the French corps' attack southeast of Cave. To make matters worse, *Tenth Army* had lost all contact with the division that afternoon and had only the vaguest details concerning the situation on its own right flank between Palestrina and Genazzano.

As darkness fell on 3 June, Field Marshal Kesselring, after studying the reports from his army commanders,

[11] MSS #'s T–1a, T–1b (Westphal *et al.*) and C–064 (Kesselring). Unless otherwise cited the following is based upon these references.

decided that only bold measures could
save the *Fourteenth Army*'s left wing from
a collapse that would open up the way
to the Aniene River crossings between
Rome and Tivoli. The army group
commander, therefore, directed the
Tenth Army's acting commander, General Wentzell, to turn his reserve division (the *15th Panzer Grenadier*) over to
General Mackensen for use on the
LXXVI Panzer Corps' sector. Kesselring
hoped thereby to keep that wing strong
enough to cover the corps' withdrawal
northward from the Alban Hills to the
Aniene and to prevent envelopment of
the *Tenth Army*'s right flank.[12]

Actually, because of General Clark's
concentration on the capture of Rome
Field Marshal Kesselring's fears were
groundless. In contrast with his earlier
concern for the enemy-occupied high
ground overlooking his left flank as the
VI Corps advanced toward Valmontone, this time the Fifth Army commander chose to ignore temporarily the
Germans in the hills north of Highway
6 as the II Corps moved along the
highway toward Rome. To be sure, as
quickly as possible Clark would move
the French Corps up onto the II Corps'
right flank as the latter wheeled left
astride the axis of Highway 6 after
capturing Palestrina and Zagarolo.
Therefore, Juin's troops would provide
a covering force to Keyes' long right
flank as it passed south of the Aniene
River.

Consequently, during the night of 3
June, with the *15th Panzer Grenadier
Division* providing a shield, General
Mackensen managed to extricate Herr's
LXXVI Panzer Corps as well as much of

Schlemm's *I Parachute Corps* from entrapment southeast of Rome. The battered *362d Infantry Division*, meanwhile,
by means of a series of hard-fought
rear-guard actions, covered the withdrawal of the remainder of the *Fourteenth Army* through the Alban Hills and
beyond the Tiber.

While the II Corps' sweep astride
Highway 6 north of the Alban Hills
seemed to Clark's eyes most promising
and to Kesselring's most threatening,
the VI Corps had also begun to move
directly into the Alban Hills. The 36th
Infantry Division and the 1st Armored
Division were to lead the way toward
Rome itself. Early on 3 June Harmon's
armor assembled along the Via Anziate
behind the 45th Division and prepared
to pass through its ranks when the
infantry division should reach the vicinity of Albano that evening. The 36th
Division, on the corps' right, had
moved beyond Velletri by noon to take
first the village of Nemi and then to
advance to the northwest as far as a
road junction just east of Lake Albano.
Nightfall found both the 1st Armored
and the 36th Infantry Divisions biv-
ouacked close by Albano and prepared
to continue their advance toward Rome
the following morning—the armored
division along Highway 7 and the infantry division along the Via Tuscolano
by way of Frascati. Meanwhile, the 34th
Division, in the corps' center, had
moved along a secondary road south of
and parallel to Highway 7 beyond
Lanuvio to a sector south of Albano,
where the division would remain until
after the fall of Rome. On the corps'
far left flank the British 1st and 5th
Divisions followed up the enemy withdrawal west of Ardea with instructions

---

[12] Greiner and Schramm, eds., *OKW/WFSt. KTB.*
IV(1), p. 500.

to advance only as far as the near bank of the Tiber southwest of Rome.[13]

Echeloned considerably to the Fifth Army's right in the upper reaches of the Sacco-Liri valley, the British Eighth Army prepared early on 3 June to launch a final attack aimed at driving the enemy beyond the Aniene and into the Umbrian highlands east of the Tiber. That this could be quickly accomplished seemed reasonable, for between Highway 6 and the Subiaco road all that stood in the path of the army's 1st Canadian and British 13 Corps were the *26th Panzer* and *305th Infantry Divisions*. These divisions, considerably understrength, held the *XIV Panzer Corps'* center and left along an east-west line extending from a point four miles west of Acuto along the Trivigliano-Genazzano road to a point one mile beyond the Subiaco road—actually the area between Highway 6 and the Subiaco road. Yet two days would pass before the Eighth Army would reach the Aniene east of Rome and pull abreast of its neighbor on the left. Caution and traffic congestion caused by the presence of two armored divisions and their numerous trains of vehicles, as well as a skillfully executed retreat on the part of General von Senger and Etterlin's *XIV Panzer Corps,* accounted for much of the delay.[14]

Even as the U.S. Fifth Army's II and VI Corps began to close in on Rome, the Eighth Army's 1st Canadian Corps,

after replacing the 1st Canadian Infantry Division with the 6th South African Armoured Division, attacked the *26th Panzer Division's* positions between Paliano and Acuto. But the Germans managed to delay the armored division behind a screen of well-placed mines and demolitions long enough to break contact and slip away in the darkness. And the British 13 Corps on the Canadian's right did no better in closing with and overwhelming the enemy. In that corps too an armored division—the British 6th Armoured—had been moved into the van to begin a pursuit, since the Germans were believed to be on the point of breaking and running for it. With two brigades—the 1st Guards and the 61st—forward, the British 6th Armoured Division advanced north and west of Alatri, forcing back the enemy's outpost line. But here too enemy rear guards and demolitions caused frequent delays which allowed the Germans to escape through the mountains to the northwest. The next morning—4 June—the British 13 Corps entered Trivigliano unopposed. At the same time, the 10th Rifle Brigade cleared Monte Justo, about half a mile to the east, while the 6th Armoured Division advanced four miles northwest of Alatri without making contact with the Germans.

The Central Apennines against which both Churchill and Alexander had hoped to pin the German *Tenth Army,* or at least a large part of it, were, in fact, not the seemingly impenetrable barriers they appeared to be on the map. Actually, through these mountains ran numerous roads and tracks over which an army could readily move and, at the same time, easily block with

---

[13] VI Corps AAR, June 44; *Fifth Army History,* Part V, pp. 153–54.

[14] Operations of British, Indian, and Dominion Forces in Italy, Part II, Sec B. Unless otherwise cited the following is based upon this source. See also, G. A. Shepperd, *The Italian Campaign 1943–45, A Political and Military Re-Assessment* (New York: Frederick A. Praeger, 1968), p. 243.

modest rearguards. When combined with the Eighth Army's cautious advance, this geographic fact and the Germans' skillfull exploitation of it enabled the *XIV Panzer Corps*, on the *Tenth Army*'s right wing to elude entrapment in the upper Liri-Sacco valley. During the past five days the corps' engineers had kept the Subiaco road open, despite efforts of Allied bombers to close it. Allied aircraft had forced the Germans to limit their activities, including road marches, to the hours of darkness, yet the entire *XIV Panzer Corps* had managed to break contact and reach the Aniene River in the vicinity of Tivoli well ahead of the British Eighth Army.[15]

Earlier, on 3 June, many miles of winding mountain roads and an elusive enemy still separated the British Eighth Army from its goal; on the other hand, the U.S. Fifth Army was almost within sight of its objective. With every passing hour the troops encountered a growing number of signs indicating that the city of Rome was not far away. During the day familiar characteristics of a large metropolitan area—a growing density of housing and an urban road and rail network—had greeted the advancing Americans, and from occasional high points the troops could see a hazy panorama that they guessed was the city of Rome itself. All of these signs and sights fueled a mounting anticipation. When the reconnaissance patrols from the 88th Division caught their first glimpse of the Roman skyline, a wave of excitement soon pervaded the entire Fifth Army. That afternoon General Gruenther observed:

The CP has gone to hell. No one is doing any work here this afternoon. All semblance of discipline has broken down. Although the G–3 War Room purposely shows only a moderately conservative picture, every pilot, everyone in fact who has come from Anzio since 1000 this morning, has brought back a pair of pants full of ants with the result that this unsuppressible wave of optimism and expectancy has swept through the headquarters.[16]

Perhaps because of Ultra's decipherment of messages between OKW and Kesselring's headquarters that Rome would not be defended, Clark realized that its fall was now only hours away. Concerned that the Germans might demolish the Tiber bridges, General Clark saw his major tactical problem as that of securing these bridges intact to enable his army to pass through Rome without pause in pursuit of the enemy. The Fifth Army commander therefore ordered the II and VI Corps commanders to form mobile task forces to make the dash into the city to secure the river crossings before the enemy had an opportunity to destroy them.[17]

Clark's concern for the bridges was groundless, for a few hours earlier Hitler had instructed Kesselring to leave the bridges intact as the Germans withdrew north of the city. Even as small detachments of Germans fought on in the southern suburbs, the Fuehrer had declared that Rome ". . . because of its status as a place of culture must not become the scene of combat operations."[18]

[15] Jackson, *The Battle for Italy*, pp. 243–44; Senger, *Neither Hope nor Fear*, p. 252.

[16] Clark Diary, 3 June 44.
[17] Winterbotham, *The Ultra Secret*, pp. 117–18; Fifth Army OI 26, 4 Jun 44.
[18] Ltr, C/S *Suedwest* to German Forces in Italy, 4 Jun 44. *Heeres Gruppe C, Ia Nr. 287/44, G.Kdos*, in *AOK 10, Ia KTB Nr. 7, Chefsachen, Anlage 12, AOK 10, Doc. Nr. 53271/2*.

GENERALS KEYES *(left)*, CLARK, AND FREDERICK PAUSE DURING DRIVE ON ROME

Entry Into Rome

The tactical progress of the Fifth Army's many spearheads during the last few hours before the army entered Rome formed confusing patterns as the small, highly mobile armor-infantry task forces leading the two corps toward the city darted back and forth through the multitude of roads and alleys veining the Roman suburbs. Accompanying infantrymen and engineers generally rode in trucks or on the decks of tanks or tank destroyers. Then came the main body of the assault divisions, some

truck-borne, some on foot. The latter were to remain on the outskirts of the city until the mobile task forces had secured the Tiber bridges.[19] *(Map 6)*

Leading the II Corps' advance to Rome along Highway 6 and the Via Prenestina were two columns under the command of the 1st Special Service Force's General Frederick. Task Force Howze made up the first column, the 1st Special Service Force the second. To each column was attached a battalion

---

[19] II Corps Opns Rpt, Jun 44; VI Corps AAR, Jun 44.

GERMAN TROOPS WITHDRAWING FROM ROME

from the 88th Division's 350th and 351st Infantry Regiments. On the left of the corps' sector another task force, built upon the 338th Infantry, led the 85th Division across the northern slope of the Alban Hills. On the corps' right the FEC had begun relief of the 3d Division's 15th Infantry in the vicinity of Palestrina. That regiment then rapidly leapfrogged the 7th, 30th, and 349th Infantry Regiments to reach positions from which it could screen Frederick's right flank as his combined force passed south of Tivoli on the way to Rome. As successive French units relieved the 7th and 30th Infantry Regi-

ments these too moved forward to join the 15th Infantry. By the morning of 4 June the entire 3d Division was deployed across the II Corps' right flank south of the Aniene River, while the FEC deployed north of the Via Prenestina and northwest of Palestrina.[20]

At the same time two companies of the 1st Special Service Force, mounted in eight armored cars of the 81st Armored Reconnaissance Battalion of Howze's task force, began moving along Highway 6 toward the suburb of Centocelle, three miles east of Rome. When

---

[20] II Corps Opns Rpt, Jun 44.

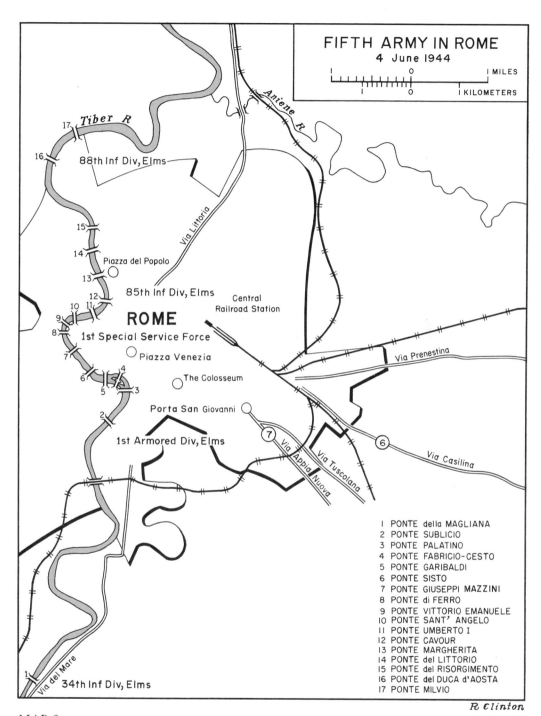

FIFTH ARMY IN ROME
4 June 1944

MILES
KILOMETERS

Tiber R

88th Inf Div, Elms

Aniene R

Via Littoria

Piazza del Popolo

85th Inf Div, Elms

Central Railroad Station

ROME

1st Special Service Force

Piazza Venezia

The Colosseum

Via Prenestina

Porta San Giovanni

1st Armored Div, Elms

Via Appia Nuova

Via Tuscolana

Via Casilina

Via del Mare

34th Inf Div, Elms

1 PONTE della MAGLIANA
2 PONTE SUBLICIO
3 PONTE PALATINO
4 PONTE FABRICIO-CESTO
5 PONTE GARIBALDI
6 PONTE SISTO
7 PONTE GIUSEPPI MAZZINI
8 PONTE di FERRO
9 PONTE VITTORIO EMANUELE
10 PONTE SANT' ANGELO
11 PONTE UMBERTO I
12 PONTE CAVOUR
13 PONTE MARGHERITA
14 PONTE del LITTORIO
15 PONTE del RISORGIMENTO
16 PONTE del DUCA d'AOSTA
17 PONTE MILVIO

R Clinton

MAP 6

ENTERING THE GATES OF ROME

the Americans attempted to advance beyond Centocelle, fire from a German parachute detachment, supported by self-propelled 150-mm. guns, brought them to a halt. The enemy guns, located in a series of strongpoints on a low ridge overlooking the town from the southwest, knocked out two of the American tanks, as the column deployed and prepared to attack with a combined tank-infantry force.[21]

While this action was taking place, the 88th Division's 88th Cavalry Reconnaissance Troop bypassed the developing fire fight to the north and sped along the Via Prenestina toward Rome. A patrol from this unit entered Rome at daybreak, but quickly withdrew to await the arrival of reinforcements before pressing on into the city to seize the bridges in the corps zone.[22] Meanwhile, the 1st Battalion of the 350th Infantry, supported by a battery of 105-mm. self-propelled howitzers of the 338th Field Artillery Battalion, a company of tanks from the 752d Tank Battalion, and a company from the 313th Engineer Battalion, had moved along Highway 6 toward Torrenova, two miles east of Centocelle. When the

---

[21] *Ibid.*

[22] 88th Div G–3 Jnl, 4 Jun 44.

battalion commander learned of the fire fight at Centocelle he too bypassed the town to reach a point overlooking the left flank of the Germans holding up Frederick's force. As the flanking force approached the enemy positions, it too was brought to a halt by heavy fire. Company C, in the lead, quickly detrucked and deployed as the rest of the battalion, accompanied by trucks, worked its way around the left flank. Only after losing three additional tanks to enemy guns did the Americans finally force the Germans to withdraw by late afternoon.[23]

While a major part of Frederick's command fought on at Centocelle, at 0615 Col. Alfred C. Marshall, Jr.'s 1st Regiment (1st Special Service Force) attacked cross-country toward the Roman suburb of Tor Pignatara, about three miles southwest of Centocelle Clinging to the decks of the tanks of Colonel Cairn's 3d Battalion, 13th Armored Regiment, the men of Company H led the way. Colonel Marshall followed in Colonel Cairn's tank. General Frederick's command half-track brought up the rear of the command group with Companies I and C following. Until this column reached the outskirts of Rome the main obstacle was a crowd of newspaper correspondents and an American field artillery battery in convoy.[24]

An hour later and one mile southeast of Tor Pignatara the column crossed the city limits of Rome. No sooner had the tanks leading the column passed the line than a well-concealed enemy anti-

tank gun opened fire. The tank-riding infantrymen quickly threw themselves to the ground, and the cavalcade of newsmen, led by a British correspondent wearing a smart-looking trench coat, disappeared to the rear. As for the artillery convoy, it simply pulled off to the side of the road as the men took cover.[25]

The enemy gun destroyed two of Cairn's leading tanks before vanishing into the maze of streets and alleys. Moving on, the column met some civilians who warned them of mines and a German tank and infantry force lurking on the road ahead. Thus forewarned, Frederick sent Companies G and I to reconnoiter a bypass. Just as Frederick dispatched the two companies, Generals Clark and Keyes arrived.

General Frederick quickly explained to his visitors his plan of maneuver, which Clark approved, although emphasizing that he wanted the column to seize the Tiber bridges as quickly as possible. Accordingly, General Keyes ordered Cairn to take a platoon of tanks and move immediately into the city without waiting for Companies G and I to complete their reconnaissance. Before starting out, Cairn wisely sent word to the two companies to continue their efforts. He then led five tanks down the highway directly into the city. No sooner had Cairn's two leading tanks, one of them his own, rounded a bend in the road, about 100 yards from where he had halted, than enemy anti-tank guns—apparently the ambush of which the Italians had warned—opened fire. The two tanks burst into flames. Hastily escaping their burning vehicles,

---

[23] 350th Inf Hist, Jun 44; 351st Inf Jnl, 4 Jun 44; FSSF S-3 Jnl, 4 Jun 44.

[24] FSSF S-3 Jnl, 4 Jun 44.

[25] Ibid.

Cairn and the surviving crew members returned to their starting point. There Cairn requested permission to abandon the frontal attack and to continue his efforts to outflank the enemy. Keyes raised no objection.[26]

Company G of the maneuvering force had in the meantime outflanked the enemy and opened fire on the self-propelled guns that had stopped Cairn. Caught completely off guard, their guns still pointed down the road toward the American lines, the Germans lost nine armored vehicles before the surviving vehicles turned and fled into the city.[27]

Company I then joined Company H and marched northward cross-country to the suburb of Acque Bollicante on the Via Prenestina. There they found Company G, which had arrived about an hour ago, just in time to see an enemy force of armored vehicles, apparently part of the force that had earlier defended Centocelle, withdrawing toward Rome. Company G's lead platoon had quickly set up an ambush on a high bank overlooking the road just as eight German tanks pulled out onto the Via Prenestina not fifty yards away. Excitedly the Americans swung their guns toward the targets, only to find that the guns would not depress far enough to hit the enemy vehicles. Nor, because of the steep bank, could the Germans elevate their own guns sufficiently to fire at Cairn's tanks. While Company G's tankers watched in dismay, the German tanks rolled right by them into the city. Company G,

however, did manage to get off a few rounds at the rear of the enemy column as it disappeared around a curve in the road.[28]

As soon as the enemy vanished, a column under the command of Colonel Howze, including his own task force as well as the 1st Special Service Force's 2d Regiment and a battalion from the 3d Regiment, arrived at Company G's position.[29] Leaving most of his infantrymen in reserve, Howze prepared to send a small tank-infantry column into the city to capture the Tiber bridges in his zone. He set H-hour at 1500 but postponed it for thirty minutes to await the arrival of a battalion from the 1st Special Service Force's 3d Regiment. At 1530 Howze's column began to move, led by numerous tank-infantry patrols, each equipped with instructions in the Italian language calling upon Romans to lead his men to the Tiber bridges.[30]

Meanwhile, on Highway 6 Colonel Marshall and a battalion of his 1st Regiment had also arrived at the Tor Pignatara. Concerned about one of the companies that had fallen behind, Colonel Marshall turned his command over to his executive officer, Major McFadden, and, accompanied by an enlisted man, set out on foot in search of the missing company. The two men had gone only about one hundred yards when enemy fire cut them down. Unaware of what had happened, McFadden and Maj. Edmund Mueller, the battalion commander, entered the city through the Tor Pignatara quarter. Close behind came a rifle company

[26] Interv, Mathews with Col Cairn, 24 Apr 50, CMH.
[27] Ibid.

[28] Ibid; Howze MS.
[29] Fifth Army History, Part V, p. 159.
[30] Howze MS.

88TH DIVISION INFANTRY RIFLEMEN PASS BURNING TANK IN ROME

commanded by Lt. William G. Sheldon. What followed appears to have been rather typical of the experiences of many of the small company-sized patrols infiltrating Rome that day. No sooner had Lieutenant Sheldon's men entered the city than they found a Mark IV tank blocking their way. Local partisans led them around the roadblock by passing through a nearby convent. A few moments later the company emerged onto a street behind the roadblock only to find another enemy tank blocking the way. This time Sheldon led his men through a store and out the rear door onto the street behind the second tank.[31]

Sheldon and his men advanced along a street leading further into the center of Rome until halted by machine gun fire from a high building overlooking an intersection. Leaving most of his men huddled in sheltering doorways, Sheldon and Mueller led a squad into the building opposite the machine gun position. Finding the elevator in order, the men rode it to the top floor, where the occupants of an apartment over-

---

[31] Interv, Mathews with Mueller, 8 May 50, CMH.

looking the enemy position offered them a vantage point from their bedroom windows. Sheldon and his men quickly silenced the gun with a burst of fire, then paused to enjoy cool drinks and sausage proffered by their hosts. After a profuse exchange of thanks and farewells the men rode the elevator down to the street and rejoined the rest of the company.[32]

Moving on to a point near the railroad yards, Sheldon's company encountered a detachment of German infantry and two self-propelled guns. Major McFadden, deciding that the company was no match for this enemy force, withdrew with his men to the Tor Pignatara to await the arrival of the rest of the battalion. Major Mueller and his battalion command detachment, in the off chance that one of his companies had already entered the city by another street, continued on toward the Tiber. Waiting in the shelter of a house until twilight, Mueller and his small party slipped by the enemy in the darkness and made their way through the dark streets to the river. There, sure enough, they found a company from the 1st Special Service Force's 3d Regiment already in possession of one of the bridges. Major Mueller and his command group remained there until noon the following day and then rejoined his battalion, which, in the meantime, had started moving through the city to meet him.[33]

The company Mueller had found on the bridge was part of Howze's column that had entered Rome at 1915. Moving to the center of the city, Howze's

men had reached the Central Railroad Station at 2000. On the way, one company had turned off from the main column into the Piazza Venezia, where the troops overtook some enemy stragglers. Individual companies fanned out to occupy two of the four Tiber bridges north of the Ponte Margherita which crosses the river just west of the Piazza del Popolo. Echeloned to the right of Howze's column, a battalion of the 351st Infantry passed through the dark streets of the city to seize a bridge already occupied by a detachment from the 1st Special Service Force. Mistaking one another for enemy in the darkness, the two units engaged in a brief fire fight. Before the error was discovered one man had been killed and several wounded, among the latter General Frederick, who had just arrived at the bridge. Following this incident, the battalion turned northward to occupy the last vehicular bridge in the corps zone, the historic Ponte Milvio. Meanwhile, a battalion of the 350th Infantry had occupied the Ponte del Duca d'Aosta, the next bridge downstream from the Ponte Milvio.[34]

As the task forces from the 88th Division, the 1st Special Service Force, and Task Force Howze led the II Corps into Rome, the 3d and 85th Divisions advanced along the corps' right and left flanks, respectively. On the left flank the 85th Division's 338th Infantry, after having taken Frascati early in the day, continued toward Rome along the Via Tuscolana well in advance of the VI Corps' 36th Division. A small motorized task force from the

---

[32] Ibid.
[33] Ibid.

[34] FSSF AAR, Jun 44; 351st Inf AAR, Jun 44; FSSF and 350th and 351st Inf S–3 Jnls, 5 Jun 44; Howze MS.

338th Infantry reached the city by 0830.[35] On corps' order, General Coulter sent the 337th Infantry, on the division's right flank, southwest toward Highway 7 with the intention of cutting off those enemy opposing the neighboring VI Corps. The regiment reached the highway at 1700 only to find the 1st Armored Division blocking its way. The resulting traffic jam delayed both units for at least an hour. Meanwhile, a small task force from the 338th Infantry, after brushing aside an enemy rear guard on the outskirts of Rome, had entered the city to occupy the Ponte Cavour, the next bridge downstream from the Ponte Margherita. On the corps' right flank the 3d Division's 30th Infantry sent patrols through the northeastern quarters of the city to seize the railway bridge over the Aniene. By 2300, 4 June, all bridges in the II Corps zone had been secured.[36]

In contrast with the helter-skelter entry of the II Corps' *ad hoc* task forces into Rome, the VI Corps' approach and entry was more systematic, less confused, but somewhat slower. This methodical approach can most likely be attributed to a widespread caution and weariness throughout Truscott's corps, fostered by the bitter combat since 26 May along the Caesar Line south of the Alban Hills. To dispel this mood and to spur a sense of competition within the corps, General Carleton, Truscott's chief of staff, sped the spearheads on their way with a challenging report that Keyes' corps, advancing in three separate columns, had already moved to

within three to five miles of Rome. "The II Corps' left flank has just crossed around us and will be in there before daylight undoubtedly," he announced.[37] Nevertheless, a weary caution prevailed on the VI Corps sector as an advance party of the 1st Armored Division's CCA, which had spent the night on the outskirts of Albano, moved slowly into the town at dawn. As the rest of the command followed two hours later, Carleton again called Harmon's command post, saying: "This is an all-out pursuit, the enemy is running away from us—put on all steam."[38] This Harmon proceeded to do. The resulting pell-mell dash by the entire armored division so crowded the roads in its zone of operations that by late afternoon a series of traffic jams had caused more delays than the scattered enemy resistance. By 1800 CCA's point moving along the Via Appia Nuova, the extension of Highway 7, had passed through the Porta San Giovanni, hard by St. John Lateran, into the inner city.

Echeloned to the left, CCB met more resistance as it advanced five miles beyond Albano. During the morning the command's spearhead encountered strong enemy rear guards whose tactics of fire and run repeatedly forced the tanks and armored infantry to deploy and fight. But by 1330 Company A, 13th Armored Regiment, finally managed to break free and, accompanied by a platoon of tank destroyers, advanced rapidly to the outskirts of Rome. The 6th Armored Infantry's 2d Battalion followed in half-tracks. Entering Rome from Highway 7 late that

[35] 85th Div G–3 Jnl, 4–5 Jun 44; FSSF G–3 Jnl, 4 Jun 44.

[36] 85th Div G–3 Jnl, 4 Jun 44; FSSF G–3 Jnl, 4 Jun 44.

[37] VI Corps G–3 Jnl, 040045B Jun 44, Tel, Carleton to Harmon.

[38] *Ibid.*, 040700B Jun 44.

ROMANS LINE STREETS AS U.S. TANK
DESTROYERS ROLL BY COLISEUM

afternoon, the battalion moved rapidly through the city to seize the Ponte Palatino. The rest of the combat command skirted the city to the south to capture two major crossings of the Tiber just outside Rome. That night the 1st Armored Division secured all bridges in its sector and by daylight on the 5th had reached Rome's western limits. "Push on to Genoa, if you want to," Truscott exultantly radioed Harmon. [39]

The 36th Division, which throughout the day had advanced toward Rome along the Via Tuscolana, also entered the city that night. But because VI Corps had given Harmon's armor priority on the roads, the infantry division was delayed while the armored division entered Rome. Shortly before midnight Walker's division too began moving through the darkened maze of Roman streets. Although street and other lights were out, moonlight helped the troops pick their way through the unfamiliar city to those Tiber bridges already in the hands of Harmon's division. "As we moved along the dark streets," Walker observed, "we could hear the people at all the windows of the high buildings clapping their hands." There was no other sound but the tramp of marching feet, and the low whine of truck motors. It was still dark when the procession crossed the Tiber.

The following morning Romans emerged from their dwellings in large numbers to give the long columns of troops still passing through their city the tumultuous, almost hysterical welcome so familiar to newsreel viewers of that time. But men who had actually captured Rome had passed through in darkness and near silence. [40]

By the morning of 5 June most of the Fifth Army had drawn up to the line of the Tiber along a 20-mile front from the river's mouth southwest of Rome to its junction with the Aniene northeast of the city. The British 1st and 5th Divisions were on the left, the U.S. VI and II Corps in the center, and on the right the FEC. Recently pinched out of line by the II Corps, the FEC covered the army's right rear, pending the arrival of the British Eighth Army on the line of the Aniene east of Rome. On the VI Corps' sector southwest of Rome the 34th and 45th Divisions faced a bridgeless Tiber. In the south-

[39] *Ibid.*, 050630B Jun 44.

[40] Walker Diary, 4 Jun 44, pp. 40–42.

ern half of the city the 1st Armored and 36th Infantry Divisions had crossed the river and advanced to the city's western outskirts. In the northeastern quarters of Rome the II Corps' 85th and 88th Divisions had also crossed the Tiber and moved to the edge of the city. The 1st Special Service Force continued to guard the bridges, and the 3d Division lay along the Aniene, prepared to enter Rome as the garrison force. Moving up on the U.S. II Corps' right, Juin's corps, after clearing Cave and Palestrina, advanced toward the Tiber east of Rome. The 1st Motorized Infantry Division and the 3d Algerian Infantry Division mopped up the area east of Rome, preparatory to relief by the British 13 Corps.[41]

The Eighth Army's I Canadian and British 13 and 10 Corps were echeloned some distance to the southeast facing north toward the Prenestini and Simbruini ranges of the Apennines. The dispositions of General Leese's forces were as follows: on the left, the I Canadian Corps with the 6th South African Armoured Division along the Anagni-Baliano road; in the center, the 13 Corps with the British 6th Armoured Division along the Alatri-Fiuggi road and the 8th Indian Division along the Alatri-Guarcino road; and, on the right, the 10 Corps with the 2d New Zealand Division forward, strung out along the Sora-Avezzano and Atina-Opi roads. On the Adriatic sector the 5 Corps came to life, as the Germans began shifting forces from that sector to the area west of the Apennines.[42]

General Clark and his Fifth Army had captured Rome two days before the Allied landings in Normandy. But contrary to Churchill's and Alexander's expectations, the German *Tenth* and a good part of the *Fourteenth Army* had escaped destruction. Ever since that first week of June 1944 the question has been debated whether the glittering prize of Rome was an acceptable alternative to the destruction of the enemy's forces in the field—the conventional object in battle.

Because Alexander in planning Operation DIADEM had the texts of all radio messages passing between Kesselring's headquarters and OKW shortly after their transmission, thanks to the code breakers in Britain, he had considerable grounds for believing that his armies would achieve that object.[43] Clark, on the other hand, believed that destruction of the enemy forces south of Rome was an impossible objective. The fact that the *Tenth Army* did indeed escape destruction without using Highway 6 tends to support Clark's position. Furthermore, when Clark recommended to Alexander that Juin's corps be allowed to move on Ferentino in the Sacco valley, there to cut off the Germans, as Alexander had hoped that Truscott's corps would do at Valmontone, the Allied commander had refused to do so. Yet Alexander still reported to Churchill on 4 June that there was not much doubt "that we have got a fair cop."[44]

On the other hand, Alexander was to observe later that "If he (Clark) had succeeded in carrying out my plan the disaster to the enemy would have been

[41] Pierre Le Goyet, *La Participation Française à la Campagne d'Italie 1943–44* (Paris: Imprimerie Nationale, 1969), p. 129.
[42] Operations of the British, Indian, and Dominion Forces in Italy, Part II, Sec. D.
[43] Winterbotham, *The Ultra Secret*, p. 118.
[44] Nicholson, *Alex*, p. 254.

much greater; indeed, most of the German forces would have been destroyed. True, the battle ended in a decisive victory for us, but it was not as complete as might have been. . . . I can only assume that the immediate lure of Rome for its publicity value persuaded Mark Clark to switch the direction of his advance."[45]

Other explanations have been offered to account for the failure of the Allied armies to destroy more of the enemy's forces south of Rome. If the four Allied armored divisions in the theater had been equipped as mountain divisions like those of the French, it has been contended, they would have been able to follow the Germans more closely through the mountains. In the Liri valley the Canadian and British armored divisions, with their vast columns of supporting vehicles, did more to slow down the Eighth Army's pursuit than the enemy.[46] Yet the difficulties encountered by the French mountain divisions after their breakthrough of the Gustav Line would indicate that divisions similarly organized and equipped would have had an equally difficult time pursuing the retreating enemy over narrow, easily blocked roads in the Apennines.

In any case the drive for Rome, which, in a sense, had begun in September 1943, had finally come to an end. Rome had been essentially an Allied victory, though only Americans savored the flavor of a triumphal entry into the ancient capital. Yet it seemed not altogether unjust that this was so,

for the Fifth Army had paid for that prize with the longest casualty lists of any of the Allied forces. Since the beginning of Operation DIADEM on 11 May, 3,145 Americans had been killed in action, 13,704 wounded, and 1,082 missing—a total of 17,931 casualties. During the twenty-four days of the May offensive, the Fifth Army had incurred one-third of its total losses in Italy since D-day at Salerno in the previous September. Yet on 4 June, thanks to a well-functioning replacement system, the Fifth Army's strength was at a peak that it had not reached before, nor would again—an effective strength of 369,356, which included 231,306 Americans, 95,142 French (mostly Algerians and Moroccans), and 42,908 British.

The French and British elements of Clark's army had also incurred relatively heavy losses during the drive on Rome. During the period from 1 April to 4 June, 520 British soldiers had been killed in action, 2,385 wounded, and 450 missing. In proportion to their total strength, the French had suffered most heavily: 1,751 of the FEC had been killed in action, 7,912 wounded, and 972 missing, for a total of 10,635 casualties.[47]

Although Operation DIADEM had given the Eighth Army the major role and the wider front, that army's casualties had been somewhat less than the U.S. Fifth Army's—11,639 as compared with 17,931. If, however, the losses of the attached French and British units are added to the Fifth Army totals, the disproportion becomes greater— 28,566—for the entire army, for the casualty figures for the Eighth Army included Dominion and Polish forces as

---

[45] John North, ed., *Memoirs, Field Marshal Alexander of Tunis, 1939–45* (New York: McGraw-Hill, 1962).

[46] Shepperd, *The Italian Campaign*, p. 43.

[47] *Fifth Army History*, Part V, pp. !66–67.

well as British. With the Eighth Army British contingents constituting the largest national elements, they quite logically had suffered the heaviest casualties—1,068 killed in action, 3,506 wounded, and 208 missing. Dominion forces listed some 910 killed in action, 3,063 wounded, and 118 missing. For the Polish corps the figure was 629 killed in action, 2,044 wounded, and 93 missing. Total Allied losses, therefore, amounted to 40,205 of all categories.[48]

For approximately the same period (10 May to 10 June) the two defending German armies had incurred a total of 38,024 casualties. Of these the *Tenth Army* lost 8,672, as compared with the *Fourteenth Army*'s 7,012. Of these 2,127 were listed as killed in action for both German armies. In addition to the casualties of the armies, *Armee Abteilung von Zangen*, opposing the British 5 Corps along the Adriatic, and *Army Group C*'s headquarters listed a total of 391 casualties of all types. The fact that within the Wehrmacht casualties were reported through two different channels, Personnel and Field Surgeon, probably accounts for a discrepancy between the totals given through the latter, 31,759, and the total of 38,024, given by the OKW War Diary.[49]

An even more significant discrepancy exists between the 15,606 prisoners of war the Allies claim to have captured during the period 1 April to 4 June 1944 and the 6,122 listed by the Germans as missing in action. The difference of 9,484 between Allied claims of enemy captured and German records of men listed as missing in action can possibly be explained as follows. The German military command generally did not record losses among non-German personnel attached to the armed forces. Many of these men were Russian and Polish prisoners of war who, to escape the rigors of life in a prison camp, had volunteered to serve as auxiliaries with the German armed forces. Known as *Hilfswillige*, or, more familiarly, as *HiWi's* among the soldiers whom they supported, these men were usually dependable when on duty in rear areas but readily deserted when caught in difficult combat situations, as was frequently the case in the defense of Rome. Dressed in German uniform, the *HiWi's* were classified as POW's by the Allies.[50]

The feelings of many on the Allied side were perhaps best summed up in the following words of a British war correspondent. "Now, at last the victory had arrived. It was good that it should come, for it had been bravely contested and in the end brilliantly achieved. But it had been a long journey, and everyone was very weary. And too many had died."[51]

---

[48] *Ibid.;* Operations of the British, Indian, and Dominion Forces in Italy, Part V; Nicholson, *The Canadians in Italy,* p. 452; Robin Kay, *Official History of New Zealand in the Second World War 1939–45,* vol. II, *Italy, From Cassino to Trieste* (Wellington, N.Z.: Historical Publications Branch, Department of Internal Affairs, 1967), p. 86.

[49] *Verluste der Wehrmacht bis 1944, Organization des Verlustmeldewesens, HI/176a Monatsmeldungen ab. 1.11.43,* photocopy in CMH; Ltr, Bundesarchiv (Militärarchiv), 18.3.1970. Az.6992/Jessup to George Blau, CMH; Greiner and Schramm, eds., *OKW/WFSt, KTB,* IV(1), p. 514.

[50] In addition to the personnel losses, the German armies reported as of 28 May, a large quantity of equipment lost or destroyed in battle. This included 500 heavy and 1,600 light machine guns, 300 artillery pieces, 60 rocket launchers, and 200 to 250 tanks of all types (approximately half of the armor on hand in the *Tenth* and *Fourteenth Armies*). See Greiner and Schramm, eds., *OKW/WFSt, KTB,* IV(1), p. 514.

[51] Christopher Buckley, *Road to Rome* (London: Hadder-Stoughton, 1945).

PART FOUR

ROME TO THE ARNO

The energy thrown into the first stage of the pursuit chiefly determines the value of the victory.

CLAUSEWITZ, *On War*

CHAPTER XII

Interlude in Rome

The View From the Capitoline Hill

As the U.S. Fifth Army moved through Rome, General Clark on the morning of 5 June summoned his corps commanders and senior staff officers to a conference in the city hall atop the Capitoline Hill.[1] Starting from the Excelsior Hotel where Clark had established his temporary command post, a procession of jeeps bearing the largest assemblage of high military rank that the Romans had seen in many months, wound its way through jubilant throngs to the city hall, at that point occupied by only a handful of anxious functionaries.[2]

The senior commanders gathered that morning on the historic hill with mixed emotions. Relief that the long drive on Rome had at last reached its goal and confidence that the enemy was at last on the run were somewhat overshadowed by an awareness that demands of other campaigns in other lands would soon obscure the Italian venture now so favorably underway. For it was the eve of OVERLORD, and

news of the Allied landing in Normandy would soon crowd Rome and the Italian campaign off the front pages of the world press and, most importantly, the campaign would drop to second place in Allied strategic planning for the Mediterranean.

On 22 May General Alexander had received assurance from General Wilson, the Mediterranean theater commander, that the Allied armies in Italy would be given "overriding priority in the allocation of resources" until the capture of Rome, but thereafter emphasis within the theater would shift to preparations for an amphibious operation to be undertaken no later than mid-September.[3]

This operation was to be either in close support of ground operations in Italy or against the coast of southern France. The force required for the latter enterprise would probably include "three United States infantry divisions and all the French divisions at present in Allied armies Italy." After the capture of Rome, one U.S. division was to be relieved by 17 June, a French division by the 24th, and three days later a second U.S. division; thereafter, the remaining formations at longer intervals. Also an "experienced U.S. Corps headquarters" was to be relieved as soon as possible. These instructions with

---

[1] Clark, *Calculated Risk*, pp. 365–66.

[2] General Clark, accompanied by his chief of staff, General Gruenther, Brigadier Georges Beucler, chief of the French Mission with the Fifth Army, and Colonel Britten of the British increment, Fifth Army, Maj. Gen. Harry H. Johnson, commander of the Rome Garrison, and Brigadier E. E. Hume, Chief of Allied Military Government, entered Rome at approximately 8 a.m. on Monday, 5 June.

[3] Alexander *Despatch*, pp. 51–52.

their uncertainties for the continued primacy of the Italian campaign in the Mediterranean took some of the edge off the victory celebrations in the several Allied headquarters, from Wilson's to Clark's, and influenced planning for operations beyond Rome.

Three days after the Fifth Army's entry into Rome, General Wilson informed his superiors in London that the success of Operation DIADEM would permit him "to mount an amphibious operation on the scale of ANVIL with a target date of 15 August." A week later Wilson directed Alexander to withdraw the U.S. VI Corps headquarters and the 45th Division immediately, the 3d Division by 17 June, and the 36th Division by the 27th. The French were to begin withdrawing one division on the 24th and a second in early July.

At the same time, Alexander also received instructions from the Combined Chiefs in London to complete destruction of the German forces in Italy south of the Pisa-Rimini Line, that is to say, south of the Arno River, with the forces remaining under his command. Until this had been done "there should be no withdrawal from the battle of any Allied forces that are necessary for this purpose." These contradictory instructions reflected the conflicting influences at work at Headquarters, Allied Armies Italy and at Allied Force Headquarters, Mediterranean. Alexander generally acted as a spokesman for Churchill's strategic views. General Wilson's headquarters, on the other hand, was dominated by the views of its largely American staff, headed by the deputy theater commander, General Devers, generally a spokesman for General Marshall's stra-

tegic views in that headquarters. Against this background of differing strategies and uncertainty the Allied commanders in Italy would undertake the pursuit of the German armies north of Rome. [4]

Planning the Pursuit

With the capture of Rome a wide gap had been opened in that part of *Army Group C* extending from Tivoli, fifteen miles east of Rome, southwest to the mouth of the Tiber. Scattered remnants of four German divisions were in the area but were too concerned with mere survival to even attempt to close the gap. General Alexander determined to exploit the situation by sending the U.S. Fifth and British Eighth Armies as quickly as possible through the gap in the hope they would reach the Northern Apennines, some 170 miles northwest of Rome, before Kesselring could once again establish his armies in terrain even more favorable for the defense than that of the Gustav Line. [5]

In planning his pursuit of the German armies north of Rome, Alexander decided to continue the classical "oblique order" in which his own armies had approached the city following the junction of the southern front with the beachhead. The oblique order now, as then, found the Allied left wing, composed of the Fifth Army and one

---

[4] Robert W. Coakley and Richard M. Leighton, *Global Logistics and Strategy: 1943–45,* UNITED STATES ARMY IN WORLD WAR II (Washington, 1968), ch. XV; Msg. MEDCOS 125 AFHQ, Wilson to COS, 7 June 44, CCS 561/5 in ABC 384 Eur, Sec. 9–A; Ehrman, *Grand Strategy,* vol. V, pp. 345–67.

[5] Operations of British, Indian, and Dominion Forces in Italy, Part II, Sec. D; Alexander *Despatch,* p. 50.

corps of the Eighth Army, advanced, in Alexander's words, *"en potence."* His right wing, made up of a second corps of Eighth Army and the 5 Corps, the latter under AAI control on the Adriatic coast, was held back. A third corps was in reserve. He expected thereby to execute a pursuit of the enemy forces by a holding attack against the still relatively strong *Tenth Army* in Kesselring's center and an all-out attack against the weakened *Fourteenth Army.* Alexander counted on this move to complete that army's destruction and enable the U.S. Fifth Army to outflank the German *Tenth Army* west of the Tiber and possibly cut off its retreat. This had been Alexander's basic strategic concept south of Rome, and it had fallen short of realization. It remained to be seen whether it would succeed north of Rome.[6]

In the Fifth Army zone of operations immediate goals were the capture of the small seaport of Civitavecchia, forty miles northwest of Rome, and Viterbo, site of an airfield complex forty miles north-northwest of Rome and thirty miles inland.[7] Possession of Viterbo would give the Allies forward bases from which aircraft of the MATAF could fly in close support of the advance to the Arno and MASAF bombers could attack cities in southern Germany. The swift capture and restoration of the port facilities at Civitavecchia were of even greater importance for ground operations, for with each passing day the Allied armies left their supply dumps farther to the rear, while gasoline consumption rates increased in

direct proportion to the distance of the armies from those dumps. For the Eighth Army the possession of the Adriatic port of Ancona, 130 miles northeast of Rome, was of equal importance.

Although in May the Peninsula Base Section (PBS), the U.S. logistics command, had launched several ambitious pipeline construction projects, the pipelines were, by 5 June, still far from Rome. The 696th Engineer Company had extended a six-inch pipeline along Highway 6 at the rate of two miles per day, and had reached a dispensing point at Ceprano, fifty-four miles southeast of Rome. Another month would pass before the pipeline would reach Rome. Along Highway 7 on the Tyrrhenian coast a four-inch pipeline under construction by the 785th Engineer Petroleum Distribution Company would not be open at its distribution point at Terracina until 9 June.[8]

Civitavecchia's eventual importance to the Allies as a petroleum distribution point lay in its role as the first port north of Naples, which since 1943 had been the Fifth Army's main supply base, capable of receiving small tankers. For some time Allied logisticians had planned to open a 100,000-barrel terminal at Civitavecchia, and construction units were poised close behind the advancing front to begin work as soon as the port was captured. In the meantime, both Allied armies would depend upon growing numbers of trucks to

---

[6] Alexander *Despatch*, p. 48.
[7] See Hq, AAI OI No. 1, 5 May 44.

[8] Lida Mayo, The Corps of Engineers: Operations in the War Against Germany, a volume in preparation for the UNITED STATES ARMY IN WORLD WAR II series, MS ch. 12 (hereafter cited as Mayo MS), CMH.

haul the vital gasoline to support their lengthening lines of communications. This increased requisition of motor transport would, in turn, reduce the number of trucks available to the engineers to haul pipeline construction material, thus delaying pipelines and completing a vicious circle which only the opening of additional ports along both the Tyrrhenian and Adriatic flanks could eliminate.[9]

Dependence upon motor transport became heavier through lack of alternative means of transport. Coastal shipping from Naples to Anzio had been practical as long as the front remained south of Rome, but with the advance to and beyond Rome the port of Anzio quickly lost its importance. Railroads offered little promise of resolving the problem since they had been systematically destroyed by the Germans and Allied bombers. The long winter stalemate along the Gustav Line and on the Anzio beachhead had given the Germans plenty of time to demolish the two main rail lines between Naples and Rome—one passing through the Liri valley and the other running along the Tyrrhenian coast. In addition to ripping up the ties, German demolition crews had also destroyed bridges, culverts, overpasses, and tunnels. Because of a shortage of manpower and construction materials railroad repairs took considerable time. Not until early June did the engineers, using captured German material, complete a 237-foot railway bridge over the Garigliano at Min-

turno. Clearing the Monte Orso tunnel through the Ausoni Mountains just south of the former Anzio beachhead was so difficult that this rail line was not opened as far as Cisterna station until 20 July. Consequently, when Rome fell on 4 June, the Allies, especially the Eighth Army, were still dependent upon a railhead at Mignano, a hundred miles southeast of Rome, and on the dumps at the former Anzio beachhead supplied by coastal shipping from Naples.[10]

The ability of the engineers rapidly to repair highways, bridges, and culverts thus had a considerable influence on the speed of the Allied pursuit. Along Highway 1, running through the Fifth Army zone, bridges and culverts averaged about one per mile and all had been systematically destroyed by the retreating Germans. Before the end of June the 1108th Engineer Combat Group, supporting first the II and VI Corps, later the IV Corps, had repaired thirty-eight culverts and graded 176 miles of roads. Fortunately, throughout Italy there was usually plenty of local material for road construction and repair.[11]

Until additional ports were opened on both coastal flanks, Alexander could hardly support more than nine divisions in the field against Kesselring's army group. Thus a race for ports, especially in the Fifth Army zone, would soon become the strategic and tactical *leitmotif* of the Allied advance to the Arno.

[9] Joseph Bykofsky and Harold Larson, *The Transportation Corps: Operations Overseas,* UNITED STATES ARMY IN WORLD WAR II (Washington, 1957), pp. 211–32.

[10] *Ibid.;* Mayo MS, ch. XV; Operations of the British, Indian, and Dominion Forces in Italy, Part II, Sec. D.

[11] Mayo MS, ch. XII.

The German Situation

The fighting south of Rome had damaged the *Fourteenth Army* more severely than it had the *Tenth* and consequently it was more hard pressed as it withdrew beyond Rome before the U.S. Fifth Army than was the *Tenth Army*, which had managed to escape virtually intact into the mountains and across the Aniene before the British Eighth Army. Aware that the Allied command would attempt to exploit this situation by pursuing the *Fourteenth Army* so vigorously as to force it to expose the *Tenth Army*'s right flank, Field Marshal Kesselring decided to cover that flank with the Tiber River, which north of Rome flows generally in a southerly direction out of the Umbrian highlands. At the same time, he also needed to reinforce the battered *Fourteenth Army* so as to delay the Fifth Army's pursuit and thereby expose as little as possible of the *Tenth Army*'s right flank. This would be almost impossible until Orvieto was reached. Between Rome and Orvieto, a Tiber crossing some sixty miles north of Rome, all bridges across the river had been destroyed either by Allied aircraft or by German engineers, acting with premature zeal. Thus for the first sixty miles beyond Rome the Allied armies would be pursuing an enemy whose main battle strength lay east rather than west of the Tiber. That this would favor the U.S. Fifth Army rather than the British Eighth Army was as evident to Kesselring in his command post near Monte Soratte on Highway 3 some twenty-two miles north of Rome as it was to Allied commanders at their 5 June conference on the Capitoline Hill.[12]

Further adding to Kesselring's woes, for the first hundred miles north of Rome the terrain offered few defensive advantages. The peninsula broadens rapidly for some eighty-five miles, until at the latitude of Lake Trasimeno it attains a width of about 140 miles. In this area the Central Apennines, after first curving eastward, begin a wide swing to the northwest to reach the sea north of Leghorn and the Arno River and become the Northern Apennines. In them Field Marshal Kesselring planned to establish a new winter line, the *Gotenstellung,* or Gothic Line, along which he expected to make another stand as he had in the winter of 1943 before Cassino and along the Rapido. The name of the line would evoke the presence of the Gothic kingdoms established in Italy by Germanic tribes in the 6th century A.D.[13]

If the German command in Italy could delay the Allied advance to the Arno and the Northern Apennines until autumn rains hampered cross-country movement, Kesselring might have a chance to turn the Gothic Line into another Gustav Line. This, then, became Kesselring's main tactical problem beyond Rome—to rebuild the shattered *Fourteenth Army* while at the same time checking the Allied pursuit and turning it once again into a slow, grinding advance as it had been from Salerno to Cassino and the Winter Line, and then to bring it to a halt for the winter along the Gothic Line.

The *Fourteenth Army* on 6 June received a new commander as Generalleutnant Joachim Lemelsen replaced General von Mackensen. Lemelsen

[12] MS # C–064 (Kesselring).

[13] Greiner and Schramm, eds., *OKW/WFSt, KTB,* IV(1), pp. 513–15.

found his command in bad shape indeed. Since the major part of the *LXXVI Panzer Corps* had escaped destruction southeast of Rome by retreating northeastward over the Aniene in the vicinity of Tivoli into the *Tenth Army*'s zone, there was left to General Lemelsen only the *I Parachute Corps* and a provisional corps. Holding the *Fourteenth Army*'s left wing, its flank resting on the Tiber, was the parachute corps. Consisting only of two battleworthy divisions, the *4th Parachute* and *3d Panzer Grenadier Divisions,* it was but a shadow of the corps that had held the Caesar Line so stubbornly in May. On the corps' right, or coastal, flank were remnants of the *65th* and *92d Divisions,* the latter a training unit originally engaged in coast-watching duties near the mouth of the Tiber. These two units had been grouped together under a provisional corps headquarters known as *Group Goerlitz.* The *Hermann Goering, 362d,* and *715th Divisions* had either experienced such severe losses as to necessitate withdrawal from action for rest and reorganization or were with Herr's *LXXVI Panzer Corps* east of the Tiber and under *Tenth Army* control.[14]

The *Tenth Army* at that point commanded three army corps—the *XIV* and *LXXVI Panzer* and the *LI Mountain Corps.* In turn, these corps controlled among them the best divisions remaining in *Army Group C.* These included the *29th* and *90th Panzer Grenadier Divisions* and the *1st Parachute, 5th Mountain,* and *44th* and *278th Infantry Divisions.* On the Adriatic flank another provisional corps, *Group Hauck,* controlled

the *114th Jaeger* and *305th Infantry Divisions.* Not yet hard pressed in that sector, these divisions could be expected eventually to provide reinforcements to the sectors west of the Tiber. In army group reserve near Orvieto were the *26th Panzer* and *20th Luftwaffe Field Divisions* and the *162d Turkomen* and *356th Infantry Divisions.* The Luftwaffe division had recently arrived from occupation duty in Denmark, and the *162d* and *356th Divisions* had been employed on coastal defense and antipartisan duties in northern Italy. The Turkomen division, of doubtful loyalty, was composed of former Russian prisoners of war from Soviet Turkestan led by German officers and noncommissioned officers.[15]

Because of the difficulties of shifting units from east to west of the Tiber south of Orvieto, Kesselring, at least for the first week following the loss of Rome, would have no recourse but to reinforce his right wing *(Fourteenth Army)* with those troops already located west of the Tiber and within marching distance of the front. These were the divisions in army group reserve near Orvieto. Kesselring decided to leave the *26th Panzer Division* at Orvieto to defend that important crossing and to send first the *20th Luftwaffe Field Division* and then the *162d Turkomen Division* southward to reinforce the *Fourteenth Army.* He hoped thereby to slow up the Allied armies enough to permit him to regroup his forces in such a way as to permit the establishment of a series of temporary delaying positions south of the Arno River. For the next

---

[14] *AOK 14, Ia KTB Anl. 3,* 7 Jun 44, *AOK 14,* Doc. 59091/1; MS # C–064 (Kesselring).

[15] Greiner and Schramm, eds., *OKW/WFSt, KTB,* IV(1), pp. 514–15.

two weeks this would become the dominant tactical theme within *Army Group C;* for in Kesselring's words, "On this everything depended."[16]

Two of the most important of these defensive lines he designated Dora and Frieda. The former began in the vicinity of Orbetello, located on coastal Highway 1 seventy miles northwest of Rome; from Orbetello it extended eastward, skirting Lake Bolsena's southern shore, thence to Narni on Highway 3 forty miles north of Rome; it then extended twenty miles southeast to Rieti on Highway 4, eastward for thirty miles to L'Azuila, then skirted the southern edge of the wild and desolate Gran Sasso d'Italia, from which the Germans had earlier rescued a captive Mussolini, and finally extended eastward to the Adriatic coast. The Frieda Line, beginning near Piombino, thirty miles northwest of Grosseto, extended about thirty-five miles northeastward to Radicondoli, thence to Lake Trasimeno, on to Perugia, an important road junction ten miles east of the lake, then twenty miles southeast to Foligno on Highway 3, and thence sixty miles eastward across the Apennines to reach the coast near Porto Civitanova.[17] For the next two weeks Allied operations north of Rome would be concerned largely with reaching and breaking through these two lines.

Rome in Allied Hands

The capture of Rome marked not only the zenith of the Italian Campaign thus far but also an important turning point in the relatively brief history of the Kingdom of Italy.[18] Not since September 1943, when the Germans had occupied Rome, had King Victor Emmanuel III, who had fled with his government to Bari in southern Italy, set foot in his former capital.[19] Several months before the Allies entered Rome, the King, his long association with Fascism having made him unacceptable either to the Allies or to the major Italian political factions, had yielded to Allied pressure and agreed to abdicate as soon as the Germans were driven from the city. Thereupon, with the approval of the Allied Control Commission (ACC), Marshal Pietro Badoglio's government had intended for the transfer of power to Crown Prince Humberto, as the Lieutenant General of the Realm. The old soldier Badoglio was then to resign, in anticipation of the Crown Prince's formation of a new government, which was to include the leaders of the Roman Committee of National Liberation (*Comitati di Liberazione Nazionale*, CLN).

As soon as the U.S. Fifth Army drew near Rome, however, the King began to have second thoughts and insisted that he should personally once again enter Rome as king. The Allied Control Commission (ACC), justifiably concerned about Rome's reception of the

---

[16] *Ibid.,* pp. 513–15; Albert Kesselring, *A Soldier's Record* (New York: William Morrow and Co., 1954), p. 247.

[17] Kesselring, *A Soldier's Record,* p. 247.

[18] The modern Kingdom of Italy was proclaimed in 1861, prior to the annexation of Venetia and Rome.

[19] Harry L. Coles and Albert K. Weinberg, *Civil Affairs: Soldiers Become Governors,* UNITED STATES ARMY IN WORLD WAR II (Washington, 1964), pp. 454–61. Unless otherwise cited the following is based upon this source. See also Charles F. Delzell, *Mussolini's Enemies: The Anti-Fascist Resistance Parties* (Princeton: Princeton University Press, 1961).

now discredited monarch, prevailed upon him to adhere to his original agreement. On 5 June, still far away in Bari, he signed the instrument transferring the royal powers to Crown Prince Humberto.

While successful in disposing of the Italian King, the Allies were less so in fulfilling the second part of their plan— forming a new government under Badoglio. Many key Italian political leaders, it developed, refused to serve under Badoglio. All factions, including the Committee of National Liberation (CLN), agreed, however, to accept the 73-year-old Ivanoe Bonomi, President of the Committee of National Liberation and a prime minister in the pre-Fascist years. In spite of the urgings by both the ACC and Bonomi, Marshal Badoglio refused to serve in this new government.

When the Fifth Army's civil affairs officer, Brig. Gen. Edgar E. Hume, arrived in the city on 5 June to become military governor, he found the city controlled by a well-organized arm of the CLN. It was led by General Roberto Bencivengo, who promptly relinquished to the Allied representative the authority the committee had exercised since the Germans had begun to evacuate the city. It was not long, however, before the first warm glow of joyous cooperation with the Allied authorities, which had accompanied the liberation of Rome, gave way to bitter recriminations as the ACC attempted to bring some order to the chaotic food and housing situations.

After formation of the new civil government, the Allied Force Headquarters (AFHQ), for military and administrative reasons, refused to authorize Bonomi's government to move to Rome from Bari for well over a month following the city's capture. Even after the return of the Italian Government to Rome a lack of effective civil administration would continue to plague Allied authorities for the remainder of the campaign.

The Allies had long since taken the position that the capture of Rome would be of greater political than military significance, and their occupation policies were therefore similar to those of the Germans. Although Rome's traditional position as the hub of the peninsula's transportation and communications network was to remain an important factor in operations, the AAI command decided not to establish advance base installations within the city. Military installations were limited to hospitals, transit camps, and a few military leave hotels. Moreover, the Vatican's neutrality was to be respected, with enemy nationals who had taken refuge there not to be disturbed. Rome was to remain, as it had been under the Germans, essentially an open city.[20]

There were other similarities too. The Allies were soon to complain bitterly, as had the German military authorities before them, that the Romans seemed indifferent to the great struggle being waged in their country, that they appeared more concerned about their own immediate interests than about the rehabilitation and reconstruction of It-

---

[20] The city of Rome was to be garrisoned by the U.S. 3d Infantry Division with attached Allied units, including a battalion of British troops and a mixed battalion of French, with one company from each of the four divisions making up the French Expeditionary Corps. See Le Goyet, *La Participation Française à la Campagne d'Italie*, p. 129.

aly.[21] As General Clark moved through the streets to the plaudits of the Romans on the morning of 5 June, he might well have meditated momentarily upon the fickleness of a populace which had submitted so often to conquerors only eventually to turn against them.

The city, with its agriculturally inadequate environs, was now cut off by the Allied victory from its traditional sources of food supply—still in German hands. Furthermore, lack of transportation facilities would greatly limit the amount of food that could be brought from the few agricultural areas in the south. The Allied cornucopia thus failed to produce the flood of food and clothing that the inhabitants had long expected. That only served to make the Romans even more restless and resentful over what they considered to be their ill-deserved misfortune. Over the coming months they would show their disappointment in a sullen hostility to the Allied military authorities and in an unconcealed and virtually uncontrollable black market, flourishing with the tacit consent of the civil authorities who refused to prosecute violators even after denunciations were made to them by the Allied Black Market Control Division.[22] In the over-all conduct of the phase of the campaign that was about to begin, the Romans would prove to be as much of a burden to the Allies as they had been to the Germans.

The capture of Rome had been the focus of Allied hopes and plans for so long that for many, ranging from private to general, the operations in the months following would appear to be a postscript to the Italian campaign. In a strategic sense perhaps they were, for after Rome and the Allied landings in northwestern France, the campaign sank to the level of a vast holding operation. But operationally considered, the eleven months between the fall of Rome and the surrender of the German armies were anything but a postscript. In terms of ground gained, of battles fought and won, and casualties incurred, the second half of the Italian campaign must be considered as equal in importance to the first half.

---

[21] Hq ACC Rpt for Jun 44, cited in Coles and Weinberg, p. 461.

[22] *Ibid.;* Harold B. Lipsius, Chief, Rome Black Market Control Division, ACC Rpt for Nov 44, ACC files 10400/153/79.

CHAPTER XIII

Pursuit North of Rome

General Alexander's order of 5 May which had set the drive on Rome in motion had also designated the broad objectives for the next phase of the campaign. General Clark's Fifth Army was to pursue the enemy northwest of Rome to capture the Viterbo airfields and the port of Civitavecchia, thereafter to advance on Leghorn. General Leese's Eighth Army was to pursue the enemy in a northerly and northeasterly direction along the general axis Terni–Perugia, thereafter to advance on Florence and the Adriatic port of Ancona.

On 7 June Alexander further refined these instructions. Both armies were to continue their advance "with all possible speed"—the Fifth Army to advance toward the western half of the Northern Apennines, comprising a triangle connecting the cities of Pisa, Lucca, and Pistoia, and the Eighth Army toward an area enclosed by a triangle connecting the cities of Florence, Arezzo, and Bibbiena. Both armies were to maintain close contact on their inner flanks, but not to wait for one another, and were to bypass strongpoints in hope of maintaining the momentum that had carried them to Rome and beyond. For Alexander, privy to Kesselring's situation and intentions, believed that if his armies could sustain that momentum they might have a second chance to outflank and destroy Vietinghoff's *Tenth Army* and breach the Gothic Line before the Germans had an opportunity to occupy it.[1]

Although traditional military wisdom at this point called for a headlong pursuit of the enemy to keep him from regrouping and re-forming his lines, Allied commanders for the next two weeks spent considerable time in shuffling units back and forth across the front. One reason is that plans for Operation ANVIL called for the Fifth Army to give up two of its four corps—the U.S. VI and the French Expeditionary Corps. Other reasons were growing logistical problems and difficult terrain. Perhaps for these reasons General Clark chose not to base his planning upon the intelligence provided by the ULTRA interception and decipherment of radio traffic between OKW and Kesselring's headquarters.

This decision at this point was unfortunate. Heavy losses in both men and materiél had rendered at least three of the *Fourteenth Army*'s divisions ineffective and reduced the remainder to half strength. Also, a wide gap had opened up between the *Tenth* and *Fourteenth Armies*. As his armies withdrew north of Rome, Kesselring intended to shift sufficient forces from the *Tenth* to the *Fourteenth Army* in an attempt to reinforce the latter and thereby close the

---

[1] Winterbotham, *The Ultra Secret*, pp. 159–60; SAC Despatch, The Italian Campaign, 10 May–12 Aug 1944, typescript in CMH.

gap. An aggressive Allied pursuit, however, would have doomed these measures.

Because he was to lose Truscott's and Juin's corps within a few weeks, Clark decided to use them in the early phase of the pursuit beyond Rome even though both corps were exhausted. The FEC, which had been covering the Army's right flank, prepared to take over from the II Corps. After a period of rest, the latter was to relieve the French in time for their withdrawal from the Army. The VI Corps, meanwhile, was to continue in line until relieved by the IV Corps.

Throughout the first day following Rome's capture, reconnaissance units ranged widely across the army's front to determine the extent of the enemy's withdrawal. Meanwhile, the 1st Armored and the 34th and 36th Infantry Divisions assembled in a bridgehead west of the Tiber. To maintain contact with the rapidly retreating Germans, Clark directed his corps commanders to form small, highly mobile task forces.[2]

After clearing Rome by nightfall on 5 June, the Fifth Army continued to advance at first on a two-corps front in the same order in which it had entered Rome: on the left, Truscott's VI Corps moving in two columns, one along the axis of Highway 1 (the coastal highway running northwestward toward Civitavecchia) and a second initially along the axis of Highway 2, roughly paralleling the coastal road some ten miles inland; on the right, Keyes' II Corps advancing to take over Highway 2 about seven miles north of Rome and continuing east of Lake Bracciano north to Vi-

terbo. The II Corps' right boundary was also the interarmy boundary and ran almost due north from a point four miles east of Rome, through Civita Castellana, thence to a point just west of Orte, forty miles north of Rome on the Tiber. *(Map VIII)*

The farther the Fifth Army moved beyond Rome, ever lengthening supply lines wreaked an inevitable burden on the hardworking trucks and drivers and exacerbated gasoline shortages at the front that could be alleviated only by opening the port of Civitavecchia. Narrow, winding secondary roads and frequent demolition of culverts and bridges by the retreating enemy contributed to delays and limited the number of troops that might advance along the axis of a single road.

Early on 6 June, General Harmon's 1st Armored Division, with Allen's CCB accompanying the 34th Division along the coastal highway toward Civitavecchia and CCA the 36th Division along Highway 2, took up the pursuit toward Viterbo. The 45th Division remained in corps reserve, while the British 1 and 5 Divisions withdrew into AAI reserve as soon as the bulk of the Fifth Army moved beyond Rome.[3] Each combat command formed a mobile task force composed of a medium tank battalion, a motorized infantry battalion, and attached engineer and reconnaissance units, as well as a battalion of self-propelled artillery. Because of difficulties involved in maneuvering and protecting the armor during the hours of darkness, motorized infantry led the way at night, armored units by day.

As night fell on the 6th, CCB had

---

[2] Hqs Fifth Army OI 28, 6 Jun 1944.

[3] *Ibid.; Fifth Army History,* Part VI, pp. 20–21.

AERIAL VIEW OF CIVITAVECCHIA

reached a point about seventeen miles southwest of Civitavecchia. Progress had been so rapid and resistance so light that Clark abandoned a plan to use the 509th Parachute Infantry Battalion to block Highway 1 behind the retreating enemy. Meanwhile, the 34th Division's 168th Infantry, mounted on trucks, consolidated gains and rounded up enemy stragglers bypassed by the tanks. Demolished bridges and culverts bore witness to the enemy's passage, but there was little physical contact with the foe. Throughout the night a motorized battalion of the 168th Infantry led the way, and by dawn on the 7th reached a

point within three miles of Civitavecchia. Entering the port, the infantry cleared it by noon.[4]

In the meantime, the 34th Division commander, General Ryder, ordered Col. William Schildroth's 133d Infantry to take up the advance in trucks along the coast toward Tarquinia, about ten miles northwest of Civitavecchia. Allen's CCB, meanwhile, turned eastward to rejoin the rest of the 1st Armored Division south of Viterbo. Against little

[4] VI Corps Opns Rpt, Jun 44; 34th Div G–3 Jnl, 5–7, 8–16 Jun 44. Unless otherwise indicated the following is based upon these sources.

opposition, the 133d Infantry, as night fell, came within five miles of Tarquinia, but the next morning, 8 June, in hilly country just south of Tarquinia the regiment encountered the first elements of the *20th Luftwaffe Field Division,* a unit that Kesselring had sent south from Orvieto to reinforce the *Fourteenth Army.* The enemy infantrymen had established themselves on the sides of a ravine overlooking the highway. Backed by mortars and artillery, they held until shortly before dark, when the Americans, using newly issued 57-mm. antitank guns as direct-fire weapons, blasted the positions. Instead of sending the 133d Infantry into Tarquinia that night, Ryder relieved it with an attached unit, Col. Rudolph W. Broedlow's 361st Regimental Combat Team, the first contingent of the 91st Division to arrive in Italy.

Early the next morning, the 9th, Truscott shifted the 36th Division, which had been advancing along the axis of Highway 2, from the VI Corps' right wing to relieve the weary 34th Division and take over the advance along the coastal highway. The 36th Division's place was taken by the 85th Division on the II Corps' left flank, which Clark had moved westward to include Highway 2. Ryder's division then retired into corps reserve in the vicinity of Civitavecchia. Two days later Crittenberger's IV Corps was to relieve the VI Corps and take command of the 36th Division and the advance along the coastal flank.

On the VI Corps' right wing Colonel Daniel's CCA, in the meantime, had advanced seven miles along Highway 2, then turned onto a good secondary road running through the corps zone west of Lake Bracciano before rejoining the main highway north of the lake. Daniel divided his unit into three small task forces, each built around an infantry and a medium tank company. Leapfrogging the task forces, Daniel, by nightfall on the 7th, had pushed his column to within fourteen miles of Viterbo. Resuming the advance the next morning, CCA headed for the point where the secondary road rejoined Highway 2. There the Germans had assembled a relatively strong rear guard from the *3d Panzer Grenadier Division,* which managed to delay Daniel's task force for three hours, long enough for the enemy to evacuate the adjacent town of Vetralla. From Vetralla, Viterbo lay only a tempting seven miles away but within the adjacent II Corps zone of operations. Not one to be overly respectful of corps' boundaries when opportunity beckoned, General Harmon, the 1st Armored Division commander, told Daniel to go on into Viterbo. Task Force C continued until halted by enemy rear guards at midnight a mile and a half south of the town. Later that night, when it became evident that the enemy had withdrawn, the task force dashed unhindered into Viterbo.

Since the beginning of the pursuit on the 6th, the II Corps front had been echeloned somewhat to the right rear of its neighbor, which was why Task Force C found no II Corps troops at Viterbo. After leaving the 3d Division behind to garrison Rome, Keyes selected the 85th and 88th Divisions to lead the II Corps along the axis of Highway 2 to the corps' objective, the road line Viterbo-Soriano-Orte. The VI Corps' units, which had been using the same highway for the first hours of their advance north of Rome, had already turned off onto a secondary road that would carry them west of Lake Bracciano. The II Corps, advancing along the axis of Highway 2, would pass east of Lake Bracciano.[5]

Early on 6 June, the 85th Division, in a column of regiments with the 339th Infantry leading and elements of the 117th Cavalry Reconnaissance Squadron screening the front and flanks, led the II Corps up Highway 2 to take over the advance on Viterbo from the 36th Division. A tank battalion and a tank destroyer battalion, attached from Task Force Howze, accompanied the lead regiment. Leapfrogging his regiments and alternating his forward elements between motorized and dismounted infantry, the division commander, General Coulter, kept his columns moving so rapidly that by dark on 8 June they had advanced to within six miles of Viterbo. There Coulter learned that the 1st Armored Division's CCA was already advancing on the town, which the army commander, General Clark, reacting to a *fait accompli,* shifted into the VI Corps' zone.

On Coulter's right, Sloan's 88th Division set out from Rome about the same time as its neighbor. Limited to secondary roads east of Highway 2, General Sloan deployed all three of his regiments. Their advance over these roads was more of a tactical march than an actual pursuit. Both to the front and on the right flank, a task force consisting of the 91st Reconnaissance Squadron

with a battalion each of tanks and tank destroyers screened the advance while the regiments followed. After the task force passed through Civita Castellana, 45 miles north of Rome, which the 6th South African Armoured Division of the British 13 Corps had captured two days before, the continued advance of the South Africans pinched out the task force.

At dawn on 9 June the French Expeditionary Corps began relieving the II Corps, whose zone of operations had been greatly reduced by the presence of the South African armor on Highway 3, temporarily assigned to use of the Eighth Army. By midmorning the 3d Algerian Infantry Division on the left and the 1st Motorized Division on the right completed relief of the 85th Division. Meanwhile, the 88th Division, pinched out by the South Africans, had also pulled out of the line.

The Fifth Army front on 11 June thus described a wide arc extending westward from Viterbo to Tuscania, thence southwest to a point just north of Tarquinia on Highway 1. Thus far casualties had been exceptionally light, each division seldom exceeding a daily average of ten in all categories.[6]

Eighth Army Joins the Pursuit

East of Rome, the Eighth Army on 6 June crossed the Tiber and its tributary, the Aniene, on a two-corps front, the 13th Corps on the left, the 10th Corps on the right. The former had the 6th South African and the 6th British Armoured Divisions, split at first by the

---

[5] *Fifth Army History,* Part VI, pp. 25–30. Unless otherwise cited the following is based upon this source.

[6] 9th MRU, Fifth Army Battle Casualties, 19 Jun 45, CMH.

southward-flowing Tiber; the latter had the 8th Indian and the 2d New Zealand Divisions. Under army group control, the 5 Corps was to follow a German withdrawal on the Adriatic flank. Operations there were to remain in low key in the hope that the Eighth Army's advance would prompt the Germans to yield the Adriatic port of Ancona without a fight. Failing that, General Alexander planned to use the 2 Polish Corps to take the port, 130 miles northeast of Rome.[7]

As with the Americans, shuffling of units helped delay the Eighth Army's advance, particularly on the left in the sector of the 13 Corps. Yet the necessity for the shifts was early demonstrated by the problems faced by the 6th South African Armoured Division, advancing, in effect, astride the Tiber River. Because the bridge to be used in the jump-off along Highway 3 was demolished, the division early on 6 June had to detour through the U.S. II Corps sector, losing several hours in the process. Reaching Civita Castellana, 25 miles to the north, as nightfall approached, the division faced the necessity of again crossing the river if progress was to continue along Highway 3 to Terni. The Tiber was as much of a barrier to intracorps movement in the attack as it was to the Germans on the defense. Furthermore, if the South Africans along Highway 3 and the 6th British Armoured Division east of the Tiber along Highway 4 continued to follow those routes, they would be moving away from their objective, the Florence-Arezzo-Bibbiena triangle.

---

[7] Operations of British, Indian, and Dominion Forces in Italy, Part II, Sec. D.

The 13 Corps commander, General Kirkman, accordingly obtained approval to put his entire corps west of the Tiber, avoiding the necessity to cross and recross the river while at the same time orienting the corps more directly toward the objective by use of Highway 71. The shift also avoided splitting the corps by another prominent terrain feature, Lake Trasimeno, which Highway 71 bypasses on the west.

The shift left the 10 Corps alone in pursuit of the stronger German force, the *Tenth Army,* east of the Tiber. The goal of that corps would be to keep enough pressure on the *Tenth Army* to forestall Field Marshal Kesselring from transferring units to reinforce the *Fourteenth Army* west of the Tiber.

Kesselring Outlines His Strategy

Even as the U.S. Fifth Army passed through Civitavecchia and Viterbo, and the British Eighth Army closed in on Orte, Narni, Terni, and Rieti, Field Marshal Kesselring began to prepare his superiors for the eventual loss of all central Italy between Rome and the Arno. On 8 June he informed the OKW that he might be able to delay the Allied armies forward of the Gothic Line for only three more weeks, and for that long only if the Allies made no attempt to turn *Army Group C*'s front with an amphibious landing on either the Tyrrhenian or Adriatic coasts, which Kesselring saw as a possibility at any time.

Both the *Tenth* and *Fourteenth Armies* were to fight delaying actions while bringing reserves from the rear and flanks, closing newly opened gaps, and establishing firm contact along the inner wings of the two armies. Loss of terrain was less important to Kesselring than overcoming the manpower losses suffered in the defeat south of Rome by rehabilitating severely mauled divisions.[8]

Compared with several delaying lines south of the Arno, the Gothic Line appeared on the map to offer a secure refuge for the German armies in the mountain fastness of the Northern Apennines, but in reality the line was far from complete. Construction of fortified positions in the relatively impregnable western sector, toward which the U.S. Fifth Army was advancing, had progressed satisfactorily, but little had been accomplished in the more vital and vulnerable central and eastern sectors, where the British Eighth Army's objectives lay. Although OKW had sent Field Marshal Kesselring additional engineer, fortification construction, and mountain battalions in order to complete the line before *Army Group C* withdrew beyond the Arno, the High Command was unable to afford him what he most needed—time. Kesselring could gain that only with his own skill and the steadfastness of his troops. While he was determined to hold the Allies as far south of the Arno as possible, unremitting pressure, especially against the *Fourteenth Army* on his right wing, delays in the arrival of reinforcements, and increasing difficulties in maintaining contact between his two armies across the barrier of the Tiber would, in Kesselring's opinion, leave little alternative to a fighting withdrawal.

Hitler disagreed. Even as Kesselring prepared on 9 June to issue new strategic guidelines to his army commanders, Hitler ordered him to stand and fight. Three days later the Fuehrer's written instructions pointed out that since another seven months were needed to complete the Gothic Line, the army group commander, if forced from his first defensive position, the Dora Line, had to be prepared to stabilize his front on the Frieda Line, forty miles farther north. Hitler also insisted that Kesselring should quickly disabuse his troops of any notion of the existence of a secure haven in the Northern Apennines into which they might eventually withdraw. The Gothic Line offered no advantages, Hitler added, for combat conditions there were less favorable than those south of the Arno. Furthermore, the hazards of flanking amphibious operations by the Allies were even greater. As if further to downgrade the importance of the Gothic Line in the eyes of both friend and foe, Hitler ordered the name of the line, with its historic connotations, changed. He reasoned that if the Allies managed to break through they would seize upon the more pretentious name as ground for magnifying their victory claims. Kesselring renamed it the Green Line.[9]

Essentially, despite Hitler's insistence on a stand and fight strategy, it developed rather that under Kesselring's command the German armies in Italy adopted a 20th-century variation of the delaying strategy associated with the

---

[8] Greiner and Schramm, eds., *OKW/WFSt, KTB*, IV (1), pp. 513–23. Kesselring's comments on *Der Feldzug in Italien*, Part II, in CMH files. Unless otherwise indicated the following section is based upon these references.

[9] Greiner and Schramm, eds., *OKW/WFSt, KTB*, IV(1), pp. 520–23. Since the Allies never adopted the new name, the text will continue to use the designation Gothic Line.

RAILROAD

HIGHWAY I
TO LEGHORN | TO ROME

GROSSETO AND TERRAIN TO THE EAST

name of the Roman general Quintus Fabius Cunctator, who, during the Punic War of the 3d century, B.C., had worn down the Carthaginian armies by a series of delaying actions. How effective was the German adaptation of that strategy twenty-one centuries later remained to be seen.

To the Trasimeno Line

As both the Fifth and Eighth Armies completed their regrouping on 11 June, the Allied front extended from a point on the Tyrrhenian coast about 20 miles northwest of Tarquinia, northeastward some thirty miles to the vicinity of Fontanile Montefiascone, thence in a southeasterly direction to Narni and Rieti, passing south of L'Aquila on the southern edge of the Gran Sasso, and on to Chieti and the Adriatic coast about seven miles south of Pescara. The Allied armies at that point were in contact with the first of the enemy's delaying lines north of Rome.

On the Fifth Army's left, Crittenberger's IV Corps held a 30-mile front between the coast and the hills overlooking it from the east and, on the right, the FEC's front stretched across twenty miles of the Umbrian highlands dominating the Tiber valley from the west. The intercorps boundary extended in a northwesterly direction from Tuscania.[10]

General Crittenberger planned for the 36th Division to make the main effort along the axis of the coastal Highway 1. To give Walker's division more punch, Crittenberger reinforced it with Broedlow's 361st Regimental Combat Team and the 753d Tank and 636th Tank Destroyer Battalions. The 117th Reconnaissance Squadron was to screen the corps front, with corps artillery to follow in general support. Two combat engineer regiments, the 36th and 39th, were also available. For the time being, the 34th Division was to remain in army reserve near Tarquinia.[11]

On the corps' right wing in the vicinity of Canino, eight miles southwest of Valentano, Crittenberger created a task force under the command of Brig. Gen. Rufus S. Ramey, with the mission of screening that flank and maintaining contact with the French Expeditionary Corps. The 1st Armored Group headquarters and headquarters company formed the command group for Ramey's task force, which included the 91st Reconnaissance Squadron, the 3d Battalion of the 141st Infantry, the 59th Field Artillery Battalion, an engineer battalion, and a medical company.[12]

The 36th Division's immediate objective was Grosseto, a provincial center approximately sixty miles northwest of Civitavecchia. Situated just north of the Ombrone River near the junction of Highways 1 and 73, Grosseto lies in the middle of a broad, flat valley formed by the Ombrone as it nears the sea. Almost fifteen miles wide, the valley is scored by a gridiron of small drainage ditches and canals.

Six miles beyond the 36th Division's front and twenty-three miles south of Grosseto lay the town of Orbetello, located at the mainland end of a causeway linking the rocky peninsula of Monte Argentario and the port of San Stefano with the mainland. San Stefano was the first of a series of small ports beyond Civitavecchia dotting the Tyrrhenian coast as far as Leghorn. The Allied command, especially the Fifth Army, hoped that with San Stefano's large liquid storage facilities in Allied hands, it would help solve the growing fuel supply problems. The gasoline shortage had been aggravated a week earlier when fire in the Fifth Army dumps near Rome destroyed large quantities of fuel.[13]

The tactical problems to be solved by the 36th Division resembled those which had been faced by the 85th along the coastal highway south of Terracina during the drive to link up the southern front with the Anzio beachhead. Between Orbetello and Grosseto the Umbrian hills stretch almost to the coast and just east of Orbetello form a defile through which Highway 1 passes.

[10] IV Corps AAR, Jun–Jul 44.
[11] *Fifth Army History,* Part VI, pp. 32–35; IV Corps AAR, Jun 44.
[12] IV Corps AAR, Jun 44.

[13] Interv, Mathews with Lt Col Charles S. d'Orsa, 10 May 48, CMH. Colonel d'Orsa was executive officer, Fifth Army G–4, during the campaign.

Since the defile had been incorporated into the enemy's Dora Line, the Germans could be expected to put up a stiff fight for the feature.

Although the 361st Infantry had been held up for most of 10 June by fire from near the defile carrying Highway 1 through the Umbrian Hills, the 141st Infantry—its 1st Battalion leading, followed by the 2d—encountered no opposition as it began moving up the highway shortly before dawn on the 11th. Yet just as the Americans had begun to suspect that the enemy had withdrawn from the defile, out of the half-light of early morning heavy automatic weapons and artillery fire stabbed at the head of the column. The lead battalion quickly deployed off the road to set up a base of fire, while the next battalion in line turned off the main road to scale the high ground flanking the roadblock to the east.

Full daylight found the 1st Battalion astride the highway, and the 2d Battalion well up the 700-foot Poggio Capalbiaccio, commanding the enemy's defenses; but during the morning two companies of German infantry, infiltrating through wheat fields east of the feature, outflanked and overran the 2d Battalion's leading company and forced the Americans to fall back to the base of the hill. Not until the afternoon, and with the help of division artillery, was the battalion on Poggio Capalbiaccio able to restore its lines. That evening, reinforced with a battalion from the 361st Infantry, the 2d Battalion once again started up the high ground. Throughout the night, fighting flared across the hillside, but dawn of the 12th found the 2d Battalion on top of Poggio Capalbiaccio and overlooking

the enemy roadblock along the coastal highway.

This feat, in conjunction with a resumption of the 1st Battalion's attack along the highway during the afternoon of the 12th, was sufficient to force the Germans to yield the Orbetello defile and fall back toward Grosetto. At that point General Walker relieved the 141st Infantry with the 143d, which had been in reserve east of Nunziatella. The 141st Infantry then shifted to the right to join Task Force Ramey and the regiment's 3d Battalion on that flank of the corps.

That night engineers accompanied the infantry across the causeway to San Stefano, where the Americans found to their delight that the fuel storage facilities were still intact, thanks to Italian engineers who had failed to carry out German orders to destroy them. An Italian diver provided information concerning the location of underwater mines placed in deep moats surrounding the tanks.

At San Stefano the Americans also discovered underground storage facilities for an additional 281,000 barrels of gasoline.[14] Yet before the first tanker could enter, the harbor had to be cleared of sunken ships and the docks repaired. That was difficult work under wartime conditions, so that not until 1 July was the first tanker to dock, but the port soon became the main POL terminal for the Fifth Army.[15]

While the 143d Infantry cleared Or-

---

[14] Mayo MS, ch. XIV.

[15] Leo J. Meyer, MS, Strategy and Logistical History: MTO, ch. XXXIX, "Extension of Communications North of Rome" (hereafter cited as Meyer MS), CMH; Interv, Mathews with d'Orsa, 10 May 48.

betello and occupied San Stefano, the 142d Infantry, accompanied by tanks, crossed the hills on the division's right wing toward the village of Capalbio. The regiment brushed aside a weak counterattack by elements of the *162d Turkomen Division* to occupy the village before noon on the 11th. That afternoon and throughout the next day the troops continued to advance—the infantry across the hills and the tanks through the narrow valleys—northwest to high ground just south of lateral Route 74.[16]

By the evening of 12 June, Walker's 36th Division was within sight of the Albegna River, which parallels Route 74 and enters the Tyrrhenian Sea five miles northwest of Orbetello. The general had planned crossings of the river that night, but it turned out that all bridges were destroyed and that the water was too deep for fording. Postponing the attack until morning, he put his engineers to work constructing footbridges in the darkness. Shortly before dawn on the 13th, the 142d Infantry, followed by the 143d on the left, began to cross.

The 143d Infantry encountered little opposition until reaching the village of Bengodi on the banks of the smaller but deeper Osa River, three to four miles north of the Albegna.[17] Not so with the 142d Infantry on the right. As that regiment neared the village of Magliano, five miles north of the Albegna, heavy fire from that village and the hills to the north brought the men to a halt. They attempted to outflank the village to the east, but resistance was

firm there as well. Nevertheless, by 1500 the 2d Battalion, supported by tank and heavy artillery fire directed against the enemy in the hills to the north, managed to win a foothold in the outskirts of Magliano. During the rest of the afternoon and throughout the night the infantry inched into the village house by house and street by street. The village's fall opened a road along which the division could outflank Grosseto from the southeast, as it had done earlier at Orbetello. Throughout the afternoon the 142d Infantry continued to move up until its leading battalions occupied high ground flanking the Magliano-Grosseto road. That night the 361st Infantry came forward to spell the 142d.[18]

Meanwhile, throughout the 14th, the 143d Infantry continued to forge ahead astride the coastal highway. Attacking at dawn, the 2d and 3d Battalions required five hours to drive the enemy from the flanking high ground north of Bengodi, in the process capturing fifty prisoners and five artillery pieces. For the rest of the afternoon the two battalions advanced against slackening opposition, as the Germans, having lost Magliano, fell back across the corps front toward Grosseto. By dark the regiment had come within twelve miles of Grosseto and the Ombrone River.[19]

Moving before dawn on the 15th, a battalion on each side of the highway, the 143d Infantry encountered no resistance in occupying the high ground

---

[16] IV Corps AAR, Jun 44; 36th Div Hist Rpt, Jun 44.
[17] 36th Div Hist Rpt, Jun 44.

[18] *Ibid.* During the battle for Magliano, S. Sgt. Homer L. Wise's fearless and skillful leadership of his rifle platoon enabled the 2d Battalion to seize its objective. For this action Sergeant Wise was awarded the Medal of Honor.
[19] IV Corps AAR, Jun 44.

overlooking the Ombrone and in flanking the highway near Collecchio, a village six miles south of the river. As the men descended into the river valley and worked their way across the network of small streams and drainage ditches scoring the valley floor, sporadic machine gun and mortar fire picked at them, but there were few casualties. Locating a ford a mile east of the main road, the troops waited until dark before attempting to cross the river. Thereupon one battalion proceeded quickly into Grosseto. The Germans had already left.[20]

To the right of the 143d, the 361st Infantry operating south and west of Istia d'Ombrone, four miles northeast of Grosseto, had more trouble in crossing the river. Unable to locate a ford, engineers toiled through the night to construct a footbridge. When the men began crossing at daylight on the 16th, enemy artillery inflicted a number of casualties. It was early afternoon before all three battalions were across the river and astride high ground overlooking the valley from the northeast.[21]

On the division's right flank Task Force Ramey had been held up since early on the 14th by resolute defenders south of Triana, a small, walled town at a road junction twenty-two miles east of Grosseto. Instead of a direct confrontation, General Ramey concentrated on clearing the neighboring villages of Santa Caterina, Vallerona, and Roccalbegna. That so threatened the enemy's line of communications to the strongpoint at Triana that the town's garrison soon withdrew.

On the morning of the 16th Ramey's men entered Triana. The fall first of Grosseto on the night of the 15th and then of Triana meant that the VI Corps was well past the Dora Line and two-thirds of the way to the Frieda Line.

Early next day, 17 June, a 9,700-man French amphibious landing force attacked the island of Elba, seven miles off the coast. Composed of two regimental combat teams from the 9th Colonial Division and a commando battalion with a group of goumiers attached, all supported by an American air task force, with a British naval task force in general support, the French approached the island over a calm, fog-shrouded sea from a base in nearby Corsica. Despite some early resistance by a 2,500-man enemy garrison, 550 of whom were Italian Fascist troops and the rest Germans, the French quickly established two secure beachheads. The next day virtually all resistance ceased. Other than to boost French morale, the capture of Elba had little immediate significance for the Allies, yet for the Germans the operation again raised the specter of an Allied amphibious operation to the German rear and made Kesselring pause before committing his reserve, the *16th SS Panzer Grenadier Division*.[22]

The IV Corps, meanwhile, continued to move northwestward, paralleling the coast beyond Grosseto. On the left wing along the coast, the 36th Division advanced on a 15-mile front to clear all

---

[20] *Ibid.*

[21] *Ibid.; Fifth Army History,* Part VI, pp. 37–40.

[22] The Allied intelligence officers had grossly overestimated the number of Italian troops on Elba; allied sources estimated 5,000 Italian soldiers to be on the island. See SAC Despatch, 10 May–12 Aug 44, pp. 37–40, and Greiner and Schramm, eds., *OKW/WFSt, KTB,* IV(1), pp. 524–25.

the high ground southeast of Route 73. On the right wing, Task Force Ramey, with the 141st Infantry attached, cut Route 73 below the town of Roccastrada, ten miles north of the coastal highway, there to await relief by the 1st Armored Division.

In ten days the IV Corps had progressed but twenty-two miles on a 20-mile front, a rate imposed by persistent German delaying action and one hardly characteristic of a rapid pursuit. Yet it then appeared that even firmer German resistance might be in the offing, possibly sufficient even to halt the pursuit; for as the corps prepared to cross Route 73, intelligence officers identified prisoners from the *16th SS Panzer Grenadier Division*.[23]

The French Advance to the Orcia

A similar threat was developing on the Fifth Army's right wing, where General Juin's French Expeditionary Corps, since relieving the U.S. II Corps on 10 June, had encountered steadily increasing resistance. In the meantime, the French had learned that they would soon be withdrawn from the front to prepare for the invasion of southern France. During the weeks to come, that knowledge would exercise, especially among the French officers of the North African legions, a strong psychological restraint over operations. Why die with the liberation of France close at hand? The dash and spontaneity that had characterized FEC operations in the mountains south of Rome thus was missing.[24]

Finding his corps again operating over the worst terrain in the army sector, General Juin formed an *ad hoc* pursuit corps headquarters to direct field operations. He placed Lt. Gen. Edgard R.M. de Larminat in command of a force that included Maj. Gen. Diego Brosset's 1st Motorized (March) Division and Maj. Gen. de Goisland de Monsabert's 3d Algerian division, all still supported by the 13th U.S. Field Artillery Brigade and its attached battalions.[25]

The first objective was Route 74, the lateral road connecting Highways 1 and 2 running east-west just north of Lake Bolsena, some nineteen miles north of the jump-off positions. Attacking on 11 June, even as the neighboring IV Corps began to head toward Orbetello and Grosseto, the French gained Lake Bolsena on the 12th. It took another two days to come up to either side of the lake and to get beyond it, at the same time that the neighboring task force cleared Route 74 between Lake Bolsena and the sea.

On the same day General Clark extended the FEC western boundary to close a developing gap between the two corps. To cover the wider front, General de Larminat reinforced General de Monsabert's Algerian division with a task force that, in proceeding diagonally to the northwest and roughly parallel to the line of the coast, soon pinched out Task Force Ramey.

By nightfall on 17 June the French had gained positions some fifteen miles beyond Lake Bolsena but for the next three days a combination of enemy resistance and worsening weather re-

---

[23] *Fifth Army History*, Part VI, pp. 38–41.
[24] Interv, Mathews with Gen Clark, 1948, CMH.

[25] *Fifth Army History*, Part VI, pp. 41–46.

stricted progress to another ten miles. By the 20th the corps was nevertheless within striking distance of the Orcia River, a westward flowing tributary of the Ombrone. As the FEC prepared to assault the obstacle, Brosset's 1st Motorized Division began to withdraw in anticipation of the invasion of southern France, while Maj. Gen André W. Dody's 2d Moroccan Infantry Division moved from corps reserve to take its place in line.

The British Sector

General Clark's concern that the British Eighth Army, facing a more capable German force and more difficult terrain, would be unable to keep pace with the Fifth Army proved needless, for General Leese's troops had maintained a momentum developed during the first week of the pursuit beyond Rome. The Eighth Army continued to advance northward on a two-corps front, the 13 Corps to the west of Lake Trasimeno via Highway 71, and the 10 Corps to the east of the lake.[26]

After some delay due to the need to squeeze through Viterbo's narrow streets at the same time the U.S. II Corps was trying to withdraw from the area, the 13 Corps by the evening of 13 June had drawn to within four miles of Orvieto, its first objective. A few days before, that move would have threatened to block the Germans' lateral communications from Terni and Todi through Orvieto to the sectors west of the Tiber; but Kesselring, too, having completed the regrouping, strength-

ened the *Fourteenth Army*'s front and no longer needed that lateral route.

The regrouping had begun on the 12th with the transfer of Senger's *XIV Panzer Corps* headquarters from the *Tenth* to the *Fourteenth Army* sector, where the panzer corps took command of the *19th* and *20th Luftwaffe Field Divisions* on the coastal flank, pending the arrival of its former divisions—the *26th Panzer* and the *29th* and *90th Panzer Grenadier Divisions* from the *Tenth Army* zone. Since 13 June the panzer and the two panzer grenadier divisions had been located west of the Tiber, where they had been steadily braking the Fifth Army's forward movement. Whether the *Tenth Army*, shorn of those units, could continue to do the same to General Leese's Eighth Army, was a question about to be answered as the Eighth Army, like the Fifth, prepared to close with the Frieda Line.

Orvieto no longer having meaning, the Germans, as the 13 Corps approached, began withdrawing into hills commanding the Paglia valley north of the town. By noon on 14 June the 6th South African Armoured Division had cleared the town of the last of the German rear guards.

East of the Tiber the 10 Corps shifted its axis slightly westward from Rieti to Terni, for enemy movements, observed by reconnaissance aircraft, had indicated that Terni had become the focus of the regrouping of General Feuerstein's *LI Mountain Corps*. For several days Feuerstein had received help in that task by terrain that had so canalized the 10 Corps' advance as to require the British 6th Armoured Division to take five days to cover the thirty miles between Passo Corese and Terni

---

[26] Operations of British, Indian, and Dominion Forces in Italy, Part II, Sec. D. Unless otherwise indicated this section is based upon this source.

on Highway 4. As on the Fifth Army front, the British armor led the way during the day and the infantry at night, and, similarly, demolitions covered by artillery and mortar fire caused most of the delays. The British armor did not reach the southern outskirts of Terni until 13 June, there to be held up for two days by a demolished bridge across a deep gorge just outside the town. The gorge at last bridged, the tankers found the enemy gone from Terni .

Kesselring Reinforces His Right Wing

From the German viewpoint, despite the successive loss of Grosseto, Orvieto, and Terni, chances of restoring an intact front had improved considerably by mid-June. In addition to returning Senger's *XIV Panzer Corps* to the *Fourteenth Army*, Field Marshal Kesselring also brought the *Hermann Goering Panzer Grenadier Parachute Division* back into action, this time on the *Tenth Army's* right flank north of Orvieto opposite the British 13 Corps.

Undoubtedly, Field Marshal Kesselring's most significant accomplishment during the first ten days after the loss of Rome had been to prevent a breakthrough along the interarmy boundary and to reinforce the *Fourteenth Army* west of the Tiber. By mid-June the *Fourteenth Army* commander, General Lemelsen, could muster nine divisions, with two others having been withdrawn for rest and reorganization. Although three of the nine critically needed relief, five of the remaining six were first-rate panzer and panzer grenadier divisions.

Opposite those divisions the U.S. Fifth Army had, by mid-June, six divisions and part of a seventh (the 91st).

On the Eighth Army left wing the British 13 Corps controlled three divisions, making a total of about nine and a half divisions against the *Fourteenth Army's* nine. Even allowing for the fact that three of the nine were understrength, the ratio of nine and a half to nine scarcely afforded a promise of a continued rapid Allied advance.[27] Opposite the equivalent of five divisions in the 10 Corps, on the Eighth Army right wing, the German situation was no more encouraging, for there General Vietinghoff's *Tenth Army* mustered eight divisions, divided between Herr's *LXXVI Panzer Corps* and Feuerstein's *LI Mountain Corps*.

The ability of the Germans, despite harassment by a daily average of 1,000 Allied air sorties, to shift major units from one sector to another and to bring important reinforcements from northern Italy to man the several delaying lines north of Rome had been largely responsible for the failure of the two Allied armies to cut off and destroy significant parts of either of the two German armies. By maintaining maneuverability, the Germans were able to re-form along new lines even in the face of Allied pressure and penetration, forcing upon the Allies a form of pursuit that had come to characterize Russian operations against the Germans on the Eastern Front. In the opinion of General von Senger und Etterlin, only if the Allies had, as at Anzio, taken advantage of the Germans' long and vulnerable seaward flanks to launch amphibious landings could that pattern have been broken. Unknown to the

---

[27] Greiner and Schramm, eds., *OKW/WFSt, KTB*, IV(1), pp. 520–21.

GENERALS BRANN, CRITTENBERGER, AND MASCARENHAS

Germans at the time, the shortage of landing craft prevented such operations.[28]

Both the specter of Allied amphibious landings and the very real fact of partisan operations against German lines of communications bedeviled German commanders. The farther north the Germans retreated the more active became Italian partisan bands, many led by former Italian Army officers. As early as 13 June, Lemelsen's chief of staff had obtained army group author-

ity to punish acts of sabotage against the German armed forces and to take ten-for-one reprisals against military-age members of the civilian population for every German soldier killed or wounded by partisans. By mid-June sabotage of the German lines of communications had nevertheless reached such proportions as to disrupt not only long-distance telephone cables, upon which the Germans had increasingly come to rely for their communications because of Allied air attacks on military signal facilities, but also to immobilize even local telephone networks. In the vicinity of Siena, some 115 miles north of Rome, partisans also cut a vital lateral supply route leading from Gros-

---

[28] See Special Investigations and Interrogation Report, Operation Lightening USDIC/SII R 30/36, 15 Mar 1947, CMH files, and Senger, *Neither Hope nor Fear*, pp. 257–58. See also Greiner and Schramm, eds., *OKW/WFSt, KTB*, IV(1), p. 519.

seto to Siena. Stung by these actions, the Germans were to take stern countermeasures in the weeks to come.[29]

The Eighth Army Closes With the Frieda Line

As the British 10 Corps resumed its advance early on 15 June, the improved stance of German units soon became apparent. The British 6th Armoured Division, leading the way, did manage to cross the Nera River over bridges recently completed at Terni and Narni during the last leg of an advance aimed at Perugia, ten miles east of Lake Trasimeno. However, Vietinghoff, the *Tenth Army* commander, had selected Perugia, a major German supply base, as the hinge of his forward defensive zone east of the lake. Although the British armor was able to go twenty miles beyond the Nera with little difficulty, unexpectedly strong resistance developed on the 16th southeast of Todi, midway between Terni and Perugia. To bypass it, the corps commander ordered the Tiber bridged about three miles northwest of Todi so that progress could continue along the west bank over terrain more favorable for armor. The bridge completed early on the 17th, the 6th Armoured Division resumed its advance along both sides of the Tiber. Moving rapidly once again, the British by nightfall drew within six miles of Perugia,[30] the goal assigned by

General Leese in the first week of June; but as was soon evident, the corps had also closed with outposts of the Frieda Line. It took another three days to conquer Perugia. After yielding the city, the Germans withdrew into their main defensive zone in hills north and northwest of the city. The next day, the 20th, in the face of the staunchest resistance since the fall of Rome, the advance ground to a halt just beyond Perugia.

In the 13 Corps sector the 6th South African Armoured Division also ran into strong defenses along that part of the Frieda Line west of Lake Trasimeno. By the 16th several fresh enemy units, taking advantage of a range of hills southwest of Lake Trasimeno, held the armor at Chiusi, on Highway 71 twenty-two miles north of Orvieto. Intelligence gleaned from prisoners indicated that the *334th Infantry Division* lay west of the highway, the *1st Parachute Division* astride the road, and the *356th Infantry Division* to the east.

Thus were signs increasing across the entire Eighth Army front that the enemy was determined to give battle along a line flanking Lake Trasimeno to the east and west. To add to the attacker's woes, heavy rains began falling on the evening of the 17th, transforming the countryside into a quagmire. By the 20th it was clear that the Germans could be dislodged only by a full-scale set-piece attack. With the 13 Corps bogged down southwest of Lake Trasimeno and the 10 Corps unable to penetrate the hills north and west of Perugia, the Eighth Army's pursuit, like that of the Fifth Army, appeared to be at an end.

Conscious that the tempo of the advance west of the Apennines was

---

[29] *AOK 14, Ia KTB Anl. 3*, 13 Jun 44, *AOK 14*, Doc. 59091/1; Ltr, R.R. Wadleigh, 2d Lt FA, 142d Inf, 16 Jul 44, to Lt Col H.E. Helsten, 2660 Hq Co Mics (reel 41–A, G–3 Div, Sp Opns files, AFHQ microfilm).

[30] Five miles southeast of Orvieto the Tiber makes a sharp bend to the northeast as far as Todi; from there it turns again northward to Perugia.

GENERALS LEESE *(left)* AND ANDERS

insufficient to induce the Germans to yield the port city of Ancona on the Adriatic coast without a fight, General Alexander accordingly decided to step up operations in the Adriatic sector. On 15 June he ordered General Anders' 2 Polish Corps back into line to relieve the British 5 Corps, which since the fall of Rome had limited its operations to proceeding on the heels of the enemy withdrawal. The next day the Poles, with a brigade-size Italian Corps of Liberation attached on the left, began to move toward Ancona, 70 miles to the northwest. Over the next five days the advance carried 45 miles to and beyond the Chienti River and within 25 miles of the goal of Ancona.

The week's rapid progress had been made possible largely by an earlier German decision to fall back on the defenses of Ancona, which constituted that part of the Frieda Line east of the Apennines. Trying to renew the advance on the 22d, the Poles too were checked. Only with sizable reinforcements, General Anders concluded, would he be able to break the enemy's hold south of Ancona. Generals Alexander and Leese approved a two-week pause to enable him to effect the buildup.[31]

The pursuit everywhere was nearing an end. At the time it had begun, General Alexander had assured General Wilson, the Mediterranean theater commander, that barring substantial German reinforcements, the Allies by the end of June would have reached a line extending from Grosseto to Perugia. Even though three additional enemy divisions had entered the line, Alexander had achieved that goal and a little more.

[31] Operations of the British, Indian, and Dominion Forces in Italy, Part II, Sec. A.

CHAPTER XIV

The Pursuit Ends

Strategic Priorities: France or Italy

As the Allied armies moved beyond Rome, the inter-Allied debate over Mediterranean strategy entered a second and more urgent phase. The first phase had ended when the American Chiefs of Staff reluctantly abandoned their plans for an Operation ANVIL timed to coincide with Operation OVERLORD. Now that OVERLORD had secured a firm toehold on northern France and Rome had fallen to the Allied spring offensive in Italy, that old question of which theater—Italy or southern France—would offer the best opportunity to contain German troops and thereby assist General Eisenhower's armies in northern France had yet to be decided.

Diversion of enemy forces from northern France was the bait that Alexander extended to his American colleagues in an effort to make his own Italy-first strategy more palatable to men whose attention for several months had been fixed on southern France rather than on Italy. The primary object of the Italian campaign was, in Alexander's words, "to complete the destruction of the German armed forces in Italy and in the process to force the enemy to draw to the maximum on his reserves."[1] The greatest assistance the Allied forces in Italy could offer the invasion of northern France was to divert large numbers of German divisions from France. Alexander's intelligence officers believed that by 6 June the Germans had already committed an equivalent of six additional divisions in Italy; actually, they had moved only four. An additional six divisions were believed to be in the country but not yet committed, although only two of those were regarded as even approximating full combat effectiveness. In reality, the Germans after the loss of Rome had withdrawn five divisions for rest and reorganization in the rear, while a sixth, the 92d, was disbanded.

At the time the Germans began to retreat beyond Rome, Field Marshal Kesselring controlled 24 divisions—19 in his two armies, 2 in army group reserve, and 3 en route into Italy. Many were understrength or inexperienced. Two, for example, were made up of Air Force personnel from airport security battalions, including antiaircraft artillery and searchlight units. Another was composed of former prisoners of war from Soviet Central Asia, while others, made up largely of overage and convalescent troops, were suitable only for coastal defense or garrison duty.[2]

---

[1] See AAI Msg, MA 1364, 6 Jun 44, AAI to AFGQ, in Operations of British, Indian, and Dominion Forces in Italy, Part II, Sec. A, App. D–2.

[2] Greiner and Schramm, eds., *OKW/WFSt, KTB*, IV(1), pp. 515–23.

Alexander concluded that by the time the Allied armies had fought their way to the Northern Apennines, Kesselring would have no more than the equivalent of ten fully combat-effective divisions with which to defend the Gothic Line. Yet Alexander believed that Kesselring would need at least twelve divisions for that task, and defense of his coastal flanks would require additional divisions of lesser caliber. Alexander believed the Germans would have to bring into Italy eight to ten fresh divisions from the nearby Western Front, rather than from the hard-pressed and more distant Eastern Front, which is what the Germans eventually did. Thus, so Alexander's argument ran, a vigorous continuation of the Allied offensive up the Italian peninsula could be expected to help the Allied drive across northern France and into Germany.[3]

Alexander calculated that after reaching the approximate line of Grosseto-Perugia (roughly, the Frieda Line), his armies during the second half of July would be prepared to mount a full-scale attack against the Gothic Line. That presupposed that Leghorn, the remaining port on the Tyrrhenian coast, and Ancona, on the Adriatic coast, would be in hand and providing necessary logistical backup for a 20-division force. Since those divisions would be full strength, they would be more than a match for twenty-four enemy divisions of lesser strength.[4]

Once past the Gothic Line, his armies, Alexander expected, would be able to continue without interruption to drive the Germans from the Northern Apennines, take Bologna, and, by late summer, establish in the Po Valley a base for operations directed most likely northeastward toward Austria and the mid-Danube basin, a long-time object of British strategic interest.[5] Airfields of great value to the Allied air forces in the western Mediterranean also could be secured, and the agricultural products of the Po Valley denied the enemy.

These long-range predictions rested upon the assumption that the Allied ground and air forces then in Italy would remain; whereas on 12 June, only a week after Alexander had made them, General Wilson had informed him that the Allied Force Headquarters' American-dominated planning staff remained firmly wedded to the ANVIL operation, which would have to be mounted out of resources already in the Mediterranean theater. That meant giving up the U.S. VI Corps headquarters, the FEC, and three U.S. and two French divisions. Although the final decision on ANVIL was yet to be made, it was evident as early as mid-June that planning for it at the theater level had advanced almost to the point of no return.

When Wilson and Alexander met again on 17 June at Alexander's headquarters in Caserta, the two tried valiantly to salvage something of Alexander's proposed strategy. Since the

---

[3] Ibid.; SAC Despatch, The Italian Campaign, 10 May to 15 Aug 44.

[4] SAC Despatch, The Italian Campaign, 10 May to 15 Aug 44.

[5] Although Alexander's recommendations also included a suggestion that operations might be mounted against France from the Po Valley, a glance at the terrain and a knowledge of British desires and intentions prompts the conclusion that this was only verbal dust to be thrown into the eyes of American advocates of Operation ANVIL (southern France).

Joint Chiefs of Staff in Washington no longer viewed the purpose of ANVIL as a diversion for General Eisenhower's armies, now that those armies were securely established in France, Wilson introduced a new variation of the diversion concept by observing that the Mediterranean theater's basic mission was to prevent the Germans from reinforcing armies in France. Alexander, in turn, elaborated on the theme by increasing his estimates of 6 June. If the Germans wished to retain the Po Valley, he maintained, they would have to reinforce their armies in Italy with ten to fifteen divisions by the end of June. Those reinforcements, Alexander reasoned, would have to come from France rather than from the hard-pressed Eastern Front or from the Balkans, long seething with partisan activity. If the Germans failed to reinforce, the Allied armies by mid-July would be in the Po Valley in a position to attack across the Adige River with ten to twelve divisions in mid-August and capture the Ljubljana Gap by the end of the month.[6]

Although this restatement of British strategic aims found support among the air force and naval commanders also present at the meeting, it found none at all with Wilson's American deputy and planning chief, General Devers, who again pointed out that diversion of enemy forces from northern France,

desirable though that might be, was no longer General Eisenhower's primary strategic requirement. The Supreme Allied Commander instead needed a major French port for bringing in American troops and supplies. Only ANVIL would satisfy that requirement.

Later in the day the U.S. Army Chief of Staff, General Marshall, who had arrived in Italy for an inspection trip following a visit to Eisenhower's London headquarters, added weight to what Devers had said. There were, Marshall noted, forty to fifty divisions in the United States ready for commitment in France. Port facilities then available in northern France were insufficient to handle such a large force and its logistical support, and to stage the divisions through the United Kingdom was impracticable. Eisenhower needed a major French port—Marseilles—through which the reinforcements could move directly. Marshall added (undoubtedly with the British interest in the Danube basin in mind) the further caveat that the divisions were, in any case, unavailable for service elsewhere in the Mediterranean theater.[7]

As for Alexander's estimate that the Germans would fight to hold the Po Valley, Marshall believed they would opt instead for defending the Alpine passes. Alexander's projected offensive through the Northern Apennines and into the Po Valley thus would cause no diversion of enemy forces from any front, east or west.

---

[6] Matloff, *Strategic Planning for Coalition Warfare, 1943–1944*; Michael Howard, *The Mediterranean Strategy in the Second World War* (New York: Praeger, 1968); Trumbull Higgins, *Soft Underbelly: The Anglo-American Controversy Over the Italian Campaign, 1939–45* (New York: The Macmillan Company, 1968). These works discuss the consequences of the military versus the political-military aspects of American versus British decision making.

[7] Never enthusiastic about a major campaign in Italy, General Marshall had agreed to operations in southern Italy and a push toward Rome only to get a firm holding position while landing craft were being shifted from the Mediterranean to England for OVERLORD. See Pogue, *George C. Marshall, Organizer of Victory, 1943–45*, p. 295.

Acknowledging the validity of Marshall's argument, Wilson pointed out that with available resources he would be unable to mount ANVIL while at the same time pursuing a major offensive in Italy. That was the theme adopted by the advocates of Italy-first when Allied commanders met two days later on 19 June to resume their discussions. This time the air commanders, Air Marshal Slessor and General Eaker, agreed with Wilson. Once the Allied armies reached the Northern Apennines and closed with the German defenses there, Eaker observed, a diversion of air power to support the attack on southern France would necessarily reduce the Italian campaign to a defensive action. Marshall countered with the observation that once the initial phase of Operation ANVIL was completed, Allied air power would be sufficient for both France and Italy.

Marshall's arguments apparently carried some weight with Wilson, for on the 19th he threw his support to ANVIL on the condition that the Combined Chiefs of Staff back Marshall's position on the paramount need for a major port in southern France.[8] The following day, in a cable to General Eisenhower in regard to future operations in the Mediterranean theater, he reiterated the familiar British position that unabated and undiminished continuation of Alexander's offensive would divert so many divisions from the path of Eisenhower's armies in northern France that the Germans would face prospects of defeat before the end of the year. If, on the other hand, Eisen-

hower preferred to proceed with the invasion of southern France, Wilson cautioned that the operation could not be mounted before 15 August. This would, of course, prevent both an immediate diversion of enemy divisions from France and an immediate offensive by Alexander's armies against the Gothic Line, thereby giving the Germans a badly needed respite.

The next day, the 21st, word arrived from London stating what Wilson already knew from his conversations with Marshall, that Eisenhower remained firmly committed to ANVIL. For the remainder of the month of June, Prime Minister Churchill would bombard President Roosevelt with frantic appeals to salvage something of British plans for "a descent on the Istrian peninsula and a thrust against Vienna through the Ljubljana Gap"; but the President held firm in support of his military advisers. For all practical purposes 21 June represented the passing of the point of no return for the ANVIL operation. Southern France it would be, and the campaign in Italy would have to suffer the consequences.[9]

In the end the dire effects so many had predicted for the Italian campaign as a result of the decision in favor of ANVIL were short-lived and far less drastic than partisans of the Italy-first theme had imagined. Even the troop withdrawals in June and July tipped the balance only slightly against the Allies in Italy, and the situation would be fully

---

[8] Matloff, *Strategic Planning for Coalition Warfare, 1943–44*, p. 470.

[9] *Ibid.*, pp. 472–75. In early August the British made a final effort to persuade the Americans to either land ANVIL forces through Breton ports or permit them to remain in Italy for an advance into the middle Danube Basin. On 1 August the code designation for Operation ANVIL was changed to Operation DRAGOON.

redressed in October. By that time the Allies were destined to have five fresh divisions in Italy, while the Germans would have moved four divisions from Italy to serve on other fronts.[10]

Breaking the Frieda Line

By 21 June the Allied armies in Italy had reached a line extending across the peninsula from a point on the Tyrrhenian coast, some 110 miles northwest of Rome, to the Adriatic coast at a point five miles north of Pedaso. The general trend of the front remained, as it had since the fall of Rome, with the Allied left advanced and the right refused.

On the left the Fifth Army was some 30 miles short of its intermediate goal, lateral Route 68, which, paralleling the Cecina River for 15 miles, connects the town of Cecina on the coastal highway with the ancient Etruscan hill town of Volterra, 20 miles to the northeast, thence another 15 miles to a junction with Highway 2 not quite midway between Siena and Florence. (Map IX) Key to the Fifth Army's program was the Tuscan Hills, a stretch of low, rolling terrain overlooking and paralleling Highway 1 from the east. Once the enemy had been cleared from those hills, the coastal corridor would provide an excellent route of advance. The crests are generally wooded and the lower, seaward-facing slopes covered with orchards and vineyards. Since it was summer, the vegetation was in full leaf and afforded the Germans, operating under Allied-dominated skies, des-

perately needed concealment. East of the hills and about five miles inland, a graveled secondary road wound northward through a series of stream valleys to a junction with lateral Route 68, eight miles east of Cecina.

About the latitude of Grosseto the trend of the coastline becomes more northwesterly, thus widening the IV Corps front and enabling General Crittenberger to employ for the first time two full divisions, the 36th Infantry and the 1st Armored. Relieving Ramey's task force, which had been screening the corps right flank, the 1st Armored Division was to clear the enemy from the hills overlooking the coastal corridor by moving along the axis of Highway 439, which joined lateral Route 68 five miles southwest of Volterra.[11]

Although Crittenberger, the IV Corps commander, realized that the hilly terrain was less favorable for armor than that assigned the 36th Division along the coast, he wanted to avoid the loss of time inherent in shifting divisions. He also believed that the Germans would concentrate on defense of the coastal flank and depend, as they had in the past, upon the more rugged hill terrain to aid them in the interior. A hard-hitting armored division with sufficient fire power could be expected to force the enemy from the hills and enable General Harmon's tanks to so threaten the flank of the Germans in the coastal corridor as to prompt their withdrawal. General Crittenberger, moreover, was aware that he soon was to lose the 36th Division and alerted General Ryder, commander of the 34th Division, to be prepared to relieve

---

[10] For a detailed analysis of this debate as it influenced the campaign in southern France, see Robert Ross Smith, The Riviera to the Rhine, in preparation for the series, UNITED STATES ARMY IN WORLD WAR II.

[11] IV Corps AAR, Jun 44.

Walker's 36th Division within the week.[12]

Learning of his latest assignment, General Harmon protested, as he had when his division had been committed in the Alban Hills south of Rome, that hill country was no place for tanks. He nevertheless again threw himself into his task with characteristic enthusiasm, gruffness, and salubrious profanity. To provide Harmon with additional infantry needed to support armor in hilly terrain where numerous defended barriers and roadblocks might be expected on narrow, winding roads, Crittenberger attached to Harmon's division the 361st Infantry (less one battalion).[13] Unfortunately, those troops had never worked closely with armor, and the result would be less than ideal.[14] To the armor Crittenberger also attached the 155-mm. guns of the 6th Armored Field Artillery Group, which were to provide reinforcing fires until the armored division had arrived at maximum range, whereupon the group was to shift westward to join the rest of the corps artillery in general support of the infantry along the coast.[15]

As the armor moved into the hills early on 21 June, Walker's 36th Division, less the attached 517th Parachute Infantry, continued along the coastal flank into a low range of hills between Highway 1 and the coast northwest of Grosseto. With the 142d Infantry on the left of the highway and the 143d Infantry on the right, the division en-

countered only scattered resistance en route to the Cornia River, about 10 miles away. In the process the advance would seal off a small peninsula and the little port of Piombino with valuable oil storage facilities.

For all the lack of determined resistance, the infantry's advance was considerably delayed by heavy rains on 22 June, but relief of Task Force Ramey during the day by the 1st Armored Division provided additional strength to assist the infantry on the 23d, both the 141st Infantry and the 517th Parachute Infantry. The paratroopers took over the 36th Division's left flank along the coastal highway, while the 141st Infantry joined the 143d Infantry for the drive toward the Cornia River. By nightfall on the 24th the two regiments had crossed the river and partially sealed off the Piombino peninsula, but the rear guard of the *19th Luftwaffe Field Division*, retreating along the coast, got away before the last escape route could be cut.

The next day, the 25th, marked the 36th Division's last participation in the Italian campaign. After having been in action almost continuously since 28 May and having covered almost 240 road miles since the breakthrough of the Caesar Line at Monte Artemisio on 1 June, Walker's division pulled out of line in preparation for its role in southern France.

As had the earlier capture of Civitavecchia and San Stefano, the capture of Piombino would soon help to relieve pressure on Allied supply lines. Located midway between Civitavecchia and Leghorn, Piombino's harbor could handle twelve ships at a time. Like Civitavecchia, Piombino, with a prewar pop-

---

[12] Interv, Mathews with Ladue, 17 Jun 48, CMH; IV Corps AAR, Jan 44.

[13] Howe, *Battle History of the 1st Armored Division*, pp. 354–55.

[14] IV Corps AAR, Jun 44; Interv, Mathews with Ladue, 17 Jul 48.

[15] Interv, Mathews with Ladue, 17 Jul 48.

ulation of 10,000, required extensive rehabilitation, but by the end of June the port was able to accommodate several ships. During the next three months, 377,000 tons of cargo and 1,477 vehicles were discharged and forwarded through the port, an amount almost twice that handled at Civitavecchia during the same period. In addition, 20,446 troops arrived there.[16] The port's main drawback was the absence of a rail connection with the main line running northward from Rome, so that all cargo had to be forwarded by motor transport until mid-August when the Fifth Army engineers established a railhead nearby at Venturina. In addition to serving the Fifth Army, the port also received and forwarded a considerable part of the Eighth Army's ration and gasoline supplies pending capture of the Adriatic port of Ancona. Yet for all the help provided by the small ports, only Leghorn, Italy's third largest port—on 25 June still 40 miles northwest of the Fifth Army front—had facilities that could sustain a major Fifth Army offensive into the Northern Apennines, and the Eighth Army would have to have Ancona.[17]

Meanwhile, General Harmon's 1st Armored Division on 22 June had begun its part in the drive toward lateral Route 68. Although the air line distance was only 40 miles, the division would have to travel 120 miles over narrow, winding secondary roads to reach its objective. Here were the Tuscan Hills with steep-sided ridges, averaging 1,500 to 2,000 feet in height. To

maintain firm contact with the French on his right, General Harmon ordered a preliminary move on the 21st by the 81st Armored Reconnaissance Battalion to establish contact with an Algerian division on the French left. Hardly had the battalion begun to move when heavy artillery fire drove the men to cover. Only after nightfall was the battalion able to accomplish its objective.

That artillery fire revealed the enemy's awareness of the armored division's presence opposite the *XIV Panzer Corps*. To forestall a possible breakthrough, the *Fourteenth Army* commander, General Lemelsen, had scraped together his remaining reserves and moved them into the corps sector.[18]

For the main attack General Harmon utilized two secondary roads: Highway 439 on the left for CCB and Route 73 on the right for CCA. As during the first week following the fall of Rome, the combat commands were subdivided into small task forces in order to facilitate using narrow side roads and trails to bypass demolitions and roadblocks on the main routes.[19]

Hardly had the armor begun to roll when General Harmon decided he needed more strength on the line. In early afternoon he inserted Task Force Howze from his reserve into the center to follow another secondary road. As it turned out, Task Force Howze made the day's longest advance: 5 miles. On the right, in the face of numerous obstacles covered by determined and accurate antitank fire, CCA managed to

[16] Leo J. Meyer, MS, Strategy and Logistical History of the Mediterranean Theater, ch. XXIX, CMH.

[17] *Ibid.*

[18] *AOK 14, Ia KTB, Nr. 3,* 22 Jun 44, *AOK 14,* 59091/1.

[19] 1st Armd Div, AAR, Jun 44.

gain only two miles. After losing heavily to an enemy ambush, CCB made even less progress. Over the next four days the rugged terrain and the enemy's roadblocks and demolitions continued to impose delays, but pushing forward doggedly, the division managed an average daily advance of five miles.

Along the coastal flank, General Ryder's 34th Division, after relieving the 36th Division on 26 June, had the 133d Infantry on the left astride the coastal highway, while in the center the attached Japanese-American 442d Regimental Combat Team took the place of the 517th Parachute Infantry, also scheduled for southern France. The 168th Infantry moved into position on the division's right.[20]

On the first day of the attack, the 27th, the 34th Division moved to within 15 miles of the intermediate objective, lateral Route 68. Paralleling that road for some 20 miles, the little Cecina River was of itself a slight military obstacle, but when defended by an enemy well established in a range of low hills beyond, it could become a formidable obstacle.

As the *Fourteenth Army* on *Army Group C*'s right wing fell back toward the Cecina River and lateral Route 68, Kesselring prepared to occupy this terrain in strength by assigning to the *XIV Panzer Corps* the newly arrived *16th SS Panzer Grenadier Division* and the *19th Luftwaffe Field Division*, the latter replacing the *20th Luftwaffe Field Division*, which then moved to the *Tenth Army*. Kesselring also relieved the *162d Turkomen Division*, which had been in action on the coastal flank almost continuously

since 8 June, with the veteran *26th Panzer Division*, thus returning the panzer division to Senger's *XIV Panzer Corps*. Two full corps, controlling between them eight divisions in line, with one in reserve, at that point manned the *Fourteenth Army* front from the Tyrrhenian coast eastward for some 35 miles to a boundary east of and parallel to Highway 2. Schlemm's parachute corps lay to the east and Senger's panzer corps to the west of that highway.[21]

Increased German strength was soon apparent to both attacking American divisions, the 34th and the 1st Armored. The 34th Division required an entire day to cover the six more miles toward Route 68 and the Cecina River and yet another to draw within two miles of the river. After dark, the 133d Infantry's Company K led the 3d Battalion in a dash for the river but in a maze of orchards and vineyards ran into an ambush that forced the rest of the battalion to halt and wait until dawn before resuming the advance. That was the first indication of the presence of the *16th SS Panzer Grenadier Division*. Although the bulk of the division lay in corps reserve near Leghorn, one of its regiments had entered the line.[22]

The 1st Armored Division took four days to achieve a comparable advance, in the process crossing the upper reaches of the Cecina River where the stream runs several miles south of

[20] IV Corps AAR, Jun 44.

[21] Greiner and Schramm, eds., *OKW/WFSt, OKW*, IV (1), pp. 525–28.

[22] IV Corps AAR, Jun 44; 133d Inf Opns Rpt, Jun 44; German *Lagekarte*, Jun–Jul 44; Fifth Army G–2 Rpts, Jun–Jul 44. Unless otherwise indicated the following section is based upon these references.

Route 68. As the division's combat commands approached the road on the 30th, sharp resistance, mainly from the *3d Panzer Grenadier Division* and newly arrived elements of the *90th Panzer Grenadier Division,* ensconced on the high ground along the road, brought the armor temporarily to a halt.[23]

Faced with evidence of German reinforcement, the 34th Division commander, General Ryder, decided to use his reserve, the 135th Infantry, to swing to the east in an effort to envelop what appeared to be the strongest defenses along the coast south of the town of Cecina. The regiment was first to relieve the attached 442d Infantry, then move along a ridge three miles inland that overlooked the coastal corridor and prepare to cross the Cecina four miles east of the coastal highway. Unfortunately for Ryder's plan, the high ground overlooking that particular sector of the river line was held by the *26th Panzer Division*, a unit that had given good account of itself in the battles south of Rome.

At dawn on the 30th, Company E led the 1st Infantry's 2d Battalion across the river to establish a modest bridgehead, but when the battalion attempted to reinforce the bridgehead, heavy fire from the high ground pinned the men to the ground. A second effort, this time with armor support, came to grief when enemy antitank gunners destroyed all but two of a force of eleven Sherman tanks. The two surviving tanks withdrew under protective fire to the south bank, leaving only the beleaguered infantry

clinging to the little bridgehead through 1 July.

Early on 2 July, the battalion tried a third time to reinforce the bridgehead. This time heavy corps artillery support and close air support from fighter bombers hammered the enemy-held high ground and carried the day. By nightfall the entire regiment had successfully crossed the Cecina and had begun to expand the bridgehead.

Resistance along the coastal route south of the town of Cecina meanwhile continued to be strong. When the 3d Battalion, 133d Infantry, resumed its attack early on the 30th, Company I in the lead required most of the morning just to recover ground lost the day before. Shortly past noon an enemy counterattack almost cut off the company from the rest of the battalion. The company saved itself only by withdrawing about 1,500 yards, thereby nullifying the gains of the forenoon. Heavy protective fires by supporting artillery finally brought the counterattack to a halt, but not before the enemy had destroyed two tanks and inflicted sharp casualties.

Since the 135th Infantry was still trying to secure its bridgehead, General Ryder saw no alternative to pressing the frontal attack by the 133d Infantry against Cecina with ever greater vigor. That the regimental commander, Colonel Schildroth, prepared to do late that afternoon when he relieved the weary 3d Battalion with the 1st Battalion, his reserve. Until darkness brought their operations to a halt, the 1st and 2d Battalions edged slowly forward, capturing six enemy guns, yet failing to drive the enemy from his positions south of Cecina.

---

[23] Howe, *Battle History of the 1st Armored Division*, pp. 356–60.

CECINA
MARINA
HIGHWAY I
TO   TO
GROSSETO LEGHORN
CECINA
RIVER
RAILROAD

AERIAL VIEW OF CECINA

The Germans managed to hold, but the effort had cost them so many casualties, mostly from Allied artillery fire, that the *Fourteenth Army* commander, General Lemelsen, decided to withdraw the right wing of the *XIV Panzer Corps* approximately five miles. Since the new position was no stronger than the one at Cecina, Lemelsen saw it as only another delaying line and told the *XIV Panzer Corps* commander to pull out the *29th Panzer Grenadier Division* on the night of 2 July and move it to an area along the Arno River about seventeen miles west of Florence, there to constitute an army reserve in prepa-

ration for an eventual Allied attack against the line of the Arno.[24]

Before daylight on 1 July, men of the 133d Infantry, unaware that the Germans were preparing to withdraw, returned to the attack. Five hours later the 2d Battalion was inside Cecina's southeastern outskirts, where the men were checked briefly by stubborn rear guards. On the left the 1st Battalion got within 500 yards of the town, then early the following morning finally cleared paths through mine fields and soon

----

[24] *AOK 14, Ia KTB Nr. 4,* 1 Jul 44, *AOK 14,* 62241/1.

after daylight joined the 2d Battalion inside Cecina.

By mid-morning the battle of Cecina was over, the costliest for an American unit since the fall of Rome. Carrying the main burden of the 34th Division's frontal attack, the 133d Infantry alone lost 16 officers and 388 enlisted men killed, wounded, or missing.

The Capture of Volterra and Siena

As the fight for Cecina proceeded, General Harmon's 1st Armored Division, operating 20 miles inland along upper reaches of the Cecina River, renewed its efforts to cut Route 68 and gain the high ground beyond. That CCB achieved during the night of 30 June, moving onto the high ground immediately north of the lateral road four miles southeast of Volterra. Enemy artillery fire halted Task Force Howze two miles south of the road, a reflection of the presence of reinforcements from the *90th Panzer Grenadier Division*. Only after Harmon had moved up the last of his reserves on 3 July was Howze's force able to drive the enemy back. In the meantime, seven miles to the southeast, CCA incurred numerous casualties in unsuccessful attempts to drive the enemy from a fortified village just south of Route 68, Casole d'Elsa. The village fell on the 4th to CCA and its attached 361st Infantry after three days of fighting that cost the armored regiment six medium tanks, three light tanks, and two tank destroyers. Over the next few days the 88th Division began to relieve the armor, which withdrew into army reserve, and one of the fresh regiments, the 350th Infantry, completed the conquest of Route 68 on

8 July by capturing the walled town of Volterra.[25]

As the IV Corps was advancing to Route 68, General Juin's French Expeditionary Corps on the Fifth Army's right wing was driving toward Siena astride Highway 2. Juin had the 3d Algerian Infantry Division on his left and, on his right, the 2d Moroccan Infantry Division.

Starting to attack on 21 June, the French soon found themselves bogged down opposite the *Fourteenth Army's* left wing, one of the most heavily defended sectors of the German front. There General Schlemm's *I Parachute Corps* had deployed from east to west the *356th Grenadier Division*, the *4th Parachute Division*, a regiment of the *26th Panzer Division*, elements of the *20th Luftwaffe Field Division*, and a regiment of the *29th Panzer Grenadier Division*. For the next five days, from 22 through 26 June, this strong enemy force held the French to a two-mile advance. Not until 26 June, after the neighboring 1st Armored Division had outflanked the enemy positions, did the Germans begin to withdraw and the French to make appreciable progress.

As the acknowledged head of all French forces fighting on the side of the Allies, General de Gaulle had assured Pope Pius XII that French troops would spare the historic city of Siena. Consequently, as Juin's corps approached the city, the French relied upon outflanking and bypassing maneuvers to cut off the enemy inside the city. While these tactics delayed entry, they succeeded in forcing the Germans

---

[25] Howe, *Battle History of the 1st Armored Division*, pp. 360–61.

GENERALS CLARK AND JUIN AT SIENA

to evacuate the city so that when the first French troops entered at 0630 on 3 July they fired not a shot and not a single historic monument was damaged.[26]

General Juin immediately regrouped his forces to continue the advance, but with the capture of Siena much of the former *élan* of the French units had vanished. Even as they entered the city, General Juin received orders detaching many of his units for service with a newly formed I French Corps then assembling in the vicinity of Naples for the forthcoming invasion of southern France.[27]

Beyond Siena, across a 15-mile front, Juin deployed two divisions, the 2d Moroccan Infantry and the 4th Moroccan Mountain. The Germans, the Moroccans found, had turned road junctions near Colle di Val d'Elsa, 12 miles beyond Siena, and at Poggibonsi, 3 miles farther north, into strongpoints,

---

[26] Le Goyet, *La Participation Française à la Campagne d'Italie*, p. 168; *Fifth Army History*, Part VI, pp. 70–76.

[27] Interv, Mathews with Ladue, 17 Jan 48, CMH.

so that the French had to fight hard over the next four days before the enemy retired during the night of 6 July from the first of the two strongpoints. Before daylight on 7 July, Colle di Val d'Elsa and the high ground overlooking the town were in French hands. That evening the French too crossed Route 68 and continued their advance over winding mountain roads toward Poggibonsi.[28]

Although thirty miles of rugged terrain remained to be crossed before the Fifth Army would reach the south bank of the Arno, the worst of the terrain between Rome and the Arno at that point lay to the rear of Clark's army. As the French Expeditionary Corps prepared to continue its drive, Crittenberger's IV Corps, having moved about five miles beyond Route 68, prepared to close with the last German defenses south of Leghorn.

The Eighth Army

While the Fifth Army advanced to and beyond Route 68, the British Eighth Army had been operating on the wider of the two army fronts and over far more difficult terrain than had the Fifth Army. The front of the Eighth Army and the separate Polish corps meandered for almost 200 miles through the fastness of the Central Apennines and the less mountainous but still challenging terrain flanking Lake Trasimeno. Yet because of a superior road net, only the 30-mile sector flanking the lake was of strategic importance. It was there that General Leese had concentrated his main strength, the 10 and 13 Corps, to the

east and west of Lake Trasimeno respectively. Because the lake divided the two corps, it was evident that in their assault on the Trasimeno Line they would at first proceed independently along separate axes fifteen miles apart. Once the waters of the lake were behind, a broad range of hills that divided the Chiana valley from the upper reaches of the Tiber River still would divide them. There would be no firm contact until they reached Arezzo, 20 miles north of the lake. The inability of each to influence the progress of the other would be a contributing factor to the success of the Germans over the next ten days (from 20 through 30 June) in holding the British to slow painstaking progress in some of the most difficult fighting encountered since crossing the Aniene and Tiber two weeks before.[29]

The Eighth Army's operational problems were further complicated after the advance beyond Rome to the Trasimeno Line had left the army's railhead and main supply base 200 miles to the rear. There were no ports on the Adriatic flank between Bari and Ancona. Although the Fifth Army's capture of the small ports on the Tyrrhenean coast helped to a degree to ease British supply difficulties, especially in gasoline, the Eighth's long lines of communication would remain until Ancona could be opened. In view of the supply problems, the Eighth Army probably would have been unable to maintain additional divisions at the front even had they been available.

---

[28] *Ibid.*

[29] Operations of the British, Indian, and Dominion Forces in Italy, Part II, Sec. D. Unless otherwise indicated the following section is based upon this reference.

General Leese, nevertheless, commanded a formidable and balanced force with which to carry out General Alexander's directive to capture Arezzo, Ancona, and Florence as bases from which to mount an offensive against the Gothic Line. On the army's left wing west of Lake Trasimeno General Kirkman's 13 Corps had an armored division, the 6th South African, and an infantry division, the British 78th, on line, and the British 4th Infantry Division in reserve. East of the lake General McCreery's 10 Corps included the British 6th Armoured and the 8th Indian Infantry Divisions. An Italian reconnaissance squadron screened the corps right flank in the foothills of the Central Apennines. There was no corps reserve.

The zone of the 13 Corps was bisected by a north-south belt of low, rolling hills overlooking two main roads on either flank—a secondary road to be followed by the South African armor on the left, and Highway 71 to serve as the axis of advance of the 78th Division on the right. The roads ran northward along the edges of what in prehistoric times had been the bed of a large lake, of which remain only Lakes Trasimeno, Chiusi, and Montepulciano, the latter two located some five miles southwest of Trasimeno. While offering terrain far more favorable than that to the east of the lakes, the region was intensively cultivated, and lush summer vegetation would conceal the enemy from Allied reconnaissance aircraft. The tactical problem of the attacking troops would be to secure a bisecting belt of hills, in the center of the corps zone, from which the enemy dominated the routes of approach to the east and west.

Opposite the 13 Corps lay the *I Parachute Corps* with three divisions in line: the *Hermann Goering*, *1st Parachute*, and *334th Infantry Divisions*. Their positions consisted mainly of field fortifications similar to those encountered elsewhere in Italy and supported by antitank guns well-sited in forward positions and supplemented by mortars and rockets. Ground and aerial reconnaissance of these positions had convinced General Kirkman, the 13 Corps commander, that he would have to employ all of his available forces when on 20 June he moved against the Trasimeno Line. While the 6th South African Armoured and the British 78th Infantry Divisions advanced on either flank, the British 4th Division was to move along secondary roads in the center and clear the dominating hills.

It took the 13 Corps eight days, until 28 June, to reach a point not quite halfway up Lake Trasimeno's western shoreline. That, nevertheless, put the corps well inside the Frieda Line, presenting the Germans with the possibility of an Allied breakthrough and prompting a slow withdrawal. The defensive battles along the Frieda Line had won for Field Marshal Kesselring an 8-day delay, but he paid a high price for it, for the Germans had lost 718 men as prisoners and probably more in dead and wounded. Over half the prisoners were from the *334th Division*, which bore the brunt of the 78th Division's attack along Lake Trasimeno's western shore. Although some favorable defensive terrain remained short of the Northern Apennines, none would be as conducive to the defense as that which the Germans were forced to relinquish.

Operating east of Lake Trasimeno,

General McCreery's 10 Corps made little progress beyond the city of Perugia, some ten miles southeast of the lake. Since north of Perugia terrain was even more favorable to the enemy, General Leese, the Eighth Army commander, adopted a strategy that Alexander had employed earlier against strong defensive positions, advancing his left (13 Corps) *en potence* and denying his right (10 Corps). To that end, priority in men and matériel would henceforth go to Kirkman's corps to reinforce its drive on Arezzo, which on 28 June lay only 28 miles away. By the end of the first week in July McCreery's 10 Corps would be reduced to the strength of a two-division holding force, the 4th and 10th Indian Divisions.

While that was going on, the 13 Corps continued to press forward through a zone of hilly terrain ten miles deep, of which the enemy took full advantage to fight a series of staunch delaying actions. On 4 July the British 6th Armoured Division, withdrawn from the 10 Corps, gave new weight to the 13 Corps attack. During the morning the British armor ran a gauntlet of fire from a ridge overlooking Highway 71 from the east to capture the town of Castiglione Fiorentino, ten miles south of Arezzo, but from this point on, progress was slow, hampered by heavy rains and frequent demolitions, the latter covered by enemy mines and artillery fire. By the end of the day it had become clear that the Germans had reached another delaying position, from which they would have to be forcibly expelled. To the east the 10th Indian Division of the 10 Corps had by 6 July advanced beyond Perugia to capture Umbertide, ten miles north of Perugia

and twenty-six southeast of Arezzo, but heavy enemy fire brought the Indians to a halt just four miles beyond the town.

Events had taken a similar course along the Adriatic flank, where, since 21 June, the Polish corps and the brigade-size Italian Corps of Liberation had reached a point twelve miles beyond Porto Civitanova, the eastern anchor of the Trasimeno Line. The Poles continued their advance during the first week of July to capture a town ten miles south of Ancona, and the Italians to reach the outskirts of another, fifteen miles southwest of the port. Thereafter, all efforts to push ahead failed in the face of resistance as determined as that before Arezzo.

Strategic Decisions

Even as the Allied advance again came to a halt, this time just short of Leghorn, Arezzo, and Ancona, an ominous directive from the Allied Force Headquarters, Mediterranean Theater, reached General Alexander. Beginning on 5 July "an overriding priority for all resources in the Mediterranean Theater as between the proposed assault on southern France and the battle [in Italy] is to be given the former to the extent necessary to complete a buildup of ten divisions in the south of France."[30] Although hardly unexpected, the directive nevertheless came as something of a shock, seemingly the final blow to a long-cherished hope, mainly British, but shared by many in Clark's headquarters as well, that the Italian campaign rather than ANVIL would somehow remain the

---

[30] SAC Despatch, The Italian Campaign, 10 May to 12 Aug 44, p. 54.

major Allied operation in the Mediterranean.

Not only the Allies but also the Germans proceeded to modify strategic guidelines that had determined their operations since the loss of Rome. Yet, unlike the Allies, the Germans were influenced more directly by events on the Italian battlefront during the preceding three weeks. The success of the British Eighth Army's 13 Corps west of Lake Trasimeno and of the U.S. Fifth Army's IV Corps along the Cecina River and Route 68, as well as the advance of the 2 Polish Corps along the Adriatic to within striking distance of Ancona, impelled Field Marshal Kesselring to summon his army commanders to a conference late on 1 July at his headquarters near Florence. There the German commander revealed that a growing shortage of both replacements and matériel forced him to modify OKW's strategic guidelines calling for maximum resistance along successive lines. While such tactics had served to delay the Allies along the Frieda Line for ten days (20–30 June), it had cost the Germans heavily in men and equipment. In view of growing demands from other fronts, there was little likelihood that those losses would be made up soon.

Instead of maximum resistance along successive lines, Kesselring said, the army group would try to hold along selected lines until the main forces had withdrawn to secondary, or switch, positions in sufficient strength to prevent a breakthrough. Along the first of those lines, there were three widely separated sectors of primary interest to the field marshal: Rosignano Solvay, 12 miles south of Leghorn; just north of Cor-

tona, covering the southern approaches to Arezzo; and along the Musone River, 12 miles south of Ancona. Kesselring expected to check the Allies in those sectors as long as his limited resources would allow before falling back to a final delaying position along the Arno. That line ran from Pisa on the Ligurian coast along the Arno to Florence, thence over the mountains and along the north bank of the Metauro River to the Adriatic. Delays along those two lines would gain time to improve the Gothic Line positions in the Northern Apennines. It was as obvious to the German commander as to his Allied opposite, General Alexander, that before the Allied armies could mount a serious threat to the Gothic Line they first would have to secure and rehabilitate the ports of Leghorn and Ancona and would also need the communications centers of Arezzo and Florence.[31]

If either commander needed further proof that his campaign had been relegated to a secondary position, that of a large-scale holding operation, the decisions required of them during the first week of July provided it. On the Allied side, the U.S. Fifth Army had been stripped of many of its best units to swell the ranks of the forces preparing to open another front in France, while the German armies would have to get along without major replacements of men or equipment, to enable the Reich to reinforce other more critical fronts. The two decisions would, in effect, cancel one another out, so that when the Allies attacked yet another German line, they would find the situation in Italy basically unchanged.

[31] AOK 14, Ia KTB Nr. 4, 1 Jul 1944, AOK 14, Doc. 62241/1.

CHAPTER XV

End of the Campaign in Central Italy

Mission

In pursuing the essential task of capturing the major port of Leghorn, the commander of the IV Corps, General Crittenberger, was determined not to repeat the tactics employed in the battle for Cecina, which had dissipated the corps strength in a frontal attack with only a belated and relatively weak attempt to outflank the objective. By intervening early in the planning stage of the operation against Leghorn, the IV Corps commander expected to coordinate the frontal and flanking operations more closely. As at Cecina, Ryder's 34th Infantry Division was to carry the main burden.[1]

To give Ryder's division additional fire power, Crittenberger reinforced it with the 442d Regimental Combat Team, the 804th Tank Destroyer Battalion, and the 363d Regimental Combat Team, the second of the 91st Division's units to be assigned to the Fifth Army to gain combat experience. To the 363d Regimental Combat Team Crittenberger gave the mission of outflanking Leghorn on the east and of threatening the enemy's route of withdrawal. That maneuver, he believed, would cause the enemy garrison, when the 34th Division approached the port from the south and east, to abandon the objective rather than attempt a last-ditch stand.[2]

The Terrain and the Plan

Before Crittenberger could execute these plans his corps, from positions in the hills some six miles north of the Cecina River, had first to cross a 20-mile stretch of terrain far more convoluted than that south of Cecina. This was infantry country and the infantry, supported by artillery, would have to do most of the fighting. From the line of the Cecina three natural routes of approach led toward Leghorn and the Arno valley. Four miles beyond Cecina, Highway 1 returned to the coast, and from that point wound along the edge of cliffs dropping abruptly to the sea. Before reaching Leghorn the highway connected several small coastal towns, the largest of which was Rosignano Solvay, seven miles north of Cecina and the site of a large chemical works. A secondary road, Route 206, led northward from the junction of Highway 1 and lateral Route 68 through a valley flanked on the left by the coastal range and on the right by a high ridge line. That road linked numerous villages and towns and passed through the largest community, Colle Salvetti, eighteen miles away on the southern edge of the Arno valley. A third, unnumbered

---

[1] IV Corps AAR, Jul 44; Interv, Mathews with Ladue, 17 Jun 48, CMH.

[2] IV Corps AAR, Jul 44.

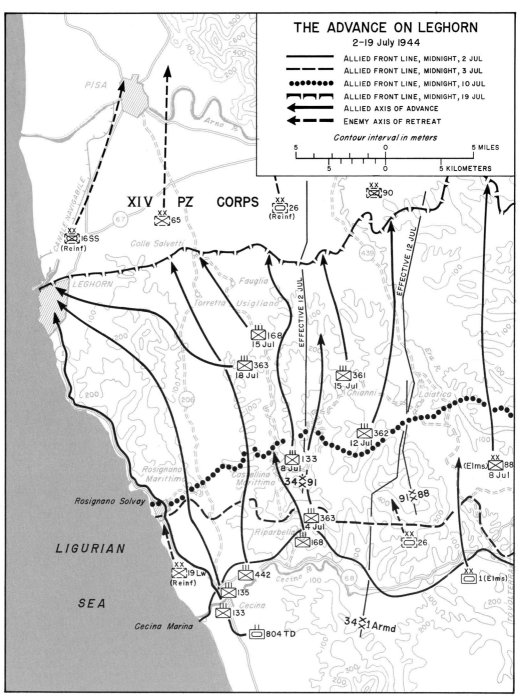

THE ADVANCE ON LEGHORN
2–19 July 1944

———— ALLIED FRONT LINE, MIDNIGHT, 2 JUL
– – – – ALLIED FRONT LINE, MIDNIGHT, 3 JUL
•••••••• ALLIED FRONT LINE, MIDNIGHT, 10 JUL
ᒡᒡᒡᒡ ALLIED FRONT LINE, MIDNIGHT, 19 JUL
◄———— ALLIED AXIS OF ADVANCE
◄– – – – ENEMY AXIS OF RETREAT

Contour interval in meters

5   0   5 MILES

5   0   5 KILOMETERS

PISA

Arno R.

CANALE NAVIGABILE

XIV PZ CORPS

XX
☒ 65

XX
☐ 26
(Reinf)

XX
☒ 90

XX
☒ 16 SS
(Reinf)

Colle Salvetti

LEGHORN

Fauglia

Torretta Usigliano

EFFECTIVE 12 JUL

EFFECTIVE 12 JUL

III
☒ 168
15 Jul

III
☒ 363
18 Jul

III
☒ 361
15 Jul

Chianni   *Laiatica*

III
☒ 362
12 Jul

Rosignano Marittimo

III
☒ 133
8 Jul

34 ☒ 91

XX
☒ 88
(Elms) 8 Jul

Rosignano Solvay

Castellina Marittimo

91 ☒ 88

III
☒ 363
4 Jul

XX
☐ 26

LIGURIAN

Riparbella

III
☒ 168

XX
☒ 19 Lw
(Reinf)

III
☒ 442

Cecina R.

XX
☐ 1(Elms)

SEA

III
☒ 135

III
☒ 133

Cecina

Cecina Marina

☐ 804 TD

34 ☒ 1 Armd

VOLTERRA

H. C. Brewer, Jr.

MAP 7

route paralleled that road about five miles to the east on the eastern side of the ridge line. The unnumbered route led northward from a junction with lateral Route 68 via Riparbella, six miles northeast of Cecina, to a junction with Route 206 at Torretta, three miles south of Colle Salvetti. Crittenberger planned to send the bulk of the 34th Division along the latter two roads while the 804th Tank Destroyer Battalion and the 34th Cavalry Reconnaissance Troop held to the narrow coastal highway.[3] (*Map 7*)

To the 34th Division's right, the 88th Division (and later also the 91st Division) was to move forward along the west bank of the Era River valley, which paralleled the coast seventeen miles inland. After the 91st Division arrived, the 88th Division was to cross the Era and proceed up its east bank toward the Arno. Thirteen miles east of the Era the French Expeditionary Corps was to continue its drive on the Fifth Army's right flank through the Elsa valley until relieved just short of the Arno by the II Corps, which General Clark for several weeks had been holding in reserve.

The terrain over which these several routes led favored the defense. Ridge lines on the flanks of the main routes of approach rose to peaks of over 1,500 feet on the left and over 2,000 feet on the right, offering the Germans vantage points from which they might rake the advancing columns with flanking fire. Seven miles north of Cecina and lateral Route 68 the reinforced *19th Luftwaffe Division* prepared to make a stand just north of a lateral road which connected

the coastal highway with Route 206, the westernmost of the 34th Division's two main routes of approach.

The town of Rosignano Marittimo, on a hilltop two and a half miles northeast of the junction of the lateral road with the coastal highway and the factory town of Rosignano Solvay, afforded the enemy a commanding view of the terrain almost as far as Cecina. On the summit of the hill in the center of the town stood a massive stone castle whose thick walls had withstood besieging armies in centuries past. The location of the town and its buildings had prompted the Germans to make it the major strongpoint of their defenses south of Leghorn.

Because of the terrain and the routes of approach, General Ryder planned to advance with three regiments abreast—the 135th Infantry on the left, the attached 442d Infantry in the center, and the 168th on the right. The 133d Infantry, which had borne the brunt of the battle for Cecina, would remain in reserve. On his left flank, the 804th Tank Destroyer Battalion, screened by the 34th Reconnaissance Troop, was to advance along the narrow, cliff-hanging coastal highway. On his right flank, Ryder would deploy the reconnaissance company of the 776th Tank Destroyer Battalion to screen the 168th Infantry's flank and to maintain contact with the 91st Division after it entered the line between the 34th and 88th Divisions. By evening of 2 July all units had reached their assigned assembly positions and were prepared to launch the drive to Leghorn early the next morning.[4]

---

[3] *Ibid*.

[4] 34th Div Opns Rpt, Jun–Jul 44.

Deployed on the high ground opposite the IV Corps front two enemy
divisions of varying quality awaited the
attack. On the *Fourteenth Army's* right
flank, General von Senger's *XIV Panzer
Corps* was controlling the *19th Luftwaffe*
and *26th Panzer Divisions*, both of which
had given such good account of themselves in the defense of the Cecina
sector, but in so doing had suffered
considerable losses. To the left and
holding a comparatively narrow front
was the *20th Luftwaffe Field Division*.[5]

Advance Toward Leghorn

At dawn on 3 July, the 135th and
168th Infantry Regiments of the 34th
Division began to advance across the
flanking ridges; at the same time in the
valley below, the 442d Infantry attacked
across a broader front. By early evening
the lead company of the 135th Infantry's 3d Battalion had reached Rosignano Marittimo's southern outskirts. A
few hours later the rest of the battalion
arrived, but was halted just short of the
town by mortar and artillery fire, including some 170-mm. rounds from
enemy guns located behind a ridge
northeast of Rosignano. Since it was too
dark to continue the assault, the battalion organized three company-sized
strongpoints and settled down for the
night. Early the next morning the battalion began the difficult task of establishing a foothold in the town. For
several hours the men inched forward
through streets made gauntlets by the
enemy's firing small arms and hurling
grenades from upper stories of the
compact stone buildings lining the
streets. After beating off a strong tank-

supported infantry counterattack, the
3d Battalion by late afternoon had at
last gained a foothold in the southern
third of the town. Despite reinforcement
by the rest of the parent 135th Infantry,
it took three more days for the men to
advance house by house through the rest
of the town. It was late on 7 July before
the men reached the northern edge of
the town, there to confront a stubborn
rear guard holding scattered
strongpoints in isolated houses along the
fringe.[6]

The remaining regiments under 34th
Division control found the fighting
equally difficult. The 442d Regimental
Combat Team, astride the valley road
in the center, and the 168th Infantry,
along the eastern ridge overlooking the
valley road, advanced in echelon to the
right rear of the 135th Infantry. Although on 4 July the corps commander
attached the 363d Infantry to the 34th
Division for use on the 168th's right,
the 442d and the 168th could do little
more than consolidate their gains across
a four-mile front. They accomplished
that only after beating off several small-
scale counterattacks by Germans infiltrating a proliferation of ravines and
gullies. So painstaking was the advance
that the 168th Infantry required four
days to reach and clear the village of
Castellino Marittimo, five miles due east
of Rosignano Marittimo.[7]

For all the difficulties, capture of
Rosignano Marittimo and Castellina
Marittimo meant that the infantrymen
had driven the enemy from the last
favorable defensive terrain south of

---

[5] *Lagekarten, Anlagen 14 AOK*, Jul 44.

[6] IV Corps AAR, Jul 44; Fifth Army G–3 Jnl and
file, 15–16 Jul 44, 105–3–2, Federal Records Center, Suitland, Md.

[7] IV Corps AAR, Jul 44.

Leghorn. That left the 135th Infantry free to move directly on the port while to the right the 34th Division's remaining regiments and attached units were to envelop the city from the east before turning west toward the coast and north toward the Arno River and Pisa, site of the famous leaning tower. They would have help from Maj. Gen. William G. Livesay's 91st Division, committed for the first time as an entire unit between Ryder's 34th and Sloan's 88th Divisions. At the same time attachment of the 363d Infantry to the 34th Division and the 361st Infantry to the 1st Armored Division terminated.

With two regiments forward—the 362d on the right and the 363d on the left—the 91st Division launched its first attack as a division early on the 12th from assembly areas three miles south of a four-mile-wide sector between Chianni and Laiatico and about ten miles northeast of Rosignano Marittimo.[8] On the 91st Division's right the 88th Division resumed its drive astride Route 439 near the Era River. Both divisions were heading for the Arno near the small industrial town of Pontedera, seventeen miles northeast of Leghorn.[9]

It would be only a matter of time before General Lemelsen's *Fourteenth Army* would have to begin a general withdrawal to the Arno. Hard pressed on the right wing, General von Senger's

XIV Panzer Corps fell back toward Leghorn. The panzer corps' left wing experienced an equally serious reverse with the loss of Volterra on 8 July to the 88th Division, which opened a wide gap in a sector occupied by the *90th Panzer Grenadier Division*. With no available reserves to close the gap, General von Senger had no alternative but to withdraw across his entire corps front. That move forced General Lemelsen to pull back the neighboring *I Parachute Corps* front as well. Even as the 91st Division during the night of 12 July prepared to attack, the *Fourteenth Army* broke contact across its entire front and fell back on the Arno.[10]

General Lemelsen was concerned not only with the persistent American ground advance but also with stepped-up Allied naval activity. For a week the Germans had been observing Allied naval units engaged in mine-clearing operations in the waters west of Leghorn and the mouth of the Arno west of Pisa. That activity rekindled both Kesselring's and Lemelsen's chronic apprehension of an amphibious operation aimed at envelopment of the *Fourteenth Army's* western, or Ligurian, flank. Lemelsen, accordingly, alerted Senger to the possibility of a landing between Leghorn and Pisa. Thus concerned, however unrealistic the threat, it was unlikely that the Germans would attempt a protracted defense of Leghorn.[11]

Over the next few days as General Crittenberger's IV Corps advanced

---

[8] On that date in severe fighting near Casaglia six miles south of the division's assembly areas, Sgt. Roy W. Harmon, Company C, 362d Infantry, so distinguished himself in combat while his battalion led the regiment toward the Chianni-Laiatico line that he was posthumously awarded the Medal of Honor.

[9] *Fifth Army History*, Part VI, pp. 85–90; IV Corps AAR, Jul 44.

[10] *AOK 14, Ia KTB Nr. 4,* 8–12 Jul 44. *AOK 14,* Doc. 62241/1.

[11] Opns Orders, *AOK 14, Ia Nr. 3015/44 g. Kdos, 1930 hrs,* 13 Jul 44, to *Hqs, LXXVI Pz Corps* in *AOK 14, Ia KTB Nr. 4, Anl. 713. AOK 14,* Doc. 62241/14. Nr. 62241/14.

across its entire front, the corps commander's attention was focused upon the columns operating southeast of Leghorn. The 168th Infantry and a newly recommitted 133d Infantry made up the force attempting to envelop Leghorn from that direction. The going for the 133rd Infantry was relatively easy, the regiment emerging from hills overlooking the Arno on 17 July; but the 168th Infantry had to fight harder for comparable gains. As the regiment on the 17th reached the outskirts of the village of Fauglia, about ten miles due east of Leghorn, the Germans in their determination to cover their main forces in a difficult withdrawal behind a bridgeless Arno mustered their remaining mortars and artillery and in the afternoon even managed a battalion-sized counterattack supported by seven Tiger tanks. It took help from all available divisional artillery for the 168th to beat off the enemy forces, but then the regiment entered Fauglia and moved on five miles beyond to Colle Salvetti, the last major town in the regimental zone of operations south of the Arno valley. Early the next morning a battalion of the 442d Regimental Combat Team to the 168th's left entered the village of Torretta, two miles west of Fauglia; and by evening of the 18th all three regiments were sending patrols deep into the Arno valley in a vain effort to regain contact with the retreating Germans.

The Capture of Leghorn

As the enveloping maneuver against Leghorn proceeded, General Crittenberger became concerned about having only one regiment, the 135th Infantry,

to assault the city frontally. That circumstance prompted him again to attach the 91st Division's 363d Infantry to the 34th Division. In concert with the 135th Infantry, approaching Leghorn from the southeast, the 363d was to attack the city from the east.[12]

Both regiments found the going easy. They readily brushed aside a weak rear guard to enter Leghorn before daylight on the 19th. Within the city they met no resistance, for the enemy garrison, concerned, as the American commander had hoped, with the columns investing the city from the east, had slipped away during the night. Meanwhile, to the south of Leghorn, the reconnaissance and tank destroyer force driving along the coastal highway had to contend with nothing more serious than destroyed culverts and widely scattered mines, and it entered the city soon after daylight. Close behind came the 442d Regimental Combat Team's 100th Battalion to take up garrison duty.[13]

Although the Germans had been forced to yield Leghorn earlier than they had planned, they managed to destroy the city's port facilities and partially block the harbor with sunken ships. All quay walls were demolished and the masonry toppled into the water. A number of ships were scuttled alongside piers and the harbor sown with mines. Allied bombing had earlier cut all rail lines and created ruins that blocked the streets in the port area. In their turn the Germans had sown the ruins indiscriminately with thousands of

---

[12] *Fifth Army History*, Part VI, p. 83.
[13] *Fifth Army History*, Part VI, pp. 83–84; Hist Rcd, 34th Cav Rcn Trp, Jul 44; 804th TD Bn AAR, Jul 44.

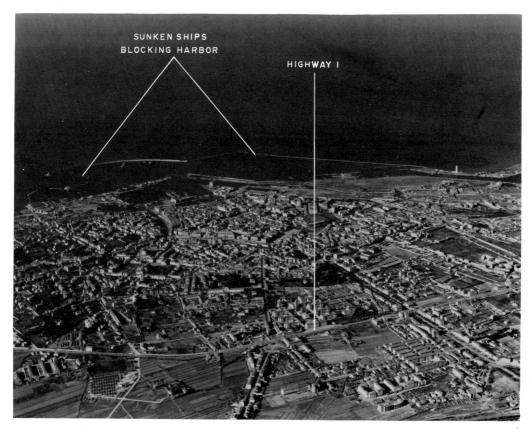

AERIAL VIEW OF LEGHORN

mines and booby traps. Hundreds of American soldiers fell victim to these devices in the early weeks following the fall of Leghorn.[14]

However monumental the task of putting the port of Leghorn in operation, it had to be done before the Fifth Army could launch major operations beyond the Arno. Surveys of the damaged harbor by Army and Navy engineers indicated that at least three weeks would be needed to provide just two

[14] Meyer MS, ch XXIX; Clark, *Calculated Risk*, p. 185.

berths for Liberty ships. Barring unforeseen circumstances the engineers estimated that it would take two months before Leghorn could meet all the needs of the Fifth Army north of Rome. The first Liberty ships carrying engineering equipment and stevedoring gear arrived at Leghorn on 20 August but had to be unloaded by lighters. Drawing upon earlier experience in rehabilitating the port of Naples, Army engineers soon bridged over the vessels sunk alongside the piers and extended the quays so that all hatches of cargo ships could be worked without reversing the vessel. By such expedients two Liberty ships were able to dock on 26 August only five weeks after the city's capture.[15]

The Capture of Ancona and Arezzo

Just as Leghorn, on the opposite coast, was vital for the Americans, so Ancona on the Adriatic coast remained a prerequisite for continued large-scale operations by the British Eighth Army. Having been halted early in July by firm resistance eight miles south of Ancona, General Anders' 2 Polish Corps prepared on 16 July to resume the drive for that port.

General Anders had two Polish divisions—the 3d Carpathian along the coast and the 5th Kresowa in the center—with the brigade-sized Italian Corps of Liberation on the left. Like General Crittenberger, General Anders hoped to envelop his objective rather than attack frontally. By simulated concentrations and movements of armor and other heavy equipment in the area of coastal Highway 16, the 3d Carpathian Division was to try to draw enemy attention away from the area of actual attack, the sector of the 5th Kresowa Division. With help of the 2d Armoured Brigade, the 5th was to attack along the axis Osimo-Agugliano in hope of turning the German defenses from the west, then to exploit eastward as far as the coastal highway above Ancona. In the meantime, an attack northward by the Italian corps was to cover the division's left flank. The Desert Air Force (DAF), the Eighth

Army's long-time air arm, was to fly in general support.[16]

During the night of 16 July four Polish infantry battalions and four armored regiments, the latter containing approximately 240 tanks, faced a front defended by an estimated three infantry battalions of the *278th Division*, plus some units of the *71st Division* that had been reconstituted after heavy losses in May during the defense of the Gustav Line south of Rome. Because the Poles planned to rely on accurate close air support, they attacked at daylight on 17 July behind the fire of approximately 300 artillery pieces and aerial bombardment by the DAF.

Early in the day some anxiety developed at Polish headquarters over the security of the left flank because of hesitation and local withdrawals by the Italians. Yet that concern was short-lived as the overwhelming weight of Allied firepower propelled the 5th Kresowa Division forward expeditiously in the center. By the end of the day the division and the tanks of the armored brigade had gained approximately four miles. The next day the Poles drove the Germans beyond the Esino River, ten miles northwest of Osimo, and on the 18th pursued the enemy beyond the river, completing the envelopment of Ancona. As the Carpathian Lancers of the 3d Carpathian Division pushed along the coastal highway to enter the city in early afternoon, they were virtually unopposed.

Over the next week the Polish corps

---

[15] Meyer MS.

[16] Operations of the British, Indian, and Dominion Forces in Italy, Part II, Sec. F, 2 Polish Corps Operations. Unless otherwise indicated the following is based upon this reference.

forced the enemy steadily northward to place the port of Ancona well beyond the range of German artillery and to give the Eighth Army a major forward supply base. No longer would British truck convoys have to make the long overland haul from Bari, over 260 miles to the south. Fortunately for the Allies, the Germans at Ancona had been unable to demolish the port as thoroughly as their confreres at Leghorn. On 23 July, only five days after the fall of Ancona, a British supply convoy steamed into the port.[17]

Meanwhile, far to the west beyond the Apennines, a major part of the British Eighth Army prepared to renew the drive against the communications center of Arezzo, a prerequisite to continuing on to Florence. Opposite the 13 Corps, which for several weeks had carried the main burden of the Eighth Army's offensive, were the same four German divisions that had earlier defended the Frieda or Trasimeno Line: the *15th Panzer Grenadier*, the *334th Infantry*, the *1st Parachute*, and the *Hermann Goering Divisions*—all under the command of General Herr's *LXXVI Panzer Corps*.[18] They were deployed along dominating heights between Monte Castiglione Maggiore and Castello di Brolio, the latter twenty miles west of Arezzo. Everywhere they enjoyed the advantage of observation and fields of fire. Only in the center, where infantrymen of the 4th Division had captured the isolated hill Poggio

al'Omo, had the Germans given ground.[19]

Checked on the left by enemy fire on 5 July, the 13 Corps at the outset failed to appreciate the strength of the German positions. Several days were lost while the leading brigades continued to probe in the belief that the positions could be penetrated through continued pressure without the necessity of a full-scale, set-piece attack. The fact that the 6th Armoured Division on the right and the 4th Infantry Division in the center continued to make some progress supported that belief, until on the 7th those divisions too encountered the full strength of the German defensive fires. On the corps right flank the tanks of the 26th Armoured Brigade, 6th Armoured Division, reached a point about a mile south of the junction of Highways 71 and 73 where they had to halt, three miles short of Arezzo. On the left the 6th South African Armoured Division also ground to a halt.

Although General Leese assumed that the 13 Corps would have to be reinforced if a breakthrough to Arezzo was to be achieved, reinforcements were less readily obtainable than they had been in June. The 10 Corps, which had earlier provided additional units for its neighbor on the left, had only one division and an armored brigade to employ against the equivalent of two or three German divisions deployed, as were those opposite the 13 Corps, on good defensive terrain; and thus the 10 Corps had first claim on reinforcements. General Leese met the claim by

---

[17] Alexander *Despatch*, pp. 60–61.

[18] On 11 July, the *715th Infantry Division* began the relief of the *Hermann Goering Division*. See *10th Army KTB Nr. 10*, 11 Jul 44, *AOK* Doc. 52991/1.

[19] Operations of British, Indian, and Dominion Forces in Italy, Part II, Sec. D. Unless otherwise cited the following is based upon this reference.

ordering forward the 4th Indian Division, which had been undergoing three weeks of training in mountain warfare. By 10 July the Indians had taken their place in line to the left of their countrymen in the 10th Indian Division.

Reinforcements for the 13 Corps had to come from theater reserves which Alexander had earlier earmarked for participation in the offensive against the Gothic Line. That development meant that the 2d New Zealand Division, resting and training south of Rome, had to be committed earlier than planned. It took until 14 July for that division to enter the line east of the Chiana Canal between the 4th Indian Infantry and the British 6th Armoured Divisions.

With the division's arrival, the 13 Corps commander, Kirkman, planned to attack at 0100 on the 15th with the 4th Infantry and 6th South African Armoured Divisions demonstrating actively on the left to conceal the main effort to be made by the New Zealanders and the British 6th Armoured Division on the right in an effort to take Arezzo from the west. The attack went slowly at first, the Germans even managing some local counterattacks while slowly yielding ground. Yet that night the Germans broke contact and withdrew. Early on 16 July the British 6th Armoured Division's 26th Armoured Brigade descended into the upper Chiana valley west of Arezzo and rapidly closed on the city and crossings of the Arno some four miles to the north. During the remainder of the day the New Zealanders and the British armor sped forward along the roads west and northwest of the objective. By evening they had crossed the Arno where it

flows westward for a short distance before turning northwestward toward Florence, 25 miles away. By dark on 16 July the battle for Arezzo had ended and the advance on Florence was about to begin.

The extended defense of Arezzo had given Field Marshal Kesselring about all the time he could hope for—an additional ten days—for improving the Gothic Line and resting and reorganizing his forces. That the respite came at a relatively low cost could be inferred from the fact that the 13 Corps counted only 165 prisoners during the ten-day flight.

Despite the heavy operational demands of the Arezzo battle, the Eighth Army continued with its administrative preparations for the Gothic Line offensive. In the vicinity of Orte and Castellana at the end of the first week of July the army opened its first railheads north of Rome. Arezzo was soon to serve as the army's main communications center and roadhead for operations in the Northern Apennines. Once that roadhead was open, the Eighth Army staff estimated, a force of thirteen and a half divisions, nine of which might be operationally employed, could be maintained north of Florence.

Pause at the Arno

As the U.S. Fifth Army drew up to the Arno west of Florence, General Clark decided against crossing the river immediately in favor of a pause to rest and reorganize his troops and assemble supplies. One of the divisions most deserving of a rest was the 34th, in action with few respites since fighting in North Africa in 1943. The 45-mile advance from Piombino to Leghorn had only been the last of a grueling battle experience that brought all ranks close to exhaustion. Even the division commander, General Ryder, was mentally and physically near exhaustion, so that on the 21st General Clark replaced him with a younger man, Maj. Gen. Charles Bolté. It was a relief without prejudice, General Ryder going on to a corps command in the United States.[20]

For French units, meanwhile, time was to run out before they could reach the Arno. Acting under orders from the Allied command, General Clark directed that all French units be relieved and assembled near Naples before the end of July. As specified by General Alexander, the British 13 Corps upon departure of the French was to shift its left flank westward to embrace the former FEC sector, thus extending the interarmy boundary to a line generally paralleling the Elsa River. As the relief neared, the French front stabilized roughly ten miles short of the Arno. The FEC's zone passed to the British on 22 July, considerably narrowing the Fifth Army's sector.

Although the French stopped short of the Arno, their contribution to the drive north of Rome was considerable. The Algerian and Moroccan divisions, for example, had captured 2,080 prisoners. The French themselves incurred 6,680 casualties, including 1,342 killed.

As the 13 Corps relieved the French, the U.S. IV Corps prepared to clear the last enemy remaining south of the Arno between Leghorn and Pisa. That task could still pose problems. A battal-

ion of the 363d Infantry, still attached to the 34th Division, ran into considerable resistance while fighting through much of the night to enter Marina di Pisa at the river's mouth before daylight on the 23d. And the 442d Regimental Combat Team and the 168th Infantry were delayed by the numerous canals scoring the broad valley. Engineers subject to harassing fire from north of the Arno had to construct numerous bridges, including one over the 100-foot-wide gap of the Canale Navigable, connecting the Arno with the port of Leghorn.

During the afternoon of 23 July, two battalions of the 363d Infantry occupied that part of Pisa lying south of the Arno. Finding all bridges destroyed, the men dug in along the south bank of the river while enemy guns and mortars poured in heavy fire. Since Pisa's famed Renaissance monuments, the Baptistry of St. John with its Campenile—the leaning tower—were north of the river, they were unaffected. From somewhere north of the Arno 280-mm. guns opened fire on Leghorn. Yet by evening the 34th Division and its attached units had occupied the entire south bank of the Arno from the sea to a point about ten miles east of Pisa. During the next two days the 91st and 88th Divisions pulled up to the south bank on the IV Corps center and right flank, respectively.

The Arno River flows through a broad valley at the foot of the Northern Apennines. From Arezzo, about forty miles southeast of Florence, it flows northward, where the Sieve River joins ten miles east of Florence. Thus enlarged, the Arno proceeds westward through Florence and Pisa for 65 miles

[20] Interv, Mathews with Ladue, 17 Jun 48, CMH; 34th Div AAR, Jul 44; Clark, *Calculated Risk*, p. 384.

before entering the Ligurian Sea at Marina di Pisa. The largest river in the Fifth Army's zone of operations, the Arno varied in width from 60 to 600 feet, with an average of from 200 to 250 feet. The depth also varied greatly, ranging from only a few feet in periods of drought to over thirty feet at flood stage. In late summer, before the autumn rains began, the river could be easily forded almost anywhere by foot troops and at numerous points by vehicles. Because of seasonal flooding in spring and late autumn, levees from 20 to 40 feet in height and 50 to 100 feet wide flanked the river for much of its length. Between Pisa and the coast the banks were about ten feet high, rising to forty feet east of Pisa, then falling off to twenty feet near Florence. As the river enters the coastal plain near Pisa, its valley widens to fifteen miles.

Since the Arno in the midsummer of 1944 represented no formidable military obstacle, General Clark's superiors both in Caserta and in Washington favored an immediate continuation of the advance beyond the river. General Alexander, in particular, was anxious to place the port of Leghorn beyond the range of enemy artillery as soon as possible. He urged the Fifth Army commander, if he found the line of the Arno weakly held, to push on immediately to seize the heights of the Monte Pisano hill mass, 14 miles northeast of Leghorn and probable haven for many of the guns harassing Leghorn. Extending from the Arno northwestward for twelve miles to the banks of the Serchio River, the hill mass might also serve as a springboard for an advance on Pistoia, 20 miles to the northeast. Since the configuration of the terrain made the

sector from the city of Prato (ten miles northwest of Florence) westward to the Ligurian coast a single tactical entity, Alexander assigned Clark's Fifth Army responsibility for all of it. After crossing the Arno, the Fifth Army would have as its objectives, after the Monte Pisano hill mass, the cities of Pistoia and Lucca, the latter about ten miles northwest of Pisa.[21]

If the Germans elected to hold along the coastal reaches of the Arno, Alexander suggested that Clark attempt instead to force a passage somewhere to the east between Pontedera, 17 miles northeast of Leghorn, and Empoli, 16 miles farther east, and from there develop two thrusts, one on Pistoia and the other on Lucca. With those cities in hand, the Fifth Army would control a four-lane *autostrada* running westward from Florence to the coastal highway, ten miles west of Lucca. That situation would give the Fifth Army an excellent lateral route over which troops might be shifted rapidly from one sector to another.[22]

Although General Alexander was aware that many of the Fifth Army's divisions needed rest and reorganization, he was also conscious that the Germans were in more serious straits and thus were unlikely to launch a major counteroffensive at any point along the river. This circumstance should enable Clark, Alexander believed, to assume the defensive on his left wing between Pontedera and the sea, thereby resting some of his divisions, while at the same time concen-

---

[21] Ltr, Marshall to Devers, 17 Jul 44, CCS 603/4, in ABC 384, Eur Sec 9–A; Ltr, Alexander to Clark, 19 Jul 44, Sub: Future Opns Hqs AAI, MA/A/470.
[22] Ltr, Alexander to Clark, 19 Jul 44.

trating his fittest units on his right between Pontedera and Empoli for the thrusts on Pistoia and Lucca. It was of "supreme importance," Alexander concluded, to go "all-out" to capture those two cities before Kesselring's armies could recover from the attrition of the past few weeks.[23]

Despite this attrition, Field Marshal Kesselring had actually achieved something of a defensive success in holding the Allied armies for so long south of the Arno. Yet there was another reason for Allied delays, not of Kesslering's making: the shift of ground and air resources during July from Alexander's armies to those forces preparing for southern France. That shift had forestalled any swift advance to and through the Northern Apennines, across the Po Valley, and into northeastern Italy.

A swift advance across the Po thus obviated, no longer was it necessary to spare the bridges of the Po. In an effort to isolate the enemy in the Northern Apennines, Alexander decided to concentrate on disrupting the enemy's lines of communication across the Po. Thus Operation MALLORY MAJOR, which aimed at destruction of all bridges across the Po, in some respects reflected less the bright hopes of early summer than an admission of frustrated expectations attributable to the events and command decisions of late June or early July.[24]

Planning for MALLORY MAJOR had begun in early June shortly after the fall of Rome, after Allied intelligence had concluded that the destruction of bridges would cause greater disruption of enemy lines of communication than the repeated bombing of railroad marshalling yards. The plan was to concentrate bombers on the destruction of the six rail bridges across the Po and one across the Trebbia, a northward flowing tributary entering the Po at Piacenza, some 34 miles southeast of Milan. The operations were to be supplemented by destruction of either the Recco or the Zoaglia viaducts on the coastal highway a few miles east of Genoa, Italy's major commercial port, about 100 miles northwest of Leghorn. The plan was later modified to include all bridges across the Po. Yet in the first weeks after the capture of Rome, expectations that Allied armies would reach the Po Valley by later summer had prompted Alexander to shelve the plans.[25]

With the decision for Operation AN-VIL, Alexander still hoped that his armies would be able to force a passage of the Northern Apennines before winter; but after Wilson's directive of 5 July, he had abandoned all hope that they would be able to do so without pause. The AAI commander therefore focused his thoughts on bringing the enemy to a decisive battle between the Apennines and a bridgeless river—thus a revived Operation MALLORY MAJOR. On 11 July Allied Force Headquarters issued orders for the operation to begin the next day.

---

[23] Ibid.

[24] Blockade: The Isolation of Italy from the Reich by the Mediterranean Tactical Air Force, 29 Aug 44–1 May 45, Hqs MATAF, July 1945, The Albert F. Simpson Historical Research Center, USAF Maxwell AFS, Ala.

[25] Operations of the British, Indian, and Dominion Forces in Italy, Part II, Sec. A, Allied Strategy; Alexander Despatch, pp. 64–65. Unless otherwise indicated the following is based upon these references.

Beginning on 12 July hundreds of medium bombers attacked the nineteen bridges from Piacenza eastward to the Adriatic, then turned westward to bomb the bridges as far west as Torre Beretti, 50 miles west of Piacenza. By the 27th all bridges between Torre Beretti and the Adriatic were destroyed, virtually cutting off Kesselring's armies from their supply bases in northern Italy.

That would appear to have been the logical time for General Clark to have crossed the Arno River, drive on Pistoia and Lucca, and force the Germans back into the Gothic Line west of Florence. Instead, the Fifth Army for almost a month after the completion of MALLORY MAJOR remained south of the river.[26] Except for a quick thrust in early August to seize Florence, so did the Eighth Army. Thus Kesselring gained more time for strengthening his defenses in the Northern Apennines and, even more important, to restore his sorely damaged lines of communication across the Po. Using pontoon bridges, ferries, pneumatic lines, and overhead cable lines, German engineers managed to keep enough supplies moving across the Po to maintain, though

not to increase, existing levels. The Germans also organized an adequate ferry service across the Po to supply Ferrara, their main communications hub behind the army group's left wing. By the end of July nineteen ferries were in service, ten of them capable of carrying twenty-four tons of cargo each.[27]

On 3 August traffic started moving again across several repaired bridges that had been knocked out in July by Allied aircraft. By 6 August the Brenner railroad line was also back in operation. Four days later the main line from the Austrian Alps to the Ligurian coast—from Brenner, via Bologna, to Genoa—was again open and the rail line to Turin, seventy-five miles northwest of Genoa, restored. On the following day the rail line from Genoa into southern France was also passable. While Operation MALLORY MAJOR was a marked success in terms of bridges destroyed, failure to co-ordinate it closely with an Allied offensive against the Gothic Line meant that in the long run it had no more than a temporary harassing effect.

---

[26] See ch. XVI, pp. 1–2, for explanation of Clark's decision to halt along the Arno.

[27] Craven and Cate, eds., AAF III, pp. 404–17; Greiner and Schramm, eds., OKW/WFSt, KTB, IV(1), pp. 542–43.

CHAPTER XVI

Along the Arno

While General Clark's decision to pause along the Arno during the second half of July had forfeited the temporary advantages provided by Operation MALLORY MAJOR through destruction of the Po bridges, timing of the aerial operation had been Alexander's responsibility rather than Clark's. Furthermore, General Clark saw several compelling reasons for holding his army south of the river, most important of which was the condition of men and equipment. The ports of Civitavecchia, San Stefano, and Piombino were just beginning to take up some of the slack caused by leaving Naples and Anzio far to the rear, but the essential port of Leghorn had yet to begin to function. Moreover, in Clark's opinion, the demands of Operation ANVIL had already deprived his army of the reserves necessary to continue the advance beyond the Arno without a pause for rest and reorganization.[1] That was a theme to which the Fifth Army commander would frequently return. Since the Eighth Army would not reach the Arno between Pontassieve and Florence until the end of the month and would, like the Fifth Army, also have to pause and reorganize before continuing, MALLORY MAJOR's brief opportunities were forfeited by the Eighth Army as well.

That Crittenberger's IV Corps, at least, was desperately weary and in no condition to continue the advance beyond the Arno without pause there seemed little doubt. Everybody was near exhaustion and in desperate need of rest, although, as Alexander reminded Clark, no more so than the enemy.

There were organizational changes too that required a pause. The 1st Armored Division, then in corps reserve, had on 17 July also acquired a new commanding general, Maj. Gen. Vernon E. Prichard, former commander of an armored division in the United States. Like Ryder, General Harmon went home to assume command of a corps. Three days later the 1st Armored Division undertook a thorough reorganization, one that had been postponed since September 1943, when the U.S. Army had adopted a new Table of Organization and Equipment for armored divisions. Although the new organization was an outgrowth of the 1st Armored Division's own experiences in the North African campaign, the division had been unable to reorganize in September, since part of the unit had been fighting in Italy and the rest was in Algeria preparing to move to Italy. In the months since Salerno some elements of the division had been in almost continuous contact with the enemy. As the Fifth Army pulled up to the Arno, the time to make the changes had come.[2]

---

[1] Clark Diary, 8 Jul 44.

[2] Howe, *The Battle History of the 1st Armored Division,* pp. 363–66.

The 1943 TOE had cut the strength of an armored division from 14,620 men to 10,937, but because the 1st Armored Division had been understrength, less than a thousand had to be transferred. In essence, the reorganization eliminated one armored regiment as well as headquarters of the other two. In their stead were three separate tank battalions and three separate armored infantry battalions, which could be thrown together in various mixes with supporting units to form two combat commands, while new small headquarters, designated division trains, controlled the division reserve and supplies. The reorganization cut the number of medium tanks from 250 to 154. The basic reasons for the reductions were control and maneuverability, the old heavy division having proved ponderous.[3]

On 25 July headquarters of the II Corps, which had been in army reserve for the past few weeks, came forward on the army right flank to take control of the 85th, 88th, and 91st Divisions. Clark, nevertheless, intended no extensive operations along the Arno since he planned to conserve Keyes' corps to carry the main burden of the army's offensive against the Gothic Line north of the river.[4]

After the capture of Leghorn, Clark began to withdraw the Fifth Army's combat divisions to afford all a rest period off the line. To make that easier, he turned over a 10-mile sector of the defensive line to four automatic weapons antiaircraft battalions converted into infantry, thereby releasing a battle-weary 34th Infantry Division. Infantry units in rest areas furnished mortars, machine guns, automatic rifles, and radios to equip the antiaircraft battalions for their new role. Tank destroyers, tanks, and batteries of 3.7-inch and 90-mm. antiaircraft guns provided heavy fire support. Brig. Gen. Cecil L. Rutledge, erstwhile commander of the 45th Antiaircraft Artillery Brigade, commanded what became known as Task Force 45.

To make up for shortages in artillery and engineers in the Fifth Army caused by earlier withdrawals for ANVIL, Clark borrowed from his British counterpart some sixty miscellaneous artillery pieces and two battalions of Royal Engineers. He also borrowed an antiaircraft artillery regiment, which he converted into infantry and assigned to Task Force 45.[5]

Meanwhile, Clark began to regroup his army across a 30-mile front between the Ligurian coast southwest of Pisa and an interarmy boundary close to the Elsa River, which enters the Arno at a point four miles west of Empoli. Crittenberger's IV Corps held a 23-mile sector on the army left flank as far inland as the village of Capanne, five miles east of Pontedera. Keyes' II Corps held the remaining seven miles. Within

[3] For detail see Mary Lee Stubbs and Stanley Russell Connor, Army Lineage series, *Armor-Cavalry*, Part I, *Regular Army and Army Reserve* (Washington, D.C., 1969).

[4] Interv, Mathews with Ladue, 17 June 48, CMH; Chester G. Starr, ed., *From Salerno to the Alps: A History of the Fifth Army, 1943–45* (Washington: Infantry Journal Press, 1948), pp. 297–98.

[5] Clark Diary, 17 Aug 44; *Fifth Army History*, Part VI, p. 99. A British AA regiment was the equivalent of a U.S. AA battalion.

the IV Corps sector Task Force 45 held the coastal flank, and the newly reorganized 1st Armored Division moved forward from reserve to take up a position on the right, while a regimental combat team of the 91st Division held the narrow II Corps front.

That disposition permitted the bulk of the Fifth Army to rest, so that by mid-August Clark would have five divisions—four infantry and one armored—ready to resume the offensive, while Task Force 45 would have received sufficient infantry experience to be useful either as a follow-up or as a holding force. Two additional units were on their way to join the army: the Negro 92d Infantry Division and the Brazilian Expeditionary Force, the latter a division-size unit consisting of the 1st, 6th, and 11th Regiment Combat Teams with attached supporting units. Because of limited training and relatively low strength, neither division was expected for the next few months to have more than a defensive capability. Even with the addition of those two units, the Fifth Army would have the equivalent of but seven divisions, only half as many as in May along the Garigliano River at the beginning of the drive to Rome. Reductions had also occurred in the number of corps artillery battalions, twenty-two as compared with thirty-three, and additional battalions were soon to be withdrawn for Operation ANVIL. For an army that had come to depend heavily upon massive artillery fire, that cutback was disturbing.[6]

By the end of July all French troops, the majority of which were

AMERICAN PATROL ENTERING PISA

Moslem, had left the Fifth Army, but the arrival of the Brazilian troops in August would give the army's G–4 little relief from long-time problems of providing rations acceptable to men of several different nationalities with widely differing dietary customs and preferences. The Brazilian menu, for example, included considerably more sugar, lard, and salt than did the American while excluding tomato juice, dried beans of all types, and rice.[7]

The Germans meanwhile faced far more critical difficulties with their rations. Long plagued with short supplies, the Germans, as they withdrew northward, were forced increasingly to live off the land, and especially to draw upon the agricultural resources of the

[6] AAI Order of Battle on withdrawal of ANVIL (DRAGOON) formations, BIGOT-ANVIL, an. II to app. D–5.

[7] *Fifth Army History,* Part VI, p. 117.

fertile Po Valley. Furthermore, among the German troops the unaccustomed heat of a central Italian summer had caused considerable hardship from heat exhaustion and illness from tainted food.[8]

The Eighth Army

While the Fifth Army paused along the Arno west of Florence, the British Eighth Army continued to advance on a two-corps front over terrain as challenging as that encountered around Lake Trasimeno. Beyond Arezzo there loomed the Pratomagno mountain massif, a region of few roads or trails, stretching almost thirty miles northwestward and filling the fifteen-mile-wide area between two arms of the Arno where the river, flowing south from the Northern Apennines, makes a large loop northwest of Arezzo before flowing northwest toward Florence, turning again, and flowing westward to the sea. Two highways extended beyond Arezzo: Highway 71 northward along the east bank of the Arno to Bibbiena, located at the foot of the Northern Apennines at the junction with Highway 70, and Highway 69 northwestward along the west bank of the Arno as far as Inciso in Valdarno, whence the highway divided into two parts, one continuing west of the river to Florence and the second east of the Arno via Pontassieve to Florence. With the 10 Corps following Highway 71 toward Bibbiena and the 13 Corps the valley of the middle Arno toward Florence, the two corps would again diverge, as they had south of Lake Trasimeno.

By the end of July the 10 Corps' 4th Indian Division had reached the entrance of the upper Arno valley, and the 10th Indian Division had secured an area in the Sansepolcro plain; but there the divisions had to pause to regroup in order to sideslip to the west toward the Pratomagno massif.[9] The 13 Corps, meanwhile, continued toward Florence without pause. General Kirkman sent the 13 Corps down the Arno valley, with the British 6th Armoured Division making the main effort on the corps right astride the river. On the corps left the 6th South African Armoured Division continued its advance west of the Chianti Hills, and in the center the British 4th Division maintained contact between the two armored forces. If the enemy continued to withdraw north of Arezzo, Kirkman intended to hold the 2d New Zealand Division in corps reserve. Otherwise, he intended to commit the New Zealanders to reinforce his main effort. The 13 Corps also had the 8th Indian Division, formerly with the 10 Corps, as well as the British 25th Tank Brigade from the army reserve and the 1st Army Artillery Group from the 5 Corps.[10]

The corps got going on 16 July on a broad front northwest of Arezzo. In a quick thrust beyond the city the 6th Armoured Division's 26th Armoured Brigade seized intact the Ponte à Buriano, a bridge across the upper Arno six miles northwest of the city, but the next day when the rest of the division attempted to cross, fire from high

---

[8] German military records frequently comment on these problems.

[9] Operations of the British, Indian, and Dominion Forces in Italy, Part II, Sec. D. Unless otherwise indicated the following is based upon this source.

[10] Tank brigades, unlike armored brigades, were designed for attachment to infantry divisions.

ground to the northwest so disrupted the column that the commander ordered a search for an alternate crossing. The search located a ford concealed from enemy observation and fire, but after only a few hours' use it deteriorated so badly that it had to be abandoned.

There the British 6th Armoured Division might have been forced to halt, except that the next day, the 17th, the 6th South African Armoured Division gained the ridge of the Chianti Hills. From the high ground the South Africans were able to direct flanking fire against the Germans opposite the 4th Division in the corps center and on the eastern flanks of the hills. That forced the Germans to fall back far enough to enable the British armor to cross the Arno in strength and, by the 20th, to capture high ground near Castiglione Fibocchi.

It was clear at that point to General Kirkman that the Germans intended to make a stand to block the middle Arno valley and the lower slopes of the Pratomagno massif east of the valley with Schlemm's *I Parachute Corps,* which had the *1st Parachute, 15th Panzer Grenadier,* and *334th Divisions* deployed opposite the 13 Corps right flank in the Arno valley. West of the valley the *715th Light Infantry Division* was in the process of relieving the *Hermann Goering Division* along a sector extending from the valley to the ridge line of the Chianti Hills. Having lost heavily in May at Anzio, the *715th Division* had been reinforced and reorganized with replacements from the Reich. Although most of the men lacked battle experience, they were deployed in terrain so devoid of roads as to favor the defend-

ers. West of the Chianti Hills, between Highway 2 and Route 222, the Germans had deployed the *4th Parachute* and *356th Divisions* across a ten-mile sector opposite the South African armored division.

After studying those dispositions and reflecting on the slight progress made thus far in the Arno valley, General Kirkman decided that the best route to Florence lay west of the Chianti Hills on his left flank, which General Leese was about to extend to take over the FEC sector from the Fifth Army. On 20 July he decided to shift the main effort to that flank and began moving there the 8th Indian Division and the New Zealand division from his reserve. The 8th Indian Division, with the armor of the 1st Canadian Tank Brigade in support, was to operate on the corps left flank, while the New Zealanders were to pass through the FEC's 2d Moroccan Division early on the 22d and drive northward toward the Arno River crossings at Signa, five miles west of Florence. To the New Zealanders' right the South Africans were to advance astride Route 222 to Impruneta, five miles south of Florence. To the South African division's right and east of the Chianti Hills, the 4th Division, supported by the 25th Tank Brigade, was to advance toward Pontassieve and cross to the north bank of the Arno at Poggio Alberaccio, seven miles east of Florence. The British 6th Armoured Division was to continue to operate on the right flank.

Thus regrouped, the 13 Corps resumed its advance on 21 July. For the next two weeks the corps battled its way through a series of well-sited and skillfully defended positions to within seven

AERIAL VIEW OF FLORENCE

miles of the Arno west of Florence. Late on 2 August the New Zealanders fought to the top of La Poggiona, high ground five miles southwest of Florence overlooking Highway 2 from the west, the last remaining favorable defensive terrain south of Florence and west of the Chianti Hills. With that loss those enemy forces still east of the highway began to thin out. By the morning of 3 August the Germans were in full retreat across the entire corps front.

Along Highway 2 during the night of 3 August the Imperial Light Horse of the 6th South African Armoured Division entered the southern portion of Florence and the next day reached the Arno. There the South Africans discovered that all of the Florentine bridges had been demolished except the picturesque Ponte Vecchio. Narrow and lined on either side with shops, the Ponte Vecchio was unsuitable for anything but foot traffic, and the Germans had blocked both ends with demolished buildings. West of the city the New Zealanders quickly closed up to the south bank of the Arno, and the 8th Indian Division secured the high ground above Montelupo, eleven miles west of the city. By nightfall of 5 August the 13 Corps was in firm control of the south bank of the river from Montelupo eastward to Florence.

The German Situation

As the British approached Florence, Field Marshal Kesselring was conscious that with Leghorn, Arezzo, and Ancona already in Allied hands, all General Alexander needed to complete a system of logistical, communications, and operational bases from which to support and control an offensive into the Northern Apennines was Florence. The city and the Arno obviously constituted an advantageous delaying line before the Apennines. On the other hand, there were important arguments for abandoning Florence and the Arno.

The main argument was Kesselring's desire to preserve, as he had Rome, the city of Florence and its irreplaceable artistic and other cultural treasures. To that end, the German commander had on 23 June designated Florence an open city and ordered his army commanders to exclude all but internal security personnel from the city. That information was communicated indirectly through Vatican officials to the Allied command. Although General Alexander, as in the case of Rome, declined to issue a similar declaration, he was equally anxious to avoid fighting within the historic city.[11]

Similarly, to fight along the Arno and at other delaying positions short of the Gothic Line was to endanger the world-renowned artistic and architectural monuments of other Tuscan cities, such as Pisa, Lucca, and Pistoia. Even the city of Prato, a few miles northwest of Florence, contained important frescos by Fra Filippo Lippi. Moreover, stored in scores of villas and warehouses over the Tuscan countryside were priceless art treasures removed for safekeeping from Florence's famed Uffizi Gallery. Should an all-out battle develop along the Arno, those too would be endangered.[12]

The argument posed for Field Marshal Kesselring a critical choice. If he allowed the Allied armies to assault the Gothic Line without first having to fight through a series of forward delaying positions, he would run the risk of facing them in the Po Valley before the end of the year. He had given orders that Pisa and Florence were to be spared, but at the same time he had directed his army commanders to make the Allies fight for every gain between the Arno and the Northern Apennines. The orders were obviously inherently contradictory, since Florence, especially, was the key to the Arno position. To yield the city would necessarily lead to a withdrawal all along the north bank of the river.[13]

While the German commander weighed the pros and cons of holding the Arno position, his Allied opponents, despite Kesselring's unilateral declaration of Florence as an open city, harbored no doubts that he would contest,

---

[11]*AOK 14, Ia Nr. 4695/44/Geh.*, 23 Jun 44, in *AOK 14, Ia KTB Nr. 3, Anl. 611.1*, 30 Jun 44, *AOK 14*, 59091/4; MS # C-095c (Senger), CMH; *Alexander Despatch*, pp. 60–61. An interesting eyewitness account as to how both sides treated the so-called open city may be found in Nicky Mariano, *Forty Years with Berenson* (New York: Knopf, 1966), Appendix: "A month with the Paratroopers in the front line."

[12]MS # C-095c (Senger), CMH.

[13]MS # C-064 (Kesselring), CMH; *AOK 14, Ia KTB Anl. 4*, 2 Aug 44, *AOK 14*, Doc. 62241/1.

as he had done so often before, every yard of defensible ground south of the city and possibly within it until forced to withdraw. Convinced that the Germans had yet to complete their defenses in the Northern Apennines, the Allied commanders believed that Kesselring still needed time and thus would attempt to hold along the Arno.[14]

As the front approached Florence, the Germans faced growing difficulties in keeping the civilian population of the city supplied with food, which had to be trucked from as far away as the Lombard plain, fifty miles to the north. The *Fourteenth Army*, in whose zone the city lay, was itself plagued by a shortage of transport to support its own operations and could spare few trucks to assist the hungry Florentines.[15]

Under those circumstances it was not surprising that, as the front neared the city, the German garrison faced mounting hostility from the population, but General Lemelsen prohibited any retaliation unless civilians engaged in hostile acts, such as guiding Allied troops over difficult terrain or informing them of the location of German positions. In such cases he did not shrink from authorizing strong punitive measures, including, in one case, reprisal by executing twenty-six civilians.[16]

On 31 July, as the British 13 Corps approached Florence, Lemelsen ordered destruction of all bridges within or near the city except the Ponte Vec-chio.[17] While that bridge is picturesque, art historians judge that it has little artistic merit in comparison with some of the others that the Germans destroyed. A consideration in Lemelsen's mind may have been that its military value was as slight as its artistic worth.

Meanwhile, after British artillery fire destroyed the electric power lines leading to Florence, conditions for the population worsened. All water supplies were cut off, thus further fanning a growing resentment toward the Germans, whom the Florentines, as the Romans before them, regarded as the authors of all their misfortunes.[18]

Evacuation of Florence

Faced with the near hopeless task of supplying a densely populated urban area with the necessities of living, Kesselring decided on 2 August to abandon the city, employing paratroopers to cover the withdrawal of Schlemm's *I Parachute Corps*. As the paratroopers fought with their backs to the Arno throughout 3 August, the fury of the battle threatened at times to engulf Florence, despite the mutual concern to spare the city. Allied artillery fire hit those quarters south of the river, and occasional long rounds smashed into the central city, hitting among other places the Piazza Museo Instituto del'Arte and the Ponte della Vittoria, one of the bridges left standing in spite of Lemelsen's order. Allied aircraft, flying close support missions, also fired into portions of the city on both sides of the Arno.[19]

[14]Msg, FX 80724, Wilson to Troopers, 9 Aug 44, AFHQ Cable Log file (OUT), 0100/4/43.

[15]*AOK 14, Ia KTB Anl. 4*, 21 Jul 44, *AOK 14*, Doc. 62241/1.

[16]*Ibid.*, 22 Jul 44; *AOK 14*, Opn. Order, *Ia Nr. 3041/44 g. Kdos*, 14 Jul 44, in *Ia KTB Anl. 4, Anl. 723, AOK 14*, Doc. 62241/4.

[17]*AOK 14, Ia KTB Nr. 4*, 26 and 31 Jul 44, *AOK 14*, Doc. 62241/1.

[18]*Ibid.*, 31 Jul 44.

The next day under strong pressure from the British, the Germans, having left combat outposts along the south bank, fell back beyond the Arno east and west of Florence. Under orders to make no stand within the city, the main body of the paratroopers withdrew to the Mugnone Canal on the northwestern edge of the city. That was to serve only as a brief delaying position before withdrawal into the Heinrich Mountain Line, another delaying position located in the Mugello Hills four miles north of Florence.[20] After first providing the Florentines with a two-day ration of bread, General Schlemm on 7 August withdrew the last of his troops. As the Germans left, local partisans swiftly occupied those quarters of the city south and east of the canal.[21]

The Ligurian Flank

While Kesselring's attention had been understandably concentrated on his central sector in the vicinity of Florence during the first week of August, he nevertheless continued to cast anxious glances toward his Ligurian flank, which he had long considered a likely site for another Allied amphibious operation. Noting that some French units had been identified in northern France, he wondered if that meant that an attack against southern France was no longer contemplated. If not southern France, perhaps the Italian Riviera? As late as 10 August intelligence officers were giving equal weight to the possibility of landings in southern France and the Italian Riviera.[22]

Kesselring's apprehension increased on the 11th when reports from German aerial reconnaissance disclosed the presence along the west coast of Corsica of two Allied convoys, totaling seventy-five ships. While the Germans believed most of that force was headed for southern France, some concern remained that at least part of it might attempt to land along the Ligurian coast where Marshal Rodolfo Graziani's Italo-German *Ligurian Army* garrisoned the coast of the Gulf of Genoa to the *Fourteenth Army's* left rear. As if to underscore the concern, Lemelsen and Graziani placed both of their commands on full alert, and Lemelsen moved a motorized battalion to Lucca, ten miles northeast of Pisa, as a security force against possible airborne or amphibious landings.[23] For the next few days the Germans waited tensely. Although a patrol captured several Americans from the 1st Armored Division, their interrogation confirmed only the obvious fact that the armored division had returned to the front.[24] The Germans also observed artillery strongpoints, heavy vehicular traffic, and the assembly of armor south and southwest of the Arno. All seemed to point to a renewal of the Allied drive northward.[25]

On 15 August Kesselring's long period of watchful waiting and wondering what the Allies were going to do with

---

[19]*Ibid.*, 3 Aug 44.
[20]*Ibid.*, 4–6 Aug 44.
[21]*Ibid.*, 7 Aug 44.
[22]Greiner and Schramm, eds., *OKW/WFSt, KTB,* IV(1), pp. 507–12

[23]The *Ligurian Army* was actually more of a provisional corps headquarters than an army, somewhat similar to *Armee Abteilung von Zangen*, consisting of the fusilier battalion of the *34th Division*, the *42 Jaeger Division*, the *3d* and *4th Italian Mountain Divisions*. See *AOK 14, Ia KTB Nr. 4*, 12 Aug. 44, *AOK 14*, Doc. 62241/1.
[24]*Ibid.*, 10 and 13 Aug. 44.
[25]*Ibid.*, 14 Aug. 44.

those troops assembling south of Rome ended when he learned of the U.S. Seventh Army's landing in southern France. Even then he expected that the Allies might yet attempt tactical landings between Genoa and La Spezia, the Italian naval base about fifty miles northwest of Leghorn. That was yet another example of Kesselring's obsession with the possibility of hostile amphibious operations against his flanks.[26]

Meanwhile, both sides continued to spar in the sectors flanking Florence, while the city itself was for several days a no-man's-land, controlled by roving partisan bands. Although German rear guards easily kept the partisans at bay along the Mugnone Canal, increasing difficulties in supplying minimum rations to the civilians in those suburban quarters still held by the Germans prompted General Lemelsen on 17 August to abandon the canal line. That night, Indian infantrymen, who had entered Florence on the 13th over the Ponte Vecchio, fanned out to take over the entire city.[27]

The Cost

With the occupation of Florence the campaign of central Italy, which had begun four months before along the Liri and the Garigliano Rivers, came to an end. The Allied drive from the Tiber to the Arno, while less costly than the major battles of the May offensive south of Rome, had taken a heavy toll nevertheless. Beyond Rome the U.S. Fifth Army captured over 16,000 Germans, while the British, Poles, and Italians added more than 7,000. The Germans listed their combat losses from mid-June to mid-August as 63,500 killed, wounded, and missing. Between Rome and the Arno the U.S. Fifth Army toll was approximately 18,000 casualties, the Eighth Army 16,000. The Allied total was about half that of the Germans, representing a much better ratio than during the drive on Rome.[28]

On a clear day one could see from the Allied front lines the distant outlines of the Northern Apennines where for months the Germans had been constructing defensive works even more formidable than those of the Gustav Line south of Rome. The withdrawals for southern France accomplished, the peninsula cleared up to the Arno, Allied commanders could turn full attention to the planning for an offensive aimed at breaking those defenses.

---

[26]*Ibid.*, 15 Aug 44.

[27]*Ibid.*, 17 and 18 Aug 44; Operations of the British, Indian, and Dominion Forces in Italy, Part II, Sec. D.

[28]*Fifth Army History*, Part VI, pp. 106 and 111; 9th MRU, Fifth Army American Battle Casualties, 10 Jun 45, CMH; *Verluste der Wehrmacht*, HI/176a, CMH. Of the 17,939 casualties in the Fifth Army, American casualties totaled 11,259: 1,933 killed, 8,777 wounded, 549 missing.

PART FIVE

THE GOTHIC LINE OFFENSIVE

In studying ancient combat, it can be seen that it was almost always an attack from the flank or rear, a surprise action, that won battles, especially against the Romans.

COLONEL ARDANT DU PICQ, *Battle Studies: Ancient and Modern Battles.*

CHAPTER XVII

Planning for the Offensive

The Allied campaign in central Italy over, some of the hardest battles and the most challenging terrain of the war in western Europe still faced General Alexander's armies as they prepared to attack in the Northern Apennines. In the months to come the character of those mountains and the soggy plain of the Romagna, northeast of the Apennines largely within a triangle formed by three major roads linking the cities of Rimini, Ravenna, and Faenza, would play an important role in determining the fortunes of friend and foe alike.

The Terrain

Extending from the Ligurian Alps just north of Genoa, Italy's major commercial port, the Northern Apennines form a great arc extending southeastward across the peninsula, almost as far as the Adriatic coast south of Rimini, before turning southward to become the Central Apennines, the rugged spine of the Italian peninsula. The northern face of the Apennines is friendly, sloping gradually and invitingly toward the Lombard plain and the valley of the Po, while the southern face is hostile, dropping sharply and formidably into the Arno valley and a narrow coastal plain south of the naval base of La Spezia, 45 miles northwest of Leghorn. (*Map X*)

Although the dominant alignment of the Northern Apennines is northwest to southeast, erosion by numerous transverse streams draining both slopes of the range has cut long and irregular spurs extending northeast and southwest and left isolated peaks along the highest ridges. The range's summits rise from an elevation of 300 feet along the edge of the Lombard plain to an average crest elevation of 3,000 to 3,600 feet. Above the ridges some summits exceed 4,000 feet and in the western part of the range, 6,000 feet.

The water divide of the Apennines is not the crest line but instead a line of high ground crossed by several passes, all over 2,700 feet in elevation. Most of the water courses run relatively parallel to one another, flowing either northeast into the Po Valley, or south into the Arno River, or the Ligurian Sea. Only a few, such as the Sieve, which flows almost due east through a valley fifteen miles north of Florence, fail to conform to the pattern. The deep valleys cut by the mountain streams, together with the irregular geology of the range, divide the Northern Apennines into countless compartments marked by broken ridges, spurs, and deep, pocket-shaped valleys providing a series of excellent defensive positions.

In contrast to the more hospitable and intensively cultivated hill country of central Italy west of the Central Apennines, the Northern Apennines afford little opportunity for cross-country or lateral movement by either wheeled or tracked vehicles. In many areas in 1944, cart tracks or mule trails were the only routes between villages. As elsewhere in Italy, grain fields, vineyards, and olive groves were spread across the valleys, hills, and lower slopes of the mountains. On the upper slopes, where there had been little erosion, chestnut, scrub oak, and evergreen forests abounded. Elsewhere centuries of erosion have exposed precipitous bare rock slopes, sheer cliffs, and razor-backed ridges.

In late September the autumn rains often turn normally small mountain streams into torrents, flooding roads and washing out culverts and bridges. With the rains in the fall of 1944 came fog and mist swirling around the mountain peaks, filling the narrow valleys, and reducing visibility to zero. At the higher elevations snow began falling in late October and in midwinter periodically blocked the passes.

Just north of Florence the foothills of the Northern Apennines extend to within a few miles of the Arno. West of the city the foothills curve northwestward, rising above a wide plain north of the river. Two spurs, extending southeast from the mountains, divide the plain into three parts. Fifteen miles west of Florence, from an elevation of 2,014 feet, the Monte Albano ridge dominates the eastern half of the plain and, four miles northeast of Pisa, the 3,001-foot Monte Pisano massif dominates the western half.

Numerous roads crossed the plain. A four-lane autostrada ran along its northern edge, connecting Florence with Pistoia and Lucca and the coastal road northwest of Pisa. A good secondary road network tied those towns with the fertile Tuscan countryside, crisscrossed by numerous drainage canals. Although in dry summer months the valley provided excellent terrain for military operations, the complex system of ditches and canals could be exploited as antitank obstacles.

The main roads that traversed the mountain range followed the dominant northeast-southwest pattern of the spurs and stream lines. An exception was the Florence-Bologna highway which followed a north-south axis. From the Arno valley twelve all-weather roads crossed the Apennines to the Lombard plain and the Po Valley, but only five figured prominently in Allied planning for the offensive against the Gothic Line. Most of the others, especially those west of Pistoia, either crossed mountainous terrain unsuited for large-scale military operations or led to points of little strategic interest. In addition, several secondary roads that would figure later in the offensive threaded across the mountains through narrow stream valleys to the Po Valley. Numerous curves, steep gradients, and narrow defiles made those roads a challenge even to peacetime motorists. Few bypasses of bridge crossings existed, and during heavy rains landslides frequently blocked the roads.

Roads available to the Allies south of the Arno were fewer than those the Germans might use for their support in the Po Valley, and heavy military traffic had left most in a bad state of repair. The U.S. Fifth Army's western sector had better lines of communications than those occupied by the British Eighth Army east of the Central Apennines, and to compound the issue, in winter the few existing roads were more frequently covered with ice and snow than those west of the Apennines.

The rail lines also favored the west coast, for two of Italy's best railroads, both double-tracked, paralleled the coast west of the Apennines. If worked to capacity the lines could deliver an estimated 10,000 tons daily to forward railheads. On the east coast north of San Severo there was only a single-track line over which a peak capacity of about 3,000 tons per day could be delivered to the railhead.

On the German side of the mountains one of the tactically most useful roads in the Po Valley and Lombard plain was Highway 9 (the old Via Emilia), which paralleled the northern base of the Apennines and ran from Rimini on the Adriatic northwestward to Milan, the industrial and population center of the region. The cities of Cesena, Forli, Bologna, Modena, Reggio, and Parma, all northern termini of roads crossing the Apennines, were located along the highway. The road thus was an important factor for enabling Kesselring to shift his forces rapidly behind his front and keep supplies moving into the mountains.

Although the valley's excellent road and rail network gave the Germans shorter and better lines of communications, Allied air superiority created serious problems, especially with the railroads. All of the frontier lines entering Italy, except those on the east and west coasts, crossed vulnerable Alpine passes and converged at the foot of the Alps at important junctions where traffic was rerouted for different parts of Italy: Genoa, Turin, Milan, Verona, Trieste, and Mestre (rail terminal for Venice). With the exception of Genoa, all of these cities lay on an east-west trunk route from Turin to Trieste and had connections with the distribution centers of Genoa and Bologna, which controlled most of the traffic from the north into peninsular Italy. Destruction of those junctions, or one of the railway bridges before the junctions, would have disrupted Italy's north-south as well as east-west rail traffic. The fact that the Italian railways had few loop lines for decentralizing the main traffic streams made them particularly vulnerable, although thus far the Germans and their north Italian allies had shown a remarkable ability to keep people and goods moving between the Alps and the Apennines.[1]

The Gothic Line

In developing the Gothic Line in the Northern Apennines, the Germans had created a defensive zone in considerable depth. The origins of the defenses actually antedated the Italian campaign. In August 1943, before the Allied landings in southern Italy, Field Marshal Rommel, then *Army Group B* commander in northern Italy, had begun reconnaissance for defensive positions in the Northern Apennines, whence the Germans might withdraw in the event of an Allied invasion of Italy.[2]

Reconnaissance for the projected defensive zone continued throughout the

---

[1] See Part V, The Railroad Situation from the beginning of January until the end of April 1945, Typescript Operation LIGHTNING. Ref. Nr USDIC/SIIR 30/S6, 15 Mar 47, Special Interrogation Rpt.

[2] MS # B–268 (Beckel and Beelitz), The Italian Theater, 23 August–2 September 1944, CMH; Greiner and Schramm, eds., *OKW/WFSt, KTB*, IV (1), pp. 16–17. Unless otherwise indicated the following is based upon these sources.

remaining months of 1943, but actual work began only in the following spring under a paramilitary German construction agency, Organization Todt, employing several thousand Italian civilians. From the vicinity of Massa on the Ligurian coast about forty miles northwest of Leghorn, the Gothic Line extended eastward along the ridge line of the main Apennines chain to foothills north of the Foglia River. From there the line ran along the crest of one of the range's many spurs to Pesaro on the Adriatic coast, some forty miles northwest of Ancona. The line covered a total air line distance of some 180 miles.

When Kesselring became senior German commander in Italy, he turned attention away from the Northern Apennines, in keeping with his plan to stand instead in the south. Until the spring of 1944 little of the Gothic Line existed except as pencil markings on maps in the German headquarters; but the rapid collapse of the front south of Rome in late May and early June, as well as instructions from the high command, finally prompted Kesselring to refocus on the Northern Apennines. In early summer antitank defenses on the more exposed sectors of the projected line were strengthened with mine fields and the civilian population was evacuated from a "dead zone" 20-kilometers deep in front of what would become the main line of resistance. Within that zone all roads, bridges, and communications facilities were either to be destroyed or prepared for demolition.

After the U.S. Fifth Army broke through the Caesar Line in June, Hitler had ordered construction work on the Northern Apennines positions accelerated. By July the western portion of the Gothic Line had been completed. That that segment was finished first was attributable not to the importance with which the Germans viewed the western portion but to its relative unimportance, so that the positions there were less complex. A breakthrough in the west would be no real attraction to the Allies, the Germans reasoned, since it would cut off no large bodies of German troops from their lines of communications with Germany. Moreover, few roads traversed the sector. The two most important, Highways 12 and 64, crossed the mountains, respectively, at Abetone Pass, about twenty-three miles northeast of Lucca, and at Porretta, some seven miles north of Pistoia. The Serchio River valley north of Lucca, the Reno valley north of Pistoia, and the Arno-Savio valley, all penetrating deep into the region, were narrow and easily defended, thus unlikely avenues of Allied attack.

The two most vulnerable sectors of the Apennines defensive zone were to be found in the central sector north of Florence, where the range is at its narrowest, and on the eastern sector south of Rimini, where the mountains fall away into low foothills and to a narrow coastal plain. In the central sector north of Florence, Highway 65 linked that city with Bologna—55 miles away—across two passes, the Futa and the Radicosa; and a good secondary road from Florence via Firenzuola to Imola, in the Po Valley twenty miles southeast of Bologna, crossed the mountains over Il Giogo Pass. On the eastern sector the coastal corridor offered a wider choice of passage to the Po Valley.

Although Kesselring had long regarded those two sectors as the most likely targets of an Allied offensive, construction on defensive works in both sectors fell behind schedule until well into the summer of 1944. On the eastern sector, an inspection in July of antitank defenses between Monte Gridolfo and the Adriatic port of Pesaro disclosed serious deficiencies. Although a complex series of antitank mine fields had been planned, only 17,000 mines, mostly of Italian manufacture, were in place by mid-July. Low brush-covered hills in that sector afforded excellent concealment and valleys and ravines at right angles to the line of defense provided covered routes of approach for troops coming from the south, yet only one antitank position had been completed. With time running out, Kesselring decided to rely instead upon a combination of antitank emplacements within the main line of resistance and a mobile reserve of self-propelled antitank guns, a tactic that had worked well in the Caesar Line south of Rome. Yet it had one serious shortcoming: vulnerability to Allied airpower. Since the Allies dominated the skies, shifting antitank guns or anything else during daylight was always hazardous. Furthermore, about 150 88-mm. guns would be needed and it was doubtful whether that many would be available in time.[3]

That this and other deficiencies were not corrected immediately was confirmed by a second inspection of the line in early August. Many defenses in no way met requirements, and a number of terrain features which permitted hostile observation deep into the defensive zone and which should have been incorporated into the main line of resistance were left undefended forward of it. In many areas no fields of fire had been cleared and, in some cases, access roads constructed in order to build the defenses would actually aid the Allies in getting into German positions.[4]

Later in the month when Kesselring himself inspected the vulnerable sectors of the line, he found that considerable late progress had been made, especially on the Adriatic flank, which earlier had bothered him so much. Yet as he pointed out to the Tenth Army commander, Vietinghoff, the antitank ditches and wire entanglements, most of which had been constructed far to the front of the main line of resistance, would have been of more value if incorporated into the main defensive zone so as to be a surprise to attacking troops.[5]

The Germans continued to improve the defenses during the last weeks of August. On the Tenth Army front an Italo-German engineer force under army command completed positions in a so-called advance zone (Vorfeld) of the Gothic Line, located along high ridges between northeastward flowing rivers, the Foglia and the Metauro. On the left flank engineers worked on a coastal defense position, the Galla Placidia Line, named by a whim of an imaginative German staff officer after the Byzantine princess whose tomb was an artistic treasure of nearby Ravenna. The line extended in a westerly direction from the Adriatic resort town of

---

[3]MS # C–095c (Senger), CMH.

[4]AOK 14, Ia KTB Nr. 4, 1 Aug. 44, AOK 14, 62241/1
[5]MS # C–064 (Kesselring), CMH.

Cattolica, ten miles northeast of Pesaro, westward for ten miles to the eastern boundary of the neutral city-state of San Marino, whose neutrality Field Marshal Kesselring had instructed General Vietinghoff to respect. From the northwest corner of the miniature state, the line continued seven miles in a northwesterly direction through the town of Sogliano to the Savio River three miles to the west, thence along the Savio valley northeastward to the Adriatic ten miles south of Ravenna. Although the line was primarily intended as a defensive zone against an attack from the sea, in some sectors, especially between Cattolica and the Savio River, it could also be used as a switch position for the Gothic Line. That possibility was important, for although a switch position designated Green Line II had been reconnoitered about eight to ten miles behind the Gothic Line, little work had been accomplished on it.[6]

German Dispositions

Following withdrawal behind the Arno, and to deploy their units to best advantage, the Germans shifted some corps and divisions, especially in the sector held by Vietinghoff's *Tenth Army* and on *Army Group C's* flanks. On 8 August the *Tenth Army's* two corps exchanged places in line. Feuerstein's *LI Mountain Corps* moved into the mountainous sector on the army right wing adjacent to the *Fourteenth Army's I Parachute Corps*, and Herr's *LXXVI Panzer Corps* moved to the *Tenth Army's* left flank where the low hills of the coastal corridor were better suited to the corps'

long experience in operations with mobile formations.[7]

In the mountains east of Florence the *LI Mountain Corps* commanded five divisions: the *715th, 334th,* and *305th Divisions and the 114th Jaeger Division*; the *44th Division* was in corps reserve. Manning the *LXXVI Panzer Corps* front were three divisions: the *5th Mountain* and the *71st* and *278th Divisions*. When the panzer corps fell back into the Gothic Line, it was to take control also of *Group Witthoeft's 162d Turkomen* and *98th Divisions*, in reserve positions guarding the coastal flank south and north of Rimini. Guarding the coastal regions at the head of the Adriatic northeast of Venice were the *94th Division* at Udine and the *188th Reserve Division* on the Istrian peninsula. The *15th Panzer Grenadier Division* and *1st Parachute Division* were in army reserve on the Romagna Plain north of Highway 9.[8]

To the *Tenth Army's* right, between Florence and Pisa, Lemelsen's *Fourteenth Army* still had two corps: Schlemm's *I Parachute* from Florence to Empoli, and von Senger's *XIV Panzer* westward from Empoli to the sea. The parachute corps controlled the *4th Parachute* and *356th* and *362d Infantry Divisions*; the panzer corps, the *65th Infantry* and *16th SS Panzer Grenadier Divisions*. In army reserve near Bologna were the *29th Panzer Grenadier* and *26th Panzer Divisions*, and along the coast fourteen miles northwest of Pisa, the *20th Luftwaffe Field Division.*[9]

---

[6]Col Horst Pretzell, Battle of Rimini, MS, CMH.

[7]*AOK 10, Ka KTB, Anl. 8,* Aug 44, *AOK 10,* Docs. 61437/1 and 61437/2.

[8]*Ibid.*

[9]*AOK 14, Ia KTB Nr. 4,* Aug 44, *AOK 14,* Doc. 62241/1.

Presence of the *Ligurian Army* under Italian Marshal Graziani along the coast farther north was testament to Kesselring's continuing concern for his vulnerable western flank. Created on 3 August, this new army replaced the former *Armee Abteilung von Zangen*, which earlier in the campaign had operated on the Adriatic flank of *Army Group C*. Graziani's *Ligurian Army* consisted of two corps: *Korps Abteilung Lieb*, a provisional corps headquarters—under the command of the *34th Division* commander, Generalleutnant Theobald Lieb—which, in addition to Lieb's division, also controlled the *Italian Division* "*San Marco,*" the *4th Mountain Battalion*, and the *Mittenwald Mountain Warfare School Battalion*. The second headquarters, Generalleutnant Ernst Schlemmer's *LXXV Infantry Corps*, originally created to guard the Franco-Italian frontier, commanded the *42d Jaeger* and *5th Mountain Divisions* and the *Italian Mountain Division* "*Monte Rosa.*" By mid-August Graziani's *Ligurian Army* had responsibility for the coastal defenses from the vicinity of the naval base of La Spezia northwestward past Genoa to the frontier.[10]

In mid-August, as the Allied forces began advancing up the Rhone Valley after DRAGOON's successful landings on the Mediterranean coast of France, Field Marshal Kesselring shifted the *90th Panzer Grenadier Division* to the Franco-Italian border to secure the Alpine passes there, for over those passes French armies under two Napoleons had invaded Italy to win control of

Lombardy on the battlefields of Marengo and Magenta. Yet in late August of 1944 Field Marshal Kesselring was more concerned about extricating from France two divisions—the *157th Mountain* and the *148th Reserve*—which OKW had transferred from Generaloberst Johannes Blaskowitz's *Army Group G* to *Army Group C*. Early in September Kesselring would relieve the *90th Panzer Grenadier Division* with the *5th Mountain Division* from the *Tenth Army*. The panzer grenadier division was then moved into *Army Group C* reserve along the Adriatic coast east of Venice. Until winter snows closed the passes from the Haute Savoie into the Italian Piedmont, the Germans would keep a watchful eye on the Franco-Italian frontier, for Kesselring believed that the Allies in France might be tempted to follow the ancient invasion trail and descend upon the Turin-Milan industrial complex of northwestern Italy.[11]

Changes in Allied Strategy

Even as Kesselring's engineers rushed to put finishing touches to their defensive works in the Apennines, Field Marshal Alexander decided upon significant changes in his plan to break through the defenses. That decision was made on 4 August at a conference among the senior British commanders gathered in the shadow of a wing of a Dakota aircraft on the Orvieto airfield at Eighth Army headquarters. The proposal to change the earlier plans had come from the army's commander,

[10]Generalleutnant Hans Roettiger and Oberstleutnant von Cannstein, *Feldzug in Italien, II Teil, Band I, Kapitel 6*; Greiner and Schramm, eds., *OKW/WFSt, KTB*, IV (1), pp. 537–38.

[11]MS # C–064 (Kesselring), CMH; Greiner and Schramm, eds., *OKW/WFSt, KTB*, IV (1), pp. 583–84. See also Smith, MS, Riviera to the Rhine, App. A, Operations Along the Franco-Italian Frontier.

General Leese, and "arose," as Field
Marshal Alexander later described it,
"from his [Leese's] judgment of his
army's capabilities and the manner in
which it [the army] could best be
employed."[12]

Alexander had originally planned for
the Fifth and Eighth Armies, their
strength concentrated on contiguous
wings, to launch a joint offensive by
four army corps, controlling fourteen
divisions, against the Gothic Line's central sector north of Florence. The armies were to attack simultaneously
along parallel axes: the Eighth along
the main routes between Florence and
Bologna and the Fifth from either
Lucca or Pistoia (preferably the latter)
toward Modena, in the Po Valley
twenty-five miles northwest of Bologna.
Since Alexander doubted that Clark's
forces would be strong enough to exploit much beyond Modena, and since
the Eighth Army was the larger, the
Allied armies commander had given
Leese's army the task of exploiting to
the Po.

Yet as the pause along the Arno
lengthened into weeks, General Leese
became convinced that the geographically vulnerable Adriatic flank and not
the central sector north of Florence
would be the most favorable point for
the main attack against the Gothic Line.
Kesselring had reached a similar conclusion and had shifted the center of
gravity of his army group to a 20-mile-
wide sector on the *Tenth Army*'s left
wing.[13]

General Leese's argument ran some-

thing like this: with the departure of
the French Expeditionary Corps, units
in the Allied armies trained and experienced in mountain warfare were few.
An offensive concentrated not in the
mountains but against the eastern flank
of the Apennines chain, where the
mountains give way to a low range of
foothills overlooking a narrow coastal
plain, would offer terrain better suited
to the Eighth Army's mobile capabilities. There Leese also could better
exploit the advantage of his superior
firepower in support of a series of set-
piece attacks against successive positions
in the low hills between the Metauro
and Foglia Rivers. Furthermore, a
breakthrough in that sector would carry
Allied troops more quickly onto the
plain north of the Apennines than in
the central sector north of Florence;
and General Leese believed, erro-
neously, that Kesselring expected no
major Allied effort in the east. An
attack in the east would also reduce the
forces needed for flank protection, for
Clark's Fifth Army represented sufficient protection for the left flank of the
main attack, and shifting eastward toward the coast would enable General
Leese to rely on the coast itself for right
flank protection, plus a small fleet of
destroyers and gunboats. The new plan
called for naval bombardment and
small-scale amphibious assaults against
the enemy's Adriatic flank.[14]

Although unstated at the time, the
shift of the main offensive would also
harmonize more closely with the strategic goals even then being persistently
upheld in Allied councils by Prime

---

[12]SAC Despatch, 13 Aug–12 Dec 44; Alexander
Despatch, pp. 65–66. Unless otherwise cited the
following is based upon these sources.

[13]MS # T–1b (Westphal *et al.*), CMH.

[14]Alexander *Despatch*, pp. 65–66; SAC Despatch,
Aug–Dec 44, pp. 5–6; Nicolson, *Alex*, p. 263.

Minister Churchill: a thrust from north-eastern Italy through Slovenia, toward which Tito and his Yugoslav partisan army were moving, and into the valley of the mid-Danube, objective of the southern wing of the Red Army. Later in the month, after the Russians over-ran Rumania, the military logic of Churchill's arguments and Alexander's eastward shift of the locale of his main offensive would seem in British eyes compelling.[15] To what degree, if any, Churchill's views influenced, or indeed, determined Alexander's decision to change his original plans for the Gothic Line offensive, can, at best, only be inferred.

In any case, Leese's argument ap-pealed to Alexander, who readily ac-cepted it.[16] Yet when he first submitted the new concept to the theater com-mander for approval, General Wilson's Joint Planning Staff, strongly influenced by General Devers, was less than enthu-siastic. The staff, for example, consid-ered the naval and amphibious opera-tions planned against the enemy's left flank too ambitious. Neither the config-uration of the coast in the Ravenna area nor the resources available would permit significant operations along the coast. Only two gunboats with 6-inch guns could be made available to supple-ment a small destroyer force already in

the Adriatic. Nevertheless, since most operational requirements, including air support, seemed well within the thea-ter's capabilities, Wilson approved the plan in principle, and on 6 August Alexander issued orders for prelimi-nary operations designed to set the stage for the main offensive to be mounted from the right flank instead of the center. Yet right up to the eve of the offensive many doubts as to the plan's feasibility lingered on at Allied headquarters, especially among the American members of Wilson's Joint Planning Staff.[17]

Preliminary Moves

On the Eighth Army front the most important problem raised by the new plan was how to continue operations in such a way as to conceal the change from the Germans. For this reason General Leese directed General Anders, the II Polish Corps commander, to resume those operations northeast of Ancona that had been interrupted on 4 August by a counterattack against the Polish bridgehead across the Misa River. The Misa was the first of a series of parallel rivers—the Cesano, the Me-tauro, and the Foglia—which the Eighth Army would have to cross in the coastal corridor. Those rivers and the military problems of crossing them had been a factor in Alexander's original decision to attack in the mountains, and changing the plan did nothing to make the problems go away.[18]

---

[15] Ehrman, *Grand Strategy,* vol. V, pp. 390–93.

[16] Whether, as has been suggested, only because of a tendency to "see the other man's point of view" seems difficult to determine, for Alexander himself has written little about the decision other than to note his own concern "at the prospect of extensive operations in the mountains without my best moun-tain troops, the French." Yet he had known for some time that these troops would not be available for the Gothic Line offensive. See Douglas Orgill, *The Gothic Line: The Italian Campaign, Autumn, 1944* (New York: W.W. Norton & Co., 1967), p. 32.

[17] SAC Despatch, Aug–Dec 44, pp. 5–6; Devers Diary, vol. II; Alexander *Despatch,* pp. 65–66; Nicolson, *Alex,* pp. 263–64.

[18] Operations of the British, Indian, and Domin-ion Forces in Italy, Part III, Sec. F, The 2 Polish Corps.

Holding the high ground north of the Misa was the *278th Infantry Division.* Concern about how much longer that division could withstand pressures from the two-division Polish corps and suspicions that General Leese might even increase those pressures had been behind General Vietinghoff's shift of Heidrich's *1st Parachute Division* from army reserve into backup positions behind the division.

Leese meanwhile had assigned Anders' corps a twofold task: to clear the ground as far as the Foglia River and to screen the assembly of the two assault forces, the Canadian 1st Corps and the British 5 Corps. With the 3d Carpathian Division on the right and the 5th Kresowa Division on the left, the Polish corps on the 9th began to expand the bridgehead beyond the Misa. Supported by generous allotments of artillery fire and aerial bombardment of enemy artillery positions by the Desert Air Force, the Polish corps by nightfall had cleared the five miles between the Misa and the Cesano Rivers and established modest bridgeheads beyond the Cesano, but most of those were lost the next day. The Polish troops could go no farther against well-organized resistance along high ground overlooking the Cesano from the north. Yet the attack had achieved a considerable advantage in placing the main lateral highway south of the Misa River well beyond the range of German artillery, making it available to the two assault corps for their assembly for the main offensive.

Conference With Clark

Until that point the discussion and the decision to change Alexander's original strategy had been limited to the British half of the Allied command in Italy. General Clark still had to be consulted and his co-operation obtained. When General Alexander requested the Fifth Army commander to come to Leese's headquarters for a conference on the afternoon of 10 August, he flew in with his chief of staff, General Gruenther, his G–3, General Brann, and Alexander's American deputy chief of staff, Brig. Gen. Lyman L. Lemnitzer. Already familiar with broad details of the new plan, Lemnitzer briefed Clark during the flight so that upon arrival Clark was no stranger to it. [19]

At General Leese's suggestion, the conference convened in a pleasant grove of trees near the headquarters. In that bucolic setting the senior Allied commanders and their chiefs of staff settled comfortably in the shade to hear General Alexander outline his new strategy. Essentially, he expanded on those arguments that Leese had used earlier. The heavy dissipation of Allied strength over the past few months, especially the U.S. Fifth Army's loss of two corps and several divisions to Anvil-Dragoon, Alexander declared, had greatly reduced the chances for success of a joint attack by both armies against the sector north of Florence. With the shift of the main attack from the central to the eastern sector on the Eighth Army's right flank, the U.S. Fifth Army, rather than attack as originally planned toward both Pistoia and Lucca, was to move only against Pistoia, for an attack against both objectives would

---

[19]Clark Diary, 10 Aug 44. Unless otherwise indicated, the following is based upon this reference.

further dissipate Clark's already greatly reduced resources.

Leese's Eighth Army was to make the main Allied effort beginning on 25 August with a three-corps attack against the German left wing along the Adriatic, to be followed at a date to be determined by Alexander by the Fifth Army's attack against the central sector of the Gothic Line. Clark's attack would begin after Alexander had determined that Kesselring had weakened the central sector by shifting forces to check Leese's attack. The operation was to be, the Allied commander observed as he had when planning the offensive south of Rome, "a one-two punch."

General Clark readily agreed that the new concept, especially on the matter of timing, seemed sound. He could easily hold on his left flank with the few forces he had there, even if the Pisano massif remained in enemy hands, and shift the rest to the central sector for the attack. His only concern was his right flank, where the distance and possible lack of co-ordination between an American attack toward Pistoia and that of the British 13 Corps on the Eighth Army's left flank constituted, in Clark's opinion, a real hazard to the success of operations in the central sector.

In raising the objection, Clark shrewdly saw an opportunity to trade off a shift of the Allies' main effort from the center to the British-controlled right for Anglo-American unity of command in the center. He appeared to be intent upon reconstructing in his own sector the concept that Alexander had just abandoned for the army group. An effective operation against the enemy's center, even if

secondary, would require that both Clark's army and the British 13 Corps be under the operational control of one commander and that their axes of attack be along the shortest distance across the mountains, that is, from Florence to Bologna.

While Clark outlined his reservations with his usual earnestness, Leese lay relaxed on the ground with his arms akimbo behind his head. Turning to Clark, he offered to meet his reservations by making McCreery, the 13 Corps commander, a provisional group commander over both 10 and 13 Corps, which would enable Clark to deal with McCreery on equal terms and thus facilitate co-operation between the two. General Leese carefully avoided any mention of placing British troops once again under Fifth Army command. Yet that was exactly what Clark was after.

Several minutes of verbal sparring followed, during which General Leese rose to his feet to argue vehemently that ultimate control of his divisions had to remain with the Eighth Army. At that point, Alexander intervened. The debate, he said, really seemed to be one of cold, logical military reasoning on Clark's part, versus strong psychological and sentimental reasoning on Leese's part, which, of course, was not to be ignored. Leese finally yielded. Thus again, as during the winter offensive of 1943–44, an entire British corps, the 13 Corps, came under the Fifth Army's command.

Clark agreed that the new strategy promised to be far more effective than the old. The only remaining drawback as he saw it, was the additional delay that would be imposed upon the Fifth

Army's attack. The American commander felt keenly the growing pressure of criticism from others in the U.S. military establishment who had long opposed extension of military operations north of Rome. Almost a month had elapsed since the Fifth Army had arrived at the Arno, and every day that passed with no effort to continue the drive beyond the river increased the urgings from the partisans of DRAGOON that the Italian campaign be abandoned altogether. The Eighth Army, the theory had it, could take over the entire front while the Fifth Army moved to France. Foremost spokesman of that viewpoint in the Mediterranean theater was General Devers, who had been named commander-designate of the 6th Army Group to assume command in southern France. A long-time opponent of British strategy in the Mediterranean, he had frequently recommended to General Marshall that the Italian venture be dropped. That the campaign seemed to have bogged down at the Arno reinforced his argument.[20]

The Allied Plan

On 13 August Alexander's headquarters distributed to the army commanders the plan for the Gothic Line offensive (Operation OLIVE) and three days later the final order. As during the spring offensive south of Rome, General Alexander envisioned turning the *Tenth Army*'s flank, this time the left and this time with the Eighth Army rather than the Fifth. Controlling 11 divisions on a relatively narrow front, Leese's

army was to drive through the Rimini Gap, consisting of approximately 8 miles of coastal plain between Rimini and the foothills of the Apennines. Once through the gap the Canadian 1st Corps and the British 5 Corps were to deploy onto the Romagna Plain, a low-lying triangular-shaped area cut by many streams and drainage ditches and bounded on the south by Highway 9, on the east by Highway 16, paralleling the coast between Rimini and Ravenna, and to the west by Highway 67, extending in a northeasterly direction from Forli on Highway 9 to Ravenna. From the Romagna the two corps were to launch a two-pronged drive to roll up the enemy's left flank toward Bologna and Ferrara. Meanwhile, the U.S. Fifth Army, with three corps controlling nine divisions on an extended front, was to move generally northward from Florence toward the Po Valley. Both armies were in time to converge on Bologna and then exploit toward the Po. Only light forces, the British 10 Corps with the equivalent of one and a half divisions, were to operate in the mountainous terrain between the two armies. On the Fifth Army's left, between the central sector and the Ligurian Sea, the U.S. IV Corps with the equivalent of two divisions on line and one in reserve was considered to be strong enough to serve as a covering force.[21]

Alexander's resources no longer afforded the luxury of an army group reserve with which to influence the offensive at a critical point. Yet that seemed no serious problem at the time, for both of his armies were to fight essentially separate battles. Moreover,

---

[20]Ltr, Gen Devers to General Marshall, 9 Aug 44, CCS 603/16, in ABC 384, Eur, Sec. 9–A; See also Devers Diary, vol. II.

[21]Alexander *Despatch*, pp. 65–66.

each army had strong corps with which to lead the assaults and sufficient forces in reserve. In a very real sense Alexander looked on the Fifth Army as his army group reserve, since under his one-two punch strategy he was to withhold Clark's army until he decided upon the most opportune moment to strike the second blow. The Fifth Army was to be prepared to move on 24-hours notice any time after D plus five.[22]

As had been the case south of Rome, there was also to be a deception plan with the Fifth Army playing the major role. Before the Eighth Army's attack, Clark's forces were to distract the enemy by simulating an imminent attack by both Allied armies along the 25-mile front flanking Florence. The fact that Alexander had originally planned to attack in that sector would lend credence to the deception. In preparation for attack along lines of the original plan, considerable shifting of troops and equipment had already taken place.

As had Alexander's strategy south of Rome, the strategy in the new offensive would require the closest co-operation between the two Allied armies and their commanders. Otherwise, Kesselring would once again be able to extricate his forces as he had in June.

Allied Regrouping

Alexander's decision to shift the main attack necessitated large-scale movement of troops and equipment to the right flank. The movement began on 15 August with long convoys of trucks and tracked vehicles passing eastward through Foligno, the main road junc-

tion on Highway 3, sixty miles southwest of Ancona. In eight days six thousand tanks, guns, and vehicles moved through the town.

By the last week of August the Eighth Army was deployed across a 25-mile front: from the coast inland, the 2 Polish Corps, the brigade-sized Italian Corps of Liberation, the Canadian 1st Corps, the British 5 Corps, and the British 10 Corps. The entire force totaled eleven divisions plus nine separate brigades.[23]

Although Alexander's decision meant the scrapping of Clark's earlier plans based upon a joint effort with the Eighth Army in the central sector, the Fifth Army commander still wanted the II Corps to make the main attack on the army's front. After Kirkman's 13 Corps had been assigned to the Fifth Army, Clark shifted the focus of his offensive eastward to a sector between Florence and Pontassieve, ten miles to the east, hoping thereby to facilitate co-operation between the American and British corps. He intended that those contingents of the 13 Corps within and east of Florence remain in place as a screening force for Keyes' II Corps until the Fifth Army offensive began, but when it became apparent that the Germans were withdrawing into the mountains to the north, Clark ordered Kirkman to cross the Arno and to regain contact.

As the II Corps relieved those Eighth Army units west of Florence, Clark also extended the IV Corps right flank eastward to afford the II Corps an even narrower front for the attack. The shift

---

[22] *Ibid.*

[23] Operations of the British, Indian, and Dominion Forces in Italy, Part III, The Campaign in the Northern Apennines, Sec. B, The Eighth Army.

left Crittenberger's IV Corps holding a 60-mile front with only the 1st Armored Division and the newly formed Task Force 45, but Clark reinforced the corps with the 6th South African Armoured Division from the 13 Corps. That left the 13 Corps with three divisions and a brigade—the British 1st Infantry and 6th Armoured Divisions, the 8th Indian Division, and the 1st Canadian Army Tank Brigade. During the first phase of the offensive, Clark planned for Crittenberger's corps to simulate a crossing of the Arno, but only after the main effort was well under way was the corps actually to cross: the 1st Armored Division to drive the enemy from the Monte Pisano massif and the area eastward to Empoli, and the South Africans to occupy the high ground just beyond the river between Empoli and the intercorps boundary.[24]

Doubts on Both Fronts

Although both the Fifth and Eighth Army commanders had enthusiastically endorsed the new concept for the Gothic Line offensive (Operation OL-IVE), a noticeable feeling of uneasiness persisted at the Allied Force Headquarters in Caserta. Less than a week before the offensive was to begin, General Devers, the deputy theater commander, had been disturbed by the jitteriness he had observed at Wilson's headquarters, "especially among the junior officers on the British side."[25]

There seemed to be widespread concern that the Americans would soon be withdrawn from Italy, leaving the British Eighth Army with a task well beyond its capabilities. At General Clark's headquarters too, General Devers had noted little optimism. Matching concern of the British at AFHQ about American intentions was a widespread lack of confidence at the Fifth Army headquarters in the British, a concern that they would "not fight hard enough to make a go of it."[26] That kind of mutual distrust hardly boded well for the coming offensive.

On the German side also arose a crisis of confidence. Why defend the Northern Apennines, some asked, when they might develop a line far shorter by withdrawing to the Alps between Switzerland and the Adriatic? Well entrenched in a similar line during World War I, the Germans and their Austrian allies had held the Allies at bay for several years, even launching a successful counteroffensive at Caporetto and driving the Italians back into the Po Valley. Withdrawal into those same alpine positions would, in the opinion of General Wentzell, the *Tenth Army's* chief of staff, enable the Germans to free three to four divisions. In a conversation with Colonel Beelitz, Kesselring's operations officer, early in August, General Wentzell let his frustrations show:

There is no insight. All is lunacy. With one wing we are up in Finland, with the other down at Rhodes; in the center the enemy is in Germany. . . . It is incomprehensible. There is an old farmer's saying that in a emergency everybody rallies around the flag. We do not even think of

---

[24]*Fifth Army History*, Part VII, pp. 21–33; Hqs. AAI, Opns Order No. 3, 16 Aug 44, AFHQ AG Sec. 0100/21/2845.

[25]Devers Diary, 20 Aug 44. Devers failed to note that the American officers on the JPS had opposed the plan when first submitted to AFHQ.

[26] *Ibid.*

this. The enemy is in Germany, the war is coming to an end, but we are still up at Murmansk. Instead of rallying around the flag the wings are extended who knows how far. I cannot understand it anymore.[27]

Wentzell's cry of despair found no echo among German commanders. Field Marshal Kesselring had his orders

to hold indefinitely in the Gothic Line. Months of planning and preparation had gone into its construction, and veteran divisions were deployed within it. To the German rear lay the rich agricultural and industrial hinterland of northern Italy, the last stronghold of Mussolini's reconstituted Fascist Republic. The German armies in Italy quite obviously would stand and fight again, this time among the rocks and crags of the Northern Apennines.

---

[27]*AOK 10, Ia KTB Nr. 8*, 5–8 Aug 44, *AOK 10*, Doc. 61437/3. (Telephone conversations, 31 Jul and 6 Aug 44.)

CHAPTER XVIII

The Gothic Line Offensive Begins

Alexander's shift of the main offensive from the central to the eastern sector created several logistical problems for the Eighth Army. In addition to combat divisions, considerable quantities of stores and ammunition that had already been amassed behind the central sector had to be moved eastward. That the Polish corps on the Adriatic flank, up to that time maintained as an independent force, passed to Eighth Army control added another responsibility. To support the British 5 Corps and the 1st Canadian Corps, which were to operate on the Adriatic flank, the Eighth Army early in August had taken over and expanded the Polish corps' line of communication, while the army's original line of communication, supporting the central sector, was to be maintained to support the British 10 and 13 Corps.[1]

The Fifth Army too had to realign and reorganize its lines of communication based on the newly captured port of Leghorn, to which the main part of the Peninsular Base Section (PBS) had moved.[2] Shortly after the capture of Leghorn on 19 July, engineers from PBS arrived to begin the hazardous task of removing approximately 25,000 mines from the harbor and nearby ruins. A man-made harbor, capable of accommodating ships with a 25-foot draft, Leghorn had been the prewar Italian navy's main base and thus had abundant facilities for the storage and distribution of petroleum products. On 3 September the first convoy of seven Liberty ships entered the harbor. As reconstruction proceeded, unloading was slow at first, only 4,242 tons of cargo during the first week of September, but in the last week of the month, those figures were to rise to 45,328 long tons. The first tankers entered the port in mid-month, by which time storage facilities for 275,000 barrels of gasoline were ready. The amount of storage for fuel would eventually almost double. Throughout this period both American and British port battalions were assigned to Leghorn, each handling ships of their respective nationalities.[3]

While developing Leghorn as a major port, logisticians backing up the Fifth Army could make only minimum use of Florence, the major communications center on the Fifth Army front. Both to conceal troop movements from the enemy and to protect the city's historical and cultural monuments, supply officers located most facilities outside the city. A Class I dump, for example, containing a million rations, was established in an olive grove several miles south of the city, while a few miles farther down the road a million gallons

---

[1] Operations of the British, Indian, and Dominion Forces in Italy, Part III, Sec. B; SAC Despatch, Aug–Dec 44.

[2] Mayo MS and Meyer MS. Unless otherwise noted the following is based upon these references.

[3] Bykofsky and Larson, *The Transportation Corps: Operations Overseas*, pp. 211–32.

of gasoline were assembled in containers concealed in a vineyard.[4]

In the final weeks before the fall offensive, the Fifth Army's combat troops spent much of their time in rest areas behind the front, there to enjoy amenities so often missing at the front. Refrigerator vans brought in large supplies of fresh meats, butter, and eggs to supplement regular rations. Shower units enabled men to dispose of long-accumulated grime. Field laundries handled over two million pounds of wash. Clothing was replaced, repaired, salvaged. It would be a well-supplied, well-fed, freshly scrubbed army that would again take the field in September.[5]

Preliminary Operations

Meanwhile, the 2 Polish Corps, which since 10 August had been halted along the Cesano River, prepared to resume its advance as a screen for the assembly of the Eighth Army's two assault corps. The corps was to cross the Metauro River and establish bridgeheads to be used by the assault corps as jump-off points for the main offensive. Although little ground action had erupted since the Poles halted on the 10th, fighter-bombers of the British Desert Air Force in a week had flown 392 sorties against German troops in the main line of resistance and supporting artillery positions.

For five days beginning on 18 August the 3d Carpathian and 5th Kresowa Divisions ground steadily forward in the kind of fighting that had come to characterize action on this part of the front. The Poles gradually pushed back the enemy's *278th Infantry Division* beyond the Metauro River, and by the evening of 22 August both divisions had drawn up to the river. The Poles counted 300 enemy dead and took 273 prisoners, but bridgeheads over the Metauro, to be exploited in the Eighth Army's main offensive, remained out of reach.[6]

Leese's Plan

Troops of the 1st Canadian and British 5 Corps moved on 24 August into assembly areas behind the Poles a little over a mile short of the Metauro. In hope of achieving surprise and making up for the lack of bridgeheads beyond the river, General Leese directed that the artillery remain silent until assaulting elements had crossed the river. The offensive was to begin an hour before midnight on 25 August.

General Leese's plan was quite simple. Both the 1st Canadian and British 5 Corps were to pass through positions of the 5th Kresowa Division on the left wing of the Polish corps. Once past the lines, the Polish division was to shift toward the coast and join the 3d Carpathian Division in a drive on the minor port of Pesaro, eastern anchor of the Gothic Line. There the Polish troops would be pinched out by the generally northwestward advance of the Canadians toward Rimini, while the 5 Corps protected the Canadian left by clearing a range of low hills. Farther west the British 10 Corps, with a strength of

[4]Ross and Romanus, *The Quartermaster Corps: Operations in the War Against Germany*, pp. 96–114.
[5]*Ibid.*

[6] Operations of the British, Indian, and Dominion Forces in Italy, Part III, Sec. F, 2 Polish Corps.

only 1 ½ divisions, was to follow up the enemy withdrawal in the mountains.[7]

German Preparations

Rather than withdraw voluntarily into the Gothic Line's main zone of resistance, the commander of the *LXXVI Panzer Corps,* General Herr, had established his divisions along a series of ridges north of the Metauro whence he could better observe Allied movements and make up for the shortages of reconnaissance aircraft. Once he had determined that the main British offensive had begun, he intended to fall back in good order into the shelter of the Gothic Line. Yet Herr ran the risk of his units being overwhelmed before they could retire should the British achieve sufficient surprise. So confident were the Germans that they would have adequate warning that General von Vietinghoff, the *Tenth Army* commander, and General Schlemm, the *1st Parachute Corps* commander, went on leave beginning 24 August.[8]

It remained to be seen whether General Leese could develop in the region of the little Metauro River the same kind of decisive victory that Roman legions of the Consul Nero in 207 B.C. had achieved against a Carthaginian army in winning the 2d Punic War in Italy. The Metauro river itself and a succession of parallel ridges and rivers between the Metauro and the Romagna Plain clearly would have an important bearing on the outcome. Thirty miles separated the Metauro from the Marec-

chia River, marking the southern edge of the Romagna Plain, the Eighth Army's objective. Within that area Allied infantrymen and tankers whose task it was to cross the rivers and drive the Germans from the ridges beyond were to become obsessed with a kind of bitter refrain: "one more river, one more ridge."

The Offensive Begins

When the Eighth Army attacked on schedule an hour before midnight on 25 August, the stratagem of artillery silence paid off. Both the 1st Canadian and British 5 Corps crossed the Metauro against little resistance. An hour later as the troops prepared to push out from their bridgeheads, the massed guns of fifteen artillery battalions fired a covering barrage. By dawn on 26 August all divisions were well beyond the river and advancing steadily behind heavy artilley fire and aerial bombardment directed mainly against enemy infantry.[9]

Throughout the day, planes of the Desert Air Force flew 664 sorties, mostly against Pesaro. Fighter-bombers also attacked enemy armor and artillery positions, while bombers hit coastal fortifications between Pesaro and Rimini as well as railroad marshaling yards to the north and northwest of Cesano, Budrio, and Rimini. Offshore two gunboats opened fire with 6-inch guns against enemy left flank positions. Even darkness brought the Germans little relief; that night, the 26th, and the next three, bombers continued to attack lines of communication around Rimini, Ra-

---

[7] Operations of the British, Indian, and Dominion Forces in Italy, Part III, Sec. B, The Eighth Army—the Gothic Line and Romagna Battles.

[8] *AOK 14, Ia KTB Nr. 4, 25 Aug 44, AOK 14 Doc. 62241/1.*

[9] Alexander *Despatch,* p. 68.

venna, Prato, and Bologna.[10] By night-fall on the 27th the Allied divisions had cleared all enemy south of the Arzilla River and prepared to continue five more miles to the northwest to reach the Foglia River, last of the waterlines before the main defenses of the Gothic Line.

German Countermeasures

The Allied offensive clearly had achieved tactical surprise. Reacting nervously to a report on 24 August of an Allied landing in the Ravenna area, Field Marshal Kesselring had canceled entrainment of the *3d Panzer Grenadier Division* for movement to France and ordered a withdrawal of the *26th Panzer Division* from army group reserve to become the *Tenth Army*'s reserve. Even after the Germans learned later in the day that the basis for the landing reports was the exceptionally heavy air attack on Ravenna, Kesselring allowed the shift of the panzer division to the eastern sector to continue. But that was more a precaution than recognition that the offensive had begun. Not until 26 August, after the Allied troops had reached the Arzilla River, did General Vietinghoff cut short his leave and hurry back to *Tenth Army* headquarters, where his staff briefed him on the developing situation. The long-awaited Allied offensive, General Vietinghoff discovered, had indeed begun. Vietinghoff immediately informed Kesselring of his conclusion. Believing the Allies had other surprises up their sleeve, Kesselring preferred to wait to see what those might be before decid-ing to react to what might be an opening or diversionary maneuver.[11]

As additional reports of Allied ad-vances along the Adriatic flank contin-ued to reach *Army Group C* headquar-ters during the 28th, Field Marshal Kesselring at last concluded that Gen-eral Alexander had indeed launched his main offensive. He authorized General Vietinghoff to withdraw Herr's *LXXVI Panzer Corps* into the Gothic Line be-hind the Foglia River and enlist from army reserve the *26th Panzer Division* to back up the Gothic Line defenses in that sector. That night the Germans opposite the Eighth Army right wing began to fall back in some disorder into the Gothic Line. Opposite the Eighth Army's left wing, General Feuerstein's *LI Mountain Corps* withdrew into the mountains to conform with Herr's ma-neuver.[12]

The Assault

Late on the 29th, across a 17-mile-wide front, the British and the Canadi-ans reached the crests of the last hills overlooking the valley of Foglia, while patrols from the Polish corps entered the southern outskirts of Pesaro. That night the last of the German troops south of the Foglia retired. The next morning Allied patrols found that in many places the river was shallow enough for fording and that a hard gravel bottom was free of mines. A study of aerial photographs and other intelligence sources indicated that the main German defenses were on a ridge

---

[10] Craven and Cate, eds., *AAF III*, pp. 443–44.

[11] *AOK 14, Ia KTB Nr. 4,* 25 Aug 44, *AOK* 14 Doc. 62241/1; *AOK 10, Ia KTB Anl.* 8, 27 Aug 44, *AOK 10* Doc. 61437/1: Pretzell, Battle of Rimini, MS in CMH.

[12] *AOK 10, Ia KTB Anl. 8,* 28–29 Aug 44, *AOK 10* Doc. 61437/1.

paralleling the river about three miles to the north. Key strongpoints appeared to have been developed around the towns of Montecalvo, Monte Gridolfo, and Tomba di Pesaro.

During the night of 30 August, the assault troops began crossing the river to move at dawn against the Gothic Line. First evidence of German reserves developed in the zone of the British 5 Corps at Monte Gridolfo where armored infantry units from the *26th Panzer Division* had occupied the town a short time before the British arrived. Poorly oriented in their new surroundings and exposed to the tremendous weight of Allied firepower, the armored infantrymen were unable to hold.

That was the story almost everywhere. Outflanking the eastern anchor of the Gothic Line, Pesaro, the Polish corps impelled the Germans in the town to withdraw on 2 September. The Canadian corps had, in the meantime, taken Tomba di Pesaro to open a gap between the *26th Panzer* and *1st Parachute Divisions* and on 3 September to advance ten miles and pinch out the 2 Polish Corps against the coast. On the Canadians' left the 46th Division of the 5 Corps kept pace.

With the defenses of the Gothic Line behind, months of hard work by German engineers had gone for naught. It was hardly surprising that a feeling of an imminent and far-reaching breakthrough permeated Eighth Army headquarters. General Leese ordered forward the 1st British Armoured Division to join the 5 Corps and prepare to follow up a German withdrawal.

Early on that same day, 2 September,

General Vietinghoff sent his chief of staff, General Wentzell, to General Herr's headquarters to evaluate the situation on the *Tenth Army*'s left wing. At the command post of the *LXXVI Panzer Corps* Wentzell found the situation even more alarming than he and others at the army headquarters had realized. After trying without success to reach army headquarters for approval to commit the *29th Panzer Grenadier Division* to close the gap between the *1st Parachute* and the *26th Panzer Divisions,* Wentzell on his own authority ordered it done. General Herr in turn brought forward his corps reserve, the *98th Division,* to help close a second gap that had developed between the *26th Panzer* and *71st Divisions.* Along the coastal sector held by the *1st Parachute Division,* General Herr formed to the rear of the parachutists a blocking position made up of miscellaneous elements from the *162d Turkomen Division,* with two artillery battalions in support.[13]

By that time it was nevertheless doubtful whether those moves would be sufficient to enable Herr's corps to hold, for they ate up the last of his reserve. Fighting for over a week against greatly superior Allied forces, the troops of the *LXXVI Panzer Corps* were close to exhaustion. The corps commander knew that for additional reinforcement he would have to depend upon General Vietinghoff's ability to persuade Kesselring to shift units from the army group center, where the Allies as yet had made no move.[14]

The Coriano Ridge

The line General Herr was attempt-

---

[13]*Ibid.,* 2–3 Sep 44.
[14]*Ibid.;* MS # T–1b (Westphal *et al.*), CMH.

ing to hold ran along the Coriano Ridge, which constituted the more prominent of two remaining hill features short of the Eighth Army's objective of the Romagna. When during the afternoon of 2 September the Canadian corps burst from a small bridgehead beyond the Conca River in the direction of the ridge, expectations at General Leese's headquarters of an imminent breakthrough burgeoned. Yet mixed in with reports of progress were disquieting indications of growing resistance. To beat back a tank-led counterattack, for example, the Canadians asked assistance from the 46th Infantry Division of the 5 Corps, whose troops crossed the intercorps boundary to help drive the enemy from high ground overlooking the Canadians' left flank. In the center and on the left wing of the 5 Corps the 56th Division and the 4th Indian Division had throughout been moving with considerably less speed aganst the enemy located in the Apennine foothills, and were becoming echeloned farther and farther to the left rear.

These setbacks were nonetheless insufficient to justify failure to try to turn what was clearly a deep salient in the enemy lines into a breakthrough, and General Leese ordered the British 1st Armoured Division into action. The armored division was to seize what appeared to be the keystone of the Coriano position, the village of Coriano.

Everything turned upon the timely arrival of the armor, yet when the division left its assembly area south of the Foglia, everything seemed to conspire against achieving that goal. The footing on the rain-soaked trails leading to the front was so poor that a score of vehicles broke down, and the rest,

grinding forward much of the way in low gear, failed to reach the south bank of the Conca River until late on 3 September. It was midmorning of the next day before the first tanks began passing through the ranks of the 46th Infantry Division.

Even then the armor had to extemporize, because the 46th Division had not yet captured the planned jump-off line in a village just over two miles short of the Coriano Ridge. By now the weary tankers had fought for five hours just to reach their starting line and by the time the move against the ridge began, the sun was in their eyes and behind defending German gunners. As night fell, the assault bogged down a mile short of the Coriano Ridge, while fire from the ridge also brought troops of the adjacent 1st Canadian Corps to a halt. The delays had given the Germans time to bring up tanks and assault guns, and the moment when breakthrough might have been achieved—if indeed such a possibility had ever existed—had passed.[15]

For three more days repeated efforts to gain the ridge got no place, partly because of the German commitment of the *29th Panzer Grenadier Division* in the gap between the *1st Parachute* and *26th Panzer Divisions* and of an infantry division, the *356th,* and partly because the rains came. Starting on 3 September while the British armor was moving from its assembly area, rain fell off and on for a week. Flash floods washed out tactical bridges along inland roads, leaving only the coastal highway as an artery for supporting those troops be-

---

[15]Operations of the British, Indian, and Dominion Forces in Italy, Part III, Sec. B.

yond the Foglia River. Until the flooding receded, operations on the Eighth Army front sloshed to a halt. While waiting for a break in the weather, General Leese could only ponder a resumption of his offensive toward Rimini and the Po Valley, and locate some 8,000 replacements for the casualties incurred since the offensive began on 25 August. German losses for the same period were approximately a thousand less.[16]

The Eighth Army's offensive had penetrated the Gothic Line but had fallen short of a breakthrough to the Romagna. The Germans had paid the penalty of early setbacks almost always exacted by surprise, but by shifting reinforcements—an infantry division and the *26th Panzer* and *29th Panzer Grenadier Divisions*—they had prevented disaster. Yet those shifts, however essential from the German viewpoint, fitted in perfectly with General Alexander's concept of a one-two punch. The time was approaching for Clark's Fifth Army to execute a left hook against the German defenses in the central sector.

The Fifth Army—Plans and Regrouping

The Fifth Army was to launch a two-phase attack against the Gothic Line north of Florence. During the first phase Clark planned for Keyes' II Corps to attack through the left half of the zone of the British 13 Corps to seize a line of hills some eight miles north of Florence, just short of the valley of the Sieve River. The 13 Corps was to assist on the right. In the second phase, the II Corps was to attack across

the Sieve and advance astride Highway 65, with the 13 Corps following several miles to the east of Highway 65 astride Route 6521, the Borgo–San Lorenzo–Imola road. Meanwhile, west of Florence on the left of the II Corps, the IV Corps was to simulate a crossing of the Arno and be prepared to follow up an enemy withdrawal.[17]

The weakest point topographically in the Gothic Line in the Fifth Army's zone of operations was along Highway 65, which crosses the Apennines at 1,200-foot Futa Pass, about twenty miles north of Florence. That fact was as apparent to German engineers as to the Fifth Army planners: the strongest man-made defenses were there, consisting of concrete pillboxes, gun emplacements, and troop shelters. In an outpost line were numerous fire trenches, barbed wire obstacles, antitank ditches, and mine fields. A ridge two miles south of the pass and the high ground flanking it were similarly fortified. Strong defenses also covered a secondary route paralleling Highway 65 several miles to the west, the Prato-Bologna road, on Highway 6620, and at a similar distance to the east, Il Giogo Pass, which carried Route 6524 across the mountains to Firenzuola.

The sudden German withdrawal during the latter days of August northward from Florence toward the Gothic Line obviated the planned first phase of the Fifth Army's offensive. Once the British in the Adriatic sector had begun to attack on 25 August, the German *Fourteenth Army* commander, General Lemelsen, had fully expected something to

---

[16] *Ibid.,* App. G; *Verluste der Wehrmacht bis 1944, Monatsmeldungen ab 1.VII.43, HI/176a,* CMH.

[17] Hqs Fifth Army, Opns Instrs 32, 17 Aug 44, in *Fifth Army History,* Part VII, Annex 1 G.

happen on his front. Kesselring's order to Lemelsen to pull back came on 29 August, and the withdrawal began two days later.[18]

IV Corps Crosses the Arno

In ordering the British 13 Corps to follow up the German withdrawal, General Clark, in effect, canceled the first phase of his planned offensive, no doubt gratified that he would be spared hard fighting on the approaches to the Apennines. He also ordered the IV Corps to cross the Arno and advance as far as the German withdrawal permitted.

When patrols during the night of 31 August found no enemy along the river, General Crittenberger ordered his forces to cross soon after daylight.[19] As the 1st Armored Division, in the center, with the 92d Division's 370th Regimental Combat Team attached, set out in midmorning, at only one point was there opposition and that only scattered small arms fire from less than determined rear guards. The armor headed for the first of the two hill masses dominating the plain north of the Arno, the Monte Pisano massif, and the city of Lucca at the foot of the mountains ten miles northeast of Pisa.

That afternoon the 6th South African Armoured Division began crossing the river on the right wing of the IV Corps, aiming at the other hill mass on the Arno plain, the Monte Albano Ridge, and to the city of Pistoia, sixteen miles to the north. The South Africans encountered some long-range artillery

[18]Greiner and Schramm, eds., *OKW/WRSt, KTB,* IV(1), pp. 550–51; *AOK 14, Ia KTB, Anl. 4,* 1 Sep 44, *AOK 14,* Doc. 62241/1.

[19]IV Corps Rpt of Opns, Sep 44. Unless otherwise noted the following is based upon this reference.

fire but found no enemy troops. General Rutledge's erstwhile antiaircraft battalions turned infantry, Task Force 45, also crossed the river to occupy that part of Pisa lying on the north bank.

For the troops the advance was a pleasant interlude, an unanticipated respite from the rigors of fighting. They moved easily as if on autumn maneuvers through countryside dotted with ocher-colored villages set amid ripening grain fields, orchards, and vineyards. On 3 September when approaching the four-lane autostrada running along the base of the Apennines, the South Africans came upon some mines, demolitions, and scattered artillery fire, while the 1st Armored Division also found demolitions and an occasional smattering of small arms fire. That night enemy aircraft, making a rare appearance, bombed two crossing points on the Arno but did little damage and caused no casualties.

On the next day, the 4th, indications developed that the unobstructed road marches might soon come to an end, but there still was no regular pattern to the enemy's resistance. Here, where the Germans might have turned to fight back sharply, they were nowhere to be seen. Southwest of Pistoia, the South Africans brushed aside half-hearted resistance to come within a mile of the autostrada, but a strong enemy rear guard denied a reconnaissance company of the 1st Armored Division entry to a town alongside the autostrada eight miles east of Lucca until late afternoon when the enemy withdrew. Farther west the 11th Armored Infantry Battalion crossed the autostrada against slight opposition, and on the division's left wing the attached 370th Infantry, nearing the autostrada just south of Lucca, met with some small arms and artillery fire. Continuing beyond Pisa, a patrol of Task Force 45 that crossed the little Serchio River was pinned down by heavy fire and succeeded in pulling back only after nightfall.

Nevertheless, by 5 September the IV Corps had occupied three of its four objectives: the Monte Pisano massif on the left, the Monte Albano Ridge on the right, and the walled city of Lucca, while Pistoia remained in enemy hands. When on the 6th heavy rains began, soon washing out tactical bridges spanning the Arno, General Crittenberger accepted growing evidence that the Germans had withdrawn as far as they intended and ordered a halt. He directed a general regrouping along a line running from the Serchio River through Lucca to the Monte Pisano massif, thence along the autostrada to the Monte Albano Ridge. Here the corps would hold until ordered to resume its advance in keeping with progress of the II Corps in the assault on the Gothic Line.

Having already established a bridgehead north of the Arno, the 13 Corps meanwhile had simply pushed forward in keeping with the rate of German withdrawal. That rate was considerably less precipitate than in front of the IV Corps, for the apparent recognition of the importance of Highway 65 to any thrust against the Gothic Line made the Germans fall back slowly. By 4 September patrol contacts provided no indication of further enemy withdrawal, so the line of the 13 Corps stabilized roughly as an extension of that of the IV Corps from five to ten miles north of the Arno.

Between the two corps, apparently as a preliminary to the planned passage of the II Corps through the 13 Corps, General Clark had assigned a narrow sector to the II Corps. The 442d Regimental Combat Team followed up the German withdrawal there until relieved the night of 2 September by a regiment of the 88th Division. The 442d was heading for southern France.

As these moves proceeded, General Clark took another look at his plan of attack on the Gothic Line. Word had just reached him through British Intelligence that Hitler had ordered Kesselring to concentrate his defense astride Highway 65 at the Futa Pass. The same message had also disclosed that the interarmy boundary between the *Tenth* and *Fourteenth Armies*, and generally the weakest point in the enemy front, lay some six miles east of the Futa Pass at Il Giogo Pass. Military logic suggested that the main effort could be more profitably made at the latter pass. A breakthrough at Il Giogo Pass would outflank the strong defenses at the Futa Pass and most likely force a German withdrawal there. From Firenzuola, five miles beyond Il Giogo Pass, he might proceed either up Highway 65 through the Radicosa Pass to Bologna or along a secondary road northeastward to Imola. Furthermore, by shifting his main effort to the right wing, the Fifth Army commander might achieve better coordination with the supporting attack of the British 13 Corps.[20]

The II Corps commander, General Keyes, planned to advance toward the Gothic Line with the 34th and 91st

---

[20] See Winterbotham, *The Ultra Secret,* p. 160.

Divisions on either side of Highway 65 in what could appear to the Germans as merely a continuation of the follow-up of German withdrawal. It would also give an impression of a main effort at the Futa Pass. Yet once the 91st Division on the right came into contact with the main defenses of the Gothic Line, the 85th Division was to pass through and make the main effort against Il Giogo Pass. Keyes' reserve, the 88th Division, was to be prepared to pass through either the 91st Division along Highway 65 or the 85th Division. To meet special supply problems to be expected in the mountains, the corps had nine Italian pack mule companies, each with 260 mules.

Despite problems posed by heavy rains and flooding, the Fifth Army by 7 September was ready, awaiting only the signal from General Alexander. "The fate of the Fifth Army," General Clark confided to his diary, was "tied up with that of the Eighth Army." Clark assumed that Alexander would delay the Fifth Army's attack until General Leese could get a renewed effort going against the troublesome Coriano Ridge, whereupon Clark would be prepared to attack "about 48 hours later."[21] "We are all set," wrote Clark, "for the thrust over the mountains toward Bologna. It is hard to wait, for we are ready and eager to go. General Alexander is holding the lanyard, and when he pulls it we will be able to jump off with less than 24 hours' notice."[22]

General Alexander was indeed about ready to pull the lanyard. On 8 September he visited Leese's headquarters to get a closer look at the stalemate at the Coriano Ridge. It would take two or three more days, he deduced, for Leese to get his stalled offensive moving again. Meanwhile, Kesselring had apparently shifted as much strength to his Adriatic flank as he could afford so that there was no point in delaying the Fifth Army's attack in hope of further shifts. Indeed, attack by the Fifth Army might loosen up the front opposite Leese's army. He told General Clark to begin his offensive on 10 September, with the Eighth Army to renew its attack two days later.[23]

The German Situation

Of the three divisions that Field Marshal Kesselring had shifted to meet the Eighth Army's offensive, only one, the *356th*, had been drawn from the *Fourteenth Army* in front of Clark's Fifth Army. Even so, committing the *26th Panzer Division* and the *29th Panzer Grenadier Division* from the *Tenth Army's* reserve had tied up two units that might otherwise have been used in the central sector. Pulling out even one division seriously weakened the defenses, for it left the *I Parachute Corps* only one division, the *4th Parachute*, with which to cover both the Futa and Il Giogo Passes in front of the U.S. II Corps, and the *LI Mountain Corps* only one division, the *715th*, to oppose the British 13 Corps. Almost on the eve of the Fifth Army's attack, Lemelsen's *Fourteenth Army* incurred another loss with departure of the *16th SS Panzer Grenadier Division* on orders from OKW to France.[24]

[21] Clark Diary, 7 Sep 44.
[22] *Ibid.*

[23] Alexander *Despatch*, p. 69.
[24] *AOK 14, Ia KTB Nr. 4*, 6–9 Sep 44, *AOK 14*, Doc. 62241/1.

Even had there been no threat of a Fifth Army offensive, General Lemelsen would have been disturbed by the shortage of troops, for partisan activity in the *Fourteenth Army*'s rear was increasing, particularly between the Ligurian coast and Highway 9, *Army Group C*'s main lateral line of communication. Almost every day some partisan band demolished a railroad, a bridge, a highway. To provide vitally needed security, Lemelsen transferred to the rear one battalion from each division in the less threatened *XIV Panzer Corps* opposite the U.S. IV Corps.[25]

In addition to harassment by partisans, the Germans were plagued by Allied bombers and fighters. Medium bombers again struck the Po River crossings to destroy bridges repaired since Operation MALLORY MAJOR in July. They also attempted to seal off the industrial area of northwestern Italy from the front by bombing five railroad bridges. Fighter-bombers harassed roads and rail lines on both sides of the Po.[26]

On 9 September the mediums, in an effort to isolate the immediate battle area planned for the Fifth Army, shifted their attacks to railroad lines leading into Bologna. By nightfall the next day they had cut all four main lines.[27]

Meanwhile, the bulk of the fighter-bombers hit the Gothic Line itself. Beginning on 9 September and continuing through the 20th, when weather would restrict operations, fighter-bombers would fly an average of 240 sorties daily against bivouac areas, command posts, and supply depots in the vicinity of Futa and Il Giogo Passes. For three days, beginning on the 9th, mediums joined the attack, flying 339 sorties against barracks, supply points, and gun positions between the front and Bologna.[28]

As the *4th Parachute* and *715th Divisions* resumed their withdrawal into the main Gothic Line defenses, General Lemelsen grew increasingly disturbed over his chances of holding the line. On 9 September his chief of staff requested Kesselring to transfer at least one depleted division from the *Tenth Army* to replace the departing *16th SS Panzer Grenadier Division*. Although Kesselring agreed, he added that he saw no reason for immediate concern, for in his opinion, the *Fourteenth Army* faced no immediate attack.[29]

[25] *Ibid.*
[26] Craven and Cate, eds., *AAF* III, pp. 445–46.

[27] *Ibid.*
[28] *Ibid.*
[29] *AOK 14, Ia KTB Nr. 4, 6–9 Sep 44, AOK 14,* Doc. 62241/1.

CHAPTER XIX

Battle for the Pass

The Approach

With the 34th Division on the left and the 91st Division to the right of Highway 65, General Keyes' II Corps on 10 September began to advance on a 15-mile front from a line of hills eight miles north of Florence toward the Sieve River, four miles away. To the right of the American corps the 1st Division of the British 13 Corps moved astride the Florence–Borgo–San Lorenzo road toward the Sieve. Since patrols had determined that the enemy had already departed, the first day's operation was little more than an approach march. Long columns of infantry moved in relative silence through narrow valleys and along crooked ridges. Ahead, shrouded in the blue haze of early autumn, were the shadowy outlines of the Northern Apennines, on whose slopes a watchful enemy lay concealed in hundreds of well-camouflaged firing trenches, gun pits, and concrete bunkers. That night the Allied troops crossed the easily fordable Sieve unopposed.[1]

Elsewhere other troops of the Fifth Army also stirred. On the coastal flank

of General Crittenberger's IV Corps, Task Force 45 followed up the enemy's withdrawal fourteen miles beyond the Arno to the vicinity of the prewar beach resort of Viareggio. Inland the 1st Armored Division and the 6th South African Armoured Division continued abreast on broad fronts. Nowhere were the Germans in evidence. Occupying Pistoia, abandoned by the enemy, the South Africans pushed on into the hills north of the city.

On the 11th the II Corps continued its approach march, but as the day wore on, indications grew that an alert enemy waited not far ahead. An occasional burst of long-range machine gun fire; a cluster of exploding mortar shells that sent forward-patrols scurrying for cover; an isolated explosion revealing a hidden mine field. The troops were obviously nearing an outpost line somewhere in low hills fronting dominating peaks overlooking the Futa and Il Giogo Passes.

Plans and Terrain

Commanded since mid-1943 by 49-year-old General Livesay, the 91st Division after crossing the Sieve veered away from Highway 65 to follow the secondary road, Route 6524, toward the main objective of the II Corps, Il Giogo Pass.

Under General Keyes' plan, once the 91st Division had fully developed the

---

[1] II Corps AAR, Sep 44; Sidney T. Mathews, "Breakthrough at Monte Altuzzo," in Charles B. MacDonald and Sidney T. Mathews, *Three Battles: Arnaville, Altuzzo, and Schmidt,* UNITED STATES ARMY IN WORLD WAR II (Washington, 1952); Chester G. Starr, *From Salerno to the Alps* (Washington: Infantry Journal Press, 1948), pp. 311–24. Unless otherwise cited the following sections are based upon these sources.

IL GIOGO PASS

enemy's outpost line, General Coulter's 85th Division was to relieve those elements of the 91st Division east of Highway 65. The two divisions then were to move against the two terrain features commanding Il Giogo Pass. These were the 3,000-foot Monticelli massif on the left of the pass and the equally high Monte Altuzzo on the right. General Keyes had also directed General Livesay to deploy one of his regiments west of Monticelli in conjunction with a holding attack toward the Futa Pass by General Bolté's 34th Division astride Highway 65. In addi-

tion to taking the key height of Monte Altuzzo, the 85th Division was also to seize neighboring Monte Verruca and other heights to the east adjoining the sector of the British 13 Corps. (Map XI)

To defend Il Giogo Pass the Germans had constructed their Gothic Line positions so as to take full advantage of a watershed 3,000 feet high. On the forward slopes, streams flowing southward into the Sieve River had cut a series of sharp irregular parallel ridges and ravines. Except where rocky outcrops and cliffs provided no foothold for vegetation, stunted pines and scattered patches of brush covered the narrow ridges, while lower slopes were generally well concealed by thick groves of chestnut and pine.

As was so often the case in the Italian Campaign, the nature of the terrain would impose strict limitations on the tactical choices open to the various commanders. Route 6524, for example, had to serve as a line of communication for both the 85th and 91st Divisions. At best the road resembled a two-lane, asphalt-covered American country road. Since its many sharp curves were under direct observation of gunners on the slopes of Monticelli and Monte Altuzzo, those portions close to the front would be unable to sustain much daylight traffic until heights flanking the Il Giogo Pass were in hand.

The Monticelli massif southwest of the pass consists of a long, steep backbone ridge with a concave southern slope. Slightly higher than Monticelli, Monte Altuzzo is a conical peak with a main north-south ridge extending southward for 2,500 yards from its summit. Numerous narrow wooded draws cut the slopes of the ridge and offered covered routes of approach for attacking troops.

Il Giogo Pass had indeed been well chosen for the American main effort, for General Lemelsen, the *Fourteenth Army* commander, and Field Marshal Kesselring shared a conviction that the Americans would concentrate on the Futa Pass and the principal crossing of the Apennines, Highway 65. Although the *4th Parachute Division* of Schlemm's *I Parachute Corps* was responsible for defense of both passes, two of its regiments focused on the Futa Pass, leaving only one, the *12th Parachute Regiment,* to

hold Il Giogo Pass, including both Monticelli and Monte Altuzzo, plus the other heights eastward to a boundary with the *715th Division* of the *LI Mountain Corps.* Reduced by heavy losses during the fighting south of Rome to a small cadre of combat-experienced troops, the *4th Parachute Division* had been fleshed out in recent weeks by inexperienced replacements, many of whom had yet to fire live ammunition. Two other divisions to the west opposite the 34th U.S. Division and the 6th South African Armoured Division were responsible for sectors of the Gothic Line averaging ten miles each, so that there was little possibility of drawing on them for reserves in the main battle. General Schlemm's corps reserve consisted of only two battalions of the *Grenadier Lehr Brigade.* [2]

Along that sector of the Gothic Line about to feel the main weight of the Fifth Army's assault, the attacking forces would enjoy a three-to-one superiority over the defenders. Before Il Giogo Pass General Keyes had concentrated half of his infantry strength, and each of the attacking divisions would have the support of an entire corps artillery group. Given those conditions, the Americans had every right to view the task ahead with confidence, in spite of the mountainous and forbidding terrain pocked with well-camouflaged positions manned by a foe with orders to defend to the last bullet.

First Contacts

During the afternoon of the 12th, Col. W.F. Magill's 363d Infantry led the

[2] *AOK 14, Ia KTB Nr. 4,* 6–8 Sep 44, Doc. 62241/1. See also *Fifth Army History,* Part VII, pp. 53–54 and 72.

91st Division toward Il Giogo Pass. Although the volume of enemy fire was steadily increasing, the 91st Division thus far had run into only sporadic opposition, prompting General Keyes to delay ordering forward General Coulter's 85th Division. The absence of determined resistance reinforced a widely held opinion in the 91st Division headquarters that the objective was only lightly manned. Colonel Magill, for his part, thought his regiment could seize both Monticelli and Monte Altuzzo without help from the 85th Division.

Late in the day Colonel Magill sent a battalion against each of the two objectives. Faced by the heaviest fire yet encountered north of the Arno and advancing in growing darkness over unfamiliar ground against defenses that would eventually absorb the efforts of two divisions, neither battalion understandably made much headway. That night local counterattacks drove one company back along the main road. Radio communication in the convoluted terrain was poor, and deployed on slopes with few features recognizable on maps, Colonel Magill's troops were unable to advise their commanders of their exact whereabouts. About all that was certain as daylight came on the 13th was that the advances had come to a halt and that both Monticelli and Monte Altuzzo were still the province of the *12th Parachute Regiment.* Until the location of the forward formations could be pinpointed, their presence was bound to inhibit the use of supporting artillery fire. [3]

The Attack on the Monticelli Ridge

The principal objective of General Livesay's 91st Division, Monticelli, was in effect a ridge line, forming a huge amphitheater whose two wings extended south from the main east-west divide. The west wing is Monte Calvi, a smooth dome-shaped hill. Monticelli itself is a long, steep-sided 3,000-foot ridge running in a northwest-southeasterly direction and forming the east wing of the amphitheater overlooking Il Giogo Pass. Stretching southward from the main ridge are two spurs, below which Route 6524 runs through Il Giogo Pass. Between those spurs are two deep, steep-sided ravines offering the only covered routes of approach to the upper slopes. On Monticelli's northwestern arms, scrub brush and a grove of chestnut trees near the hamlet of Borgo offered the only concealment. Narrow foot trails led to Borgo from the mountain's lower slopes, but beyond Borgo there were no trails, and the steep upper slopes would make supply and evacuation of wounded extremely difficult. [4]

So cleverly concealed were the Gothic Line defenses that they were almost invisible to the approaching troops. Many had been constructed of reinforced concrete or blasted into the rock. Roofed with three feet of logs and earth, each position could accommodate five men. In front of the defenses the Germans had strung at 100-yard intervals bands of barbed wire a foot high

---

[3] 363d Inf Jnl and Opns Rpt, Sep 44.

[4] Capt. Lloyd J. Inman, Inf., The Operation of Company B, 363d Infantry, in the Attack on Monticelli, Study, The Infantry School, Ft. Benning, Ga. Unless otherwise indicated the following is based upon this source.

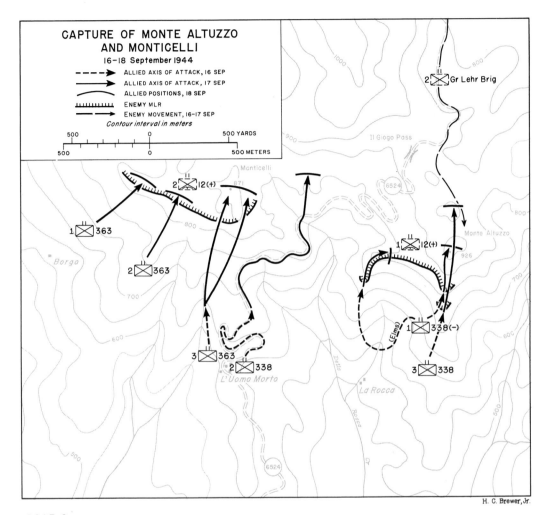

CAPTURE OF MONTE ALTUZZO
AND MONTICELLI
16-18 September 1944

- - - ▶ ALLIED AXIS OF ATTACK, 16 SEP
——▶ ALLIED AXIS OF ATTACK, 17 SEP
——— ALLIED POSITIONS, 18 SEP
⊥⊥⊥⊥⊥ ENEMY MLR
━ ━▶ ENEMY MOVEMENT, 16-17 SEP
Contour interval in meters

MAP 8

and twenty-five feet deep. They had
also placed mines in the two ravines
leading to the upper slopes, for they
too saw the ravines as logical routes of
approach. On the reverse slope the
Germans had built large dugouts extending seventy-five feet or more into
the mountain, capable of accommodating up to twenty men, and 300 yards
north of the Monticelli ridge they had
blasted a 50-man shelter out of the

solid rock.[5]

On 13 September two battalions of
the 363d Infantry began to climb toward Monticelli's western ridge. Heavy
and accurate enemy mortar concentrations, punctuated by machine gun fire,
soon slowed the advance and caused so
many casualties that the regimental
commander committed his reserve. The

_____
[5]91st Div Opns Rpt, Sep 44.

ARTILLERY BATTERY IN ACTION

pattern of the fighting for Il Giogo Pass was set that first day on the slopes of both Monticelli and Monte Altuzzo and those less towering crests to right and left.[6] (*Map 8*)

The terrain and the nature of the enemy's defenses, the men soon discovered, would permit no grand over-the-top assault by co-ordinated formations. Of a mighty attacking army numbering over 262,000 men, those who would

bear the brunt of the fighting at critical points sometimes constituted a platoon or less, seldom more than a company or two. Little clusters of men struggled doggedly up rocky ravines and draws separated by narrow fingers of forested ridges, isolated, climbing laboriously squad by squad, fighting their way forward yard by yard, often not even knowing the location of the closest friendly unit. Only a massive fire support, provided by the artillery of division, corps, and army, by the tubes of tanks and tank destroyers firing in battery in the manner of artillery, and

---

[6]Maj. John Brock, Inf., Operations of the 363d Infantry at Monticelli, Monograph, The Infantry School, Ft. Benning, Ga. The following section is based upon this source.

by fighter-bombers, gave to the many isolated firefights any real unity; but it was that very unity, however difficult to discern, that was in the end to decide the battle.

The experience of Company B, 363d Infantry, commanded by Capt. Lloyd J. Inman, was indicative of the kind of fighting that characterized the struggle for Il Giogo Pass. As the 363d Infantry renewed the attack on 14 September, Captain Inman's company was to lead one of two attacking battalions behind a rolling barrage fired by the 34th Field Artillery Battalion. The initial objective was the hamlet of Borgo on Monticelli's southwestern slope. From there the company was to gain the crest of the western ridge and push on to the summit.

A platoon of heavy machine guns from Company D was to support the attack with overhead fire from positions on one of the lower ridges extending southeastward from the Monticelli hill mass. When those fires became masked, the platoon was to displace forward one section at a time. Starting 20 minutes before the ground attack, the supporting artillery and 81-mm. mortars were to fire twenty minutes of preparatory fire against predetermined targets. Thereafter the artillery was to shift its fires to the base of the mountain, then commence a rolling barrage, lifting it 100 yards per minute as Company B's leading platoons followed at a distance of a hundred yards.

At 1400 Company B, with Technical Sgt. Charles J. Murphy's 1st Platoon on the left and 1st Lt. Bruno Rossellini's 2d Platoon on the right, crossed the line of departure. Off to the right Company C began to move. For the first half hour all seemed to go well as Captain Inman's men filed slowly up narrow trails. Suddenly a voice claiming to be that of the Company C commander broke into the battalion's SCR–300 channel, complaining bitterly that friendly artillery fire was falling on his troops. Although both Captain Inman and his artillery forward observer could see from their observation post that that was not the case, they were unable to convince the artillery battalion commander, who immediately halted the barrage. It was obviously an enemy ruse. No sooner had the barrage lifted than Germans who had been taking shelter in the innermost recesses of their dugouts returned to their guns and opened fire on Company B's forward platoons.

Yet in spite of that fire men of the two platoons, using every fold and wrinkle of the ground for cover, managed to reach Borgo and by nightfall had moved beyond the hamlet about a third of the way up the mountain. There grazing machine gun fire at relatively close range stopped them. In the deepening twilight it was impossible to locate well-camouflaged enemy positions. With ammunition running low and casualties heavy, Captain Inman ordered his men to dig in for the night. In the darkness the wounded made their way or were carried to the rear, while porters struggled forward with ammunition and rations.

Determined to locate the guns that had stopped his company, Captain Inman sent 1st Lt. John C. Kearton and six volunteers from the 3d Platoon in search of the enemy positions. Concealed by darkness, the seven inched up the mountainside until halted by barbed wire. Suspecting that the goal was near, Lieutenant Kearton wormed his way through twenty-five yards of barbed wire to the base of an enemy bunker before hand grenades drove him back. Satisfied that he had found the exact location of the enemy machine guns, Kearton withdrew with his men to report his find to his company commander.

The following morning—15 September—as soon as it was light enough to observe, Inman called in artillery fire on the enemy position. Firing a few rounds to adjust for range, the Company B forward observer brought in the fires of a battery of 155-mm. guns, partially destroying the enemy gun emplacement and breaching the wire entanglements before it. Hardly had the firing stopped when Lieutenant Rosselini and ten of his men assaulted the bunker and forced five dazed occupants to surrender. Accompanied by Sergeant Murphy's 1st Platoon, the rest of Rosselini's men came forward and both platoons deployed beyond the captured enemy position.

In that isolated little action, Company B had scored the first important breach in the defenses of Monticelli and the first in that sector of the Gothic Line. Although flanking units had failed to keep pace, the company pushed doggedly on toward the crest of the Monticelli ridge, but with both flanks exposed casualties were heavy, among them the company executive officer and the forward observers for both artillery and 81-mm. mortars.

By 1800 Murphy's and Rosselini's platoons nevertheless reached the comparative safety of a low embankment a few yards from the crest of the ridge.

Only a foot high on the left where Sergeant Murphy's platoon sought cover, the embankment gradually increased in height as it extended to the right at a slight angle to the crest until, in Rosselini's sector, it reached a height of three feet. Sergeant Murphy realized that his platoon, huddled behind the lowest part of the embankment, had to move quickly or else risk certain discovery by the enemy. Ordering his men to fix bayonets, Murphy led them in an assault up the last fifty yards to the crest of the ridge. There they routed enemy soldiers from two dugouts and took five prisoners. Pinned down by heavy flanking fire from the right and the right front, Rosselini's platoon remained in the shelter of the embankment.

Captain Inman and his radio operator followed Murphy to the crest and immediately began adjusting artillery fire on groups of enemy soldiers withdrawing down the reverse slope. When Murphy drew his company commander's attention to a group of Germans to the right, apparently assembling for a counterattack, Inman called for artillery fire, but hardly had he asked for the support when enemy machine gun fire damaged his radio and drove him and the radio operator to cover.

Company B had reached its objective, the northwestern end of the Monticelli ridge, but enemy fire had reduced the company strength to about seventy men and again ammunition was running low. Committing his 3d Platoon to extend and cover his right flank, Inman ordered his men to dig in and defend in place. The attached machine gun platoon, following the assault platoons, had already come forward and began to set up firing positions along the edge of the embankment just below the crest while Captain Inman signaled his battalion headquarters for a new radio battery, ammunition, and reinforcements.

The men were still digging in when approximately a score of Germans launched a small counterattack against Sergeant Murphy's positions on the company's left flank on the northwestern end of the ridge. In apparent response to Captain Inman's call for reinforcements, a 17-man detachment from Company A, consisting of riflemen and a light machine gun section under 1st Lt. Ross A. Notaro, arrived just in time to help repulse the enemy thrust. An hour later another small group of Germans mounted a second counterattack, but by that time Lieutenant Notaro and his men were well dug in on Murphy's left and halted the move before it could gain momentum.

Early that evening the Germans mounted their third and heaviest counterattack. Following a mortar and artillery barrage, the enemy scrambled over the ridge and headed again toward Company B's left flank. Inman called for previously registered defensive fires from the 81-mm. mortars, the regimental cannon company, and supporting artillery. As the counterattacking Germans neared his foxholes, Inman adjusted the fires so closely that occasional rounds fell within the company's perimeter. Although the Americans suffered no casualties, the fire took a heavy toll of the Germans, some of whom were so near that when hit their momentum carried them into the American positions. Anticipating hand-to-hand fighting, Inman ordered his men to fix

CARRYING SUPPLIES TO MOUNTAIN POSITIONS

bayonets, but the artillery barrage insured that no live enemy got inside the perimeter.

Individual soldiers using their own weapons aggressively and courageously also played a major role in checking the counterattack. On the company's far left flank Lieutenant Notaro's detachment was particularly hard pressed, but suddenly, Sgt. Joseph D. Higdon, Jr., section leader of the light machine guns, leaped to his feet and, cradling a light machine gun in his arms, ran toward the enemy, firing as he went. That bold and unexpected action sent the Germans fleeing back down the reverse slope. Severely wounded, Sergeant Higdon tried to return to his own position but collapsed thirty yards short of it. When his companions reached him, he was dead.

The counterattacks halted, Company B, despite severe casualties, continued to hold on the western end of the Monticelli ridge. To conserve his company's dwindling strength, Captain Inman consolidated his force, pulling back Murphy's platoon from its exposed position and placing it nearer Rosselini's platoon, but Notaro and his small detachment remained for the night in their exposed positions on the left. Throughout the night, by the light of German flares, the two sides exchanged small arms fire and hand grenades.

At dawn on the 16th, men whom Inman had sent back during the night for supplies returned with ammunition and a new battery for the company radio, which despite three bullet holes in its chassis had continued to function. As yet no battalion carrying party had reached the company. Although two attached litter bearer teams worked all night trying to evacuate the wounded, morning found some wounded still in the company area. The large number of casualties and a long trek over rugged terrain to the battalion dressing station had been more than the two teams could handle.

Meanwhile, to Company B's right, Company C, after breaching a mine field and overcoming an enemy position bypassed earlier by Inman's company, had reached a point within 200 yards of Company B, while on the left, Company G, attached from the 2d Battalion, took up position to Company B's left rear. That was the situation when soon after daylight a sudden burst of enemy small arms fire struck and wounded Captain Inman. Command of Company B passed to Lieutenant Rosselini.

The coming of daylight revealed that during the night the Germans had moved into the positions on the left flank held previously by Sergeant Murphy's platoon. That made Lieutenant Notaro's detachment on the extreme left flank even more vulnerable than before and also jeopardized Murphy's platoon. Reduced to 17 men, Sergeant Murphy gained reinforcements by integrating into his defenses seven men of a mortar section that had fired all its ammunition.

Throughout the 16th and well into the following day, the Germans attacked again and again against Company B's vulnerable left flank in desperate attempts to regain control of the ridge. Yet somehow the little band of Americans held. The successful defense owed much to Pfc. Oscar G. Johnson, one of the seven mortarmen that Sergeant Murphy had deployed as riflemen. Standing at times to get a better view of the enemy, Private Johnson directed a steady stream of fire at each of the counterattacks. During lulls in the fighting he crawled around the area gathering up all available weapons and ammunition from the dead and wounded and then returned to his own position to resume firing. When weapons malfunctioned, he cannibalized those he had collected for replacement parts. By the afternoon of the 16th Johnson was the only man left in his squad alive or unwounded. Nevertheless, he continued to fight through the night, beating back several attempts to infiltrate his position. Twice the intense fire drove back or wounded men sent to help him. Not until the next morning did help finally arrive. For his steadfast defense of Company B's left

CAPTURED GERMAN POSITION IN GOTHIC LINE

flank Private Johnson later received the Medal of Honor.[7]

Early on 17 September two enemy soldiers carrying a white flag emerged from an emplacement a hundred yards away. Ordering his men to cease fire, Lieutenant Rosselini went forward to meet them. Identifying himself as commanding officer of the paratroopers defending that sector of Monticelli, one of the Germans requested a truce so that the wounded of both sides might be evacuated. Rosselini immediately got in touch with his battalion headquarters for a decision, but before he received an answer, two dozen German soldiers, apparently unaware of the purpose of their commander's parley with the Americans, came down the slope and gave themselves up. Seeing his men surrender, the officer too submitted. That obviated any need for a truce.

Although the surrender took some of the pressure off Company B, reduced

---

[7] See *The Medal of Honor of the United States Army* (Washington: Government Printing Office, 1948), p. 343.

85TH DIVISION TROOPS ON MT. VERRUCA

could pour flanking fire on men of the 85th Division struggling slowly up the slopes of Monte Altuzzo.[8]

After holding the 3d Battalion in reserve for three days, Colonel Magill had committed it during the afternoon of the 16th to move up the eastern slope of the Monticelli ridge, only to see the battalion seriously disrupted by heavy enemy fire, minefields, and the broken terrain. By dawn on the 17th the battalion was so thoroughly disorganized that the division commander himself, General Livesay, felt impelled to go to the battalion command post in an effort to restore control and morale. Yet so reduced in strength were the other two battalions that the 3d remained the only hope for responding to pressure from the II Corps commander, General Keyes, to get on with the task of securing Monticelli's crest.

at that point to 50 men, heavy fire still prevented Rosselini and his men from clearing and occupying all of the Monticelli ridge in their sector. That afternoon after making plans with Capt. Edward J. Conley, commander of the neighboring Company G, for a final assault to sweep the ridge, Lieutenant Rosselini was returning to his command post when enemy fire cut him down. Since Rosselini had been Company B's last surviving officer, Captain Conley absorbed the remnants of Company B in his own command.

For four days all the 363d Infantry's rifle companies had at one time or another been drawn into the fighting, yet the Germans still held Monticelli's summit. From there they could fire not only on men of the 363d Infantry but

A rolling artillery barrage again was to precede the assault. Just at dawn, Company K, commanded by Capt. William B. Fulton, led off while an anxious General Livesay waited in the background. Because the hard-pressed troops on Monticelli's western ridge could cover Company K's left flank, the task was easier than that faced earlier by Company B. Within half an hour after the jump-off Captain Fulton's company was within 600 yards of the summit but receiving heavy fire. Not until midafternoon of the 17th was tension in Colonel Magill's command post eased with word that Fulton and six of his men, including a radio opera-

---

[8] 361st Inf Regt Hist, Sep 44; 363d Inf Hist, Sep 44. Unless otherwise indicated the following is based upon these references.

tor, were at the top of the summit. An hour later the rest of Fulton's company and of the 3d Battalion also made it.

Taking advantage of the excellent observation atop Monticelli, Fulton directed artillery fire that broke up a series of counterattacks while the rest of the regiment gradually consolidated its grip on the mountain. After nightfall, as wounded were still being evacuated, a company of the 361st Infantry, which had been attacking west of Monticelli, arrived to clear the enemy from Monticelli's western crest, where the intrepid Private Johnson was still holding almost singlehandedly what had once been Company B's left flank. Denied the honor of reaching Monticelli's summit, Company B had nevertheless played the key role in the breakthrough, for the company's determined advance up the mountain's western ridge and its dogged defense had made possible the 3d Battalion's final and successful assault on the summit.

More than 150 enemy dead were to be counted in Company B's sector along with at least 40 attributable to Private Johnson's steadfast defense of the company's left flank; the company also took 40 enemy prisoners. Company B lost 14 men killed and 126 wounded.

By 18 September the western height overlooking Il Giogo Pass was firmly in American hands, while in the meantime just to the east of Highway 6524 the 85th Division's 338th Infantry had reached the top of Monte Altuzzo after a five-day fight similar to that experienced by the 363d Infantry. Farther to the east, the 339th Infantry had by noon of the 17th captured the neighboring peak of Monte Verucca and during the afternoon the 337th Infan-

try on the corps right flank occupied Monte Pratone.[9]

Once the 363d Infantry had captured the summit of Monticelli, the 361st Infantry followed enemy withdrawal onto the hills west of Monticelli. Meanwhile, slightly farther to the west, a two-regiment containing attack had carried the 34th Division to within striking distance of the Futa Pass. By fostering the illusion that the Futa Pass was the focus of the Fifth Army offensive, as noted earlier, the 34th Division had assured that no enemy forces from that sector would be shifted to Il Giogo Pass. That ruse undoubtedly contributed to the breakthrough at Il Giogo Pass.[10]

East of Il Giogo Pass and the II Corps sector the British 13 Corps, constituting the Fifth Army right wing, had played a similar role by pinning down enemy troops that might otherwise have been shifted westward to oppose the army's main effort. As were units west of the pass, the British corps was echeloned to the rear of the II Corps. The flank units nevertheless had advanced sufficiently to afford favorable jump-off positions for exploiting what amounted to a breakthrough of the Gothic Line seven miles wide astride Il Giogo Pass, and troops on the Fifth Army's extreme west wing had drawn up to the line.

The six-day fight had taken an inevitable toll of the three assault divisions of

---

[9] See Mathews, "Breakthrough at Monte Altuzzo," in *Three Battles* for a detailed account of the breakthrough operation in the 85th Division sector.

[10] In the course of the attack, 2d Lt. Thomas W. Wigle, Company K, 135th Infantry, distinguished himself in action on 14 September on Monte Frassino. He was posthumously awarded the Medal of Honor.

LOOKING NORTH FROM FUTA PASS

the II Corps: a total of 2,731 casualties. Yet those could be considered light in view of the results achieved. German losses, although unrecorded, were unquestionably far greater. While the isolated, fierce little engagements at close quarters between opposing infantrymen on the steep slopes and mountaintops were costly to both sides, the Germans lost considerably more men to American supporting fires. Hardly any of the little batch of reinforcements moving into the line got through unscathed.

From the first the Germans had been faced with a dilemma. So great was the pressure exerted by General Bolté's 34th Division in what was actually a holding attack against the Futa Pass that German commanders never divined that the main effort was directed against Il Giogo Pass. The *Fourteenth Army* commander, General Lemelsen, and the *I Parachute Corps* commander, General Schlemm, saw the main effort extending across a nine-mile front encompassing both passes. Yet even had they discerned the American plan from the start, they could have done little about it. Once the *4th Parachute Division* had committed every possible man to the fight as infantry—antitank gunners, engineers, even men of an untrustworthy Lithuanian Labor Battalion—all that was left were the two battalions of the *Grenadier Lehr Brigade.* Although Field Marshal Kesselring on 15 September authorized commitment of those battalions to help defend Il Giogo Pass, he stipulated that they had to be released three days later to reinforce the Adriatic front.[11]

In thus displaying greater concern for the Adriatic front, Kesselring revealed a recognition that a breakthrough by the British Eighth Army might have a more far-reaching effect than one by the American Fifth Army.

There were other positions in the mountains that still might be used to delay the Fifth Army, but a breakthrough by the British might outflank the entire German army group.

That the German command recognized that American penetration at Il Giogo Pass was inevitable became apparent in early evening of 17 September when General Lemelsen ordered the *I Parachute Corps* to abandon the Gothic Line and fall back to build a new defense in the heights north of Firenzuola.[12] That move meant that General Clark's plan had succeeded. A breakthrough at Il Giogo Pass had indeed outflanked the more utilitarian Futa Pass and prompted German withdrawal from the Futa Pass.

---

[11] *AOK 14, Ia KTB,* 12–18 Sep 44, *AOK 14,* Doc. 62241/1.

[12] *Ibid.*

CHAPTER XX

A Diversionary Operation

Having breached the Gothic Line, Allied commanders were confident that they would soon sweep a broken and defeated enemy into the Po Valley. They were soon to learn that, to the contrary, heavy fighting still lay ahead. Even before the Fifth Army had begun its assault on Il Giogo Pass, the Eighth Army got its first bitter taste of what lay ahead as the army attempted to exploit its penetration of the Gothic Line on the Adriatic flank.

Since the start of the Eighth Army's phase of the offensive on 25 August, the Germans, skillfully defending along a series of ridges extending in a northeasterly direction from the Apennines, had exacted for each ridge a heavy toll in Allied personnel and materiel. Yet General Leese still had a reserve of uncommitted units: the British 4th and the 2d New Zealand Divisions and the 3d Greek Mountain and British 25th Tank Brigades. He also had ample reserve stocks with which to replenish materiel losses.

The Eighth Army nevertheless continued to be plagued by the superior armor and firepower of German tanks. Even the introduction of ammunition that increased the firepower of the British tanks failed to compensate for their deficiencies *vis-à-vis* the heavier armor and more powerful guns of the German Panther. During the lull after the futile attempt to take the Coriano Ridge, Eighth Army logistical staffs had made strenuous efforts to bring forward new heavy British Churchill tanks, which were just beginning to arrive in Italy. At the same time, new 76-mm. U.S. Sherman tanks and 105-mm. self-propelled guns were arriving from the United States. Although U.S. units had priority on deliveries, the British received some of the new equipment. However, it would take considerable time to forward replacements to units still in close contact with the enemy.

When the heavy rains of the first week in September and a determined enemy had brought the Eighth Army to a halt before the Coriano Ridge, the army was still eight miles short of the Marecchia River, which marks the southern boundary of the Romagna Plain for which the British were striving. Ahead of the army lay three more of the northeastward extending ridges or spurs that had been serving the Germans as alternate lines of defense: the Ripabianca, a mile north of the Coriano Ridge, covering the crossings of the Formica Creek; the San Patrignano, from which the enemy could dominate the crossings of the Marano, two miles beyond the Formica; and two miles farther, the San Fortunato Ridge overlooking the Ausa River. Eighth Army aerial reconnaissance indicated that the enemy had developed field-works only on the latter ridge and thus could be expected to conduct only delaying operations on the Ripabianca and the San Patrignano Ridges.[1]

To the fieldworks along the San Fortunato Ridge the Germans had given the designation, the Rimini Line. The positions included dug-in tank turrets reminiscent of the fortifications of the Hitler Line in the Liri valley. Because the Rimini Line was the last possible defensive position short of the Romagna plain, the Germans could be expected to defend it stubornly.

Leese's Plan

Since 8 September General Leese had shifted the burden of operations to the 5 Corps on his left flank, in order to permit the 1st Canadian Corps to rest and regroup, for he planned to use the latter to make the main assault on the Coriano Ridge, the key to Rimini. Extending northeastward for five miles, from the village of San Savino to a point on the coast five miles southeast of Rimini and near the fishing village of Riccione, the Coriano Ridge covered the southern approaches to Rimini. To assist the Canadian corps, General Leese had reinforced it with three of his four reserve units; the British 4th Division, 3d Greek Mountain Brigade, and British 25th Tank Brigade. The fourth, the 2d New Zealand Division, was to remain in reserve with the 2 Polish Corps.

On 9 September the Eighth Army commander outlined a revised plan of

operations designed to carry the army northward thirty miles beyond Rimini to Ravenna and provide control of the Romagna Plain. From there General Leese expected to be able to turn the German *Tenth Army*'s left flank and roll it up toward Bologna and to make a junction with Clark's Fifth Army.

In the first phase of the revised plan Leese intended both the British 5 Corps and 1st Canadian Corps to converge upon the Coriano Ridge—the British from the left and the Canadians frontally. During the lull General Leese had reversed the operational roles of the British 5 and 1st Canadian Corps. The 5 Corps was to work its way around the western flank of the ridge to divert enemy attention from preparations being made by the Canadian corps to make the major assault against its eastern extremity. The 700 guns that had signaled the opening of the Gothic Line offensive on 25 August were to fire in support of the 5 Corps' three infantry divisions as they advanced beyond the Conca River toward the town of Croce, five miles southwest of Coriano, while the 1st Canadian Corps' 5th Canadian and British 1st Armoured Divisions were to exploit capture of the ridge and secure bridgeheads over the Marano River. During the third phase the Eighth Army (the 1st Canadian Corps then leading the way) was to cross the Marecchia and deploy onto the Romagna Plain. The 1st Canadian Corps commander, General Burns, planned at that time to employ either the 2d New Zealand Division or the 5th Canadian Armoured Division as an exploiting force. To help the main effort by the Canadians, General Leese impressed upon the 5 Corps commander, General

---

[1]Operations of British, Indian, and Dominion Forces in Italy, Part III, Sec. B, The Eighth Army and the Gothic Line and Romagna Battles. Unless otherwise noted the following is based upon this source.

Sir Charles Allfrey, the importance of maintaining enough pressure in his sector to prevent the enemy from shifting forces to check the Canadian thrust on the coastal flank.[2]

Resuming the Offensive

Even as the Fifth Army's II Corps on 12 September began its assault against the Gothic Line north of Florence, the British 5 and 1st Canadian Corps—their way prepared by the fires of the 700 guns supplemented by an offshore naval force of gunboats and destroyers and by hundreds of sorties by bombers of the DAF—resumed the Eighth Army offensive on the Adriatic flank. Although priority on air support had been shifted to the central sector to support the Fifth Army, the Eighth Army still had the full support of the DAF. On 13 September that consisted of more than 500 tons of bombs during 900 sorties, 700 of which were flown in close support of ground operations.

Helped by that firepower, the Canadian infantry and armor managed during the first day to establish a secure foothold on the Coriano Ridge just south of the town of Coriano. Throughout the 13th and on into the night, troops of the Irish Regiment of Canada drove a battalion of the *29th Panzer Division* from the town, house by house. Many of the defenders withdrew only to fall into the hands of troops from the British 5 Corps' 4th Division, coming up on the left of the ridge.

Without pausing to consolidate their newly-won positions, the Canadians hastily tackled their next objective, marking the second phase. By evening of the 14th they had reached the south bank of the Marano River, two miles northwest of the Coriano Ridge, and during the night established several bridgeheads beyond the river.

Despite having to relinquish the Coriano Ridge, General Herr, *LXXVI Panzer Corps* commander, still maintained the integrity of his front by withdrawing his troops to delaying positions along the San Patrignano Ridge, midway between the Marano and Ausa Rivers. There the Germans delayed the Canadians throughout the 15th and gained time to improve fieldworks along the Rimini Line, especially those on the San Fortunato Ridge, two miles north of the Ausa. As at Coriano, the Germans turned the village of San Fortunato into a strongpoint. South of the Ausa River and three miles from the San Fortunato strongpoint, the Germans developed a second strongpoint around the monastery of San Martino, situated on a small knoll overlooking Route 16, the coastal road leading to Rimini from the southeast. Well-concealed artillery in defilade behind the San Fortunato Ridge supported the positions.[3]

Since the main highway and railway serving the coastal flank and connecting with the major routes across the Romagna Plain had to be cleared before any large-scale operation could be undertaken beyond the Marecchia River, General Burns directed his attention to

[2]General Leese had earlier placed the New Zealand division and the 3d Greek Mountain Brigade under the Canadian corps for planning purposes. See Nicholson, *The Canadians in Italy,* pp. 532–35. Unless otherwise indicated the following is based upon this reference.

[3]*AOK 10, Ia KTB Anl. 8,* 17–18 Sep 44, *AOK 10* Doc. 61437/1; Horst Pretzell MS, The Battle of Rimini, in CMH files.

the San Martino strongpoint. As the Canadian armor and infantry approached on the 16th, defending troopers of the *1st Parachute Division,* veterans of the Cassino battle many months before, disappeared into well-prepared bunkers and called down heavy artillery fire immediately in front of their lines. Caught in the open plain between the Marano and the Ausa, the Canadians had to fall back to their starting point, the bridgeheads over the Marano.

The action was costly. Instead of renewing the assault immediately, Burns spent the next day regrouping and reorganizing. Trusting to darkness to conceal the next assault, he attacked again during the night of the 17th. A diffused light, created by beams from searchlights on the reverse slope of the Coriano Ridge thrown against low-hanging clouds, helped troop commanders maintain control. Yet so well registered were the German guns on open ground over which the attackers had to pass that the darkness was but a small handicap. The fire left the Canadians "sweating and bleeding on the low ground" south of the Ausa River.[4]

For all the damage inflicted by German artillery, the two successive Canadian assaults had taken a sharp toll among the defenders. Lacking replacements, the German commanders realized that they would soon have to yield the positions south of Rimini, regardless of whether artillery support remained intact.[5]

Along the entire Pisa-Rimini line the battle of attrition, for such it had become, had reached a climax. The

U.S. II Corps had broken through Il Giogo Pass across a seven-mile front on the 18th, and the next day the neighboring British 13 Corps stood on the threshold of a breakthrough of both the Casaglia and San Godenzo Passes, on the Faenza and Forli roads. Along the Adriatic front, as well as in the Apennines, the Allies had pushed back both flanks of the *Tenth Army,* so that, to General Vietinghoff, the army's front resembled a dangerously bent bow. Doubting that the bow could bend much further without breaking, the *Tenth Army* commander urged Kesselring to allow him to relieve tension by withdrawing in the center. With units thus made available, Vietinghoff expected to shore up the army flanks. Although Kesselring agreed in principle, he told Vietinghoff that an authorization to withdraw would be given only if the situation grew worse. That afforded little consolation for the *Tenth Army* commander.[6]

As it turned out, neither Kesselring nor Vietinghoff had long to wait for the situation to worsen. During the night of the 19th the 1st Canadian Corps, behind a heavy bombardment from land, sea, and air, crossed the Ausa River and stormed the slopes of the San Fortunato Ridge to seize Villa Belvedere, a large country mansion only 600 yards from the village of San Fortunato and command center of the enemy strongpoint. Bypassed by the successful Canadian assault to the west, the paratroopers abandoned the San Martino position and slipped away. Again it seemed as if the bow would snap and the Canadians break through,

---

[4]Nicholson, *The Canadians in Italy,* pp. 550–51.
[5]*AOK 10, Ia KTB Anl. Nr. 8,* 17–19 Sept. 44, *AOK 10 Doc. Nr.* 61437/1.

[6]*Ibid.,* 19 Sep 44.

but again the elements were destined to intervene. In a heavy rain the Germans broke contact and withdrew beyond the Marecchia, some four miles away. Bogged down by muddy roads and halted by swollen streams, the Canadian armor was unable to exploit the capture of the San Fortunato Ridge.[7]

The Capture of Rimini

Over the next forty-eight hours the waters of the flood-swollen Marecchia and its muddy flood plain became more effective barriers to Allied forces than anything the Germans were capable of throwing in their path. The loss of the San Fortunato Ridge and the San Martino strongpoint, last German defenses south of Rimini, meant nevertheless that General Herr could no longer expect to hold the city. On the 19th Kesselring authorized Vietinghoff to withdraw Herr's left wing beyond the Marecchia and evacuate Rimini the next night. In doing so, the *Tenth Army* commander, perhaps moved by the aura of history which permeated the peninsula, elected to forfeit some of the flooded Marecchia's tactical advantages by sparing the only remaining bridge across it, a 1,900-year-old stone structure built during the reign of Emperor Tiberius but still usable in 20th century warfare.[8]

As troops of the 3d Greek Mountain Brigade, operating on the coastal flank of the Canadian corps, prepared to enter Rimini's outskirts, the men could hear through the darkness the sound of heavy explosions as the Germans aban-doned the city. Early on the 21st a motorized patrol from the Greek brigade entered. By 0800 the Greeks had reached the main square to raise their battle standard over the town hall.[9] Seventy-five percent of the city lay in ruins, but among the surviving structures stood the Triumphal Arch of Augustus built in 27 B.C. With multiple bridges soon spanning the Marecchia, the Canadians the next day deployed onto Highway 9 and the Romagna Plain, "the plains so long hoped for and so fiercely fought for . . . [whose] clogging mud and brimming water-courses" would soon confront the Eighth Army with obstacles as challenging as the mountains and ridges.[10]

By 21 September the Eighth Army, having covered over thirty miles in twenty-six days, hardly a pell-mell pursuit, was well established in the eastern terminus of the Pisa-Rimini line. Operation OLIVE, which General Alexander had outlined to his army commanders in early August, had been completed but far behind schedule. After the fall of Rome in early June Allied commanders had confidently expected to reach that line by the end of July, but, in the months since then, the transfer of much Allied strength to other fronts with higher priority as well as a series of skillful enemy defenses had caused both the Fifth and Eighth Armies to lag behind projected timetables. To make matters worse, the heavy rains soaking the low-lying plains in the Eighth Army sector would soon turn to ice and snow in the Apennines where the Fifth Army

---

[7]Nicholson, *The Canadians in Italy.* pp. 556–57.
[8]*Ibid.*, p. 558; *AOK 10, Ia KTB Anl. 8,* 21 Sep 44, *AOK 10,* Doc. 63437/1.

[9]Nicholson, *The Canadians in Italy,* p. 558. The Greeks gallantly requested the Canadians to furnish a Canadian flag to be flown alongside their own.
[10]Alexander *Despatch,* pp. 70–71.

GENERALS CLARK AND KEYES STUDY THE II CORPS SITUATION MAP NEAR FIREN-
ZUOLA, SEPTEMBER 1944.

was resolutely fighting from one mountain to another.

Toward Imola

Even as the Eighth Army crossed the
Marecchia and deployed onto the Romagna Plain, Clark's Fifth Army moved
through Il Giogo Pass and prepared to
exploit its capture. Keyes' II Corps soon
crossed the Santerno River and advanced to the road junction at Firenzuola, five miles north of the pass. The
once formidable defenses of the Futa

Pass, thus outflanked, lay five miles to
the southwest, so that not only Highway
65 but also Highway 6528, a secondary
road five miles to the east that led from
Firenzuola down the valley of the Santerno to Imola on Highway 9 in the Po
Valley, would soon be open.

The situation offered General Clark
a choice between two courses of action:
either to concentrate, as originally
planned, all of the II Corps' efforts
along the axis of Highway 65 toward
Bologna via the Radicosa Pass, seven
miles beyond the Futa Pass, or divert a

portion of the corps northeastward toward Imola. The breakthrough at Il Giogo in itself pointed to a change in that it suggested a very real weakness along the boundary between the *Tenth* and *Fourteenth Armies,* which roughly followed the Firenzuola-Imola road. A rapid descent into the Po Valley in the vicinity of Imola, General Clark deduced, might take advantage of that weakness and assist the Eighth Army's operations along Highway 9 where General Leese's troops were at that point heavily engaged seventeen miles northwest of Rimini. Once established in Imola, the Fifth Army units could, Clark believed, "dispatch forces as far to the east as possible to gain contact with the rear of the German elements, demolish roads and cover other Fifth Army units that must be immediately sent out to take positions across the main highways to prevent the withdrawal of German forces." General Clark's projected plan envisioned eventual debouchment into the Po Valley at Imola of at least two American divisions, heavily reinforced with tanks and artillery, although the size of the force would depend upon the condition of the road.[11]

As it turned out, the condition of the Santerno valley road was to be the determining factor. Route 6528 was an inferior road, capable in the autumn of 1944, Clark soon learned, of serving as a line of communication for not more than one division under combat conditions. Although Clark told General Keyes to divert a division toward Imola, Bologna and not Imola remained the II

Corps' main objective. The bulk of the II Corps—the 34th, 91st, and 85th Divisions—would continue along the axis of Highway 65 via the Radicosa Pass. As a possible reinforcement to exploit beyond Imola should the lone division moving along Route 6528 get there quickly, he shifted the 1st Armored Division's CCA from the IV Corps to army control.

In turn, General Keyes selected Brigadier General Kendall's 88th Division, which since early September had been in corps reserve, to undertake the drive to Imola. Kendall was to attack early on 21 September through the right wing of Coulter's 85th Division. Attached to the 88th Division for the operation were the 760th Tank Battalion and a company each of the 805th Tank Destroyer and 84th Chemical Battalions. Because of the paucity of roads and trails in the region, Keyes also gave the division two and a half pack-mule companies.[12]

The 88th Division's left flank was to tie in with the right flank of the 85th Division, west of and parallel to the Imola road. The 88th Division would advance at first on a three-mile front that would widen to five miles at the critical point just before descent into the Po Valley. The remainder of Keyes' forces—the 85th, 91st, and 34th Divisions, in that order from a point just east of Highway 65 westward to the Prato-Bologna highway—was to bypass the Futa Pass, if possible, and concentrate on capturing the Radicosa Pass. The 91st Division's 363d Infantry

---

[11] Clark Diary, 21 Sep 44; Jackson, *The Battle of Italy,* p. 276.

[12] *Fifth Army History,* Part VII, pp. 89–91. Unless otherwise indicated the following is based upon this source.

would, in the meantime, deal with any enemy troops still left around the outflanked Futa Pass.

For all the promise afforded by the Santerno valley and Route 6528 as a route over which the Fifth Army might come more quickly to the aid of British forces east of Cesena, the mountainous terrain flanking the valley soon proved to be the most formidable the 88th Division had yet faced in the Italian Campaign. For over half of the thirty miles between Firenzuola and Imola the black-topped road followed the winding Santerno River through a narrow gorge flanked by high mountains with steep slopes cut by narrow ravines through which small streams descended to the river. As far as the village of Castel del Rio, ten miles northeast of Firenzuola, and a road junction beyond it, the last important road junction before Imola, only a few trails led from the main road into the mountains.

Since passage through the Santerno valley hinged upon control of Castel del Rio, General Kendall, who had been in command of the division since July when an ailing General Sloan had returned to the United States, focused from the first on taking the village and nearby road junction. That feat depended on gaining the flanking high ground, a task which he assigned to Colonel Fry's 350th Infantry and to Colonel Crawford's 349th Infantry. The high ground in hand, Kendall planned to send Colonel Champeny's 351st Infantry down the main road to Castel del Rio.[13]

---

[13] 88th Division Opns Rpt and Jnl, Sep 44. Unless otherwise indicated the following is based upon this source.

Battle For the Mountains

During the night of 20 September, Colonel Fry's and Colonel Crawford's regiments moved through the 85th Division right wing from an assembly area near Monte Altuzzo. At dawn on the 21st the two regiments, in columns of battalions, began advancing over narrow mountain trails generally toward Castel del Rio, ten miles away. An intermittent misty rain, interspersed with patches of fog, made movement difficult and at times hazardous for men, mules, and vehicles. Under those conditions it was particularly fortunate that neither regiment encountered significant resistance. Indeed, the two regiments forged so far ahead of the British 1st Division, the adjacent unit of the 13 Corps, as to expose the 88th Division's right flank. That night an infiltrating enemy patrol taking advantage of the gap surprised and captured an entire battalion command post.

Despite that incident Colonel Fry's troops, by the 23d, had captured Monte della Croce, three miles southeast of Castel del Rio, and to the left Colonel Crawford's regiment held Monte la Fine, three miles west of the village. Those successes prompted General Kendall to release Colonel Champeny's 351st Infantry and send it down the main road with the mission of bypassing Castel del Rio and taking the road junction beyond the village. Dawn on the 24th found all three of the 88th Division's regiments deployed across a five-mile front from Monte La Fine to Monte della Croce. (*Map XII*)

The *Tenth Army* left flank had been pushed back to within fifteen miles of the Po Valley, yet there had been no breakthrough. Despite the American success, the enemy still held Castel del Rio and some of the high ground flanking the village and appeared determined to hold. Until the high ground was cleared there could be little additional progress toward Imola.

Just how determined were the Germans began to become apparent on the afternoon of the 24th when the 350th Infantry's 3d Battalion, from positions on Monte della Croce, two miles east of Route 6528, attempted to occupy Monte Acuto, 1,200 yards to the north. For the first time since the operation had begun three days before, heavy fire forced the men to ground. As the fighting intensified, Colonel Fry moved his command post onto Monte della Croce for better control of his forward units in the rugged terrain. Although General Kendall pressed for speedier progress, a chill and damp darkness found the 3d Battalion still well short of its objective. Litter bearers, hampered by uncertain footing on the rain-soaked mountain trails, could scarcely keep up with the battle's casualties.[14]

The Germans Reinforce

The unexpected stiffening of the enemy defense resulted from General Lemelsen having persuaded Field Marshal Kesselring to shore up an admittedly weak sector astride the interarmy boundary, where, since 19 September, contact between the *Tenth* and *Fourteenth Armies* had been limited to radio and telephone. The left wing of the *Fourteenth Army* was in a particularly

difficult situation. For a week it had borne the full weight of the Fifth Army offensive, which, in the words of Lemelsen, the *Fourteenth Army* commander, had "sucked the army dry of available reserves." Unless *Army Group C* provided reinforcements to the *I Parachute Corps* on the *Fourteenth Army*'s left wing, that corps would have to yield more ground.[15]

No doubt remained that all or part of three German divisions then manning the parachute corps front were insufficient to hold much longer against the U.S. Fifth Army's offensive. The *334th Division* held the right wing west of Highway 65; in the center was the *4th Parachute Division*, hard hit in defending Il Giogo Pass; and astride the Imola road, bearing the brunt of the 88th Division's attack, were elements of the *362d Division*, which Lemelsen had shifted from the *XIV Panzer Corps*. All three divisions were sorely in need of rest and replacements.[16]

The situation was serious enough to convince Kesselring to authorize transfer of two additional divisions from the *Tenth Army* to the *Fourteenth Army*. For the *Tenth Army* their loss at that time would not be critical, for the divisions were to come from the relatively quiet mountainous sector of the *LI Mountain Corps* opposite the British 10 Corps on the Eighth Army's left wing. The two, the *715th Infantry* and *44th Reichsgrenadier Divisions*, began moving westward between 19 and 21 September. Meanwhile, Kesselring extended the left flank of the parachute corps eastward

---

[14] 350th Inf Opns Rpt, Sep 44; 88th Div Opns Rpt, Sep 44.

[15] *AOK 14, Ia KTB Anl. 4*, 20–21 Sep 44, *AOK 14*, Doc. 62241/1.
[16] *Ibid.*

GERMAN PRISONERS CAPTURED NEAR CASTEL DEL RIO

in an effort to close the gap between the *Fourteenth* and *Tenth Armies.* [17]

Those measures, however, had come too late to prevent the American 88th Division from thrusting seven miles north-northeastward from Firenzuola to capture the heights of Monte la Fine and Monte della Croce. By 25 September the 351st Infantry had pushed to

within two and a half miles south of Castel del Rio to take the village of Moraduccio. Meanwhile, a battalion each from the *362d* and *44th Reichsgrenadier Divisions* were in place on the summits of hills overlooking the village from the north. [18]

On the same day, General Keyes widened the neighboring 85th Division's front two miles to include Monte la Fine, thereby relieving Colonel Crawford's regiment of responsibility for that feature and slightly narrowing the 88th

[17] *Ibid.* A veteran of the Stalingrad and Cassino battles, the *44th Division* was made up largely of Austrian levies. In recent months it had been brought up to strength with replacements from Germany. The *715th Division* had experienced heavy losses the previous May and June in the battles for the Anzio beachhead.

[18] *AOK 14, Ia KTB Anl. 5,* 26 Sep 44, *AOK 14,* Doc. 62241/1.

Division's front. The corps commander's action underlined for the division commander the determination at both corps and army that his troops reach their objective quickly. General Kendall that afternoon sent General Ramey, his assistant division commander, to Colonel Fry's command post to emphasize the importance attached to a rapid descent into the Po Valley before the Germans could move sufficient reinforcements to parry the thrust. In short, keep moving.

Possibly in reaction to the command pressure, the 350th Infantry the next day captured not only Monte Acuto but also Monte del Puntale on the intercorps boundary, which would facilitate contact with the British 1st Division.

West of the Imola road Colonel Crawford's 349th Infantry captured Monte Pratolungo, then moved a mile northward to take another height west of Castel del Rio. With so much of the flanking high ground in American hands, the Germans had no choice but to abandon Castel del Rio. On their heels, troops of the 351st Infantry moved into the village.[19]

An even more impressive gain developed the next day when men of Lt. Col. Corbett Williamson's 2d Battalion, 350th Infantry, moved two miles beyond Monte Acuto to Monte Carnavale, there to surprise an enemy company digging in on the reverse slope. Driving the Germans from the mountain, the battalion continued toward Monte Battaglia, a mile and a half to the northeast. Passing the night short of the objective, the men on the next day, the 27th, encountered a group of partisans

Monte Battaglia

who claimed to be already in possession of Monte Battaglia. Guided by the partisans along a narrow mule trail, the battalion saw no evidence of the enemy other than sporadic artillery fire.

Reaching Battaglia's crest in mid-afternoon, Colonel Williamson established his command post on the reverse slope. Because he was well in front of the rest of the division, he posted only one company on the summit and deployed the rest to cover a long and tenuous line of communications to the regimental command post. While a few of the partisans remained with the Americans, the others vanished into the mountains, presumably to harass the enemy. From the II Corps commander came the message, "Well done," to which General Kendall and Colonel Fry added their congratulations. Of the

[19] 88th Div Opns Rpt, Sep 44; *Fifth Army History,* Part VII, pp. 93–94.

high ground in the vicinity of Castel del Rio, there remained to the enemy only Monte Capello, two miles west of Monte Battaglia.

The surprising ease with which the 2d Battalion, 350th Infantry, had occupied Monte Battaglia quickly proved deceptive. Hardly had Williamson's battalion consolidated its positions than the Germans, supported by mortar and artillery fire, launched two successive counterattacks. By dark both were repulsed, but through the night enemy artillery fire continued to pick at the American positions.

The gains of the past two days had extended the gap between the 350th Infantry and the adjacent unit of the British 1st Division. Dismounted tank crews of the 760th Tank Battalion, which since the 21st had been engaged in covering the II Corps right flank, tried unsuccessfully to close the gap, which by nightfall on the 27th had grown to almost 5 miles. To close it and assure the integrity of the 350th Infantry's supply lines, General Keyes had to draw upon two armored infantry battalions of the 1st Armored Division's CCA, made available from the Fifth Army reserve.

However vulnerable the open flank, the Germans were unable to take advantage of it. Except for Monte Capello, the Americans at that point held all the dominating heights around the Castel del Rio road junction, and from Monte Battaglia northward the ground descended as the Santerno threaded its way to the Po Valley. In the German rear, partisan units, such as the one that had led the way to Monte Battaglia, increased the tempo of their harassment with each passing day, briefly knocking out communications between the parachute corps and *Fourteenth Army* headquarters. Everything seemed to favor the notion that the admittedly diversionary operation might produce an Allied breakthrough to the Po Valley, a view widely held at Clark's headquarters.[20]

Meanwhile, the main effort of the II Corps had made gratifying, though less dramatic, progress. There the 34th, 85th, and 91st Divisions had gained an average of six miles to close with the high ground flanking the Radicosa Pass. To the east of the II Corps sector, the British 13 Corps' 1st Division, 8th Indian Division, and British 6th Armoured Division, all echeloned to the southeast of the II Corps, pressed on at a somewhat slower pace toward Castel Bolognese and Faenza, four and nine miles respectively southeast of Imola.[21]

Like the Eighth Army, the Fifth Army seemed again to be on the threshold of a breakthrough, but the change in the weather that had brought the Eighth Army to a halt was to have a similar effect on the Fifth Army. For several days rain and fog grounded virtually all Allied aircraft, especially the ubiquitous artillery spotter planes, and sharply limited the effectiveness of Allied artillery fire. The *I Parachute Corps* and *Fourteenth Army* commanders, as had their colleagues on the Adriatic flank, quickly took advantage of the fortuitous break in the weather to reinforce their front.[22]

---

[20]Clark Diary, 21 Sep 44.

[21]*Ibid.*

[22]*AOK 14, Ia KTB Anl. 5*, 28 Sep 44, *AOK 14*, Doc. 62241/1.

The Defense of Battle Mountain

With a battalion each atop Monte Carnevale and Monte Battaglia, or "Battle Mountain" as the troops called it, Colonel Fry's 350th Infantry remained slightly ahead of the rest of the 88th Division. To the left, about a mile beyond Castel del Rio, Colonel Champeny's 351st Infantry had been stalled for several days, and for the next two would try in vain to drive the Germans from Monte Capello, two miles northeast of the road junction. Farther to the left, a mile west of Castel del Rio, Colonel Crawford's 349th Infantry had no more success in its efforts to push forward.[23]

To Colonel Fry the 2,345-foot Monte Battaglia seemed at first an excellent position; its northwestern slopes and those of a northeastward extending spur, the directions from which the enemy might be expected to counterattack, were quite steep. Yet there were some disturbing features. Deeply indented by ravines and gullies, a grass-covered eastern slope seemed to invite the infiltration tactics at which the enemy was so adept. Monte Battaglia's treeless summit offered little cover or concealment; holes and trenches hacked out of the thin soil and an ancient ruin afforded the only shelter from either the elements or enemy fire. Almost from the moment of arrival on the summit, Colonel Williamson's men had spent their time between enemy artillery barrages and counterattacks in digging dugouts and fire trenches. Each passing hour made it clearer to Colonel Fry how difficult Monte Battaglia might

[23] 350th Inf S–3 Jnl, Sep 44. Unless otherwise cited the following is based upon this source.

MEN, MULES, MUD

prove to hold. Well ahead of the other regiments and leading the remaining battalions of the 350th Infantry, the 2d Battalion was exposed to fire from three sides. Supplies and reinforcements could reach the men only over the narrow mule trail along a steep-sided ridge connecting Monte Battaglia and Monte Carnevale. To insure use of that trail, Colonel Fry had to deploy his other two battalions along it, enabling the 2d Battalion to concentrate on the summit. This left him little with which to reinforce if the 2d Battalion got into trouble. Rain and fog closing in on the high ground increased the likelihood of enemy infiltration and made footing on the steep trail doubly hazardous.

Hardly had Colonel Fry on 28 September completed moving his command post forward—to within 400 yards of Monte Battaglia—when a message from Colonel Williamson atop Monte Battaglia told of a "terrific counterattack" and a situation that was "desperate." It was the work of troops of the *44th Reichsgrenadier Division, [Hoch und Deutschmeister]*, a competent unit composed largely of Austrian levies. Supported by intense concentrations of artillery fire, the grenadiers struck in approximately regimental strength from three directions. The worst of it appeared to hit Company G, whose commander, Capt. Robert E. Roeder, led his men in a desperate hand-to-hand struggle against Germans swarming over the positions. When Roeder fell, seriously wounded, his men carried him to his command post in the shelter of the ancient ruin. After allowing an aid man to dress his wounds, Captain Roeder dragged himself to the entrance of the old building. Bracing himself in a sitting position, he picked up a rifle from a nearby fallen soldier and opened fire on attacking Germans closing in on his position. He killed two Germans before a fragment from a mortar shell cut him down. Encouraged by their captain's example, the men of Company G rallied to drive the enemy off the summit and back down Monte Battaglia's slopes.[24]

With reinforcement from a company of another battalion sent forward by Colonel Fry, the 2d Battalion by 1700 had beaten back the counterattack, but throughout the night German artillery fired intermittently on Colonel Williamson's positions. Although painful to the men undergoing it, the fire could in no way compare with that put out by

American guns. The number of enemy rounds falling on Monte Battaglia rarely exceeded 200 a day or a maximum of 400 rounds for the entire regimental sector. On the other hand, on 1 October, when clear skies permitted artillery spotter aircraft to fly, the 339th Field Artillery Battalion alone fired 3,398 rounds.

Fighting erupted again on Monte Battaglia on 30 September, when Germans carrying flame throwers and pole charges with which to burn and blast paths through the American defenses again stormed up the mountain. For a second time they penetrated the 2d Battalion's perimeter and briefly occupied the ruins of the summit, but as before, Williamson's men rallied to drive the enemy back down the mountain. By that time the position of the men on Monte Battaglia had improved through achievements of adjacent units. On the 30th the 351st Infantry at last captured nearby Monte Capello, and elements of the British 1st Division came up on the 88th Division's right flank.

The Imola Drive Abandoned

Despite the 88th Division's improved position, the thrust represented nothing more than a narrow salient achieved at considerable cost. Still, if General Clark should choose to pour in fresh troops to expand the salient into a breakthrough to Imola and Highway 9, it could pose a genuine threat to the Germans. Nevertheless, the Fifth Army commander still saw the Firenzuola-Imola road as incapable of carrying the increased traffic reinforcements would generate. Nor had the thrust shown any indications of softening resistance

---

[24] Captain Roeder was posthumously awarded the Medal of Honor.

in front of the Eighth Army, at that point apparently checked by determined German defenders in the vicinity of Faenza. In view of that situation and of the limited capability of the single road, General Clark had no desire to divert strength from his main effort. What he apparently did not know was that the German command was unable to afford more troops to throw against the salient, and those that had been doing the fighting were close to collapse.[25]

The 88th Division having run into what appeared to be serious opposition and reinforcements having been ruled out, General Clark abandoned the secondary drive on Imola. He now took steps aimed at eventual shift of the left flank of General Kirkman's 13 Corps westward to take over the Santerno valley sector and enable General Keyes to concentrate on the capture of Bologna. The first step was to attach the 1st Guards Brigade of the British 6th Armoured Division, on the 13 Corps right flank, to the British 1st Division to relieve the 350th Infantry on Monte Battaglia. Later the U.S. 88th Division was to be relieved by the British 78th Division from the Eighth Army sector, while the British 6th Armoured Division took its place on the Adriatic flank. The 88th Division was then to join the other divisions of the II Corps in the drive toward Bologna astride Highway 65.

Meanwhile, Colonel Fry had received word that relief for his men on Monte Battaglia was on the way. If all went well, the British might be able to begin

replacing the 350th Infantry the following night. The promise of relief had come none too soon for the 2d Battalion: all officers of Company G had either been killed or wounded and the company was down to only fifty men; Companies E and F were in little better shape.

Although relief was in sight, the 2d Battalion's ordeal was yet to end. Early on 1 October enemy artillery again began falling on Monte Battaglia. After twenty minutes the artillery lifted, and out of the semidarkness the Germans once again attacked up fog-shrouded slopes. This time, however, the sun soon burned off the fog, and a clear sky enabled artillery spotter planes to take to the air to direct defensive fires. With that support the 2d Battalion by midday was able to repel the counterattack and send some 40 enemy prisoners rearward. Shortly after midday officers from the Welsh Guards (1st Guards Brigade) arrived at Colonel Fry's command post to make a reconnaissance before relieving the 350th Infantry.[26]

With the arrival of the British advance party, the defenders of Monte Battaglia had reason to expect they would be off the mountain within twenty-four hours, but that was not to be. Despite aerial bombardment and counterbattery fire, enemy artillery continued to shell the summit, seriously interfering with movement of incoming troops of the 1st Guards Brigade. Three days would pass before the relief was completed and the last of the Americans trudged wearily down the trail from Monte Battaglia. Before the

---

[25] *AOK 14, Ia KTB Anl. Nr. 5*, 3–7 Oct 44, *AOK 14*, Doc Nr. 65922/1.

[26] 350th Inf Opns Rpt, Oct 44.

last men departed on 5 October, the Germans delivered yet another counter-attack, but this time the relieving British troops joined in repulsing it.[27]

Reflecting not only the fighting on Monte Battaglia but also that in the hills west and north of Castel del Rio, where since the 28th the 349th and 351st Regiments had attempted with scant success to extend their gains beyond Castel del Rio, losses were high. Since General Kendall's division had re-entered the line on 21 September until the last man left on 5 October, the 88th Division's three regiments incurred 2,105 casualties. That was almost as many as the entire II Corps had sustained during the six-day break-through offensive against Il Giogo Pass and the Gothic Line. Losses were high too from injury and sickness attributed to the rugged terrain and inclement weather. Fortunately, the Fifth Army replacement pool system, so effective since the beginning of the campaign, still functioned well. Within a few days replacements and hospital returnees brought the 88th Division's regiments back up to strength.[28]

The Germans Take Stock

On the German side, a week after the British 1st Guards relieved the 88th Division, the *98th Division,* recently transferred from the *Tenth Army,* replaced the *44th Reichsgrenadier Division.* Although the *98th Division* earlier had suffered considerable casualties during the battle for the Rimini Line, the division absorbed some replacements during about two weeks out of line.

The division's low combat capability nevertheless remained of concern to General Lemelsen, the *Fourteenth Army* commander. Fortunately for Lemelsen and the *98th Division,* General Clark's decision to concentrate his operations along Highway 65 promised some relief for the *Fourteenth Army's* hard-pressed left flank. The *44th Reichsgrenadier Division,* meanwhile, was moved into army reserve.[29]

As evidence accumulated at Lemelsen's headquarters that Clark had abandoned the thrust toward Imola, the *Fourteenth Army* commander concluded that the Allied command had shifted the focus of its offensive from the Adriatic flank to the central sector south of Bologna, and that as a result, pressure from the Eighth Army might ease to some degree. Field Marshal Kesselring, for his part, was not so sure. He soon realized that Clark had sufficient strength within his own army to mount a major effort against Bologna without any drawing upon the Eighth Army.[30]

Shift Back to Highway 65

Kesselring was right in any case, but particularly so because in blocking the road to Imola the Germans had gravely jeopardized their chances at the Radicosa Pass. There three prominent peaks, Monti Bastione and Oggioli west of the pass and Monte Canda to the east, were potentially formidable defensive positions. Higher than the summits in the Gothic Line, they also presented generally bare, treeless slopes. Yet two

---

[27] *Ibid.*
[28] *Fifth Army History,* Part VII, p. 97.

[29] *AOK 14, Ia KTB Anl. Nr. 5,* 7 Oct 44, *AOK 14,* Doc. 65922/2.
[30] *Ibid.*

of the three enemy divisions defending the pass—the *334th* and *362d Infantry Divisions* (the *4th Parachute Division* was the third)—had taken considerable losses when contingents of the divisions had shifted hastily eastward to help shore up the defenses of the Imola sector. Thus when the three divisions making the American main effort—the 34th advancing on Monte Bastione, the 91st on Monte Oggioli, and the 85th on Monte Canda—converged on the Radicosa Pass, General Schlemm, whose *I Parachute Corps* controlled the sector, saw no alternative to withdrawal. Taking advantage of the fog and rain, which there as elsewhere enveloped the front, the Germans broke contact on 28 September and fell back along the axis of Highway 65 to establish a new line based on the village of Monghidoro, three miles north of the pass.

During the night the 91st Division occupied the Radicosa Pass without opposition, and for the rest of the day, on the 29th, two regiments pushed about two miles north of the pass through a thick fog that reduced visibility to a few yards. To the flanks the 34th and 85th Divisions kept pace in their sectors. All three divisions patrolled, as actively as the persistent fog would allow, in an effort to locate the enemy's new line and determine its strength.[31]

[31] *Fifth Army History*, Part VII, pp. 100–102; Starr, *From Salerno to the Alps*, pp. 138–40.

By the end of September the Fifth Army's objective of Bologna lay a tempting twenty-four miles north of the forward positions of the II Corps astride Highway 65, and on a clear day the British troops atop Monte Battaglia could see the Po Valley only about ten miles away. Yet for all the strategic position of the II Corps, the rest of the Fifth Army was less well situated. To the right, the British 13 Corps, after taking over the Santerno valley sector from the U.S. 88th Division, held a 17-mile front, wider than at the start of the offensive and so extended that the corps' three divisions could make only limited advances. The same could be said of General Crittenberger's IV Corps with a 50-mile front. Already thinly spread, the corps had been weakened more when General Clark had withdrawn part of the 1st Armored Division into Army reserve. Although the IV Corps had been pushing ahead gradually, so that with the exception of Task Force 45 along the coast all units by the end of September had passed through the Gothic Line, the pace was too slow to prevent Field Marshal Kesselring from shifting units from the *XIV Panzer Corps* to reinforce more threatened sectors opposite the U.S. II Corps. With the approach of winter weather, the IV Corps in the coming months could hardly be expected to pick up the pace.

PART SIX

IN THE NORTHERN APENNINES

However highly we must esteem courage and firmness in war, and however little prospect there is of victory to him who cannot resolve to seek it by exertion of all his powers, there still is a point beyond which perserverance can only be termed desperate folly, and therefore can meet with no approbation from any critic . . . .

CLAUSEWITZ, *On War*

CHAPTER XXI

From Ridge to Ridge

In mid-September, while the Fifth and Eighth Armies were battling through the Gothic Line, the Combined Chiefs of Staff met in Quebec for a second time in order to prepare plans for what was then thought to be the final phase of the war against Germany. The Americans, believing that Eisenhower's armies in northwestern France stood on the threshold of victory over the Germans, were at that point inclined to lend a more sympathetic ear to British pleas for bringing the campaign in Italy to a successful conclusion. General Marshall took pains to reassure his British counterpart, Imperial Chief of Staff General Sir Alan Brooke, that the U.S. Fifth Army would not be withdrawn "until General Wilson had completed the campaign then under way to defeat [Kesselring]." The Joint Chiefs of Staff therefore gave tacit support to British proposals for trans-Adriatic operations designed to outflank the Germans in the Po Valley. Landing craft that had been employed earlier in the landings in southern France would be made available for an amphibious operation against the Istrian peninsula; but since that same shipping would soon be needed for the Pacific, the Americans placed a time limit on its availability. For that reason, SACMED (General Wilson) had to make up his mind by 10 October whether to undertake an amphibious assault in the Adriatic.[1]

Heartened by the turn in the fortune of strategies long deferred in the Mediterranean, Churchill summoned Wilson and Alexander to meet with him on 8 October during a brief stopover at Naples en route to Moscow for a conference with Stalin. At Naples the British made a preliminary survey of ways to take advantage of the American offer to support a trans-Adriatic amphibious operation. The survey disclosed two possible courses of action: a seaborne attack on the Istrian peninsula, including the capture of Trieste; or a landing south of Fiume followed by a thrust northward toward that city. Which to choose, the conferees agreed, would depend upon the situation in Yugoslavia and the state of Allied resources in the Mediterranean Theater.

In Yugoslavia the military situation was unclear. German *Army Group E*, commanded by Generalfeldmarschall Maximillian von Weichs and consisting of about 240,000 men divided among 15 German, Bulgarian, Croatian, and Cossack divisions, had withdrawn from Greece to hold temporarily along the line of the Athens-Salonika-Belgrade railroad. Opposing the Germans and their allies were approximately 180,000

---

[1] Matloff, *Strategic Planning for Coalition Warfare, 1943–1944*, pp. 510–11.

guerrillas, mostly under the leadership of Marshal Tito.[2]

As for Allied resources, the situation was equally obscure and full of drawbacks, such as a growing shortage of infantry replacements and the rather short time limit the Americans had placed on the use of the sealift in the Mediterranean Theater. Wilson was asked to undertake a study concerning the feasibility of an amphibious operation in the light of those factors and report his conclusions and recommendations as soon as possible to the CCS in London.[3]

Two days later Wilson submitted a report that offered little comfort to the advocates (Churchill and Alexander being those most prominent) of amphibious operations on the Adriatic flank. For the next few months there seemed, in Wilson's view, little likelihood that the Allied armies in Italy could contribute directly to the outcome of the campaign in northwestern Europe. It seemed more likely that a Russian drive into Hungary would have a far greater chance of forcing Kesseling's withdrawal from northern Italy than anything Alexander's armies might accomplish in the immediate future. Moreover, a Russian advance would very probably cause the Germans to withdraw from the Balkans as well and leave Tito's partisans in control of the Dalmatian coast.

If current Allied operations in Italy continued at their existing pace through November, not until December at the earliest could troops be withdrawn from the front to prepare for a seaborne assault. In Wilson's view, an amphibious operation against the Istrian peninsula was thus out of the question before early spring of 1945. To mount an assault even at that time, Wilson believed, would require reinforcements in the form of three fresh Allied divisions before the end of 1944; for unless the Russians forced Kesselring to withdraw during the winter, the Allies would have to husband existing strength in Italy in order to mount a spring offensive. As originally planned, an amphibious operation against Istria was to be accomplished with one airborne and two seaborne divisions in the assault phase and a fourth division in the follow-up.

As for the second course of action— landing south of Fiume followed by an overland advance on that city—it would depend largely upon German movements in Yugoslavia over the next few months. Even without an airborne division, that operation would nevertheless need the same amount of assault shipping, although possibly somewhat less than an assault against Istria.

Wilson's rather cautious forecast was enough to convince the CCS that hope for a trans-Adriatic amphibious assault had to be abandoned. In the event the Germans failed to capitulate before the end of the year, Eisenhower would need all of his divisions for a major offensive in early 1945. November and December would therefore be crucial months, during which the enemy had to be kept fully engaged on all fronts.

---

[2] DA Pamphlet 20–243, Aug 51, *German Antiguerrilla Operations in the Balkans, 1941–44*; Earl F. Ziemke, *Stalingrad to Berlin: The German Defeat in the East*, Army Historical Series (Washington, 1968), p. 367.

[3] Ehrman, *Grand Strategy*, vol. VI, pp. 37–51. Unless otherwise cited the following is based upon this source.

It was thus vital that the armies in Italy maintain strong pressure against Kesselring "and that," in the words of the CCS, "could be done only by continuing to fight hard in the peninsula itself." Under those circumstances, troops hardly were to be spared from the main battlefront for a major amphibious assault.

In taking their position, the CCS concluded "that the overland offensive in Italy should be relentlessly pursued until the major offensive in northwestern Europe had been launched, probably at the end of December." They recommended that the American sealift be retained no longer in the Mediterranean and that no additional divisions be moved into the theater. The latter point was driven home with additional force two days later when President Roosevelt personally intervened to reject a request from Churchill to divert to Italy two, or possibly three, American divisions about to leave the United States for Europe.

There the matter might have rested but for the Prime Minister's return to the fray on 21 October. On that date, during a stopover on return from Moscow, Churchill once again conferred with his commanders in Naples. The British Prime Minister's appetite for a mid-Danube or Balkan venture apparently had been whetted by the Red Army's recent successes in Czechoslovakia and Hungary and, only the day before the meeting, by the capture, with the assistance of Tito's partisans, of Belgrade. Henceforth the Yugoslav partisans, their ranks swelled to over 200,000, would fight as organized units alongside the Red Army, and Tito and his partisans would no longer be as dependent as before upon Allied aid.[4]

Acting on Churchill's instructions, Wilson proposed to the CCS on 24 October that as soon as the U.S. Fifth Army had captured Bologna, the Allied armies would pass to the defensive along or near the La Spezia–Bologna–Ravenna line. Alexander then could withdraw from the front up to six divisions with which to mount an amphibious operation or an administrative landing along the Dalmatian coast, depending upon the degree of control over the area then exercised by Tito's partisans. Once the Allied landing force had established a beachhead at Zara, three or four divisions could pass through to begin, during the first week of February, 1945, an overland advance on Fiume and Trieste. After the divisions captured Fiume, Wilson projected increasing the Allied force in Yugoslavia to six divisions and with them continuing northward to cut Kesselring's line of communications with Austria and Weichs' *Army Group E* in the Balkans. At the same time, Allied air forces in Italy, with assistance of a partisan uprising, would cut the German escape routes across the Alps, while the remaining Allied forces in Italy crossed the Po Valley. In order to preserve at least the threat of trans-Adriatic operations, Wilson requested permission to keep in the Mediterranean for the time being amphibious shipping for at least one division. Meanwhile, Wilson suggested switching the major air effort from Italy to harass the remaining Germans out of Yugoslavia.

---

[4] DA Pamphlet 20–243; Ziemke, *Stalingrad to Berlin*, p. 367.

Unfortunately for the expectations of Alexander and his staff, that plan found no more favor with the CCS than had the former. Actually, the plan's failure to provide either for a full engagement of Kesselring's armies during December and January, or even a compensating threat to his lines of communications, cost the Mediterranean command its major support within Allied planning circles. Churchill too was deeply disappointed by Wilson's apparent inability to undertake operations across the Adriatic before the end of 1944. On 30 October the Prime Minister observed that "one of the absurd things in all the plans which are submitted by the Mediterranean Command is the idea that if they move in February they will be in time to affect anything."[5]

The Prime Minister at that point somewhat reluctantly threw his support to the Imperial Chief of Staff's proposal that the Allies limit themselves beyond the Adriatic to increasing their support to the Yugoslav partisans. Since Wilson's plan to move on Trieste in February 1945 would be too late to provide the necessary support for Eisenhower's offensive in northwestern Europe, SACMED should, in Churchill's opinion, give up this plan unless somehow he, Wilson, could mount it before the end of the year, and that was manifestly impossible. On the 31st, the JCS concurred in the British proposal and added a recommendation that Wilson be directed to make Bologna his immediate objective. Once having reached the line La Spezia–Bologna–Ravenna, the Allied armies should continue to maintain pressure on Kesselring's armies in order to keep as many Germans as possible tied down in northern Italy.

The German high command, for its part, had a reasonably good notion of Allied capabilities and limitations in the Mediterranean. Allied schemes for trans-Adriatic operations were known to the Germans, but had not been taken seriously. Since the British intervention in the Greek civil war in October, the *WFSt (Armed Forces Operations Staff)* believed that Allied forces in the Mediterranean area lacked the strength to support landings either at Fiume or Trieste while at the same time supporting the Greeks and maintaining an active front in northern Italy. There was also a question whether either the Russians or Tito's partisans, after their capture of Belgrade on 20 October, would still welcome large-scale Allied operations in Yugoslavia and, even more doubtful, in the mid-Danube region, which the capitulation of Rumania in August and of Bulgaria in September had placed in the Red Army's zone of operations. Indeed, the German intelligence officers had accumulated considerable evidence indicating that they would not be welcome.[6]

Oblivious to the strategic debates and analyses in Allied and German planning circles throughout October, the combat troops on both sides attacked and counterattacked in the foggy mountain valleys and ridges of the Apennines and in the flooded plain of the Romagna where September had sloshed to an end with brimming water courses and washed-out roads vying with enemy fire

---

[5] Ehrman, *Grand Strategy*, vol. VI, p. 51.

[6] Greiner and Schramm, eds., *OKW/WFSt, KTB,* IV(1), pp. 566–67.

as obstacles to Allied progress. On the Fifth Army's front Keyes' II Corps had passed through the Radicosa Pass on the heels of a withdrawing enemy, and its four infantry divisions prepared to close the twenty miles separating them from Bologna and the Po Valley. On the Army's right flank the British 13 Corps had assisted its neighbor, as the fall offensive moved into October, by taking over several miles on the right of the II Corps to give the latter a narrower front on which to concentrate its strength. To the II Corps' left Crittenberger's IV Corps had continued, through a series of limited-objective operations, to try to hold enemy divisions on its front and thereby prevent Kesselring from shifting troops eastward to oppose the II Corps. Yet all those efforts had had only limited success, for the flanking units were themselves holding wide sectors with minimum forces and were unable to apply much pressure.

Although September had seen both the Fifth and Eighth Armies make impressive gains by breaking through the Gothic Line and driving, respectively, to within sight of the Po Valley and moving northwestward along Highway 9, some seventeen miles from Rimini to a point just east of Cesena, both were still far from their original goals of destroying the *Tenth Army* south of the Po and pushing the *Fourteenth Army* north of the river. The worsening weather and attrition of the September battles made it seem, at least to General Alexander, that those goals could not be gained in the near future.

On 21 September Alexander informed the Chief of the Imperial General Staff that, although the Allied armies in Italy had inflicted severe losses on the enemy, Allied losses also had been heavy. The Allied commander added that the nature of the terrain in the mountains as well as in the Romagna Plain necessitated a three-to-one superiority in troop strength for successful offensive operations. Since his armies were not likely to achieve that ratio in the foreseeable future, General Alexander believed that decisive victory in Italy was no longer possible before the end of the year—a conclusion that the U.S. Army's Chief of Staff, General Marshall, had reached in August. Five days later Alexander returned to the same theme in a message to the theater commander, observing that "the trouble is that my forces are too weak relative to the enemy, to force a breakthrough and so close the two pincers. The advance of both armies is too slow to achieve decisive results unless the Germans break, and there is no sign of that."[7]

Shortages of replacements had been felt first among Eighth Army units. The Greek 3d Mountain Brigade, which had captured Rimini, had been withdrawn from the front for eventual movement to Greece for use in a civil war then wracking that recently liberated country. An Indian division was also to be withdrawn by the end of October for shipment to the Allied Southeast Asia Command. There was little likelihood that replacements for those units would be forthcoming, for Allied strategic attention, especially that of the Americans, was focused on northwestern Europe, so that Alex-

[7] Ehrman, *Grand Strategy,* vol. VI, p. 37; SAC Despatch, 13 Aug–12 Dec 44, p. 34.

ander had little choice but to somehow raise the needed manpower through reorganization of his own command.

As part of the reorganization, he reduced the British 1st Armoured Division to nonoperational status and transferred its infantry to the British 56th Division to bring it up to strength. Some help was also coming from outside Eighth Army resources. Two infantry brigades, recruited among refugee Poles, joined the 2 Polish Corps, adding approximately ten thousand men to Eighth Army ranks. In October, Clark finally wrung from a reluctant War Department 3,000 American infantrymen. Originally scheduled as replacements for northwestern Europe, they arrived too late to take part in the fighting during that month. General Marshall also repeated his earlier assurances that all U.S. troops then present in Italy would remain until the enemy had been defeated. That at last laid to rest the chronic concern at Alexander's and Leese's headquarters that the U.S. Fifth Army might be moved from Italy and the British left to carry the campaign alone.[8]

In spite of reinforcements for the Polish corps, American replacements, and assurances that U.S. troops would remain in Italy, General Alexander continued to be skeptical about the prospects for his armies. Their great autumn offensive, he reported to General Wilson on 2 October, was "a slow and costly process, and my fears are now that we may not be just quite strong enough to carry it through. I am reinforcing [Clark's] Fifth Army by giving them the [British] 78th Division for 13 Corps. It is my last remaining fully fresh division"[9]

Welcome though the 78th Division was to General Clark, a lone division could not suffice to alleviate the Fifth Army's chronic shortage of infantry replacements, a shortage made increasingly acute with the attrition of each passing day of combat and worsening weather. During the first week of October the II Corps' four infantry divisions had endured a daily average of 550 casualties over and above returns to units from hospitals. At that rate those four divisions, upon which rested the burden of continuing the Fifth Army's fall offensive, could maintain their T/O strength only through 10 October. Without additional replacements, the infantry strength of the divisions would be reduced by approximately 500 men for each day of fighting after that date. Under those circumstances the offensive would eventually have to come to a halt short of its goal.[10]

Keyes' Plan

In spite of the discouraging estimates, Allied commanders saw no alternative to maintaining pressure against the Germans on all fronts. General Clark therefore ordered the II Corps to resume a full-scale effort along the axis of Highway 65 toward the village of Monghidoro, about three and a half miles north of Radicosa Pass.

North of the pass the terrain would be similar to that already encountered by the 88th Division in the Santerno valley. The drainage patterns of the

---

[8] SAC Despatch, 13 Aug–12 Dec 44, p. 34; *Fifth Army History*, Part VII, p. 163.

[9] SAC Despatch, 13 Aug–12 Dec 44, p. 46.
[10] Clark Diary, 6 Oct 44.

streams flanking the highway tend generally northward, with the main ridge lines paralleling the streams. Tributary streams and major transverse ridges cut across those patterns at intervals of three to four miles. Monghidoro, to which the Germans had withdrawn on 28 September, lay on the first of those ridge lines beyond the Radicosa Pass. Four miles to the north of Monghidoro the Germans had prepared a second and even stronger defensive zone along an east-west ridge line running through the village of Loiano. Work on similar defenses had also begun on two other ridge lines at Livergnano and Pianoro, ten and fourteen miles, respectively, north of the Radicosa Pass. To the II Corps commander, General Keyes, it appeared likely that the enemy would attempt to hold each ridge line until forced to withdraw, thereby forcing the Americans to pause and regroup before launching a set-piece attack against each of the positions.[11]

General Keyes planned to employ all four of his infantry divisions. Since that left him no reserve, he instructed each division commander to hold out a regiment and rotate his three regiments in line approximately once every five days. The corps commander had developed that plan to permit launching of coordinated attacks against the successive enemy defensive lines at intervals corresponding to the five-day rotation system. Thus, despite the shortages of infantry replacements, each phase of the offensive would be led by relatively fresh regiments returning to action after a period of rest in reserve.

During the first phase, the 85th and 91st Divisions were to make the main effort east of Highway 65 with the focus in the 85th Division's zone. General Coulter's 85th Division was to attack on a four-mile front whose left flank rested upon the Idice River [a mile east of Highway 65] and whose right flank rested upon the Sillaro Creek, some five miles east of the highway. From positions just north of the Radicosa Pass, General Livesay's 91st Division was to advance on a four-mile front astride the highway. To Livesay's left, General Bolté's 34th Division was assigned a secondary role to cover the corps left flank along the Setta Creek six miles west of the highway. West of the Santerno valley on the corps right flank, General Kendall's 88th Division was to cover that flank and maintain contact with elements of the British 13 Corps in the Santerno valley.

To further secure the flanks of the Fifth Army's main effort and enable Keyes to concentrate solely upon the Bologna sector, Clark removed the 6th South African Armoured Division from IV Corps control and placed it, together with CCB of the U.S. 1st Armored Division, under army control. That change would enable Clark to coordinate the reinforced division's advance more closely with that of the II Corps. Furthermore, the move of the British 78th Division from the Eighth Army to the 13 Corps would enable that division eventually to take over the U.S. 88th Division's sector in the Santerno valley.

As Keyes prepared to resume the drive to Bologna, he was to find some of his logistical problems somewhat eas-

---

[11] II Corps G–3 Jnl and AAR, Oct 44. Unless otherwise indicated the following is based upon these sources.

ier to solve; gasoline, for example, would be more readily available. By 3 October, Fifth Army engineers had completed a 4-inch pipeline as far as Pontedera, eighteen miles east of Leghorn. During the rest of the month the engineers extended the line thirty-six miles farther to the northeast to Sesto, and from there it would be extended during November to the Futa Pass, some twenty miles away.[12]

II Corps Resumes Its Advance

Hard on the heels of a heavy artillery preparation, the U.S. II Corps at 0600 on 1 October attacked across a ten-mile front. For the first hours low clouds and fog concealed all troop movements, but later in the morning the sun broke through and gave both ground and airborne artillery observers excellent visibility. After a week of inactivity, aircraft of the tactical air command also returned to the battle. (*Map XIII*)

The *4th Parachute* and *362d Grenadier Divisions* of the *I Parachute Corps* took the main shock of the American attack along the defensive line hinged on the village of Monghidoro. Both divisions had sustained heavy losses during the earlier battles in defense of the Gothic Line, but they held their ground until the night of 4 October. Then under cover of darkness they broke contact and fell back four miles to the parachute corps' next planned defensive position, based on a ridge running approximately east-west through Loiano.[13]

The next day, the 5th, General Clark

flew to the 91st Division's headquarters, then located in Monghidoro, where he expressed his pleasure over the 91st Division's performance. Well might he have been pleased, for from Monghidoro he caught his first glimpse of the Po Valley and the snow-covered Alps beyond. His goal was at last in sight, however long it yet might take to get there.[14]

Although Schlemm's parachute corps had held Keyes to a four-mile gain in as many days, the Germans had paid a high price. The Americans captured 858 men, and several times that number fell to American fire. But being on the defensive, the Germans could expect their losses to diminish as they fell back into successively stronger positions.

During the first four days of the attack beyond the Radicosa Pass, U.S. casualties had increased over the previous week to a total of 1,734. To that total, worsening weather, rugged terrain, and fatigue added an equal number of nonbattle casualties. Yet unless these figures increased markedly, the II Corps staff calculated that the corps still might debouch into the Po Valley and capture Bologna before the winter snows began.

As the II Corps offensive began its second phase early on 5 October, the focus shifted from Livesay's 91st Division to Coulter's 85th, which was to exploit a salient that had developed during the first phase along a ridge between the Idice and Sillaro Rivers. The division bumped almost immediately into a strong defense based on Hill 578, highest point in the Monterenzio hill mass, five miles east of Liv-

---

[12]Mayo MS, Chapter XV.
[13]*AOK 14, Ia KTB Anl. 5,* 4–5 Oct 44, *AOK 14,* Doc. 65922/1.

---

[14]Clark, *Calculated Risk,* p. 396.

ergnano on Highway 65. Corps intelligence officers identified the defenders as elements of the *362d* and *65th Infantry Divisions* supported by the *98th Infantry Division's 117th Infantry Regiment.* Only on the 85th Division's left, near the Idice River, were significant gains made. There the 338th Infantry drew within striking distance of Monte delle Formiche, the highest ground on the enemy's third line of defense, an east-west escarpment running through the village of Livergnano on Highway 65 eight miles north of Monghidoro.

Meanwhile, along Highway 65, Livesay's 91st Division moved against the village of Loiano, three and a half miles north of Monghidoro. With General Keyes' approval General Livesay temporarily modified the plan for rotating regiments and kept all three on line in order to mount a stronger assault until Loiano was taken.

Overcast skies grounded fighter bombers and most artillery spotter aircraft as the 91st Division attacked at dawn on 5 October behind a 12-minute artillery concentration of a thousand rounds. Thirty minutes later the 362d Infantry's 2d Battalion entered Loiano, where Company L led the battalion house by house through the shattered village. One tank was lost to enemy fire, and that afternoon the assault company called for additional artillery fire to beat off a vigorous counterattack; but by nightfall the battalion had established an outpost line beyond the village and the 363d Infantry moved into reserve for its delayed rest.[15]

Before proceeding against the enemy's next defensive line, the 91st Division had to deal with a secondary delaying position two miles beyond Loiano based on a height, Monte Castellari, that constituted in effect an outpost for the next major defensive line. Hoping to surprise contingents of the *4th Parachute Division* on the height, the 362d Infantry early on 7 October attacked without artillery preparation. Although the terrain was fairly open, frequent spells of rain and fog had the effect of isolating the attacking companies and subjecting them to a deadly mosaic of unsupported fire fights. So poor was visibility that not until the second day was a lone observation aircraft able to get into the air. Nevertheless, using data obtained from shellbursts, partisan reports, and previously collected photo intelligence, supporting artillery fired a daily average of 4,500 rounds. Although unobserved, the fire apparently had effect, for early on 9 October patrols from the 1st Battalion managed to emplace rope ladders on Monte Castellari and reach its crest without serious opposition. Within a few hours the Americans had occupied the last high ground between Loiano and Livergnano, the latter the hinge of the enemy's next defensive zone, four miles beyond Loiano.

Since 5 October the center of the corps front had advanced about three miles, a rate slower than during the first phase of the operation. Although casualties remained high, they totaled some 300 less than during the first four days of the month. Furthermore, evidence was accumulating that the Germans too were having serious manpower problems.

---

[15] 91st Div Opns Rpt, Oct 44. Unless otherwise indicated the following is based upon this source.

The Livergnano Escarpment

The Germans were indeed in a difficult situation, for Schlemm's *I Parachute Corps* had sustained considerable losses during its withdrawal from Monghidoro to the Livergnano escarpment. Kesselring could no longer close his eyes to the fact that Lemelsen's *Fourteenth Army* was facing a major offensive directed against the sector south of Bologna. Although Lemelsen had managed while falling back to keep his front intact, the cumulative effect of combat losses was telling. If the Allied offensive continued undiminished, the situation of the *Fourteenth Army's I Parachute Corps* would soon become critical and that of the *Tenth Army's LXXVI Panzer Corps*, slowly falling back before the Eighth Army on the Romagna Plain, was little better. In a series of visits to corps and division command posts, Kesselring emphasized the importance of defense in depth, rather than continuation of the traditional and costly tactic of trying to cling to the main line of resistance through a succession of counterattacks. If a first counterattack failed, withdrawal to the next defensive position was to follow.[16]

Fortunately for the Germans, by moving into positions along the Livergnano escarpment, they were occupying the strongest natural defensive line since departing the Gothic Line. The escarpment extended eastward about ten miles, from the Monterumici hill mass in the 34th Division's zone to Monte delle Formiche and the Monterenzio hill mass in front of the 85th Division, and ended at Monte delle Tombe and the Gesso Ridge on the II Corps right flank in the 88th Division's zone.

Because the escarpment was particularly forbidding in the central sector flanking Highway 65, General Keyes decided to continue to place the main emphasis of his offensive east of the highway in the 85th Division's zone. The 91st Division astride Highway 65 before Livergnano and the 88th Division in the western edge of the Santerno valley were both to maintain pressure to prevent the enemy from shifting troops to oppose the 85th.[17]

The 85th Division's immediate objective was bald-crested 2,092-foot Monte delle Formiche, atop which stood a tower affording observation as far west as Highway 65 and eastward across the Idice valley. As at Livergnano, an almost perpendicular escarpment blocked the southern and southeastern approaches to the objective, with only a narrow trail that passed through a wooded ravine near the hamlet of Casa del Monte on the southwestern slope to provide a gradual route of ascent. Intelligence had identified the elements of three enemy divisions, the *94th*, *362d*, and *65th Infantry Divisions*, deployed in the vicinity of the objective. The 85th Division commander, General Coulter, planned to employ the 338th Infantry, assisted on the left by a battalion of the 363d Infantry, attached from the neighboring 91st Division.

At 0800 on 10 October the 338th Infantry's 2d Battalion attacked toward Casa del Monte. For the first time in a

---

[16] *AOK 14, Ia KTB Anl. Nr. 5,* 8–9 Oct. 44, *AOK 14,* Doc Nr. 65922/1.

[17] II Corps G–3, Jnl, Oct 44; 85th Div G–3 Jnl & file, Oct 44; 88th Div G–3 Jnl & file, Oct 44. Unless otherwise indicated the following sections are based upon these sources.

week, clear skies enabled tactical aircraft and corps and division artillery to support the attack fully. With the way cleared by overwhelming firepower, Company E encountered little resistance in scaling the escarpment through the ravine to enter Casa del Monte in early afternoon; but then the Germans counterattacked, cutting off part of the company and driving the remainder from the hamlet. While Company E fought to retake Casa del Monte, Company G came through the ravine, swung to the right and by late afternoon had worked up the slopes of Monte delle Formiche to occupy the crest and capture 53 Germans in the vicinity of a small chapel on top of the mountain. Company F arrived in time to help repulse an enemy attempt to regain the position. At that point a fresh battalion took over to continue the advance, but so staunchly did the Germans contest every foot of ground that three days later the battalion was still only a mile beyond Monte delle Formiche.

On the eastern side of the Idice valley the 337th Infantry, with a battalion of the 338th Infantry attached, fought up Hill 578, the highest point in the Monterenzio hill mass. It was midday on 13 October before the objective and 23 prisoners were in hand. Shortly thereafter the battalion captured the hamlet of Poggiolo, a thousand yards northeast of Hill 578. As the 339th Infantry relieved the 337th, German resistance stiffened. As on the western side of the valley, the 339th Infantry could push forward no more than a mile. Having established a firm foothold on the escarpment, the 85th Division could go no farther.

Meanwhile, after the British 78th Division relieved the 88th Division in the Santerno valley, General Keyes shifted the axis of the 88th Division's attack to the northwest, paralleling that of the 85th Division. Encountering increasing resistance in the new sector, the division commander, General Kendall, brought forward his reserve regiment, the 350th Infantry. That regiment's attack early on the 10th got off to a good start but soon ran into difficulty. For the better part of three days neither of the two attacking battalions made any headway until the night of the 13th after a patrol located a gap in the enemy's defenses. Passing through the gap, one battalion crossed the little Sillaro River and by the 15th had advanced over a mile beyond it. That unhinged the opposition holding up the other battalion. As the Germans fell back in some disarray, both battalions were able to pull abreast of the forward positions of the 85th Division just beyond Monte delle Formiche.

The 85th Division's limited success at Monte delle Formiche probably could be attributed in part to the 91st Division's feat in holding the enemy on the Livergnano sector astride Highway 65. It was there that the Germans had expected the Americans to make their main effort and had concentrated most of their strength. An escarpment 3 miles long and nearly 1,800 feet high made the position all the more imposing, but there were two openings through that wall, one at the village of Livergnano where Highway 65 passed, and another a wooded ravine over a mile east of the highway near the hamlet of Bigallo. It was to those two openings that General Livesay, the 91st

Division commander, turned his attention.[18]

To make the attack, General Livesay selected the 361st Infantry. Because of the enemy's strong position, he planned to employ all three battalions in line; the 1st on the left to launch a holding attack against Livergnano, the 2d to pass through the ravine near Bigallo and gain a foothood on the escarpment, the 3d on the right to cover that flank and tie in with the 85th Division's 337th Infantry, attacking Monte delle Formiche. After gaining the escarpment near Bigallo, the 2d Battlion was to turn westward to cut in behind the enemy defending Livergnano, while at the same time the 1st Battalion launched a frontal attack against the town. Because of sharply compartmented terrain, each of the battalions would have to operate pretty much on its own.

As the 1st Battalion prepared to make its holding attack against Livergnano early on 9 October, the Germans countered with an attack of their own, throwing the battalion off balance and off schedule. Although the Americans soon drove the enemy back into the town, the operation was delayed until midmorning. Since the 2d Battalion had already begun its approach march to the Bigallo ravine, it was vital for the 1st Battalion to make up in vigor what it had lost in time. That may have explained why the 3d Platoon of Capt. Chatlain Sigman's Company K, without waiting for artillery support, boldly stormed into Livergnano only to be driven to cover by heavy enemy fire.

Instead of scattering pell mell, the entire platoon except for ten men dashed for cover into the largest building in the town, a four-story house. The other ten men took cover in a nearby pigsty. After dark Captain Sigman led the rest of his company into Livergnano and set up a defense in the four-story house.[19]

Just before dawn the Germans, apparently having pinpointed the company's location, attacked the building but were repulsed. In mid-morning they came back, accompanied by two tanks. Opening fire, the tanks blasted gaping holes in the walls. As the tanks lifted their fire, the German infantry stormed the ruins to overrun and capture Sigman's entire company, except for the ten men still hidden in the pigsty. That night those men managed to slip back to American lines with the story of what had happened to the rest of Company K.

The 2d Battalion, meanwhile, fared better in its efforts to pass through the ravine near Bigallo and reach the top of the escarpment. As the men of Companies E and G prepared to move, a heavy ground fog rolled in. Their approach well concealed, the two companies passed through the ravine early on the 9th and gained the escarpment without opposition. As the men prepared to continue to Hill 592, which overlooked the highway and Livergnano, the providential fog began to disperse. They had gone no more than 500 yards when heavy fire from the flanks pinned them to the ground.

The two companies had come to a halt in what resembled a tilted saucer

---

[18] 91st Div Opns Jnl, Oct 44. Unless otherwise indicated the following is based upon this source.

[19] See Robert A. Robbins, *The 91st Division in World War II* (Washington, 1947), pp. 175–180 (a war correspondent's account of the action).

surrounded on three sides by enemy-held high ground, which included Hill 592 and the village of Santa Maria di Zena on the slopes of Monte delle Formiche, not yet occupied by the neighboring 85th Division. Throughout the day of 10 October the Germans poured small arms, mortar, and artillery fire at the companies. Although the battalion commander tried to get the attack moving again by committing his reserve, Company F, that company by nightfall had still to get beyond the hamlet of Bigallo at the foot of the escarpment. With one company presumably lost in Livergnano, two pinned down on the plateau above the escarpment, and a fourth stalled in Bigallo, the 361st Infantry plainly was in trouble. The only bright spot was that the 85th Division captured Monte delle Formiche to spare Companies E and G from enemy fire from at least that direction.

Early on the 11th fighter-bombers and corps artillery began pounding Livergnano's northern outskirts, apparent keystone of the enemy defenses, but when the stalled companies tried to resume their advance, resistance was much the same as before. In the hope of breaking the stalemate, General Livesay late in the day decided on an envelopment on a wider scale by sending the 1st Battalion, 361st Infantry, farther to the northwest of Livergnano and the 363d Infantry, which had reached the base of the escarpment, to the northeast. Those maneuvers, he hoped, would force the enemy to release his grip on the high ground overlooking Livergnano.

All the while, the situation of Companies E and G atop the escarpment continued to deteriorate. Even though Company F also at last reached the top of the escarpment, most of the men had to be employed in supplying the other two companies and evacuating their wounded. Evacuation was a 12-hour ordeal for both wounded and carriers over a path too steep and narrow for litters; instead, relays of men carried the wounded down the steep draw on their backs. Even an unimpeded company runner required four hours to make the trip.

Concerned that the 91st Division's lack of success at Livergnano was at least part of the reason that the 85th Division had stalled just beyond Monte delle Formiche, General Clark late in the day personally intervened to order General Livesay to reinforce the companies on the escarpment that night. Spurred by command pressure that increased as it moved down the chain of command, the 363d Infantry's Companies A and C began shortly after dark on the 11th to climb laboriously up the escarpment. They made it around dawn, to be followed later in the morning by the same regiment's 3d Battalion. West of Livergnano, the 1st Battalion, 361st Infantry, had at the same time launched its wide flanking attack, but only one platoon managed to scale the escarpment and then had to fall back in the face of an enemy counterattack.

The stubbornness and success of the enemy's defense of the Livergnano sector owed much to the arrival on the scene of the *65th Infantry Division*, a relatively fresh unit that General Lemelsen had shifted from the *XIV Panzer Corps* sector opposite the U.S. IV Corps. Shortly after the II Corps began its attack, the *65th Infantry Division* had entered the line in the center of the parachute corps sector between the *4th Parachute* and *362d Divisions.* [20]

Some dramatic intervention, bringing substantially greater weight of firepower, was needed if the enemy was to be blasted from his strong positions along the Livergnano escarpment. A fortuitous break in the weather made that possible. After having been grounded for much of a week, observation aircraft and fighter-bombers returned to the air in large numbers on the 12th, and for the next four days Fifth Army artillerymen enjoyed their first extended period of observed fire since the breakthrough of the Gothic Line on 17 September. Between 12 and 14 October, for example, the 91st Division artillery fired over 24,000 rounds. Other divisions in the II Corps enjoyed similar support.

Medium and heavy bombers of the MATAF and MASAF also moved to the attack, joining forces to launch an aerial assault code-named PANCAKE against enemy defenses in the Bologna sector. As the skies began to clear, B–26's from the 42d TAC Wing bombed bridges and a factory in the enemy rear area. On the 12th, 177 B–25's dropped over a thousand 500-pound bombs on German supply dumps and barracks areas, while 698 heavy bombers dropped over a thousand tons of bombs on ten enemy targets. Between the 11th and 13th, the XXII TAC flew 880 sorties in support of ground troops. [21]

Behind the impressive artillery fire and air support, General Livesay's 91st Division at last began to extend its precarious foothold on the escarpment. On 13 October the 1st Battalion, 361st Infantry, finally scaled the escarpment to complete the wide outflanking maneuver of Livergnano from the west, and on the following day, the 2d Battalion took Hill 592, outflanked the town from the east, and proceeded westward to reach Highway 65 in the afternoon at a point just north of Livergnano. As might have been expected, the enemy abandoned the town. [22]

To provide a fresher force for bearing the brunt of the continuing drive on Bologna, then only ten miles away, General Keyes directed General Bolté's 34th Division to begin taking over a portion of the front just east of Highway 65 then occupied by a regiment each of the 85th and 91st Divisions. In anticipation of the shift, Keyes earlier had provided General Bolté with the 1st Armored Division's CCA, which enabled the 34th Division to begin the shift even while continuing a relatively low key attack with one regiment against the Monterumici hill mass about two miles west of Highway 65, an extension of the Livergnano escarpment. By nightfall on the 15th the 34th Division was in position in the corps center to lead the fourth phase of the offensive, scheduled to begin the next morning. [23]

[20] *AOK 14, Ia KTB Anl. 5,* 9–11 Oct 44, *AOK 14,* Doc. 65922/1.

[21] In early October the XII TAC's operational strength was increased by addition of the 27th and

79th Fighter Groups. On 19 October the command was officially redesignated the XXII Tactical Air Command (XXII TAC). See Craven & Cate, eds., *AAF III,* pp. 450–54.

[22] 91st Div Opns Rpt, Oct 44.

[23] *Fifth Army History,* Part VII, pp. 137–39.

Action on the Flanks

While the II Corps was extending and widening its salient south of Bologna during the first two weeks of October, the roles of its flanking units—the 6th South African Armoured Division on the left shoulder and the British 13 Corps on the right shoulder of the salient—increased in importance. As evidence of enemy build-up opposite the nose of the salient accumulated, General Clark deemed it vital that enemy units elsewhere be tied down to prevent further shifts to the defense of Bologna.

After taking over the bulk of the Santerno valley sector from the American 88th Division, the British 78th Division had continued to move gradually northward. Elsewhere on the 13 Corps front the British 6th Armoured Division's 1st Guards Brigade in the Monte Battaglia sector, the British 1st Division astride Highway 934 (running down the Senio valley toward Castel Bolognese in the Po Valley), and the 8th Indian Division operating astride Highway 6521, which follows the Lamone valley to Faenza on Highway 9, made scant progress. Reduced by detachments to only one brigade, the British armored division could do little more than cover the 13 Corps' right flank and maintain a tenuous contact with the Eighth Army's 10 Corps. The 13 Corps commander, General Kirkman, had been forced to draw so heavily on his less important right flank to reinforce his left that the armored units in the mountains on the right could do little more than follow up enemy withdrawals.

To the II Corps' left the 6th South African Armoured Division under Fifth Army control held a five-mile sector from the Setta Creek, on the corps' left boundary, westward to the Reno River, right boundary of the IV Corps. Advancing mainly astride Highway 6620, about two miles west of the Setta Creek, the South Africans kept the 34th Division left flank well covered during the first half of October. On the 13th they launched a set-piece attack to gain control of a ridge between the Setta Creek and the Reno River, the key to which was Monte Stanco, a 2,200-foot summit at the midpoint of the ridge. Well supported by corps and army artillery, the division made its heaviest attack since the desert campaign of El Alamein. By nightfall Monte Stanco was in hand, along with more than a hundred prisoners from both the *94th Grenadier* and the *16th SS Panzer Grenadier Division.* A relatively modest gain, the capture of Monte Stanco nevertheless opened up the eastern portion of Route 6424, a lateral road connecting Highways 64 and 6620 so that trucks no longer had to make the long haul over a tortuous secondary road. The division's right was at that point securely tied in along the Setta Creek with the U.S. 1st Armored Division's CCA, holding the 34th Division's former sector on the II Corps left flank. On the South African division's left flank the attached 1st Armored Division's CCB maintained contact with the U.S. IV Corps along the Reno River.

Holding a 50-mile front extending from the Reno valley to the coast just north of Viareggio, the IV Corps during the first half of October had the mission of covering the Fifth Army's vital supply line from the port of

INDIAN INFANTRY IN NORTHERN APENNINES

Leghorn to the central sector north of Florence, and tying down enemy units that otherwise might move against the II Corps. That was all the corps could hope to accomplish, for after losing the 6th South African Armoured Division and the 1st Armored Division's CCB to army control, the corps had a strength of little more than a reinforced division.

The Personnel Problem

In mid-October the prospect loomed ever larger that unredeemed battle

losses would ultimately bring both the Fifth and Eighth armies to a halt. During the six days from 10 through 15 October, for example, the four infantry divisions of the II Corps sustained 2,491 casualties. When combined with even larger losses of the first nine days of the month, the prospects for the future were disturbing. While some of the losses could be made up by men returning to duty from hospitals and by replacements trickling into the theater, the theater's replacement pool that had served so well since the beginning of the Italian campaign was for the first time showing signs of depletion. If losses continued at their current rate and the replacement pool was not replenished, Clark warned Alexander, the Fifth Army's offensive toward Bologna and the Po Valley would fall short of its goal.[24]

As for the Eighth Army, the battles to turn the Gothic Line, break into the Romagna Plain, capture Rimini, and push beyond had been, in the words of General McCreery, the new Eighth Army commander, "as bitter as at Alamein and Cassino." A total of 14,000 combat casualties since the beginning of the Gothic Line offensive bore witness to the truth of his observation.[25] Yet after the capture of Rimini the Eighth Army's losses had declined sharply, while American losses had increased (13,082 American and 2,451 British).

Even as General Clark launched the third phase of his attack toward Bologna on 10 October, British Prime Minister Churchill made his appeal to his American ally for "two, or better still, three" American divisions with which to sustain the Italian campaign.[26] General Marshall's negative response to the plea rested upon the same strategic principle that had supported his espousal of Operation ANVIL in early 1944. Northwestern Europe and not the Mediterranean was the main theater of operations, and a "diversion of divi-

6TH SOUTH AFRICAN ARMORED DIVISION TANKS ASSEMBLED FOR ATTACK

sions to Italy would withhold needed fresh troops from southern France while committing those forces to the high attrition of an indecisive winter campaign in Italy." In any case, in Marshall's opinion, additional men would no longer affect the outcome of the Italian campaign in 1944, for by mid-October the time had already passed when the Allied armies could drive the Germans from the peninsula and cross the Alpine passes along the Italo-German frontier, already blocked with snow.[27] No matter what successes Alexander scored before the end of 1944, the strategic picture in the Mediterranean at that stage of the war would not, in Marshall's opinion, be altered. Yet campaigns, like other human enterprises, once undertaken, often claim their advocates long after

---

[24] Clark Diary, 15 Oct 44.

[25] Alexander, *Despatch,* p. 71. On 1 October General Sir Oliver Leese had handed over command of the Eighth Army to General Sir Richard L. McCreery, former commander of 10 Corps. General Leese then departed to command British forces in Burma.

[26] SHAEF Diary, Bk. XIII, 10 Oct 44, pp. 1775–76, Msg. PM to Eisenhower for Marshall.

[27] *Ibid.*, 17 Oct 44, Msg. Marshall to Eisenhower.

the undertaking has served its purpose. That was the case in Italy.

Unrealistic Strategies

Against this somber background and in spite of General Marshall's pronouncement, the Allied command in Italy, in a mood reminiscent of that of army commanders on the western front during World War I, prepared in mid-October to have one more try at capturing Ravenna and Bologna. General Alexander's plan called for the Fifth Army, after debouching from the mountains, to join with the Eighth Army in encircling and destroying the elusive *Tenth Army*. The hope was utterly forlorn. Neither south of Rome, during the pursuit to the Arno, nor following the breakthrough of the Gothic Line had the two Allied armies succeeded in so disorganizing the enemy as to cut off and destroy any significant portion of the German armed forces. In mid-October, following several weeks of minor advances won at the expense of numerous casualties and at the end of ever-lengthening supply lines, that possibility seemed even less likely than before.

By that time not only Allied but also German strategy in northern Italy had come to assume an air of unreality. Instead of withdrawing to the line of the Alps, a superb natural defensive barrier from which the Austro-German armies had kept the Allies at bay through much of World War I, the German high command continued to employ in defense of northern Italy many units whose presence on other fronts, while not sufficient in themselves to turn the tide of battle, could at least

have won for the Germans needed time to extricate their armies. Hitler's determination to keep alive Mussolini's shadow republic and to maintain a grip on the admittedly large agricultural and industrial potential of the Po Valley seems to have been among the reasons for Kesselring's back-to-the-wall defense in the Apennines and along the swollen rivers of the Romagna Plain. As with the Allies, there was also possibly the additional factor, as already noted, that campaigns often tend to develop their own partisans; the German armed forces too had their Mediterranean faction.

Falling back on what surely seemed to the Allied commanders an interminable series of defensive positions, Kesselring's strategic and tactical problems presented him with fewer difficulties than those of his Allied counterparts. But he had other problems, among them the unexpected loss of one of his army commanders. In mid-October General Lemelsen, his *Fourteenth Army* commander, became ill and was evacuated to a hospital. To take command of the *Fourteenth Army* until his recovery, Kesselring selected the *XIV Panzer Corps* commander, General von Senger und Etterlin.[28]

Taking stock of the situation, Senger compared the situation on the Bologna sector to a thick cloth incessantly jabbed by a spear. For a time the cloth's elasticity would prevent the spear from breaking through, but eventually the cloth would give way.[29]

To prevent the fabric of the Bologna sector from being pierced, von Senger

---

[28]*AOK 14, Ia KTB Anl. 5,* 14 Oct 44, AOK 14, Doc. 65922/2.

[29]Senger, *Neither Hope nor Fear,* p. 276.

promptly reinforced with the *16th SS Panzer Grenadier* and *94th Divisions* from his own corps, where those units had been engaged defending against the attacks of the South African armoured division. On 15 October the two German divisions entered the line south of Bologna, thereby increasing to six divisions the German forces opposing the U.S. II Corps. When General Clark's G–2 informed him that, in addition to those two divisions, the *29th Panzer Grenadier* and the *90th Division* were also

on their way from the *Tenth* to the *Fourteenth Army* sector, the Fifth Army commander noted despairingly in his diary, "this seems more than we can stand." Clark might also have added a dictum attributed to the elder von Moltke: no plan survives contact with the enemy.[30]

---

[30]*AOK 14 Ia KTB Anl. 5*, 14–15 Oct 44, *AOK 14,* Doc. 65922/1; Clark Diary, 17 Oct 44. See also Correlli Barnett, *The Swordbearers*, (New York, 1964), p. 24.

CHAPTER XXII

Toward a Winter Stalemate

The Eighth Army Advance to the Ronco

However gloomy General Clark's assessment on 17 October of his army's situation, he could take some comfort in a decision by the Eighth Army commander two days earlier to reinforce his army's left wing south of Highway 9. Deducing that the foothills of the Apennines offered better operational terrain than the waterlogged plain and flooded rivers north of the highway, General McCreery decided to relieve the British 10 Corps on his left—which had the 1st Armoured Division in line with the 4th Indian Division in reserve—with the relatively fresh 2 Polish Corps, controlling the 3d Carpathian and 5th Kresowa Divisions. After several weeks in army reserve, the Polish corps could be expected to add considerable strength to the advance on the better drained ground south of the highway where the British 5 Corps and its 10th Indian and British 46th and 56th Divisions were currently operating. The 1st Canadian Corps, with an armored and two infantry divisions, continued to hold the remainder of the Eighth Army's front from Highway 9 to the coast, seven miles to the northeast.[1]

Starting from the vicinity of Galeata, twenty miles southwest of Cesena, the Polish corps' two divisions proceeded in a northerly direction along two roads running through the Rabbi and Bidente river valleys toward Highway 9, just east of Forli. Even as General Clark made his pessimistic assessment on 17 October, the 5th Kresowa Division led the 2 Polish Corps in a night attack from Galeata toward Montegrosso, a 2,100-foot peak three miles north of Galeata dominating the area between the two river valleys. Realizing that an Allied success at Montegrosso would threaten to turn the front east of Cesena opposite the Canadian corps and British 5 Corps, the Germans fought stubbornly. Polish troops nevertheless drove the last of the Germans from Montegrosso on 21 October and cleared the way for an advance by the 3d Carpathian and 5th Kresowa Divisions toward Forli, on Highway 9. Even so, it took the Poles five days to cover the six miles from Montegrosso to the town of Preddapio Nuova, on the banks of the Rabbi River nine miles south of Forli. Although the Polish troops swept into the town without opposition on the 26th, a strong German counterattack forced them to yield it later, so that not until the next day was the town retaken and secured. That was as far as the Polish corps could advance for the rest of the month.

Even as the Poles had moved against Montegrosso, the British 5 Corps to the right, from a line just beyond the Rubicone River some 7 miles southwest of Cesena attacked toward Cesena and the Savio River flowing west of the town in a northerly direction. Astride

---

[1] SAC Despatch, Aug–Dec 44. Unless otherwise indicated the following is based upon this source.

Highway 9, the Carleton and York Regiments of the 3d Infantry Brigade on the Canadian corps left flank also moved towards Cesena. On 19 October the 5 Corps' 46th Division entered the town from the south, while the Canadians came in from the southwest. There was no opposition, for the *LXXVI Panzer Corps* was already withdrawing beyond the Savio. The next day the British 4th Division relieved the British 46th Division to make an assault crossing of the Savio, but long-range enemy artillery prevented British engineers from bridging the river until the 23d. In the meantime, the 4th Division held its bridgehead while the Canadians pulled up along the east bank of the Savio. During the same period, the remainder of the Canadian corps, including the 2d New Zealand Division, advanced to the Savio north of Cesena and on the 20th captured the seaport of Cesenatico, nine miles northeast of Cesena.

On 23 October the British 4th Division crossed the Savio over recently completed bridges south of Cesena to begin an advance toward the Ronco River, nine miles to the northwest. Reaching the river late on the 25th, the British waited until dark before crossing in assault boats to establish bridgeheads on the west bank; but German counterattacks over the next two days forced the British to retire to the east bank. From then until the end of the month, the 4th Division lay there, while heavy rains washed out bridges and roads to the rear, disrupting lines of communication.

To the 4th Division's left and on somewhat higher ground, the 10th Indian Division had somewhat more to show for its efforts. After crossing the Savio on the 20th, the Indians swung northwestward toward Meldola on the Ronco River some six miles south of Forli. Since the high water had swept down to the plain below, the Indian division was able to ford the Ronco near Magliano, two miles north of Meldola. Unlike their neighbors on the right, the Indians retained their bridgehead beyond the Ronco. On the 26th, they widened their bridgehead to include the town of Meldola, where resistance continued until Indian successes on high ground to the north forced the Germans on the 30th to abandon their last foothold in the town.

After capturing the port of Cesenatico on 20 October, the Canadian Corps pushed on for the next three days along the coastal road (Highway 16) as far as the Savio and the town of the same name, located near where the river enters the sea. That advance outflanked defenses northeast of Cesena and hastened the enemy's withdrawal toward the Ronco, seven miles to the northwest.

As the Eighth Army's three corps pulled up to the Ronco, General McCreery decided that the time had come to relieve the 1st Canadian Corps, which had been in contact with the enemy since the beginning of the Gothic Line offensive on 25 August. The relief took place on 28 October just short of the Ronco River by Porter Force, the task force commanded by Lt. Col. A. M. Horsbrugh Porter and composed of the 27th Lancers and 3d Canadian Armoured Reconnaissance Regiments, supported by some armor as well as by Canadian artillery and engineers. The task force's mission was to demonstrate vigorously along the Ronco to conceal withdrawal of the Canadians.[2]

The next day the British 5 Corps began extending its right flank northeastward as far as the coast to take over the Canadians' former zone of operations. That would ultimately give the 5 Corps a 20-mile sector, with the 4th British and 10th Indian Divisions and Porter Force in line. The 2d New Zealand Division, in the meantime, moved into 5 Corps reserve. Since the Germans were only too anxious to keep the Ronco between themselves and the Allied forces, the relief of the Canadian corps apparently went undetected.

The end of October found the Eighth Army with three instead of four corps in contact and at a standstill across a 30-mile front extending from the Adriatic coast about eight miles south of Ravenna, southwestward along the Ronco, to within sight of Forli on Highway 9 and ten miles southwest of Faenza, longtime goal of the British 13 Corps, operating on the U.S. Fifth Army's right wing.

The state of the weary Canadian corps was symptomatic of the Eighth Army's plight. General McCreery no longer had fresh formations to throw into battle. Of his reserve divisions, the British 1st Armoured and the 56th were non-operational because of lack of replacements, the 4th Indian Division was scheduled to leave shortly for Greece, and the 46th Division had just been relieved from the line. Instead of armor exploiting across the Romagna Plain as envisioned in the plan for Operation OLIVE, the Eighth Army's

push from the Marecchia to the Ronco had been a frustrating trial by mud from one brimming water course to another.

The II Corps' Plan

General Clark's Fifth Army meanwhile continued its equally frustrating ordeal in the high mountains of the Northern Apennines. There the main terrain problems continued to be the dearth of roads and trails and a seemingly endless series of ridges and peaks dominating narrow valleys. Against three peaks making up a ridge extending from Monte Adone (three miles northwest of Livergnano) via Monte Belmonte in the center to Monte Grande (eight miles northeast of the village), General Keyes, the II Corps commander, focused his attention. He planned to attack the mountains in turn, starting on the 16th with Monte Belmonte two miles northeast of Highway 65 overlooking the Zena Creek valley; then Monte Grande, dominating a narrow valley leading to Highway 9 in the vicinity of Castel San Pietro; and finally Monte Adone, just west of Highway 65.

General Keyes planned to employ against Monte Belmonte General Bolté's 34th Division, yet to play a major role in operations of the II Corps. With Monte Belmonte occupied, the division was to continue down the Idice valley to cut Highway 9 southeast of Bologna. The division was to have first priority on artillery and tactical air.[3]

Since other divisions of the corps had

---

[2] Nicholson, *The Canadians in Italy*, p. 596.

[3] II Corps Opn Rpt, Oct–Nov 44; *Fifth Army History*, Part VII, pp. 149–51. Unless otherwise cited the following sections are based on these sources.

already borne so much of the battle, General Keyes had little choice other than to employ the 34th Division, even though that move boded ill for the success of the new phase of the offensive. The division was, in General Clark's opinion, "diseased," suffering from the chronic malaise of battle weariness. Overseas for two and a half years and veterans of some of the hardest fighting since the previous winter, surviving old-timers in the division had long been clamoring to go home, and replacements soon sank into a similar state of low morale. Yet the 34th Division, even without the detached 135th Infantry, was still numerically strong.[4]

Artillery of the adjacent 85th and 91st Divisions was to support the 34th Division until Monte Belmonte was captured, whereupon emphasis was to shift to the 88th Division for an attack against Monte Grande, thence to the 91st Division and the third objective, Monte Adone. In the last attack the 1st Armored Division, on the 91st's immediate left, was to assist by a holding attack on the left flank of the corps.

General Bolté planned to attack with his remaining two regiments abreast. On the right and holding the widest portion of the division sector, the 168th Infantry, in a daylight operation, with a company of the 757th Tank Battalion in support, was to lead the attack astride a broad ridge forming a divide between the Zena Creek and the Idice River. The regiment's objective was Monte della Vigna, a 1,512-foot knob a little over a mile north of Monte della Formiche and a mile and a half south

of the division's objective, Monte Belmonte. General Bolté expected that timely capture of Monte della Vigna would assist a later attack planned for the 133d Infantry. Assigned a narrower sector for greater concentration of firepower, that regiment was to make the main attack against Monte Belmonte by night.

As the II Corps completed preparations to make the last thrust toward Highway 9 and the Po Valley, both Generals Clark and Keyes looked to Kirkman's British 13 Corps to continue its role of tying down the *334th, 715th,* and *305th Infantry Divisions.* That was about all Kirkman's corps was capable of. Its right flank remained virtually stationary below Route 67, where rugged terrain and modest combat strength permitted little movement, and its left wing was being constantly extended northward to keep pace with the 88th Division and to cover the II Corps' right flank.

The II Corps' Attack Renewed

From a line of departure about a half mile north of Monte della Formiche, the 168th Infantry, with three battalions abreast, attacked at 0500 on 16 October. Hardly had the attack begun when a German antitank gun disabled the lead tank of the supporting company from the 757th Tank Battalion. The disabled tank blocked the narrow road and prevented other tanks from coming forward, breaking up the closely knit tank-infantry team upon which battlefield successes had come to depend. A heavy volume of enemy mortar and small arms fire prevented the infantry from continuing alone. By nightfall only the regiment's 2d Battal-

---

[4] Clark Diary, 16 Oct 44. See also General Keyes' report on 34th Division cited in Truscott, *Command Missions,* pp. 461–62.

ion had managed any penetration of the enemy's positions.

While that fight raged, men of the 133d Infantry assembled for their night attack. As the battalions moved into assembly areas late in the afternoon, fighter-bombers of the XII TAC dropped hundreds of high explosive and newly-introduced napalm bombs in a saturation assault against Monte Belmonte. The aircraft flew 137 sorties and dropped 72 tons of high explosive bombs and 94 napalm fire bombs against known enemy positions on and near the objective. Shortly after the aerial attack, all guns of the supporting corps artillery opened fire.

As darkness fell over the shattered terrain, searchlights of antiaircraft units illuminated the sky to provide artificial moonlight. At 2000 the 133d Infantry attacked in a column of battalions with the 2d leading. Hardly had the first men crossed the line of departure when a heavy mortar and artillery concentration fell on one company, disorganizing the platoons and causing several casualties, among them the company commander. The battalion commander shifted that company to become his reserve.[5]

That was to be the enemy's sole interference that night. By dawn on the 17th Company G had almost reached the crest of Hill 401, the southernmost spur of the Monte Belmonte ridge, without physical contact with the enemy. Then suddenly, out of a thick fog that had enveloped the objective, the Germans counterattacked. Overrunning Company G, the enemy inflicted numerous casualties and captured four

officers and over a score of enlisted men. The counterattack also cut off the commander of Company E and twenty of his men, who would have to wait for nightfall before infiltrating back to the 2d Battalion command post. When night came all survivors fell back to reorganize in a small ravine on Monte Belmonte's southwestern slope. Meanwhile, to the left rear, the 1st Battalion had gained a little over a mile to reach the village of Zena, near which a bridge crossed the Zena Creek, while the 3d Battalion came to within supporting distance on the 2d Battalion's right.[6]

Reports of the 133d Infantry's setback on Monte Belmonte's fog-shrouded slopes reached General Clark shortly after he learned of the arrival of the *29th Panzer Grenadier Division* opposite the II Corps and of the coming commitment of the *90th Panzer Grenadier Division*. The Fifth Army commander telephoned General Alexander that night to complain bitterly that his army would soon reach the limits of its endurance unless the Eighth could siphon off some of the enemy's strength. The appeal was in vain, for the Eighth Army already was fully committed.

The combined pressures of the Allied forces was insufficient to force the Germans to relax their grip on the ridges and summits south of Bologna, as became clear when at dawn on 18 October the 34th Division's 133d Infantry renewed the assault on Monte Belmonte. Again the regiment attacked in a column of battalions, with the 2d still leading. Because of persistent fog and rugged terrain, the battalions had about as much difficulty determining their

---

[5] 133d Inf Opns Rpt, Oct. 44.

[6] *Ibid.*

own locations as those of the elusive enemy. Under these circumstances, the 133d Infantry's experienced commander, Colonel Braun, decided in mid-afternoon to halt, to reorganize, and to replenish supplies before renewing the attack after nightfall.[7]

For the renewed assault, Colonel Braun committed the 1st Battalion, which since the morning of the 18th had been in reserve near the Zena bridge. To cover the regiment's left flank, the 1st Battalion was to seize high ground north of Zena, while the 2d and 3d Battalions continued toward Monte Belmonte.

Hardly had nightfall come when the enemy revealed that he had used the interval to reinforce his positions. A heavy mortar and artillery barrage hit two companies of the 3d Battalion, whereupon enemy tanks moved to within 100 yards of the lead battalions to deliver point-blank fire. Plagued by mud and poor trails, Braun's own supporting tanks and tank destroyers were too far to the rear to be of any assistance, and enemy guns matched the artillery supporting the regiment round for round. In the face of that kind of opposition, General Bolté on 20 October directed both the 133d and 168th Regiments to halt in place and regroup, the latter having at last completed clearing the enemy from Monte della Vigna but too late to be of much help to the 133d Infantry.

On the 34th Division's left, the 91st Division had also encountered heavy enemy fire—the heaviest since September—as that division attacked along the axis of Highway 65 to assist the operation against Monte Belmonte. In General Livesay's sector much of the fire seemed to be aimed at the Livergnano bottleneck with the purpose of blocking the flow of supplies along the highway. By nightfall on 19 October the 91st Division had managed to advance only three miles beyond Livergnano. West of the highway enemy forces in the vicinity of Monte Adone, two miles northwest of Livergnano, also checked General Prichard's 1st Armored Division.

The enemy's success in thwarting all three divisions comprising the left wing of the II Corps was all the more disturbing because of gathering evidence that either the enemy's *16th SS* or *29th Panzer Grenadier Division* was approaching or already in the area. Lacking reserves, General Keyes deemed he had little choice but to order the three divisions to assume what he called "an aggressive defense."[8]

Progress on the II Corps right wing meanwhile showed greater promise. There General Coulter's 85th Division had moved rapidly along a ridge east of the Idice Valley and on the 19th captured Monte Fano, one of the spurs of a ridge three miles northeast of Monte della Formiche. From that position the division was in a favorable position to assist General Kendall's 88th Division on the right during its forthcoming operation against Monte Grande, three miles to the northeast.

German Countermeasures

The growing resistance the II Corps had encountered since 17 October

---

[7] 133d Inf Opns Rpt, Oct 44. Unless otherwise indicated the following is based upon this source.

[8] *Fifth Army History,* Part VIII, pp. 155–56.

stemmed largely from Field Marshal Kesselring's calculated risk (taken in mid-October) to thin out Senger's *XIV Panzer Corps,* opposite the IV Corps, by shifting major combat units to the sector opposite the U.S. II Corps. For the time being the *Tenth Army* reserve would have to be prepared to support the remaining sectors of *Army Group C's* front.[9]

Underlying Kesselring's decision was the belief that the most immediate threat to the integrity of the front lay in the Bologna sector, where an Allied breakthrough would menace the rear of that part of the *Tenth Army* falling back northwestward along the axis of Highway 9. In the Bologna sector itself the greatest hazard was a deteriorating situation east of Highway 65, especially along the interarmy boundary where, for the past few weeks, contact between the *Tenth* and *Fourteenth Armies* had been only intermittent.[10]

It had also not escaped Kesselring's attention that on the Bologna sector American operations for a month had been carried out by the same four divisions. Since their cumulative losses had undoubtedly been heavy, the German commander confidently expected that if his troops could only hold out a bit longer, the Fifth Army offensive would soon lose momentum.[11]

Since the beginning of October the *16th SS Panzer Grenadier Division* (its departure for France delayed) and the *65th, 94th,* and *334th Divisions* had been moving from the *XIV Panzer Corps* to the *I Parachute Corps* south of Bologna.

From the *Tenth Army* had come the *29th Panzer Grenadier Division,* while the *90th Panzer Grenadier Division* had already been ordered from Italy's northwestern Alpine frontier and could be expected to arrive in the central sector by 22 October.[12]

While those changes were taking place, Senger (in Lemelsen's absence still acting commander of the *Fourteenth Army*) had also shifted all available artillery from his panzer corps to support the Bologna sector. Only one battery remained to protect the Abetone Pass on Highway 12 that runs from Lucca in the Arno valley to Modena on Highway 9. That fact caused neither Kesselring nor Senger concern, for they were well aware of the IV Corps' weaknesses and were confident that, in the off chance that the IV Corps should spring to life, the *XIV Panzer Corps* could afford to yield considerable ground before reaching terrain critical to the integrity of the *Fourteenth Army's* front.[13]

New Plans for II Corps

On 19 October General Clark determined to make a third attempt to break through to Highway 9, this time on Keyes' right wing southeast of Bologna where the operations of the 85th and 88th Divisions—the Castor and Pollux of the Fifth Army—had uncovered a weak point. Clark also hoped to force the *Fourteenth Army* commander to spread his forces over a wider front by stepping up efforts by the IV and 13 Corps on the II Corps flanks. Meanwhile, General Lemelsen had returned from the hospital to resume command

---

[9] *AOK 14, Ia KTB Anl. 5,* 17 Oct 44, *AOK 14,* Doc. 65922/1.

[10] *Ibid.,* 18 Oct 44.

[11] *Ibid.,* 19 Oct 44.

[12] *Ibid.,* 17 Oct 44.

[13] MS # C–064 (Kesselring).

of his army, and Senger reverted to his corps command.

In accordance with Clark's instructions Keyes worked out a three-phase operation with Kendall's 88th instead of Bolté's 34th Division making the main effort in the first phase—this time to capture Monte Grande, three miles east of Monte Fano and only six miles southwest of Castel San Pietro on Highway 9. Reinforced by the 85th Division's 337th Infantry, the 88th Division was to attack on the night of 20 October. In the second phase Kirkman's 13 Corps was again to shift westward to take over Monte Grande while the 88th Division reverted to corps reserve for a well-deserved rest. The 34th Division, in the meantime, was to continue its efforts to capture Monte Belmonte, and the 91st Division was to improve its positions east of the Savenna Creek.[14] In the third phase, emphasis was to shift back to the corps left wing as the 91st Division attacked Monte Adone, two miles northwest of Livergnano, and continued on to Pianoro, four miles north of Livergnano and only eight miles from Bologna. With Monte Adone in hand, Keyes expected the harassing artillery fire on Livergnano and Highway 65 to cease and permit a concentration of arms and men along the highway for a final drive on Bologna.

Thus far the II Corps had failed to take any of the three objectives Clark had designated on the 15th. In hope of breaking the impasse by conquest of Monte Grande, General Keyes during the night of 19 October assembled all the firepower available, including

tactical aircraft that hammered at the enemy positions in and around Monte Grande throughout the day. Taking off at 15-minute intervals, fighter-bombers of the XXII TAC flew 158 sorties and dropped tons of napalm and high explosives on targets marked by divisional artillery with colored smoke. Beginning at 1700, the 88th Division's artillery, reinforced by two medium batteries each from the 248th and 178th Field Artillery Battalions, as well as seven light batteries and a medium battery from the 85th Division, began preparatory fires. The guns fired steadily for an hour against 42 selected targets while 23 supporting tanks and destroyers fired harassing missions against targets north and east of Monte Grande. That made for a total of 8,400 rounds fired in one hour. As that fire ceased, corps artillery took up the chorus with an extensive counterbattery program against all known enemy gun positions. In hope of stimulating the division commander's zeal, General Clark on the eve of the attack visited the 88th Division's command post to assure Brigadier General Kendall that his second star of rank was waiting atop Monte Grande.[15]

Morale heightened by the vast display of firepower, the infantrymen of the 349th Infantry set out in darkness and through a driving rainstorm toward Monte Grande and Monte Cerrere, the latter the high point of a spur a thousand yards southeast of Monte Grande. On the left, Company A, commanded by 1st Lt. John Ernser, met no resistance as it led the 1st Battalion up

[14] II Corps Opns Rpt, Oct 44.

[15] 88th Div Opns Rpt, Oct 44. Clark, *Calculated Risk,* p. 400.

Monte Cerrere. The approach concealed by the heavy downpour and darkness, Ernser's men shortly before dawn quietly surrounded a large building on the crest, believed to be the hiding place of any surviving enemy soldiers. When daylight revealed the American presence, eleven haggard Germans filed out of the building with hands high in surrender.[16]

On the right, the 2d Battalion meanwhile made the main attack against Monte Grande. Under fire from the time of crossing the line of departure a mile south of the objective, Company G three hours after midnight nevertheless occupied Hill 581, an intermediate knob just south of Monte Grande. From there the company was able to cover the advance of Companies E and F as they in turn came up on the left to assault the main objective. As the companies advanced, supporting artillery fire continued to crash onto the enemy's positions on the mountainside and his line of communications.

The effectiveness of that close fire support was amply demonstrated when at first light Company F's 1st Platoon leader, 1st Lt. Jack S. Parker, led his men onto Monte Grande's summit without firing a shot. The rest of the company followed to move quickly over the crest and occupy the northern slope, while Company E dug in on the reverse slope. As the inevitable counterattack ensued in no more than platoon strength, the Americans handily repulsed it, killing four of the enemy and scattering the rest back down the northern slopes of Monte Grande.

---

[16] 349th Inf Jnl and file. Unless otherwise cited the following section is based upon this source.

By midday on the 20th the 349th Infantry's thrusts on Monte Grande and Monte Cerrere had driven a deep salient into the *I Parachute Corps* from southeast of Bologna and advanced the Fifth Army's front to its closest point yet to the city. That afternoon General Kendall, his second star assured, widened the salient by sending the 350th Infantry, assisted by the 85th Division's 339th Infantry, against Montecuccoli on a ridge extending westward from Monte Grande into the 85th Division's sector. That objective soon fell to the 350th Infantry, whose 2d Battalion shortly after dark secured the village of Farneto, a mile west of Monte Grande. Over the next two days General Kendall moved the attached 337th Infantry up on the 350th Infantry's left to take over that part of the 350th Infantry's sector west of Farneto, leaving the 349th and 350th Regiments with narrower fronts for exploiting north from Monte Grande.

General Clark underscored the first real success the II Corps had achieved since mid-October by visiting the 349th Infantry's command post, where he personally congratulated Colonel Crawford and his men. With the example of Monte Battaglia still fresh in mind, Clark cautioned Crawford to be prepared to defend against almost certain German efforts to retake the height.

Clark's disappointment with the 34th Division's failure to take Monte Belmonte was as acute as his delight with the 88th Division's triumph on Monte Grande. Thus far, every effort by the 34th Division either to drive the enemy from Monte Belmonte or to proceed along the ridge south of Zena Creek had failed. There were, moreover, ominous signs of enemy buildup opposite the II Corps' left wing west of Highway 65.

Since the current offensive had taken only one of three planned objectives, Clark decided to forego taking Monte Belmonte and Monte Adone and instead to concentrate strength on the corps right, where the enemy seemed to be weakest. On 22 October Clark directed Keyes to advance his right wing as far as Monte Castelazzo, some three miles to the northeast of Monte Grande, to a general line extending from Monte Castelazzo in the 88th Division's zone of operation northwestward three miles to Ribiano Hill in the 85th Division's zone. Those two heights, three and four miles respectively, southwest of Castel San Pietro on Highway 9, represented the enemy's last possible defensive positions short of that highway and the Lombard plain. If Keyes' corps could occupy those features before the end of the month, the Fifth Army might yet be able to debouch onto the plain before winter's snows prevented further operations in the Northern Apennines. Clark meanwhile instructed Kirkman to assist Keyes' thrust beyond Monte Grande by massing at least four brigades of the 13 Corps west of the Santerno River and by taking Monte Spaduro and a line of hills southwest of the Sillaro to increase pressure along the road between Castel del Rio and Imola.

In preparation for this final effort, Keyes instructed the 34th and 91st Divisions and 1st Armored Division to regroup to enable the 91st Division to withdraw two regiments into corps reserve, which Keyes might draw upon to repel a possible spoiling attack against

the II Corps left flank. If no spoiling attack developed the reserve of six battalions might be used to exploit the expected capture of Monte Castelazzo and Ribiano Hill. Three divisions were to make only holding attacks, to include continuing efforts by the 34th Division to take Monte Belmonte.

Shortly after dark on 22 October, the 85th and 88th Divisions began the new main effort toward high ground northeast of the three heights of Monte Grande, Monte Fano, and Monte Cerrere that the divisions had previously captured. Coulter's 85th Division on the left wing was to take Hill 459, a mile northeast of Monte Fano. Kendall's 88th Division on the right was to capture Hill 568, about a thousand yards northeast of Monte Grande. Control of Hill 568 would enable Kendall to dominate Montecalderaro, a hamlet at the junction of two secondary roads leading to Highway 9, about five miles away. From the hill Kendall was to send a force a mile and a half to the northeast to occupy high ground overlooking the hamlet of Vedriano within a mile of the division's final objective, Monte Castelazzo. A second force, moving northeast from Monte Cerrere, was to cover the division's right flank along the Sillaro River.

Since Colonel Crawford's 349th Infantry had just taken Monte Grande and Colonel Fry's 350th had seen considerable action since the heavy fighting on Monte Battaglia earlier in the month, Kendall selected Colonel Champeny's 351st Infantry to lead the attack toward Hill 568. Crossing the line of departure on Monte Grande's forward slope shortly after nightfall, the 351st Infantry's 3d Battalion slipped through the fog and darkness to reach the objective before the enemy awoke to what was happening. By 0730 on the 23d the battalion had rounded up twenty-eight Germans and sent them to the rear as prisoners. Hill 568 was in hand.[17]

Meanwhile, the fog that had helped the Americans gain Hill 568 concealed the arrival of first units of the *90th Panzer Grenadier Division*. Two counter-attacks followed, but by 1015 both had been repulsed, and Hill 568 remained in American hands.[18]

The unexpected show of enemy strength nevertheless disturbed Colonel Champeny, who decided to continue the attack with a fresh unit, the 2d Battalion, while the 3d defended Hill 568. That night the 2d Battalion, in a column of companies with Company G leading, set out for Vedriano, a mile and a half to the northeast. Evading harassing fire from two bypassed enemy strongpoints, the company entered the village early on the 24th. Forty Germans surrendered, including two officers, but when the other companies sought to join Company G in the village fire from the now alerted defenders of the two strongpoints stopped them outside.[19]

That hindrance meant that Company G alone would have to defend Vedriano against almost certain enemy efforts to retake it. The company seemed at first to be quite capable of doing the job, for after repulsing one small counterattack during the forenoon, Company G's commander reported that everything was under control. Yet soon

thereafter an intercepted German radio message, expressing concern over Vedriano's loss and noting that the village was a vital point in the German defenses, struck an ominous note.

In early afternoon the regimental executive officer, Colonel Yeager, telephoned Colonel Champeny from the 2d Battalion command post that Company G in Vedriano had just received a German parliamentary. As events unfolded, the Germans claimed to have surrounded Vedriano, but they would allow Company G to withdraw in exchange for the 40 prisoners captured that morning. Colonel Champeny brusquely rejected the offer and began planning to relieve the beleaguered company with his reserve battalion supported by tanks. Companies E and F at the same time continued their efforts to reach Company G. Tactical aircraft also flew over the area to bomb and strafe the enemy's position.

While all that was going on, Company G's radio went off the air. An intercepted German radio message revealed the company's fate. Vedriano had been retaken and 80 Americans captured.

From the 1st Battalion in reserve on Monte Grande, Colonel Champeny brought forward a company to assist Companies E and F in their efforts to retake Vedriano; but intense small arms, artillery, and mortar fire brought all three companies to ground at the western base of the hill mass on which Vedriano stood. As withering fire produced numerous casualties, Champeny reluctantly accepted that the enemy had so reinforced that his regiment unassisted would be unable to regain the village.

[17] 351st Inf. Jnl and file, Oct 44.
[18] *AOK 10, Ia KTB Anl.* 9, 23–24 Oct 44, AOK 10, Doc Nr. 63426/1.
[19] 351st Inf Jnl and file, Oct. 44.

Kesselring Hospitalized

The vigorous enemy reaction at Vedriano stemmed largely from two factors: the arrival during the night of 22 October of the *90th Panzer Grenadier Division* and the shifting of the *Tenth Army's* boundary westward to bring the *I Parachute Corps* under that army's control. The latter move put the army group's two most active fronts under a single commander and through the remaining days of October facilitated the German defense.[20]

After overseeing the boundary change, Field Marshal Kesselring left by auto during the evening of 23 October for a conference with General Vietinghoff, the *Tenth Army* commander. Traveling under blackout conditions through heavy fog over roads crowded by military traffic, the field marshal's car collided with a towed artillery piece. Gravely injured, Kesselring was taken to the nearest field hospital and later transferred to a general hospital at Ferrara, where he was to remain for several months.[21]

Kesselring's abrupt departure necessitated further command changes. On 27 October General Vietinghoff took over Kesselring's place in command of *Army Group C.* General Lemelsen then moved over from his *Fourteenth Army* command to take over the *Tenth Army,* while von Senger und Etterlin again moved from the *XIV Panzer Corps* to command the *Fourteenth Army.*[22]

The Attack Continues

While those changes occurred on the German side, General Kendall prepared to resume the effort to retake Vedriano. Throughout the 25th, the 351st Infantry's 1st and 2d Battalions assembled west of Vedriano, while from Hill 568 Colonel Champeny's tanks and tank destroyers, together with division artillery, shelled the enemy in the hope of softening up the objective for a night assault by the 1st Battalion. Early that evening, with the 2d Battalion covering the left flank, the 1st Battalion moved against Vedriano, Company A advancing astride a road directly toward the village, Company B trying to outflank it from the west. Company C remained in reserve.[23]

Company B managed to work its way halfway up the western slope of the hill before heavy machine gun fire forced a halt. Most of the company, made up largely of recent replacements, scattered, leaving behind only a handful of veterans, some of whom joined forces with a company of the 2d Battalion while others drifted over to Company A, which also came to a halt short of the objective.

Out of an early morning fog on the 26th, the Germans counterattacked. Overwhelming one of the companies of the 2d Battalion and the handful of survivors of Company B that had joined the company, the enemy slipped away into the mist with their prisoners before anybody could come to the rescue. Only one man escaped capture.

Except for the 3d Battalion's success on Hill 568, Colonel Champeny had little other than severe losses to show

---

[20] *AOK 14, 1a KTB Anl. 5,* 24 Oct 44, *AOK 14,* Doc. 6922/1. Effective the evening of 25 October, *XIV Panzer Corps* took over the sector formerly held by *LI Mountain Corps,* which then assumed control of the panzer corps' former sector on the *Fourteenth Army's* front.

[21] *AOK 10, KTB Anl. 9,* 23 Oct 44, *AOK 10,* Doc. 6345/1.

[22] *Ibid.,* 27 Oct 44.

[23] 351st Inf Jnl and file, Oct 44. Unless otherwise cited the following is based on this source.

Truck Crossing a Steel Truss
Bailey Bridge in Apennines

for his drive toward Monte Castelazzo.
Three rifle companies had been severely crippled, while the enemy still
held Vedriano. Furthermore, adjacent
units had fared no better. Crawford's
349th Infantry had been unable to
advance much beyond Monte Cerrere
and the 85th Division's 337th Infantry
had its hands full merely holding onto
its newly won position just north of Hill
568. Four miles southeast of Monte
Grande troops of the British 13 Corps
had taken Monte Spaduro on the night
of 23 October but had been unable to
advance farther down the Santerno
valley.

During the morning of the 26th,
torrential rains began to fall. Within a
few hours rising waters had washed out
three bridges across the Sillaro. That, in

effect, severed the line of communications of General Kendall's 88th Division
and forced General Keyes to cancel
plans for the 91st Division's 362d Infantry to pass through the 88th Division's
349th Infantry for an advance down
the Sillaro valley. The washouts spelled
trouble for all the troops, for only small
amounts of ammunition and rations
could be hand-carried across hastily
constructed footbridges. From there
jeeps could carry the supplies as far as
Monte Grande, but the last moves
would have to be by pack mules. Under
the circumstances little possibility existed
of maintaining a volume of logistical
support sufficient to sustain the offensive toward Castel San Pietro and
Highway 9. That afternoon, after obtaining General Clark's approval, General Keyes directed Coulter and Kendall to withdraw their troops to defensible ground and dig in.

The sudden deluge of rain caused
similar difficulties for the Germans. In
the *I Parachute Corps* sector rising waters
in the Idice River valley on 27 October
collapsed a dam near the village of
Budrio, ten miles northeast of Bologna,
flooding a wide area behind the German lines. For the next three days all
work on defensive positions came to a
standstill while German engineers and
Italian civilians toiled day and night to
divert the flood waters and repair the
dam. Other streams washed out bridges
and isolated units. For a full week
troops on both sides would be able to
pay less attention to fighting each other
than to repairing the ravages of
weather.[24]

---

[24] *AOK 10, Ia KTB Anl. 9,* 27 Oct 44, *AOK 10,*
Doc. 63426/1.

An effective combination of determined enemy defenders, adverse weather, and irreplaceable personnel losses had brought the II Corps to a halt on the northern slopes of the Apennines within sight of the Po Valley, which during rare intervals of clear weather weary American infantry could glimpse just over four miles away. From the beginning of the offensive on 10 September until 26 October, the four infantry divisions that bore the main burden of the offensive had incurred 15,716 casualties, most of them in the combat arms. Of those, 5,026 were from the 88th Division, which had fought so hard, but in vain, for Vedriano. At about the same time that Keyes ordered Kendall to go on the defensive, the 88th Division commander had reported that his division was understrength by 1,243 officers and men. The already strained theater replacement pool would be hard put to make up such shortages. Furthermore, the long periods of cold, rainy weather had sapped the strength of the combat troops and brought a steady increase in nonbattle casualties; indeed respiratory diseases, trench foot, and psychiatric disorders had exacted a heavier toll than had enemy fire. Even so, the battle casualty rate had been higher than for any comparable period since the Salerno landings in September 1943. Allied commanders generally agreed that the Fifth Army's replacement system would soon break down with this casualty rate.[25]

Compounding the difficulties, significant shortages developed toward the end of October in artillery ammunition, forcing General Clark to impose especially severe restrictions on the use of medium caliber artillery ammunition. Heavy caliber ammunition was less of a problem, for early in the month the II Corps had lost its last two heavy battalions to the campaign in southern France, and the Fifth Army's remaining heavy artillery was in the attached British 13 Corps.[26]

Washed-out bridges might be rebuilt and weary units reformed after a few days' rest, but what could not be quickly restored was the diminished offensive power of four infantry divisions, understrength and exhausted after more than six weeks of almost uninterrupted combat. The predictions Clark had made on two occasions in early and mid-October that the Fifth Army's offensive could not be maintained beyond the end of the month without additional infantry replacements appeared now to have been fulfilled.[27] To make matters worse, the Eighth Army advance along the axis of Highway 9 had bogged down along the Ronco River at about the same time as Clark's army came to a halt southeast of Bologna. As General Clark was later to observe, "We didn't fully realize it then, but we had failed in our race to reach the Po Valley before winter set in. Our strength was not enough to get across the final barrier to which the enemy clung."[28]

As October came to an end, the II Corps settled down into defensive posi-

[25] *Fifth Army History*, Part VII, pp. 163–64; Charles M. Wiltse, *The Medical Services in the Mediterranean* (Washington, 1965), p. 427; Devers Diary, 19 October 1944, in CMH.

[26] *Fifth Army History*, Part VII, pp. 165 and 258–59.

[27] Clark Diary, 6 and 15 October 1944.

[28] Clark, *Calculated Risk*, p. 401.

tions encompassing Monte Grande and Monte Belmonte that afforded control of the commanding heights east of Highway 65. Monte Belmonte finally had fallen to the 133d Infantry after loss of Monte Grande and Hill 568 prompted German withdrawal. West of the highway control of the heights was reversed, for the Germans still held Monte Adone and the Monterumici hill mass.

To the west the positions of the II Corps tied in with those of the 6th South African Armoured Division, under Fifth Army control. Throughout the month the South Africans, reinforced by the 1st Armored Division's CCB, had covered the left flank while the 13 Corps' 78th Division covered the right. Given the limited strength of those units and the unfavorable terrain over which they had to operate, they could do little more than try to keep up enough pressure to prevent the enemy from shifting units from their fronts to reinforce the sector opposite the II Corps. Since most, if not all, of the German units moving to halt the II Corps had come either from the *Tenth Army* opposite the Eighth Army, or the *XIV Panzer Corps* opposite the U.S. IV Corps, they apparently fulfilled their mission.

Operations on the IV Corps Front

Still holding an elongated 50-mile front, extending from Forte dei Marmi on the Ligurian coast to a line just short of the Reno River in the east, General Crittenberger's IV Corps had two general missions: protecting the Fifth Army's left flank and organizing and training the two recently arrived divi-

sions—the Brazilian Expeditionary Force's 1st Division, commanded by Maj. Gen. J. B. Mascarenhas de Morales, and the American 92d Division. As part of that training, regimental size combat teams were to participate during October in limited-objective type operations.

The operations began on 6 October when the BEF's 6th Regimental Combat Team attacked a sector held by the Italian *Monte Rosa Alpine Division*. Crossing the Lima Creek at Bagni di Lucca, 12 miles north of Lucca, the Brazilians advanced northward up the Serchio valley for eight miles against light resistance. Showing little eagerness to stand and fight, the Italians fell back slowly into the high mountain fastness they knew so well. On the 11th the Brazilians captured the town of Barga, and at the end of the month the operation came to an end.[29]

At the same time, Maj. Gen. Edward M. Almond's Task Force 92 began an attack on the coastal flank to afford combat experience for a contingent of the 92d Division. The task force consisted of the 92d Division's 370th Regimental Combat Team and the 2d Armored Group made up of the 434th and 435th Antiaircraft Artillery Battalions, converted into infantry and supported by the 751st Tank Battalion and the 849th Tank Destroyer Battalion. The mission was a limited objective attack toward the town of Massa, six miles northwest of Forte dei Marmi, but rather than launch a frontal attack against the still intact Gothic Line de-

[29] J. B. Mascarenhas de Moraes, *The Brazilian Expeditionary Force by Its Commander*, 2d Ed., Rio de Janeiro, 1965, pp. 57–73.

fenses south of Massa, General Almond decided first to seize Monte Cauala and Monte Castiglione, overlooking the coastal corridor from the east.[30]

In a driving rain on 6 October the two antiaircraft battalions first launched a diversionary attack along the coastal plain but managed only to reach the outskirts of Querceta, a mile from their starting point at Forte dei Marmi. In the mountains overlooking the coastal plain the 370th Infantry, plagued as were all units of the 92d Division with a long-standing malaise growing from mutual distrust between mainly white officers and black enlisted men, made only slight progress on Monte Cauala's slopes. After several days of desultory fighting during which the 370th Infantry twice won and twice lost its objective, the regiment at last regained Monte Cauala's summit on the 12th and held. After General Almond called off the attack on 23 October, the sector settled down to relative inactivity for the next month and a half.[31]

The Offensive Is Halted

Although the weather that had helped bring the Allied ground forces to a halt had also impeded operations of the supporting tactical air force, aerial strikes against enemy lines of communications had continued throughout October. During the month MATAF dropped 4,500 tons of bombs, claimed 44 bridges destroyed and another 83 damaged, rail lines cut in 240 places, and a large number of locomo-

tives and rolling stock destroyed. In the same period, MASAF dropped 2,500 tons of bombs on strategic targets throughout northern Italy, including the Alpine passes. As for the Luftwaffe, there was virtually no sign. Except for occasional forays over Allied lines by not more than two or three aircraft, the German Air Force had vanished from the skies of Italy.

Yet Allied domination of the air could not disguise the stalemate on the ground. In tacit recognition of that fact, General Wilson directed the Allied armies in Italy to halt their offensive on 27 October with little chance that the situation would change before winter. Operations in northwestern Europe had first call on replacements, and a worldwide shortage of ammunition among the Allies meant Italy with its low strategic priority would suffer most. Chronic personnel and ammunition shortages, as well as the onset of winter weather in the mountains, the SACMED informed the Combined Chiefs of Staff, would prevent the Allied armies from carrying offensive operations on the Italian front beyond the line Ravenna–Bologna–La Spezia, and if that line were not reached by mid-November, the Allied offensive might have to be brought to a halt short of even that objective. That report hardly could have filled the hearts of the Combined Chiefs with dismay, for even though La Spezia, Bologna, and Ravenna remained in German hands, the Allied armies in Italy had already gone beyond the goal set for them at the Teheran Conference in November 1943: the Pisa–Rimini Line.[32]

---

[30] *Fifth Army History*, Part VII, pp. 172 and 178; Ulysses Lee, *The Employment of Negro Troops*, UNITED STATES ARMY IN WORLD WAR II, (Washington, 1966), pp. 544–51.

[31] *Ibid.*

[32] SAC Despatch, Aug–Dec 44, p. 48; Matloff, *Strategic Planning for Coalition Warfare, 1943–44*, p. 353.

Another factor ameliorated the failure to reach the Po Valley before winter set in: a serious food shortage in the Allied-occupied regions of Italy that threatened the civil population with the prospect of near starvation. Having to feed the population of the yet unconquered regions of northern Italy as well would have further stretched already inadequate foodstocks.

As early as July, General Wilson, at the suggestion of the Allied Control Commission, had taken note of the growing seriousness of the food situation by announcing his intention to increase the daily bread ration from 200 to 300 grams per person. When that increase was projected to include the regions of northern Italy still under German control, it became clear to Allied planners that the grain import program would have to be heavily augmented, even though the area normally exported food. Since under the most favorable conditions the Italian harvest would provide only 160 grams of the requirement, imports of over a million and a half tons would have been needed to meet the 300-gram goal for all Italy, and a world-wide shortage of both wheat and shipping made that an impossible task.[33]

Under those circumstances the Combined Chiefs saw the failure of General Alexander's armies to occupy northern Italy, with its heavily populated industrial region, as something short of regrettable. The Allied command could take some comfort in the fact that the enemy would have to draw upon its own limited resources to sustain the region through the winter.

---

[33] Coakley and Leighton, *Global Logistics and Strategy, 1943–45*, pp. 773–779.

CHAPTER XXIII

Stalemate in the Mountains and on the Plain

Alexander Develops His Strategy

By the end of October it seemed unlikely that the Allied armies would wrest control of the Po Valley from the Germans before winter set in. Except on the Adriatic flank, the Allies still faced the enemy in the Apennines. The Eighth Army had been checked along the Ronco River, and south of Bologna the Fifth Army had been ordered to go onto the defensive. For the latter there loomed the uninviting prospect of yet another winter in the mountains.

Yet the situation, oddly enough, best served the overall Allied strategy for the Italian Theater—that of containing the maximum number of German divisions. For to hold in their present positions, the Germans would have to use all of the divisions presently in northern Italy. If driven from these positions, the German armies would fall back first to the Po, then the Adige, river lines. These formidable natural obstacles could be held with considerably fewer troops than the existing line in the Apennines and along the Ronco. Divisions spared by more favorable defensive lines then could be released to other more threatened fronts. Thus, instead of the Allies containing the Germans, the latter would be containing the Allies.

Looking forward to resumption of a full-scale offensive in the spring, General Alexander hoped to avoid such a reversal of roles by reviving his earlier concept of a trans-Adriatic operation by the Eighth Army. He envisioned such an operation as a large-scale turning maneuver to outflank the German forces in northern Italy and to open up the road into the mid-Danube basin and possibly reach Vienna before the Russians.[1]

According to General Alexander's calculations, the Germans should be able to hold the line of the Adige with eleven divisions, and the U.S. Fifth Army would be adequate to fully engage them. This would free the Eighth Army for operations across the Adriatic. Belgrade had fallen to the Russians and their partisan auxiliaries on 20 October, and Tito's partisans were clearing the Dalmatian coast of the enemy. General Alexander believed he would soon be able to occupy the Yugoslav ports of Zadar, Split, and Sibenik with light forces. In February, as part of the final Allied offensive, the Eighth Army could pass through these ports and advance rapidly on Fiume and Ljubljana and thence into lower Austria. Thus would Alexander bring the Germans to decisive battle on

---

[1] Alexander *Despatch*, pp. 76–78; Operations of the British, Indian, and Dominion Forces in Italy, Part III, Sec. B, pp. 62–97. Unless otherwise indicated the following is based upon these sources.

ground of his choosing rather than along fortified river lines, such as the Po or the Adige. Important to the realization of this strategy, however, would be the early capture of Bologna, needed as a base for the Fifth Army's operations against the Po and the Adige lines, and the capture of Ravenna, required as a base, along with Ancona and Rimini, for the Eighth Army's trans-Adriatic operations. Thus it was, that instead of settling down into defensive positions at the end of October, the two Allied armies would prepare for or continue offensive operations in their respective sectors for another month.

As his armies paused in the mountains and on the plain, General Alexander presented to Generals Clark and McCreery his plan for the capture of Bologna and Ravenna. The Eighth Army left wing was to move first, crossing the Ronco and capturing Forli, four miles to the northwest. This feat would open up Route 67 between Florence and Forli and improve lateral communications between the two armies. At the same time, the Eighth Army right wing was also to continue astride Highway 16 (the coastal road) to capture Ravenna, the northeastern terminus of Route 67. These operations on the Eighth Army's front could be expected to siphon off enemy strength from before the U.S. Fifth Army, which, in the meantime, was to withdraw units from the line to rest and prepare for resumption of the drive on Bologna. On army group order, General Clark was to return these units to the line as secretly as possible to make what was expected to be the final effort to capture Bologna before winter set in. On 29 October, at a conference with

his two army commanders at army group headquarters, General Alexander agreed to extend the cut-off date for the forthcoming operations from 15 November to 15 December. This would give Clark more time to rest his exhausted divisions, and McCreery more time to take Forli and Ravenna. General Alexander's only caveat—but an important one—was that the operations were to be undertaken only if the weather were favorable and if they (the two armies) had "a good chance of success."[2]

The Capture of Forli

For the Forli operation, General McCreery planned to employ only two of his four corps, the British 5 and the Polish 2. The remaining corps, the Canadian 1st Corps and the British 10 would be given an opportunity to rest, the former eventually to be used against Ravenna and the latter to be moved before the end of the year to Greece, together with the British 4th and 46th Divisions and the Indian 4th Division, to enhance the British role in the escalating civil strife in that recently liberated country.

Since 27 October, through a series of limited-objective operations, the 5 Corps had managed to improve its position along the Ronco. The most important of these, on 31 October, had been the 4th Division's crossing of the river east of Forli and the 10th Indian Division's crossing of the Ronco at Meldola, six miles southeast of Forli. The latter division, after crossing the river, turned northwest and made its way as far as Collina, halfway to Forli. On 2 Novem-

---

[2] Alexander *Despatch*, p. 76.

ber the British 46th Division came forward to relieve the Indian division and to join the 4th Division in a final converging assault on Forli from the southeast and the east. (Since both British divisions were slated eventually for duty in Greece, McCreery wanted to make full use of them before their relief.)

On the 5 Corps' left in the Apennines foothills south of Highway 9, the 2 Polish Corps, meanwhile, prepared to resume its advance in the direction of Faenza, thirteen miles northwest of Preddapio Nuova where the corps had halted on 27 October. General McCreery had assigned the Poles the task of clearing high ground south of the highway between Forli and Faenza, eight and a half miles northwest of Forli.

A period of clear, cold weather moved into the area on 6 November, and the fighter-bombers of the DAF emerged in force to support the Eighth Army across its entire front. As the bombs rained down on the enemy lines, the 4th Division initiated the 5 Corps' main attack from the vicinity of Carpena, just southeast of the Forli airport, a little over two miles from the city. On the division's left, the 46th Division attacked from a point about two miles south of Forli. As a diversion to these two operations, a brigade from corps reserves, the 56th Division, launched a holding attack along Highway 9. Southwest of the 5 Corps the Polish 5th Kresowa Division had reached Monte Maggiore and the village of San Zeno in Volpinara, two and a half miles northwest of Predappio Nuova. This advance outflanked the Forli sector to the south and gravely threatened the integrity of the German defense of Forli. Now threatened on three sides, the Germans in Forli broke contact and withdrew during the night of 8 November to the line of the Montone River where it turns northward some three miles northwest of the city. The 4th Division entered Forli early on the 9th.

When the British attempted to exploit beyond the city, however, they were checked briefly by the Germans who, in the meantime, had established themselves behind the flooded Montone. Nevertheless, by the 12th the British managed to cross the river at Ladino, four miles southwest of Forli. Two days later they overran Villagrappa two miles northwest of the bridgehead. But by the 16th growing enemy resistance had brought the 5 Corps' advance to a halt seven miles southeast of Faenza, the corps' next objective.

Forli and the high ground immediately southwest of it were now in Allied hands. This had been an important gain for the Eighth Army. Located at the junction of Highway 9 and Highway 67, Forli, in Eighth Army control, would open up the Florence-Forli road and thereby facilitate lateral communications with the Fifth Army.

Meanwhile, six miles northeast of Forli, the 5 Corps' flanking unit, the 12th Lancers, aided by local partisans, had routed the Germans from Coccolia, their last stronghold along the Ronco on 15 November. Eight miles northeast of Coccolia, Task Force Porter, which held the former Canadian sector, occupied the Ravenna airport, despite local flooding caused by the enemy's opening the flood-gates of the Uiumi Uniti Canal. With the line of the Ronco breached at three places, the Germans northeast of Forli would have no choice but to fall back on the Montone, which parallels the Ronco two to three miles to the west and forms the last possible defense line before Ravenna.

Since Eighth Army's growing threat to Ravenna might cause the Germans to shift units from the Faenza sector to protect their northeastern flank, McCreery decided to take advantage of this shift by mounting a set-piece attack on Faenza. On the west bank of the Lamone River, ten miles northwest of Forli, Faenza, an ancient center of ceramic manufacturing, still lay unscathed behind its 15th century ramparts when on 18 November General McCreery issued his orders for an attack on the city. As they had during the operation against Forli, the 5 Corps' 4th and 46th Divisions would avoid a frontal assault on the city and attempt to invest it from the Apennines foothills to the south. On the corps' left flank this maneuver was extended as the 2 Polish Corps' 3d Carpathian Division sent patrols as far as Modigliana, ten miles southwest of Faenza where contact was made with the Fifth Army's 13 Corps. As before, the 4th and 46th Divisions were to make a converging attack, the former advancing south of Highway 9 and the latter astride the highway. On the 5 Corps' right a holding attack would be set in motion by the 10th Indian Division, which had, meanwhile, replaced the 12th Lancers. For the present the British 56th Division remained in corps reserve.

By 21 November the 5 Corps had completed preparations for the assault on Faenza. On that day clear skies permitted 500 aircraft, including medium bombers, to roar into the air above the front to bomb and strafe enemy positions on the Faenza sector over the next two days. Shortly before the divisions began to move corps artillery opened fire across the front.

In spite of this firepower the Germans clung to the line of the Montone until nightfall on the 23d. Under the concealment of darkness they broke contact and fell back three miles, first to the line of the Marzeno, then an additional three miles to the Lamone.

On the 25th the 5 Corps pulled up to the Lamone on a broad front. The next day heavy rain began to fall, flooding the river and tributary streams. Despite the fact that southwest and northeast of Faenza the 4th and 46th Divisions were now within easy assault distance of the city they could do little until the weather cleared and the rains abated. In the interval the corps commander, General Keightley, relieved the 4th Division with the 2d New Zealand, which, after several weeks in reserve, would be comparatively fresh for the next phase of the offensive.

Meanwhile, to 5 Corps' left, General Anders' Polish corps had made good progress on the 16th in the valley of the Marzeno southwest of Faenza.

Capturing Montefortino, the high ground northeast of Modigliana, the 5th Kresowa Division lost it to a counterattack on the following night. On the 18th the 3d Carpathian Division relieved the 5th Kresowa Division and went on to recapture Montefortino on the 21st. On the Polish corps' left a screening force entered Modigliana on the 15th. Over the next nine days this force patrolled beyond Modigliana as far as the upper Lamone. On the 24th the patrols probed to within six miles southwest of Faenza.

Reorganization and Planning on the Fifth Army's Front

While the Eighth Army's 5 Corps and Polish corps fought their way northwestward from one river line to the next, the U.S. Fifth Army's commander, Clark, had taken advantage of the November respite to rest his divisions, assemble supplies, and prepare for a resumption of the U.S. II Corps' offensive toward Bologna and the Po Valley. Kendall's 88th Division was the first to be withdrawn. To do this Clark on 2 November once again shifted the left boundary of Kirkman's 13 Corps to the northwest, this time to take over Monte Grande and Monte Cerrere from Kendall. This further thinned out the 13 Corps' front and made it difficult for that corps to give the Eighth Army's drive on Faenza much support. On the other hand, the shift further narrowed the II Corps front, thereby increasing its impact when the attack resumed. Clark also imposed strict rationing of artillery ammunition throughout his army to build up stocks for resuming the offensive in December. Finally, the November hiatus enabled the Fifth Army to integrate replacements who had arrived too late for the October battle.[3]

Following their relief, the troops of the 88th Division enjoyed a few weeks rest before returning to the lines on 22 November to relieve the 85th Division

and elements of the 34th Division. The remainder of the 34th and all of the 1st Armored Division then took over the 91st Division's sector so that unit could join the 85th Division in corps reserve, where both divisions were to prepare themselves to make the main effort in the forthcoming offensive.

On 4 November the IV Corps resumed command of the 6th South African Armoured Division and its attached units. At the same time in the coastal sector north of Viareggio, General Almond's 92d Infantry Division, under army control, replaced Task Force 92.

During November additional units continued to arrive in the Fifth Army. General J. B. Mascarenhas de Morales Brazilian Expeditionary Force was brought up to division strength with the arrival of the 1st and 11th Infantry Regiments and the 92d Infantry Division's ranks were swelled by the attachment of a fourth regiment—the separate 366th Infantry—and the 758th Light Tank Battalion. In addition to these units, 5,000 infantry replacements arrived in Italy and were quickly integrated into the several combat divisions. In spite of these arrivals the Fifth Army was, by the end of November, still 7,000 understrength in the combat arms, mainly infantry.

Considerable juggling and reorganization had to be done to maintain the army's artillery strength. Although the 8th Antiaircraft Artillery Group had been transferred to the Seventh Army during November, the loss was partly made up by retaining several inactivated antiaircraft artillery units and re-equipping them with self-propelled 105-mm. howitzers to form the 1125th

---

[3] Clark Diary, 27 Oct 44, citing Ltr, Alexander to Clark, and latter's comments thereon; *Fifth Army History*, Part VI, p. 175ff.

Armored Field Artillery Battalion. Some of the heavy artillery taken away were partially replaced by the attachment to II Corps of a battery of the British 54th Super-Heavy (8-inch) Gun Regiment.

As the time set for the II Corps' renewed assault on Bologna drew near, General Clark began to wonder whether it would ever take place. Early in November, before the CCS finally laid to rest Alexander's plans for a trans-Adriatic operation, Clark had become convinced that the British, eager for a morale-lifting victory, would, in spite of mutually agreed upon plans for a double-pronged offensive against Bologna, concentrate instead on preparations for the Balkan venture and leave the U.S. Fifth Army alone in opposing the bulk of the German forces in Italy.[4] This was indeed Alexander's intention, but at that time he considered the Fifth Army fully adequate for the task.

Chronically suspicious of British intentions, Clark also tended to overestimate enemy strength in Italy. Instead of the eleven divisions he assumed Vietinghoff had on the *Tenth Army's* front, the Germans actually had only ten, most of them greatly understrength. These divisions, moreover, were not massed opposite the U.S. II Corps' front, as Clark believed, but rather were spread out opposite the II and 13 Corps fronts, as well as that of the Eighth Army's.[5] General Clark was also worried whether the forthcoming drive on Bologna would have sufficient tactical air support. What the Fifth Army commander had in mind was

something approaching the massive carpet bombing that had paved the way for the breakout of General Omar Bradley's First Army at St. Lo, France, in July. Then a series of blunders and misunderstandings had caused over 900 casualties among the American ground troops and had wrung from General Eisenhower the declaration that he would never again employ heavy bombers in a tactical role.[6]

General Cannon, the senior Allied air officer in Italy, shared these misgivings, for he was mindful of even greater technical difficulties in Italy where winter weather and mountainous terrain would present serious challenges to airmen attempting to provide close support for ground operations. General Clark, however, was willing to accept such risks and insisted that the Fifth Army's renewed offensive, scheduled for early December, receive close and continuous support from strategic as well as tactical bombers. General Cannon reluctantly agreed.[7]

Outside Influences on Strategy

Meanwhile, events had taken place elsewhere in Europe that would help keep Allied attention in Italy focused upon the front in the Apennines and the Po Valley rather than on the far shores of the Adriatic. By the third week in November the Germans had

---

[4] Clark Diary, 5 Nov 44.

[5] Clark Diary, 30 Oct 44. See also *AOK 14* and *AOK 10, Ia KTB's.*

[6] He would do so, however, in Operation QUEEN during the Siegfried Line campaign. See Charles B. MacDonald, *The Siegfried Line Campaign* (Washington, 1963). For an account of Operation COBRA at St. Lo see Martin Blumenson, *Breakout and Pursuit* (Washington, 1961), pp. 228–38. Both are volumes of UNITED STATES ARMY IN WORLD WAR II. See also Clark Diary, 30 Oct 44.

[7] Clark Diary, 30 Oct 44.

regained control over the western half of Yugoslavia. This meant, barring an advance by the Red Army beyond Budapest, that the Germans would probably continue to defend their present front in northern Italy well forward of the Austrian frontier. In addition to restored German control in western Yugoslavia, Tito's partisans, now fighting alongside the Red Army, had indicated that additional Allied personnel would no longer be welcome in Dalmatia.[8]

Therefore, on 22 November, Wilson reported to the Combined Chiefs of Staff in London "that recent developments obliged him now to concentrate primarily on the campaign in Italy." He proposed to Alexander that the Allied armies ". . . exploit to the limit of [their] resources with the object of destroying or containing the maximum enemy forces remaining in the peninsula." The once-vaunted trans-Adriatic venture would then be reduced to a mere threat, possibly mounted from an Allied air base at Zara and designed simply to contain those Germans still in Yugoslavia. The assault shipping Wilson had requested in October was now no longer needed in the Mediterranean. SACMED's recommendations found favor with the CCS who agreed to provide Wilson with a new directive concerning future operations.[9]

Command Changes

As planning for the joint offensive neared completion, the entire Allied command picture changed. On 25 No-vember Clark received word that he had been selected to command the Allied Armies in Italy, now redesignated the 15th Army Group. This change in command had been occasioned by the untimely passing of Sir John Dill, head of the British Military Mission in Washington. SACMED, General Sir Henry Maitland Wilson, had been selected to take Dill's place in Washington, and Field Marshal Alexander would move into the position of theater commander. Clark's place at Fifth Army would be taken by General Truscott, who since mid-August had been in command of VI Corps in France. Another important change reflected the needs of inter-Allied relations. Unlike Alexander's, Clark's new headquarters was to be tactical only. This would permit Eighth Army to deal directly with AFHQ (Alexander's headquarters) for administrative matters, rather than clearing through Army Group. These changes, however, were not to become effective until mid-December.[10]

Alexander's Orders

On 28 November, Alexander issued orders for resumption of the joint offensive in early December. The Eighth Army, with its 1st Canadian Corps once again in line and with supplies adequate for another three or four weeks of offensive operations, depending upon the intensity of the fighting, was to continue its current operations aimed at capturing Ravenna in the northeast and

[8] SACMED *Despatch*, Aug-Dec 44; Ehrman, *Grand Strategy*, Vol. VI, pp. 50–56.
[9] SACMED *Despatch*, Aug-Dec 44.

[10] In Clark's diary, 23 Nov 44, the date given for the change in command is 16 December; Alexander *Despatch*, p. 78, gives it as 12 December 1944. Clark, *Calculated Risk*, pp. 404–05.

Faenza in the northwest and at driving toward a junction with the Fifth Army near Imola by 7 December. Thereafter, the Eighth Army's main thrust was to turn slightly northwest along the Imola-Budrio axis—Budrio lying eight miles northeast of Bologna. A subsidiary thrust was to be directed northwestward beyond Ravenna in the direction of Ferrara, if favorable opportunities beckoned in that direction.[11]

The appearance of the Eighth Army before Imola was to be Fifth Army's signal to begin its phase of the joint offensive toward Bologna. On the Fifth Army's right flank, General Kirkman's 13 Corps had been stretched so thin by frequent westward shifts of its left flank to take over more and more of the II Corps' sector, that it was unlikely that the 13 Corps could provide as much help to the Eighth Army's advance along Highway 9 as General Alexander had expected when outlining his original plan.

In the Fifth Army's center, Keyes' II Corps was to continue to make the army's main effort, this time along the axis of Highway 65. The Fifth Army's participation in the December offensive was to begin on Alexander's order anytime after 7 December and on three days' notice. Everything, however, would depend upon the weather. The coming of severe winter storms was expected to restrict operations to the main roads, and unless ground and weather conditions were favorable, Alexander declared there would be no offensive.

The Desert Air Force was once again to support the December offensive. Since the beginning of the campaign in North Africa this force had been the Eighth Army's constant companion and would fly again in its support. The XXII Tactical Air Command would support the Fifth Army. In response to General Clark's insistence, General Cannon had agreed to the use of heavy as well as medium bombers in direct support of the ground forces.

An Allied Directive

Meanwhile, on 2 December, Wilson received from the CCS the long-awaited directive that would govern the operations of the Allied Armies in Italy until the spring of 1945. After stating that no major Allied forces (other than those British units already earmarked for Greece) were to be introduced into the Balkans, the directive spelled out once and for all that the first and immediate mission of Alexander's armies "should be to capture Bologna, then to secure the general line Ravenna–Bologna–La Spezia and thereafter continue operations with a view to containing Kesselring's army. Withdrawal of forces from the line for rest, rehabilitation, and rotation should be consistent with the above mission."[12]

Although the new directive ruled out large-scale trans-Adriatic operations, it had left open the door for the introduction of light forces through those Dalmatian ports still in partisan hands "in order to harass, and exert pressure and attrition on the Germans withdrawing from Yugoslavia." But in view of the changed attitude of Tito's partisans

---

[11] Hq AAI Opns O No. 1, 28 Nov 44, 0300/6/55. Unless otherwise indicated the following section is based upon this reference.

[12] Ehrman, *Grand Strategy*, Vol. VI, p. 56.

toward the Allies, this seemed a remote possibility. The directive further fanned within Alexander's headquarters faint sparks of hope for operations other than on the main front; forces and resources made available as a result of withdrawals from the line were to "constitute a strategic reserve well placed to reinforce the effort against Kesselring and facilitate the rotation of tired units *to be available for prompt employment in other operations as the changing situation permits.*"[13]

Whether or not this slight nod toward the now vanished British designs for Balkan ventures satisfied General Alexander is difficult to determine. In any case, until spring returned to the battlefields of Europe such operations would be, at the most, limited to local offensives and possible counteroffensives.

The Eighth Army's Advance Continues

Inasmuch as the CCS directive was consistent with Alexander's operational plan for early December, he made no changes in Eighth Army's phase of the attack, scheduled to be resumed on 2 December. Since intelligence reports had indicated that in order to hold the threatened Faenza sector, the Germans had thinned out their defenses in the northeastern coastal flank, McCreery had decided to replace with the 1st Canadian Corps the relatively weak Porter Force, a task force that had relieved the Canadians late in October. Operating on the coastal flank, the Canadians were to attack across the Montone River, which joins the Ronco

a mile south of Ravenna. After establishing a bridgehead near San Pancrazio, five miles southwest of Ravenna, and capturing Godo, three miles northwest of the crossing, the corps was to continue its advance in three columns— the first to turn northeastward to cut in behind Ravenna; the second to cut Highway 16 north of Mezzano, five miles north of Godo; and the third to advance on Russi, three miles southwest of Godo, and cross the Lamone River.[14]

While the 1st Canadian Corps took its place on the Eighth Army's right wing, in the center the British 5 Corps, having secured Forlì, prepared to resume its advance on Faenza. To take advantage of the well-drained ground in hills south of Highway 9 and to avoid a frontal attack over the soggy terrain north of the highway, the corps was first to seize the high ground near Pideura, four miles southwest of Faenza, then bypass the city and take Castel Bolognese, five miles beyond. The 2 Polish Corps on the Eighth Army's left flank was meanwhile to conform to the 5 Corps' advance.

As General Alexander had stipulated, the resumption of operations would depend upon the weather, for as already indicated, the Allies were relying greatly upon the support of their air force. Fortunately, the skies were clear on 2 December, as the aircraft of the DAF bombed and strafed the enemy across the front. On the ground the Canadian corps advanced to the northnorthwest in the face of heavy resist-

---

[13] *Ibid.* Italics supplied.

[14] Operations of British, Indian and Dominion Forces in Italy, Pt. III, Sec B. Unless otherwise indicated the following is based on this source.

ance. Two days later the Canadian 5th Armored Division rolled into Godo and further tightened the noose around Ravenna by cutting Highway 16 six miles to the northwest.

Inasmuch as a partisan uprising had already driven the Germans from the city, the Canadians had little difficulty entering on 4 December. This event marked the first appearance on the Allied front of a major, well-organized partisan unit, for hitherto partisans had played only a peripheral role but would henceforth take a more active part in operations. With Ravenna's capture, the 900-man Communist-led 28th Garibaldi Brigade took a place in the Eighth Army's ranks somewhat comparable to that of a Regular unit, receiving logistical support in the form of ammunition, food, and clothing through army supply channels. For the balance of the winter the brigade would hold a quiet sector of the army's front but would eventually take an active part in the spring offensive to the Po.

Unlike Rimini, Ravenna offered the Eighth Army no logistical advantages other than to provide some shelter for the winter months. Centuries earlier Ravenna had been an important seaport, but in 1944 it was connected to a harbor only by a canal. Shallow and heavily mined, the harbor was ignored by the Eighth Army, which depended instead on a recently opened railhead at Cesena, seven miles west of Rimini. The army's logistical system would be improved even further when a pipeline and oil storage facilities were completed on 10 December as far as Forlimpopoli, six miles beyond Cesena. These developments eliminated much of the long truck haul from Ortona, far to the

army's rear, and greatly shortened and simplified the army's line of communications.

Elsewhere on the Canadian Corps sector the Canadian 1st Infantry Division, on the 5th Armored Division's left, encountered stronger resistance on 4 December as it moved toward Russi, eight miles southwest of Ravenna. Bypassing the town, the Canadian infantry rushed to reach the Lamone, two miles to the west where they were halted by the Germans dug in along the far bank. The next day, however, the Canadians managed to establish a precarious bridgehead across the river.

Southwest of the Ravenna sector the 2d New Zealand and the British 46th Infantry Divisions began the first phase of an outflanking maneuver against the Faenza sector. During the night of 2 December the New Zealanders feinted toward the Lamone to hold the enemy on that sector, while four miles south of Faenza in the Quartolo San Ruffilo area the British division established a bridgehead across the river. On the following day, however, the Germans checked all attempts by the British to enlarge the bridgehead in the direction of the Pideura Ridge, two miles to the west and covering the southern approaches to the city.

On the 46th Division's left, the Polish corps supported the 5 Corps' attack on Faenza by clearing the Marradi-Faenza road as far as the town of Strada, twelve miles southwest of Faenza. After crossing the upper reaches of the Lamone on 5 December, the Polish infantry advanced two miles to the west, where they captured the village of Montecchio on Monte San Rinaldo and all the high ground to the south of it, thereby securing the left flank of the Eighth Army's offensive.

German Reactions

The acting *Army Group C* commander, General Vietinghoff, had believed that he could hold the Canadians south of Ravenna at least temporarily. But the partisan uprising, which had seized control of the city, upset his calculations and forced him to request permission from OKW to fall back in the Ravenna sector to avoid the necessity of drawing reserves from the Bologna sector, where the Americans could be expected to resume their offensive at any time. In spite of his earlier orders to the army group to hold in place in northeastern Italy, Hitler now reluctantly authorized Vietinghoff to withdraw the *Tenth Army* to a line northwest of Ravenna to prevent that army's right wing from being cut off.[15]

Although willing to authorize a withdrawal in the northeast, the German leader was adamant about holding in place on the Faenza sector. As Herr's panzer corps dug in along the west bank of the Lamone, Hitler personally intervened on 7 December to order Vietinghoff to stand fast at Faenza and to yield no ground there. To help *Army Group C* in this effort OKW promised to send 2,600 replacements to Italy. On 9 December, first the *90th Panzer Grenadier Division*, then the *98th Infantry Division* appeared on the *LXXVI Panzer Corps'* front to back up the Fuehrer's order. As the British widened and eventually joined their bridgeheads west of the Lamone on the 11th, Hitler

modified his original order by authorizing Vietinghoff to fall back slightly, but cautioned against a temptation to withdraw into the illusive security of the so-called Genghis Khan switch position, which ran northeast from Bologna thirty miles to Lake Comacchio on the Adriatic coast.

Attack on Faenza Resumed

Even before Hitler ordered his troops to defend Faenza at all costs, the British 5 Corps had encountered growing resistance as it attempted to turn the successive enemy defense lines by advancing northwestward through the Apennines foothills south of Highway 9. In addition to increasing resistance, broken country and a lack of roads made it hard for the 46th Division to maneuver in trying to clear the Pideura Ridge. And for a few days high water made the bridges over the Lamone impassable. Consequently, it was not until 7 December that the British finally cleared the enemy from Pideura village. The Germans, in the meantime, having received Hitler's order to hold in place, stubbornly defended high ground to the north of Pideura. Poor weather, which restricted tactical air support over the battle area, even enabled the Germans to launch several local counterattacks, thereby preventing the British from exploiting Pideura's capture.

There was another factor limiting the momentum of the British advance—the necessity to pull units out of line to be sent to Greece. Although all counterattacks were thrown back with considerable loss to the enemy, Major General C. F. Keightley, the 5 Corps commander, was forced to halt his attack to pull the Greece-bound 46th Division out of the

---

[15] Greiner and Schramm, eds., *OKW WFSt, KTB*, IV(1), pp. 570–76. Unless otherwise indicated the following section is based upon this source.

line. This forced him to regroup his remaining divisions across the corps' sector. Regrouping was completed by 14 December, as two relatively fresh units, the 10th Indian and 2d New Zealand Divisions, moved into the bridgeheads across the Lamone. The Indian division assembled in the left half of the bridgehead and the New Zealand division in the right and along the line of the river east of Faenza. North of the city lay the 5 Corps reserve—the 56th Division, now committed to a quiet water-logged sector east of the Lamone.

While General Keightley regrouped his corps, the 2 Polish Corps' 5th Kresowa Division advanced beyond Brisighella onto the high ground seven miles southwest of Faenza. When patrols reached the Sintria River, three miles northwest of Brisighella, they found that high water made the river unfordable.

Taking advantage of concealment offered by darkness, the 5 Corps, in the meantime, launched its assault on Faenza during the night of 14 December. To support the assault General Keightley had massed more than 400 guns to cover the advance of the New Zealanders from the southwest and the Indians from the east of the city. On the 5 Corps' left the Polish troops crossed the flooded Sintria and closed up to the Senio River, two miles to the west. Faced now with the prospect of being trapped in Faenza, the German garrison withdrew to the northwest, where they re-established themselves along the Senio, three miles away. On the heels of the retreating Germans the 43d Motorized Indian Infantry Brigade (10 Indian Division) rolled into the

city. By dawn on the following day the Indians had established two small bridgeheads across the Senio at a point west of Faenza.

Before the line of the Senio could be forced in any strength, a bridge carrying Highway 9 across the Lamone at Faenza had first to be rebuilt. But north of the city opposite the 56th Division, the Germans still held positions where flooded fields enabled them to take their time about withdrawing in the sector. From these positions enemy fire made completion of the bridge impossible until the Germans finally withdrew on the 22d. While the engineers worked on the bridge, the 5 Corps tried consolidating its positions in and around Faenza. Meanwhile the Eighth Army's advance along Highway 9 had come virtually to a halt.

On Eighth Army's coastal flank, the 1st Canadian Corps encountered less trouble reaching the Senio in its sector. After having consolidated its positions beyond Ravenna and along the east bank of the Lamone River, the Canadians patrolled northward toward the Comacchio Lagoon, a large coastal body of water nine miles north of Ravenna. On 11 December the Canadians established two large bridgeheads over the Lamone, following on the 12th with a third, six miles northwest of Ravenna near Mezzano on Highway 16. After linking all three bridgeheads, the Canadians advanced against relatively little opposition toward Bagnacavallo, six miles southwest of Mezzano, as the Germans, with the Canadians following closely, fell back to the next river line, the Senio, five miles west of the Lamone river.

The Fifth Army Plans and Waits

All this time, other than reorganization of units, resting of weary men, and planning for coming operations, the only activity on the Fifth Army sector had taken place on the flanks. To the right, the British 13 Corps helped Eighth Army's operations south of Highway 9 through pressure against the enemy opposite its sector. The 8th Indian Division, on the corps' right flank, proceeded along the Marradi-Faenza road, following the valley of the upper Lamone toward Brisighella, seven miles southwest of Faenza. On the 13 Corps' center, the British 6th Armoured Division pushed 5 miles beyond Castel del Rio along the Santerno valley road to capture the village of Fontanelice on 30 November. This brought the British armor to within ten miles of Imola. On the corps' left wing, the British 1st Infantry was less fortunate, for not only did it make no gains but during the night of the 28th was driven from Monte Castellera near Monte Grande by troops from the *1st Parachute Division.*

There was far less action in the west, on the Fifth Army's left flank, where some Brazilian units received their baptism of fire. This was a brief set-piece operation on the Bombiana-Marano sector by the 6th Regimental Combat Team of the BEF. Thereafter that sector too settled down to sporadic patrolling, as was the case elsewhere on the army's front.

During this period Army and Corps headquarters, however, bustled with activity as planning for resumption of the drive on Bologna continued. Much of the Fifth Army's earlier crippling personnel shortages had largely been re-plenished. Enough replacements had arrived to bring the divisions up to full strength. The 91st Division had returned to the front on 3 December. Keyes' II Corps now had four divisions on line; from left to right, the 1st Armored, the 91st, the 34th, and the 88th Infantry Divisions. The 85th Division lay in corps reserve, enjoying a well-deserved respite from combat.[16]

To reach Bologna, Clark planned a three-phase attack astride Highway 65. During the first two phases Keyes' corps was to clear the enemy from the high ground in the vicinity of Pianoro, eight miles south of Bologna. In the last phase the corps was to sweep down from the last of the Apennines into the Po Valley and capture Bologna. While the II Corps advanced along Highway 65, Crittenberger's IV Corps was to maintain pressure against the enemy by continuing the series of limited objective operations initiated earlier by the Brazilians on the Bombiana-Marano sector. On the right of the II Corps, Kirkman's 13 Corps was to continue to exert pressure down the Santerno and Lamone valleys against the flank of the *LXXVI Panzer Corps,* opposing 5 Corps on Highway 9.

The Fifth Army was ready to move, but the Eighth Army had not yet reached the objectives that Alexander had set for it on Highway 9, and Allied meteorologists were unable to forecast the necessary minimum of three days of good flying weather to assure Clark of the close air support he so strongly desired. On 7 December, therefore, General Alexander, instead of giving

---

[16] *Fifth Army History,* Part VIII, pp. 12–16. Unless otherwise indicated the following is based upon this citation.

the signal for Fifth Army to attack, announced the first in a series of postponements of the Fifth Army's offensive. Despite plans and revision of plans, followed by preparations and alerts, postponement followed postponement.

Were these postponements necessary? Was Alexander's decision not to unleash Clark's Fifth Army militarily valid or unduly cautious? Both Allied armies had broken through the Gothic Line on their respective sectors. In the mountains the U.S. II Corps lay within nine miles of the center of Bologna and five miles from Highway 9. And the attached British 13 Corps was within ten miles of Imola. In the plain the Eighth Army's three corps had reached the east bank of the Senio and at one point were within seven miles of Imola. Furthermore, the enemy divisions had been weakened by considerable casualties. Might not one last mighty effort by both Allied armies have carried them through to Bologna and the Po Valley on a broad front? Possibly. But the offensive that had been under way since August on the Eighth Army's front and since September on the Fifth's had left the troops near exhaustion by the beginning of December. Faced with the need to rest the weary divisions, Alexander had no choice but to call the offensive to a halt.[17]

For the rest of the year most of the Fifth Army's front remained dormant. The Allied command believed that the German armies in Italy would adopt a similar posture. But when the Germans in northwestern Europe precipitated a large-scale counteroffensive against Ei-

senhower's forces in the Ardennes, General Alexander had to revise his earlier assumptions. He concluded that if the enemy undertook a similar enterprise in the Italian theater, the likeliest to be attacked would be the weaker of the two Allied armies—the Fifth Army. The logical location of an attack on that army's front would, of course, be that sector held either by the Brazilian Expeditionary Force or the newly arrived and largely untested 92d Infantry Division, both on the Army's left flank.

In mid-December major changes of command took place among the senior Allied commanders in the theater. General Alexander, promoted to Field Marshal, took over General Wilson's headquarters as Supreme Allied Commander, Mediterranean (SACMED), whereupon General Clark moved up to take command of the Allied Armies, Italy; and General Truscott returned from his command in France to head the Fifth Army. The problem of how to deal with a possible enemy counterattack on the Italian front now passed to Alexander's successors.

One of the first papers to reach General Truscott's desk was an intelligence report of a buildup of enemy forces opposite the Fifth Army's left flank in IV Corps' sector. The *148th Infantry Division* and two Italian units, the *Monte Rosa* and *San Marco Marine Divisions,* had been reported in the La Spezia area, and there were some indications that the *157th Mountain Division* might be moving into the sector as well. There was also some evidence that the Germans might take advantage of the lull on the central front by shifting the *16th SS Panzer Grenadier,* the *26th Panzer,* or the *5th Mountain*

---

[17] Nicholson, *Alex,* p. 266.

Division to their Ligurian flank. Moreover, aerial reconnaissance had confirmed partisan and prisoner of war reports that bridges and roads destroyed earlier in the upper Serchio Valley had been repaired. Even as the vital Allied port of Antwerp seemed to be the ultimate objective of the German counteroffensive in the Ardennes, so now it seemed to the Fifth Army's intelligence officers that the port of Leghorn might become the objective of a similar operation in the northern Apennines on the Fifth Army's left flank.

Such speculations seemed not without substance, for at the beginning of December all that stood in the way of a German thrust toward Leghorn was General Almond's relatively inexperienced 92d Infantry Division, holding a 6-mile-wide front from the coast inland to the village of Barga in the upper Serchio valley. This division, made up entirely of Negro enlisted men, with officers from both races, had been activated at Fort McClellan, Alabama, in October 1942, from a cadre of officers and men drawn from the 93d Infantry Division, the first Negro combat division to be organized in World War II.[18]

Since its activation, the 92d Division's ranks had been characterized by unusually high percentage of poorly educated men. At the end of January 1944, the division's General Classification Test score percentages disclosed that none of

the enlisted men assigned was in Class I, 10 percent were in Class II, 15 percent in Class III, 41 percent in Class IV, and 21 percent in Class V. Thirteen percent had received no score at all because they were illiterate and unable to take the test. Obviously the men of the 92d Division had come into the Army with far fewer educational and cultural opportunities and from homes with significantly lower socio-economic status than men in other combat divisions. This situation was widely known throughout the army and, even before December 1944, had given the division a reputation as an undesirable assignment for white officers.

Only one of the division's regiments, the 370th, had seen any action, that as part of Task Force 92. Although the division commander, General Almond, had nothing but praise for his unit's artillery, communications, supply, medical service, and transportation troops, he was less enthusiastic about the performance of the combat infantry, which had shown little steadiness in its first encounter with the enemy. The very limited battle experience gained by the 370th Infantry since October had, in Almond's opinion, "been no compensation for the loss of key leaders incurred." On 18 October the second of the regiments, the 371st Infantry, had arrived at Leghorn and relieved the 370th Infantry on 31 October. After the 365th Infantry had completed its deployment on 8 November, the 92d Division took over a 6-mile front in the Serchio valley on the II Corps' left flank.

It was hardly surprising, therefore, that one of General Truscott's first decisions as Fifth Army commander

---

[18] See Lee, *The Employment of Negro Troops,* for the details on the division's training and organization difficulties. See also Paul Goodman, *A Fragment of Victory,* a special monograph (hereafter cited as Goodman Monograph), written at the Army War College, Carlisle, Pa., 1952; and IG file on 92d Div. Unless otherwise indicated the following section is based upon these sources.

was to shift additional units to IV Corps where they would be in position to back up the 92d Division as a precaution against an enemy counteroffensive. On 23 December Truscott attached the 85th Division's 339th Infantry to IV Corps. At the same time, he shifted the 85th Division's 337th Infantry from II Corps reserve and two brigades of the 8th Indian Division from 13 Corps reserve to back-up positions in the IV Corps' rear. Meanwhile, Truscott also returned the 92d Division to army control. He also detached from II Corps the 84th Chemical Battalion, the 755th and 760th Tank Battalions, two 155-mm. howitzer and one 155-mm. gun U.S. Field Artillery battalions, and two regiments (battalions) of British 5.5-inch guns and sent them to IV Corps in the vicinity of Lucca. By 25 December both Indian brigades had closed into reserve position near Lucca. The 85th Division's remaining regiment, the 338th Infantry, remained in II Corps reserve to help repel any counteroffensive directed against either the 1st Armored Division's or the 91st Division's sectors.

A German Counterattack

General Truscott's precautionary moves were well justified, for the *Fourteenth Army,* then under the command of General der Infanterie Kurt von Tippelskirch, had on its own initiative made plans to deliver on 26 December, a limited objective attack under the code Operation *WINTERGEWITTER* (Winter Thunderstorm). The primary purpose of this operation was to relieve pressure on the Italian Alpine division, *Monte Rosa,* which had been engaged earlier by the Brazilian Expeditionary

Force in the Serchio valley. The *LI Mountain Corps,* which had replaced the *XIV Panzer Corps* on the *Fourteenth Army's* right wing, had assembled a miscellaneous group of units for Operation *WINTERGEWITTER.* They included a battalion each from the *148th Infantry Division's 285th* and *286th Infantry Regiments,* the *Alpine Training Battalion (Mittenwald)* (a school battalion from the German mountain warfare school at Mittenwald), and the *4th Alpine Battalion.* The mountain units were first-rate troops. A motorized artillery battalion of the *51st Artillery Regiment* and one heavy and two light battalions of the *1048th Artillery Regiment* were to provide fire support for the operation. The mission of this force was to initiate a limited objective operation against the U.S. 92d Division with the intent of destroying its effectiveness for further offensive operations. This was an ironic twist, for, in the eyes of its own commander, the division already lacked a capacity for such operations.[19]

The euphoria of Christmas Day at the snow-covered front had just begun to fade when, early on the 26th, Operation *WINTERGEWITTER* broke over the Serchio valley. Behind a screen of mortar and artillery fire, the Germans attacked along the slopes flanking the valley. West of the river, from the vicinity of Castelnuovo, twenty miles north of Lucca, the enemy struck, simultaneously, the 1st Battalion of the 370th Infantry, located near the village of Molazzana four miles south of Castelnuovo, and the 2d Battalion, in the village of Calomini, a mile south of

---

[19] *AOK 14, Ia KTB Anl. 5,* 11–27 Dec 44, *AOK 14,* Doc. 65922/1.

Molazzana. East of the Serchio, the enemy attack also hit outposts of the 366th Infantry's 2d Battalion, attached to the 370th Infantry and garrisoning the villages of Sommocolonia, Bebbio, and Tiglio—all lying just east of Molazzana.[20]

Feinting first at the American positions west of the Serchio the *2d Battalion* of the *285th Infantry Regiment* advanced from one to two miles to capture the villages of Calomini and Gallicano early in the day. Some hint that the thrust west of the valley might be a mere feint became apparent when the Germans recoiled quickly in the face of a weak American counterattack in that area.[21]

Operation *WINTERGEWITTER*'s main effort was actually concentrated east of the Serchio, where the *286th Infantry Regiment*'s *2d Battalion* overran the area west of Barga, a mile and a half south of Sommocolonia, and beat back several American counterattacks launched from Barga. After bitter house-to-house fighting, the *4th Alpine Battalion* finally drove the Americans from Sommocolonia northeast of Barga, and to the northwest occupied the high ground at Monte Vano. To the grenadiers' east the *Mittenwald Battalion* captured the village of Tiglio.[22]

When General Crittenberger, the IV Corps commander, learned of the German attack, he immediately moved the two Indian brigades into backstop positions behind the 92d Division. Sharing the corps commander's concern for that division's steadfastness and uncertain of enemy intentions, General Truscott also detached Prichard's 1st Armored Division from II Corps and moved it westward to the vicinity of Lucca. The 34th Division's 135th Infantry followed to take up a reserve position near Viareggio.[23]

By the afternoon of the 26th German successes seemed to threaten a breakthrough on the 92d Division's Serchio valley front. The threat was especially evident east of the valley where Company G of the 366th Infantry had fallen back in disarray, opening up a 500-yard gap through which the enemy troops rushed toward the village of Barga.[24] Despite steadfast resistance by a handful of heroic men, the village fell to the Germans on the following morning. Continuing their attack throughout the 27th, the Germans pushed a few miles beyond Barga, then concluded the operation by mopping up the area between the village and the Serchio River. Since their mission had been accomplished, and they had not intended to advance any further, they now began to withdraw, leaving, for the next few days, only a screening force in contact with U.S. IV Corps.[25]

In the meantime, the 8th Indian Division's 19th Brigade had been moved five miles northwest of Bagni di Lucca to establish a line to the 92d

---

[20] The 366th Infantry, a separate all-Negro regiment, had been assigned to the 15th Air Force from 6 May to 19 November 1944, during which time the regiment had been used to guard airfields. Assigned to the Fifth Army on 19 November, the regiment was attached to the 92d Division until 25 February 1945. See *Fifth Army History*, Part VII, p. 17.

[21] *AOK 14, Ia KTB Anl. 5*, 26 Dec 44, *AOK 14*, Doc. 65922/1.

[22] *Ibid.*

[23] *Fifth Army History*, Part VIII, pp. 17–19.

[24] Lee, *The Employment of Negro Troops*, pp. 62–67; Goodman Monograph, p. 76.

[25] *AOK 14, Ia KTB Anl. 5*, 27 Dec 44, *AOK 14*, Doc. 65922/1.

Division's rear; the line extended from Coreglia Antelminelli in the northeast, southwest four miles to San Fomano, a mile south of the Serchio River and about four miles south of Barga. During the night of the 26th the disorganized survivors of the 2d and 3d Battalions of the 370th Infantry passed through the Indians' lines on their way to the rear, where the men believed they might find safety from enemy fire. After rounding up these men, General Almond had them moved west of the Serchio, where they took up positions on the Indians' left and to the rear of the 370th Infantry's 1st Battalion. Late that same night the Indian patrols ran into the German screening force.[26]

The skies were clear and bright on the 27th as the aircraft of the XXII TAC appeared over the front to pound the withdrawing enemy troops. For the next four days, the supporting aircraft flew a total of 1,330 sorties while the two Indian brigades, driving the screening force before them, cleared Barga on the 29th and Sommocolonia the following day. As the year 1944 drew to a close, the Indians met little resistance as they retook in turn Gallicano, Bebbio, and Molazzana to recover virtually all of the ground lost to the enemy since the 26th.[27]

Contrary to the Fifth Army G–2's belief, Operation WINTERGEWITTER had no connection with the Ardennes offensive. As a matter of fact, after the operation in the Serchio valley had run its course, Hitler's chief of staff cautioned the Army Group C commander

not to undertake such operations in the future without prior approval from supreme headquarters.[28]

The Fifth Army command was not alone in being somewhat puzzled over enemy objectives in the Serchio valley— the German supreme command itself had questioned the operation—but General von Tippelskirch, acting Fourteenth Army commander, harbored no doubts as to its desirability and purpose. The brief offensive had, in his opinion, improved troop morale by giving his men a needed victory over the Americans. Moreover, the units participating had received valuable training and combat experience. Most importantly, the U.S. Fifth Army had been forced to withdraw troops from the critical II Corps' sector south of Bologna in order to support the sagging Serchio valley sector.[29] Both General von Tippelskirch and his superiors would have been even more pleased had they known that Operation WINTERGEWITTER had also thrown the Fifth Army off balance to such an extent as to contribute to a fourth and, what proved to be, a final postponement, until spring, of the assault on Bologna.[30]

The Stalemate

Not only on the Fifth Army's front, but also on the Eighth Army's, all military operations now came to a halt. Although the Germans had been driven from Ravenna on 4 December, from Faenza on the 16th, and Bagnacavallo,

[26] Lee, Employment of Negro Troops; Goodman Monograph; Fifth Army History, Part VII, pp. 17–18.
[27] Fifth Army History, Part VIII, pp. 17–18.

[28] Greiner and Schramm, eds., OKW/WFSt, KTB, IV (1), p. 569.
[29] AOK 14, Ia KTB Anl. 5, 31 Dec 44, AOK 14, Doc. 65922/1.
[30] Msg 06006, Hq 15th Army Group to AFHQ, 28 Dec 44, MOSTEL 44, 0100/4/26.

two miles to the northeast, on the 21st, these were to be the Eighth Army's last significant advances in 1944. The Lamone River had been crossed on a broad front, but three miles beyond it the Germans had re-established themselves along the west bank of the Senio. In spite of these limited successes, time had run out on the Eighth Army's operations for 1944. Imola and the Santerno River, necessary springboards for a co-ordinated assault on Bologna by both armies, still lay well behind enemy lines. The weather had meanwhile worsened, grounding aircraft and making it impossible even for tracked vehicles to operate off hard-surfaced roads. Although the ground had begun to freeze, it was not yet firm enough to support armor. Once again a change in the weather would deprive the Eighth Army of the advantages of its superiority in armor and airpower. Commenting on this fact before leaving to take up his new post in Washington, Wilson had observed that "the terrain and weather were all in [Kesselring's] favor; these discounted our superiority in armor and restricted the use which could be made of our powerful Air Forces, thus bringing the enemy's resources in the battle area to a level more comparable to our own." [31]

There were other factors operating to reduce Allied strength and to bring the opposing armies more into balance during the winter of 1944–45. Before the end of the year the Eighth Army would lose a corps headquarters and three divisions to the growing civil strife in Greece. And, in February, a decision that had been debated since September

and finally had been made in January would be implemented, as the 1st Canadian Corps and its two divisions left to join other Canadian forces in northwestern Europe. Under these circumstances, there was little the Eighth Army could do but to dig in along the Senio and there await the coming of spring and perhaps better days for the fortunes of Allied arms in Italy. [32]

The failure of the two Allied armies to reach the Lombardy plain had placed them at some disadvantage, when compared with the Germans, who had in Highway 9 an excellent lateral road with relatively short distances between it and their front lines. The Allies had no comparable lateral road network. In some instances forward units on the Fifth Army's front lay eighty miles from a railhead or advance base, and usually the last thirty miles to the front could be traversed only by jeeps for the stretch and generally ended with mule trains or back-packing by the men themselves.

Although the Allies, anticipating mountain operations, had assembled and organized considerable mule transport, the operational demands during November and December far exceeded anything foreseen. A school to train additional muleteers had been established by the Allied armies at Orvieto, after efforts to recruit them from among the civilian population had been less than satisfactory. But as the Fifth Army settled down for another winter in the mountains, the supply of both men and animals never quite kept up with the demands of combat troops, for mud and cold would take a high toll.

---

[31] SAC Despatch, Aug-Dec 44, p. 58.

[32] Alexander *Despatch*, pp. 76–78.

ITALIAN MULE TRAIN TRANSPORTING
SUPPLIES TO THE FRONT

General Truscott had meanwhile informed his corps commanders on the 28th that all troops were to remain on a nine-day alert pending resumption of offensive operations. General Crittenberger's IV Corps was to continue to cover the army's lines of communications between the central front south of Bologna and the base at Leghorn, while General Keyes' II Corps was to be prepared to move on short notice, and General Kirkman's 13 Corps was to maintain pressure in the Santerno valley along the Imola road and assist, if possible, any further Eighth Army movement along Highway 9. General Prichard's 1st Armored Division was to remain at Lucca in army reserve.[33]

This dogged optimism could not be long maintained, however, in the face of the present reality of a winter stalemate. General Clark, after conferring on 30 December with his army commanders, did cling for awhile to his determination that Bologna must be captured that winter, and refused to abandon the offensive until ammunition stocks were rebuilt. But he, too, finally capitulated to reality a week later, when at a meeting with Field Marshal Alexander at the 15th Army Group headquarters in Florence, Clark at last acknowledged that resumption of the Bologna offensive was no longer feasible before spring. The two men, therefore, agreed that the Fifth and Eighth Armies were to remain on the defensive while building up strength for a spring offensive, tentatively scheduled to begin on 1 April.[34]

Despite two months of planning and shifting of units, the Fifth Army's front line would remain for the rest of the winter approximately where it had come to a halt in late October. An enemy counterattack in the west had forced Truscott to thin out the II Corps' front in order to strengthen the IV Corps' sector. The 17th Indian Brigade had taken over the support tasks formerly accomplished by the 8th Indian Division (less 17th Brigade) which returned to the 13 Corps. East of the Serchio, Task Force 45 (the retread antiaircraft artillerymen who had become infantrymen) and the Brazilian Expeditionary Force sectors remained unchanged, and the 6th South African Armoured Division held its old sector

_____

[33] Truscott, *Command Missions*, pp. 456–68.

[34] Msg FX 81059, AFHQ to Br COS, 8 Jan 45, MEDCOS 228, 0100/4/671.

GENERAL CLARK VISITS BRITISH 13 CORPS SECTOR WITH GENERAL KIRKMAN,
DECEMBER 1944

between the II and IV Corps and under Fifth Army control. The 1st Armored Division and the 85th Division moved over to the IV Corps' zone, where they were to rest and prepare for the spring offensive. The 34th Division withdrew into II Corps reserve, while the 91st and 88th Divisions took over the entire II Corps front.[35]

Even as the Allies abandoned for the winter their plans for resumption of offensive operations against Bologna, the Germans also reduced their forces, defending that sector with a force far below the October strength of nine divisions. Since 15 December, only four understrength divisions—the *65th* and *362d Infantry* and the *42d Rifle* and *1st Parachute Divisions,* all under the *XIV Panzer Corps*—remained on the front south of Bologna. Secure in their belief that a winter stalemate had settled over the front, the Germans had no immediate concern for that city.[36]

[35] *Fifth Army History,* Part VII, p. 19.

[36] MS # C–095 (Senger), CMH.

CHAPTER XXIV

Through the Winter

Sustaining the Armies

Except for three relatively brief, limited-objective operations, one in the Eighth Army and two in the Fifth, most of the front from sea to sea during the final winter of the war lay dormant beneath a coat of snow and ice. Even the wide-ranging and largely unchallenged Allied air arm was grounded much of the time as frequent fog or storm covered much of the country. Yet deep in the rear areas of both armies the countless activities required to keep modern field armies alive and functioning continued at an undiminished pace.

The numerous rear echelon units of both Allied armies had three main tasks: to sustain and nourish their forces, repair and salvage equipment, and assemble and forward supplies for the pending spring offensive. The U.S. Army Transportation Corps, for example, moved vast quantities of supplies from port to depot; army signal units manned switchboards, often handling as much daily traffic as a small city, and maintained a vast network of telephone and radio communications; and quartermaster units employed thousands of Italian civilians to repair and manufacture nonstandard items of winter clothing. Except for those abundant reserves of civilian manpower, there were few other indigenous resources in the Allied-occupied zone of Italy from which

to draw to maintain the armies.[1]

The U.S. Fifth Army was sustained largely by a 5,000-mile supply line extending from the United States across the Atlantic, the western Mediterranean, and miles of rugged Italian terrain. Convoys of freighters brought their cargoes from the United States to the Peninsular Base Section at either Naples or Leghorn, the latter having become after mid-November the army's main supply base in Italy. From the ports transportation corps units moved the supplies to dumps located in the vicinity of Lucca, Pistoia, and Florence, with shipments from Naples moving by rail. After March 1945 the service was extended from Leghorn to Florence.

Important though the railroads were for long distances, the burden of short haul movement of supplies fell largely to motor transport. From the major dumps in the Arno valley long truck convoys moved day and night up and down fifty miles of steep, winding mountain roads to deliver supplies to the forward elements of the II Corps. From there jeeps, and in the end, mules and men took over. During the winter 15 Italian pack mule companies with an approximate strength of 3,875 animals operated in support of the Fifth Army.

---

[1]*Fifth Army History,* Part VIII, pp. 21–51. Unless otherwise noted the following section is based upon this reference.

The unsung heroes of the supply operations were the engineer, transportation, and quartermaster units. Transportation units kept traffic moving over roads that engineers not only kept open but even managed to improve for the heavy traffic scheduled for future operations. Thousands of Italian civilians helped. In addition to providing warmer clothing and improved rations, the quartermaster units operated and maintained rest centers in the Arno valley, including centers at historic Florence and at Montecatini, where the troops could enjoy the therapeutic properties of sulphur springs long famed among European upper classes. Soft beds were among the amenities that a fashionable watering place could offer, even in wartime.

Even at the front life became more endurable. An army-wide campaign to winterize living quarters, made possible by a static front, gave the infantrymen a few more creature comforts. Although men actually manning the forward positions remained in foxholes, they made them as comfortable as human ingenuity could devise. In support and reserve positions troops constructed snug dugouts, and in some cases enjoyed the comparative comforts of pyramidal tents equipped with oil- or lignite-burning stoves. For evacuation hospitals, Nissen huts and other prefabricated buildings replaced the tents. The men would spend the winter in as comfortable circumstances as possible for a field army in a war-devastated land.

Strengthening the Army

The winter lull also afforded Allied commanders an opportunity to rein-force their armies. On 27 December, about the time the Germans made their brief foray into the Serchio valley, the first units of the U.S. 10th Mountain Division, under the command of Maj. Gen. George P. Hays, landed in Italy, and within two weeks the entire division was ashore.[2] In late March the Japanese-American 442d Infantry, with attached units, returned from France, where the regiment had served since September of the preceding year. At the same time the Legnano Combat Group, an Italian infantry unit of about brigade strength, one of five trained and equipped by the British, was assigned to the Fifth Army. The remaining four Italian combat groups composed of veteran soldiers of the old Italian army, joined the Eighth Army. There were also a number of Italian engineer, quartermaster, and medical units assigned or attached to various Allied commands.[3]

Also in March the 536th and 527th Field Artillery Battalions, both equipped with powerful 8-inch howitzers, arrived from the United States. Those were later joined by the 530th Field Artillery Battalion (155-mm. guns), the 765th and 766th Field Artillery Battalions (155-mm. howitzers), and headquarters of the 428th Field Artillery Group. In addition there also arrived the 679th Tank Destroyer Battalion, equipped

---

[2] *Fifth Army History,* Part VIII, pp. 72–73 and 91–93; Alexander's Rpt to the CCS, The Italian Campaign, 12 Dec 44 to 2 May 45, p. 24; Opns Instructions No. 2, Hq. Fifth U.S. Army, 9 Jan 45, annex F. to above. Unless otherwise indicated the following section is based on these references.

[3] See Coakley and Leighton, *Global Logistics and Strategy,* 1943–45, pp. 716–720, for details concerning Allied use of Italian manpower following the Italian surrender in September 1943.

MOTOR TRANSPORT IN NORTHERN APENNINES

with towed 3-inch guns. To those American units were added a section (4 guns) of the British 11/54 Super Heavy Regiment and a 240-mm. howitzer unit. Further reinforcements came from the 15th South African Field Artillery Regiment and from the 111th Field Regiment, the latter recently returned from duty with the Yugoslav partisans.

To ease supply and administration all attached British artillery units, except the heavy artillery, were placed under the operational control of IV Corps. The four guns of the 11/54 Super

Heavy Regiment remained with II Corps in the Highway 65 sector. To make a more equitable distribution of heavy artillery for the spring offensive, Clark would later transfer the British 61st Heavy Regiment (7.2-inch howitzers and 155-mm. guns) from the II Corps to Eighth Army.

The need to build ammunition reserves, a factor in the decision to postpone resumption of the offensive until spring, was, with the increase in artillery units, all the more essential. From November in the Fifth Army and January in the Eighth, severe restrictions were placed on the use of artillery to enable both armies to begin accumulating large stocks of ammunition. With the arrival of regular shipments from the United States, ammunition dumps in both army areas were by March at last filled to overflowing. Regular depots, operated by the Peninsular Base Section in the vicinity of Pistoia and Leghorn, could store no more ammunition, necessitating the retention of 20,000 additional tons at Naples. The U.S. II Corps also had built up large stocks in forward areas. By the first of March ammunition stocks were so large that daily allotments per gun were increased about one-third throughout the Fifth Army to make room for subsequent shipments. By the end of March supplies of ammunition in the Fifth Army had reached the 60-day reserve level authorized by the War Department.[4]

Regrouping the Army

In addition to maintaining and strengthening the Fifth Army, General Truscott regrouped his divisions in order to rest the troops and reorganize and train units for the spring offensive. The process went on throughout the month of January in the Fifth Army. Most of the units that had been detached from the II Corps in December to reinforce against the German counterattack in the Serchio valley were returned to the central sector including the 135th Regimental Combat Team from Viareggio to its parent division, the 34th, and the entire 85th Division.

---

[4]*Fifth Army History*, Part VIII, pp. 30–32.

SOLDIERS RELAXING DURING LULL IN BATTLE

The 92d Division's 365th Regimental Combat Team, which had been attached temporarily to the II Corps as additional relief for the infantry divisions east of Highway 65, moved back to control of its parent division in the Serchio valley sector, formerly held by the 8th Indian Division. The Indian division then moved into a corps rest area near Pisa. The 10th Mountain Division's 86th Mountain Infantry Regiment, the first unit of that division to arrive, was attached to the IV Corps and relieved the 434th and 900th AA Battalions and the British 39th Light AA Regiment in the division-sized Task Force 45's sector northwest of Pistoia. In turn, the two American antiaircraft battalions, functioning since the previous autumn as infantry, became part of a newly formed 473d Infantry Regi-

ment.[5] By 28 January the 10th Mountain Division's other two regiments had
arrived and joined the first regiment in
the Reno valley on the IV Corps' right
wing where the division was attached to
Task Force 45. At that point the IV
Corps front was held from left to right
by the 92d Division, Task Force 45,
including the 10th Mountain Division,
and the division-sized Brazilian Expeditionary Force, with the 8th Indian Division constituting a reserve. (*Map XIV*)

Similar shifts of major units also took
place on the II Corps front. Early in
January the 85th Division began relieving the British 1st Division in the
Monte Grande area on the left flank of
the 13 Corps, thus extending the right
flank of the II Corps eastward. With
the return of the British 13 Corps
to the operational control of the Eighth
Army on 18 January, the Fifth Army's
new boundary paralleled the Firenzuola-Imola road two miles to the east
as far as a point opposite Castel del Rio,
where it turned northward to skirt the
eastern edge of Monte Grande and
reach Highway 9 at Castel San Pietro,
seven miles northwest of Imola. The
British 1st Division, formerly under 13
Corps, came under control of Allied
Force Headquarters and eventually was
transferred to the Middle East. That
left the 13 Corps in control of only the

British 6th Armoured and 78th Infantry Divisions.[6]

During the month a round robin of
relief of one division by another gave
all a brief rest out of the line. At the
end of January the II Corps held its
sector from left to right with the South
African 6th Armoured Division and the
88th, 34th, and 85th Infantry Divisions,
the latter on the right flank adjacent to
the British 13 Corps. The 91st Division
lay in II Corps reserve; the 1st Armoured Division and the 8th Indian
Division were in Army reserve.

Eliminating Enemy Bridgeheads on the Eighth Army Front

The British Eighth Army commander, General McCreery, meanwhile
was similarly turning his attention to
strengthening and tidying his front,
which except for two potentially troublesome enemy bridgeheads, lay along
the east bank of the Senio River. Cessation of the army's offensive in mid-
December had left the *714th Jaeger
Division* in possession of a bridgehead
some five miles northwest of Ravenna,
while the *278th Infantry Division* held a
second bridgehead to the southwest of
the first, between the towns of Cotig-
nola and Franarola. Eliminating those
bridgeheads was to occupy the Eighth
Army for the next few days.[7]

The separate 473d Infantry Regiment, activated on
14 January 1945 at Montecatini was formed from the
434th Antiaircraft Artillery (Automatic Weapons)
Battalion, the 435th Antiaircraft Artillery (AW) Battalion, and the 900th Antiaircraft Artillery (AW) Battalion. Headquarters and Headquarters Company of
the 2d Armored Group constituted the Headquarters
and Headquarters Company of the newly formed
473d Infantry Regiment.

[6]The 17th Indian Brigade, since December holding the extreme right of the Fifth Army's line, was
in the meantime moved to Pisa, where it rejoined its
parent, the 8th Indian Division, in reserve.
[7]Nicholson, *The Canadians in Italy, 1943–45*, pp.
644–51; Operations of the British, Indian, and
Dominion Forces in Italy, Pt. III, Sec. B. Unless
otherwise indicated the following section is based
upon these sources.

The first of the two bridgeheads lay opposite the Canadian Corps and could be used as a springboard for a counterattack on Ravenna, while the second and smaller of the bridgeheads lay opposite the British 5 Corps. Less of a threat than the first, the second had thus far been tenaciously defended, and the existence of both extended the length of the front and the troops needed to hold it. General McCreery determined to eliminate the two bridgeheads as soon as the frozen earth afforded firm footing for tanks and the weather enabled tactical aircraft to go aloft.

The opportunity came on the morning of 2 January when a period of clear, cold weather set in. Along the Adriatic flank the Canadian 5th Armoured Division moved against the bridgehead north of Ravenna by way of a dry river bed, making use of dikes for a covered route of approach. The town of Conventello fell during the first morning and despite a small German counterattack, the armor on the third day crossed a canal to gain access to the rest of the area still held by the Germans south of the Reno River. By evening of 5 January almost all the territory was under Canadian control. The Italian Cremona Battle Group subsequently assumed responsibility for the sector.

Meanwhile, on 3 January the British 5 Corps attacked the other bridgehead and took only two days to eliminate it. By the end of the first week in January the Eighth Army was drawn up along the east bank of the Senio from the mountains to the sea. At the same time General McCreery withdrew the headquarters of the Polish corps for a period of rest, its former sector passing to the British 5 Corps. Until the final offensive began in April McCreery made no significant changes on a generally inactive front.

German Dispositions

In spite of the relative inactivity of the winter months, the German, as did the Allies, experienced steady attrition through combat as well as noncombat causes, which the *Army Group C*'s replacement system would never be able to make good. In January, for example, losses totaled 13,526, of which 1,299 were killed, 3,132 wounded, 1,417 missing, and 7,678 sick from various causes, mostly respiratory ailments. Yet during the month only 5,600 replacements arrived in northern Italy from the Reich. Among the returnees to *Army Group C* in January was Field Marshal Kesselring, who, after a short convalescent leave, arrived on 15 January to resume command of the German forces in Italy. General Vietinghoff, who had commanded the army group during his absence, left to take command of an army group on the Baltic front.[8]

In January the Germans took advantage of poor flying weather for Allied aircraft to move entire divisions in and out of northern Italy. First to depart, the *356th Infantry Division*, moving to a beleaguered Hungarian front, managed

---

[8]Greiner and Schramm, eds., *OKW/WFSt, KTB,* pp. 1396ff. Lemelsen remained in command of *Tenth Army* until 17 February, when he replaced Tippelskirch in command of the *Fourteenth Army.* Herr, the *LXXVI Panzer Corps* commander, then took Lemelsen's place in command of the *Tenth Army.* Unless otherwise cited the following section is based on the above source.

to traverse the Brenner Pass by rail without incident. At the end of February the *16th SS Panzer Grenadier Division* left for the same sector, while several companies of mountain troops moved to the western front. To take the place of the two departing divisions, the *278th Infantry Division* arrived from Belgium, where it had organized the previous year, and the *710th Infantry Division* arrived from occupation duty in Denmark.

As both Allied armies in Italy closed up to positions from which a co-ordinated attack might be launched against Bologna, General Vietinghoff, then still *Army Group C* commander, reacted by shifting the *Tenth Army* boundary westward from the Santerno to the Reno valley, thus bringing von Senger's *XIV Panzer Corps* into the *Tenth Army* and uniting under one command the most active battle fronts. That move brought the number of corps operating under the *Tenth Army* to five: the *LXXIII* and *XCVII Corps* with four divisions between them, guarding the Adriatic flank and the coastal areas of the Gulf of Venice to the Istrian peninsula; Herr's *LXXVI Panzer Corps* with four divisions, holding a relatively narrow sector from, Bagnacavallo, ten miles northeast of Faenza, to a point just south of Highway 9; and Schlemm's *I Parachute Corps* with six divisions east of Highway 65 and Senger's *XIV Panzer Corps* with four divisions west of the highway, the two jointly holding the critical Bologna sector. To the *Tenth Army*'s right the *Fourteenth Army* commanded two corps, the *LI Mountain Corps* with two German and two Italian divisions, and the *Corps Lombardia* with the equivalent of two Italian divisions and elements of a Ger-

man division. The *Army Group Liguria,* commanded by Mussolini's Defense Minister Rodolfo Graziani, held the coastal defenses of the Gulf of Genoa to the *Fourteenth Army*'s right rear with three German divisions and one Italian division. Two divisions each were in *Tenth Army* and *Army Group C* reserve.

Scattered throughout the *Army Group* rear areas were several miscellaneous units, mostly non-German, including Italian police units totaling about a hundred thousand men. They were of little value other than for local security.[9]

Although the German commanders foresaw no major Allied military operations in Italy before the spring, they were less certain of whether the Allies might attempt limited objective attacks during the winter. While Field Marshal Kesselring assumed that Allied commanders wanted to rest their troops, he also believed they wanted to prevent him from doing the same. Thus the Eighth Army's attacks to eliminate the German bridgeheads over the Senio River in January came as no real surprise. Nor did limited attacks by the U.S. Fifth Army in February. What was surprising was the timing and strength of the attacks.[10]

Operation Fourth Term

As early as 28 December, as an aftermath of the limited German operations in the Serchio valley, General

---

[9]*Schematische Kriegsgliederung*, Stand 26.1.45. Gen. St. d H/Op. Abt. III. MS # C–064 (Kesselring); *Die Hoeheren Dienstellen der Deutschen Wehrmacht, 1933–45* (Munich: Institut fuer Zeitgeschichte, 1953); Greiner and Schramm, eds., *OKW/WFSt, KTB*, pp. 1399–1400; Alexander, Rpt to the CCS, *The Italian Campaign*, pp. 17–18.

[10]MS # C–064 (Kesselring).

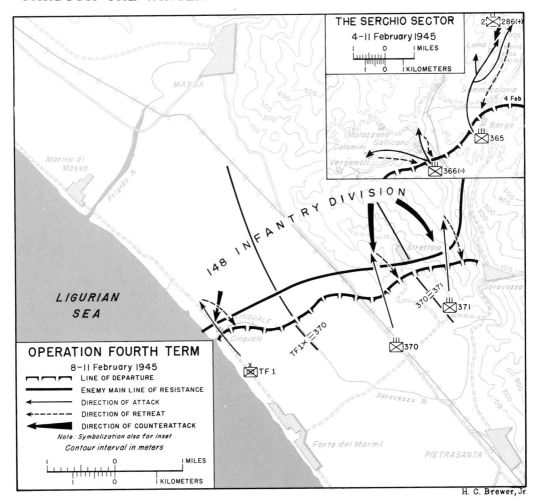

MAP 9

Truscott told the IV Corps commander, General Crittenberger, to get
ready to clear the valley as far north as
Castelnuovo and the coastal area as far
as La Spezia.[11] After reflecting upon a
shortage of combat-worthy units available for the drive and the fact that the
Gothic Line defenses in that area were
still intact, General Truscott two weeks
later lowered his sights considerably. At

that point he called for only limited
attacks "in order to improve positions,"
particularly in the sector of the 92d
Division.[12]

In response, General Almond and his
staff of the 92d Division planned a two-
phase operation given the code name
FOURTH TERM. The first phase, a diversion for the second, was to take the
division up the Serchio valley as far as

[11]Hqs Fifth Army, Opns Instr No. 38, 28 Dec 44,
in *Fifth Army History,* Part VIII, ann 1.

[12]Hqs Fifth Army, Opns Instr No. 2, 9 Jan 45,
Fifth Army History, Part VIII, ann 2.

the Lama di Sotto Ridge, four miles northwest of Tiglio. Then the main attack was to be aimed at securing the Strettoia Hill mass, about three miles northeast of Forte dei Marmi, overlooking both the coastal corridor and the approaches to the town of Massa, five miles north of Forte dei Marmi. Capture of the hill mass could be expected to open up the coastal roads as far as Massa and bring corps and division artillery within range of Italian naval guns at La Spezia.[13]

The Serchio valley operation began on 4 February as the 365th Infantry set out along a ridge east of the Serchio, while the attached 366th Infantry kept abreast west of the river. (*Map 9*) All went well at first as the 366th occupied the village of Gallicano, and the 365th pushed far ahead to reach the foot of its objective, the Lama di Sotto ridge. After only token resistance, opposing Italian units simply melted away into the mountains. Then over the next two days, as the 366th Infantry moved into the next village of Calomini and the 365th moved onto the ridge itself to capture the village of Lama, signs developed that German units had begun to replace the faltering Italians. A counterattack during the night of 7 February by a battalion of the *148th Division's 286th Infantry Regiment* confirmed the fact. Striking at troops of the U.S. 365th Infantry east of Serchio, the Germans forced them to withdraw from Lama and back down the slope of the ridge to within three-quarters of a mile of the original starting point of the

operation. To maintain contact, the 366th Infantry withdrew a similar distance. When the Germans made no effort to press their advantage, both sides contented themselves with eyeing each other warily. A diversionary operation, the attack in the Serchio valley had gained little ground in the end but had at least demonstrated that the two inexperienced American regiments could attack and seize high ground against moderate resistance, even though they failed to hold it.

The 92d Division's real test came in the coastal corridor to the west where General Almond planned for the division's 370th Infantry to capture the Strettoia Hills, three peaks three miles inland overlooking the coastal corridor. The regiment's three battalions were to leapfrog in turn from one hill to the next in hope of maintaining momentum while at the same time providing a defense in depth against counterattack. On the right flank the 371st Infantry was to keep abreast, while on the coastal flatlands a tank-infantry task force built around the 366th Infantry's 3d Battalion was to cross the Cinquale Canal between the coastal highway and the sea four miles south of Massa.

Early on 8 February, as the limited offensive began, Generals Truscott and Crittenberger, along with General Almond, watched from an observation post in the hills northeast of Forte dei Marmi. Unfortunately, from the very beginning the plan began to fall apart. After covering only 800 yards, the 371st Infantry stumbled into an enemy mine field and came to a halt, thereby exposing the 370th Infantry's right flank. Supported by aircraft of the 86th Fighter Squadron, the leading battalion

---

[13]Lee, *Employment of Negro Troops*, pp. 568–72; Goodman Monograph, pp. 92–114. Unless otherwise noted the following is based upon these sources.

AREA NORTH OF CINQUALE CANAL, 92D DIVISION ZONE

of the 370th Infantry nevertheless continued to press ahead and by late afternoon had occupied its initial objective. Hardly had the men dug in when a shattering barrage of mortar fire signaled a sharp counterattack. The Germans quickly overran the forward company and forced the second to withdraw down the eastern slopes of the Strettoia Hills. Units of another battalion proceeding according to plan to leapfrog to the next peak, ran into men falling back under enemy fire. In the resulting confusion the attack broke down completely. At dawn on the third day an urgent message to the battalions from the regimental command post disclosed the regiment's plight: "We have no reserve except our command post . . . It is very important that we let nothing stop us from getting every available man together. Search all houses and places for stragglers. We can expect pressure today and be ready for it. Report every hour on progress and number of men rounded up."[14]

---

[14]Goodman Monograph, pp. 102–03.

That pattern of failure was repeated on the narrow coastal plain to the left of the Strettoia Hills. After three days of costly but inconclusive fighting a task force composed of the 366th Infantry's 3d Battalion with attached armor and engineers failed to get beyond the shallow Cinquale Canal. Large caliber naval guns firing from the Italian coastal defenses at Punta Bianca ten miles northwest of the canal contributed to the failure.

So widespread were disorganization and straggling throughout the 92d Division and its attachments that further attempts to continue the operation seemed futile. General Almond canceled it on the third day, the 11th. The limited thrust had cost the 92d Division 47 officers and 659 enlisted men killed, wounded, and missing, among them two battalion commanders and many of the more capable company grade officers. That had been a high price to pay for 145 enemy captured and virtually no ground gain. Combined with the shortcomings demonstrated earlier in the reverse in the Serchio valley, the disproportionately high losses among officers and the rampant straggling convinced General Truscott that he would be unable to count on the division as then constituted for further offensive action.

A Forecast of Spring

A week after the ill-fated operation by the 92d Division, General Crittenberger's IV Corps began the second of its mid-winter limited offensives, one designed to win better positions for starting the spring offensive, which was no longer to focus, as it had earlier, on

capture of Bologna. With the passing of cold weather the city's attraction as winter quarters also would pass, and no longer was Bologna needed as a communications center for exploitation into the Po Valley. Allied commanders had come to think beyond a deliberate thrust into the valley—to wide-sweeping movements by both the Fifth and Eighth Armies aimed at encircling not only Bologna but also entire German armies.[15]

General Crittenberger had selected for the major role in the limited operation his only fresh, untried division, the recently arrived 10th Mountain Division. Because of specialized mountain training and comparatively light organic artillery—there were only three battalions of 75-mm. pack howitzers as contrasted with the three battalions of 105-mm. howitzers and one of 155-mm. howitzers in the standard infantry division—commanders in other theaters had declined the division's services, but the specialized training enhanced the division's attractiveness to an army engaged in mountain warfare.[16]

Activated in the summer of 1943 at Camp Hale, Colorado, the 10th Mountain Division included the 85th, 86th, and 87th Mountain Infantry Regiments. With its 75-mm. pack howitzer artillery support and few motor vehicles, the division resembled a German *Jaeger* or light infantry division. In sharp contrast to the unfortunate 92d Division, or, for that matter, almost any other U.S. division, the ranks of the 10th Mountain Division contained a high percentage of

---

[15] Alexander, Report to the CCS, pp. 32–33.

[16] Interv, Sidney T. Mathews with Gen. Marshall, 25 Jul 49, CMH; Truscott, *Command Missions*, p. 464.

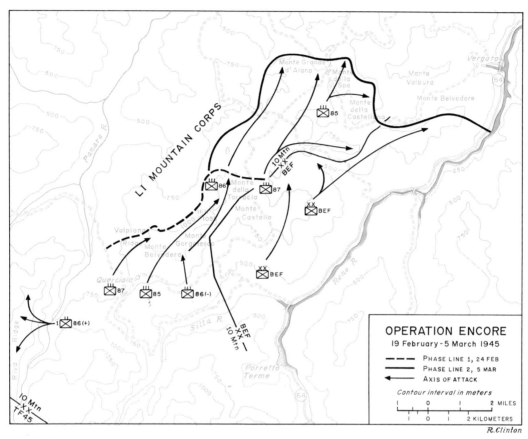

MAP 10

college-trained men, including winter sports enthusiasts and members of mountain climbing and skiing clubs, most of whom had volunteered for service with the division through an unorthodox recruitment campaign conducted by the civilian National Ski Patrol System.

The division commander, General Hays, had come favorably to General Marshall's attention during World War I when during a heavy artillery barrage Hays had ridden on horseback through enemy fire to locate targets for his artillery. For this action Hays had received the Medal of Honor. In World War II Marshall had transferred him from command of the 2d Division artillery in France to command of the mountain division just before its departure for Italy. Truscott would later rate him as one of his ablest battle leaders.[17]

Plans for the new offensive—code named Operation Encore—were initiated at army instead of corps level. Truscott's intention was to secure high

---

[17]Truscott, *Command Missions,* p. 465.

SKI PATROL, 10TH MOUNTAIN DIVISION

ground dominating a ten-mile section of Highway 64. Averaging about 3,800 feet in height, the objective consisted of a series of mountain peaks and ridges about five miles west of the highway. From it the Germans had excellent observation over a large section of Highway 64 and into the American positions east of the Reno River. In American hands, the terrain would provide observation almost as far as the Po Valley, about twenty miles away. North of Vergato the terrain, though still mountainous, descends gradually to-

ward Highway 9 and the Lombardy Plain. Inherent in General Truscott's concept for the limited objective operation was the possibility of an eventual westward shift of the main axis of the Fifth Army's spring offensive into the Po Valley.[18]

In early February the 10th Mountain Division held positions in the valley of the Silla River not far from its confluence with the Reno River, through

---

[18]Opns Instr No. 4, Hq Fifth Army, 16 Feb 45, in *Fifth Army History*, Part VIII, ann. 1.

APENNINES, IV CORPS SECTOR

whose valley Highway 64, one of the two main routes leading to Bologna on the Fifth Army's front, runs. (*Map 10*) Dominating the region were two ridges whose highest peaks rose between three thousand to nearly five thousand feet. Known to American troops as the Riva Ridge, the first of the two overlooked the mountain division's left flank and dominated routes of approach to the second: the Monte Belvedere–Monte della Torraccia Ridge.

The Riva Ridge paralleled the left flank of the division's zone of operations for four miles. The side of the ridge facing the division was a cliff, rising in some places almost 1,500 feet above the valley floor. Since the ridge would have to be cleared before the main attack could move toward Monte Belvedere, the mountain troops would have to scale that cliff. Once the Monte Belvedere–Monte della Torraccia ridge was in hand, the division was to open a second phase of the attack to continue northeastward about four miles and

ARTILLERY AMMUNITION BEING BROUGHT
FORWARD, 10TH MOUNTAIN DIVISION

occupy a series of lower ridges from
which roads descended into the Po
Valley.[19]

General Hays had secretly assembled
his troops some two to three miles
south and east of the two ridges.[20] To
the right was the Brazilian Expeditionary Force, holding with its three regiments a three-mile sector between the
mountain division's right flank and the
Reno River. The Brazilians were to
cover the mountain division's right
flank. To make up for the mountain
division's lack of heavy fire support,

General Crittenberger attached the
175th Field Artillery Battalion with 105-
mm. howitzers, the 84th Chemical (4.2-
inch) Mortar Battalion, two tank destroyer battalions, and a tank battalion.

For the men of the 10th Mountain
Division, crossing the snow-covered
ground would be especially difficult
because of limited concealment provided by nothing more than scattered
clumps of stunted trees. Vehicular
movement also would be difficult because the few roads and trails crossing
the area were narrow and in poor
condition. The burden of transport
would fall mainly upon pack mules,
full-tracked "Weasels," and jeeps. Tanks
could, by skillful handling, be brought
forward in small groups as far as the
village of Querciola, a little more than a
mile southwest of Monte Belvedere.

Through interrogation of enemy
prisoners, the mountain division's G–2
had determined that the peaks and
ridges opposite both the mountain division and the Brazilians were lightly held
by troops of the *232d Infantry Division*,
with all three regiments in line across
an 18-mile front. Originally intended
only for rear area duty, most of the
division's troops were either older men
or convalescents intercepted en route to
their former units on the Eastern front.
In reserve were a fusilier battalion and
elements of a mountain battalion.[21]

Into the Mountains

In the bitter cold, as darkness settled
over the valley below Monte Belvedere,
teams of picked rock climbers slung

---

[19]*Fifth Army History*, Part VIII, pp. 78–88; IV
Corps Opns Rpt, Feb 45; 10th Mountain Division
G–3 Jnl and file, regimental jnls and historical
narratives. Unless otherwise cited the following is
based upon these references.

[20]Arrival of the division in the theater was not
announced to the Allied press until 23 Feb 45.

[21]*Order of Battle of the German Army* (Washington:
Military Intelligence Division, War Department,
1945), pp. 210–11.

coils of ropes over their shoulders and hung clusters of pitons and snap links to their belts. For long months these men had trained in the Rocky Mountains for just this kind of action—scaling the face of 1,500 Riva Ridge. Setting out soon after dark on 18 February, a climbing team from each of the three rifle companies of the 86th Mountain Infantry's 1st Battalion and another from the 2d Battalion was to prepare the way. Climbing in the darkness, the men drove steel pitons into the rock, hooked snap links to them, then fastened ropes to the snap links to provide fixed hand lines for the main body of climbers to follow.

When the climbing teams reached the rim of the ridge, they signaled to the main body of the 1st Battalion, 86th Infantry, in the valley below. The battalion set out in a column of companies toward the base of Riva Ridge, each company to take a different route up the cliff to a series of peaks along the ridge. Aided by the ropes, the men scaled the cliff without difficulty. Before dawn, virtually the entire battalion had reached the top undetected.

The mountain infantry may have been aided by the fact that even as the men were working their way up, the *232d Fusilier Battalion* was relieving a battalion of the *1044th Infantry Regiment* on the ridge. Discovering the Americans with the coming of daylight, the enemy managed to mount three minor counterattacks, but the mountain infantry repulsed them without much trouble. As indications of enemy withdrawal developed in the afternoon, a patrol probed along the ridge, encountering only a seven-man enemy detachment. Three were captured, four killed. By the end of the day the entire ridge was secured.

The division's left flank protected by capture of the Riva Ridge, troops of the 85th and 87th Mountain Infantry Regiments set out that night in silence for a forward assembly area at the base of the Monte Belvedere–Monte della Torraccia hill mass. Eschewing an artillery preparation in hope of achieving surprise, the regiments attacked an hour before midnight. While the 85th Mountain Infantry moved frontally against Monte Belvedere and adjacent Monte Gorgolesco, the 87th moved up the western slopes toward a trio of villages lying between Belvedere and the Riva Ridge, and from there was to proceed to the Valpiana Ridge, northwestern spur of Monte Belvedere. Gaining the Valpiana Ridge would have the effect of outflanking defenses on the crest of Monte Belvedere.

Dispensing with an artillery preparation apparently paid off, for men of the 87th Mountain Infantry were virtually atop the enemy's outposts before they met resistance. From a line of bunkers, machine gun positions, and fortified houses, the Germans fought back sporadically, while extensive minefields created further hitches. Both leading battalions nevertheless made steady progress, so that within a few hours the Valpiana Ridge and two of the three villages were in hand.

The story was much the same with the 85th Mountain Infantry in the frontal drive against the two heights. At Monte Belvedere the first resistance developed 300 yards short of the summit, but during the next three hours the mountain infantrymen fought their way to the top. Others had a similar

MONTE BELVEDERE

MONTE BELVEDERE MASSIF FROM LIZZANO, 10TH MOUNTAIN DIVISION SECTOR

experience on Monte Gorgolesco. Protecting the division's right flank, a battalion of the 86th Mountain Infantry occupied a village on Monte Gorgolesco's northeastern slope.

As the advance continued northeastward toward the last peak of the hill mass, Monte della Torraccia, the mountain division's artillery and its supporting guns came into play, with counterbattery fire that partially neutralized enemy guns. With the coming of daylight, L–5 artillery spotter aircraft adjusted fires with marked accuracy while

also directing fighter-bombers to targets, some within 600 yards of the American positions. During the first two days British Spitfires and U.S. P–47's flew a total of 412 sorties in support of the attack.

Despite the artillery and aerial support, the enemy early on the 21st managed a counterattack by a reinforced battalion against the 3d Battalion, 85th Mountain Infantry, on Monte Belvedere. The counterattacking force represented first commitment of troops of the *714th Jaeger Division*, which by

EVACUATING CASUALTIES OVER MOUNTAIN TRAIL

chance had been en route from the Adriatic flank to the Monte Belvedere sector even before the 10th Mountain Division's attack had begun. Reinforcing were portions of a battalion of the *1043d Infantry Regiment,* the *232d Division*'s local reserve. Although the Germans failed to regain any of the lost ground the counterattack prompted a temporary pause in the American advance toward Monte della Torraccia.

Meanwhile the troops of the Brazilian Expeditionary Force entered the fight to protect the 10th Mountain Division's right flank by seizing Monte Castello, about a mile southeast of Monte della Torraccia. Unknown to the Brazilians, the American drive toward Monte della Torraccia had precipitated an enemy withdrawal from Monte Castello. Behind a 15-minute artillery preparation, the Brazilian 1st Regiment converged on the objective from south and southwest and quickly gained the summit. Soon after nightfall the last resistance from a small rear guard ceased.

The counterattack on Monte Belvedere at an end and the Brazilians moving on Monte Castello, the 85th Mountain Infantry during early afternoon of the 21st renewed the drive for Monte della Torraccia. A fresh battalion, the 2d, led the way and quickly discovered that the Germans intended to make a fight of it. In the heavy combat that followed, casualties were high, including the 2d Battalion commander and his heavy weapons company commander. Three salvos from enemy artillery fire were particularly devastating until counterbattery fire silenced the guns. Throughout the night and well into the next day the battalion clung to positions 400 yards short of the objective, unable to push farther. By late afternoon of the 22d the battalion was down to some 400 effectives and was low on ammunition, food, and water. The battalion's condition prompted General Hays to relieve the 85th Mountain Infantry with the 86th.

During the afternoon of the 23d the 3d Battalion, 86th Mountain Infantry, came forward to make the final assault against the crest of Monte della Torraccia. As the battalion began to attack the next morning, tactical aircraft strafed and bombed hedgerows sheltering and concealing enemy gunners. Company I was atop the objective within an hour, and by early afternoon all of Monte della Torraccia and ridges north and northeast of it were in friendly hands. Although a battalion of German mountain troops from the *232d Division's* reserve counterattacked vigorously, the 3d Battalion with strong artillery support held fast. By nightfall the entire complex of heights from the Riva Ridge to Monte Castello was firmly in hand.

In a first full-scale battle action, men of the 10th Mountain Division had fought with courage and determination,

wresting a stretch of rugged terrain from the enemy at a cost of just over 900 casualties, of which 203 were killed. However deplorable any losses at all, that was hardly an alarming figure for a first engagement. Field Marshal Kesselring would later call the division "outstandingly efficient."[22] From General Crittenberger came the message: ". . . you have done a wonderful job. All eyes are on you. You are carrying the ball." That was a statement that General Truscott could heartily endorse, for carrying the ball was exactly what he expected the division to do when the army's offensive resumed in the spring.[23]

The Second Phase

For the next step of the limited objective operation, the 10th Mountain Division and the Brazilian Expeditionary Force were to advance on a more northeasterly axis, generally toward the road junction town of Vergato, on Highway 64, twelve miles northeast of Monte Belvedere. The objective was another line of hill crests or peaks roughly 4 miles to the north and northeast of the positions gained in the first phase, whence the terrain the rest of the way to the Po Valley was downhill. The peaks would serve as the jump-off line in this sector for the spring offensive. From west to east, they were Monte Grande d'Aiano, Monte della Spe, Monte della Castellana, and Monte Valbura.

Although scheduled to begin on 1 March, the drive had to be postponed for two days because of poor weather.

[22] MS #C–064 (Kesselring).
[23] 10th Mtn Div Opns Rpt and Jnl, Feb 45.

It produced few surprises. Again General Hays employed two regiments abreast—the 86th Mountain Infantry on the left, the 87th on the right—while the Brazilians kept pace with the mountain infantry to protect the right flank. As before troops of the *232d Infantry* and *714th Jaeger Divisions* fought back from every crest and village until forced out by the combined force of artillery, air, and aggressive foot troops. Where tank destroyers could negotiate the rugged terrain, they proved of particular value, especially when the Germans holed up in thick-walled stone houses. Almost inevitably the Germans counterattacked, but in no case were they successful.

In two days—3 and 4 March—the two assault regiments took all intermediate heights and also captured Monte Grande d'Aiano, whereupon early on 5 March General Hays sent his third regiment, the 85th, to seize Monte della Spe and Monte della Castellano. Despite the heaviest defensive fires of the three-day drive, the 1st Battalion by late afternoon stood on top the summit of Monte della Spe. The 2d Battalion, meanwhile, encountered such heavy fire on the slopes of Monte della Castellana that the men had to withdraw and take another approach, but the second try carried the position.

Those heavy defensive fires on 5 March were the first indication that the Germans were attempting to reinforce the sector. Aware of heavy losses in both defending divisions during the first phase of the American drive, Field Marshal Kesselring had been intending to replace the two with a fresh division, but the second phase opened before he could accomplish it. The renewed thrust disturbed Kesselring. Was this the beginning of a major offensive aimed at encircling Bologna from the west?

Unable to determine for sure, Kesselring deemed he could ill afford to take a chance. He saw no choice but to rush his major reserve, the *29th Panzer Grenadier Division,* then undergoing reorganization, to the threatened sector. It was, he observed, "a grim decision [but] unfortunately . . . absolutely unavoidable."[24] However limited the scope of the operation from the American viewpoint, the Germans saw it as a serious threat. The fight appeared to have developed into "a battle for possession of the gateway into the Po Valley at both the operationally and tactically most unfavorable point."[25]

Shortly before midnight on 5 March the *15th Panzer Grenadier Regiment,* first contingent of the *29th Panzer Grenadier Division* to arrive, mounted the first in a series of four counterattacks against the 1st Battalion, 87th Mountain Infantry, on Monte della Spe, the apex of the American salient. Although the German infantrymen actually penetrated the battalion's positions at one point, the Americans drove them back in fierce hand-to-hand fighting. When the fourth counterattack failed, the Germans backed off and contented themselves with harassing artillery fire.

Truscott Halts the Attack

Anxious lest Kesselring become so alarmed that he would develop defensive positions astride Highway 64 as formidable as those on Highway 65,

---

[24] MS # C–064 (Kesselring), p. 149.
[25] *Ibid.*

Truscott ordered the IV Corps to halt in place. The objectives of the limited offensive were in hand in any case. At a cost of another 549 casualties, including 106 killed, the mountain division had brought the right wing of the IV Corps abreast of the II Corps and in control of excellent jump-off positions for the spring offensive.[26]

Over the next few days the Brazilians

shifted position to the 10th Mountain Division's left, while the mountain troops extended their control to embrace two additional features on the right, Monte Valbura and a second Monte Belvedere. The 10th Mountain Division now held a six-mile front between Monte Grande d'Aiano and Highway 64, the favorable jump-off point they had been seeking for an offensive down the Reno valley and Highway 64.

---

[26] 10th Mt Div AAR, Mar 45.

PART SEVEN

THE LAST OFFENSIVE

Thus a victorious army wins its victories before seeking battle; an army destined to defeat fights in the hope of winning.

SUN TZU, *The Art of War*

The commander in war must work in a medium which his eyes cannot see; which his best deductive powers cannot always fathom; and with which because of constant changes he can rarely become completely familiar.

CLAUSEWITZ, *On War*

CHAPTER XXV

Strategies and Plans

German Strategic Problems

Except for the setback dealt the U.S. 92d Division on the westernmost sector of the Italian front, the German command could take little comfort from the last winter of the campaign except in that the front was still intact. At a superficial glance, the overall military situation of the Germans in the west, including Italy, did not appear hopeless. There had been, to be sure, a threatening penetration of the western front in the vicinity of Aachen in the Rhineland, but elsewhere the German armies still held the Allies at bay from the North Sea to Switzerland. In northern Italy, except for the newly won positions of the U.S. IV Corps on the high ground west of the upper Reno River, *Army Group C* still maintained an unbroken defensive line from the Romagna Plain to the Tyrrhenian Sea. Yet in fact Germany's military situation was deteriorating rapidly. In late August 1944 Rumania had capitulated to the Russians, and in early September of the same year Bulgaria had followed. Only German arms prevented a third ally— Hungary—from collapsing before the Red Army.

After mid-January 1945 the time had passed when divisions from the Italian front could be used to influence decisively the course of the war on other fronts. Although in January and February Kesselring had moved four divisions out of Italy to other fronts, by March the railroads leading out of the peninsula were in such poor condition that it would have taken months to move additional divisions, even if they had been available. For the Germans the time had long since passed for a strategic withdrawal from Italy.[1]

On 8 March Hitler summoned Kesselring to Berlin to tell him that he was to leave Italy to command the Western Front where, following the failure of the Ardennes counteroffensive in December 1944, Allied armies under General Eisenhower were pressing the Germans back into the Reich itself. When asked whom he would recommend as his successor in Italy, Kesselring named Vietinghoff. When Hitler readily agreed, Vietinghoff, since January in command of *Army Group Kurland* on the Baltic front, returned to Italy and the command of *Army Group C*.

Kesselring was less successful in obtaining the Fuehrer's agreement to giving the new army group commander more flexibility in the conduct of operations when the Allies resumed their offensive in the spring. That lack of flexibility had long acerbated relations

---

[1] Yet in late March 1945 Stalin was to complain bitterly to his western allies that covert negotiations between the Americans and Germans in Switzerland were a smoke screen to permit German troop movements to take place. See Herbert Feis, *Churchill, Roosevelt, Stalin: The War They Waged and the Peace They Sought* (Princeton, 1957), pp. 588–89.

between *Army Group C* and OKW and
was to hang like a heavy cloud over the
army group headquarters as Vietinghoff prepared plans for defensive measures to be taken when the Allied armies
resumed the offensive.[2]

In early February OKW had informed Kesselring that under no circumstances was he to abandon major
portions of his front voluntarily. To
that directive he replied that, while he
had no such intention, he would like to
be free to pull back in certain sectors
even in advance of an Allied attack
when an attack appeared imminent, for
he lacked the manpower to hold every
sector of the front in its present location against heavy Allied pressure. Kesselring observed that had he been given
that kind of freedom prior to the U.S.
10th Mountain Division's recent attack
at Monte Belvedere, he might have
been spared the necessity of committing
the *29th Panzer Grenadier Division* from
his army group reserve. Yet the most
OKW would grant was permission to
fall back only in those sectors against
which a large-scale Allied operation was
already under way.[3]

That concession hardly afforded the
field marshal or his successor much
strategic flexibility. If the Allied spring
offensive forced Kesselring to abandon
his positions in the Apennines, he saw
no alternative to fighting a series of
delaying actions along each of the many
river lines as he withdrew into the Alps.
Although the German high com-

mand at first frowned on the plan,
Kesselring remained convinced that as
long as he was commander-in-chief in
Italy, he could, as he so frequently had
done in the past, obtain the Fuehrer's
approval to disengage before the situation became catastrophic. While *Army
Group C's* commander had no intention
of ordering an immediate large-scale
withdrawal, neither did he intend to
fight the decisive battle for northern
Italy along the river lines south of the
Reno, since to do that would stake the
future of the entire campaign on one
card, a card that offered him little
chance of saving his armies from destruction. Regardless of the high command's views, Kesselring believed his
only choice to be the plan he had
developed: withdrawal under pressure
of an Allied offensive while fighting
delaying actions along a succession of
favorable defensive positions based on
those river lines. That defensive strategy had worked well in the past and
could, if followed, make the last offensive costly for the Allied armies.

On 22 February, however, a directive
from the Fuehrer dashed Kesselring's
hopes for even that much freedom of
action. Hitler acknowledged that although *Army Group C's* over-all strength
was admittedly weak, the solution lay
not in Kesselring's plan but rather in
deployment in greater depth in the
sector facing the greatest threat. While
Hitler would raise no objection to
planned withdrawals to stronger positions in the face of a large-scale Allied
offensive, he would never consent to
voluntary withdrawals by means of a
series of delaying actions. That, Hitler
believed, would destroy the morale of
the troops. On the eve of the Allied

---

[2] Greiner and Schramm, ed., *OKW/WFSt, KTB,*
IV(2), 1394–99; MS # C–064 (Kesselring), pp. 123–
30; Jodl Diary, 9 Mar 45.

[3] Greiner and Schramm, ed., *OKW/WFSt,* IV(2),
p. 1394. Unless otherwise cited the following is
from this source.

offensive Hitler was destined to reiterate his antipathy to voluntary withdrawals when he refused to authorize *Army Group C* to implement Operation *HERBSTNEBEL,* a long-standing plan for large-scale withdrawal to prepared defensive positions along the line of the Ticino and Po Rivers. That refusal, observed the *Fourteenth Army*'s chief of staff, was tantamount to a death sentence for the army group in Italy.[4]

Those differences failed to dampen either Vietinghoff's or Kesselring's optimism and obvious loyalty to their Fuehrer. Yet there were senior officers within the German command structure in northern Italy who took quite a different view of the Reich's military situation and agreed with the judgment of the *Fourteenth Army*'s chief of staff. As exchanges between the OKW and *Army Group C* over strategic and tactical plans for meeting the anticipated Allied offensive gradually assumed an air of unreality, several senior SS officers in Italy took advantage of their unique position within the Reich's military hierarchy to establish covert contacts with Allied agents. On 21 February, the day before the Fuehrer's directive binding the German armies in Italy to a stultified strategy was received at Kesselring's headquarters, an Italian businessman, Baron Luigi Parrilli, an intimate of SS General Karl Wolff, senior SS officer in command of the security forces, arrived in Zürich to make contact with American intelligence agents.

Within the German forces in northern Italy perhaps no one group had a

better picture of military and civilian morale than did the SS police and security units. It was thus natural that they had a more pessimistic and yet more realistic picture of the over-all situation than did many of their counterparts in the Army whose eyes were focused more specifically on the battlefronts. Yet in the weeks to come what amounted to their incipient treason would have no influence on the course of battle. Most commanders and the rank and file of the German armies in Italy would remain steadfastly at their posts until ordered to withdraw or until the tide of battle overwhelmed them.

The German armies in Italy faced a more immediate problem: a rapidly deteriorating transportation system without which a modern field army cannot operate. A general shortage of vehicles of all types and a shortage of motor fuel, complicated by a wide-ranging Allied aerial interdiction of road and rail traffic, was largely responsible.

To keep essential military traffic moving, the Germans had commandeered hundreds of civilian passenger cars, trucks, and buses. For several months even oxen had been employed to move heavy equipment, including artillery. In many motor convoys every third truck was employed to tow two others. Substitute fuels such as methane gas, fairly abundant in many areas of the Po Valley, were inadequate for combat vehicles, but were widely used to power administrative vehicles. Such fuels as alcohol and benzol were mixed with gasoline and diesel oil on a one-to-three ratio in order to stretch limited fuel supplies. A few small oil wells in northern Italy, some producing as little

---

[4] MS # T–1b (Westphal *et al.*), *Feldzug in Italien, II Teil, Kapitel 11a (Die Abwehr kampfe der 14. Armee im u. noerdlich des Apennin im Fruejahr 1945* (Wolf-Rudiger Haüer, Gen Maj a.D.).

SS GENERAL WOLFF

as 1,000 gallons a day, contributed small amounts of fuel.[5]

Even winter failed to give the Germans the respite from Allied aerial harassment they so sorely needed. Although snow secured the *Army Group C* flank in the western Alps and hampered military operations in the Apennines, it failed to halt air attacks against the German lines of communications. In December alone there were 900 major breaks in those lines, only fifty of which had not been repaired by the beginning of the year. Only through careful organization of motor transport and husbanding of dwindling resources had the Germans in Italy been able to keep their logistical system from collapsing before the end of 1944.[6]

Up until the end of the year, 50,000 tons of supplies per month, mostly coal shipments, arrived in Italy from Germany, but after January 1945 all coal shipments came to a halt. That impelled the Germans to make intensive efforts to achieve complete self-sufficiency for their armies in northern Italy. Those efforts, in turn, placed the economy of the region under severe inflationary pressures and caused increased unrest among the population. Food shortages and widespread unemployment inflicted considerable hardship.

A shortage—almost a dearth—of reconnaissance aircraft had long made it difficult for the Germans to obtain intelligence on Allied intentions. For almost a year the Germans had been unable to make anywhere near adequate aerial reconnaissance, which contributed to making it difficult to see through Allied deception plans.[7]

Late in March Allied intelligence learned through the Enigma Code that those plans were apparently succeeding, for it seemed that the *29th Panzer Grenadier Division* had been moved from the Bologna sector, where it had been in army group reserve, to overwatch the Adriatic coast northeast of Venice. Aware that enemy fuel stocks were low, the Allies believed that only a conviction on the part of the German command that an actual threat existed on the Adriatic flank could have prompted such a move.[8]

From the German point of view there seemed to be considerable grounds for giving credence to numerous indications of a forthcoming Allied amphibious operation north of the

[5] MS # T–1b (Westphal *et al.*), *Part II, Feldzug in Italien; Fifth Army History*, IX, 12–13.
[6] MS # C–064 (Kesselring).

[7] *Ibid.*
[8] Alexander, Report to the CCS, The Italian Campaign, pp. 37–41.

mouth of the Po. By early April Tito's partisans had reached Senj, only thirty miles southeast of Fiume, a major Italian port on the northeastern corner of the Istrian peninsula. To the Germans it seemed logical that to take advantage of this development the Allies might land somewhere to the west of the peninsula and thrust overland to effect a junction with the Yugoslavs and together advance via Ljubljana toward Vienna. Inasmuch as the Red Army also threatened that city, that course of action seemed an even more likely possibility.[9]

In an effort to counter the threat, the German high command in early April extended *Army Group C*'s long eastern flank northward to include the Austrian provinces of Vorarlberg, Tyrol, Salzburg, and the western half of Styria and Carinthia. Because of that added responsibility, *Army Group C*'s eastern boundary was withdrawn westward an average of twenty miles from the prewar Italo-Yugoslav frontier to the line of the Isonzo River, which flows southward through the easternmost Italian province of Gorizia to enter the gulf of Trieste some twelve miles west of that city. Since the partisans under Tito's leadership had long claimed the Isonzo as the legitimate postwar frontier between the countries—it had been the pre-World War I boundary between the Austrian Empire and Italy—the German action had, perhaps deliberately, cast an apple of discord into the midst of Allied councils. As a result of the boundary shift between Vietinghoff's *Army Group C* and von Weich's *Army Group E*, the *XCVII Corps* with two

divisions passed to command of *Army Group E*.[10]

On the eve of the Allied offensive Vietinghoff's command included 26 divisions of all types, of which 21 were German and five Italian. Sixteen were actually deployed across the front from the Adriatic to the Tyrrhenian Sea. The remainder were either in reserve or on coastal defense or rear area security duty. The *Tenth Army*, since February commanded by General Herr, continued to hold the army group's left wing with two corps: the *LXXVI Panzer Corps* with four divisions and the *I Parachute Corps*, also with four.[11]

Two of the best of the divisions of the *I Parachute Corps*, the *4th Parachute* and the *26th Panzer*, were astride Highway 9, which the Germans still considered to be the most likely approach to Bologna from the southeast. The sector in the Apennines foothills was held by the *1st Parachute Division* opposite the 13 Corps Monte Grande sector, and the *278th Division* opposed the 10 Corps. Defending the *Tenth Army*'s front that would eventually bear the brunt of the Eighth Army's offensive, the *LXXVI Panzer Corps* employed the *42d Jaeger (Light Infantry)*, the *362d Infantry Division*, defender of Cisterna at Anzio the previous spring, and the *98th Volksgrenadier Divisions*. Since those divisions occupied positions on which they had been working since January, they could expect to be fairly well sheltered from all but direct hits by artillery fire or aerial bombs. All, however, had incurred heavy losses during the fighting

---

[9] MS # T–1b (Westphal *et al.*), vol. 2, part II.

[10] *Ibid.* Unless otherwise indicated the following section is based upon this source.

[11] Greiner and Schramm, ed., *OKW/WFSt, KTB*, IV(2), 1400.

of the previous autumn and winter in the mountains and were still considerably understrength, as, indeed, were all German combat divisions in the last months of the war. A fourth division, the *162d Turkomen*, was deployed along the Comacchio Lagoon's northeastern edge and on a spit separating the lagoon from the sea.[12]

The front opposite the Fifth Army was held by Lemelsen's *Fourteenth Army*, with two corps deployed across a front extending approximately 50 miles southwestward from the Idice valley southeast of Bologna to the Serchio valley. The *LI Mountain Corps* held the western half with the *232d Reserve Division*, made up largely of older men and convalescents; the *714th(114th) Jaeger Division*, composed largely of ethnic Germans from Poland, Czechoslovakia, and Alsace; and the *334th Infantry Division*, which had taken heavy casualties while bearing the brunt of the Fifth Army's drive through the Futa Pass in October. Senger und Etterlin's *XIV Panzer Corps*, long a familiar antagonist of the Fifth Army, held the remainder with the *94th Division*, since the fighting south of Rome a frequent, if somewhat battered, opponent of the Fifth Army; the *8th Mountain Division;* and the *65th Division*, also long engaged on the Italian front. Since the beginning of April the *90th Panzer Grenadier Division* had been assembled in army reserve behind the panzer corps sector and northwest of Bologna.

Except for the *8th Mountain Division*, which had over 3,000 combat infantrymen, all divisions were understrength in front-line soldiers. The *714th [114th] Jaeger Division* was in the worst condition with only 984 combat infantry as of the end of March 1945; the other divisions were in somewhat better condition with strength ranging from 1,766 to 2,542.

From those figures it is evident that Lemelsen had concentrated his strength south of Bologna on the *XIV Panzer Corps* sector and opposite the U.S. II Corps rather than the U.S. IV Corps. The Italo-German *Ligurian Army*, under the command of Marshal Graziani, composed mostly of fortress and coastal defense units, was deployed along the gulf of Genoa as far as the Franco-Italian frontier.[13]

The German Defenses

The German front line from sea to sea simply represented the line along which the Allied offensive had ground to a halt during the winter. Only on the western coastal plain did it still embrace portions of the Gothic Line.

Opposite the Eighth Army German defenses were in considerable depth to protect Bologna from an attack coming from the southeast. They were based upon a series of river lines, beginning with the Senio, then the Santerno, the Sillaro, a switch position along the Sellustra, and, finally, the so-called Genghis Khan Line, based on the Idice River and anchored in the east in the flooded plain west of the Comacchio Lagoon. At their northern extremities those river lines were linked to another line of defense based on a stretch of the Reno River that flowed eastward from

[12] Heinz Greiner, GLT, a.D., *Kampf um Rom, Inferno am Po,* pp. 150–58.

[13] Records of German Field Commands, Army Groups, *Heeresgruppe C*, Microfilm Roll T–311, National Archives, Captured Records Division.

a great bend twelve miles southwest of Ferrara. The latter line gave some depth to the defenses of the line of the lower Po and was an essential element of the German defensive system. The Germans saw it as the pivot upon which the central and western sectors of their front had to swing toward the lines of the Po and the Adige Rivers and the northeastern passes leading into Germany.

Throughout the winter months over 5,000 German engineer troops and additional thousands of civilian laborers toiled at preparing field works along the Po and the Adige Rivers. The line along the Adige was reinforced with naval gun batteries from the Ligurian coast, while the line of the Po was continued westward along the Ticino River to cover the withdrawal of Marshal Graziani's *Ligurian Army* on the German western flank.

Behind those two defensive lines—the Po and the Adige—the Germans developed yet another line, a so-called *Voralpenstellung* (the forward position of the Alps). Extending east and west of Lake Garda, that line represented an outwork of the almost impregnable bastion of the Alps. In a manner somewhat similar to the way the river lines southeast of Bologna were tied in with the Reno, the river lines of the Brenta, Piave, Tagliamento, and Isonzo, all flowing from the Alps in a generally southerly direction toward the Adriatic, were tied in with the *Voralpenstellung*. Those lines were intended to cover a possible withdrawal by the German forces northeastward toward the Ljubljana Gap.[14]

Allied Strategy and Plans

As Field Marshal Alexander and his staff studied the situation map at the Mediterranean theater headquarters showing those defenses and, thanks to decipherment of the German code, an accurate picture of the enemy's troop dispositions, they considered the possibility that the Germans might ignore those lines and withdraw from northern Italy directly into a so-called "National Redoubt." That consideration arose from an idea that earlier had gained some acceptance within SHAEF and among some Allied commanders. The idea rested upon an assumption that Hitler and the survivors of his legions might fall back into an Alpine defense zone extending from Salzburg and Klagenfurt in the east to the Swiss frontier in the west and including the cities of Innsbruck, Bolzano, Landeck, and Bregenz. There the fanatical remnants of the Third Reich might attempt a last-ditch stand of indefinite duration. Although British intelligence circles, to which Alexander was privy, remained skeptical of the redoubt's existence, no commander could afford to ignore the possibility.

There were some within the Allied command in Italy who believed that Marshal Kesselring had no alternative, other than outright surrender, to retreat into the Alps. There the Germans might find refuge in former Austrian fortifications that had survived World War I. Constructed along the former Austro-Italian frontier, many had been left intact by the Italians and could prove quite formidable if manned.[15]

---

[14] Greiner and Schramm, eds., *OKW/WFSt, KTB,* IV(2), 1389–1400.

[15] For details on the National Redoubt, see Rodney G. Minott, *The Fortress That Never Was, the Myth of Hitler's Bavarian Stronghold* (Toronto & New York: Rinehart & Winston, 1964).

As planning proceeded for the spring offensive, the same divergent strategies that underlay the Anglo-American controversy over ANVIL again came to the surface. As they had since the beginning of the Italian campaign, the British continued to look upon the peninsula as a promising road into eastern Europe and the mid-Danube basin. The Americans, for their part, still regarded the Italian campaign as a sideshow to the main drama moving to a denouement on the plains of northwestern Europe. For the closing months of the Italian campaign, the Americans would continue to think, as their President had once reminded Churchill during the ANVIL debates, in terms of the shortest distance between two points—in short, a drive aimed directly at the Alps. A direct thrust northward via Bologna, Verona, and Lake Garda to the Brenner Pass would trap those still considerable enemy forces left in northwestern Italy and afford entry to the National Redoubt before the enemy had an opportunity to get set there.

Thinking in terms of the post-war balance of power in Europe, the British continued to focus much of their attention on northeastern Italy. Even if there should be no drive into the mid-Danube basin, a thrust to the northeast still might thwart long-held Yugoslav ambitions to acquire territory along Italy's northeastern frontier. The Italian ports of Trieste, Fiume, and Pola lay within the region coveted by Marshal Tito and his communist-oriented partisans, and the British were determined to keep the ports out of communist hands lest they become naval bases from which a Soviet fleet might dominate the Adriatic. For several months the British had been intervening actively in the civil war in Greece in an effort to keep that strategic Mediterranean land from falling into communist hands, and loss of Trieste and control of the Adriatic would jeopardize that effort. Furthermore, the British would need the port of Trieste to support the occupation forces they eventually expected to deploy in Austria. The requirements of British strategy in the Mediterranean area in general, and the Italian theater in particular, were, as they had been since the beginning of the war, considerably more comprehensive and complicated than those of the Americans.

Inter-Allied differences were further complicated when early in the planning for the spring offensive it became evident that changes in command had also altered attitudes and relationships among command and staff at the three major Allied headquarters in Italy. Formerly, Alexander and his Eighth Army commander had tended to think along similar lines in developing their operational concepts, especially during planning for the offensive south of Rome and for the Gothic Line, while Clark as Fifth Army commander sometimes found himself a lone dissenter in the triumvirate. When Clark moved up to become the 15th Army Group commander in mid-December, that close identity of views that had so long characterized relations between that headquarters and the Eighth Army soon came to an end. Clark and the staff that accompanied him from the Fifth Army continued to see their former command as the dominant partner in the Italian enterprise and to view the Fifth Army's role in the forthcoming offensive as essentially a continuation of that played during the long quiescent Bologna offensive.

Yet Truscott, Clark's successor in command of the Fifth Army, would soon demonstrate that he too was as determined to develop his own operational concepts independently of Clark as the latter had been *vis a vis* Alexander. Thus Clark would, as before, frequently find himself holding a minority viewpoint—although, as army group commander, the prevailing one—in Allied planning councils. As planning progressed at the several headquarters, he would on occasion be forced to compromise long-held views to make allowance for the particular operational concepts being developed at his two army headquarters. The plan that would eventually emerge from the 15th Army Group headquarters would represent a rather loosely worded compromise allowing the two army commanders to carry out cherished operational concepts that Clark had initially opposed.

Indications that that would happen surfaced even as Field Marshal Alexander and his staff turned to the task of laying out characteristically broad operational guidelines for the coming offensive. As Alexander and his staff considered the zone of operations that lay between them and the distant Alps, they concluded that by occupying the historic "Venetian Quadrilateral"—Mantua, Peschiera, Verona, and Legnano—the Allies had a good chance of destroying many of the German forces in northern Italy and of quickly reaching the northeastern frontier and the Alps.[16]

Thirty miles southeast of the Quadrilateral and defending the approaches to it, the northward-flowing Reno River made a sharp bend to the east and, passing southeast of Ferrara, entered the sea south of the Comacchio Lagoon. It was along the northward-flowing tributaries of that section of the Reno that the Germans had constructed their defensive positions east of Bologna. If the Allies could cross the Reno near its mouth, those successive lines might be turned with relative ease by an advance northwestward along the Reno's northern bank. That would afford a good chance of trapping a major part of the *Tenth Army* south of the Reno as it flowed to the southeast and of preventing the Germans from using the Reno as another defensive line to cover a withdrawal to the Po and the Quadrilateral.

Uninterrupted by large water courses and endowed with an excellent road system, the plain north of the Reno also offered the Eighth Army favorable terrain for maneuver. Since the key to the area lay not in the Fifth Army's zone of operations south of Bologna but in the Eighth Army's, Alexander and his staff no longer focused attention on Bologna. In the Allied theater commander's words, ". . . we were . . . no longer thinking merely of the capture of Bologna, nor, indeed, of any objective on the ground, but of more wide-sweeping movements which would encircle as many of the Germans as possible between the converging blows of the two armies." Drawing

---

[16] The Venetian Quadrilateral comprising those four fortress cities had been until 1866 the key to Austrian military control of northern Italy. It was in a sense an outwork of a bastion formed by the mountains of the Tyrol and divided northern Italy strategically into two parts, east and west.

frequently upon earlier experience on the arid plains of North Africa, General Alexander had never lost his enthusiasm for the "wide-sweeping movement" and the "double-fisted" blow.[17]

Since the U.S. Fifth Army's IV Corps occupied favorable positions west of the Reno as it flows northeast toward the great bend southwest of Ferrara, the Fifth Army might serve as the left fist of the maneuver. The Americans might advance along the axis of Highway 64 and, remaining west of the highway and river, debouch into the Lombard plain west of Bologna, thereby avoiding the defenses south of the city. Once in the valley the Fifth Army could fulfill the goal of cutting off enemy forces in the northwest by driving directly toward the Alps along the Ostiglia-Verona axis (Highway 12). As for the right fist, the Eighth Army after crossing the Reno as close to its mouth as possible could advance along the axis of Highway 16 to Padua, thence via Highway 14 into northeastern Italy and the frontier, as well as join with the Americans to cut off those enemy forces defending Bologna to the east and the area south of the Po.[18]

A prerequisite to the success of Allied plans was that the Germans continue to defend in place. Yet both Alexander and Clark were aware of the possibility that the Germans might at any time break contact and fall back beyond the Po into their suspected Alpine redoubt. That remained a source of nagging concern with Clark throughout the planning period, for such a maneuver would adversely affect American stra-

tegic goals more than those of the British. Alexander, at least, was confident that wide-ranging Allied aerial reconnaissance and partisan informers would provide sufficient early warning of any withdrawal. Thus Allied planning proceeded on the assumption that the Germans would continue to fall back only under overwhelming pressure.[19]

That Alexander's broad operational concepts were somewhat different from those taking form in General Clark's mind would become apparent when in early January the army group commander began a series of planning conferences with his two army commanders. The first took place on 8 January when McCreery met with Clark at the latter's headquarters in Florence. McCreery arrived convinced that, inasmuch as the integrity of the northeast Italian frontiers *vis-à-vis* communist ambitions was as significant a challenge as defeating the German armies in Italy, the Eighth Army should be the vehicle for the main Allied effort and as such have first claim on Allied resources in the theater. Moreover, despite a chronic shortage of replacements and transfer of troops to Greece, the Eighth Army in January was still the larger of the two Allied armies. In spite of McCreery's arguments, which Clark agreed had some merit, the army group commander maintained long-held private reservations about the Eighth Army. Long convinced that the British could not be depended upon "to carry the ball," he was determined not to yield to McCreery as Clark believed Alexander

[17] Alexander's Report to the CCS, The Italian Campaign, p. 32. Nicolson, *Alex*, p. 277.
[18] *Ibid*.

[19] *Ibid*.; Intervs, Sidney T. Mathews w/Gen Clark 10–21 May 48, Pt. I.

MONTE ADONE

THE LAST HEIGHTS BEFORE BOLOGNA

had done in the case of Leese on the eve of the Gothic Line offensive in August.[20]

On 12 February Clark presented to his commanders his own operational concept for the offensive with instructions to prepare plans for its implementation. The army group commander's plan essentially followed the same pattern that Alexander had outlined for the fall offensive. The main axis of the 15th Army Group's offensive would be along a line extending from Bologna to

Verona in order to cut in two the German forces north of the Apennines. The offensive was to be divided into three phases: the first to capture the area in and around Bologna; the second to advance to the Po and prepare a set-piece attack against that enemy line; and the third to cross the Po and advance on Verona, the capture of which was expected to seal the main escape route out of Italy to the northeast for those enemy forces still in northwestern Italy. At the same time, a so-called Venetian Line along the Adige River was to be attacked. If the enemy

---

[20] Clark Diary, 19 Jan 45.

failed to defend that line, both armies were to cross the Adige and continue without pause—the Fifth to the Alps and northwestern Italy, the Eighth to Trieste and the northeastern frontier.[21] Inherent in Clark's concept was that the Fifth Army would at first throw its main effort against the formidable enemy defenses astride Highway 65 south of Bologna and take the city while the Eighth Army resumed its methodical advance northwestward astride Highway 9 toward Bologna.

The 15th Army Group Operations Plan

Taking into account the differing views of the two army commanders, the army group commander's staff prepared a detailed three-phase plan that General Clark presented at a conference at his headquarters on 18 March. During the first phase, the Eighth Army in a secondary role was to cross the Senio and push on to establish bridgeheads beyond the Santerno. Until the Santerno was crossed, all available air support, including heavy bombers, was to be allotted the Eighth Army. Thereafter priority would shift to the Fifth Army, which was to make the main effort by advancing into the Po Valley either to capture or isolate Bologna. The wording would leave Truscott free to bypass the city, if he wished, and downgraded the earlier priorities that Clark had placed on its capture. Emphasis in the second phase was to be placed, as both Alexander and McCreery had argued, on encircling major enemy forces south of the Po, rather than on Clark's earlier emphasis on a

rapid thrust through the enemy's center to divide the enemy and develop the line first of the Po and then of the Adige.[22]

If the major goals of the first two phases were realized, those of the third would be relatively easy: to cross the Po, capture Verona, and develop the line of the Adige, which, if major enemy forces were destroyed south of the Po, probably would be lightly defended. As Clark saw it, the Eighth Army's role in the third phase was primarily to assist the Fifth Army in trapping the enemy south of the Po. Following establishment of bridgeheads over the Santerno, the Eighth Army was to continue to advance in two columns, one in the direction of the Bastia Bridge and the other toward Budrio. The former, a crossing of the Reno, lay three miles south of Argenta, while Budrio was located nine miles northeast of Bologna. Clark expected Budrio to draw McCreery northwestward in the direction most advantageous to the Fifth Army. Only if he appeared to be making good progress in that direction was he to launch an amphibious operation across the Comacchio Lagoon. If thereby he managed to outflank the Argenta Gap, which Clark doubted he would be able to do, the two commanders would then decide whether to redirect the army's main effort in a more northerly direction toward Ferrara, as McCreery had originally planned and desired. Only then would Budrio and the entrapment of major enemy forces between Budrio and Bologna be relegated to the status of secondary objectives. In short, if all

---

[21] 15th AGp, Opns Instr. No. 3, 12 Feb 45, ann. A; Truscott, *Command Missions*, p. 480.

[22] Hq 15th AGp, Opns Instr. No. 4, 24 Mar 45, in *Fifth Army History*, Part IX, ann. B.

went well along the Santerno, McCreery would be given an opportunity to make his right hook against the Argenta Gap, which the British envisioned as the first major step on the road to Trieste.[23]

In the matter of the selection of D-day for the offensive, General Clark insisted, despite objections from Mc-Creery, on 10 April. Clark's meteorologists had assured him that by mid-April the ground in the Po Valley would be firm enough for tracked and wheeled vehicles; and even though the winter had been bitterly cold, there had been less snow than usual at higher elevations, thus lessening the danger of flooding in lower reaches of the rivers during April. Clark was also concerned lest the Red Army marching up the Danube and the U.S. Seventh Army advancing through southern Germany should reach Austria's alpine frontier before the 15th Army Group should get there. After the long, arduous advance northward from Cassino, Clark was determined to be in on the kill when the war ended and not be left bogged down either in the northern Apennines or in the Po Valley.[24]

General McCreery objected to the April date because LVT's (Landing Vehicle, Tracked, called by the British "Fantails" or "Buffaloes") that he hoped to use in an amphibious right hook over the Comacchio Lagoon had yet to arrive, and he doubted whether enough vehicles would be on hand and crews trained to operate them before May. When in mid-March it appeared that enough vehicles and crews would be available in early April to lift at least

one infantry brigade, he agreed to the 10 April date.[25]

The 15th Army Group Commander's operational guidelines left General Truscott somewhat greater freedom to realize his own operational concepts than they had General McCreery. For example, Clark had downgraded the isolation or capture of Bologna to a secondary mission. Truscott was to debouch into the Po Valley, presumably west of Bologna. Once in the valley, the army was to exploit rapidly toward the Po as well as toward a junction with the Eighth Army in the vicinity of Bondeno to complete the encirclement of enemy forces in the central sector. Clark's failure to insist upon the axis of Highway 65 represented a significant concession to Truscott's views that the sector west of Highway 64 "was most promising for breaking through the German positions and into the Po valley." The Fifth Army commander was determined, he recalled later, to retain that concept in his plans and "did not want Clark, because of his predilection for PIANORO (Highway 65), to interpose a restriction which would make it impossible. I had not forgotten the change of direction in the breakout from Anzio."[26]

Truscott also drew the assignment of launching a preliminary attack. Before the Fifth Army moved, the 92d Division was to capture Massa and exploit via Carrara toward the naval base at La Spezia. That, Truscott expected, would draw some enemy strength from the central front toward the west, thereby easing the task of the IV and II Corps.

---

[23] Ibid.
[24] Clark Diary, 2 Mar 45.

[25] Ibid.
[26] Truscott, Command Missions, pp. 478–79.

The Eighth Army's Plan

As General McCreery and his staff studied the situation after the Eighth Army had closed to the line of the Senio in January, they realized that they had a choice of one or two axes for that army's main effort. The first, along Highway 9, fitted in well with General Clark's strategic concepts and led directly to Bologna. The second led 13 miles northwestward along Highway 16, to Argenta. If the main effort were made along the Argenta axis it would avoid the numerous defended river lines that lay east of Bologna and would enable the army to outflank the east-west stretch of the Reno upon which those lines were anchored, but there was a major disadvantage to that axis: much of it lay under water. The Germans had blown the dykes and dismantled numerous pumping stations, thereby flooding all but a narrow, readily-defended corridor (the Argenta Gap) through which ran Highway 16, and the immediate vicinity of Argenta itself.

The disadvantage called for extraordinary measures and saw the genesis of the British plan to use LVT's to outflank the corridor by moving across the Comacchio Lagoon and its adjacent flooded lowlands. That idea had long appealed to Eighth Army engineers, but for long they had lacked the necessary topographic data, such as the depth of the water and soil conditions of the bottom and shore line. The information, it developed, could be supplied by friendly Italian fishermen slipping through British lines.[27]

---

[27] Operations of the British, Indian, and Dominion Forces in Italy, Part IV, Campaign in Lombardy.

For such an operation to succeed the enemy had to be kept ignorant of the presence of the LVT's and induced to commit his reserves to another sector before the amphibious move began. To do that, the Eighth Army devised a cover plan designed to suggest to the Germans that the main Allied effort would again be made along the axis of Highway 9, while a secondary operation, an amphibious landing, would be launched north of the Po in the gulf of Venice in a manner somewhat reminiscent of the Anzio landing south of Rome. Concealing the presence of the LVT's from the enemy presented few immediate difficulties since only a few had arrived in Italy, and their crews would be trained on Lake Trasimeno far to the south.

After the withdrawal in February of the Canadian corps and its two divisions to northern Europe, General McCreery had extended the right flank of the 5 Corps to take over responsibility for the former Canadian sector on the Adriatic flank. With one armored and five infantry divisions, Maj. Gen. C. F. Keightley's corps was by far the largest of the army's four corps and thus a logical choice for the assignment. Manning the sector from right to left from Highway 9 were the British 56th Division, with the 24th Guards, the 9th Armoured, the 2d Commando, and the Italian 28th Garibaldi Brigades attached. Next in line were the Italian Cremona Battle Group, the 8th Indian, the 78th British, and the 2d New Zealand Divisions. The 21st Tank, 4th New Zealand, and 2d Armoured Brigades were in corps reserve awaiting an opportunity for armored exploitation. The units had recently been reinforced with several items of new equipment, including modified flame-throwing Churchill tanks (Crocodiles), armored infantry carriers (Kangaroos), and regular medium tanks modified for use in stream crossings.[28]

The 2 Polish Corps, with two infantry divisions—the 3d Carpathian and 5th Kresowa—and the equivalent of one armored division—the 2d Polish Armoured and 7th Armoured Brigades and the 43d Lorried Gurkha Brigade—held the sector astride Highway 9 near Faenza. For a brief period at Eighth Army headquarters after it got news of the Yalta agreements that determined the future of Poland, there had been some concern that the Polish forces in their despair might decide to sit out the last offensive. For a time General Anders considered giving up his command and requesting that the western Allies accept him and his corps as prisoners of war rather than accept the Yalta decision. How to replace the Polish corps was for a time of serious concern to Clark. Only after consulting with the Polish government in exile in London did Anders finally decide to stick it out until victory.[29]

The Eighth Army's two remaining corps, 10 and 13, controlled between them the equivalent of only two divisions and held that part of the army front still in the mountains south of Highway 9. Along a sector extending from the upper Senio to south of Imola, the 10 Corps, recently returned from Greece, had only the Jewish He-

bron Brigade and Italian Friuli Battle Group. The 13 Corps held the remainder of the Eighth Army front to the Monte Grande sector with the 10th Indian Division and the Italian Folgore Battle Group.

Salient features of McCreery's battle plan included a two-pronged attack toward the north and northwest. The first and main attack was to be made by the 5 Corps in the direction of Lugo, two miles west of the Senio and nine miles north of Faenza on Highway 9. With Lugo in hand, the corps was to drive on Massa Lombarda, four miles to the west, before turning northward toward the Bastia Bridge and Argenta. The former was the key to the Argenta Gap. Spanning the lower Reno thirteen miles west of the Comacchio Lagoon, the Bastia Bridge represented the most desirable crossing point of the Reno opposite the 5 Corps right wing. Once a crossing had been made there the line of the lower Reno would be turned, thereby permitting the 5 Corps to move along the river's north bank to turn the successive enemy river lines anchored on that stretch of the Reno.

Preceding the 5 Corps attack, the 56th Division was to launch a series of preliminary operations to gain control of a wedge of flooded lowland at the southeastern corner of the Comacchio Lagoon and several small islands in the middle of the lagoon, as well as to clear the enemy from a spit of land separating the lagoon from the sea. If those operations succeeded, the corps would gain control of the lagoon and of favorable sites along its western shore from which to mount attacks against the seaward flank of the Argenta Gap. The enemy's attention might thereby be

---

[28] *Ibid,* Sec. B, The Final Offensive. Unless otherwise indicated the following sections are based upon this reference.

[29] Clark, *Calculated Risk,* pp. 421–22.

drawn away from the main sector opposite Lugo and the Bastia Bridge.

In preparation for the main attack,
McCreery planned to concentrate six
divisions behind his center, from a
bend of the Senio near Lugo where the
river turns toward the northeast to, but
exclusive of, Highway 9. The sector had
the advantage of several good crossing
sites, and the highway along which the
Germans had concentrated at least two
of their best divisions, the *4th Parachute*
and *26th Panzer*, might be avoided.
Once the attacking divisions had
crossed the Santerno, about five miles
beyond the Senio, they were to turn in
a more northerly direction toward Argenta. By holding the enemy in place
and drawing units away from the
coastal flank, the maneuver was expected to assist those forces making an
amphibious right hook against the Argenta Gap.

The 5 Corps operation against Lugo
was to be made by two divisions: the
8th Indian, passing to the right, and
the 2d New Zealand, to the left of the
town. By D plus 2 both divisions were
expected to have established a large
bridgehead beyond the Santerno near
Massa Lombarda. At that point the
78th Division, having moved beyond
Lugo, was to relieve the Indian division,
then continue the attack toward the
Bastia Bridge. While that was in progress, a brigade of the 56th Division,
transported in LVT's, was to cross the
flooded plain as far as the Menate
pumping station, on the Comacchio
Lagoon's shore eleven miles east of the
Bastia Bridge. The New Zealand division, meanwhile, was either to cover the
78th Division's left or, in co-operation
with the Polish corps, to advance west-

ward toward Budrio, seventeen miles
northwest of Massa Lombarda, depending upon the success of the thrust in
the direction of the Bastia Bridge. The
8th Indian Division and the Cremona
Battle Group were to round up bypassed enemy forces before passing into
5 Corps reserve.

The 2 Polish Corps to the left of the
5 Corps was to form the second prong
of the Eighth Army's offensive. First
Polish objectives beyond the Santerno
were the towns of Medicina, eighteen
miles northwest of Faenza, and Castel
San Pietro, a similar distance from the
Polish front on Highway 9. Eventually
the Polish corps was expected to co-
ordinate closely with the U.S. Fifth
Army's II Corps in the capture or
isolation of Bologna, and in the event
the 5 Corps failed to break through the
Argenta Gap, to keep open General
McCreery's option for switching the axis
of his main effort toward Budrio.

If McCreery's plans succeeded, he
intended to continue his offensive in
two separate battles: the first, a battle of
annihilation against the enemy south of
the Po, the second an exploitation as
far as Ferrara. Both were to be followed by pursuits, the first beyond the
Po and the Adige and the second along
the south bank of the Po to prevent
enemy forces still south of the river
from reaching it.

On the other hand, if the 5 Corps
had difficulty in forcing the Argenta
Gap, the 13 Corps headquarters was to
come around from the army's left flank
to take control of those divisions fighting the first of the two battles in the
direction of Budrio. That would leave
the 5 Corps free to concentrate on the
Argenta sector. Once the corps broke

through there, the 10 Corps headquarters was to come around from the left to take control of a special engineer task force. Passing through the gap in the wake of the 5 Corps, the 10 Corps was to move up on the right to prepare for the first crossings of the Po.[30]

Developing the Fifth Army's Plan

By the end of March, Truscott had just about completed regrouping his forces for the spring offensive. The British 13 Corps having been returned earlier to Eighth Army control, the Fifth Army was left with a somewhat narrower front. Crittenberger's IV Corps continued to hold the widest segment, 50 miles from the Reno to the sea. Within the IV Corps, Crittenberger extended the sector of the 92d Division and its attached units, the 473d and 442d Regiments, as far as the Cutigliano valley, where the 365th Infantry, detached from the division, held an independent command in the former sector of Task Force 45. East of the 365th Infantry lay the 1st Brazilian Division (BEF), occupying a mountainous sector stretching northeastward from the Riva Ridge past Monte Belvedere to the U.S. 10th Mountain Division's left boundary west of Pietra Colora. With the exception of a narrow sector held by the 81st Cavalry Reconnaissance Squadron on the corps right flank south of Vergato, Hays' mountain division held the remainder of the IV Corps front.

Dispositions within the II Corps reflected Keyes' plan again to use the 85th and 88th Divisions to spearhead

the renewed drive to Bologna and the Po Valley. The 1st Armored Division, with the 91st Reconnaissance Squadron attached, held a five-mile sector on the left wing just east of the Reno River. The 34th Division lay astride Highway 65 in the center. On the right wing the 91st Division and attached Legnano Battle Group occupied positions in the Idice valley and on Monte Belmonte. Three divisions—the 6th South African Armoured and 85th and 88th Infantry—were assembled in rear areas for rest and training.

In contrast to Clark, Truscott had long ceased to focus his attention on Bologna. He intended instead to concentrate the Fifth Army's main effort in the IV Corps sector west of Highway 64 between the Samoggia and the Reno Rivers. An advance on that axis by the IV Corps would, he expected, outflank from the west the admittedly strong defenses south of Bologna. When the IV Corps debouched into the valley, the II Corps west of Bologna would sidestep to the left from the axis of Highway 65 to that of Highway 64. Once out of the mountains, the two corps would advance abreast from Modena northward toward the Po, the IV Corps capturing Ostiglia, where Highway 12 crossed the river, and the II Corps, Bondeno, eighteen miles to the southeast near where the Panaro joins the Po. There contact was to be made with the Eighth Army advancing from Ferrara, thus completing the encirclement of German forces still within the bend of the Reno.

After crossing the Po at Ostiglia, the IV Corps was to advance as far as Verona and then to Lake Garda, and, if things went well, cut off those enemy

---

[30] W.G.F. Jackson, *The Battle for Italy* (New York, 1967), pp. 303–04.

forces still in northwest Italy. In co-operation with the Eighth Army's drive to the northeast, the II Corps was to cross the Po and advance to the Adige. Meanwhile, the 92d Division on the army's left flank, operating directly under the Fifth Army, was to continue its advance along the Ligurian coast to Genoa, Italy's major seaport, and thence northwestward to an eventual link-up with French forces along the Franco-Italian frontier.[31]

The Fifth Army's Operation BIG GAME was designed to create the illusion that the II Corps was moving eastward to join the Eighth Army in making the main Allied effort along the Adriatic flank and that the IV Corps would take over the Fifth Army's entire front. Dummy radio nets were established for some units, and radio silence imposed upon others. While most of the movement was simulated, some units, their divisional markings removed from personnel and equipment, actually shifted but only within the army sector.[32]

To avoid having to divide air support equally between the two armies, Clark instructed Truscott to delay his phase of the offensive until about D plus 3 when the Eighth Army would have crossed the Santerno River. Thus the full weight of the tactical and strategic air forces could be thrown in support first of the Eighth Army on the right, then of the Fifth Army on the left.

Truscott developed a similar scheme for allotting air support between his two corps. Attacking first, Crittenberger's

IV Corps would at first receive the Fifth Army's entire allotment of airpower, then 36 hours later all air support was to be shifted to support of Keyes' II Corps. Staggering the army's attack in that manner also had the advantage of placing greater firepower alternately behind each of the two army corps rather than dividing it between them as McCreery had done with the Eighth Army. While assigning one of the Fifth Army's two armored divisions to each corps, Truscott nevertheless managed to assure a concentrated armored thrust by positioning both divisions side by side on the interior wings of the corps: the U.S. 1st Armored Division on the IV Corps' right and the South African 6th Armoured on the II Corps' left.[33]

Within the Fifth Army's main zone of operations opposite the IV and II Corps only two highways, 64 and 65, led through the 12-mile belt of remaining mountainous terrain between the front and the Po Valley. Long favored by Clark, Highway 65 offered the most direct approach. Except for two rugged peaks, Monte Sole and Monte Adone, rising above north-south running ridge lines bordering the Setta valley between Highway 65 and the Reno River to the west, the terrain was favorable and permitted movement and support of up to five divisions. The main disadvantage of Highway 65 lay in that the Germans had concentrated their strongest positions astride it in defense of the southern approaches to Bologna. A major offensive along that route might involve

[31] Hq, U.S. Fifth Army, Opns Instr. No. 7, 1 Apr 45, in *Fifth Army History*, Part IX, ann. E.; Truscott, *Command Decisions*, pp. 478–79.

[32] *Ibid.*, IX, 26.

[33] Opns Instr. No. 7, 1 Apr 45, Hq Fifth Army, in *Fifth Army History*, Part IX, ann. E. Unless otherwise indicated the following sections are based upon this source.

a repeat of the costly experience of the previous winter.[34]

Highway 64, on the other hand, held out the possibility of enveloping Bologna from the southwest instead of assaulting the defenses frontally. That route too would permit passage of up to five divisions. Following the course of the Reno River, the highway was defiladed from the west for much of its length through the mountains by a 15-mile ridge paralleling the highway from Monte Belvedere to Monte Pigna, four miles northwest of Vergato, a heavily fortified road juction just north of American lines. An advance along Highway 64 would require a simultaneous effort to clear the remainder of that ridge line as well as Monte Sole, which overlooked the highway some five miles to the northeast of Vergato.

The Plan

By mid-March all but a few of the minor details of a greatly modified Operation PIANORO, newly designated Operation CRAFTSMAN, had been completed. CRAFTSMAN outlined an attack with two corps abreast; the IV Corps attacking first on D plus 3 and the II Corps on army command on 24-hour notice. From a line just south of Vergato, Crittenberger's corps was to advance northeasterly on a 10-mile front, bounded by the Samoggia River in the west and the Reno in the east. The IV Corps was expected to debouch into the Po Valley in the vicinity of Bazzano, some thirteen miles west of Bologna. Deployed essentially along the same line where the winter offensive had come to

a halt, Keyes' II Corps was to advance at first directly toward Bologna along the axis of Highway 65, but after the IV Corps had captured the road junction of Praduro, on Highway 64 some fifteen miles north of Vergato, most of the II Corps was to shift westward to the axis of Highway 64, so that the two corps would debouch abreast into the Po Valley west of Bologna. Only a minor effort was to be made frontally against Bologna, mainly to hold the enemy there in place.[35]

For purposes of control, Truscott designated three phase lines—Green, Brown, and Black. During the Green phase, Crittenberger was to send the 10th Mountain Division toward Monte Pigna and Monte Mantino, two miles northeast of Monte Pigna, and the 1st Armored Division along the axis of Highway 64 against Vergato and Monte Pero, a mile northwest of town. The IV Corps left flank was to be covered by the Brazilian Expeditionary Force and the 365th and 371st Regiments, detached from the 92d Division. Those units were to follow up any enemy withdrawal along the axis of Highway 12, roughly paralleling Highway 64 some fifteen miles to the west. The order for the II Corps to attack was to be given when the IV Corps reached the Green Line.

Once the offensive was under way, Truscott planned to form a mobile reserve of his armored divisions with which to exploit the most promising opportunities. When his troops reached the Po Valley, he intended to create,

---

[34] *Fifth Army History*, IX, 21–22; Truscott, *Command Missions*, pp. 477–78.

[35] Operation Craftsman, Fifth Army Opns. Instr. #7, 1 April 1945. See also Truscott, *Command Missions*, p. 482. Unless otherwise indicated the following sections are based on these references.

from the mobile reserve, infantry-armor task forces to lead the dash first for the Panaro, then the Po.

In the Brown phase the two corps were to advance abreast: the IV Corps continuing in a northeasterly direction west of Highway 64, the II Corps capturing Monte Sole, Monterumici, and Monte Adone, the high ground between Highways 64 and 65. Truscott believed that his counterpart, General Lemelsen, would have to weaken these otherwise formidable positions to deal with the IV Corps advance west of Highway 64. On the II Corps right flank, the Italian Combat Group Legnano was to patrol aggressively and maintain contact with the British 13 Corps on the Eighth Army's left.

At the beginning of the Black phase, the 85th Division from the Army reserve was to pass through the 1st Armored Division and come under II Corps control. That would be made possible by a shift in the corps boundary from just east of Highway 64 to four miles west of the highway south of Praduro. During that phase the armored exploitation force was to begin assembling: the 1st Armored Division just west of Vergato and the South African armored division to the southeast of the town. Truscott planned to employ both divisions to exploit an expected breakthrough west of the highway, thrusting into the Po Valley as far as the Panaro River 22 miles northwest of Bologna. The American armored division was to operate in the direction of Modena, on Highway 9, 22 miles northwest of Bologna, and the South African northeastward in the direction of the Eighth Army's left flank and Bondeno, on the Panaro

River 27 miles north of Bologna. It was expected that the Fifth and Eighth Armies would link up at Bondeno.

There was to be no artillery preparation, in hope of surprise. Instead, the army was to fire a 20-day program of gradually increasing intensity, building to a crescendo during the final week preceding D-day, a procedure bearing some similarities to the Anzio breakout offensive. To support the program Truscott authorized an increase of 328,090 rounds over the basic rate for the 20-day period preceding the offensive. Stocks assembled in depots during the winter and early spring were more than adequate.

To support an exploitation beyond the Po, Truscott's G–4 planned on building up a 15-day stock of all classes of supply in the Bologna area as soon as the city had been captured. Reserve rations, sufficient to feed 400,000 prisoners for thirty days, were also stocked in anticipation of large-scale enemy surrenders, although captured enemy stocks were to be used first.

As the time for the beginning of the spring offensive drew near, Allied commanders could look with considerable satisfaction on their overwhelming domination of the skies, both over the battlefront and the enemy-occupied regions north to the Alps. In no other arm did the Allied armies have such complete superiority, for the once powerful Luftwaffe had all but vanished from the skies of Europe. Except for scattered concentrations of antiaircraft batteries defending a few vital targets, the Germans in the spring of 1945 had virtually nothing with which to fend off Allied aircraft. As a result, the XXII TAC, which during March had concentrated on communications targets, had by the end of the month virtually run out of suitable targets in northern Italy. At the same time, the heavy bombers of the Strategic Air Force (MASAF) had also run out of targets outside of Italy. This meant that, in addition to the aircraft of the XXII TAC, the B–17's and B–24's of the MASAF would be free for close support of the spring offensive, as Clark had long insisted.[36]

The staggered nature of the ground attack meant that the Eighth Army offensive would be supported by a greater mass of airpower than ever before in the Italian campaign. On the afternoon of D-day 800 heavy bombers employing 175,000 20-pound fragmentation bombs were to lay a lethal carpet on enemy artillery and reserve positions in front of each of the two assaulting corps. More specifically, from 1350 to 1420 the bombers were to attack a two-square-mile L-shaped area in front of the 5 Corps and west of Lugo. At the same time, 120 medium day bombers were to attack three gun areas opposite the Polish sector, and an additional 48 medium bombers a gun area opposite the 5 Corps. That assignment completed, 500 fighter-bombers of the DAF and 200 of the XXII TAC, normally flying in support of the U.S. Fifth Army, were between 1520 and 1930 to attack a total of 56 hostile batteries and 64 strongpoints, mortar positions, and command posts across the enemy front. Any traffic on roads into the battle area was to be strafed. During the same period, on the 5 Corps front, there was to be a series of five 42-minute "false-alarm" bombardments by artillery and

mortars. Between each there was to be a 10-minute interval during which fighter-bombers were to attack close-in targets along the western floodbanks of the Senio. At H-hour, after the final artillery bombardment, the aircraft were to fly a dummy run along the floodbanks. From 1830 to 1930 the fighter-bombers would also attack the floodbanks in front of the Polish corps. Even H-hour and darkness would bring the enemy no respite, for from 2030 to 0400 on D-day and D plus 1, counter-battery fires were to be integrated with attacks by 100 light night bombers, while 100 heavy night bombers were to attack Santerno defenses identified by artillery night marker shells. On D plus 1, from 1100 to 1230, 800 heavy bombers were to saturate with fragmentation bombs a 10½-mile-square target area just beyond the Santerno.

The magnitude of the planned air support is apparent from the total numbers of bombs—148,556—and over-all tonnages—16,924.[37] Similar tonnages were planned for the Fifth Army's attack, but because of the mountainous terrain there was to be no carpet pattern to the bombing.

Allied Preponderance in Material and Manpower

Not only were the Allied armies to possess overwhelming air support but also a two-to-one preponderance over the enemy in artillery, including towed antitank guns, enemy infantry cannon, and Nebelwerfers. A similar ratio existed in combat infantrymen, and an even greater ratio—three-to-one—in ar-

---

[36] Craven and Cate, eds., *AAF III*, 482–83; Truscott, p. 483.

[37] Operations of the British, Indian, and Dominion Forces in Italy, IV, Sec. B, Eighth Army—the Final Offensive.

mor, including self-propelled antitank assault guns. The Eighth Army, for example, had 1,017 artillery pieces in support of the two assault corps and an additional 256 pieces in support of the two holding corps, for a total of 1,273 pieces. Compared with the 187 field and medium guns and 36 Nebelwerfers that the Germans had deployed in positions from which they might engage the Eighth Army's attack, the advantage was almost as impressive as that enjoyed in the air. Similar ratios also existed in the Fifth Army.[38]

Although both Allied armies contained a similar number of divisions, the Fifth Army's divisions had much larger assigned overstrengths and far larger replacement pools from which to draw than the Eighth Army's. Of the nine divisions and the equivalent of a tenth in the Fifth Army, there were six American infantry divisions, one Brazilian infantry division, two armored divisions (one South African and one American), and miscellaneous American and Italian units to the equivalent of a division. As advancements on future replacements, more than 7,000 officers and enlisted men had been assigned as overages to those divisions to enable the men to receive some training and experience before the offensive began. In addition, there awaited in replacement depots in Italy 21,000 white officers and enlisted men, 2,000 black replacements for the 92d Division, 5,000 replacements for the Brazilian Expeditionary Force, and 1,200 Nisei for the Japanese-American 442d Infantry Regiment.[39]

Not only did the Germans face an overwhelming force at the front, but behind German lines there lurked in northwestern and northeastern Italy, as well as in the Apennines, approximately 50,000 partisans, organized into companies, battalions, and brigades, poised and ready to strike at the enemy's rear areas whenever the Allied command gave the word. Allied support of the Italian resistance movement had begun shortly after its spontaneous inception in September 1943, following the Italian surrender and the Allied landings in southern Italy. Since then a total of about 2,400 tons of military supplies had reached partisan bands either by air drop or by covert landings along the coasts. Five hundred tons had been delivered during March alone. When the autumn offensive had begun in August 1944, a combination of stepped-up Allied assistance and a wave of enthusiasm, caused by an ill-founded anticipation of early liberation, had prompted an estimated 130,000 men to flock to the guerrilla standards, but during the long winter months, after the Allied offensive bogged down, discouragement and vigorous enemy counteraction reduced the number of partisans to approximately 50,000 by spring of 1945. Those men, however, represented a hard core, or cadre, capable of rapid expansion should the Germans be forced into a large-scale retreat. At the time of the spring offensive there were some 200 Allied personnel divided into sixty mission teams in contact with and assisting the partisan formations behind the enemy lines.[40]

---

[38] *Ibid.*

[39] *Fifth Army History*, IX, 4.

[40] AFHQ G–3 Memo to COS, 24 Jan 45, sub: Appreciation by G–3 of Future Support and Employment of Italian Resistance, in AFHQ Records file, Microfilm Reel 38A, Federal Records Center; *Fifth Army History*, IX, 12.

CHAPTER XXVI

Breakthrough on the Eighth Army Front

In the East

The first of the two preliminary operations scheduled for each of the coastal flanks began on the night of 1 April when a flotilla of LVT's carrying the British 2d Commando Brigade set out across the Comacchio Lagoon's shallow waters on the Eighth Army's Adriatic flank. That operation was to be the first of a series of three designed to give the British forces advance positions from which to cover an amphibious right hook against Argenta.

The lagoon's waters were indeed shallow—too shallow, for shortly after launching, all of the LVT's mired down in a muddy bottom. Only after the troops transferred to storm boats were the lightened vehicles pulled free. The assault then continued in the boats against the spit of land separating the lagoon from the sea.[1] Despite a shallower draft, many of those craft ran aground as well, some as far as a thousand yards from the landing site; but all troops were able to wade ashore, albeit in some instances through knee-deep mud.

Surprisingly, those mishaps failed to arouse the small garrison of Turkomenian troops on the spit. Catching the

enemy completely by surprise, the brigade by 4 April had pressed over five miles north to clear the spit as far as Porto Garibaldi, a small fishing village off the lagoon's northeastern corner, yielding some 800 prisoners. The next day a squadron of the Special Boat Service, a small amphibious force, completed the second action by quickly capturing a group of small islands in the center of the lagoon.

In the meantime, the 2d Commando Brigade and its newly acquired sector passed under the control of the British 56th Division. On 6 April that division launched the third and last of the actions near the mouth of the Reno to capture the wedge of ground at the Comacchio Lagoon's southwestern corner, appropriately designated "the Wedge." In spite of strong opposition, the division by nightfall of the second day had cleared that area and captured another 700 prisoners. That time the LVT's performed perfectly, easily crossing the flooded fields and putting to rest concern raised by the earlier groundings in the operation against the Spit. In no great force, British troops were nevertheless established on the north bank of the Reno.

In the West

Meanwhile, some 120 miles to the west on the Fifth Army's Ligurian

---

[1] The assault boats were light-weight, shallow-draft craft powered by outboard motors, used primarily for river crossings.

flank, the 92d Division jumped off on 5 April in a second preliminary operation. Appropriately named Operation SECOND WIND, it was aimed at the capture of Massa, on the south bank of the Frigido River, five miles northwest of the division front and the last enemy-held strongpoint of the old Gothic Line.

Since the ill-starred Operation FOURTH TERM of the previous winter, the 92d Division had been reorganized. Two of its former regiments (the 365th and 371st) had been detached to cover the long left flank of the IV Corps. By shifts within the division, Almond had gathered together the best men of the three original regiments into the 370th Infantry, commanded by Col. Raymond G. Sherman. To take the place of the detached regiments, Truscott attached the Japanese-American 442d Regimental Combat Team, under the command of Lt. Col. Virgil R. Miller, and Col. William P. Yarborough's 473d Infantry, the unit made up of former antiaircraft artillerymen. Thus the 92d Division at that point was a vastly different unit from the one which had performed so unfortunately during the previous winter.[2]

This time Almond decided to risk no repetition of the abortive operation across the Cinquale Canal on the coastal plain. Rather would the division's main effort be made across the high ground overlooking the plain from the east. The 370th Infantry was to cross the flanks of the Strettoia Hills to the east while the 442d Infantry operated on the right over the higher summits just below the jagged peaks of the Apuan Alps, where the 371st had fought in February. The 473d Infantry was at first to remain in the Serchio valley on the division's right flank. By gaining control of the high ground as far as Massa, Almond expected to force the enemy to yield the objective without a costly frontal attack. The question yet to be answered was how would the reconstituted 370th Infantry perform over the same terrain that had been the scene of the regiment's debacle in Operation FOURTH TERM.

Early on 5 April planes bombarded enemy positions, including the naval guns at Punta Bianca, followed by a 10-minute artillery preparation aided by British destroyers offshore. The two regiments on the left wing attacked from a line of departure five miles southeast of Massa astride the coastal highway. Getting off to a good start, the 370th Infantry's leading company covered more than two miles to occupy a height halfway to the objective of Massa, but when the enemy counterattacked, as was his custom, the company and its supporting armor yielded most of the gain. Undaunted, the regimental commander, Colonel Sherman, reorganized and attacked again; but to no avail, for mediocre leadership and endemic straggling persisted. For the next few days the 370th Infantry continued to lag behind the 442d on the right.[3]

---

[2] *Fifth Army History*, Part IX, pp. 35–43; Goodman Monograph, pp. 129–46; Thomas D. Murphy, *Ambassadors in Arms* (Honolulu, 1954), pp. 263–67. Unless otherwise indicated the following sections are based upon those sources.

[3] Truscott, *Command Missions*, p. 485. In the reorganization of the 370th Infantry Regiment, white officers replaced all black company commanders, in spite of the fact that there were in the division a number of black officers with superior ratings. The effect upon the blacks, officers and

The 370th's lagging at first had little effect on the progress of the 442d Infantry. After passing through the 371st Infantry's lines on Monte Cauala, three miles northeast of the mouth of the Cinquale Canal, the 442d led by the 100th Battalion pushed forward about a mile and a half in a wide flanking attack against 2,800-foot Monte Fragolita,· three miles southeast of Massa. By nightfall on the 5th, the Japanese-Americans had driven the enemy not only from Monte Fragolita but also from several surrounding heights.[4] For the next two days the regiment pursued a retreating enemy over narrow mountain trails made even more treacherous by rain and fog and captured 3,000-foot Monte Belvedere, two miles northeast of Massa.

As the Japanese-Americans pressed forward, Almond relieved the lagging 370th Infantry with the 473d, which he brought from the Serchio valley. The 370th then took up positions to protect the division's right flank. The 442d

Infantry having outflanked Massa from the east, Almond believed he needed a more aggressive unit to team with that regiment and make a frontal assault on the town, for the enemy showed no inclination to yield it without a fight. The antiaircraft artillerymen turned infantrymen would not disappoint him: they pushed steadily northward astride Highway 1 through extensive mine fields, artillery, and mortar fire to reach the outskirts of Massa by midday on the 9th. Supported by tanks of the 758th and 760th Tank Battalions, the 473d Infantry prepared to assault the town the next morning; but the enemy, already outflanked, at last chose to slip away during the night. The Americans occupied the town on the morning of the 10th. The same day, northeast of Massa, the 442d Infantry forded the Frigido River to capture Monte Bruguana, two and a half miles north of Massa, then continued another two miles early on the 11th to occupy the famed marble quarry of Carrara.

By that time increasing difficulties in supplying the forward troops as well as growing enemy resistance, including long-range harassing fire, especially against the 473d Infantry in the coastal corridor from the Italian coastal batteries at Punta Bianca, near the naval base of La Spezia, indicated that the relatively swift advances would soon come to an end. For the next week, until 19 April, the 92d Division would be brought to a virtual standstill by enemy forces well dug-in just behind the Carrione Creek, seven miles north of Carrara.

Operation SECOND WIND had nevertheless served its purpose, for in order to check the division's advance beyond

---

men alike, was to create an impression of a continuing lack of confidence in the fighting qualities of blacks. That helped explain the continued poor performance of the 370th Infantry. (See Notes on Interview with Truman K. Gibson, Civilian aide to Sec. War, by Bell I. Wiley, 30 May 1945, DA CMH files.)

[4] The sacrifice and teamwork inherent in this bold and successful maneuver was exemplified by Pfc. Sadao S. Munemori, who, after his squad leader had been wounded, took command. Leading the squad in several assaults against troublesome machine gun positions and silencing two with hand grenades, Private Munemori sought shelter in a shell crater already occupied by two of his men. Just as Munemori reached the crater an enemy grenade struck his helmet and bounced unexploded to the ground. Without hesitation he threw himself on the missile, taking its full blast with his body, thereby losing his life but saving the lives of his comrades. Munemori posthumously received the Medal of Honor. See *Medal of Honor*, p. 359.

Carrara, the enemy had been forced to dip into his main reserves. In spite of harassment from Allied aircraft and severe fuel shortages, a regiment of the *90th Panzer Grenadier Division* managed to move in sufficient strength from its reserve position in the vicinity of Modena to the Ligurian flank to help bring the 92d Division's advance to a halt. Yet that meant that General Vietinghoff had committed an irreplaceable part of his reserves against what was only a diversionary effort. He had taken the risk because he considered himself still bound by the long-standing OKW order to yield no part of the Winter Line.[5]

Well-designed Allied deception plans and the two preliminary attacks had succeeded in drawing off at least a part of the German reserves. Anticipating an Anzio-type amphibious operation somewhere along the Adriatic coast north of the mouth of the Po, Vietinghoff had earlier shifted half of his army group reserve, the *29th Panzer Grenadier Division*, to watch that flank, separated by several river lines from what was soon to become the main battle area. Then he had sent a regiment of the remaining half of his army group reserve, the *90th Panzer Grenadier Division*, to shore up his Ligurian flank. Thus when the Eighth Army attacked on 9 April in the first of two blows against Vietinghoff's *Army Group C*, a major part of the enemy's reserve would be ill-positioned to reinforce the main arena.

German Indecision

Shortly before the Eighth Army opened its offensive against the *Tenth*

Army, General Herr, whose troops had been on alert since the beginning of April, recommended to General Vietinghoff the adoption of a tactic employed by both the Germans and the French on the western front in World War I. Known to the Germans as the "false front maneuver," the tactic called for withdrawal under the cover of an artillery barrage as close as possible to the actual beginning of the attack by the opposing side. If the *Tenth Army* withdrew from the Senio to the Santerno in that manner, the Eighth Army's attack would strike thin air, and quite likely be thrown off balance, which was exactly what Clark and McCreery feared might happen. If it did, the Eighth Army would be forced to pause to reorganize. Because the Fifth Army's entry into the battle was tied to the Eighth Army's advance, the entire Allied plan might be jeopardized.

The tactic appealed to Vietinghoff, who readily gave his assent, despite the fact that a voluntary withdrawal ran counter to OKW's directive to stand fast and fall back only under overwhelming pressure. Because of the directive, he first had to obtain authorization from OKW. Although Hitler had considered employing the same tactic a year earlier on the eve of the U.S. VI Corps breakout from the Anzio beachhead, he refused to permit his commander in Italy to use it.[6]

Deprived of the one opportunity that might have provided an extended lease on life, the German armies in northern Italy had no choice but to brace themselves to meet the Allied onslaught in place. Herr nevertheless ordered a cov-

---

[5] MS # T–1b (Westphal *et al.*), CMH; Truscott, *Command Missions*, p. 485.

[6] MS # T–1b (Westphal *et al.*), Feldzug in Italien.

ering barrage fired during the night of 6 April to conceal a thinning of the sectors held by the *98th Division* of the *LXXVI Panzer Corps* and the *26th Panzer Division* of the *I Parachute Corps* along the line of the Senio. Anticipating that the Eighth Army's main attack would fall upon the intercorps boundary, Herr believed that the Allies might be checked briefly at the Santerno if the main resistance were encountered between the two rivers instead of along the line of the Senio. In spite of OKW's orders, he decided to employ an attenuated version of the false front tactic. What he had not reckoned on was that his maneuver would result in exposing the shifting German troops to the massive carpet bombing attack that was to precede the Eighth Army's offensive.[7]

The Eighth Army Attack

Shortly after midday on the 9th General Clark and his chief of staff, General Gruenther, left 15th Army Group headquarters near Florence on a short flight to an airfield at Forli, on Highway 9 southeast of Faenza. From there the American officers motored to Faenza, where the Eighth Army commander joined them, then continued a few miles west of the town to an observation post in a farmhouse with a fine view of the front some 2,000 yards away. Assembled were the commanding generals of the MASAF, the Twelfth Air Force, the XXII TAC, and the DAF, come to witness the first mighty blow in the fruition of weeks of planning by their respective staffs—the most impressive aerial bombardment of a campaign already marked by such awesome spectacles as the destruction from the air of the Abbey of Monte Cassino.[8]

Meanwhile, several formations of heavy bombers had taken off from airfields in central Italy and flown northward parallel to the Adriatic coast, as if pursuing a normal long-range mission north of the Alps. Reaching the latitude of Cesenatico, seventeen miles east of Forli, they turned westward over the Italian mainland. Passing relentlessly and in seemingly endless procession over the enemy's main defensive zone parallel to the Senio River, the heavy bombers began releasing their bombs. For the next two days 1,673 heavy bombers completely carpeted specific target areas between the Senio and the Santerno. During the same period some 624 medium bombers, in close co-ordination with the heavy bombers, first attacked enemy defenses and troop concentrations along both sides of Highway 9, between the two rivers, then turned to the area opposite the 5 Corps, astride Highway 16 northwest of Ravenna. After the heavy aircraft completed their tasks on the 9th, fighter-bombers of the DAF and XXII TAC launched their planned close-support missions, while the ground troops, supported by over a thousand pieces of artillery and hundreds of tanks, began moving toward the banks of the Senio just as the sun disappeared below the western horizon.[9]

H-hour had been set for 1930 to spare the tank gunners the ordeal of a setting sun in their gun sights and to give the infantrymen the advantage of the concealment of dusk, heightened by

---

[7] *Ibid.*

[8] Clark Diary, 9 April 45; See also Blumenson, *Salerno to Cassino*, p. 411n.

[9] Craven and Cate, eds., *AAF III*, pp. 484–85.

billowing clouds of dust raised by the bombers. The dust also had the effect of making it difficult for the tactical aircraft to find many of their close-support targets. Just before the infantrymen began to advance from assembly areas 200 yards east of the Senio, several flights of fighter-bombers roared across the army front in dummy runs in an effort to convince the enemy to remain under cover while infantry and armor moved toward the crossing sites along the east bank of the river.

First came flamethrowing Churchills, searing the far bank with fiery jets of napalm, then the assault infantry bearing assault boats and kapok bridges to provide men and equipment a way across the river. (*Map XV*) In spite of the massive aerial bombardment and flaming napalm, some German automatic weapons opened fire from positions along the western floodbank of the Senio, but supporting artillery and mortars silenced the enemy gunners and enabled the Allied infantrymen to launch their small boats and push their assault bridges into place.[10]

After eight hours of almost continuous bombardment from the air and the ground, that the enemy could resist at all was a tribute to the courage and discipline of the German infantryman. Yet resist he did from well-prepared positions worked on throughout the winter. As was often the case, heavy Allied bombardment did less damage to front-line positions than to communications to the rear, though that forced the Germans to fight independent and

unco-ordinated small unit actions all along the front. Under those conditions resistance could only be short-lived. More than 1,300 prisoners rounded up by the 5 Corps during the first twenty-four hours reflected, in part, the degree of disorganization among the enemy units caused in large measure by disruption of their communications.

The main assault on the Eighth Army's right wing, made by the 2d New Zealand and the 8th Indian Divisions of the 5 Corps, established bridgeheads beyond the Senio during the night. Dawn on the 10th found contingents of both divisions firmly established in their new bridgeheads, and by evening the New Zealanders had pushed three miles beyond the Senio to gain the east bank of the Santerno. Encountering somewhat greater resistance, the Indians came within a mile of the Santerno in their sector.

Although the attack by the 2 Polish Corps between Highways 9 and 16 began about the same time as that of the 5 Corps, the Polish units ran into considerably stronger resistance, for opposite them lay the relatively fresh battalions of the crack *26th Panzer Division*. It took two brigades of the 3d Carpathian Division until the morning of the 10th to establish a bridgehead beyond the Senio. Yet the attack gathered momentum during the day, and by evening a strongpoint at Solarolo on the Lugo Canal, two and a half miles west of the Senio and five miles northwest of Faenza, had fallen, although the Santerno still lay three miles to the west.

During the first twenty-four hours of the offensive the enemy's *98th* and *362d Divisions* bore the full brunt of the

---

[10] Operations of the British, Indian, and Dominion Forces in Italy, Part IV, Sec. B. Unless otherwise indicated the following sections are based upon that reference.

attack. The *362d Division* did manage a counterattack south of Lugo against the Allied right wing; but the purpose appeared to be only to enable the division to extricate itself from positions at the bend of the Senio, southeast of Lugo, before abandoning Lugo itself later in the day. By evening of the 10th, across a three and a half-mile front, both German divisions had withdrawn to the Santerno. The next day continued pressure finally forced them back across the river, uncovering the left flank of the *26th Panzer Division*, which also withdrew behind the Santerno. South of Highway 9 in the foothills of the Apennines the *4th Parachute Division* of the *I Parachute Corps* also began withdrawing to confirm to the retrograde movements on its left.[11]

By morning of 12 April, both the British 5 Corps and the 2 Polish Corps had established shallow bridgeheads beyond the Santerno. That afternoon the 2d New Zealand Division burst from its beachhead and advanced two miles beyond the river to capture the town of Massa Lombarda, while on the flanks of that thrust the Indians and the Poles continued to strengthen and deepen their bridgeheads.

While that encouraging progress developed, the British 56th Division on the Eighth Army's right wing launched the first of a series of amphibious attacks from the "Wedge," won during the preliminary operation, to expand positions north of the mouth of the Reno. Carried by a flotilla of Fantails, an infantry brigade landed near the hamlet of Menate, three miles beyond

the mouth of the Reno and seven miles northeast of the Bastia Bridge. Not expecting an attack from that direction, the enemy was taken by surprise. Within a few hours both Menate and Longastrino, three miles to its south, were in British hands. Simultaneously, a second brigade pushed westward along the north bank of the Reno to link up with the first. The two brigades soon joined to open a route over which armor and artillery could advance along dikes paralleling the Reno's northern bank to lend additional weight to the attack. Yet at the same time resistance stiffened as the defending *42d Jaeger Division*—threatened also by envelopment on the right by Allied advances beyond Massa Lombarda—fought desperately to withdraw from a salient created by the 56th Division's thrust at Alfonsine, near where Highway 16 crossed the Senio ten miles southeast of the Bastia Bridge.

Breakthrough at the Argenta Gap

The crossing of the Santerno in the west and the outflanking of the line of the Reno to the east marked completion of the first phase of the Eighth Army's offensive. General McCreery believed nevertheless that the situation had yet to develop sufficiently to enable him to decide whether to concentrate on a westerly thrust toward Budrio or on a northerly drive toward Argenta. Deciding to force the issue, McCreery brought forward the British 78th Division. Passing through the 8th Indian Division's bridgehead, the 78th Division moved northward along the Santerno's west bank in the general direction of the Bastia Bridge, while the 56th Divi-

---

[11] MS # T–1b (Westphal *et al.*); Greiner and Schramm, eds., *OKW/WFSt, KTB*, IV(1), pp. 160–65.

sion prepared to move on Bastia from the east. The 78th Division's left flank was to be covered by the 2d Commando Brigade, advancing in Fantails across flooded fields south of Argenta. To the right of the 56th Division the 24th Guards Brigade prepared to launch yet another Fantail-borne assault, setting out across the flooded lowlands toward the Chiesa del Bante, three miles northeast of Argenta.

One Allied division advancing frontally on the Bastia Bridge and another outflanking it from the east over flooded areas hitherto regarded impassable convinced both Vietinghoff and Herr that the Eighth Army no longer intended a major amphibious operation north of the mouth of the Po. That prompted the army group commander to relieve the *29th Panzer Grenadier Division* from its pointless vigil and commit it to defense of the Argenta Gap.[12]

After only a brief check at the village of Conselice, five miles north of Massa Lombarda, the 78th Division reached the Reno River and captured the Bastia Bridge early on the 14th before the retreating *42d Jaeger Division* could demolish it. Yet when the British attempted to expand their bridgehead, they found the *Jaegers* well-entrenched within the village of Bastia. Southeast of the Bastia sector the *Jaegers* also checked the 56th Division's second amphibious operation, launched on the morning of the 13th, short of its goal.

Despite those local defensive successes, it was obvious from the loss of the Bastia Bridge that the check would be brief. Once more General Vieting-

hoff recommended to OKW limited withdrawals in less threatened sectors in order to obtain reinforcements to prevent a breakthrough on Herr's left wing. After pointing to the courage and steadfastness of the embattled troops attempting to hold the Argenta Gap, Vietinghoff called the Supreme Command's attention to the imminent threat of an Allied breakthrough into the Po Valley, which if successful would endanger the "entire east flank of the [*Army Group C*] front. . . If we do not succeed in stopping the enemy at the northwestern corner of Lake Comacchio (the Comacchio Lagoon)," the army group commander continued, "a breakthrough into the Po Valley will be inevitable. All necessary forces to stop this move must be available at once. They can only be taken from the *I Parachute Corps* sector and only if the salient [at Imola] is reduced by a fighting withdrawal." Any other solution, Vietinghoff went on, could bring only temporary relief and raised the specter of entrapment.[13]

As for the Genghis Khan positions along the Idice River, the last before Bologna, Vietinghoff observed that they "will likewise not be defended for any length of time, since, as far as can be judged by this headquarters, neither new units nor replacements of personnel and materiel, particularly gasoline, can be supplied in sufficient quantities." Even that estimate was optimistic, for the Eighth Army had already penetrated the line several days before.

---

[12] MS # T–1b (Westphal *et al.*).

[13] Cable, *OB Army Group C* to OKW, 14 Apr 45, quoted in Operations of the British, Indian, and Dominion Forces in Italy, Part IV, Sec. G, Ann. F. Unless otherwise indicated the following section is based on that source.

Despite OKW's earlier rejection of a large-scale withdrawal to the Po, Vietinghoff again returned to the theme, stating:

If the Supreme Command of the Army Forces continues to maintain its intention of keeping the Anglo-Americans as far and as long as possible from the borders of the Reich, its aim can only be achieved if we defeat the known intentions of our enemies, the annihilation of the German armies. This can be done only if we avoid decisive battles by retreating, if necessary, to our prepared Ticino-Po defense positions. This decision must be made soon in order to allow for the necessary and difficult moves from the western Alps and from the Ligurian coast. As these moves will require at least two weeks, we must act quickly in order to prevent the enemy from reaching the Po on our eastern flank. This means that *Tenth Army* would have to hold its sector at least two weeks after the commencement of our withdrawal from the western and alpine sectors of the army group's front. This is considered the only way in which the north Italian areas, so important to our war industry, can be preserved for the German Army until the day of our decisive battle.

Without waiting for OKW's reply, Vietinghoff risked Hitler's opprobrium by withdrawing the *I Parachute Corps* from the Imola salient and pulling it back into the Genghis Khan Line. Meanwhile, he continued to reinforce the Argenta Gap as best he could.

Vietinghoff had little time to lose, for Keightley's 5 Corps was closing in on the gap and McCreery, deciding to strengthen his center, started shifting the British 13 Corps with its 10th Indian Division from the army right wing to a sector between the 2 Polish Corps and the British 5 Corps. Unaware of that decision but anticipating it as likely, General Herr ordered the entire *29th Panzer Grenadier Division* to the defense of Argenta and the *278th Volksgrenadier Division* from the *I Parachute Corps* to the *LXXVI Panzer Corps*, where the volksgrenadier division was to relieve the *98th Division*, reduced by casualties to the size of a battle group. He then pulled the *26th Panzer Division* from the line opposite the 2 Polish Corps to provide a mobile reserve for the Reno line.[14]

By 15 April the *278th Division* had taken over from the *98th Division* the sector astride the Medicina–Massa Lombarda railroad; but the change came too late to do more than momentarily check the momentum of the New Zealanders' thrust from their bridgehead over the Sillaro. South of that sector the *4th Parachute Division* also briefly held up those elements of the Polish corps advancing astride Highway 9. Brief though it was, that rear guard action nevertheless enabled the *I Parachute Corps* to withdraw those forces still in the Imola salient to the temporary—but as it turned out, illusory—security of the Genghis Khan Line.

Confronted by elements of the *29th Panzer Grenadier Division* instead of battered survivors of the *42d Jaeger* and *362d Divisions*, General Keightley decided to throw in everything that the relatively narrow Argenta sector could accommodate. All three of his separate infantry brigades were to continue their efforts to outflank Argenta: the first to drive northeastward toward Portomaggiore, a second to pass directly east of Argenta, and a third to assist the 78th Division in reducing the strongpoint at Bastia village. The 2d Commando Bri-

---

[14] MS # T–1b (Westphal *et al.*).

gade was at the same time to continue its advance southwest of Argenta.

General der Panzertruppen Gerhard Graf von Schwerin, new commander of the *LXXVI Panzer Corps*, had in the meantime pressed deployment of the *29th Panzer Grenadier Division* in the Argenta Gap; but it was too late. Because the northward advance of the British 78th Division was threatening collapse of the central sector, held by the *362d Division*, which would uncover the *29th Panzer Grenadier Division*'s right flank, von Schwerin formed survivors of the *42d Jaeger* and *362d Divisions* into two battle groups with orders to hold until early on the 16th. Although forced to yield Bastia village on the 15th, the *42d Jaeger* by its stubborn defense gave the *29th Panzer Grenadiers* some time to dig in north of the Marina Canal, about a mile and a half south of Argenta. To enable von Schwerin to extricate remaining units of his *LXXVI Panzer Corps* still south of the Reno, the panzer grenadiers had to hold that line for at least twenty-four hours, for once Allied forces took the Argenta Gap, they would be in a position to move rapidly northwestward along the Reno's north bank, turn successive river lines, and expedite the advance of those divisions attacking astride Highway 9.

By the evening of 16 April the British 78th Division struck the line of the Marina Canal on the *29th Panzer Grenadier Division*'s right flank. Although the panzer grenadiers fought gamely, the leading British battalion managed early on the 17th to secure a small bridgehead. The Marina Canal line had not held quite as long as von Schwerin had hoped it would, but the rear guard action nevertheless enabled

him to straighten out his front south of the Reno preparatory to withdrawing to the Reno itself.

While supporting artillery guided by wide-ranging observation aircraft pinned down those troops still deployed along the Marina Canal line, tactical aircraft of the DAF again took to the air at dawn on the 17th to strike at anything that dared move north of Argenta. During the morning the 78th Division burst out of the bridgehead and passed east of Argenta, while a brigade of the British 56th Division, mounted in Fantails, moved up on the right across the flooded lowlands to the near bank of the Marina Canal southeast of Argenta. To the 78th Division's left the 2d Commando Brigade, also in Fantails, crossed a flooded area west of the Reno to pull abreast of the center. Those advances so stretched the enemy's defenses that two fresh battalions of the 78th Division reached Argenta without difficulty, one bypassing it on the right, the other moving directly into the town. While the lead battalion cleared the last German from Argenta, a second brigade of the 78th Division came forward, and early afternoon of the 18th found two of the division's brigades advancing northwest of Argenta along Highway 16. As Vietinghoff had warned OKW four days earlier, a breakthrough of the Argenta Gap threatened to turn the line of the Reno.

OKW's reply to Vietinghoff's message of the 14th warning of that threat arrived at *Army Group C* headquarters on the 17th even as the threat became a reality. Although the reply bore Generaloberst Alfred Jodl's signature, the order was Hitler's:

All further proposals for a change in the present war strategy will be discontinued. I wish to point out particularly that under no circumstances must troops or commanders be allowed to waver or to adopt a defeatist attitude as a result of such ideas apparently held by your headquarters. Where any such danger is likely, the sharpest countermeasures must be employed. The Fuehrer expects now, as before, the utmost steadfastness in the fulfillment of your present mission, to defend every inch of the north Italian areas entrusted to your command. I desire to point out the serious consequences for all those higher commanders, unit commanders, or staff officers, who do not carry out the Fuehrer's orders to the last word.[15]

More than draconian orders and thinly veiled threats were needed to check the momentum of the Eighth Army's offensive. While the 78th and 56th Divisions pushed through the Argenta Gap on the right, in the center and on the army's left the 2d New Zealand Division of the 5 Corps, the 10th Indian Division of the 13 Corps, and the Carpathian and Kresowa Divisions of the 2 Polish Corps advanced along the Medicina-Budrio axis and Highway 9. The main burden of defense there fell upon the *4th Parachute Division*, for the *278th Division* had been steadily falling back before the New Zealanders ever since arriving in the sector on the 15th. The parachutists gradually fell back to the line of the Gaiano Canal, about midway between Medicina and Budrio and a mile and a half beyond Castel San Pietro on Highway 9. By the 18th, the 2 Polish and British 13 Corps had closed up to the canal, some five miles east of the Idice River, which formed the Genghis Khan Line in that sector. Although the *Tenth Army* commander hoped to delay the Eighth Army's advance there long enough to allow his forces to reach the line of the Po in good order, the end of the battles south of the Po was by 18 April in sight. Meanwhile, just four days before, the U.S. Fifth Army had launched its phase of the spring offensive.

---

[15] Cable No. 2, 17 Apr 45, *OKW to OB Army Group C*, in Operations of the British, Indian, and Dominion Forces in Italy, Part IV, Sec. G. Ann. F.

CHAPTER XXVII

Breakthrough on the Fifth Army's Front

Originally scheduled for 12 April, D-Day for the Fifth Army's phase of the spring offensive was postponed when heavy fog rolled in over the airfields and forced cancellation of all flights. When meteorologists could forecast no clearing for the next day, Truscott set D-Day for the 14th, H-hour for 0600.

Before dawn on the 14th the army commander and members of his staff sat anxiously drinking coffee and smoking in their headquarters at Traversa while awaiting the latest weather reports. Presently telephones began to ring. All air bases repeated the same story: fog-shrouded runways. Truscott telephoned his IV Corps commander, General Crittenberger, to tell him to delay his attack but to be prepared to move on an hour's notice. The officers in the headquarters tent then settled back glumly over more coffee and cigarettes.

Only a few minutes passed before a call from the air base near Grosseto revealed that the fog might be lifting there. Again more coffee and cigarettes while calls went out to other bases. Then at 0800 Grosseto reported the end of the runway visible. Fighter-bombers were taking off. Elated, Truscott telephoned Crittenberger: "The attack is on for 0900." Messages from other air bases reporting clearing weather confirmed the decision. For the critical first day of attack the IV Corps would be assured of air support.[1]

Precisely at 0830 wave after wave of heavy bombers droned over the mountains from the south. For the next forty minutes the sky was filled with hundreds of aircraft dumping thousands of tons of high explosive, fragmentation, and napalm bombs on the enemy's positions. Eventually, over four days, some 2,052 heavy bombers flew, first in support of the IV Corps, then of the II Corps. That number exceeded the 1,673 heavy bombers that had supported the Eighth Army's attack four days before: all in all, "the beginning of the most sustained heavy bomber close support effort ever undertaken in the Mediterranean."[2]

As the heavy bombers completed their first day's missions, medium and fighter-bombers of the XXII TAC, engaged since the 10th in operations against enemy communications and supply depots, appeared over the front to attack the enemy's main line of resistance. The aircraft flew over 459 sorties, mostly in flights of four planes each against gun positions, strongpoints, troop areas, and other defensive works

---

[1] Truscott, *Command Missions*, p. 486.

[2] Craven and Cate, eds., *AAF III*, pp. 486–87; *Fifth Army History*, Part IX, pp. 91–92; IV Corps History, pp. 614–15. Unless otherwise indicated the following is based upon those references.

immediately opposite the IV Corps front. Many of the sorties were napalm attacks against the 10th Mountain Division's first objective of Monte Pigna, four miles northwest of Vergato, the latter at the junction of Highway 64 and the lateral road connecting the highway with the Panaro valley ten miles to the west.

No sooner had the aircraft completed their missions than supporting artillery opened fire at 0910. For thirty-five minutes over 2,000 pieces, ranging from the 10th Mountain Division's 75-mm. pack howitzers to the Fifth Army's 8-inch howitzers, fired a devastating barrage. The smoke and dust raised by the massive aerial and artillery bombardment turned the morning into a gray twilight, whereupon the mountain division's infantrymen began moving to a line of departure on the forward slopes of Monte della Spe, just northeast of Castel d'Aiano overlooking the northernmost of two lateral roads connecting Vergato with Castel d'Aiano and a secondary road that was to be the axis of advance for the division in carrying "the brunt of the attack to the Po Valley—and beyond."[3] (*Map XVI*) With all three regiments moving abreast, the division's immediate goal was a mountain mass extending northeastward for about seven miles from the 2,500-foot Rocca Roffeno massif in the southwest through Monte Pigna and terminating at Monte Mantino and Monte Mosca, the latter overlooking both the Lavino and Reno river valleys.[4]

Capture of the Roffeno feature would provide early control of the lateral road running west-northwest from Vergato and thence down the Samoggia valley to Modena. Most importantly, with the massif in American hands the mountain infantry would be able to turn the flank of the *94th Infantry Division*, which with the *334th Infantry Division* was holding that sector of the *Fourteenth Army* front between the Samoggia and the Reno Rivers. The Roffeno massif was, observed the *94th Division*'s operations officer, the Achilles heel of that sector.[5]

Although both German divisions had prepared positions capable of withstanding all but direct hits by heavy artillery and aerial bombs, both were understrength. Each had three grenadier regiments of only two battalions each, and neither had more than company-sized local reserves. Reinforcements could come only from the *Fourteenth Army*'s reserves, i.e., the *90th Panzer Grenadier Division* southwest of Bologna, but one regiment of that unit had already moved to the west to reinforce the Ligurian flank.

Artillery support for the sector held by the two divisions totaled only 240 pieces of all types, hardly a match for the 381 pieces that the U.S. IV Corps alone controlled, not to mention artillery under Fifth Army control. Furthermore, the American phase of the offensive would occur approximately along the intercorps boundary between the *LI Mountain Corps* on the west and the *XIV Panzer Corps* on the east, traditionally a weak point. The *334th Division*, in whose sector lay the Roffeno massif,

---

[3] Truscott, *Command Missions*, p. 487.
[4] 10th Mtn Div Rpt of Opns, Apr–May 45.

[5] MS # T–1b (Westphal *et al.*). Unless otherwise cited the following section is based on that source.

was the left flank unit of the mountain corps, and the *94th Division* the right flank unit of the panzer corps.

As the aerial and artillery bombardment ceased, the 85th Mountain Infantry on the 10th Mountain Division's left moved down into the Pra del Bianco basin, a small bowl-shaped valley just northeast of Castel d'Aiano. Across the flanks of the hills overlooking the basin from the west the Germans had constructed an intricate system of bunkers and covered gun emplacements. Yet in the basin itself outposts were manned only at night so that men of the 85th Mountain Infantry had no difficulty bypassing them in the half light of early morning. Widespread antipersonnel and antitank mine fields along the basin's western edge were another matter. In addition to causing numerous casualties among the infantrymen, the mines also prevented the 751st Tank and 701st Tank Destroyer Battalions from staying close to the mountain infantrymen and providing support against well-sited enemy automatic weapons overlooking the basin. The mine fields thus enabled the Germans to gain time to man their weapons within the main line of resistance. With a surprisingly heavy volume of fire, considering the bombing and artillery that had preceded the attack, they were able to check the advance just short of the crest of the hills overlooking the basin.

Although the 85th Mountain Infantry's commander, Col. Raymond C. Barlow, called for artillery fire to counter the enemy's mortars and artillery beyond the range of his infantry, credit for finally silencing the enemy's automatic weapons was attributable to the mountain infantrymen themselves, stubbornly fighting their way forward despite the fire. One man, for example, Pfc. John D. Magrath of Company G, armed only with a rifle, charged an enemy machine gun position, killing two enemy soldiers and wounding three others and capturing their machine gun. Arming himself with the captured piece, Magrath continued across an open field to neutralize two more machine guns. Circling behind still another, he destroyed it from the rear. Noticing a fourth position, Magrath opened fire on it, killing two and wounding three of the enemy. Meanwhile the men of Company G followed Magrath, to occupy the ground he had cleared. Volunteering to check on casualties, Magrath fell mortally wounded. He was posthumously awarded the Medal of Honor.[6]

As the men of the 2d Battalion inched forward, the 3d Battalion surprisingly met little resistance and moved quickly to the crest of Hill 860, part of the high ground overlooking the basin. From that vantage point the battalion, with support from guns of the 604th Field Artillery Battalion, fired on the enemy flank, thereby relieving some of the pressure on the 2d Battalion. Soon after noon two additional crests along the high ground were in hand, and the two battalions turned northeastward along the ridge line to clear the rest.[7]

Meanwhile, at 0945, the 87th Mountain Infantry, under Col. David M. Fowler, crossed a line of departure on Monte Spicchione's forward slopes. In a column of battalions, the regiment trav-

---

[6] *Medal of Honor*, pp. 359–60.
[7] 10th Mtn Div Opns Rpt. Apr–May 45.

ersed the lateral road leading northeast from Castel d'Aiano to enter the village of Serra Sarzana, a mile to the northeast of Castel d'Aiano and two miles southeast of Monte Pigna, one of the major features of the Roffeno massif. When the mountain infantry attempted to continue, heavy enemy artillery fire forced them to shelter in the ruins of the village, while from the high ground to the west, not at that point cleared by the 85th Mountain Infantry, enemy machine guns probed with fire. Only when that fire ceased, probably as a result of the regiment's advance, was the 1st Battalion able to lead the way into the neighboring village of Torre Iussi. While the battalion fought through the village house by house, Colonel Fowler sent the 2d Battalion to bypass the village and capture Hill 903, high ground overlooking Torre Iussi. The maneuver was sufficient to convince the Germans that to fight any longer invited envelopment. They promptly withdrew from both village and hill.

On the 10th Mountain Division's right wing the 86th Mountain Infantry, under Col. Clarence Tomlinson, attacked with the 2d Battalion forward toward the northern slope of the Rocca Roffeno. Those men too came under heavy fire from the enemy on Hill 903, but once that feature fell to the 87th Mountain Infantry, men of the 86th Mountain Infantry were able to scale a nearby height and by late afternoon take the height of Rocca Roffeno.

Continued resistance and the coming of darkness nevertheless prevented further advance. Yet unknown to the men of the 10th Mountain Division, they had opened a serious breach between

MOUNTAIN INFANTRY IN TOLE AREA

the *334th* and *94th Divisions*. Any further American advance to the northeast, the Germans feared, would outflank the *94th Division*. In an effort to prevent that, the *94th Division* commander, General Steinmetz, rushed forward his reserve battalion to close the gap. It was too late. The plight of the defenders of the Rocca Roffeno position became evident that night via a radio message from the survivors: "Fire on our position. . . ." Then the radio fell silent.[8]

The Americans, meanwhile, had settled down on their newly-won ground to await the customary counterattack, but none came. Instead only sporadic artillery fire and occasional flares indicated that an enemy still waited in the

[8] MS # T-1b (Westphal *et al.*), Part II, *Die 94th Grenadier Division*.

dark hills and valleys to the north. Key ground had been won, but the first day had been costly, with 553 mountain infantrymen killed, wounded, or missing. Although the Americans had a foothold on the Roffeno massif, Monte Pigna still remained in enemy hands.

At dawn on 15 April a 20-minute artillery barrage, including the guns of supporting tanks and tank destroyers, opened the second day of the IV Corps attack. Twenty minutes later the leading battalions of the 87th Mountain Infantry moved out from Torre Iussi and Hill 903 toward Monte Pigna about a mile to the north. Resistance was spotty, and just over an hour later the Americans were on the crest preparing to continue their advance northward toward the town of Tole, four miles northwest of Vergato commanding a network of secondary roads leading into the Samoggia and Lavino valleys.

About the same time, the 86th Mountain Infantry in the center began moving from Rocca Roffeno toward the hamlet of Amore, a battered collection of stone cottages a thousand yards to the north. There too resistance was weak. Passing through Amore in mid-morning, the men continued along a ridge terminating at Monte Mantino and just as darkness fell occupied that height without opposition.

The situation was far different on the division's left flank where the 85th Mountain Infantry, advancing from the high ground overlooking the Pra del Bianco toward Monte Righetti, two and a half miles west of Monte Pigna, ran into such heavy resistance that the division commander thought it prudent to bring forward a special unit for flank protection, the 10th Mountain Infantry

Antitank Battalion, formed from the antitank companies of the division's three regiments. Noting the contrast with fading resistance on the right, the corps commander, General Crittenberger, directed a shift of the division's main effort to the right.

The enemy commander in that sector, General Steinmetz of the *94th Infantry Division*, was fully aware that his front was crumbling. Having requested *XIV Panzer Corps* headquarters in vain for permission to withdraw his left flank regiments, he decided on the 16th to take matters into his own hands. That afternoon he ordered the troops on his center and left to fall back during the night to new positions. But he had waited dangerously long, for the Americans had already cut the few roads leading from that sector. Steinmetz's troops had to withdraw cross-country in the darkness over mountainous terrain, abandoning much of their heavy equipment along the way and falling prey to harassing American artillery fire. So cut up was the division's left flank battalion as to become virtually useless.

The 10th Mountain Division was on the verge of a breakthrough of the enemy front between the Samoggia and Lavino Rivers, and progress over the next three days confirmed it. As the *94th Infantry Division* continued to withdraw behind smoke screens and artillery fire, the 86th and 87th Mountain Infantry Regiments, moving in column of battalions following a 20-minute artillery barrage, jumped off at 0620 on the 16th. Despite the efforts of a determined rear guard, the 86th Mountain Infantry in the early afternoon occupied hills just north of Monte Mantino,

GERMAN PRISONERS CAPTURED BY 10TH MOUNTAIN DIVISION

then with the help of tanks from the 751st Tank Battalion advanced another four miles to the hamlet of Montepastore. Meanwhile, the 87th Mountain Infantry advanced via Tole toward Monte Croce and Monte Mosca, the latter five miles northeast of Monte Pigna and the last high point along the eastern ridge line. Progress over the next two days was just as steady, so that by nightfall on the 18th the troops of the 10th Mountain Division had almost reached the edge of the mountains overlooking Highway 9 and the plain.

Five days of attack had cost 1,283 casualties, and the surviving infantrymen were close to exhaustion. Of the first men to enter the village of Montepastore, an officer of the 86th Mountain Infantry observed that they were "incredibly weary . . . . Wherever the men dropped their packs they fell asleep. They slept in barns, cowstalls, bedrooms, any place they could find. After a rest [they] looked for food and found chickens, onions, some captured

German cheese and bologna. Fires sprang up all over town, and soon [they] were eating their first food, other than K-rations, in four days."[9]

Droves of German prisoners meanwhile streamed back to the division rear. A not uncommon sight was one weary American infantryman shepherding a column of 40 to 50 equally weary Germans. Among the prisoners were the staff and commanding officer of the *2d Battalion, 361st Panzer Grenadier Regiment*, thus confirming rumors circulating among the Americans for the past two days that the *90th Panzer Grenadier Division* was on its way to the front opposite the IV Corps. On the same day, elements of the *190th Reconnaissance Battalion* and the *200th Panzer Grenadier Regiment* of the same division were also identified. Thus did the Americans learn of Vietinghoff's decision to commit his remaining reserve to plug the widening gap in the *Fourteenth Army* front between the Samoggia and the Lavino Rivers.[10]

As the *90th Panzer Grenadier Division* came forward, the Germans began to fall back slowly toward a so-called *Michelstellung*, an east-west switch position passing through Monte San Michele, some five miles north of Montepastore. Last of the prepared positions in the hills south of the Po Valley, the *Michelstellung* was less a continuous line than a series of lightly held strongpoints. Like the Americans, the German infantry would reach the new positions in a state of virtual exhaustion.

Armor Joins the Battle

While the 10th Mountain Division pushed rapidly over the mountain ridges in its zone of operations, units to the left and right were advancing abreast. On the left the Brazilian division occupied the village of Montese and surrounding hills three miles northwest of Castel d'Aiano, while on the right General Prichard's 1st Armored Division, beginning on 14 April soon after the mountain division's attack started, moved against Vergato and the hills to the northwest of that town.[11]

On the armored division's right wing, on the heels of TOT fired by the 105-mm. guns of the 27th Armored Field Artillery Battalion, dismounted cavalrymen of the 81st Cavalry Reconnaissance Squadron stormed an enemy strongpoint at Vergato. Within two hours the Americans had fought through the town's southern outskirts to occupy what remained of the railroad station, while so occupied was the enemy in defending Vergato that the 14th Armored Infantry Battalion encountered little resistance in coming up on the cavalrymen's left to attack the village of Suzzano, two miles to the northwest. Following repeated bombardment by planes of the XXII TAC and supporting artillery and armor, tank-infantry teams moved rapidly into Suzzano late on the 15th. The next day men of the 11th Armored Infantry Battalion passed through to capture Monte Mosca, three miles to the northeast.

---

[9] IV Corps History, p. 623; 9th MRU, Battle Casualty Reports of Fifth Army, 10 Jun 45.
[10] MS # T–lb (Westphal *et al.*),Part II, annex to Ch 11a.

[11] Howe, *Battle History of the 1st Armored Division*, pp. 407–08; *Fifth Army History*, Part IX, pp. 50–51; IV Corps AAR, Apr 45. Unless otherwise cited the following sections are based upon these references.

The only real opposition was in the ruins of Vergato. In the smoldering town the Germans fought through the night, and only with the coming of daylight on the 15th and arrival of a trio of tanks and an armored bulldozer were the men of the 81st Cavalry Reconnaissance Squadron able to get on with a systematic clearing of the ruins, house by house. Another night passed before resistance was completely eliminated.

Over the next two days—16 and 17 April—men of the armored division made systematic advances in several columns. By nightfall of the 17th the 81st Cavalry had reached a point nearly five miles beyond Vergato, while the 6th Armored Infantry Battalion passed beyond Monte Mosca to capture Monte d'Avigo, three miles to the northeast. A 30-minute artillery preparation discouraged meaningful resistance by a reinforced German company. To the right the 11th Armored Infantry Battalion gained Monte Milano overlooking the Reno valley.

On the left the Brazilians, on the right the armor had come abreast of the 10th Mountain Division. On the IV Corps front all was going well.

The II Corps Attacks

Not so on the II Corps front, for there the advance toward Bologna seemed at first agonizingly reminiscent of the fighting in November 1944 in the same area. The problem lay not only in the difficult terrain, but in the fact that there the enemy had concentrated his strongest defenses. Yet in the conviction that Keyes' corps would face greater challenges than its neighbor west of Highway 64, General Truscott had placed the majority of his divisions under the II Corps between Highway 64 in the west and Highway 65 in the east.

The Germans had developed their defense on the central sector south of Bologna around four clearly defined geographic features. The first—and most important in terms of Truscott's intention to concentrate his main effort in the Reno valley—was Monte Sole, six miles northeast of Vergato midway between the Reno River and Setta Creek. The capture of Monte Sole, together with the IV Corps' operations west of the Reno valley, would open the way for an advance to the Praduro road junction on Highway 64 where the Setta enters the Reno. The second and third features were Monterumici and Monte Adone, overlooking Highway 65 from the west, and a series of hills just north of Monte Belmonte, overlooking the same stretch of Highway 65 from the east. Clearing the enemy from the high ground would permit an advance to the town of Pianoro, the fourth feature, on Highway 65 only eight miles from Bologna. Possession of Pianoro would enable Keyes to put considerable pressure on the enemy's defenses south of Bologna.

Extensive reconnaissance had disclosed that the strongpoints developed around those four features were mutually supporting. That being the case, it was evident to Keyes that the capture of one would not necessarily lead to a breakthrough, so that it would be necessary to attack simultaneously across the entire corps sector. That, Keyes hoped, would prevent the enemy from shifting local reserves from one threatened point to another. With the enemy pinned down, Keyes would be free to exploit his vast superiority in manpower and materiel to concentrate sufficient strength at one point to achieve a breakthrough.[12]

To defend south of Bologna, General Lemelsen had assembled slightly more than four divisions. Although that constituted more units than the U.S. II Corps controlled, in terms of manpower the Germans were far inferior. Opposite the inter-army boundary to the II Corps right lay the *1st Parachute Division*, then the *305th Infantry*, followed by the *65th Infantry* and *8th Mountain Divisions*, with part of the *94th Division* opposite the II Corps left. The *65th Infantry* and the *8th Mountain Divisions* were especially well positioned between the Reno River and Highway 65, the main route through the sector.[13]

The four divisions of the II Corps held a 15-mile front running northeasterly from the Reno River eastward to a ridge line about two miles east of the Idice River. The 6th South African Armoured Division was in position opposite Monte Sole across the high ground between the Reno and the Setta Creek. Next in line was the 88th Division facing Monterumici. The 91st Division stood astride Highway 65 facing Monte Adone and the high ground flanking Pianoro. East of the highway was the 34th Division, whose objectives were the Savizzano and Gorgognano ridges northeast of Monte Belmonte. The Italian Legnano Combat Group on the far right flank was to demonstrate

but not attack when the II Corps' phase of the offensive began.

As Keyes prepared for that phase, the full weight of available air support shifted to his corps. On 15 April, the afternoon preceding the attack, 765 heavy bombers attacked targets along both highways between the front and Bologna. Medium bombers followed to attack installations and troop assembly areas in the vicinity of Praduro. The next day the heavy bombers repeated their attacks, while the medium bombers shifted to the enemy's lines of communications in the vicinity of Bologna. Meanwhile, in late afternoon of the 15th, 120 fighter-bombers in waves of four to eight aircraft continuously attacked the enemy in the Monte Sole sector. Just before dusk fighter-bombers turned their attention to other strongpoints across the corps front, dropping tons of flaming napalm on known enemy emplacements and illuminating the darkening landscape with pillars of fire. In addition to the aerial bombardment, 548 artillery pieces fired counterbattery and antipersonnel barrages immediately prior to the first moves by the ground forces. To all that the Germans replied only weakly: only just over a thousand rounds of enemy artillery fell across the entire II Corps front during the first two days of the attack.

On 15 April, while smoke and dust from the bombs and shells hung heavily over the rugged terrain or drifted into the narrow valleys, the 6th South African Armoured Division and the 88th Division on the corps left wing attacked soon after nightfall. Four and a half hours later, at 0300 on 16 April, the 91st and 34th Divisions launched their operations on the corps right wing.

---

[12] II Corps AAR, 1 Apr–2 May 45; Starr, *From Salerno to the Alps*, pp. 410–12; *Fifth Army History*, Part IX, pp. 50–87; Truscott, *Command Missions*, pp. 488–89. Unless otherwise indicated, the following is based upon those references.

[13] MS # T–1b (Westphal *et al.*).

The preliminary aerial and artillery barrages had sent the Germans scurrying deep into their bunkers, but as was soon apparent to the attackers, they quickly reoccupied their gun positions. German fire, supplemented by mine fields and the difficult terrain, limited the 88th, 91st, and 34th Divisions to slow, costly advances, so familiar to the veterans of the previous autumn's operations. Only on the left flank could Keyes report success: there the South Africans, in a series of gallant assaults, supported by a devastating 35,000 rounds of artillery, before daylight on the 16th captured Monte Sole.

On the second day, as the German defenses west of Highway 65 began to waver, the 88th Division finally drove the last enemy from Monterumici. The Germans continued nevertheless to hold firm astride Highway 65. Only on the third day did signs develop that the enemy's defenses were about to crumble there as well, as the 91st and 34th Divisions cleared the high ground flanking the highway. The IV Corps, meanwhile, continued to widen its penetration west of the Reno and Highway 64, and the Eighth Army's Polish corps threatened Bologna from the southeast. Isolation of the German sector south of Bologna seemed imminent.

Sensing that a breakthrough was at hand, General Truscott decided the time had come to shift the weight of his army's attack and the intercorps boundary westward. By so doing he would place the important Praduro road junction and eventually Highway 64 and the Reno River within the zone of operations of the II Corps. The latter was then to make the army's main drive to the Po.

Anticipating the army commander's decision, General Keyes had already begun moving his divisions westward. He first shifted the 88th Division to the corps left flank between the 6th South African Armoured Division and the Reno River. Again the 88th was to team up with the 85th Division, which on the 16th had begun to move from reserve positions on the Arno to an assembly area in the vicinity of Vergato. There the division prepared the next day to relieve the 1st Armored Division west of the Reno. Although Truscott had originally planned to assign the 85th Division to Keyes, he gave it instead to Crittenberger for use on the 10th Mountain Division's right flank, where the progress of the preceding four days had suggested an important enemy weakness.

As the 85th Division completed relief of the 1st Armored Division, the armor moved to positions along the Panaro River, ten miles to the west, where the terrain was more favorable for armored operations. The armor could also cover the extended left flank of the 10th Mountain Division, which was to become the spearhead of the Fifth Army's offensive. To fill the gap created by shifting the 88th Division to the left flank, the 91st and 34th Divisions also sideslipped westward. That move served to widen the relatively inactive sector of the Legnano Group and set Highway 65 as the boundary between the Italians and the 34th Division. The regrouping completed, Truscott expected that the next two days would produce a break out from the mountains onto the Lombardy (Po) plain.

Breakthrough to the Plain

At 0930 on the 18th the 10th Mountain and the 85th Divisions led off the

INFANTRYMEN ENTERING PO VALLEY

renewed IV Corps attack. From the first the 85th Division on the right experienced no contest. Trying to withdraw, the Germans had become so disorganized that they found it difficult to make a stand anywhere. By nightfall of the first day the two leading regiments of the 85th Division had advanced five miles to hills north of the village of Piano di Venola, halfway between Vergato and Praduro.

Men of the 10th Mountain Division had slower going at first. In early afternoon the Germans fought back with heavy artillery and mortar fire, prompting the front-running 85th Mountain Infantry to hold up for the night short of the initial objective of Mongiorgio. Yet as the mountain infantrymen determined early on the second day, the 19th, that spurt of resistance was but a screen for continuing enemy withdrawal. When the 85th Mountain Infantry took the lead in a drive to Monte San Michele, a dominating height northeast of Mongiorgio and key to a position the Germans had hoped to hold at length—the *Michelstel-*

34TH DIVISION INFANTRYMEN PAUSE IN BOLOGNA

lung—the German defense collapsed. Around noon Monte San Michele was in hand and a request went back for every available tank and tank destroyer to join the attack, for the enemy withdrawal had become a rout. The leading troops stopped for the night three miles beyond Monte San Michele but only to allow supporting troops and reserves to catch up. To the left a battalion of the 87th Mountain Infantry occupied another height, Monte San Pietro, again in the face of virtually no opposition. General Truscott's hope for a break-

through onto the plain in two days had fallen short but not by much. Debouchment was bound to come on the 20th.

The 1st Armored Division meanwhile had one combat command ready to attack on the 18th up the valley of the Samoggia to protect the left flank of the corps. The next day the remainder of the division joined the drive. That was fortunate, for in a desperate effort to stop a breakthrough onto the plain, the Germans threw in tanks of the *90th Panzer Grenadier Division*. As tank fought tank, the advance of the American armor was restricted, but the desperate effort to prevent a breakthrough had come too late. With the 1st Armored Division obviously capable of handling the nuisance on the flank, the 10th Mountain and 85th Divisions had no cause for concern.

At long last, on 20 April, the bitter struggle to break out of the northern Apennines finally reached a climax. Fighting was still intense on occasion, as at the village of Pradalbino where the Germans made a determined stand, culminating in a bitter house-to-house struggle with the 87th Mountain Infantry. Yet that and other attempted stands were futile. In mid-afternoon the 86th Mountain Infantry broke across the arrow-like concrete ribbon that was Highway 9 in the vicinity of Ponte Samoggia, ten miles northwest of Bologna, while men of the 88th Division crossed the intercorps boundary athwart the axis of the II Corps advance in their eagerness to reach the flat country of the Lombardy plain beckoning ahead. In the resulting confusion the latter division became "the bottom of a gigantic T trying to punch through a top which was the 10th and 85th divisions."[14] The situation however was soon straightened out by having the 88th Division's units "relieve in place all 85th Division units as they were overtaken."[15]

The II Corps immediately south of Bologna had in the meantime also begun to move. The 6th South African Armoured Division throughout maintained close contact with the right flank of the IV Corps, on the 20th gaining the town of Casalecchio alongside the 88th Division at Riale, while that night troops of a battalion of the 34th Division's 133d Infantry clambered aboard tanks of the 752d Tank Battalion and set out in darkness along Highway 65 for Bologna. Proceeding cautiously, the little force nevertheless reported entering the city at 0851 the next morning. All but a few German stragglers had departed.

Progress on the Flanks

To the east and northeast of Bologna the Polish corps also participated in the general advance, pushing back the enemy along a series of stream lines to within ten miles of Bologna, while southwest of Budrio the Poles crossed the Quaderno River midway between Medicina and Bologna to pinch out the 10 Corps and take over the Eighth Army's left flank. Early on the 21st the Poles entered Bologna to join the U.S. 34th Division and the Italian Legnano Group in occupying the city.[16]

On the Eighth Army's right flank General Keightley of the 5 Corps committed the British 6th Armoured Division in pursuit of a retreating enemy along the axis of Highway 16. By 20 April the division had pushed to within ten miles of Ferrara. West of the highway the 10th Indian Division outflanked Budrio to the east while a mile north of the town the New Zealand division established a bridgehead beyond the Idice. Those advances had carried the entire corps through the

[14] John P. Delaney, *The Blue Devils in Italy* (Washington: Infantry Journal Press, 1947), pp. 203–04.

[15] *Ibid.*

[16] Operations of the British, Indian, and Dominion Forces in Italy, Part IV.

Genghis Khan Line, breaching the last defenses south of the Po.

On the western side of the peninsula the U.S. 92d Division had also resumed an advance that had been limited since the 14th to relatively modest gains by several battalion-strength counterattacks by the *90th Panzer Grenadier Division*'s *361st Panzer Grenadier Regiment*. On the 17th, the U.S. 473d Infantry advanced astride the coastal road, Highway 1, crossed the Parmignola Canal, and closed in on Sarzana, near the junction of the coastal road with Highway 62 ten miles east of the naval base of La Spezia. To the regiment's right the Japanese-American 442d Infantry tried repeatedly, but in vain, to break through defenses running north and south from the mountain strongpoint of Fosdinovo, five miles northeast of Sarzana.[17]

The reinforcements from the *90th Panzer Grenadier Division*, however, were never intended to stop the Americans indefinitely but only to cover a slow German withdrawal into Sarzana and La Spezia. Coastal batteries, firing from Punta Bianca, three miles south of La Spezia, harassed the Allied-held towns of Massa and Carrara and the routes of approaches passing through them. In spite of frequent attempts by tank destroyers, fighter-bombers, and even an 8-inch howitzer to silence the guns, those on the eastern side of the peninsula continued to fire until the 19th, when, presumably, the Germans destroyed them just before withdrawing. The guns on the western side, however, continued to fire for another day, until

the enemy, faced with the necessity for a rapid withdrawal, because of the Allied breakthrough on the central front on both sides of Bologna, abandoned the batteries to the 92d Division.[18]

The 20th of April thus marked the turning point in the Allied spring offensive across the entire front. From that point the operation was to become a pursuit with fighter-bombers of the MATAF flying in close support of wide-ranging Allied columns fanning out across the Lombardy plain. The aerial harassment, which would soon make of the Po River as much of a barrier to the retreating Germans as they had hoped it would be to the Allies, represented the culmination of 11,902 Allied sorties of all types, flown over the battle area since 14 April. The six days since the Fifth Army's phase of the Allied offensive had begun had witnessed the greatest single week's air support effort of the entire Italian campaign and was a fitting climax to the long months of Allied air operations in the theater.[19]

Meanwhile, five days earlier, the U.S. 6th Army Group under Lt. Gen. Jacob L. Devers, operating north of the Alps, had begun moving south and southwest into western Austria toward the Austro-Italian frontier. On 15 April the SHAEF commander, General Eisenhower, had issued an order sending General Devers' army group, which included the First French Army and the U.S. Seventh Army, through Bavaria and into western Austria toward an eventual link-up with the Allied

---

[17] *Fifth Army History*, Part IX, pp. 42–43; Goodman Monograph, pp. 162–63.

[18] Goodman Monograph, pp. 162–63.
[19] *Ibid.*; Craven and Cate, eds., *AAF III*, pp. 486–89.

armies in Italy. At the same time, Eisenhower sent Patton's Third Army southeastward down the Danube Valley into Austria for eventual link-up with the Russians advancing from Vienna. Thus, from three directions an Allied ring was closing around the German armies in the southwest, forcing them into an Alpine fastness from which there was no escape—and no hope of survival.[20]

Hitler's Strategic Decisions

For the Germans, 20 April had also been a turning point. Until that time the *Tenth Army*'s *I Parachute* and *LXXVI Panzer Corps* had managed, except for the Argenta Gap, to keep their fronts intact while skillfully withdrawing northeastward beyond the Reno. Once again it seemed as if the elusive *Tenth Army* would escape the Eighth Army's grasp. But the failure of the *Fourteenth Army*'s *XIV Panzer Corps* to prevent a breakthrough west of Bologna, first by the U.S. IV Corps and then by the U.S. II Corps, threatened to open a gap between the two German armies and jeopardize the ability of the *Tenth Army* to continue its retrograde movement. Faced at that point with a threat to the integrity of his entire army group, General von Vietinghoff, even without obtaining authorization from OKW, ordered the long-deferred Operation *HERBSTNEBEL* into effect on the night of 20 April. As he did so, he

dutifully reported his decision to his Fuehrer, together with congratulations on Hitler's birthday.[21].

It had been anything but a happy birthday for the Fuehrer, for on that very day Hitler had ordered his headquarters to disperse. Command of the western front was to pass to a northern group under Grand Admiral Karl Doenitz, with his headquarters at Flensburg on the Baltic, and a southern group under Field Marshal Kesselring, with headquarters near Berchtesgaden. The Fuehrer and the remainder of OKW were to continue to command the eastern fronts from the Reichschancellery bunker in Berlin.

Hitler had actually made the decision to divide his headquarters nine days earlier, when it became clear that the advance of the Allied armies on all fronts made it virtually impossible to continue direction of the war from a central headquarters. When the Russians crossed the Oder River on the 20th, Hitler realized that he could delay no longer and ordered the northern and southern sections of the OKW to depart at once. The motor convoy carrying the headquarters that was to operate under Kesselring left the Air Defense School barracks at Wannsee on the outskirts of Berlin on 20 April and arrived at Berchtesgaden on the 23d. It would be under the command of the latter headquarters that the German forces in southwestern Europe, includ-

---

[20] SCAF 281, FWD in SHAEF, Post OVERLORD Planning File, 381, IV. See also, *The Last Offensive*, by Charles B. MacDonald, Wash. D.C., 1973, pp. 433–42, for the account of the Allied sweep from the Danube to the Alps.

[21] Greiner and Schramm, eds., *OKW/WFSt, KTB*, IV(2), pp. 1438–39; Cable No. 3, 20 Apr 45, Vietinghoff to the Fuehrer, reprinted in Operations of the British, Indian, and Dominion Forces in Italy, Part IV, Sec. G, App. F; Walter Warlimont, *Inside Hitler's Headquarters, 1939–45* (New York: Progress, 1964), p. 513.

ing *Army Group C*, would fight their last battles.[22]

Implicit in Hitler's decision to disperse OKW was a change in his strategy—if such it can be described. In the weeks immediately preceding the decision the German leader had clung stubbornly to the hope that his armies in the west and south could somehow hold the American and British armies at bay long enough for the German forces on the eastern front to check the Russians and possibly persuade the Western Allies to join forces with the Germans to turn back the Red tide threatening to spill into central Europe. The Russian crossing of the Oder changed all that, prompting the Fuehrer to abandon all hope of persuading the Western Allies to turn against the Russians. The German armies in the west and south were instead to hold out long enough to permit those retreating before the Russians in the east to reach the zones of the Western Allies and thereby avoid mass surrenders to the Red Army.

That strategy, or procedure, quickly became the *leitmotif* of Kesselring's operations, but not of Vietinghoff's. For within *Army Group C*'s headquarters there soon surfaced a conflict between the partisans of Hitler's strategy of desperation and those who had adopted an attitude of *sauve qui peut*, convinced that continued resistance in Italy or, for that matter, anywhere else, no longer served a valid purpose. That conflict would help explain the con-

fused moves and countermoves that were to take place within *Army Group C* headquarters in the closing days of the campaign in Italy.[23]

The Byzantine atmosphere at the German headquarters in Italy would become murkier with the maturing of covert surrender negotiations between the senior SS commander in Italy, General Wolff, and the head of the American OSS apparatus in Switzerland, Allen Dulles. Under way since early March, those negotiations, like the military operations on the battlefront, had also taken a sharp turn on 20 April. For on that date the Allied Combined Chiefs of Staff ordered Field Marshal Alexander and Mr. Dulles to terminate the negotiations. "You should," the CCS informed the Allied commander, "consider the matter as closed and so inform the Russians."[24] After 20 April a crushing military victory over the Germans seemed in sight, not only in Italy but on all battlefronts. To the Allied High Command there seemed little to be gained in accepting a capitulation in one of the war's secondary theaters of operations at the risk of alienating one of the major Allied governments—the Soviet Union.

---

[22] Greiner and Schramm, eds., *OKW/WFSt, KTB*, IV(2), pp. 1438–39; Warlimont, *Inside Hitler's Headquarters*, p. 513.

[23] In his commentary on the OKW War Diary, Percy Ernst Schramm observed that in the last months of the war Hitler's ". . .leadership had become more and more an 'Illusionsstrategie,' outlined in red and blue markings on situation maps but having no relationship to reality, even if executed." (*OKW, KTB, LV[1], 1944–45*, p. 32).

[24] Msg WX 70553, CCOS to Alexander, 20 Apr 45, AFHQ 0100/11c/58. For a narrative of the negotiations between Dulles and Wolff, see Chapter XXX. It seems doubtful whether these instructions were known to Hitler at the time he made his change of strategy on the 20th.

PART EIGHT

PURSUIT TO THE ALPS

Now, in the combat all action is directed to the destruction of the enemy, or rather of his fighting powers, for this lies in the conception of combat. The destruction of the enemy's fighting power is, therefore, always the means to attain the object of combat.

CLAUSEWITZ, *On War*

CHAPTER XXVIII

Race for the Po

As Allied forces debouched onto the Lombardy plain and the Germans began to withdraw in keeping with Operation *HERBSTNEBEL*, one terrain feature dominated the thinking on both sides: the Po River. Allied commanders still hoped to trap sizeable contingents of the German forces south of the river, while if the Germans were to survive as a fighting force in northern Italy, they had somehow to get their heavy equipment, artillery, transport, and troops beyond the river.

From turbulent beginnings in the Alps of northwestern Italy, the Po meanders for 250 miles in a series of great bends dotted with numerous islands and sand bars. finally to enter the Adriatic through a large delta twenty miles northeast of the Comacchio Lagoon. Halfway in its course the river increases from 1,000 feet upstream from Ferrara to four time that width at a point north of Parma, sixty miles to the west, with the actual wet gap varying between 400 and 1,500 feet. Both east and west, of that stretch the wet gap was considerably narrower but still too wide to be spanned by field-type military bridges. There was another difficulty: the danger of flooding. Along almost the river's entire length stood a vast system of dikes, rising 15 to 25 feet above the level of the surrounding countryside and in places bringing the water level to a point higher than the valley floor. If the river were high, breaching the dikes could cause widespread flooding and make the Po a more formidable barrier.

Traversing generally flat terrain, the best highways in Italy crossed the Po Valley, and most secondary roads were graveled and well drained, affording alternate routes to almost any point. Thus, other than fighting delaying actions along watercourses crossing the axes of advance, the fleeing enemy could do little to block his pursuers. German difficulties were further compounded by seemingly omnipresent Allied aircraft. Every day Allied planes swept the length of the river to attack both crossing sites and the troops and equipment streaming toward the Po.

Before the spring offensive the Fifth Army engineers had made thorough aerial and map reconnaissances of that part of the Po crossing the axis of the army's advance. From those surveys the engineers had determined that the best crossing sites within the army's zone lay along a 20-mile stretch of the river between Borgoforte on Highway 62 (the Parma-Mantua road) eastward to Ostiglia on Highway 12. Midway between those two points lay the San Benedetto crossing site. The western half, between San Benedetto and Borgoforte, appeared to be more favorable than the eastern, where a large marshy area near Ostiglia would constrict military operations.[1]

---

[1] See Mayo MS, The Corps of Engineers: Operations in the War Against Germany.

AERIAL VIEW OF PO RIVER CROSSING

The engineers had selected twelve likely sites for assault crossings, an equal number of sites for ferry crossings, and nine possible sites for floating bridges. Most importantly, nearly all sites were suitable for all three types of river-crossing operations. Expecting that Keyes' II Corps would reach the Po first, General Truscott had placed the 39th Engineer Group of that corps in charge of preparing the river crossings, but when late on 22 April it appeared likely that Crittenberger's IV Corps would reach the Po first, Truscott shifted most of the engineers to the IV Corps.[2]

Well aware of the tactical problems of withdrawing across a broad river while under attack from air and ground, the Germans months before had begun preparations for re-crossing the Po. Their engineers had selected several favorable crossing sites, understandably the same ones later picked by Allied engineers. At each site they had cached the necessary materiel, including large

[2] Ibid.

GERMAN EQUIPMENT DESTROYED ALONG PO

and small ferry boats suitable for use with any of three possible water levels, for during early spring and summer the Po in this was unpredictable. Yet as had so often been the case in the Italian campaign, nature would intervene to upset carefully made preparations.[3]

Despite the heavy snows of the previous winter, spring of 1945 found the Po at its lowest level in half a century. Although that condition removed the danger of flooding, it left the water too

shallow for larger ferries on which the Germans had counted for transporting their heavy equipment and vehicles. Often running aground, the ferries became easy targets for Allied fighter-bombers, leaving the Germans no choice but to use smaller, shallower draft ferries with greatly reduced carrying capacity. That inevitably meant abandoning much heavy equipment south of the river.

Plans for withdrawing behind the Po were further jeopardized when many German engineer units, originally detailed to operate the crossing points,

---

[3]MS # T–1b (Westphal *et al.*). Unless otherwise indicated the following is based upon this reference.

were committed as combat troops to reinforce rear guard operations. Deprived of engineer assistance, unit commanders frequently had no choice but to improvise on the spot.

Moreover, by 21 April it appeared already too late for many of the German units even to reach the Po, let alone to cross it. One such unit was the ill-starred *94th Infantry Division*. That night its commander, General Steinmetz, received orders from the *XIV Panzer Corps* to assemble survivors of his division in the vicinity of Mirandola on Highway 12 about midway between Modena and the Po River crossing point at Ostiglia. At Mirandola the *94th Division* was to prepare a delaying position, but even as the hapless Steinmetz was reporting to corps headquarters to receive the order, the U.S. 88th Division entered Mirandola. The *94th Division*'s survivors, generally in small detachments, made their way to the Po as best they could. Meanwhile, the division's operations officer was wounded and captured while making reconnaissance for crossing the river, and Steinmetz himself was cut off from his troops. Lacking essential signal equipment to control the divisions of the corps, General von Senger und Etterlin saw no alternative but to dismiss his headquarters staff with orders to reassemble at Legnano on the Adige some ten miles to the north. Thus it was that early on 23 April the corps commander and his staff joined the precipitate flight across the Po.[4]

Imminent German collapse was clearly evident at U.S. Fifth Army headquarters. As early as 21 April Truscott's

G–2 had noted in his journal that "no front line in the formal sense exists."[5] Truscott planned at that point to thrust virtually his entire army into the gap caused by the disintegration of the *XIV Panzer Corps*. Crittenberger's IV Corps was to seize crossing sites along a 20-mile stretch of the Po extending from Borgoforte on Highway 62, just seven miles south of Mantua, eastward to Ostiglia on Highway 12, twenty-seven miles south of Verona; while Keyes' II Corps on the right was to capture additional sites on a narrower sector extending from Ostiglia to Sermide, ten miles to the east.[6] (*See Map XVI.*)

The Pursuit

The IV Corps continued to lead the way. In the center, Hays' 10th Mountain Division progressed rapidly throughout 21 April against only scattered resistance. To take advantage of the situation, Hays formed a tank-infantry task force composed of a battalion each of the 85th and 86th Mountain Infantry Regiments, the 91st Cavalry Reconnaissance Squadron, an engineer company, a light tank company, and a tank destroyer platoon, all under the assistant division commander, Brig. Gen. Robinson E. Duff. The task force reached the Bomporto bridge on the Panaro River at dusk. Although the Germans had prepared the bridge for demolition, the task force captured it intact. In the 85th Division sector, the leading regiment also seized intact the bridge over the Panaro at Camposanto, near where over a century before a

---

[4]MS # C–095e (Senger).

[5]Hq Fifth Army G–2 Rpt, 21–22 Apr 45, G–2 Jnl, 105–2.2.
[6]Fifth Army OI 9, 19 Apr 45.

12,000-man Austrian-Piedmontese army under Field Marshal Count Abersberg von Traun fought to the draw a 15,000-man Spanish army under General Don Juan, Count de Gages.[7] There was no chance of a draw in the current campaign as the two American corps swept almost unimpeded over the broad Po Valley. If the corps could maintain their rate of advance for the next twenty-four hours, Generals Crittenberger and Keyes assured the army commander, both would be drawn up along the south bank of the Po by the 23d.[8]

The 1st Armored Division, however, advancing as a covering force along the IV Corps left flank, encountered considerable resistance, as the *LI Mountain Corps* began to swing back like a great gate toward the northwest. After the collapse of the panzer corps front, that was the only course of action open to General Lemelsen, the *Fourteenth Army* commander. To the armored division's right rear the Brazilian division, choosing not to press the Germans too closely, followed up the enemy withdrawal, while the 34th Division temporarily garrisoned Bologna.[9]

At dawn on 22 April, after having crossed the Panaro at Bomporto the previous day, Task Force Duff, its tanks and tank destroyers leading the way, resumed the march northward. What followed was typical of the enemy's many small delaying actions that day, although few others were as effective in gaining time for the Germans. Since the task force had run into little opposition during the past twenty-four hours, General Duff relaxed flank security in order to accelerate a dash for the crossing point at Ostiglia, some thirty miles away. The task force was thus an easy mark for an enemy ambush just beyond Bomporto. Allowing half of the column to pass, the Germans opened fire on the tanks and tank destroyers in the middle of the column with panzerfausts, destroying and damaging several vehicles. Infantry following in trucks quickly dismounted and deployed. Although the enemy detachment was dispersed within an hour, that meant that much more time for enemy forces to escape across the Po.[10]

Determined to reach the Po by nightfall, General Duff roamed the column like an anxious sheep dog, hurrying the men and vehicles through occasional small arms fire from isolated enemy rear guards firing one last volley before vanishing into a maze of roads, trails, and villages. About an hour before Task Force Duff reached San Benedetto, the main crossing point in the 10th Mountain Division's sector, an antitank mine exploded near General Duff's jeep, seriously wounding him. The division commander, General Hays, came forward to take command of the spearhead. By 1800 San Benedetto was in hand, while the remainder of the mountain division arrived during the night and deployed along the south bank of the Po in preparation for crossing the next day.[11]

While Hays' division drew up to the Po, Prichard's armored division, with two combat commands forward, ad-

---

[7]See Spenser Wilkinson, *The Defense of Piedmont, 1842–1848, A Prelude to the Study of Napoleon* (Oxford, 1927), pp. 73–81, for details of that battle.

[8]IV & II Corps AAR, Apr–May 45.

[9]*Ibid.;* IV Corps History.

[10]IV Corps History.

[11]10th Mtn Div AAR, ʌpr 45; IV Corps AAR, Apr–May 45.

vanced throughout the 22d along the mountain division's left flank, but at a somewhat slower pace. That afternoon CCA on the right bypassed Modena, 23 miles northwest of Bologna, and crossed the Secchia River just beyond the city. With its tank battalion leading the way throughout the night, the combat command reached the Po on the morning of the 23d at the town of Guastalla. Throughout the 22d resistance met by CCB, moving up on the left, so delayed it that it reached the Po several hours after its neighbor.[12]

In the II Corps sector, the 88th Division led the drive to the Po, primarily because other units constituting the right wing of the corps encountered relatively strong delaying positions manned by contingents of the *I Parachute Corps*. Troops of the *1st* and *4th Parachute Divisions* made a particularly strong stand along the Panaro River, which cut diagonally across the zone of advance, thus delaying the 6th South African Armoured and the 91st Infantry Divisions. The 88th Division gained the Po late on 23 April, reaching the river at a point where thousands of Germans were assembling in hope of crossing to the north bank. A mammoth haul over the next two days of 11,000 prisoners, including the *362d Infantry Division*'s Maj. Gen. Friedrich von Schellwitz, the first German division commander captured during the campaign, surrendered to the troops of the 88th Division.[13]

On the Eighth Army's front also breakthrough and pursuit were the order of the day. There, however, the general northwestward orientation of the British drive meant that General McCreery would be unable to use his entire force, for a main effort by the 5 British Corps northwestward from Argenta toward Ferrara and juncture with the Americans of the II Corps would soon pinch out both the 13 British Corps and General Anders' 2 Polish Corps.[14]

Next to reaching the Po, the basic objective of the main effort was to trap the *I Parachute Corps*. That task fell primarily to the British 6th Armoured Division, which on 21 April had lunged forward to Passo Segni, nine miles south of Ferrara, to establish a bridgehead over a lateral canal between the Reno and a southeastward flowing arm of the Po. After hurling back a series of small but vigorous counterattacks, the armor burst from the bridgehead to rush forward another seven miles to Poggio Renatico, eight miles southwest of Ferrara, there to close the last escape route for survivors of the *278th Infantry Division*, until then acting as the left flank pivot for withdrawal of the *I Parachute Corps*. That action forced the parachutists to continue their withdrawal toward the northwest and assured a complete break between the paratroopers and the *LXXVI Panzer Corps*.

Even northwesterly withdrawal was soon denied. The next day, the 22d, the British armor drove on to Bondeno, only a few miles from the Po, and on the 23d not only reached the river but linked with the 6th South African Armoured Division of the U.S. II Corps at the village of Finale. For

[12] IV & II Corps AAR's, Apr–May 45; Howe, *The Battle History of the 1st Armored Division*, p. 419.

[13] Starr, *From Salerno to the Alps*.

[14] Operations of the British, Indian, and Dominion Forces in Italy, Part IV, Sec. B.

many of the Germans of the *I Parachute Corps* the village's name signified their fate. While the cordon thrown up by the two Allied armored divisions was sieve-like, it nevertheless served to trap thousands of Germans, and many escaped only by the expedient of swimming the sprawling Po.

On the same day, the 23d, the 8th Indian Division gained the Po three miles north of Ferrara. By mid-day all organized resistance on the Eighth Army's front west of that point had ceased, but farther east the *LXXVI Panzer Corps* was still south of the river, remnants of its *26th Panzer* and *29th Panzer Grenadier Divisions* still posing problems for the British infantry. Yet the position of the units of the *LXXVI Panzer Corps* was less than enviable, for they were in effect hemmed in south of the Po between strong British formations on the west and the Adriatic coast on the east. About the only way for them to get across the river was to abandon everything and swim for it.

Crossing the Po

By 22 April engineers of the IV Corps had already brought forward fifty 12-man assault boats for an early morning crossing by the 87th Mountain Infantry's 1st Battalion. It was to be the first major river crossing by any contingent of the mountain division, and the troops had received little amphibious training.[15]

In view of the nature of the opposition, that made little difference. Just before the crossing was to begin enemy 20-mm. and 88-mm. guns opened fire

---

[15] 10th Mtn Div AAR, Apr–May 45. Unless otherwise cited the following is based upon this source.

from the north bank, causing some casualties among troops assembled for the operation and delaying it, but supporting artillery located the enemy guns and drove them off. When the engineers propelled the assault boats across the river, not a man was lost.

On the far bank the assault troops found little but abandoned weapons emplacements. Only an hour had passed before the 1st Battalion reported the beachhead secure and ready to receive the remaining battalions. After nightfall, as engineers worked to build a ponton bridge, the rest of the 10th Mountain Division crossed the river, so that at daylight on the 24th all but the division's heavy equipment was deployed north of the Po.

About the time the mountain infantry began crossing the river, a regiment of the 85th Division reached the Po on the IV Corps right flank, while the 1st Armored Division continued to cover the west flank. His "wildest hopes" exceeded by the bold thrust to the Po, General Truscott prepared to take advantage of it by bringing up the 34th Division from garrison duties at Bologna to free part of the armor to exploit the crossing of the Po. Combat Command A then moved eastward to San Benedetto to join the 10th Mountain and 85th Divisions in a dash to the Adige River and Verona, whose capture would further restrict the avenues of escape still left to those German forces in the western half of Italy. Meanwhile, Combat Command B and the 81st Reconnaissance Squadron assembled near Reggio, midway between Modena and Parma, to assist the 1st Brazilian Infantry Division in rounding up the remnants of the *LI Mountain*

AMERICAN TROOPS STORM ASHORE AFTER ASSAULT CROSSING OF PO RIVER

Corps trapped between the Apennines and the Po.[16]

As demonstrated by the hordes of Germans eager to surrender, by the debris of a once-proud German Army that choked the roads leading to the Po, and by the easy crossing of the river by the 10th Mountain Division, no need remained for any formal set-piece attack to get across the Po. With that in

mind, General Truscott ordered all divisions to cross on their own as quickly as possible.

Close alongside the mountain division, the 85th Division began crossing on 24 April, and by noon of the 25th the IV Corps had a treadway bridge in operation, followed four hours later by the opening of a ponton bridge. Having relinquished engineers, assault boats, and bridging equipment to the IV Corps, units of the II Corps had to improvise. A regiment of the 88th Division stole a march on 24 April by

---

[16] Truscott, *Command Missions*, pp. 439–95; II Corps AAR, Apr–May 45; IV Corps AAR, Apr–May 45.

PLACING A STEEL TREADWAY BRIDGE ACROSS THE PO

sending a detail of men and then an entire battalion across the ruins of a railroad bridge. Others followed in captured rubber assault boats, while men of another regiment shuttled across in a few DUKW's and Alligators. The next day, the 25th, both the 91st Division and the 6th South African Armoured Division also crossed in DUKW's and on makeshift rafts and barges. Nowhere was the opposition more than token.

On the Eighth Army front, as troops of the 5 British Corps gained the Po after having pinched out other contingents of the Eighth Army, General McCreery moved to readjust his formations to bring other corps headquarters back into action. A first step was to transfer the 6th British Armoured Division from the left wing of the 5 Corps to the 13 Corps to afford a second corps at least limited frontage along the Po. Having anticipated a set-piece attack in order to get across the river, McCreery had formed a "Special Po Task Force" to make the attempt under the aegis of the 10 Corps, but the extent and rapidity of the enemy's disintegration and a sudden serious illness of the 10 Corps commander changed that plan.[17] Splitting the task force between the 5 and 13 Corps, McCreery told both to take the river on the run.

Meanwhile, the commander of the enemy's LXXVI Panzer Corps, General von Schwerin, whose troops still maintained a semblance of organization in what was in effect a bridgehead south of the Po, came to the conclusion that nothing could save his corps. As long ago as the preceding summer in Normandy and then in September along Germany's western frontier, von Schwerin had evidenced disenchantment with the war and conviction that continued fighting merely deepened his country's misery; he had survived Hitler's wrath only because he was a respected member of the old German nobility. At this point all was so patently lost that he instructed his troops— including men of the 26th Panzer and 29th Panzer Grenadier Divisions—to abandon tanks, artillery, and other heavy equipment and make for the river to try to swim to safety. General von Schwerin himself surrendered the next morning, 25 April, to the British.[18]

Contingents of both the 5 and 13 Corps crossed the Po on 24 April against no opposition. A race for the next likely enemy delaying position, the Adige River, was on, but from all indications the Germans had nothing left with which to make a stand at the Adige or anywhere else.

---

[17] The commander, Lt. Gen. J. L. T. Hawkesworth, died a few days later.

[18] Operations of the British, Indian, and Dominion Forces in Italy, Part IV, Sec. B. See also MacDonald, The Siegfried Line Campaign, pp. 81–82, and Blumenson, Breakout and Pursuit, pp. 462–63, for details of von Schwerin's earlier disagreements with his superiors on the battlefield.

CHAPTER XXIX

To the Alps

The Fifth Army's immediate goal beyond the Po, 27 miles away, was the fabled city of Verona astride the Adige River on the main road to Trento, the Alps, and the Brenner Pass. The swiftly flowing Adige River was at this point 300 to 500 feet wide, potentially a formidable obstacle. Even so, the possibility of a sturdy German defense here or elsewhere gave Allied commanders little pause, for the enemy's final collapse was obviously imminent.

As the 10th Mountain Division led the IV Corps and the Fifth Army across the Po on 23 April, Truscott assigned his two corps commanders missions that aimed at reaching the Alps and clearing northern Italy of the enemy. General Keyes' II Corps, after crossing the Po at Ostiglia, was to continue as the Fifth Army's right wing along the axis of Highway 12 to occupy the south bank of the Adige between Verona and Legnano, 20 miles to the southeast. General Crittenberger's assignment was more complex. He was to send three divisions of the IV Corps northward along the axis San Benedetto–Mantua–Verona, with Verona and its airfield in the suburb of Villafranca, ten miles to the southwest, as initial objectives. At the same time, the IV Corps commander was to round up the enemy forces in northwestern Italy. That job he was to accomplish by sending tank-infantry task forces to the Po Valley's northern edge, thence northwestward along the base of the Alpine foothills to block exits from the Po Valley leading to the Italian lakes region and the Swiss frontier. General Crittenberger was also to send the Brazilian Expeditionary Force and the 34th Division northwestward astride Highway 9 along the southern reaches of the valley to seal the *LI Mountain Corps* and its three divisions in the Apennines.[1]

In that assignment the BEF and the 34th Division were to be assisted by the 92d Division on the Fifth Army's left flank unit, which by 23 April had passed through the last of the Gothic Line defenses along the Ligurian coast and sent columns northwestward and northeastward. One consisting of two infantry regiments raced along the coastal highway toward the port of Genoa 35 miles away, while the other composed of one regiment moved along Highways 62 and 63 on the heels of the *148th Infantry* and the *Italia Bersaglieri Divisions* as they withdrew from the mountains toward Highway 9 and into the trap to be formed by the Brazilians and the 34th Division.

For the main drive to the Adige, General Crittenberger again called on General Hays' mountain division to lead the way. Screened on the left by the 91st Reconnaissance Squadron, the 10th Mountain Division was to bypass Mantua and cut the highway connecting Verona with Lake Garda. On the right

---

[1] *Fifth Army History*, Part IX, pp. 108–22; II Corps AAR, Apr–May 1945. Unless otherwise indicated the following is based upon these references.

General Coulter's 85th Division was to strike directly for Verona. To provide armored support for the drive, the 1st Armored Division's CCA was to cross the Po at San Benedetto, while the rest of the armored division turned to the northwest to support the thrust toward Milan and other populated centers of the upper Po Valley.

Race for Verona

As before, General Hays decided on a mobile task force to lead the mountain division's advance. By chance he obtained for it a new commander to replace the wounded General Duff. An old friend of General Hays, Col. William O. Darby, who earlier had commanded a Ranger unit in Italy but had since been reassigned to a staff job in Washington, appeared at Hays' command post in mid-April as an escort officer for several War Department dignitaries. Much to Darby's pleasure, General Hays persuaded Generals Truscott and Clark to request Darby's assignment as assistant division commander. When the War Department acquiesced, Task Force Darby came into being.[2]

The task force consisted of the 86th Mountain Infantry, the 13th Tank Battalion from the 1st Armored Division's CCA, a company each of light tanks and tank destroyers, three battalions of field artillery, and small engineer and medical units. The tank battalion was to spearhead the column, while light tanks and tank destroyers were dispersed along its length to provide protection or to fall out along the way to establish

COLONEL DARBY

roadblocks on the flanks. Hays motorized his own command post to bring up the rear of the task force, followed in turn by the 85th and 87th Mountain Infantry Regiments to mop up bypassed enemy troops.[3]

When the task force could move depended on getting a bridge over the Po to enable tanks, tank destroyers, and artillery to cross. That was not to be available until the afternoon of the 25th. Meanwhile, beginning on the 24th, the 85th Mountain Infantry probed the northern limits of the division's bridgehead without making contact with the enemy. Concluding that the Germans had withdrawn, General Hays, not waiting for Col. Darby's task force, sent the regiment off in pursuit.

The 85th Mountain Infantry's 1st

---

[2] Truscott, *Command Missions*, p. 493; Clark, *Calculated Risk*, p. 435.

[3] 10th Mountain Division AAR, Apr–May 1945.

Battalion started out early on the 25th for the Villafranca airport some 20 miles away. Because there were innumerable mines to clear from roads, culverts, and bridges, it took the head of the column an hour to move the first five miles, but from that point the pace quickened. Around 0900 the column entered Mantua, found Italian partisans already in control, and passing quickly through continued heading for the airport. With no more mines to clear, the column covered the 15 miles in less than an hour. Quickly dispersing a small German rear guard detachment, the battalion set up a defensive perimeter to await the tanks and artillery of Task Force Darby.

On the mountain infantry's right, General Coulter's 85th Division, after crossing the Po early on the 24th, also set out in the direction of Verona at about the same time. Proceeding warily, two forward regiments reached the vicinity of the Villafranca airport around dusk, there to bivouac for the night. At dawn the division continued to move cautiously in a column of regiments for Verona, seven miles away. This, however, proved unnecessary because the troops soon discovered that other Americans, men of the 88th Division, were already in control of the city.

Unlike the 85th Division's cautious approach in its belated assault on Verona, the 88th had won the race by a headlong pursuit. Its commander, General Kendall, had instructed his troops not to wait for heavy equipment to cross the Po but to strike out boldly for the city. Early on the 25th the 351st Infantry, its 2d Battalion leading the way along Highway 12, left the Po bridgehead at Ostiglia. Using any transporta-tion they could lay hands on—captured trucks, jeeps, even bicycles—the men raced pell mell, undeterred either by rear guards or mines, for Verona, about 30 miles away. Late that afternoon five light tanks and seven tank destroyers, the first to cross on a newly completed ponton bridge, caught up with the forward troops to form a small tank-infantry assault force to lead the way into Verona. Although resistance was spotty, some squads and platoons occasionally had to engage in sharp fire fights until enemy delaying detachments could salve their consciences with a show of resistance before surrendering.

The worst setback ironically came not from the enemy but from Allied aircraft. As the column paused on the outskirts of Verona, two Allied planes attacked, apparently in the belief that a small force so distant from other Allied units had to be German. Despite identification panels prominently displayed and frantic efforts by a radio operator to reach air-ground control, the aircraft strafed the column repeatedly with cannon and machine guns. Before the aircraft finally flew away, five men of a radio crew were killed and several jeeps destroyed.[4]

The 2d Battalion's task force entered Verona at 2210, 16 hours after leaving the Po bridgehead. Within the hour the remainder of the regiment arrived to help clear the city. Only from contingents of the *4th Parachute Division* holed up in Verona's ruined railroad station was there any real defense attempted,

---

[4] John P. Delaney, *The Blue Devils in Italy, A History of the 88th Infantry Division in World War II* (Washington: Infantry Journal Press, 1947), pp. 211–12.

91st Reconnaissance Squadron Moves Through Verona Railroad Station

and by daylight on 26 April that was at an end.

Clearing the Po Valley

As troops of the 88th Division cleared Verona, Colonel Darby's task force came forward after crossing the Po, passed west of the city, and turned toward Lake Garda to begin an advance along its eastern shore toward Trento and the Brenner Pass. At the same time, General Crittenberger detached the 1st Armored Division's CCA from the task force and sent the combat command northwestward in the direction of Brescia, Bergamo, and Como to close along the way the remaining escape routes from the Lombardy Plain to the Swiss frontier. At the same time the 85th Division passed through Verona to clear hills beyond the Adige before continuing toward the Alpine foothills. To the east the 88th and 91st Divisions of the II Corps, with the 6th South African Armoured Division screening on the right, closed up to the Adige between Verona and Legnano and that afternoon the two infantry divisions crossed without opposition. Beyond the river a brigade of the

South African armoured division screened their flank while the rest of the armor remained south of the river until the bridgehead could be expanded.

Elsewhere the 34th Division, the Brazilian Expeditionary Force, and the 1st Armored Division's CCB, all under IV Corps control, rounded up those Germans still south of the Po in northwestern Italy. The 34th Division, with the Brazilians on the left, continued along the axis of Highway 9. Two of the 92d Division's regiments, the 371st and the 365th, attached to corps and army respectively, had other tasks: the first to advance northward on Modena along the axis of Highway 12, the second to guard the swelling numbers of prisoners streaming into stockades in the rear.

On the Ligurian flank the attached 473d Infantry led the 92d Division's continued thrust along the coastal highway toward Genoa. Encountering only scattered opposition along the way, the regiment entered the city early on the 27th. There as no resistance, for Genoa's 4,000-man garrison had surrendered to partisans the day before. Only a small detachment of German marines, dug in on a hill top overlooking the harbor, held out until the Americans arrived, when the marines too laid down their arms. By 0930 on 27 April the ancient port city was in American hands.

Like the advance of most of the Fifth Army's units to the Adige, that of the Eighth Army resembled less a combat operation than a tactical march. Aside from the fact that the Eighth Army was moving into the gap between the *I Parachute Corps* and the *LXXVI Panzer*

CROSSING THE ADIGE

Corps, the surrender of the panzer corps commander, General von Schwerin, and his order to his troops to abandon their equipment and swim for their lives further insured that there would be no real fight north of the Po.

Having crossed the Po without opposition during the night of 24 April, two divisions of the 13 Corps on the Eighth Army's left pushed somewhat cautiously toward the Adige, 10 miles away. The 2d New Zealand Division made it in late afternoon of the 26th, followed shortly by the 6th South African Armoured Division. Some 250 Italian volunteers dropped by parachute in small groups throughout the Eighth Army's zone in an effort to add to German confusion.

Having crossed the Po without opposition the night of the 24th, the 8th Indian Division of the 5 Corps also headed toward the Adige, assisted by the 56th Division, after brushing aside a brief flurry of resistance in crossing just before noon on the 25th. By early evening of the 26th both divisions were on the Adige: the night before, the Italian Cremona Combat Group had crossed the Po on the Eighth Army's right and with the aid of partisans had cleared the countryside near the coast.

When, on the 27th, units of both the 5 and 13 Corps crossed the Adige with no difficulty, the last major river barrier in both army zones in northern Italy lay behind. All that now remained, Allied commanders believed, was to receive the surrender of a defeated enemy, but that was not how it was to be. The fighting yet to be done would in no way affect the outcome of the long campaign, but it continued nonetheless to exact a bitter toll of dead and wounded men. The fighting was all the more frustrating and the casualties all the more tragic because they came at a time when the end was clearly in sight.

Army Group C's Situation

East of Lake Garda the enemy had only two routes of escape: one, opposite the Eighth Army, led northeastward toward southeastern Germany and Yugoslavia; the other, opposite the Fifth Army, led northward along the shore of Lake Garda and the axis of Highway 12 toward the Brenner and Reschen passes into Austria. What was left of General Herr's *Tenth Army,* following the surrender of von Schwerin's *LXXVI Panzer Corps,* would in the next few days attempt to retreat along the first route, which was the objective of Marshal Tito's partisans; and von Senger's

XIV Panzer Corps—all that was left of Lemelsen's *Fourteenth Army* east of Lake Garda—would withdraw along the second toward the rugged terrain of the Austrian Arlberg, which was the objective of the U.S. Seventh and the French First Armies driving through southern Germany. The German situation thus was utterly desperate.

Yet for the German commander, General von Vietinghoff, and his army group headquarters, a choice—however dismal—still remained: he could fall back through the zone of the *Tenth Army* or of the *Fourteenth.* Vietinghoff chose the latter and the zone of the *XIV Panzer Corps,* for only there existed the slightest chance of maintaining for a few days longer at least some semblance of resistance. Moreover, the French and Americans coming in the back door of that route were somehwat more predictable adversaries than the Yugoslav partisans and their Red Army allies. Through the last week of April the *Army Group C* command post would relocate successively along the axis of Highway 12.[5]

On 24 April General von Senger and his panzer corps staff had set out in search of the peripatetic army headquarters for new orders. Coming upon General Lemelsen at Ala, some 23 miles north of Verona, Senger learned that the *Fourteenth Army* commander wanted the *XIV Panzer Corps* to defend the sector between Lake Garda and Highway 12. The next day von Senger established his own headquarters at Ala after Lemelsen moved on to the north.

During the next two days small

---

[5] MS # C-95e (Senger), CMH; MS # T-1b (Westphal *et al.*).

groups of officers and enlisted men straggled into von Senger's headquarters, among them elements of a signal battalion with critically needed communications equipment and wire. By the evening of 26 April, *XIV Panzer Corps* headquarters was again operational, but all that it controlled were three *Kampfgruppen,* made up of the consolidated remnants of four divisions, all together not more than 2,000 men. This small force was to hold a 20-mile sector extending from the Pasubio pass, southeast of Ala on Highway 46, westward to Lake Garda. Since the pre-World War I Austro-Italian frontier had run approximately along that line, some of the old border fortifications could be used. Assigning *Group Klotz* to the right, *Group Steinmetz* to the center, and *Group Schricker* to the left, General von Senger prepared to fight his last battle. As General von Vietinghoff outlined it, the objective was to gain time so that the capitulation of *Army Group C* woud coincide as closely as possible with that of *Army Group G* north of the Alps and *Army Group E* withdrawing through Croatia to the Julian Alps.[6]

The plan was Vietinghoff's, the strategy Kesselring's. Since 27 April the former commander of German forces in Italy had been commander-in-chief of all German forces in southwestern Europe, including *Army Groups C, G,* and *E.* Kesselring meant for all three army groups to fall back on the Alpine massif, there to hold out long enough to allow those forces retreating before the Russians to reach the American and British armies and surrender not to the dreaded Russians but to the Western Allies.[7]

Victory on the Flanks

As German forces retreated toward the Alps, Allied headquarters issued a call for a general uprising throughout northern Italy. In most towns and cities of Lombardy neo-Fascist authority had all but ceased to exist, in any case. Town after town fell under partisan control, often days before the arrival of the Allied forces. In many places the Allied advance involved much less fighting than it did a series of enthusiastic civic receptions.

The 88th Division on 28 April entered Vicenza, northeast of Verona, to find that city already held by partisans. Passing quickly through crowded streets, the division continued its march toward the valleys of the Brenta and Piave Rivers, flowing southward from the Alps to enter the Adriatic near Venice. On the 30th, Truscott shifted the 85th Division from the IV to the II Corps where it deployed alongside the 88th, which was to advance up the Brenta while the 85th moved up the Piave to an eventual junction on 4 May with the U.S. Seventh Army. The two divisions thus would end the campaign in Italy as they had begun it twelve months before, moving forward side by side.

To the right of those two divisions in the corps center the 91st Division ad-

---

[6] MS # T–1b (Westphal *et al.*).

[7] Kesselring, *A Soldier's Record,* p. 87. Although Kesselring's strategy had nothing to do with a so-called National Redoubt, it tends to lend credence to that myth among Allied commanders. For a discussion of the National Redoubt and final operations in Germany and Austria see MacDonald, *The Last Offensive.*

AMERICAN INFANTRY ENTER VICENZA

vanced astride Highway 53 to cross the
Brenta on the 29th and the next day to
race 25 miles eastward to Treviso, just
north of Venice. The 6th South African
Armoured Division stayed roughly
abreast on the corps right flank. As
April came to an end, both divisions
had reached the limits of their assigned
zones. While the 91st Division rounded
up scattered enemy units, the South
Africans assembled southwest of Treviso in preparation for a move far to the
west to garrison the city of Milan.

In the southern reaches of the Po
Valley, units of the IV Corps continued
their assignment of rounding up a
beaten enemy. In capturing in succession the cities of Parma, Fidenza, and
Piacenza, the 34th Division cut off the
line of withdrawal to the northeast of a
major part of Marshal Graziani's *Ligurian Army*. Only the *232d Grenadier Divi-*

sion managed to slip past. Assembling in
a bend of the Po south of Cremona,
the grenadiers defended their bridgehead long enough to allow some troops
to cross the river, but most opted for
surrender.[8]

Marshal Graziani himself took refuge
in an SS-held strongpoint near Cernobbio on Lake Como, some 27 miles
north of Milan, while his headquarters
personnel, left under Graziani's German deputy, Generalmajor Max Pemsel, fought through converging partisan
units to reach Lecco on Lake Como's
southeastern arm. Surrounded there by
partisans but unwilling to surrender to
irregulars, Pemsel held out until 28
April, when the U.S. 1st Armored
Division's CCA arrived.[9]

The next day tanks of the American
armored division entered Milan, already
in the trigger-happy hands of excited
partisans. Anxious to be clear of the
turbulent city, General Prichard quickly
hustled his troops through to assume
positions to the north and east and
block all routes to the Alpine frontier.
On the same day, General Truscott
shifted the 34th Division and the Italian
Combat Group Legnano northward to
Brescia, midway between Milan and
Verona, to strengthen control of the
northern exits from the Po Valley.
Meanwhile, to the west, the 442d Infantry, operating under the command of
the 92d Division, raced some 40 miles
across the Lombard plain to capture
Alessandria and a 3,000-man garrison.
Two days later the Japanese-Americans
took Turin, 50 miles farther west. The

[8] MS # T–1b (Westphal *et al.*).
[9] AFHQ Cable, Nicholson to Bern for 110, 30
Apr 45, in AFHQ SAC Negotiations, Vol. II, 0100/
4.

473d Infantry went forward along the coastal highway twenty miles beyond Genoa and made contact with elements of the French 1st March Infantry Division, Army Detachment of the Alps, at Savona, over 60 miles east of the Franco-Italian frontier crossing at Monaco. That penetration by French troops was matched 65 miles to the northwest when on 1 May troops of the French 27th Alpine Division made contact with the 442d Infantry at Turin. At that point the commander of the 6th Army Group, General Devers, under whose command the French divisions operated, ordered the French to cease all offensive operations in northwestern Italy. General Devers may possibly have been unaware of the extent of French territorial claims in the region dating back to the military campaigns of the 18th century.

PARTISANS BEFORE THE CATHEDRAL OF MILAN

The Last Engagements

With the Po Valley's northern exits closed, enemy forces west of Lake Garda had no alternative but surrender, which they began to do on a large scale on 29 April. That was pretty much the case in northeastern Italy as well but not on a narrow sector east of Lake Garda where the 10th Mountain Division's Task Force Darby moved along the lake's eastern shore toward final defensive positions of the *Fourteenth Army's XIV Panzer Corps*.

Because there had been little fighting in the Fifth Army zone since 18 April, men of the 10th Mountain Division started out on the 28th with little doubt that the enemy would merely continue his withdrawal. That was figuring without knowledge of the three *Kampfgrup-*

pen still left in the *XIV Panzer Corps* and the line they had established running from Highway 46 in the east across Highway 12 to a western anchor at the town of Riva at the northern end of the lake.

General Hays did anticipate that as a delaying tactic the enemy might attempt to block the eastern shore road where it passed through several tunnels. With that threat in mind, he arranged for several companies of DUKW's to cruise on the lake slightly to the rear of his infantry, ready to transport infantry in attempts to outflank and bypass enemy roadblocks. It was a wise precaution, for on the first afternoon the 86th Mountain Infantry, the lead element in Task Force Darby's column, ran head-on into heavy automatic weapons fire at the

ENGINEERS REPAIRING APPROACH TO TUNNEL, LAKE GARDA

first of a series of tunnels located about five miles south of Torbole.[10] (*Map 11*)

In spite of the enemy fire, the lead battalion of the column with fire support from accompanying tanks cautiously worked toward the tunnel. As the Americans approached, the Germans set off demolitions, collapsing the entrance to the tunnel and effectively blocking the road. To continue the assault along the road was out of the

question. Early that afternoon a rifle company clambered into the DUKW's and moved out onto a lake whipped by strong winds. From the far shore enemy guns opened fire, killing two men aboard the craft and wounding several others. Although the enemy gunners persisted, the DUKW's scurried along the shore to outflank the demolished tunnel with no further losses.

As General Hays expected, the outflanking maneuver forced enemy withdrawal, but as the Germans fell back, they demolished bridges and blocked other tunnels. By midafternoon the 2d

---

[10] 86th Mtn. Inf. AAR, Apr–May 45. Unless otherwise cited the following is based upon this document.

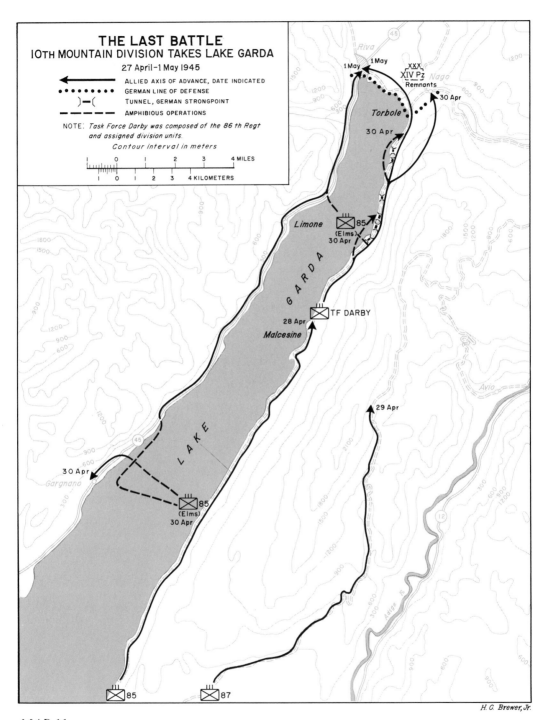

THE LAST BATTLE
10TH MOUNTAIN DIVISION TAKES LAKE GARDA
27 April–1 May 1945

⬅———— ALLIED AXIS OF ADVANCE, DATE INDICATED
•••••••• GERMAN LINE OF DEFENSE
)—(TUNNEL, GERMAN STRONGPOINT
– – – – AMPHIBIOUS OPERATIONS

NOTE: *Task Force Darby was composed of the 86th Regt and assigned division units.*

Contour interval in meters

MAP 11

H. C. Brewer, Jr.

Battalion had bypassed four tunnels and was about to attack a fifth when a demolition charge exploded prematurely, killing about fifteen of the enemy detachment defending the tunnel. Taking advantage of the resulting confusion, the American infantrymen rushed foward to capture the position. As one tunnel after another was outflanked and captured, engineers cleared them of debris to open the road to vehicular traffic.

As the 86th Mountain Infantry advanced along the east shore, General Hays sent the 85th Mountain Infantry across the lake in DUKW's to occupy the town of Gargnano, reputed hiding place of ranking Italian officials. Finding neither Italian officials nor German soldiers, the regiment continued along the western side of the lake toward Riva and eventual junction with Task Force Darby. Hays meanwhile sent his third regiment, the 87th Mountain Infantry, over a narrow mountain road five miles east of the lake to outflank the enemy's main positions from the east.

Early on the 29th, as the 86th Mountain Infantry, continuing as Task Force Darby's lead element, approached the last of the tunnels and the anchor of the German defenses at the northern end of the lake, resistance stiffened. Just as the mountain infantry started to pass through the tunnel, German guns began firing from the vicinity of Riva. One round exploded just inside the northern end of the tunnel, killing four Americans and wounding fifty. The regiment quickly took to the DUKW's to bypass the tunnel, and soon after midday patrols entered the town of Torbole. Along with Riva at the northern end of the lake, that and the

adjacent town of Nago constituted the main strongpoints of the enemy's last defensive position.

Signs of German determination became increasingly evident when German tanks and self-propelled artillery, located northeast of Torbole, forced the 86th Mountain Infantry to pull its forward battalions out of that town. Darby's men then had no choice but to wait for supporting artillery before attempting to retake it. When the artillery arrived two hours later to silence the enemy guns, the 3d Battalion pushed back into the town and by midnight reported it cleared of Germans.

Still the Germans refused to cede the town. Shortly after midnight they counterattacked with the support of tanks. Seeing no need to take heavy losses with the end of the war obviously at hand, General Hays ordered his troops again to withdraw. Only after the regimental and battalion commanders assured him the men could hold without appreciable risk did he rescind the order.

Having bypassed Torbole on the right, the 1st Battalion after 14 hours of painstaking slipping and sliding over rain-swept shale slopes, scaling cliffs, and threading through narrow ravines, had come to within a mile of Nago, close enough to launch an assault against it. Because the assault would have to be made through a narrow ravine whose northern exit lay under German guns, the battalion commander delayed until darkness.

At dusk, passing in single file through the ravine, men of Company B had moved to within 200 yards of Nago without attracting enemy fire when an attack came suddenly from an unexpected direction: the air. A single aircraft—its nationality was never determined—dropped eight antipersonnel bombs, killing nine men and wounding several others. Shocked by the incident, the company commander withdrew his men into the hills to spend the rest of the night on a cold, wet, windswept ridge overlooking the objective.

As it turned out, no fight had to be made for Nago. Ammunition virtually exhausted, the German garrison during the night of 29 April withdrew. The next morning when Company B returned cautiously to the narrow ravine, patrols pushing ahead reported the town abandoned. That afternoon the 86th Mountain Infantry's reserve battalion occupied Riva without a fight. The Germans had abandoned the entire line.

Other than to send patrols to determine the extent of the enemy withdrawal, Colonel Darby chose to hold his troops in place for the rest of the day. During the afternoon he and Lt. Col. Robert L. Cook, who had recently assumed command of the 86th Mountain Infantry, strolled to a broad promenade along Lake Garda to discuss plans for taking up the pursuit the next day. While they talked, a single artillery shell, presumably the enemy's parting shot from somewhere north of Riva, burst in the air above them. Cook and another officer standing nearby were wounded, an enlisted man was killed, and Colonel Darby fell mortally wounded. Carried into his command post, he died forty-five minutes later.

The stubborn and futile last-ditch defense of Torbole and Nago and the round that killed Darby and one of his men were the enemy's last defiant gestures. By last light on 30 April all survivors were fleeing toward Trento, Bolzano, and the Alpine frontier.

The Eighth Army Crosses the Adige

Task Force Darby's experience was in marked contrast to that on the Eighth Army front, where, as already noted, the 5 and 13 Corps had crossed the Adige. Because of long lines of communication and shortage of transport, the Eighth Army could maintain no more than two divisions beyond the river, but that turned out to be enough. As the 56th Division of the 5 Corps and the 2d New Zealand Division of the 13 Corps crossed the river, resistance was almost nonexistent. As one division set out for Venice, some thirty-five miles to the northeast, and the other for Mestre, Venice's mainland neighbor, and thereafter for the port of Trieste at the head of the Adriatic, they only encountered small groups of enemy soldiers who appeared only too willing to surrender. On the 29th the 56th Division entered Venice and the 2d New Zealand Division captured Padua.[11]

General Clark had originally decided that the Eighth Army alone would occupy all of northeastern Italy, but the army's logistical difficulties and the need for a large force in case of friction with the Yugoslavs in the disputed territory of Trieste and Venezia Giulia prompted him to change his mind. To make room for an additional division within the Eighth Army's zone, he

---

[11] Operations of the British, Indian, and Dominion Forces in Italy, Part IV, Sec. B. Unless otherwise cited the following is based upon this reference.

shifted the interarmy boundary westward and on 1 May altered his longstanding practice of not placing American units under British command. Attaching the U.S. 91st Division to the Eighth Army, while leaving responsibility for the division's support with the Fifth Army, he strengthened the sector while imposing no additional logistical burden upon the Eighth Army.

That same day the 2d New Zealand Division sped along the coastal road leading to Trieste to make contact in the afternoon with Yugoslav partisans 17 miles northwest of the city. Pausing for the night, the New Zealanders entered Trieste in the afternoon of 2 May to accept the surrender of a German garrison that had refused earlier demands for capitulation by the Yugoslav partisans. Meanwhile, with the port of Venice available, General McCreery felt free to commit additional forces. He sent the British 6th Armoured Division in two columns into the foothills of the Dolomites, one toward Udine and the other toward Belluno.

Since the beginning of the spring offensive, the two Allied armies in Italy had taken 145,000 prisoners from the *Tenth* and *Fourteenth Armies*. Their scattered survivors were either surrendering *en masse* or withdrawing in small groups toward the only exits still open to the German forces in Italy, the Brenner and Reschen passes. Graziani's Italo-German *Ligurian Army* had surrendered to Crittenberger's IV Corps, and the Italian marshal, Mussolini's last defense minister, was himself in Fifth Army custody.

Only in the western Alps, in the Aosta and Susa valleys, and along the Gulf of Genoa, where French forces by their thrust into Italian territory gave signs of having designs on it, and at Trieste in the Venezia Giulia region of northeastern Italy, where Yugoslav partisans seemed bent on a similar enterprise, were there clouds on an otherwise bright horizon on 1 May. On a personal note, the day was also General Clark's forty-ninth birthday.[12]

Next day company-size patrols from the 86th Mountain Infantry moved five miles along the Riva-Trento road through a landscape bright with blossoming orchards and greening vineyards to occupy the town of Arco in midmorning, then continued northward to occupy by noon a succession of villages a few miles closer to Trento. No enemy were to be seen. Meanwhile, patrols from the 85th Mountain Infantry fanned out in search of enemy stragglers in hills overlooking Riva from the west. Only a few were found, each pathetically eager to surrender to regular military formations rather than to Italian partisans.

Late that afternoon radios of the 10th Mountain Division picked up a signal from the BBC announcing unconditional surrender of the German armies in Italy. That gave substance to rumors of an enemy capitulation that for over a week had been in the air.

---

[12] Clark Diary, 1 May 45.

CHAPTER XXX

The Capitulation

The campaign in Italy would end as it had begun in early September 1943—with weeks of intrigue and behind-the-scenes negotiations. Known only to a small group of senior commanders and staff officers on both sides, covert contacts to bring about a separate surrender of the German forces in Italy had been under way since February.

They began late in January when an Italian businessman, Baron Parrilli, a former head of the Fascist information bureau in Belgium, applied for a Swiss visa to travel to Switzerland for the avowed purpose of visiting a long-time friend, Dr. Max Husmann, director of an exclusive private school on the outskirts of Lucerne. Only after Professor Husmann had posted a bond of ten thousand Swiss francs as guarantee that Parrilli would make no attempt to remain in Switzerland was the baron able to obtain a visa.[1]

In Switzerland Parrilli informed his host that the Germans were reported to have prepared large-scale demolition plans which, if carried out, would make an economic desert of northern Italy.

Such a catastrophe might be averted, the baron suggested, for there were in Italy high-ranking German officers opposed to the plans and willing to discuss the problem with responsible officials on the Allied side. Although Parrilli mentioned no names, he did assert that there were certain well-placed SS officers in Italy who had hopes of persuading the Allies to join forces with the Germans to keep the Russians out of Europe.

Although Professor Husmann saw no possibility of meaningful contacts with the western allies on that basis, the possibility of somehow averting the destruction of northern Italy was compelling. He telephoned an old friend, Col. Max Waibel, chief of the Italian section of Swiss Army intelligence, reaching him at St. Moritz where Waibel had gone for a winter vacation. To Colonel Waibel Husmann's information was serious enough to prompt him to cut short his holiday and return to Zurich the following day.

As Parrilli and Waibel talked, Waibel revealed that he had heard a somewhat similar story from other sources. In answer to the colonel's questions as to Parrilli's sources of information, the baron gave the names of no high-ranking German officers—only that of *SS Obersturmfuehrer* Guido Zimmer of the Milan office of the foreign intelligence branch of the *Reichssicherheitshauptamt (RSHA)*. Like Husmann, Waibel dismissed the idea that the Americans

---

[1] Col Max Waibel, GSC, Swiss Army, The Secret Negotiations Concerning the Surrender of the German Armed Forces in Italy, 21 February to 2 May 1945, MS (hereafter cited as Waibel MS), CMH. Also Office of Strategic Services Memoranda file on same subject, National Archives, Washington, D.C., John Kimche, *Spying for Peace* (London: Weidenfeld and Nicolson, 1961) pp. 126ff; Allen W. Dulles, *The Secret Surrender* (New York: Harper and Row, 1966). Unless otherwise cited the following is based upon these references.

and the British would negotiate at the expense of their Russian ally. Yet the situation, in Waibel's words, "seemed to open vast perspectives," and he declared himself willing to act as an intermediary.

On the evening of 25 February, Colonel Waibel and his assistant, Dr. Bernhard Mayr von Baldegg, met Allen Dulles, ostensibly an official of the American Embassy but in reality chief of the Office of Strategic Services (OSS) intelligence network for Central Europe, and his assistant, Dr. Gero von Gaevernitz, at Husmann's villa near Lucerne. Knowing nothing about Baron Parrilli, Dulles approached the matter with caution, but he sanctioned Waibel's sounding out the German unofficially on his own responsibility. Only if the Germans gave evidence of genuine sincerity about ending the war in Italy would Dulles enter the picture.[2]

The Widening Circle

Two days after the Waibel-Dulles meeting and after arranging with Professor Husmann for a secret password to permit less formal arrangements for re-entry into Switzerland, Baron Parrilli returned to Italy. Meanwhile, *Obersturmfuehrer* Zimmer reported to *SS Obergruppenfuehrer* Karl Wolff, highest SS and Police Commissioner with the German Forces in Italy, and Rudolf Rahn, German Ambassador to the neo-Fascist Republic, on the results of Parrilli's first mission. According to Rahn, Wolff was eager to make contact with the Allies. He selected *SS Standartenfuehrer* Eugen

Dollmann, Wolff's liaison officer at Kesselring's headquarters, to lay the groundwork for possible negotiations.

Wolff had formerly been Heinrich Himmler's adjutant and confidant. In his capacity as senior SS official in Italy, he reported directly to Himmler and thus enjoyed a command channel to the highest levels independent of the *OB Suedwest*, Field Marshal Kesselring. After mid-1944 Wolff was also designated General Plenipotentiary of the Armed Forces in Italy, a strategic post in the channel between the OKW and Mussolini's neo-Fascist Republic.[3]

Ambassador Rahn for his part was no stranger to covert negotiations by military leaders behind the backs of their civilian counterparts, for when he had first arrived in Rome to present his credentials in September 1943, members of the Italian high command were busily putting the finishing touches to secret operations designed to get Italy out of the war. Even so, in negotiations aimed at ending hostilities with the Allies the key role from the beginning apparently belonged to Wolff.[4]

From the end of February to the first week in April the circle slowly widened on the German side to include, in addition to Wolff and his confidants, General von Vietinghoff and his chief of staff, Generalleutnant Hans Roettiger, and on the Allied side Field Marshal Alexander's military representatives, Generals T.S. Airey (British)

---

[2] The Germans had known of Dulles' presence and mission since the previous autumn. See Walter Hagen, *Die Geheime Front* (Wien, 1950), p. 455.

[3] Rudolf Rahn, *Ruheloses Leben* (Dusseldorf, 1949), p. 282.

[4] Details of these negotiations are to be found in the AFHQ CROSSWORD Cable file, 0100/4, AFHQ SACS, Negotiations for German Surrender in Italy, Feb–Apr 1945 (Waibel MS). See also Dulles, *The Secret Surrender*.

and Lyman Lemnitzer. Nonetheless, outside that circle there were others less favorably disposed to the negotiations. Both Heinrich Himmler and his deputy, Dr. Ernst Kaltenbrunner, had begun to suspect the nature of Wolff's Swiss contacts. Reaching Soviet agents, news of the contacts had also aroused latent suspicions among the Soviet leaders that their western partners were surreptitiously dealing with the Germans. To allay the suspicions the western allies began in mid-March to keep their eastern allies informed of the conversations with Wolff's agents.[5]

GENERAL VON VIETINGHOFF

German Reservations

On 9 April Parrilli, accompanied by Maj. Max Wenner, Wolff's adjutant, went to Chiasso on the Italo-Swiss frontier with a message from General Wolff. The message asked "an honorable capitulation," including permission for the German forces to withdraw into Germany with military honor and for *Army Group C* to maintain a modest contingent "as a future instrument of order inside Germany." That had been the German Army's role following the Armistice in 1918 and reflected General von Vietinghoff's influence on the drafting of the message.[6]

Vietinghoff's request accorded with a soldierly honor and tradition largely alien to Wolff and his SS associates.

Although Wolff and the men close to him had all sworn fealty to the Fuehrer as head of state, they, unlike Vietinghoff, would have little compunction in betraying the Fuehrer and deserting his ally, Mussolini. Opportunists to the core, they were anxious to save anything that could yet be salvaged, including their lives and fortunes.

The terms requested by Vietinghoff were in any event foredoomed, for they ran counter to the Allied political and military decision to extirpate German military traditions and institutions. Surrender, it had been agreed, was to be unconditional and, unlike 1918, no German forces would be allowed to march back to their fatherland in military formation.

Baron Parrilli nevertheless urged his Allied contact not to reject Vietinghoff's request out of hand, for as a soldier of the old school the general would no doubt continue to fight rather than act contrary to what he deemed his military

---

[5] For details of Russian reaction and Allied response see Winston S. Churchill, *Triumph and Tragedy* (Boston: Houghton-Mifflin Publishing Co., 1953), p. 446; William D. Leahy, *I Was There* (New York: Whittlesey House, 1950), pp. 334–35; Feis, *Churchill, Roosevelt, Stalin.* See also 00100/4, AFHQ SACS, Negotiations for German Surrender in Italy, Vols. 1–4.

[6] See Harry R. Rudin, *Armistice 1918* (New Haven; Yale University Press, 1944), pp. 395ff.

code. Wolff himself pointed out in his message that while he believed he could keep his promise to deliver northern Italy to the Allies by 16 April, Vietinghoff's insistence upon points of military honor constituted a serious obstacle.[7]

Concerned lest the Germans might be attempting to draw out the negotiations, Field Marshal Alexander refused to give Wolff and his colleagues anything in writing. He instructed Dulles instead to tell the Germans that a draft copy of the capitulation would be handed the German plenipotentaries only after their arrival at Allied headquarters fully empowered to act in Vietinghoff's behalf. With that reply in hand, Parrilli returned on 10 April to Wolff's headquarters at Fasano. After hearing the baron's report Dulles and Gaevernitz concluded that the German commanders in Italy would actually capitulate only after *Army Group C* had been effectively cut off from communication with the Reich. At that point even the most fanatical units would have no alternative to surrender.

The next day, 16 April, two days after the Fifth Army had launched its phase of the final offensive, Zimmer arrived at Chiasso, where he informed the Swiss agents who acted as liaison with Dulles that Himmler had been pressuring Wolff to come to Berlin. Wolff, Zimmer added, urged the Allies not to "make useless sacrifices with their intensified offensives," for a surrender was imminent. Although Dulles transmitted that information to Allied head-

quarters at Caserta, Alexander dismissed it, convinced that it was only an attempt to relieve the mounting pressure of Allied operations against the German forces or to delay the progress of the offensive. One bit of information that did invite the Allied commander's consideration was that OKW had placed the territory east of the Isonzo River under Generaloberst Alexander Loehr's heterogeneous German-Croat-Cossack *Army Group E*, then withdrawing before Tito's partisans and the Russians. That meant that the Trieste area, lying east of the Isonzo, would not be included in any surrender of *Army Group C*. The establishment of a new interarmy boundary also raised the possibility, the Allies believed, that OKW might use Loehr, who had had no part in the surrender negotiations, to pressure Vietinghoff into not surrendering prematurely. In reality, Vietinghoff had already taken precautions against that possibility by directing **his air commander, General Erich Ritter von Pohl, who had been informed of** the covert contacts, to move troops under his command west of the Isonzo in order to cover *Army Group C*'s rear. Pohl also sent artillery to the Alpine passes east of the Brenner Pass to block movements by either Yugoslav partisans or German units opposed to a capitulation.

The labyrinthine maneuverings within the German command were actually of no more than minor interest to Field Marshal Alexander. With the Eighth Army's phase of the spring offensive favorably under way and the Fifth Army about to unleash its second phase, the Allied commander was confident that no matter what the Germans

---

[7] General von Schwerin, following his surrender on 25 April, said that Vietinghoff "will continue to obey the Fuehrer's orders as long as a telephone line exists between his headquarters and OKW." See Operations of British, Indian, and Dominion Forces in Italy, Pt. IV, Sec. G, App. B.

did, their defeat was only a matter of weeks. Thus, he cautioned Dulles and his representatives to avoid giving the Germans an impression that the Allies were negotiating; the Allied commander's sole interest was in arranging for safe passage of enemy parliamentaries to his headquarters "with full powers to arrange details of unconditional military surrender."[8]

Parrilli meanwhile arrived at Chiasso on 17 April with the disturbing news that, at Himmler's insistence, Wolff had finally gone to Berlin for a face-to-face confrontation with Hitler and the Reichsfuehrer SS. Two days later Wolff, proving an exception to the rule that those summoned peremptorily to the Fuehrer's headquarters rarely came back, returned to Italy with assurances that nothing had been compromised. As the general explained to Dulles through his intermediaries, he had convinced Hitler that the discussions with the Allies had been only a ploy to gain time and divide the Allied coalition. Apparently satisfied, the Fuehrer ordered him back to his post with no restrictions other than to forbid travel to Switzerland.

Preparations for a Cease-Fire

Aware that his movements would be carefully watched from Berlin, Wolff nevertheless continued to try to talk his colleagues into reaching an immediate cease-fire agreement. Impelled by a growing sense of urgency, he met on 22 April with Vietinghoff, Pohl, Rahn,

and Franz Hofer at army group headquarters, then located at Recoaro. Gauleiter of the Tyrol, and a confidant of Kaltenbrunner, Himmler's deputy, Hofer affected an extremely defeatist position in an effort to draw out the conferees so that he could later betray them to Kaltenbrunner. The war was lost, Hofer declared, and further fighting would produce senseless slaughter. If Hitler himself should come to the Tyrol and order a last-ditch resistance in the Alpine Redoubt, Hofer added, he would place the Fuehrer in a sanitorium. It took the conferees little time to agree that the tempo of contacts with the Allied agents in Switzerland should be stepped up.

As prepared by Rahn, guidelines for final negotiations specified that from that point *Army Group C* was to act independently and, in particular, no orders originating from Himmler were to be followed. All present bound themselves on their word of honor to support the effort to bring the fighting in northern Italy to the earliest possible end.

Von Vietinghoff then wrote out instructions for his representative, Oberstleutnant Victor von Schweinitz, "to conduct negotiations [with Allied authorities] within the meaning of my instructions . . . [and] to sign binding agreements in my name."[9] He inserted the phrase "within the meaning of my instructions" to help ensure that von Schweinitz would do everything possible to secure honorable conditions for the troops.

As senior political representative, Hofer sought to look out for his own

---

[8] Msg. AGWAR for CCS from Alexander SACMED, ref. no. FX–59004, 12 Apr 45. In 0100/4, AFHQ SACS, Gen McNarney's Papers Concerning Negotiations for German Surrender in Italy, Mar–Apr 45 (127–132SP), ser. 412.

[9] Waibel MS, p. 69.

interest by insisting that certain political questions concerning the Tyrol and upper Austria also be included in the instructions, possibly a reflecton of a strong undercurrent of Austrian separatism which was surfacing among Nazi functionaries from that part of the Reich. In any event, Hofer's efforts were futile, for Wolff was determined to ignore them.[10]

Unknown to the German emissaries as they prepared to set out for the Swiss frontier, the climate for negotiations on the Allied side had changed. Convinced by SACMED's reports that the German command in Italy had no real intention of surrendering on terms acceptable to the Allies, the Combined Chiefs of Staff directed Field Marshal Alexander on 20 April to tell Dulles to break off contact with the Germans. He was to "regard the whole matter as being closed" and so inform the Russians through the Allied mission in Moscow.[11]

On 22 April Baron Parrilli arrived at Chiasso with word that General Wolff, accompanied by his aide, Major Wenner, and Oberstleutnant von Schweinitz, entrusted with full powers to conduct surrender negotiations in Vietinghoff's name, were on their way to the frontier and would arrive the next day. For Dulles that posed a dilemma. Three enemy plenipotentiaries were on their way to surrender the German armies in Italy, yet Alexander and Dulles were under unequivocal orders to cease all contacts with them.

The Swiss intermediaries, Major Waibel and Professor Husmann, under no such restrictions, meanwhile prepared to meet the Germans at the frontier. Although aware of the Allied decision to end negotiations, they decided against telling the Germans of it as did Dulles himself, for he could have informed them by secret radio.

Learning on the morning of 23 April that Wolff and his party had arrived, Waibel and Husmann hastened to Chiasso, making part of the trip by train because snow still blocked the St. Gotthard Pass. They had to hurry in order to pick up the Germans and return in time to catch the last train of the day through the St. Gotthard tunnel and bring the Germans to Waibel's home near Lucerne, for under the circumstances they could hardly be lodged in a public hotel.[12]

Waibel and Husmann found Parrilli, Wolff, and his party waiting for them. Still reluctant to reveal the Allied order to break off negotiations lest the news throw Wolff into the arms of the bitterenders in Italy, Waibel nevertheless considered that it had to be done. Choosing his words carefully, in an attempt to prepare Wolff for the blow, he explained that there had been some difficulties on the Allied side and that Dulles had been instructed temporarily to break off contact with Wolff.

Waibel quickly added that he would use his influence to get the talks started again. Meanwhile, he invited them to come to his country home, Villa Doerrenbach near Lucerne, and there await

---

[10] *Ibid.*, Rahn, *Ruheloses Leben*, p. 289.
[11] Msg. U.S. Mission, Moscow, from Alexander, ref. No. F–63542, 21 Apr 45, in 0100/4, AFHQ SACS, Gen McNarney, Papers Concerning Negotiations for German Surrender in Italy, Mar–Apr 45, (128–132SP), ser. 412.

[12] Waibel MS. The following section is based upon this source.

the results of his efforts. When Wolff and his companions wearily accepted the invitation, Waibel telephoned Dulles to ask him to come to Lucerne that evening. Although Dulles agreed to meet with Waibel, he pointed out that he would be unable to see Wolff.

Sure enough, about the same time that Waibel and his companions arrived from Chiasso, Dulles, accompanied by Gaevernitz, drove to Lucerne from Bern. Calling on Dulles at his hotel, Waibel laid before him Vietinghoff's written statement naming von Schweinitz as his plenipotentiary. Dated 22 April and written on the official stationery of *Der Oberbefehlshaber Suedwest und der Heeresgruppe C,* the document stated that von Schweinitz was empowered to conduct and conclude binding agreements "within the framework of the instructions which I have given him." The document bore von Vietinghoff's signature.

In Dulles' view the statement of authority contained in the document changed matters, for no such authority had entered into earlier negotiations. Dulles cabled Caserta for new instructions, and Alexander, in turn, cabled the CCS that enemy officers had appeared in Switzerland with full powers to act for the German commander-in-chief in Italy in bringing about an unconditional surrender.

Wolff and the two plenipotentaries meanwhile waited restlessly at Villa Doerrenbach. Early on 24 April, not quite 24 hours after their arrival, word arrived from Caserta via Bern that while Alexander awaited a reply to his request to the CCS, Dulles was free to refer the matter to higher political authority, which prompted General Wolff to observe wryly to Husmann that he himself was acting without his superiors' permission. Indeed, he was in Switzerland in defiance of them. Because of the delay Wenner and von Schweinitz at that point were ready to abandon the project and return to Italy, but Wolff would not permit them to do so.[13]

During a luncheon conference later that day, Waibel, Husmann, and Wolff agreed that without waiting for Dulles' reply, Wolff should return to his headquarters where he could keep watch over the situation and, if necessary, try unilaterally to bring about a cessation of hostilities. Although Waibel doubted whether that was practicable, he thought it worth trying, even if it brought about only a partial end to the fighting.

Before leaving the villa Wolff gave Wenner full authority in writing to sign binding agreements in the name of the highest SS and Police Commander and General Plenipotentiary of the Wehrmacht in Italy. At Waibel's insistence he deleted the words "to negotiate." Accompanied by Husmann, Wolff on 25 April returned to Chiasso.

General Wolff had motored only four miles from Chiasso when bands of partisans forced him to take refuge in an SS command post in the Villa Locatelli near Cernobbio on the shores of Lake Como, to await the arrival of a military convoy. There Wolff found several neo-Fascist dignitaries, among them Mussolini's defense minister, Marshal Graziani, and the Italian Air Force

---

[13] Waibel MS; Msg. Alexander to AGWAR for CCS, ref. no. FX65020, 24 April 45, 0100/4 AFHQ SACS.

commander, General Ruggero Bonomi. Learning of Wolff's plans, they readily authorized him to surrender their forces. Meanwhile, the hoped-for convoy never came.

Deterred by partisans and the Allied offensive, General Wolff was able only through intervention of the Swiss intermediaries and an American agent serving with the partisans to return to the frontier, where Major Waibel met him. Since the circumstances made it impossible to go directly from Chiasso to *Army Group C*'s headquarters at Bolzano, Waibel arranged for Wolff and Guido Zimmer, who had joined Wolff, to return to Bolzano by way of Austria. Just as Wolff was leaving Switzerland on the 27th he learned that Dulles had received word lifting the ban on contacts with the Germans.[14]

Vietinghoff and his senior commanders gathered in Bolzano on the afternoon of 28 April at his headquarters to hear Wolff's report. What Wolff had to say was brief and to the point. Schweinitz and Wenner, acting as plenipotentiaries for Vietinghoff and Wolff, were on their way to Caserta, perhaps were already there. Although Wolff had not even bothered to mention Hofer's political conditions to Allied representatives in Switzerland, yet he told his colleagues that he had done so but that the Allies had refused to consider them.[15]

Expressing keen disappointment at that news but still determined to retrieve something for his pains, Gauleiter Hofer insisted that Vietinghoff place

him in control of all military units in the Tyrol, which, in effect, would give him control of most of the forces still under Vietinghoff's command. The army group commander's immediate and violent reaction to the demand revealed a widening gap between the military and political authorities in the southwestern theater. At that point Vietinghoff's chief of staff, Roettiger, who thus far had been quietly biding his time, became spokesman for the opposition to Hofer and his fellow die-hards in the German camp. The Gauleiter's demands, Roettiger said, were completely out of line with the military situation. After five hours of fruitless discussion turning on that point, the conferees dispersed to await the return of Schweinitz and Wenner.[16]

Although Hofer found himself in a minority at army group headquarters, he still had a powerful ally in Field Marshal Kesselring. Having hosted a meeting with Kesselring, Vietinghoff, and Rahn at his estate near Innsbruck on the 27th, Hofer knew as well as the others that Kesselring at that time had flatly rejected a capitulation in northern Italy. It was also well known how harshly the field marshal had dealt with officers involved in an abortive uprising near Munich the day before.[17]

Kesselring's reaction had puzzled Wolff, who only a few days earlier had sent one of his staff, *SS Standartenfuehrer* Dollmann, to the field marshal's headquarters on the Western Front to sound

---

[14] Msg.Alexander to Military Mission to Dean and Archer, ref. No. FX66435, April 45, file 0100/4 AFHQ SACS.

[15] Waibel MS; Crossword Cable File.

[16] Memo, Wolff, in Crossword Cable File.

[17] *Ibid.* This was a premature attempt on the part of the garrison at a cantonment to seize control of Munich and order a cease-fire prior to the arrival of Allied forces. The officers involved had been summarily executed.

him out concerning surrender in Italy. The field marshal, according to Dollmann, had at that time declared that he would raise no objections to the capitulation of *Army Group C,* although he himself could take no active part in it until the Fuehrer's death should release him from his soldier's oath. (It is possible, of course, that Dollmann interpreted Kesselring's remarks in such a way as to encourage Wolff in his enterprise.)

The field marshal's seeming change of heart and unyielding stand apparently arose from his own estimate of the military situation. A premature surrender of Vietinghoff's *Army Group C,* Kesselring believed, would create an untenable situation for General Schulz's *Army Group G,* still fighting north of the Alps, and Loehr's *Army Group E,* falling back before the Russians and Yugoslavs through Croatia to the Isonzo. A surrender in Italy, he believed, would also adversely affect troops still fighting in Berlin and along the Eastern Front. To that line of reasoning none of the conferees at the earlier Innsbruck meeting had raised objections.[18]

Recalling that conference strengthened Hofer in his conviction that in the developing confrontation with Wolff and Roettiger, Kesselring would be on his side. Without consulting either Vietinghoff or Wolff, Hofer telephoned Kesselring to give what Wolff would later describe as "a dangerous stab in the back" to the military command in northern Italy. Thus in the last four days of *Army Group C*'s existence the fantastically unrealistic political hopes of the Kaltenbrunner-Hofer faction joined

with the Doenitz-Kesselring faction. Their strategy represented a desperate hope of saving as much as possible of the German armed forces from capture by the Red Army and their east European partisan allies.[19]

The Surrender at Caserta

However much difficulty Wolff's plans for a separate peace had encountered within the German command structure, these plans were moving smoothly toward realization. Late on the 28th, an airplane bearing the two German plenipotentiaries and Dulles' assistant, von Gaevernitz, arrived at Caserta, where they were met by General Lemnitzer and General Airey, who had taken part in the earlier conversations with the Germans in Switzerland. The party then drove to a camp especially prepared for the visitors in a secluded corner of the palace grounds at Caserta.[20]

Late that evening Lt. Gen. Sir William D. Morgan, since December 1944 Alexander's chief of staff, together with representatives of the Allied air forces and naval commands, met with the Germans. This time there was none of the outwardly informal, sometimes cordial conversation marking the clandestine sessions in Switzerland. It was a meeting of conqueror and conquered; for as far as the Allied command was concerned, the sole purpose of Caserta was to receive an unconditional military surrender and instruct the defeated army in the steps for an orderly capitulation. After receiving the German

---

[18] Kesselring, *A Soldier's Record,* p. 341.

[19] Waibel MS; Crossword Cable File.

[20] See AFHQ SACS file 0100/4; Waibel MS; Dulles, *The Secret Surrender.* Unless otherwise cited the following section is based on these sources.

GERMAN REPRESENTATIVES SIGN SURRENDER DOCUMENT

emissaries, General Morgan handed them three copies of the instrument of surrender and told them to withdraw to their quarters to study it.

Three hours later General Morgan summoned the Germans to a second conference. For the first time a representative of the Russian armed forces, Maj. Gen. Aleksey Pavlovich Kislenko, Soviet delegate to the Allied Control Commission in Rome, was present as an observer. Morgan opened the meeting by asking the Germans to state whether the general instrument of surrender was acceptable. After some hesitation they agreed that it was. Assured that all who surrendered would be treated as prisoners of war, von Schweinitz also asked assurance that Germans would be interned in Italy rather than be transferred to either Great Britain or to the United States. Allied representatives refused such assurance. Schweinitz failed to bring up Vietinghoff's desire, expressed earlier, that the German troops be allowed to retain belts and bayonets and march back into Germany as in 1918.

The Germans did ask that all officers and military police be permitted to retain side arms in order to maintain discipline during the interim between cease-fire and internment. Conceding that some units might refuse to accept the cease-fire order, Morgan acceded to that request.[21] He also agreed to let Schweinitz, before signing the surrender terms, radio them and the results of the discussions to Vietinghoff, who could then indicate a time for cessation of hostilities.

Following the meeting, General Lemnitzer and Dr. von Gaevernitz accompanied the Germans to their quarters, where the four spent most of the rest of the night discussing technical details of the appendices to the surrender document, point by point. By 0400 on 29 April they had drafted a mutually acceptable cable for transmission to Vietinghoff via Dulles' office in Switzerland.

The message, which reached Bern later that morning, was garbled by atmospheric conditions so that Vietinghoff's headquarters did not receive a clear text. Anxious to forward a complete and ungarbled version of the surrender terms to Vietinghoff as soon as possible, Dulles decided to parachute a member of his staff near the German headquarters at Bolzano. By the time plans had been completed and an aircraft obtained, it was already too late in the day.

When neither an acknowledgement nor a reply came from *Army Group C's* headquarters, Wenner, General Wolff's representative, who had been instructed to sign a surrender document no matter what the terms, indicated his willingness to do so. Schweinitz for his part refused to proceed without word from Vietinghoff and at the same time continued to argue for a promise of internment of German troops in Italy. Not until late in the morning of the 29th did Schweinitz finally agree to sign without waiting for Vietinghoff's reply. Even then he insisted that he was exceeding his instructions.

At 1400 that afternoon the two German emissaries entered Morgan's office to sign the surrender document. Both Schweinitz and Wenner appeared somewhat ill at ease in the glare of floodlights, popping of flash bulbs, and whirring of movie cameras. Quickly recovering their composure, they turned to face a room filled with high-ranking Allied officers gathered to witness the ceremony. General Morgan stepped forward to ask formally if the two were prepared to sign an instrument of surrender on behalf of their respective commanders. When they replied affirmatively, an aide to General Morgan placed five copies of the document before them.

Breaking an awkward silence that followed, Schweinitz—speaking in German, although he was able to discourse fluently in English—reiterated that in signing without guarantees concerning internment of German prisoners of war in Italy, he would be exceeding his authority. Nevertheless, he declared, he would sign on his own reponsibility and on the assumption that his superiors would approve, although he could give

---

[21] General Clark, apparently unaware of the concession, was incensed that von Senger had surrendered while wearing his side arm. He ordered the German general to remove it. Von Senger did so, throwing the weapon and belt to the ground. Clark ordered a guard to retrieve it for his souvenir collection. See *Calculated Risk*, p. 440.

GENERAL MORGAN RECEIVES GERMAN REPRESENTATIVES

no absolute assurance to that effect. The mild caveat failed to deter Morgan, who replied that he was prepared to accept the signature under that condition. In reality, Schweinitz's declaration was no more than an empty gesture, for the Germans in Italy had no alternative to surrender.

Shortly after 1400, 29 April, Schweinitz and Wenner signed the document, which stipulated that the capitulation was to be unconditional and that hostilities were to cease, beginning at noon, GMT, on Wednesday, 2 May 1945. The Germans thus had four days to get

word of the capitulation to their troops.[22]

Because of difficulties in radio communications and the need for security, the text of the surrender document had to go to von Vietinghoff as soon as possible. Immediately following the surrender ceremony, the German emissaries, accompanied by von Gaevernitz and an American staff officer, headed to Switzerland. The emissaries went on to Bolzano. They got there late in the

[22] See Garland and Smyth, *Sicily and the Surrender of Italy*, pp. 435–552.

evening of 30 April. Thirty-one hours had elapsed since the two officers had left Caserta; only 36 remained before the cease-fire was to take effect.

Army Group C's Last Hours

Army Group C, Schweinitz and Wenner discovered upon reaching Bolzano, was no longer under von Vietinghoff's command. Hofer having by telephone charged von Vietinghoff and his chief of staff, General Roettiger, with treasonable contact with the Allies, Kesselring had relieved both officers and placed *Army Group C* under the *Army Group G* commander, General Friedrich Schulz. Kesselring referred SS General Wolff's case to the chief of the RSHA, Dr. Kaltenbrunner, for disciplinary action. Kaltenbrunner had, in the meantime, left Berlin to take refuge in upper Austria, where he was engaged in a wild and hopeless effort to take over surrender negotiations and arrange, through conservative clerical circles, a separate peace for Austria.[23]

At noon on the 30th General Schulz and his chief of staff, General Wentzell, had arrived to assume command of *Army Group C.* Von Vietinghoff immediately turned over his command to Schulz, but Roettiger, unwilling to abandon the scene, decided to remain in his office for a day or so, ostensibly to "orient" his successor. Determined to carry out Kesselring's intent for *Army Group C* to continue to resist in hope of gaining time for other forces elsewhere to elude the Russians, General Schulz ordered all subordinate units to fight on.

The situation on 1 May was such that the order was manifestly impossible to execute. In northwestern Italy virtually all resistance had already ceased and north of Lake Garda and in the Brenta and Piave valleys the remnants of the two German armies were backed up against the Alps.

At that point Roettiger emerged as the key figure in an attempt to force Kesselring to abandon his plan and permit the capitulation to take place at the appointed hour. Instead of allowing von Schweinitz and Wenner to report directly to the new army group commander, Roettiger had them brought to his own quarters were they were joined by General Wolff and *SS Standartenfuehrer* Dollmann. All agreed that without Kesselring's authorization neither Schulz nor Wentzell would order the cease-fire. If there was to be an immediate cease-fire, there was no alternative, Roettiger and Wolff agreed, to taking Schulz and Wentzell into custody and themselves issuing a cease-fire order.

Events at *Army Group C* headquarters thus acquired the character of *opéra bouffe.* To prevent word from reaching Kesselring, Roettiger and Wolff, with the co-operation of the army group intelligence officer, blocked all communications between Bolzano and the Reich. Moving rapidly, they thereupon seized Schulz and Wentzell soon after daylight on 1 May and confined them to their quarters under house arrest.

In *de facto* command of *Army Group C,* Roettiger issued the cease-fire order, but he had failed to reckon with the hold that military protocol and tradition still had on his fellow officers. When two of the army commanders, Lemel-

---

[23] AFHQ SAC Negotiations, file 0100/4, Vol. II, Msg Bern to AFHQ, 30 April 45.

sen and Herr, learned that Schulz and Wentzell were under house arrest, they refused to implement Roettiger's orders even though they had agreed in principle with the decision to surrender. That left Roettiger with no choice but to release Schulz and Wentzell and attempt to win them over by argument. At Wolff's insistence, Schulz called a meeting of all the senior commanders for 1800 at army group headquarters, which Roettiger and Vietinghoff would be allowed to attend.

While that bizarre drama was being played out, the *XIV Panzer Corps* commander, General von Senger, had moved with his corps staff to Mattarello, three miles south of Trento. There, "in a pretty country house with a baroque garden and a wide view into the Adige valley," he awaited word of the capitulation.[24]

That afternoon Senger received a call from Lemelsen asking him to take his place at the army command post because he had just been summoned to a meeting at army group headquarters. Arriving at army headquarters that evening, von Senger learned details of the capitulation that had been signed at Caserta on the 29th and that Lemelsen and Herr, as well as General Pohl, the air force commander in Italy, and *SS Obergruppenfuehrer* Wolff, had all concurred in the action.[25]

In the meantime, a teletype message from Admiral Doenitz reached *Army Group C* headquarters, telling of the Fuehrer's death in Berlin and announcing that, in accordance with the Fuehrer's will, Doenitz was Chief of State and Commander-in-Chief of the Armed Forces. Doenitz's message also ordered the German armies to continue to fight against the Western Allies so long as they interfered with the battle against Bolshevism.[26]

In view of that order—or exhortation—Schulz hesitated to support the pro-capitulation faction at army group headquarters. Yet from the two army commanders he learned that they no longer considered their armies capable of meaningful resistance, so that continuation of the war in Italy no longer made sense. Wolff and Pohl added that with partisans already in control of wide areas of German-occupied Italy, the political situation there was equally hopeless. Even so Schulz merely agreed to pass that information on to Kesselring; he still refused to issue a ceasefire order without the field marshal's approval.

Unaware of the machinations within the German command and concerned that the emissaries might not have reached Bolzano, Field Marshal Alexander, meanwhile, in another message to von Vietinghoff demanded an unequivocal answer to whether he accepted the terms of surrender and whether his force would cease fire at the agreed time. The message arrived at *Army Group C* at 2130 on 1 May. Its stern tone convinced even Schulz that a final decision could no longer be deferred.[27]

After advising the Allied commander that a decision would be made within the hour, Schulz telephone Kessel-

[24] MS # C–095f (Senger).

[25] *Ibid.*

[26] Records of the Reichsfuehrer SS and Chief of the German Police, Microfilm T–175, Roll # 225.

[27] Msg Alexander to AGWAR for CCS, 2 May 45, AFHQ SACS, file 0100/4.

ring's headquarters only to learn after he finally got through that he field marshal was at the front and that his chief of staff was unwilling to make a decision. Wolff then got on the telephone and angrily insisted that since all were agreed that further resistance was futile, one of *Army Group C*'s senior commanders should be given authority to issue the cease-fire order. To that the chief of staff lamely replied that he would lay the matter before the field marshal when the latter returned that night.

When by 2200 no word had been received from Kesselring's headquarters, Lemelsen and Herr at last agreed to issue the orders on their own responsibility. Later that night Lemelsen telephoned von Senger to tell him to order a cease-fire as of 1400 on the 2d—two hours later than the time agreed upon at Caserta—and to halt all troop movements except those necessary for supply. Von Senger immediately transmitted the orders to the *LI Mountain* and the *XIV Panzer Corps,* as well as to the *I Parachute Corps,* which in the confusion of the past week had come under the control of the *Fourteenth Army.* [28] The *Tenth Army*'s *LXXVI Panzer Corps* having surrendered a week before, Herr had little trouble communicating the orders to the few troops still under his command.

While there were no objections or demands for explanation from any of the corps headquarters, it soon became evident at army group headquarters that many younger officers were determined to fight on. To avoid a showdown with the young zealots, Wolff, Pohl, and the two army commanders

[28] MS # C–095f (Senger), CMH.

GENERAL LEMELSEN AND COLONEL VON SCHWEINITZ

took refuge in Wolff's headquarters where the SS general had prudently assembled seven tanks and 350 SS troops.

They acted just in time, for at 0115 on 2 May an order arrived from Kesselring for the arrest of Roettiger, von Schweinitz, and von Vietinghoff. Although the order made no mention of the army commanders, both Herr and Lemelsen found it prudent to depart for the relative security of their own headquarters. A similar order from Kesselring's air officer for the arrest of General Pohl reached Pohl's adjutant, who quietly ignored it.

Before the arrests could be carried out, Kesselring telephoned Wolff in his barricaded headquarters and upbraided him for attempting to usurp his, Kesselring's, authority as commander of the

GENERAL HERR LEAVES BOLZANO FOR SURRENDER

southwestern theater. For two hours the two officers argued bitterly until connections became bad, whereupon the chiefs of staff of the two commanders resumed the argument. Toward the end of the marathon and sometimes acrimonious debate, even Schulz joined in, supporting Wolff's contention that since further resistance was impossible Kesselring would only be agreeing to a *fait accompli.*

Not until 0430 on 2 May did Kesselring finally agree to authorize Schulz to issue a cease-fire order—limited to the sphere of command of *OB Suedwest.*

Wolff then sent word of Kesselring's acceptance of the "written and verbal conditions of the Armistice Agreement" to Alexander with a request that public announcement be withheld for forty-eight hours. The Allied commander agreed to relay the request to his superiors but insisted that Wolff was "to carry out your agreement to cease hostilities on my front at 12 noon GMT today [2 May]."[29] The Germans, after a two-hour delay, broadcast cease-fire or-

[29] Msg Alexander to AGWAR for CCS, ref. No. FX–69224, 2 May 45, in AFHQ SACS, McNarney file 0100/4.

ders to their troops at 1400. When the Allied command picked up their broadcast, Alexander announced the ceasefire four and a half hours later at 1830.[30]

Field Marshal Kesselring meanwhile placed himself at Grand Admiral Karl Doenitz's disposal for "this arbitrary and punishable action."[31] At the same time, he asked Doenitz's authority to arrange for surrender of the remaining two army groups, *G* and *E*. Alhough the Admiral approved Kesselring's action in regard to *Army Group C,* he refused to authorize capitulation of the two other army groups.

Back at headquarters of the *XIV Panzer Corps* on the morning of 2 May, General von Senger, explaining the surrender, fully emphasized that Kesselring had approved it, for the field marshal's name still enjoyed considerable prestige among the officers and men. "It was," von Senger noted in his diary, "a tragic moment, the complete defeat and the imminent surrender after a fight lasting six years, tragic even for those who [like himself] had foreseen it for a long time."[32]

At *Army Group C*'s behest von Senger then left to head a mission to the Allied 15th Army Group headquarters at Florence to arrange for implementation of the surrender agreement. Under the escort of Brig. Gen. David L. Ruffner, deputy commander of the 10th Mountain Division, and a British colonel, von Senger and a small party that included von Schweinitz traveled south along Lake Garda's eastern shore, taking to the windswept waters in DUKW's to bypass the damaged tunnels, and at about 2100 arrived cold and wet at the 10th Mountain Division's command post. Transferring to staff cars and exchanging General Ruffner for General Hays, the party set out for Verona, where they spent the night, then flew to Clark's headquarters at Florence.

At 1030 on 4 May the German commander appeared before his longtime adversary in the van that Clark used as an office.[33] Von Senger presented a gaunt and haggard appearance. Saluting Clark and other senior American commanders crowded into the little van, he reported formally in English that as General von Vietinghoff's representative he had come to receive his instructions consistent with the terms of surrender signed at Caserta. Did he have full authority to implement the terms of unconditional surrender, Clark asked. Von Senger replied that he had. Handing him detailed instructions for the surrender, Clark told him to withdraw with General Gruenther and other members of Clark's staff for full explanation of these instructions.

During the conference with Gruenther, von Senger and his staff pointed out that until the Allied forces arrived in the German-held areas, armed bands of partisans roaming the countryside would make it difficult, if not impossible, for the Germans to lay down their arms and at the same time protect their supply depots, which by the terms of surrender were to be

---

[30] Msg Alexander to AGWAR for CCS, Ref. No. FX–69417, 2 May 45, AFHQ SACS, McNarney file 0100/4.

[31] Kesselring, *A Soldier's Record*, p. 342.

[32] MS # C–095f (Senger), CMH.

[33] Clark Diary, 4 May 1945. Unless otherwise noted the following is based upon this reference.

GENERAL VON SENGER SURRENDERS TO GENERAL CLARK AT FIFTEENTH ARMY GROUP
HEADQUARTERS

turned over to the Allied forces and not to irregulars. That was a crucial point, for General Clark was anxious to prevent additional arms from falling into the hands of Communist-controlled partisans who constituted one of the largest and most active groups in the Italian resistance.[34]

The problem was deemed serious enough to refer back to Clark. What von Senger essentially wanted was for the Allied commander to restrain the partisan bands. That Clark agreed to do, although he noted that, having just given them a "signal to go in for the kill," it would be pretty hard to squelch all that ardor through radio messages.[35] The best solution would be to get the American troops as quickly as possible into those areas still occupied by the Germans.

This had to be carefully arranged, for to rush American troops into German-occupied areas before all German

[34] MS # C–095f (Senger).

[35] Clark Diary, 4 May 45.

GERMAN REPRESENTATIVES RECEIVE INSTRUCTIONS FROM GENERAL GRUENTHER

units had gotten word of the surrender was to invite possible bloodshed. General Truscott had thus held Keyes' II Corps in place since early on 2 May to allow the German command in the area east of Lake Garda and in the Piave and Brenta valleys ample time to get word of the cease-fire to all units, many isolated and lacking regular military communications with their headquarters. Some German units took advantage of the delay to attempt escape through the Alpine passes into Austria, in spite of a standfast order. Aerial reconnaissance reported over a thousand horse-drawn vehicles and more than 500 motor vehicles mixed with civilian traffic passing through Bolzano in the direction of the Brenner pass. Deterred by poor weather conditions and reluctant to cause further bloodshed, Allied pilots made no effort to attack the columns.

Satisfied by 3 May that all German units had received the cease-fire order, Truscott let Keyes' II Corps resume roundup operations. Northeast of Lake Garda the 85th and 88th Divisions sent small task forces up the Piave and Brenta valleys toward the Austrian

PRISONERS OF WAR ASSEMBLE AT FOOT OF ALPS

frontier. Early on 4 May the 339th Infantry crossed the frontier near Dobbiaco, forty miles east of the Brenner pass, and a few hours later a reconnaissance unit from the 349th Infantry met troops from the Seventh Army's VI Corps at Vipiteno, nine miles to the south of the Brenner. Later in the day, the 338th Infantry, advancing astride Highway 12, reached the frontier at the Brenner pass. The next day, 5 May, the 10th Mountain Division, after passing through Bolzano, turned northwestward via Merano and reached the Austrian frontier over the Reschen pass. Just beyond the pass, at the Austrian village of Nauders, the mountain infantrymen made their first contact with those German troops retreating before

the U.S. Seventh Army. Aware that the Seventh Army had already received a surrender delegation from *Army Group G,* General Hays halted his men just outside Nauders. On 6 May, following surrender of *Army Group G* at noon, elements of the 10th Mountain Division continued northward to establish contact with troops of the Seventh Army's VI Corps, Truscott's former command.[36]

In northwestern Italy throughout 3 May the divisions of the IV Corps—the 1st Armored and the 34th, 91st, and 92d Infantry Divisions—had continued to accept the capitulation of isolated enemy units that had not yet received word of the general surrender. Faced with a choice of surrendering to the French, the Americans, or partisans, most of the Germans gave themselves up readily, even eagerly, to the Americans.

Meanwhile, on 1 May, the Eighth Army had contacted Tito's partisans at Montfalcone, about 17 miles northwest of Trieste. Although for many months an uneasy confrontation would remain between the Western Allies and the Yugoslavs along the Isonzo and at Trieste, northeastern Italy rapidly settled down to welcome though tense peace. By 6 May the occupation of all Italy from the Straits of Messina to the Alps had been completed. The eastern, western, and northern frontiers were closed, with all major exits under Allied control.

In spite of the protracted negotiations, which had reached a point of dramatic tension through frequent covert comings and goings across interna-

---

[36] *Seventh Army Report of Operations,* pp. 856–61.

88th Division in Alpine Pass

tional frontiers, the end came in Italy, as it would in northern Europe, only after the German forces, defeated in the field, had been backed into corners of Europe from which there was neither escape nor hope of survival. Only then did the Germans finally lay down their arms.

CHAPTER XXXI

An Assessment

In the evaluation of the Italian campaign three questions must be asked: What were its objectives, or rather what was the campaign's place in Allied grand strategy? Did the campaign achieve its objectives or fulfill its intended role in that strategy? Finally, were those objectives worth the cost and effort expended? Or, from another viewpoint, could those objectives have been achieved at less cost? In each case the student of military history is faced with a bewildering variety of answers. Judgments of the campaign range all the way from a harsh characterization as "tactically the most absurd and strategically the most senseless campaign of the whole war," to the more benign, "without Italy [the Italian campaign] OVERLORD might have bogged down as had Anzio and Cassino."[1]

At the QUADRANT Conference in late summer of 1943 the Allied chiefs of staff decided, among other things, that military operations in Italy would aim at holding the maximum number of German divisions as far away as possible from what was expected to be the main scene of operations in northwestern France. Measuring how well that objective was accomplished is clouded by the fact that assessing comparative strength on the basis of mere size gives a false picture. The value of a division as a fighting force, never constant, depends on such imponderables as the nature of the fighting morale and on a variety of purely local considerations as much as on numerical strength, mobility, firepower, and equipment. In the absence of other measurable criteria, however, a comparison of the number of available divisions is the only feasible means of arriving at even a rough approximation of relative strength.[2]

At one time or another in the Italian campaign the Allies employed a total of 30 divisions. When separate brigades and attached Italian units, mainly combat groups, are reckoned in their divisional equivalents, the total comes to about 33. The Germans committed 36, of which 3 were Italian and 1 Russian.

Since at the time of the Allied invasion of Italy in September 1943, the Germans had only six divisions, then south of Naples, the Allies appear to have drawn some 30 enemy divisions from other more critical fronts. Though on the surface it seems that the same could be said of the 30 Allied divisions engaged on the peninsula, in reality there was a marked difference. Most of the Allied divisions were already in the Mediterranean area—indeed, one of the reasons underlying a campaign in Italy was to utilize the resources which had already been assembled in North Africa and Sicily.

---

[1] See J.F.C. Fuller, *The Second World War, 1939–45: A Strategical and Tactical History* (New York: Duell, Sloan and Pearce, 1947), p. 265; and Blumenson, *Salerno to Cassino*, pp. 455–56.

[2] AFHQ, G–2, 11 Nov 1944, Review of Enemy Strength in Italian Combat Zone as of 7 Nov 1944, 0100/11E/77.

Because of limited port capacity in the United Kingdom, the divisions in Italy could have been moved there only by delaying the arrival of divisions from the United States. But such a move was not warranted. By remaining in Italy rather than shifting to an as yet inactive front, the American forces played a worthwhile role. The Germans, on the other hand, kept divisions in Italy that could have been deployed along relatively short interior lines on either the western or eastern fronts, which in both cases had critical need for additional forces.

They failed to send such forces even during the two major crises in the war in northwestern Europe: they pulled no division-size units from Italy to bolster either their defenses against OVERLORD or their counteroffensive in the Ardennes, although in preparation for the latter Field Marshal Walter Model did ask for three or four panzer divisions from other theaters. Hitler refused the request, even though at the time the excellent *26th Panzer Division* lay in army group reserve in the Po Valley. All Field Marshal Model got were two third-rate *Volksgrenadier Divisions* from within the Reich itself.[3] Not until the Red Army drove to the approaches of Budapest in March 1945 did the Germans move any divisional-size unit from Italy to reinforce another front.

A question arises, nevertheless, whether the Allies could have contained just as many German divisions if they had managed to bring the campaign to a halt along any of a number of satisfactory holding positions in Italy—

the Naples-Foggia area, for example. Naples provided a large enough port through which sufficient forces could have been supported to hold southern Italy, including the Foggia airfield complex. Strategic bombers flying from those fields could reach enemy targets in southern Germany, Austria, northern Italy, and the Balkan peninsula.

The city of Rome and the Viterbo airfield complex, some 20 miles north of Rome, would have been another position from which the Allied armies could have maintained a satisfactory holding operation. Rome would have been an adequate communications center for all of southern Italy, and from the Viterbo airfields Allied bombers could have reached even more enemy targets than from Foggia.

In the Northern Apennines the Allied armies had their last opportunity to halt while still containing large numbers of enemy divisions in Italy with relatively few Allied divisions. For beyond the Apennines the country widens and also beyond the Apennines lies the Po and finally the Alps. The latter offered naturally strong positions which the Germans could themselves have held quite economically, so that it would have been the Germans who would have contained the Allies along that line. It made no strategic sense to drive the Germans from the Apennines and into the Alps unless the Allies had sufficient strength to break through the Alpine defense line and into the mid-Danube basin and southern Germany. An alternative strategy would have been to trap the Germans south of the Po by an aerial assault on bridge and ferry sites, then to encircle and destroy the enemy armies on the Lombard plain.

---

[3] See Hugh M. Cole, *The Ardennes: Battle of the Bulge,* U.S. ARMY IN WORLD WAR II (Washington, 1965), p. 671.

Another course, one advocated by some senior American officers, would have been to leave a minimum of troops in Italy holding the most favorable defensive position and shift the remainder to southern France.

Until the last offensive in May 1945, the Allies, of course, adopted none of those possibilities. Instead, following the capture of Rome, Alexander's armies conducted a desultory pursuit to the Arno, restricted by the decision already made to shift two army corps and several divisions from the Fifth Army for operations in southern France. When the Allies finally made an effort to drive the enemy from the Northern Apennines with an offensive against the vaunted Gothic Line, Alexander's armies managed to break through but soon bogged down in a campaign of attrition against a series of enemy positions, each about as strong as the other. In late autumn of 1944 in the midst of this frustration the British command shifted several divisions from the Eighth Army to reinforce a British operation to shore up the Greek government in its civil war with communist partisans. And just before the spring offensive in 1945, the Allied command further weakened the Eighth Army by moving several Canadian divisions with a corps headquarters to northwestern Europe. Not surprising then that only two of the major Fifth Army offensives—the drive on Rome in May 1944 and the spring offensive into the Po Valley in April 1945—went according to plan. On the other hand, throughout the entire campaign the Germans were able to go on the offensive on an army-wide scale only twice—at Salerno and Anzio—and they failed both times.

After the Allied armies became established on the Italian mainland in September 1943, Churchill, who resented the American tactic of limiting strategic choices in the Mediterranean to only one of two possibilities—either southern France or Italy—sought to enhance the status of the latter and so keep alive both strategic choices. At British insistence in February 1944 the Americans agreed to delay ANVIL and concentrate on pushing the campaign in Italy at least as far as the capture of Rome.[4] That goal achieved in early June 1944, the British became even more preoccupied with the potential of the Italian campaign, preferring to employ available resources in the Mediterranean theater for a thrust into northern Italy and an advance, via Venezia Giulia, through the Julian Alps, Ljubljana Gap, and into the mid-Danube basin, there to join forces with (or possibly confront) the Russian troops advancing toward that region.[5] With the exception of Gen. Devers, senior Allied commanders in Italy, possibly recalling the success of the Napoleonic armies in northern Italy, shared this view. Yet what was possible for lightly equipped 18th and mid-19th century armies was not feasible for the heavy formations of the mid-20th century, which, given the global requirements of Allied strategy, were beyond Allied capabilities.[6]

Stalin, Roosevelt, and de Gaulle, on the other hand, opposed the mid-Danubian venture, each for his own reasons.

[4] Ehrman, *Grand Strategy*, Vol. V, p. 361, app. vii, Ismay's memo to P.M. 28 Apr 44.

[5] *Ibid.*, pp. 347–356; Forrest C. Pogue, *The Supreme Command*, U.S. ARMY IN WORLD WAR II (Washington, 1954), p. 218.

[6] See Le Goyet, *La Participation Française a la Campagne d'Italie*, pp. 189–91.

Stalin, because he had long since staked out the Balkans, including the Danube basin, as a Russian zone of influence. Roosevelt, with the prospects of major operations still looming in the Far East, was intent on driving directly into the heart of the Reich and getting the war in Europe over with as quickly and cheaply as possible. As for de Gaulle, the political situation in France itself led him to focus his attention there rather than seek further glory for French arms in foreign parts. He was determined that troops loyal to him participate in the liberation of French territory, particularly in the south of France where well-organized Vichyites and a Communist-dominated resistance might attempt to block his efforts to gain control of France.[7]

Able to buttress their own views with such formidable support, Marshall and Eisenhower never yielded to British blandishment or argument. In their eyes France remained the decisive theater, and any attempt to enhance the status of the Italian campaign *vis-à-vis* that in northwestern Europe the American command saw as an attempt to change a grand strategy already agreed to at the QUADRANT Conference.[8]

Eventually the American (and majority) view prevailed. Alexander, Clark, and Juin reconciled themselves to the campaign's secondary role in the Mediterranean, Alexander observing in the process that the success of the Allied armies in Italy henceforth would have to be judged not upon ground gained, for that was vital neither to the Allies nor the Germans, but rather "in terms

of its [the campaign's] effect upon the war as a whole."[9]

Thus bringing to battle the maximum number of German divisions and denying their use on other, more critical fronts, would from that point constitute the sole mission of the Allied armies in Italy. Actually, as far as the Americans were concerned, that had always been the mission, certainly since the QUADRANT Conference of 1943. In American eyes the British had finally been brought around to recognition of a long-standing reality.

Again, whether this strategy was the right one has been the subject of bitter debate since the war. Americans have contended that it was the correct strategy while the British have generally taken the opposite view.[10] The campaign should have accorded equal status with the one in northwestern Europe, they have argued. Also, according to these British analysts, Alexander's armies in the summer of 1944 should have been kept intact for a drive northward to the Po Valley, thence through the Alps to the mid-Danube basin. That, they claim, would have placed the postwar line of demarcation between the west and the Russian-dominated states of Europe much further east than as finally drawn.[11]

Whatever the validity of that line of reasoning, its weakness lies primarily in failure to take into account the logistical limitations, particularly the chronic

---

[7] *Ibid.*

[8] Ehrman, *Grand Strategy*, pp. 349–50.

[9] Quoted in *The Battle for Italy,* by W.G.F. Jackson, New York, 1967, p. 317.

[10] Two distinguished British historians of the Second World War, however, have argued that the strategic mission was essentially correct. See Ehrman, *Grand Strategy*, vols. V & VI, and Howard, *The Mediterranean Strategy in the Second World War.*

[11] See Clark, *Calculated Risk,* pp. 370–72.

shortage of shipping that plagued the Allies in the Mediterranean. Under that handicap, it is hardly likely that during the winter of 1944–45 the Allies could have supported such a large-scale advance. No valid grounds seem to exist, furthermore, for believing that the Allied armies could have crossed the Alps and deployed into the mid-Danube region before the late spring of 1945. By that time the Soviet forces had already seized Vienna and lay astride the mid-Danube basin, so that an Allied presence would have served no useful purpose. As one British historian has observed, "an effective case has still to be made out that there could have been any more rapid or economical way of winning the war" than that adopted by the Allies in western Europe.[12]

German Strategy

The Germans too had their difficulties in developing a meaningful and viable Mediterranean and Italian strategy. After the Italians, in an expansion of the war contrary to Germany's overall strategic interests and without any fixed plan, became hopelessly bogged down in an ill-conceived Balkan venture, the Mediterranean soon became for the Germans a theater "of fateful importance for the conduct of the war."[13]

As for the Italian campaign, after Allied landings on the mainland, military wisdom dictated a step by step withdrawal up the peninsula to the Alps, where, during World War I, a relatively small Austro-German force had held a larger Allied force at bay for three years. Instead, Hitler elected to hold all of the peninsula, even as he had done in the Balkans, including the off-shore islands in the eastern Mediterranean, which for several years tied down large numbers of German troops to no purpose.[14]

Once the Allies had regained control of the western Mediterranean and ably demonstrated this fact through three successive amphibious operations— HUSKY, AVALANCHE, and SHINGLE—the Germans had no alternative but to assume that the Allies could mount a third or even a fourth amphibious assault elsewhere along either the Ligurian or Adriatic coast and shaped their strategy accordingly. The ANVIL/DRAGOON landings in August 1944 only confirmed the Germans in their assumption. Until the last Allied offensive in 1945 was well advanced, the German command in Italy continued to divert important reserves to watch over what had long since become nonexistent threats to their coastal flanks. Thus did the German High Command play into Allied hands and tie down in the Mediterranean—both in the Balkans and in Italy—German divisions of high fighting quality at a time when they were urgently needed on other fronts, especially after June 1944 in northwestern France.

Architect of the strategy to defend all of Italy, Field Marshal Albert Kesselring by virtue of his personality and skill largely determined the stubborn nature of the German defense. Tagged with

---

[12] Howard, *The Mediterranean Strategy*, p. 71. See also Le Goyet, *La Participation Française a la Campagne d'Italie*, pp. 189–91.
[13] Concluding Remarks on the Mediterranean Campaign, by Albert Kesselring MS # C–014, typescript in CMH files.

---

[14] *Ibid.*

the sobriquet "Smiling Al," Kesselring throughout the long campaign maintained, in spite of every ground for despair, that indomitable optimism so important to a commander of troops. Brilliant soldier that he was, however, his optimism never blinded him to the realities of the battlefield.[15]

In support of his strategy, the German commander argued that to have evacuated the peninsula without a fight and withdrawn to the line of the Alps would not have allowed the Germans to release a significant number of troops for other fronts. In view of the defensive potential of the alpine terrain, that argument seems a tenuous one. A possibly more valid argument is that abandonment of the peninsula would have given the Allies untrammeled freedom of movement either in the direction of France or of the Balkans. Here again, at least as far as France was concerned, the Allied command of the western Mediterranean had already made it possible to invade southern France whenever desired. As for the Balkans peninsula, it turned out that except for British intervention in Greece following German withdrawal from that country, the Allies chose to do little in the area other than to supply Tito's partisans with arms, ammunition, and foodstuffs.

The argument that to yield the Italian peninsula would mean the sacrifice of an indispensably deep battle zone and unleash the air war on Austria and southern Germany ignores the fact of Allied control of the Foggia airfields and later those in Sardinia and Corsica.

Those fields had already opened up all of Italy and the southern regions of the Reich to Allied aerial attack. Nevertheless, Kesselring never lost his conviction that the Italian campaign "was not only justified but even imperative, and the problem one of simply doing whatever seemed best for one's own theater irrespective of the general strategic plan."[16]

A marked parochialism characterized the approaches of both sides to Mediterraean strategy in general and the Italian campaign in particular. Both the Allied and the German commands became so locked into their respective campaigns that they appeared incapable of turning away from their own operation maps long enough to reflect upon just what part the continuation of operations in the peninsula played in the overall strategic plan of their respective high commands.

The Commanders

In contrast with Allied operations in northern Europe, those in the Mediterranean theater were under overall British command. The American strategic viewpoint, however, was represented by Devers, the theater commander's deputy, and by Lemnitzer, Alexander's deputy chief of staff. Clark, on the other hand, was eventually to become an advocate of the British belief in the primacy of the Italian campaign in the Mediterranean.

Clark saw no need for the landing in southern France in August of 1944. American and French divisions withdrawn from the Fifth Army for that purpose could, he claimed, have been

[15] B.H. Liddell-Hart, *Why Don't We Learn From History?* (New York: 1971), p. 25.

[16] Kesselring, *A Soldier's Record*, p. 267.

employed to better advantage in Italy. Although in the advance from Rome to the Arno the Fifth Army's narrow front would have permitted the employment of no more divisions than Clark already had in Italy, he nevertheless contended that the divisions given up could have been used to alternate with those in line to afford his weary troops much needed rest. That would have enabled the Fifth Army, he argued, to maintain the momentum of the pursuit and drive the Germans more rapidly from central Italy. As for General Marshall's position that the port of Marseilles was needed for funneling additional divisions into France for Eisenhower's use, Clark later observed that the port could have been captured just as readily by sending troops into southern France from northwestern Italy. Had the momentum of the Allied spring offensive been sustained beyond Rome, the Fifth Army, he claimed, would have been in a position to do so by the end of July 1944.

The Alexander–Clark entente on strategy did not, however, extend to tactical matters. Yet differences in this area, while chronic, never threatened to rupture the close working relationship between Allied Armies headquarters and the U.S. Fifth Army. The relationship between Alexander and Clark resembled the one between Alexander and Montgomery in the North African campaign, during which Alexander gave his talented subordinate what was almost tantamount to free rein in the conduct of military operations and exercised only a general, albeit decisive, control over strategic planning. That was Alexander's style of command—a style which undoubtedly helped account

for the success of Allied coalition warfare in the Italian campaign.

Inter-Allied tactical disagreements during the course of the campaign arose mainly from a British determination to avoid a repetition of the large-scale frontal attacks typical of World War I, whose enormous costs Britain could no longer afford to pay. Those differences came to a head in May after Truscott's VI Corps had broken free of the Anzio beachhead and prepared for the final drive on Rome.

Operation BUFFALO, based upon Alexander's predilection for the wide-swinging outflanking maneuver—the one-two boxing punch, the phrase so often used by Alexander—assumed that the maneuver would entrap large numbers of enemy troops south of Rome. With attention focused on Rome, Clark had objected to that assumption (and the plan) on the grounds that there were just too many avenues of escape available to the enemy for a thrust from the beachhead to Highway 6 to cut off major German units in the Liri-Sacco valley. Furthermore, Clark regarded Truscott's VI Corps as insufficiently strong to cut and effectively block the highway in the first place. Even after the bulk of Truscott's corps had turned northward into the Alban Hills, however, General O'Daniel succeeded in cutting the highway, even if only with artillery fire.

Earlier Clark had refused Alexander's request that elements of the Fifth Army slip behind the Germans opposing the Eighth Army and thereby weaken the enemy's resistance to the British advance up the Liri valley, observing that Allied aerial reconnaissance had shown that the enemy had already withdrawn the bulk of his forces from the valley and that very few Germans would be trapped by sending the Fifth Army, or a major part of it, toward the Liri. That argument was similar to the one Clark was to use later against Operation BUFFALO. The most that Clark had been willing to agree to was to send the FEC toward Ceprano, even though he was convinced, apparently correctly, that few enemy troops would be trapped by the move.

While acknowledging that the Eighth Army had a tough assignment in the Liri valley and that Alexander's request thus had some justification, Clark intimated both in his wartime diary and in postwar interviews that, in his view, the Eighth Army was simply not trying as hard as it should. For that, Clark was inclined to blame what he called poor leadership, although the British had to work within far greater manpower restrictions than did the Americans and were therefore more chary about casualties.

Underlying much of Clark's reluctance to divert part of his Fifth Army to assist the Eighth Army's advance was a determination not to share with others the glory of the capture of the first of the Axis capitals. After being told the approximate date of the Normandy invasion, General Clark was anxious to take Rome before the invasion captured world attention.

Even though both French and British wanted to be in on the capture of Rome, Clark was determined to make it exclusively an American show. So strong was his determination not to allow his allies to share in the capture that, he revealed in a postwar interview, he told Alexander he would, if ordered

to permit the Eighth Army to participate, not only refuse but would fire on any Eighth Army troops who tried to do so. At any rate, in keeping with a long-standing tendency to go along with the desires of his more assertive subordinates, Alexander did back down, and Clark had his Roman triumph.[17]

Allied Tactics

Except for invaluable air artillery control techniques and refinements in the use of the tank-infantry team, the Allies developed few tactical innovations during the campaign. They usually resorted to the frontal assault, for despite Alexander's partiality for the wide-sweeping outflanking maneuver, the rugged, sharply compartmented Italian terrain imposed upon operations characteristics reminiscent of World War I—slow, grinding, costly battles of attrition—and undoubtedly helped account for Kesselring's success in holding the Allies to a long, slow advance up the peninsula.

In the rare instances when the Allies did resort to less conventional tactics, such as several skillfully devised deception plans and an occasional unorthodox use of troops and equipment, as during the final offensive in the Po Valley, the results were rewarding. Field Marshal Alexander's reliance on deception, for example, on several occasions drew German reserves far out of position. These tactics were aided by the intelligence that came from breaking the German code and by the fact that enemy commanders lacked reconnaissance aircraft to detect large-scale

---

[17] Interv. Mathews with Gen. Clark, 18 May 1948, in CMH files.

Allied troop movements preceding an operation. This proved especially valuable in Operation DIADEM in the spring of 1944 and Operation OLIVE in the autumn of the same year. In the same way the Eighth Army imaginative use of amphibious-tracked (Fantails) vehicles as in crossing the flooded plains near the mouth of the Reno to outflank a very formidable enemy position in the Argenta Gap, helped assure success in the early stages of the final offensive. That tactic was matched in ingenuity by the Fifth Army's employment of mountain troops to move across rugged terrain so rapidly as to confound the Germans, who did not expect such an Allied move. The consequent surprise, much like that achieved by the FEC over similar terrain in the Aurunci mountains a year before, resulted in a breakthrough into the Po Valley.

Although tactical innovations were few, the Italian campaign did see the development and testing of several technical innovations that later were to prove their worth in northwestern Europe. Among these were artificial harbors (Mulberries), first employed during the landings in Sicily and later vital in the Normandy invasion, and highly specialized airborne direction of artillery fire by spotter aircraft.[18]

Another technical innovation was the proximity fuze for artillery shells. Long used in antiaircraft fire, it was first released for ground use in the Ardennes counteroffensive (in December 1944) and was also employed in Italy in the latter stages of the campaign. Still another, radar-directed bombing

through darkness and overcast, stripped the enemy of his only remaining protection from Allied aerial harassment. In situations where practicable, Allied ground forces effectively employed offshore naval gunfire support requiring a high degree of interservice co-ordination.

An assessment of the role of airpower in the campaign leads to the conclusion that, while it was helpful, it was not decisive, either in close support of ground operations or in tactical interdiction and isolation of the battlefield, as in Operation STRANGLE. General Clark, for one, pointed out that air force claims that close air support would assist the taking of objectives at little cost to ground forces was not demonstrated at Monte Cassino.[19]

The Surrender Negotiations

In the closing weeks of the war the German High Command, or what remained of it, sought grimly to avoid large-scale capitulation to the Russians. On this effort hung the fate of over two million German soldiers, including *Army Group E* in Croatia and *Army Groups South* and *Center* in Czechoslovakia. (Trapped along the Baltic and already lost to the Russians were the 230,000-man *Army Kurland* and the 150,000-man *Army Ost-Preussen*.) Aware that Soviet suspicions had already been aroused by the protracted and covert negotiations leading to the German capitulation in Italy and by oft-repeated attempts by the common foe to divide the Allies, the British and the Americans pointed out to the Russians that a German surrender in Italy was

---

[18] Although the Germans had been the first to use these, they were unable to continue to do so after losing control of the skies to the Allies.

[19] Interv. Mathews with Gen. Clark, 10–21 May 1948, in CMH files.

little different from a separate German surrender on the Russian front, as, for example, at Stalingrad.

At the same time, the western Allies sought further to avoid friction by emphasizing that where feasible, surrender in every instance had to be made to representatives of all the major Allies. In the end, however, the Germans succeeded in extricating the bulk of their forces from the Eastern Front, with the exception of *Army Group Center,* by surrendering them to the western Allies.

The German surrender in Italy set a pattern for a series of piecemeal surrenders to the British and Americans. On 2 May, the same day that Vietinghoff capitulated, Grossadmiral Doenitz sent emissaries to Field Marshal Montgomery's headquarters with an offer to surrender to the British the German forces remaining in northwestern Germany, Denmark, and the German islands. Two days later, General Eisenhower told Montgomery to accept the offer in much the same way as Alexander had reacted to the offer in Italy.

On the same day, 4 May, emissaries from the German *19th Army* to General Patch's U.S. Seventh Army headquarters near Munich offered to surrender what would eventually include all of *Army Group G* in southern Germany. Three days later the final German surrender took place at Rheims and on 9 May the ceremony was restaged in Berlin for the benefit of the Russians.[20]

---

[20] For details of the several surrenders see Pogue, *The Supreme Command,* pp. 480 ff; MacDonald, *The Last Offensive,* Chapter XXIX; *The Seventh Army, Report of Operations,* pp. 856–65; Schramm, *KTB/ OKW,* Vol. IV (2), pp. 1478 ff.

Rightly regarded as a secondary or subsidiary operation, the Italian campaign in terms of the number of men involved, casualties, ground gained, and materiel consumed was nonetheless a major undertaking. Allied forces in Italy advanced 1,140 miles by road from Cape Pessaro on Sicily's southernmost tip to the Brenner Pass on Italy's Alpine frontier. From the first landings on the mainland in September 1943, they traveled 480 airline miles, about the same distance covered by Eisenhower's armies from Normandy to the Elbe. Because of the winding roads that vein much of the Italan peninsula, the actual ground distance was of course much longer. In the advance the two Allied armies crossed some of the most challenging terrain in Europe, alternating between hot and humid plains, forested mountains, and high, rocky, almost pathless summits. The weather ranged rom the oppressive summer heat of the Mediterranean littoral to the almost arctic cold of the Central and Northern Apennines. During the campaign the Allied forces completed four assault landings and three major offensives.

Counting both sides, approximately a million men were at one time or another involved. Allied strength ranged from 400,000 to 500,000 men, the Fifth Army from a high of 370,000 men at the time of the capture of Rome in June 1944 to a low of 266,000 at the beginning of the final offensive in April 1945. German strength generally was somewhat lower, declining more or less steadily throughout the campaign as the manpower situation in the Reich grew desperate.

Enemy losses, mainly men taken prisoner, were much higher than Allied. From September 1943 to May 1945 the two Allied armies incurred 312,000 casualties of all types, 188,746 of them by the Fifth Army.[21]

German casualties for the campaign totaled 434,646, of which 48,067 were killed and 214,048 missing. Generally forced to yield the ground fought over, the Germans were unable to determine how many of the missing had been killed, although the percentage probably was high.[22]

---

[21] Compared to 766,294 Allied casualties in northwestern Europe, of which American casualties were 586,628. See MacDonald, *The Last Offensive*, Chapter XX.

[22] The official German sources for battle losses, *Der Heeresartz Oberkommando des Heeres*, Gen. St.d. H/ Org. Abt., 26 Apr 45, lists only casualties for the army. Casualties for the *Waffen SS*, the *Luftwaffe*, and the *Kriegsmarine* are unavailable but would constitute a much smaller percentage since the bulk of German forces in Italy was army.

When the Germans laid down their arms, the longest sustained Allied campaign of World War II came to an end. **A total of 602 days had passed from** the landings in Italy on 9 September 1943 to the capitulation on 2 May 1945. Each day had seemed an eternity, as many a veteran of the campaign on both sides has testified. Almost always at a foot-slogger's pace—a pace rendered all the more interminable by the infrequent exhilaration of pursuit—and seemingly always approaching precipitous heights controlled by a well-concealed enemy, Allied troops, under a broiling sun or in numbing cold, had slowly pushed ahead. Nowhere on the far-flung battlefronts could the end have brought more relief than to those who fought the prolonged fight in a cruel, bitter campaign that all too often seemed to be going nowhere.

Appendix A

Table of Equivalent Ranks

U.S. Army	German Army and Air Force	German Waffen-SS
None	Reichsmarschall	None
General of the Army	Generalfeldmarschall	Reichsfuehrer-SS
General	Generaloberst	Oberstgruppenfuehrer
Lieutenant General	General der Infanterie	Obergruppenfuehrer
	Artillerie	
	Gebirgstruppen	
	Kavallerie	
	Nachrichtentruppen	
	Panzertruppen	
	Pioniere	
	Luftwaffe	
	Flieger	
	Fallschirmtruppen	
	Flakartillerie	
	Luftnachrichtentruppen	
Major General	Generalleutnant	Gruppenfuehrer
Brigadier General	Generalmajor	Brigadefuehrer
None	None	Oberfuehrer
Colonel	Oberst	Standartenfuehrer
Lieutenant Colonel	Oberstleutnant	Obersturmbannfuehrer
Major	Major	Sturmbannfuehrer
Captain	Hauptmann	Haupsturmfuehrer
Captain (Cavalry)	Rittmeister	
First Lieutenant	Oberleutnant	Obersturmfuehrer
Second Lieutenant	Leutnant	Untersturmfuehrer

Note on Sources

The main body of records upon which this volume is based is to be found in the Modern Military Records Division of the National Archives in Washington. They consist for the most part of monthly after-action reports together with supporting documents such as staff journals, message files, telephone logs, and periodic reports. The after-action reports are narrative summaries of operations prepared by every unit from army down to regiment and separate battalion. Varying in quality from unit to unit, they must be checked against the accompanying journals and message files; nevertheless, these reports provide a valuable framework in fitting information contained in the supporting document—often fragmentary—into place.

For operations above the army level, records of Allied Force Headquarters (AFHQ), consisting of a vast collection of reports, messages, planning papers, and correspondence, are an important primary source. They are to be found on microfilm at the Modern Military Records Division.

The National Archives Records Service is also the repository for microfilm of captured German records; the originals, including maps, having been returned to Germany. An index, *The Guide to German Records Microfilmed at Alexandria, Virginia,* consists of many volumes.

The most useful of the German records are the War Diaries (KTB) of the *Tenth* and *Fourteenth* Armies. In addition to daily summaries of operations, the diaries contain messages and transcripts of telephone conversations between commanders. These transcripts, especially, offer valuable insights into the thinking of senior German commanders in Italy, for in most cases they, unlike American telephone logs, are not summaries but are complete and candid. The wealth of the army records in large measure makes up for the fact that those of *Army Group C* are missing, probably lost in the war.

The War Diary of the German high command has been published as *Kriegstagesbuch des Oberkommando der Wehrmacht (Wehrmachtführungsstab),* edited by Helmuth Greiner and Percy Ernst Schramm, Vols. 1–4, Frankfurt a/Main, 1961. Volume IV, parts 1 and 2, are most useful for the Italian campaign. Unfortunately, the diary for the last month of the war is missing.

Unofficial Records (Allied)

Three American generals—Devers, Clark, and Walker—made their wartime diaries available to the author. General Clark lent that part of his diary relating to the campaign from May 1944 to May 1945, while the other two diaries are on file in the Center of Military History. The diaries include observations, comments, summaries of meetings, and correspondence dictated, generally on a daily basis, to each individual's aide de camp, who actually kept the diary. Frequently there are candid comments on events and personalities not to be found elsewhere in the record.

Also on file in the Center of Military

History are numerous interviews with key participants in the Italian campaign in two broad categories: combat and after-action. The first were conducted by professional historians on the staff of the Fifth Army Historical Detachment during or shortly after a military operation; the second were generally made after the war by historians of the Center of Military History. The combat interviews, as to be expected, add color to the official record and give historians a better feel for the operation and the individual soldier's reactions to it. The postwar interviews also helped round out the narrative with insights and recollections not often found in the official record.

In addition to the unpublished records, the Supreme Allied Commander, Mediterranean, and the commander of the Allied armies in Italy published reports for submission to the Combined Chiefs of Staff. They are essentially operational summaries and should, of course, be checked against the unpublished official records.

Although the records of the headquarters of the British Eighth Army and its subordinate units have not been available to the author, the British Historical Section, Central Mediterranean, prepared a multivolume narrative covering all aspects of the Eighth Army's operations during the Italian campaign. In manuscript form, the narrative represents a large-scale preliminary collection of studies for a subsequent official history. Entitled "Operations of British, Indian, and Dominion Forces in Italy, 3 September 1943–2 May 1945," this manuscript is in the U.S. Army Military History Research Collection, Carlisle Barracks, Pa.

In the postwar period several of the U.S. Army's combat arms schools, most notably the Infantry School, published studies prepared by students, usually company grade officers, who played key roles in combat operations. The studies are primarily useful for detail generally at or below the regimental level.

G–3 Section, Headquarters, 15th Army Group, published shortly after the cessation of hostilities a work entitled *A Military Encyclopedia, Based on Operations in the Italian Campaign, 1943–45.* Printed in a limited edition, it contains detailed information concerning all arms and the technical services as they related to Fifth Army operations.

Unofficial Records (German)

Soon after the war, the Historical Division, European Theater of Operations, U.S. Army, undertook a project whereby captured German officers turned out a series of historical studies embracing virtually every phase of German military operations during World War II. The results of the project, which continued for about a decade, are catalogued in *The Guide to Foreign Military Studies, 1945–54,* published under the auspices of the Historical Division, Headquarters, United States Army, Europe. The guide includes a comprehensive subject index and may be consulted either at the National Archives or the Center of Military History. Among the narrative studies is a lengthy manuscript in two volumes entitled *Feldzug in Italien* (MS T–1a and 1b) prepared by senior commanders and staff officers of the German armies in Italy. When used in co-ordination with the War Diary of the *Oberkommando der Wehrmacht,* the studies are extremely useful accounts of operations from the German point of view.

Additional studies, based largely upon those prepared by the German officers and upon interviews with the officers themselves, were produced by staff historians with the Foreign Military Studies Section of the Center of Military History. Grouped in a so-called R–Series, they total 165, but only a few are concerned with the campaign in Italy.

Published Works

Also available are a large number of published works covering the entire gamut of military and diplomatic operations relating to the Allied campaign in the Mediterranean and in Italy. The following is a partial list of those consulted in the preparation of this volume:

Official Histories, U.S.
The United States Army in World War II

The War Department

Leighton, Richard M. and Coakley, Robert W. *Global Logistics and Strategy, 1943–45* (Washington, 1969).

Matloff, Maurice. *Strategic Planning for Coalition Warfare, 1943–44* (Washington, 1959).

The Mediterranean Theater of Operations

Blumenson, Martin. *Salerno to Cassino* (Washington, 1969).

Howe, George F. *Northwest Africa: Seizing the Initiative in the West* (Washington, 1957).

Garland, Lt. Col. Albert N. and Smyth, Howard McGraw. *Sicily and the Surrender of Italy* (Washington, 1965).

The European Theater of Operations

MacDonald, Charles B. *The Last Offensive* (Washington, 1973).

The Technical Services

Kleber, Brooks E. and Birdsell, Dale. *The Chemical Warfare Service, Chemicals in Combat* (Washington, 1965).

Ross, William F. and Romanus, Charles F. *The Quartermaster Corps: Operations in the War Against Germany* (Washington, 1965).

Special Studies

Lee, Ulysses. *The Employment of Negro Troops* (Washington, 1966).

MacDonald, Charles B. and Mathews, Sidney T. *Three Battles: Arnaville, Altuzzo, and Schmidt* (Washington, 1952).

Weinberg, Albert K. *Civil Affairs: Soldiers Become Governors* (Washington, 1964).

American Forces in Action Series (available on microfilm).

The Fifth Army at the Winter Line (15 Nov 43–15 Jan 44) (Washington, 1945).

Small Unit Actions (Washington, 1946).

Anzio Beachhead (22 Jan–25 May 1944) (Washington, 1947).

The U.S. Army Air Forces in World War II

Craven, Wesley Frank and Cates, James Lea, eds. Vol. III, *Europe: Argument to V–E Day* (January 1944–May 1945) (Chicago: University of Chicago Press, 1951).

Official Histories, Allied

Nicholson, Lt. Col. G.W.L. *The Canadians in Italy, 1943–45.* OFFICIAL HISTORY OF THE CANADIAN

ARMY IN THE SECOND WORLD WAR, Vol. II (Ottawa: Queen's Printer, 1956).

Kay, Robin. *From Cassino to Trieste.* NEW ZEALAND IN THE SECOND WORLD WAR (1939–45), Vol. II (Wellington, N.Z.: Historical Publications Branch, Dept. of Internal Affairs, 1967).

Pal, Dharm. *The Campaign in Italy, 1943–45.* OFFICIAL HISTORY OF THE INDIAN ARMED FORCES IN THE SECOND WORLD WAR, 1939–45 (New Delhi. Combined Inter-Services Historical Section [India and Pakistan], 1960).

Ehrman, John. *Grand Strategy.* Vol. V, *Aug. 1943–Sept. 1944.* Vol. VI, *Oct 1944–Aug. 1945.* Butler, J.R.M., ed. HISTORY OF THE SECOND WORLD WAR, UNITED KINGDOM SERIES (London: Her Majesty's Stationery Office, 1956).

Molony, Brigadier C.J.C. *The Mediterranean and Middle East.* Vol. V, *The Campaign in Sicily and the Campaign in Italy, Sept. 1943–March 1944.* HISTORY OF THE SECOND WORLD WAR (London: Her Majesty's Stationery Office, 1973).

Le Goyet, Col. Pierre. Ministere des Armees, Etat-Major de L'Armee de Terre, Service Historique. *La Participation Française A La Campagne D'Italie (1943–1946)* (Paris: Imprimerie Nationale, 1969).

Unit Histories

Fifth Army History, Vols. I–IX. Published shortly after the war and covering the period from the army's activation to the end of the war in Italy in May 1945, this history was prepared by members of the Fifth Army's Historical Section, initially under the direction of Col. John D. Forsythe, later succeeded by Lt. Col. Chester G. Starr. In a sense, the history resembles a large-scale after-action report. When consulted along with journals and message files, it is a very useful source.

The best of the division unit histories are:

Howe, George F. *The Battle History of the 1st Armored Division* (Washington, 1954).

Taggart, Donald G., ed. *The History of the 3d Infantry Division in World War II* (Washington, 1947).

Others, varying in quality, are:

Böhmler, Rudolf. *Fallschirmjaeger, Bildbuch u. Chronik* (Bad Nauheim: Podzun-Verlag, 1961).

Delaney, John P. *The Blue Devils in Italy, A History of the 88th Infantry Division in World War II* (Washington: Infantry Journal Press, 1947).

Heargon, Capitaine. *La Victoire, sous Le Signe des Trois Croissants.* Vol. I, *Les Peines, et les Gloire de la 3eme D.I.A. en Italie* (Algerie, 1946).

De Moraes, Marshal J. B. Mascarenhas. *The Brazilian Expeditionary Force. By Its Commander,* trans. from 2d Edition, Revised and Enlarged (Rio de Janeiro, 1965).

Robbins, Maj. Robert A. *The 91st Infantry Division in World War II* (Washington, 1947).

Schultz, Paul, L. *The 85th Division in World War II* (Washington, 1949).

Strootman, Capt. Ralph E. *History of the 363d Infantry, One Regiment of the 91st Division in World War II* (Washington, 1947).

Published Works, General

Adelman, Robert H. and Walton,

Col. George. *The Devil's Brigade* (Philadelphia: Chilton Books, 1966).

Carpentier, Gen. Marcel. *Les Forces Allies en Italie: La Campagne d'Italie.* Editions Berger-Levrault (Paris, 1949).

Churchill, Winston S. *Closing the Ring* (Boston: Houghton Mifflin, Co., 1951).

Clark, Mark W. *Calculated Risk* (New York: Harper and Brothers, 1950).

Dulles, Allen W. *The Secret Surrender* (New York: Harper and Row, 1966).

Greiner, Heinz Glt.a.D. *Kampf am Rom, Inferno am Po*, Die Wehrmacht im Kampf, Band 44 (Neckargemund: Kurt Vowinckel Verlag, 1968).

Higgins, Trumbull. *Soft Underbelly, The Anglo-American Controversy Over the Italian Campaign, 1939–1945* (New York: The Macmillan Company, 1958).

Howard, Michael. *The Mediterranean Strategy in the Second World War* (New York: Frederick A. Praeger, 1968).

Jackson, W.G.F. *The Battle for Italy* (New York: Harper and Row, 1967).

Jackson, W.G.F. *The Battle for Rome* (New York: Charles Scribner's Sons, 1969).

Kesselring, Albert Generalfeldmar-schall a.D. *Kesselring, A Soldier's Record* (New York: William Morrow & Company, 1954).

Nicholson, Nigel. *Alex, The Life of Field Marshal, Earl Alexander of Tunis* (New York: Atheneum, 1973).

Orgill, Douglas. *The Gothic Line, The Italian Campaign, Autumn 1944* (New York: W.W. Norton & Co., 1967).

Scrivener, Jane. *Inside Rome with the Germans* (New York: The Macmillan Company, 1945).

Shepperd, G.A. *The Italian Campaign, 1943–45, A Political and Military Reassessment* (New York: Frederick A. Praeger, 1968).

Truscott, Lucian K. *Command Missions* (New York: E. P. Dutton & Co., 1959).

Westphal, Siegfried. *Heer in Fesseln, aus den Papieren des Stabschefs von Rommel, Kesselring, und Rundstedt.* (Bonn: Athenaum-Verlag, 1950).

Winterbotham, F.W. *The Ultra Secret* (London: Weidenfeld and Nicholson, 1974), p. 187.

References to additional published works will be found in the footnotes of this volume.

Glossary

AAF	Army Air Forces
AAI	Allied Armies, Italy
AAR	After action report
Abn	Airborne
ACC	Allied Control Commission
ACMF	Allied Central Mediterranean Forces
ACofS	Assistant Chief of Staff
Admin	Administrative
AFHQ	Allied Force Headquarters
AG	Adjutant General
AGp	Army group
Armd	Armored; armoured
AOK	Armee Oberkommando (Army High Command)
Bd	Board
CCA	Combat Command A
CCB	Combat Command B
CCS	Combined Chiefs of Staff
CG	Commanding general
CinC	Commander in Chief
CofS	Chief of Staff
CLN	Comitate di Liberazione Nazionale (Committee of National Liberation)
Comd	Command
Comdr	Commander
Corresp	Correspondence
COS	(British) Chiefs of Staff
CMH	Center of Military History
CP	Command post
DA	Department of the Army
DAF	(British) Desert Air Force
DCofS	Deputy Chief of Staff
DSC	Distinguished Service Cross
DUKW	$2^{1}/_{2}$ ton, 6×6 amphibious truck
Engr	Engineer
ETOUSA	European Theater of Operations, U.S. Army
Exec	Executive
ExecO	Executive officer
FA	Field Artillery
FO	Field order

FEC	French Expeditionary Corps
G–2	Intelligence section of division or higher staff
G–3	Operations section of division or higher staff
G–4	Logistics and supply section of division or higher staff
Hiwis	(Hilfswillige) Russian and Polish prisoners volunteering for service with German forces
Incl	Inclosure
Inf	Infantry
Instr	Instruction
Intel	Intelligence
Interv	Interview
JCS	Joint Chiefs of Staff
JPS	Joint Staff Planners
KTB	Kriegstagebuch (War Diary)
LVT	Landing vehicle, tracked
MAAF	Mediterranean Allied Air Forces
MACAF	Mediterranean Allied Coastal Air Force
MATAF	Mediterranean Allied Tactical Air Force
MASAF	Mediterranean Strategic Air Force
Maint	Maintenance
Min	Minutes
Msg	Message
Mtg	Meeting
MTOUSA	Mediterranean Theater of Operations, U.S. Army
NATOUSA	North African Theater of Operations, U.S. Army
OBSW	Oberbefehlshaber Suedwest (Headquarters, Commander in Chief, Southwest)
OI	Operations instructions
OKH	Oberkommando des Heeres (Army High Command)
OKL	Oberkommando der Luftwaffe (Air Force High Command)
OKW	Oberkommando der Wehrmacht (Armed Forces High Command)
OPD	Operations Division, War Department General Staff
Opn	Operation
OSS	Office of Strategic Services
PBS	Peninsula Base Section
Prcht	Parachute
RAF	Royal Air Force
Regt	Regiment

Rep	Representative
RN	Royal Navy
SACMED	Supreme Allied Commander, Mediterranean
SHAEF	Supreme Headquarters, Allied Expeditionary Forces
S–2	Military intelligence section of regimental or lower staff level
S–3	Operations and training section of regimental or lower staff level
Sec	Section
Sitrep	Situation report
SOS	Services of Supply
Teleconv	Telephone conversion
TF	Task force
WFSt	Wehrmachtfuehrungsstab (Armed Forces Operations Staff)

Code Names

ANVIL	Early plan for invasion of southern France
AVALANCHE	Allied amphibious assault near Salerno to capture Naples, 9 September 1943
CROSSWORD	Covert operation leading to German surrender, 2 May 1944
DIADEM	Allied offensive in Italy, 11 May 1944
DRAGOON	Allied invasion of southeastern Mediterranean coast of France, 15 August 1944; name changed on 27 July 1944 from ANVIL
ENCORE	IV Corps limited objective operation against Monte Belvedere, February 1945
FOURTH TERM	IV Corps limited objective operation in Serchio Valley, February 1945
HERBSTNEBEL	German operational plan for withdrawal beyond the Po river
HUSKY	Allied invasion of southeastern Sicily, 10 July 1943
NUNTON	Allied cover and deception plan, March 1944
OLIVE	Allied Gothic Line offensive, September 1944
OVERLORD	Allied cross-Channel invasion of continent of Europe on the Normandy coast of France, D-day, 6 June 1944
QUADRANT	U.S.–British conference at Quebec, August 1943
SEXTANT-EUREKA	Allied conferences at Cairo and Teheran, November–December 1943
SHINGLE	Amphibious operation at Anzio, 22 January 1944
STRANGLE	Allied air operation to interrupt and destroy enemy road, rail, and sea communications in Italy, March–May 1944
TRIDENT	U.S.–British conference at Washington, May 1943
WINTERGEWITTER	German limited objective counterattack against U.S. IV Corps, 26 December 1944

Basic Military Map Symbols*

Symbols within a rectangle indicate a military unit, within a triangle an observation post, and within a circle a supply point.

Military Units—Identification

Antiaircraft Artillery . . . .

Armored Command . . . .

Army Air Forces . . . .

Artillery, except Antiaircraft and Coast Artillery . . . .

Cavalry, Horse . . . .

Cavalry, Mechanized . . . .

Chemical Warfare Service . . . .

Coast Artillery . . . .

Engineers . . . .

Infantry . . . .

Medical Corps . . . .

Ordnance Department . . . .

Quartermaster Corps . . . .

Signal Corps . . . .

Tank Destroyer . . . .

Transportation Corps . . . .

Veterinary Corps . . . .

Airborne units are designated by combining a gull wing symbol with the arm or service symbol:

Airborne Artillery . . . .

Airborne Infantry . . . .

*For complete listing of symbols in use during the World War II period, see FM 21–30, dated October 1943, from which these are taken.

Size Symbols

The following symbols placed either in boundary lines or above the rectangle, triangle, or circle inclosing the identifying arm or service symbol indicate the size of military organization:

Squad . . . . ●

Section . . . . ●●

Platoon . . . . ●●●

Company, troop, battery, Air Force flight I

Battalion, cavalry squadron, or Air Force squadron . . . . I I

Regiment or group; combat team (with abbreviation CT following identifying numeral) . . . . I I I

Brigade, Combat Command of Armored Division, or Air Force Wing X

Division or Command of an Air Force XX

Corps or Air Force XXX

Army XXXX

Group of Armies XXXXX

EXAMPLES

The letter or number to the left of the symbol indicates the unit designation; that to the right. the designation of the parent unit to which it belongs. Letters or numbers above or below boundary lines designate the units separated by the lines:

Company A, 137th Infantry . . . . A ⊠ 137

8th Field Artillery Battalion . . . . ▣ 8

Combat Command A, 1st Armored Division . . . . A ▭ 1

Observation Post, 23d Infantry . . . . △ 23

Command Post, 5th Infantry Division . . . . ⊠ 5

Boundary between 137th and 138th Infantry . . . . —¦¦¦—
137
138

Weapons

Machine gun . . . . ●→

Gun . . . . ●

Gun battery . . . . ⊥⊥⊥

Howitzer or Mortar . . . . ◆

Tank . . . . ◇

Self-propelled gun . . . . ▰●

UNITED STATES ARMY IN WORLD WAR II

The following volumes have been published or are in press:

Index

☆ U.S. GOVERNMENT PRINTING OFFICE: 1993   331–886